AF245522

INFORMATION MODELLING AND KNOWLEDGE BASES IX

Frontiers in Artificial Intelligence and Applications

Series Editors: J. Breuker, R. López de Mántaras, S. Ohsuga and W. Swartout

Volume 45

Previously published in this series:

ISSN: 0922-6389

Information Modelling and Knowledge Bases IX

Edited by

Pierre-Jean Charrel
University of Toulouse, France

Hannu Jaakkola
Tampere University of Technology, Finland

Hannu Kangassalo
University of Tampere, Finland

and

Eiji Kawaguchi
Kyushu Institute of Technology, Japan

IOS
Press

Ohmsha

Amsterdam • Berlin • Oxford • Tokyo • Washington, DC

ISBN 90 5199 396 X (IOS Press)
ISBN 4 274 90221 8 C3000 (Ohmsha)

Publisher
IOS Press
Van Diemenstraat 94
1013 CN Amsterdam
Netherlands

Distributor in the UK and Ireland
IOS Press/Lavis Marketing
73 Lime Walk
Headington
Oxford OX3 7AD
England

Distributor in Germany
IOS Press
Spandauer Strasse 2
D-10178 Berlin
Germany

Distributor in the USA and Canada
IOS Press, Inc.
5795-G Burke Center Parkway
Burke, VA 22015
USA

Distributor in Japan
Ohmsha, Ltd.
3-1 Kanda Nishiki-cho
Chiyoda-ku
Tokyo 101
Japan

LEGAL NOTICE
The publisher is not responsible for the use which might be made of the following information.

PRINTED IN THE NETHERLANDS

Preface

Information modelling is the essential part of information system design. Design methods, specification languages, and tools tend to become application dependent, aiming at integration of methodologies stretching traditional database design to advanced knowledge bases, and including use of logical languages, and process oriented system description.

This book is the ninth volume in the series "Information Modelling and Knowledge Bases". This series dates back in 1990 with annual publications now amounting to more than 250 reviewed articles. The articles introduce results of the work and collaboration in a geographically wide researcher network originating from the Finnish-Japanese research initiative begun in 1988. The published papers are formally reviewed by an international programme committee and selected for the annual conference forming a forum for criticism, which is taken into account in the final published versions.

The topics of the articles cover a wide variety of themes in the domain of information modelling, specifications of information systems and knowledge bases, ranging from foundations and theories to systems construction and application studies. The contributions represent the following major themes:

(1) the use of ontologies in knowledge modelling,

(2) concept modelling and conceptual modelling,

(3) database modelling: applications of object-oriented modelling,

(4) view integration and consistency checking,

(5) modelling multimedia and multimedia models,

(6) design methods,

(7) process modelling,

(8) formal systems,

In the first group, *G. Steve, A. Gangemi* and *D. M. Pisanelli* describe an experience of conceptual integration of terminological ontologies in a medical domain, while *A. Goñi, E. Mena* and *A. Illarramendi* use domain ontologies as a tool for query processing strategies of heterogeneous and distributed data repositories. The contribution of *C. Reynaud, N. Aussenac-Gilles* and *F. Tort* discusses the use of the entity-relationship model in domain knowledge modelling with a case study.

In the second group of articles, *E. Compatangelo* and *G. Rumolo* describe a framework for concept modelling and conceptual modelling combining ontological, methodological and operational aspects. Then, *A. Cardon*'s contribution deals with a multi-agent based model of communication and information systems to manage crisis and emergency situations, which represents intentions and judgements of actors. The article written by *S. Ohsuga* presents a general problem solving model based on a multi-layer representation principle and its applications to automatic programming. *J. F. Nilsson* and *J. Palomäki* discuss how to handle intensional aspects of concepts with the use of a meta-logical system based on a binary relational algebraic logic. *M. Duzi* and *J. Pokorný* develop an approach based on intensional logic for the study of data semantics in the context of conceptual modelling. *T. B. Ho, T. D. Nguyen, H. Shimodaira*, and *M. Kimura* specify an interactive-graphic system for discovering and using conceptual knowledge based on methods, which induce knowledge in the form of concept hierarchies.

Three papers are grouped in the third category. First, *D. Massart* and *J. Richelle* present an experiment of integrating experimental and reference information about biological macromolecular data in an object-oriented conceptual model. *M. Matskin* and *D. Montesi* specify a graphical rule language for active database modelling. The contribution of *M. Akaishi* and *Y. Tanaka* is a new query processing method for large multi-media object databases.

The fourth group of papers begins with *M. Kirikova*'s analysis of different aspects of consistency checking in a process of requirements engineering. *P. Eden* presents a solution to the integration of alternative user views in a database conceptual model based on a new integrity constraint. *Y. Kiyoki, A. Miyagawa* and *T. Kitagawa* specify and experiment a system which provides personalised interfaces for multidatabase system users, based on a multiple view mechanism with a new learning method for semantic associative search.

M. Kangassalo begins the fifth group by describing an experiment based on matching simulation-based models of a natural phenomenon with a method to learn conceptual modelling. *E. Kawaguchi* and *M. Niimi* present their method to model digital images, which separates informative and noise-like regions by means of a complexity measure. The next co-authors, *T. Tokuda, C. Ritthongpitak* and *K. Kawai* deal with a completely codeless model for algorithm animations. At last, *Y. Yasumura, K. Orimoto, N. Babaguchi* and *T. Kitahashi* contribute with an automatic acquisition of the model of a class of three dimensional objects.

K. Nakata's represents the only paper dealing with design methods, owing to his application of temporal logic to represent and reason about physical systems in the design task.

Process modelling is also represented by one paper, written by *S. Nurcan* and *C. Rolland*. They specify a method to represent co-operative work processes based on a process meta-model.

The last two papers are written by *N. Harada, S. Arikawa* and *H. Ishizaka* who develop a new prover of elementary formal systems, and by *A. Ligeza* and *P. Fuster-Parra* who present a multi-level knowledge-based model of diagnostic reasoning.

The Editors

CONTENTS

Integrating Medical Terminologies with ONIONS Methodology

Geri Steve, Aldo Gangemi, Domenico M. Pisanelli
Reparto Informatica Medica, Istituto Tecnologie Biomediche, CNR
Viale Marx 15-I 00137 Roma
{geri,aldo,nico}@color.irmkant.rm.cnr.it

ONIONS helps terminological ontology construction from existing, contextually heterogeneous terminologies. It is a methodology for integrating the context-dependent conceptualizations underlying conceptually heterogeneous terminology systems. We describe an application of this methodology to the medical domain with an example extracted from the UMLS system. We also give a short description of the current ontology library produced by means of ONIONS, and of its metaontology.

Introduction

Integration of large knowledge bases is a relevant issue and is gaining a constantly raising attention in literature (see for example: [Gruber, 93] [Gennari, Tu, Rothenfluh, Musen, 94] [Neches et al., 91] [Fankhauser, Kracker, Neuhold, 91] [Sujanski, Altman, 94] [EPISTOL, 94] [van Heijst, Schreiber, Wielinga, 97]).

Although much work has been already devoted to integration of data formats and even to integration of representation formalisms, a more challenging integration issue comes from the heterogeneity of intended meaning of concepts.

We introduce ONIONS (ONtologic Integration Of Naïve Sources), a methodology for the integration of terminological knowledge from repositories with heterogeneous conceptualizations. This methodology is founded on a philosophically account to a semantic theory (i.e. our theory of meaning) which drives the structure of the methodology itself [Gangemi, Steve, Rossi Mori, 95], [Steve, Gangemi, 96], [Gangemi, Steve, Pisanelli, Giacomelli, 97].

ONIONS creates a common framework to generalize and integrate the definitions that are used to organize a set of terminological sources. In other words, it allows to work out coherently a domain terminological ontology (a terminological ontology is usually defined as the explicit conceptualization of a vocabulary) for each source, which can be then compared with the others and mapped to an *integrated ontology library*.

Terminological ontologies are commonly distinguished into domain, generic and representation ontologies:
- domain ontologies concern specialized knowledge in a domain or subdomain: medicine, cardiology, clinical administration, protocols, etc. Some examples concern concurrent engineering, planning, medicine, law, military applications [McGuire, Kuokka, Weber et al, 93] [Tate, 96] [Gangemi, Steve, Giacomelli, 96] [Rossi Mori, Gangemi, Steve, et al., 97] [Valente, Breuker, 96] [Swartout, Patil, Knight, Russ, 96]. Also, some restricted generic and domain terminological ontologies have been defined as part of KBS development within the projects GAMES-II [Falasconi, Stefanelli, 94], Protégé-II [Gennari, Tu, Rothenfluh, Musen, 94], Kactus [Martil, Turner, Terpstra, 95] [Laresgoiti, Anjewierden, Bernaras, et al., 96].
- generic ontologies concern general, foundational aspects of knowledge: processes, part/whole structure, connexity, kinds of objects, quantities; good examples are [Sowa, 95] [Varzi, 96] [Borgo, Guarino, Masolo, 96] [Cohn, Randell, Cui, 96] [Gerstl, Pribbenow, 96] [Borst, Akkermans, Top, 97];
- representation ontologies specify the conceptualizations that underly knowledge representation formalisms [Guarino, Carrara, Giaretta, 94]; the frame-ontology [Gruber,

93] defined by the designers of Ontolingua is a typical example; a representation ontology is also considered a metaontology (it defines "meta-level" categories, §4.);

ONIONS has been applied to medicine, that can be itself seen as the integration of many heterogenous subdomains. The current resulting medical ontology is ON9 (§3.).

Our research is related to others in the same domain, such as vocabulary standardization [CEN, 95], natural language (lexical) processing [Bateman, 97], terminology server design [GALEN, 94] [Humphreys, Lindberg, 92] [Rector, Gangemi, Galeazzi, Glowinski, Rossi Mori, 94], conceptual modeling of subdomains [Rossi Mori, Gangemi, Steve, et al., 97], knowledge integration, sharing, and reuse [Evans, Cimino, Huff, Bell, 94] [Gennari, et al, 94] [Falasconi, Stefanelli, 94] [Swartout, Patil, Knight, Russ, 96] [Valente, Breuker, 96], [Steve, Gangemi 97] and multi-agent system development [Falasconi, Lanzola, Stefanelli, 96].

1. Some premises

There exist very few methodologies for terminological ontology construction (for example, Uschold, King, 95] [Valente, Breuker, 96]). In fact, in recent years ontological frameworks concentrated mainly on formal languages for expressing ontologies (*ontology representation*). We argue that the main reserve in discussing the methodology issue is linked to the difficulty of solving such problems as *context dependency, conceptual relevance* and *detail level*. We briefly summarize an assessment to these problems (an extensive discussion is in [Gangemi et al, 97]).

Context-dependency   The analysis conducted on medical terminologies has shown that the conceptualization of a term is context-dependent, where "context" has to be intended in a wide sense, including:
- the text in which the term appears;
- the possible terminological repositories in which the term is classified.
- the historical evolution of the use of the term;
- the spatio-temporal situation in which an agent uses the term; etc.
- the belief space of an agent which uses the term;
- the particular viewpoint an agent chooses on the use of the term;
- the disciplinary domain in which the term mainly occurs;
- the particular viewpoint inside a domain (e.g. morphology, physiology in medical domain);

For example, in the definition of *viral hepatitis*: «inflammation of liver caused by virus», we have to consider that *inflammation* may mean in different — or within a same — terminological source:
- a *physiological function* performing segregation of external agents;
- a *portion of a body part* which embodies that physiological function;
- a specific *abnormal morphology* (texture, color, shape, other abnormalities) of that portion.

One or more of these intended meanings are acceptable in a given context. Context dependency (or "situatedness", cf. [Menzies, 96]) is consequently troublesome when different contexts are to be integrated in the same ontology.

Conceptual relevance   How to assess what is conceptually relevant? For example, if we are faced with the task of conceptualizing the term *inflammation*? Should we conceptualize all the possible meanings or only some, and what criterion should guide us?

Within AI, relevance problems in terminology conceptualizations have appeared mainly in the description logics domain, where the classic distinction between *terminologic* and *assertional* knowledge tried to impose a formal criterion on an ontological problem. What is terminological? How to state the border?[1] An interesting study on the difficulty of representing domain (medical) knowledge in such an environment is [Haimowitz, Patil, Szolovits, 88]). Among the others, assessments of the issue are in [Owsnicki-Klewe, 89]. For a general assessment of relevance in information modelling, see [Marjomaa, 93].

Since we claim, with [Davidson, 86], that «linguistic ability [...] is the ability to converge on a passing theory from time to time» (p.173), we can conclude that conceptual relevance itself is context-dependent (Davidson's passing theory is what we may call a conceptualization).

---

[1] Usually, only some rule-of-thumb is suggested, such as "encode in terminologic knowledge only what appears 'obviously' taxonomic".

Detail level   A related problem to relevance is the *detail level*: when to stop detailing the explicitation of a conceptualization? If relevance is context-dependent, detail level implies a judgment on the refinability of a conceptualization without loosing the reference to the context (without "overcommitting"). For example, deciding about the conceptualization of the term *ulcer of stomach* as *inflammation of stomach* vs. *inflammation of the wall of stomach* vs. *inflammation of the mucosa of the wall of stomach*, is a detail level issue.

Our responses   Although context-dependency is a problem to conceptual integration, it is also a guide as far as relevance and detail are concerned: in fact, we have to conceptualize only what is relevant in a context, and we do stop over there.

This leads to the problem of catching the specifities of different kinds of context and the way to conceptualize them. This is an ongoing research, too complex to present here; we can provide a minimal framework:[2] a *non-symbolic* context (e.g., spatio-temporal regions, situations, time spans, cultural systems) can be opposed to a *symbolic* context (e.g. linguistic texts, formal models), which is a representation of a non-symbolic context (cf. also [Sowa, 96]).

The symbolic context is the target of our method of terminological ontology construction. Namely, we take symbolic contexts to be the direct contexts of terminologies. Consequently, our solution to the relevance question in ontology integration is to integrate terminology repositories which have been developed by experts for given tasks with consequent contextual relevance and significant detail.

Such a solution is performed in our methodology in this way: firstly, after the direct symbolic context of a term is explicitated, we interpret the minimal intended meaning in that context. Thus, we have got a minimal local conceptualization. Secondly, we trigger one or more generic ontologies which can provide the coding of non-symbolic contexts for the local conceptualization: what are its situational, spatio-temporal, and cultural coordinates? Thirdly, we build an ontology library comprising the generic ontologies, as well as the domain ontologies which explicitate our conceptualization. In few words, we place a local conceptualization inside a more global knowledge context.

These responses have a philosophical background. Elsewhere [Steve et al., 96] [Gangemi et al., 97], we have explained in detail a semiologic theory of meaning, based on [Saussure, 80] [Eco, 84] [Peirce, 80], which underlies the way we treat context-dependency. The main features of this theory include the recognition of terms as *expressions* of arbitrary complexity within a *text*. Their interpretation is provided by other expressions, called *interpretants*, which are found in the same or a different text. The set of interpretants for an expression is called the Interpretant Field (IF). When we delimit (with a selection criterion) the set of texts which act as interpretant sources, the resulting set of interpretants is called the Qualified Interpretant Field (QIF). If we trigger some interpretation frameworks made of general knowledge, i.e. the so-called "paradigms", cf. [Kuhn, 62], and put the interpretants within such frameworks, the resulting structured field is called Ontologized Field (OF). OFs are used to construct our ontology libraries; in particular, paradigms are specified in the generic ontologies.

In Figure 1 we give an analogical intuition of this theory. The local analysis and definition of an expression can be represented as an onion section in which the dissected leaves represent the *definientes* i.e. the interpretants actually used in the definition. Different subjects can carry on different analyses and different definitions in the same way one can make different sections of an onion. However, we can figure out that different definitions are equivalent if one can find out correspondences between their definientes. In the onion metaphor this equivalence is analogous to the correspondence between pairs of dissected onion leaves belonging to the same leaf. To catch the core of the concept means to find out all the highly specific interpretants (leaves) necessary to distinguish the concept from all similar concepts: two conceptualizations can be equivalent only if they substantially catch the same leaves.

Another issue should be addressed here: if "paradigms" govern the interpretation framework for QIFs, how to assess the relevance of a paradigm? On this point, we adopt a special "grounding" philosophy which is variously inspired by a bunch of psychologic, linguistic, and philosophic works ([Harnad, 90] [Petitot, Smith, 91] [Talmy, 95] [Varzi, 96], etc.). We do not detail such a philosophy here; we only say that paradigms are constrained on their turn by:

---

[2] The following distinction corresponds to the one adopted in linguistics between "context" and "co-text".

• the actual *structure of the world* that interacts with human behavior: the ordinary, or *common sense structure*. This concerns the *universals*, or *invariants*, of cognitive perception, such as *wholeness* and *parthood* of objects [cf. Simons, 87], *connectedness*, *strata* of reality (material, biologic, psychological, socio-cultural) [cf. Hartmann, 66]; and
• the *cognitive schematization* [Lakoff, 90] [Langacker, 91], which bounds perception and develops to make humans efficiently interact with world; examples are the kinaesthetic image schemata, such as *up/down, front/back, containment, configuration, path, link, force dynamics*.

Therefore, a set of generic ontologies should be provided which contains theories about these two constraints. Such generic ontologies should not be "absolutely" right: they are good as far as ontology integration is successfully performed and intersubjectively acceptable.

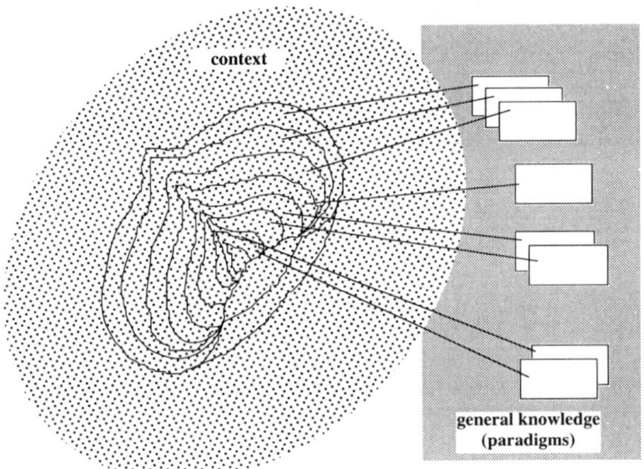

Fig.1: The onion metaphor: leaves represent interpretants in a local definition of an expression, linked to paradigms (rectangle).

2. The ONIONS methodology

2.1 An overview We developed ONIONS (ONtologic Integration On Naïve Sources) in order to analyse and to integrate domain ontologies. We consider ONIONS a methodology that constrains and explicits "intellectual activities", such as conceptual analysis and modeling choices, which cannot be reduced to sequences of "elementary actions" to be accomplished. The goal of our methodology is to transform the potential arbitrariness of such intellectual activity in a trasparent organization according to guidelines coherent with our theory of meaning (§1.); this means that the great amount of subjectivity inherent in this activity is not eliminated nor hidden, but it is made completely explicit step by step, such that it becomes intersubjective if one agrees with it. Partial agreements are possible depending on the modularity of the resulting system. Here we summarize the five main phases of ONIONS:
• M_0: Creating a corpus of validated textual sources of a domain. Sources must be individuated together with an assessment of their diffusion and validation inside the domain community.
• M_1: Taxonomic analysis. If lacking, taxonomies are constructed.
• M_2: Local source analysis. The conceptual analysis of terms in order to locate their free-text descriptions and other constraints (local definitions).
• M_3: Multi-local source analysis. The conceptual analysis of the descriptions allows to link the local definitions with multi-local concepts and general knowledge (paradigms).
• M_4: Building an integrated ontology library. An ontology library covers all the local definitions and the paradigms that have been used in building multi-local, integrated definitions.
• M_5: Implementing and classifying the library. These steps pertain to the diffusion, use, classification, and validation of the model.

Extension, partial acceptance/rejection, refinements, updating, integration with other sources can be carried out iteratively using ONIONS. The ontologies resulting from previous integrations can furtherly play the role of source to be analysed and integrated with its appropriate degree of relevance.

In Figure 2 we introduce in an abstract and schematic form the basics of ONIONS methodology. It describes a methodology with six phases and a set of input and output states in the analysis or in the construction of a terminology system. Such states are described by a set of structural and ontologic properties. We name a property "ontological" if it concerns the principles of conceptual organization of a terminology system.

Each ONIONS phase M_i makes a terminology system or repository evolve from a state S_i into a state S_{i+1}. P_i and O_i are respectively the structural and ontological properties of S_i systems. Hence, such properties also allow a classification of existing terminology systems according to their structural and ontological properties.

2.2 Phase M_0: Creating a corpus of validated sources

At state S_0 domain knowledge is formally unstructured (P_0) as well as ontologically opaque (O_0: no explicit conceptualization). Phase M_0 aims at collecting a validated terminological corpus for a domain. Such a phase has hooks to corpora formation techniques and textual types definition and acquisition (not examined in this paper).

For example, our primary experiment of medical terminological integration has taken into account five terminology systems: the UMLS Semantic Network (UMLS-SN) [Humphries, 92] (all 215 semantic types and relations, and the ~1400 "templates" defined on them), SNOMED-III [Coté, Rothwell, Brochu, 94] (~600 most general concepts and links) and GMN [Gabrieli, 89] (~700 most general concepts) nomenclatures, ICD10 [WHO, 94] classification (~200 most general concepts), and the CORE model developed by the GALEN project [GALEN, 94] (version 5g, all ~2000 concepts).[3]

Other specialized corpora of medical terms have been conceptualized by the ONIONS methodology (e.g. surgical procedures [Rossi Mori, Gangemi, Steve, et al., 97]).

At state S_1 domain knowledge is represented by a list of valid expressions (P_1), which are meant to be conceptually plausible (O_1). Term lists compiled by experts and standard bodies, or extracted from free text, can be classified as such.

The next phases of ONIONS are designed to build and ontologize qualified interpretant fields (§1.) for such expressions.

A practical example of how qualified interpretant fields are retrieved and ontologized is followed in this overview. It concerns the interpretant field of *viral hepatitis type A*. Several terminology systems in our medical corpus contain interpretants to build a qualified interpretant field concerning *viral hepatitis type A*. We employ here only the UMLS system, which in its 'Metathesaurus' part (a collection of terminology systems) includes "viral hepatitis type A" from SNOMED-II, indicated as synonymous to "hepatitis A" from MeSH.

UMLS system includes the UMLS-SN, which has a hierarchical structure, includes "types" and "relations", and provides free-text definitions and template-like combinations of types and relations. It has a browser but does not allow to create new concepts. Its types are used as "categories" assigned to the UMLS Metathesaurus concepts, which comprise the MeSH thesaurus [NLM, 96] and other nomenclatures (SNOMED-II, ICD-9-CM, etc.).

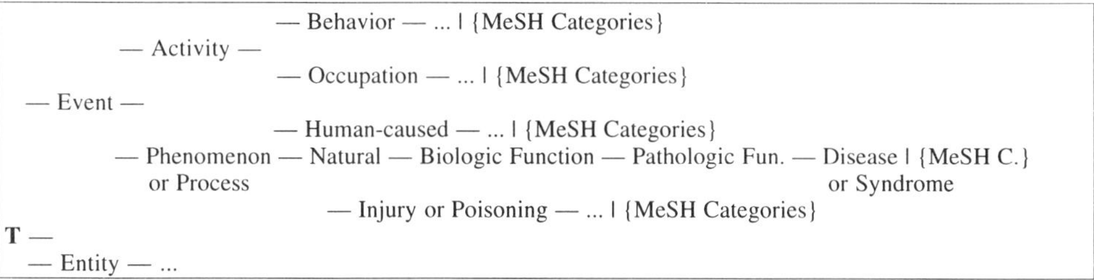

Frame 1: The UMLS (semantic network) taxonomic context for "Disease or Syndrome".

---

[3] For a description of the sources used in our experiment or quoted here: [Gangemi, Steve 96; Steve, Gangemi, 96].

2.3 Phase M_1: Taxonomic analysis

Phase M_1 aims at finding out the main taxonomic structure within term lists. At the beginning, we select the most relevant sets of expressions (*source expressions*).

Given a corpus, the taxonomy of expressions contained in each single source is inferred. The taxonomy is exploited to identify the top-level concepts in the source, and then top-level concepts are used to choose a depth limit (for example, in the medical ontology application, we chose to truncate the *body part* taxonomy — within the *vessel* branching — to kinds of vessel, not including instances of arteries, veins, etc.). Since our main scope was to integrate general medical terminologic knowledge, the most detailed taxa for anatomy were excluded. This seems to be sound to the extent that a specialized microdomain integration could be done in a further research (for example, an extension of the current medical ontology ON9 to *angiology*).

As far as our example is concerned, UMLS-SN makes some distinctions (*Frame 1*). In the Metathesaurus, *viral hepatitis type A* is classified as an instance of UMLS-SN "Disease or Syndrome". In fact, the "Phenomenon or Process" type hierarchy branching in UMLS-SN stops at "Disease or Syndrome". To find the actual taxonomic position of *viral hepatitis type A* we have to search down the UMLS Metathesaurus and look at the MeSH hierarchies and at the other taxonomies referred there (ICD9-CM, SNOMED-II, etc.). The result of such investigation is summarized in *Frame 2*.

<table>
<tr><td valign="top">

UMLS Semantic Network
Event [*see description in* frame 3]
•Phenomenon or process [*see description*]
••Natural phenomenon or process [*see description*]
•••Biologic function [*see description*]
••••Pathologic function [*see description*]
•••••Disease or syndrome [*see description*]
    (subsumes:
    1) MeSH "Virus diseases" hierarchies *entirely*,
    without linking to taxonomy
    2) ICD9-CM item: "Viral hepatitis A without
    mention of hepatic coma"
    3) SNOMED-II hierarchies *entirely*, without
    linking to taxonomy)

Entity [*see description*]
•Conceptual entity [*see description*]
••Finding [*see description*]
    (subsumes: 1) MeSH "Symptoms and general
         pathology" hierarchy
    2) ICD9-CM item: "Viral hepatitis A without
    mention of hepatic coma")

MeSH
Diseases
•Virus diseases [*see description*]
••Hepatitis, Viral, Human [*see description*]
•••Hepatitis A [*see description*]
•••RNA virus infections
••••Picornaviridae infections [*see description*]

</td><td valign="top">

•••••Enterovirus infections
•••••• ^Hepatitis A
••Digestive system diseases
•••Liver diseases
••••Hepatitis [*see description*]
•••••^Hepatitis A
•Symptoms and general pathology <NON-MeSH>
••Disease [*see description*] <NON-MeSH>

ICD9-CM
Diseases and injuries
•Diseases of the digestive system
••Other diseases of the digestive system
•••Other disorders of liver
••••Hepatitis
•Infectious and parasitic diseases
••Other diseases due to viruses and chlamidiae
•••Viral hepatitis
••••Viral hepatitis A without mention of hepatic coma

SNOMED-II
Disease Axis
•Infectious and communicable diseases
••Diseases caused by viruses
•••Viral hepatitis
••••Viral hepatitis, type A <D-0521>
•Diseases and syndromes of the digestive and urinary tract
••Diseases and syndromes of digestive system
•••Diseases and syndromes of liver and bile ducts
••••Disease of liver

</td></tr>
</table>

Frame 2: The UMLS (Metathesaurus) taxonomies involving the conceptualization of "viral hepatitis type A".

Therefore, at state S_2 the lists have an order induced by IS_A inclusions, namely, the lists are mono- or multi-hierarchical taxonomies (P_2), as shown in *Frame 2*. From an ontological perspective we could ask how many and which meta-classes further organize the taxonomies: in other words we assess which kind of taxonomy we have got (O_2). For example, the lists in *Frame 2* are all homogeneous taxonomies. Most 'classic' terminology systems (ICD10, SNOMED-II, GMN, etc.) can be classified as such.

2.4 Phase M_2: Local definitions analysis

Once a relevant set of concepts from each source is available, we focus on the criteria of classification, namely on the *local definitions* of concepts, in order to create a qualified interpretant field. We have to work out an answer to the "definitional" question: which is the difference within a group of homogeneous concepts from the same source, typically between two children-concepts of the same parent concept?

From a definitional viewpoint, concepts to be defined are "definienda", and defining concepts are "definientes". The problem is that very often sources have informal, or poor definitions, and sometimes they lack at all.

When definitions are lacking, we create a sound explicit definition, exploiting all hints that a terminology system can provide (hierarchy, grouping, free text definitions, boolean combinations, axioms, frames, meta-linguistic modifiers, etc.), as well as additional definitional sources (dictionaries, glossaries, encyclopaedias) and experts.

Additional texts are provided to explicitly construct the qualified interpretant fields of the sources. For instance, ON9 (§3.) exploited dictionaries [Dorland's, 94] [Stedman, 95] and expert physicians from partner institutions. We have also proposed a scale of explicitness for sources [Steve, Gangemi, 96] which is based on the availability of these hints.

Back to our guiding example, UMLS provides a fine environment for comparing various taxonomies from the same or different sources. Only, this environment does not provide explicit conceptualizations, except for a natural language description provided to all UMLS-SN types and to some MeSH items in the UMLS Metathesaurus. We should collect such natural language descriptions to get two results: 1) the explicitation of subsumption criteria and 2) the possible additional constraints that the terminology system has decided to include.

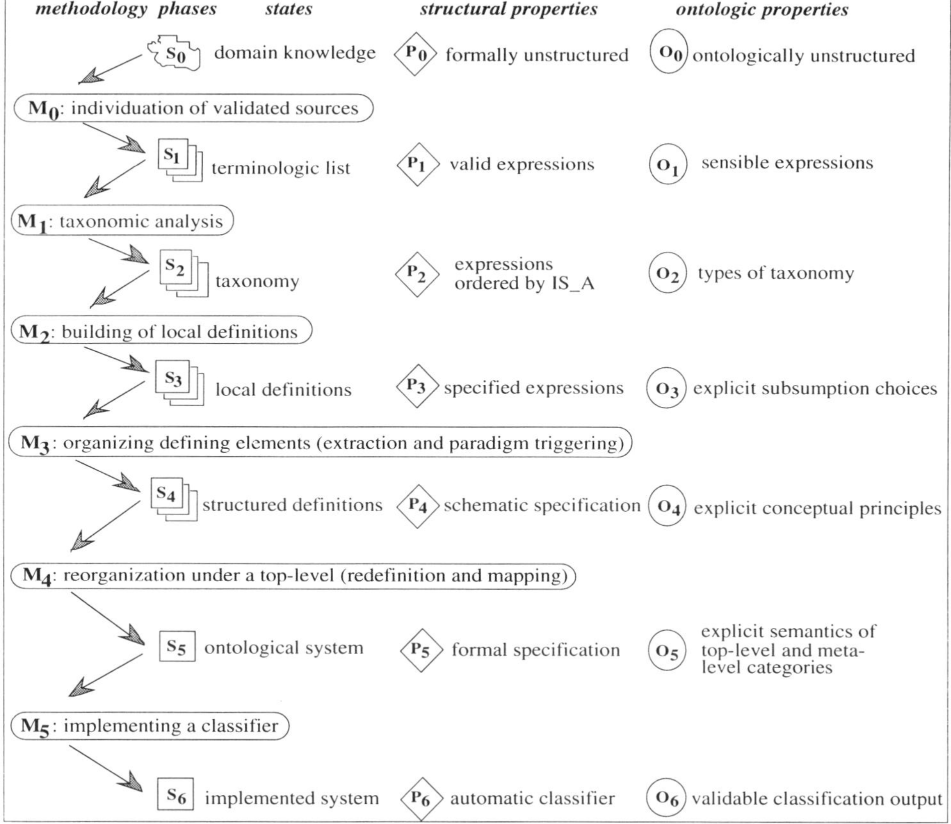

Figure 2. The phases of ONIONS. The output of any phase is a special state of a terminology system, described by both structural and ontological properties. Such states are independently re-usable for a specific purpose.

In *Frame 3* all the UMLS descriptions available for the concepts listed in *Frame 2* are presented. An analysis of such a collection (*Frames 2* and *3*) leads to the following issues:

- top-level concept descriptions are extensionally given, namely they do not provide subsumption criteria, e.g. "Event" is "*a broad type for grouping activities, processes and states*"
- many descriptions show lexical gaps. For example, "Pathologic Function" is described as "*a disordered process, activity or state*", while its child-concept "Disease or Syndrome" is "*a condition*", but "*condition*" is not a UMLS-SN concept: we are obliged to infer that a condition is "*a disordered process, activity or state*" as well. Another example is "*a broad type for grouping activities, processes and state*": neither "*activity*", "*process*", nor "*state*" are concepts in UMLS taxonomies. A more comprehensive example is the following: since "Hepatitis A" is an "Enterovirus Infection" (see taxonomy in *Frame 2*), which is subsumed by "Picornaviridae Infection", which is subsumed by "RNA Virus Infections", we can infer — with the help of additional expertise sources (experts, dictionaries, etc.) — that "Hepatovirus" in the description of "Hepatitis A" is actually the "Hepatitis Virus A", belonging to the genus "Enterovirus", family "Picornaviridae", order "RNA Virus", etc.

On the other hand, when filling gaps, we should not be tempted to overcommit: for example one might want to include a dictionary definition of "Picornaviridae" [Stedman's, 95]: "a family of very small ether resistant, nonenveloped viruses having a core of single-stranded RNA enclosed in a capsid of icosahedral symmetry with 32 capsomeres". In fact there is no hint that UMLS terminology system has a similar commitment, at least as far as "Hepatitis A" is concerned. If we want to activate the interpretant field of "Hepatitis Virus A", thus we should have to check what the real commitment is. By the way, we would discover that the UMLS commitment for "Picornaviridae" is limited to: "small RNA viruses comprising some important pathogenes of humans and animals". In other words, commitment depends on some variety of non-symbolic context. Non-symbolic contexts are the only guide in decisions concerning a detail level problem (see §1.).

---

original UMLS-SN type descriptions:

Event $\approx_{df}$ *a broad type for grouping activities, processes and states*

Phenomenon or Process $\approx_{df}$ *a process or state which occurs naturally or as a result of an activity*

Natural Ph. or Pr. $\approx_{df}$ *a phenomenon or process that occurs irrespective of the activities of human beings*

Biologic Function $\approx_{df}$ *a state, activity or process of the body or one of its systems or parts*

Pathologic Function $\approx_{df}$ *a disordered process, activity, or state of the organism as a whole, of a body system or systems, or of multiple organs or tissues. Included here are normal responses to a negative stimulus as well as pathololologic conditions or states that are less specific than a disease. Pathologic functions frequently have systemic effects*

Disease or Syndrome $\approx_{df}$ *a condition which alters or interferes with a normal process, state, or activity of an organism. It is usually characterized by the abnormal functioning of one or more of the host's systems, parts, or organs. Included here is a complex of symptoms descriptive of a disorder*

Entity $\approx_{df}$ *a physical or conceptual entity*

Conceptual Entity $\approx_{df}$ *a broad type for grouping abstract entities or concepts*

Finding $\approx_{df}$ *that which is discovered by direct observation or measurement of an organism attribute or condition, including the clinical history of the patient*

original MeSH categories descriptions:

Virus Diseases $\approx_{df}$ *diseases produced by viruses*

Hepatitis $\approx_{df}$ *infection of the liver and liver disorder involving degenerative or necrotic alterations of hepatocytes*

Hepatitis, Viral, Human $\approx_{df}$ *viral hepatitis in man*

Picornaviridae Infections $\approx_{df}$ *virus diseases caused by the picornaviridae*

Hepatitis A $\approx_{df}$ *hepatitis caused by hepatovirus. It can be transmitted through fecal contamination of food or water*

Frame 3: The available UMLS descriptions for the taxonomies in Frame 2.

- some descriptions include meta-linguistic constraints, eg " *Included here is a complex of symptoms descriptive of a disorder*", which signals that also syndromes are instances of "Disease or Syndrome";
- some descriptions have default or modal expressions, eg " *It is usually characterized by ...*";
- cxccpt for UMLS-SN and partly MeSII, taxonomies do not provide a description for each concept in the taxonomy;

• several viewpoints emerge from the taxonomies (see *frame 2*): "Hepatitis A" results to be subsumed in both the "Disease or Syndrome" and "Conceptual Entity" branchings, and in the "Disease or Syndrome" branch it results to be subsumed in both the "Hepatitis, Viral, Human", "RNA Virus Infections", and "Digestive System Diseases" branchings. This is a good feature indeed, since non-multihierarchical taxonomies of some terminology systems (SNOMED, ICD) preclude explicit different views of the same concept. On the other hand, the relationships between the subsumption criteria to different views are not given.

A merging process, which takes into account the taxonomical information and the descriptions we have shown, and applies gap filling and subsumption criteria to undescribed concepts, leads to a more compact description to *viral hepatitis type A* (*Frame 4*).

Typically, the merging process ignores extensional descriptions and meta-linguistic constraints, and produces some explicit viewpoints.

Once we consider only the characteristic description of *viral hepatitis type A* (the features not inherited from being a human liver disease, a morphology, and a finding), we can assess the "differentia specifica" of *viral hepatitis type A* within UMLS (*Frame 5*).

---

as human liver disease $\approx_{df}$ it alters or interferes with a normal phenomenon or process of a human organism, usually characterized by an abnormal functioning of the organism as a whole, of a body system or systems (the digestive system), or of multiple organs or tissues (the liver), and which occurs naturally

as aetiology $\approx_{df}$ caused by hepatovirus A, belonging to the genus Hepatovirus, family Picornaviridae, order RNA Virus

as morphology $\approx_{df}$ an infection of the liver involving degenerative or necrotic alterations of hepatocytes

as transmission $\approx_{df}$ it can be transmitted through fecal contamination of food or water

as finding $\approx_{df}$ an abstract entity which is discovered by direct observation or measurement of an organism feature, including the clinical history of the patient

---

Frame 4: A concise collection of the UMLS descriptions for the viewpoints to the concept "viral hepatitis type A".

---

viral hepatitis type A $\approx_{df}$ *"the disease of human liver involving a degenerative or necrotic alteration of hepatocytes; it is caused by hepatitis virus A and is transmitted by fecal contaminated food. It can be viewed as a morphology of liver as well as a finding"*

Frame 5: A concise paraphrase of the conceptual viewpoints in Frame 4.

Frame 5 provides an intuition of what is the minimal situated commitment of the UMLS sources for the QIF of *viral hepatitis type A*.

As the examples show, at state S_3 the taxonomies are coupled with free text descriptions of terms (P_3); conceptually, these definitions explicitate (O_3) taxonomic constraints (the so-called *differentia specifica*). Most dictionaries and glossaries in medicine are classifiable as S_3.

2.5   Phase M_3: Multi-local definition analysis: triggering paradigms   The methodological phase M_3 consists in 1) the schematization of the elements produced during the M_2 description, in order to provide some "weak" constraints, and in 2) the "triggering" of the conceptual principles (paradigms) which motivate the description.

This schematization can be performed through the construction of domain ontologies for the QIFs produced in phase M_2. Such domain ontologies do not require an axiomatization, but only a set of "templates". This amounts to say that elements ("fillers") used in the description of an expression have explicit relationships ("slots" or "roles") with the described term (the "frame"). In logical terms, a frame gives constraints on the domain and the range of the relations applicable in a certain context of knowledge. Ontologically, a frame should have explicit conceptual principles. For instance, a conceptual principle may concern *part-whole* relationships, another the *teleology* of processes, still others the *quantities*, the *topology* of objects, the *physical* properties, and so on. In other words, we should make a call for some valuable and practicable generic ontology.

The *viral hepatitis type A* description from M_2 (from *frame 5*) may be schematized by encoding it in some frame language with loose formal constraints. Here we create a local definition written in the Ontolingua "frame-ontology" [Gruber, 93]:

```
(in-theory 'o-umls)                                                          (1)

(define-class viral-hepatitis-a (?vh)                                        (2)
  "the disease of human liver causing a degenerative or necrotic alteration of
   hepatocytes; it is caused by hepatitis virus A and is transmitted by fecal
   contaminated food or water. It can be viewed as a morphology of liver as
   well as a finding"
  :axiom-def (and (subclass-of viral-hepatitis-a human-liver-disease)
                  (subclass-of viral-hepatitis-a finding)
                  (subclass-of viral-hepatitis-a morphology)
                  (caused-by viral-hepatitis-a hepatitis-virus-a)
                  (involves viral-hepatitis-a degenerative-alteration-of-hepatocytes)
                  (involves viral-hepatitis-a necrotic-alteration-of-hepatocytes)
                  (transmitted-by viral-hepatitis-a fecal-contaminated-food)
                  (transmitted-by viral-hepatitis-a fecal-contaminated-water)))
```

Constructs (1) and (2) say that in a theory named `o-umls`, the concept `viral-hepatitis-a` is subsumed by (inherits the constraints from) the concepts: `human-liver-disease`, `finding`, and `morphology`, and features five specific constraints (the syntax is: *template ::= slot frame filler*).

This is the schematization part: a minimal structure has been overimposed to the free text description by conjoining all the minimal constraints and unpacking the "or-expressions".

The complete account for the UMLS *viral hepatitis type A* QIF calls for constructs for all the concepts involved: `human-liver-disease`, `finding`, `morphology`, `hepatitis-virus-a`, `degenerative-alteration-of-hepatocytes`, etc. These, on their turn, would require other constructs for their respective QIFs, and so on.

For the ontological part, we have to trigger the paradigms which underly the specific constraints. Many routes can be taken at this point. Our reasoning steps included:

(a) since `_caused-by_`, `_involves_`, and `_transmitted-by_` all concern relationships between objects and processes, and since some valuable cognitive paradigms ("actantial" paradigms) claim for a uniform treatment of all relations involving some object carrying some process and the related dynamics, we make a call for some theory of actants;

(b) moreover, what allows to keep all these constraints together? how does a transmission of contaminated food concern alteration of hepatocytes? these leads to the recognition of the part-whole structure of the objects and processes involved; therefore, we make a call for some part-whole theory;

(c) the explicitation of part-whole structure requires an explicit reference to an organism in which such structure makes sense.

These reasoning steps are encoded as explicit calls for generic theories in the `:issues` field of an Ontolingua construct, which is added to the definition (2):

```
:issues ((:generic-theories  "_caused-by_, _involves_, and _transmitted-by_      (3)
          require a theory of actants and a paradigm of functions (natural
          processes)" "the patient status is not mentioned" "anatomy is not
          mentioned: at least, a part-whole theory is required")))
```

As an output of M_3, at state S_4 definitions are framed (P_4) and have explicit hooks to paradigms (O_4).

Few terminology systems have S_4 properties: the UMLS Semantic Network is one, the GRAIL models in the GALEN project are another example of S_4 (the GRAIL implementation also features an automatic classifier (P_6), see below phase M_5). At present, no terminology systems in medicine fulfil O_4. How to fulfil O_4 as well? For ONIONS-produced ontologies, we have developed a library of generic ontologies (see next phase and §3.).

2.6 Phase M_4: Building an integrated ontology library We have seen that for each source, local definitions have underlying paradigms (see §1.). Our purpose is the enrichment of local definitions by constructing domain ontologies which explicitly include other ontologies specifying such paradigms, for example [Sowa, 95] [Bateman, 90] [Hartmann, 66] [Simons, 87] and many others. Such an enrichment is not an arbitrary choice: it is made in order to connect heterogeneus local definitions by explicitating their paradigms (usually through the application of generic ontologies). Therefore it requires a minimal increase of commitment: only to the extent that we get the raising of definitions from the status of *local* to *multi-local*. Namely to the extent that we have constructed a library of domain and generic ontologies which contains (or allows the construction of) all the heterogenous definitions.

Since generic ontologies are not built with having in mind all their possible specifications in domain ontologies, phase M_4 comprises a lexical gap-filling process. Gap-filling is performed at M_2 to make local taxonomies complete, while in M_4 it is performed to raise the status of taxonomies to multi-local.

A "lexical gap" is better understood when two different languages are compared: for example, where English has *wood*, Italian has *legno* (as *matter*), *bosco* (as *aggregate of trees*), *foresta* (as *wide, heterogeneous aggregate of trees*). Not that English lacks the Italian ontology: it only does not let it emerge in the lexicon of words, in fact English is capable to paraphrase the three Italian meanings through multi-word noun phrases. But to paraphrase the Italian meanings, English needs the explicitation of the paradigms which guide the interpretation of the three meanings (a paradigm for *matter*, another for *parts and aggregates*, another for *heterogeneity*, another for *qualitative sizes*, etc.).

In terminology systems (in the same language), the phenomenon, though less evident, is the lexical correlate of conceptual heterogeneity: for any two formally equivalent expressions (for example, "viral hepatitis type A" in SNOMED and "hepatitis A" in MeSH), the interpretant fields are the same (they are 'synonymous'), but the qualified interpretant fields are different, because the two terminology systems explicitly encode only certain taxonomical constraints. In short, we could define an M_4 *lexical gap* as follows: «when we compare two allied (referrable to the same interpretant field) QIFs gathered from two different lexica, the absence in one QIF of a concept present in the other is a *lexical gap*».

Gap-filling is a finite, decidable work, thus the detail level problem (§1.) is not resurrected in the form: "how much comprehensive a generic ontology should be?". In the *wood* example, a generic ontology concerning parts and aggregates should contain all and only the definitions useful to integrate Italian and English, not a maximally comprehensive ontology.

On the other hand, it is not so easy finding pretty generic ontologies which are ready to be chunked each time for our special purpose of the moment. Above all, could we call such chunks a response to context-dependency? Well, there are two answers to this difficulty: the first is operative: chunking must be made attentively and explicitly; namely, if we want to buy a section of Nelson Goodman's mereology, we must refer explicitly this paradigm and the possible modifications we make. Also, we should include in our generic ontology inspired by that paradigm at least the most general concepts, in order to maintain a minimal soundness to the paradigm formalized in the generic ontology. The second answer is not a short term one: we envisage the creation of 'common good' data bases containing a huge amount of paradigms expressed as (formal) generic ontologies. In this ideal situation, the ontological engineer can buy a piece of a data base and provide the reference to that piece when creates its own ontology.

We summarize the methodological phase M_4 as follows:

(1) the construction (or the reuse, if available) of a library of generic ontologies to account for the `(:issues (:generic-theories))` requirements memorized during M_3 phase; this equals to build a well-grounded *top-level*;

(2) the enrichment of domain ontologies from M_3 phase. This requires the inclusion of the generic ontologies in the domain ontologies;

(3) the assignment of sound meta-level categories to the classes and relations in the library.

As far as the guiding example is concerned, *frame 3* gives us an informal description of the minimal UMLS commitment for *viral hepatitis type A*.

In phase M_3, with construct (3) we have also kept explicit track of the paradigms required to integrate the viewpoints present in *frame 3*. On the other hand, we still lack:

• a formal explicit conceptualization (an ontology) for each viewpoint in the *viral hepatitis type A* (UMLS) QIF;

• an explicit specification of the generic ontologies to be used to specify the QIF (to make it an Ontologized Field, cf. §1.) for *viral hepatitis type A* in the context of an ontology library.

Making an Ontologized Field of the above descriptions for *viral hepatitis type A* would be quite difficult if we had to start from scratch. Luckily, we can define it on the basis of the integrated ontologies already developed by applying ONIONS.

For example, in ON9 (see §3.), we can trace back `viral-hepatitis-type-a` to `viral-hepatitis`, `human-liver-disease`, `disease`, `pathologic-function`, `physiologic-function`, `biologic-function`, `function`, `process` (by the way, this backtracing is an extensive M_4 gap-filling). All these concepts are contained in explicit ontologies, thus `viral-hepatitis-type-a` is automatically inserted in a wide network of ontologized fields (the ON9 ontology library). Consequently, in the multi-local definition (4) only the specific constraints (the "differentia specifica") are listed:

```
(define-class viral-hepatitis-a (?vh)                                          (4)
  "the disease of human liver causing a degenerative or necrotic alteration of
   hepatocytes; it is caused by hepatitis virus A and is transmitted by fecal
   contaminated food or water. It can be viewed as a morphology of liver as
   well as a finding"
 :axiom-def (and (subclass-of viral-hepatitis-a viral-hepatitis)
                 (subclass-of viral-hepatitis-a finding)
                 (!type viral-hepatitis-a ))
 :def (exists (?liv ?pat ?vir ?vec ?pro ?hep ?inf)
              (and (liver ?liv) (*patient ?pat)
                   (part ?liv ?pat) (is-embodied-in ?vh ?liv)
                   (virus-a ?vir) (has-a-cause ?vh ?vir)
                   (or (fecal-contaminated-food ?vec) (fecal-contaminated-water ?vec))
                   (contains ?vec ?vir) (trasmitted-through ?vh ?vec)
                   (or (degeneration-process ?pro) (necrotic-process ?pro))
                   (induces ?vh ?pro)
                   (hepatocyte ?hep) (plurality ?hep) (element ?hep ?liv)
                   (is-embodied-in ?pro ?hep)
                   (inflammation ?inf) (is-morphology-of ?inf ?liv)
                   (is-a-cause-of ?pro ?inf)))))
```

(4) differs deeply from (2). Firstly, the frame definition in (2) is become an axiomatization:
• subclass declarations have been maintained, but with updated subsumptions;
• a !type meta-level assignment has been added (see §4.);
• the existentially quantified first-order sentence gives a clear focus to the vague templates in (2);
• in particular, the compact expressions of (2) have been expanded into well-connected assertions; e.g., `degenerative-alteration-of-hepatocytes` is expanded according to the minimal commitment of ON9: it is now a `degeneration-process` which `is-embodied-in` a `plurality` of `hepatocytes` which are explicitly `element` of any `liver` which `embodies` a `viral-hepatitis-a`. The morphological meaning of `degenerative-alteration-of-hepatocytes` is encoded in the last three conjuncts.

These features are the result of the application of a more formal language as well as they originate from the inclusion of the generic ontologies called for in (3). For example:
• from theory: actants[4] we used the relations: `is-embodied-in`, `has-a-cause`, `induces`. The axiomatizations in theory: actants mainly rely on results obtained in cognitive science, linguistics and narratology investigations [Miller, Johnson-Laird, 76], [Prince, 82], [Fillmore, 71];
• from theory: epidemiology (dependent on theory: actants), we used the relation `trasmitted-through`, which is axiomatized with respect to the object which has the capability of conveying a pathogenic agent to the organism;
• from theory: meronymy[5] we used the relations: `part` and `element`, that, with `plurality` (from theory: quantities), allow to model `hepatocytes`, which are (a plurality of) elements of the liver;

As an output of M_4, at state S_5 definitions are axiomatized (P_5); ontologically, definitions have an *explicit semantics* (O_5) of both the *top-level concepts* (the concepts provided by generic ontologies) and of the *meta-level categories* (the concepts in a representation ontology, §4.).

In Fig. 2 only one system is in the state S_5 (only one square frame), in order to represent that it can integrate the previous ones. Of course, we can get different integrated systems according to the particular generic ontologies that one decides to include or use.

---

[4] see the WWW site; http://saussure.irmkant.rm.cnr.it/HOME/ON9/actants/index.html.
[5] see the WWW site: http://saussure.irmkant.rm.cnr.it/HOME/ON9/meronymy/index.html

2.7 Phase M₅: Classifying the library The methodological phase M_5 consists in the implementation of a domain ontology in a system which allows automatic classification. Obviously, the generated classification should pass a validation control.

At state S_6, a domain ontology is implemented in an automatic classifier (P_6), e.g. Loom [Mac Gregor, 94]. Some terminology systems are currently implemented with an automatic classifier, for example the GALEN Core Model. Our method is to export a library of ontologies from the Ontolingua [Gruber, 93] or OCML [Motta, 95] form into Loom and to make Loom classify the library (e.g., see the translation of (4) in the following (5):

```
(defconcept viral-hepatitis-a :is-primitive                                      (5)
    (:and finding viral-hepatitis
     (:some is-embodied-in (:and liver (:some part *patient)))
     (:some has-a-cause virus-a)
     (:some transmitted-through
      (:and (:or fecal-contaminated-food fecal-contaminated-water)
       (:some contains virus-a)))
     (:some induces
      (:and (:or degeneration-process necrotic-process)
       (:some is-embodied-in (:and hepatocyte plurality (:some element liver)))
       (:some is-a-cause-of (:and inflammation (:some is-morphology-of liver)))))))
```

WWW-available, collaborative modelling tools are currently exploited to support phases M_4 and M_5, and to manage the byproducts of the earlier phases [Gangemi, 97].

3. The ON9 ontology library

ON9 is a library of ontologies designed by means of the ONIONS methodology (some part of it is available at: http://saussure.irmkant.rm.cnr.it/HOME/ON9/index.html).

ON9 has been defined as the multi-local integration of a corpus of medical sources (§2.2). It includes a detailed representation ontology and it is written in Ontolingua. It has been translated to Loom and it will be soon available through the Ontosaurus HTTP interface [Swartout, Patil, Knight, Russ, 96]. Its top-level thus governs a large set of representation, general and domain ontologies. It can be summarized by the tuple:

$$< s , p , c , r >$$

$s \in S$: the domain of *object sorts*: static, atemporal entities;

$p \in P$: the domain of *process sorts*: kinematic, temporal entities;

$c \in C$: the domain of possible *context sorts* arising as complements of the sum of other intensional entities: regions, domains, time spans, situations, texts;

$r \in R$: the set of intensional *structuring concepts* (the dimensions which give structure to the

concepts in an Interpretant Field): $\bigcup (Ar, As, Sc, Ph, La)$ where:

- Ar is the set of *Actantial roles*: it includes relations such as 'agent', 'patient', 'instrument', 'goal', 'cause', etc. This should map the notions of 'scene', 'verb frame', 'script', etc. from Fillmore, Schank, Lagendoen, etc. Such structuring concepts are useful in the definition of contexts and meta-level categories (§4.);
- As is the set of *Assessment: relations,* it includes concepts of 'assessment' or 'judging', such as typicality, conventionality, relevance, representation. Such concepts deserve a deeper understanding, for example in terms of more basic cognitive properties;
- Sc is the set of *Schematic relations* of space, time, quantity, etc. (governed by a cognitive schema: such schemata can be taken as 'forms of the intuition', in a kantian fashion, as well as 'a-priori forms of perception', as gestalt psychology proposes). This set is rich: for example spatial ontologies comprise mereological, topological, locative relations;
- Ph is the set of *relations expressing Physical (substantial) concepts*, such as matter features, morphologies, physical states and dimensions, etc.
- La is the set of *ontological Layers*: the realms in which the continuum of the human knowledge about reality can be segmented (material, biologic, psychologic, social,

abstract). This set includes granularities as well: molar, molecular, atomic, sub-atomic, etc. (cf. §1.). This is the primary dimension for defining objects.

We could also consider a variable $m \in M$: the set of Meta-level categories, namely the concepts which mediate between the formal and conceptual properties of an ontology. While previous concepts and relations are usually defined within generic ontologies, meta-level categories are defined in representation ontologies, sometimes called 'metaontologies' (see §Introd. and §4.).

Figure 3 shows an inclusion lattice of some ON9 ontologies: the representation ontologies provided by default in Ontolingua are "frame-ontology" and the set of "kif-ontologies". We defined the ontologies: "structuring-concepts", "meta-level-concepts" and "semantic-field-ontology", to link the representation ontologies with the generic ontology library. The sets of "structural ontologies" and of "structuring ontologies" contain generic ontologies. Generic ontologies are variously included in domain ontologies. In particular, the integrated-medical-ontology includes all the generic ontologies which have been used to integrate the terminological ontologies of the five terminology systems.

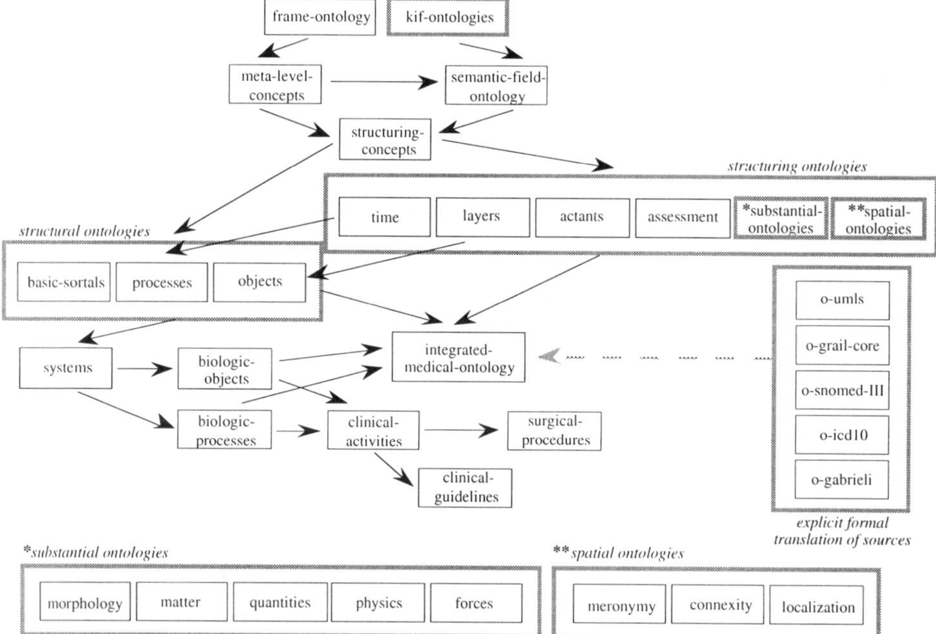

Figure 3. A significant subset of the inclusion lattice of the ON9 library of ontologies. Ontologies are represented by black circles. Thick grey frames or circles are sets of ontologies (some explictly show the elements). The semantics of black arrows is *included-in* (applied according to a system constraints, for example Ontolingua inclusion is looser than Loom's). The dashed grey arrow means *integrated-in* .

The analysis perfomed to build our ON9 ontology library allowed us to explicitly formalize important interpretant fields which have heterogeneous conceptualizations in the sources described in §2.2, for example:
* disease as *pathological function* or as *outcome of an inferential process*, and diagnosis as inferential process or as *outcome of an inferential process*. For example, SNOMED or ICD identify disease and diagnostic outcome, because they are oriented to statistics, records and reports. UMLS-SN is oriented towards scientific knowledge, and disease is considered a pathologic function, while diagnosis is an inferential process; SNOMED or ICD diseases have to be mapped here as diagnostic outcomes.
* morphology as *form* vs. *outcome of a function* vs. *structure in a given condition*, in particular when a structure is the outcome of a surgical procedure or a pathological process;
* regions, spaces, holes as *conceptual arrangements of structures* (e.g. in UMLS-SN) vs. *structures* themselves (*immaterial objects*).

4. Metaontological issues

We have reused terminology systems, also assuming that they contain the *basic concepts* of a domain [Steve et al., 96] [Rosch et al., 78] [Lakoff, 90].

The basic concepts and gap-fillers (cf. §2.2.5) in the resulting ontology library are called the *structural concepts*, while the concepts which provide the relational structure are called the *structuring concepts*, mostly coming from the paradigmatic sources.

If an order-sorted logic is adopted, we suggest to represent structural concepts with *sorts* and structuring concepts with *relations* of various arity.

If a more refined meta-ontology is wanted, one should look for a theory specifying a representation ontology (cf. §Introduction). There is no general agreement on the necessity of a detailed representation ontology; we suggest that it should be part of an ontology library, but should not be implemented in a formal language. In other words, we want to be free to use a fomal language with a minimal meta-level commitment, but we also want the capability of assigning Meta-Level Categories (MLC) to concepts (independently from the formal language used). A MLC (such as slot, concept, sort, relation, etc.) is a predicate which assigns a precise semantics to a (object-level) predicate.

In the following we summarize some issues in the design of MLC.

Guarino and co-workers [Guarino, Carrara, Giaretta, 94] introduce some MLC for unary predicates on the basis of some criteria (*Tab. 1*):

* *type, quality, indep-role* and *dep-role* are *sortal* (countable) unary predicates: for example, *book* is countable because a part of an instance of book is not a book (compare to *object*); *roles* must be subordinated to some *type/kind*;
* *category* and *mass-like* are *pseudo-sortal* unary predicates: these are stable and rigid (an instance of such a predicate is always an instance of it, but it is uncountable;
* *property* and *state* are *non-sortal* unary predicates: these are uncountable and non-rigid (predications are not necessary);

M L C	countable	temporally stable	ontologically rigid	independent from another predicate	*Examples*
TYPE/KIND	Y	Y	Y	Y	apple, person
QUALITY	Y	Y	Y	N	color, length
INDEP-ROLE	Y	Y	N	Y	fat-person
DEP-ROLE	Y	Y	N	N	son, student
CATEGORY	N	Y	Y	Y	event, object
MASS-LIKE	N	Y	Y	Y	gold, sand
PROPERTY	N	Y	N	Y	red, great
STATE	N	N	N	Y	studies, closed

Table 1: A set of meta-level categories for unary predicates (adaptation from [Guarino, 92] [Guarino et al, 94]).

Criteria for MLC definition of unary (and binary) predicates have been formalized in a modal logic in [Guarino, 92] [Guarino, Boldrin, 93]; for a summary, [Steve et al., 96].

4.1 ON9 meta-ontological commitment

Our *sorts* divide into *types, categories,* and *reified properties*, which roughly map to Guarino's *sortal* predicates. Our *reified properties* map to Guarino's *roles*, which is non-rigid, say it is an accidental specification of a type. From a converse path, we defined types as motivated by validated basicality in a domain, and our *reified properties* are thus non-basic, although from a local viewpoint.

The uncountable topmost layers of ON9 are the *categories*. A cognitive counterpart of countability is the basicality prototype for common language (for criteria, see [Steve, Gangemi, 96]). In particular, categories are less reidentifiable than types: what's the mental image for "object", or "process"? On the other hand, categories seem to be highly schematizable: imagine a simple diagram for "process" (eg, a path) or "object" (eg, a configuration).

Among reified properties, we can follow the dependent/independent distinction. Its cognitively-based counterpart can be *actantiality*, the property of being able to take a special part in a situation change: agent, patient, instrument, goal, cause, etc. The special status of these categories has been acknowledged in ancient grammars ("complements"), in recent frame grammar ("cases"), in narratology, etc.

Meta Level Categories			basic	field structuring	one, image	accessible schema	actantial	*Examples*
SORT	TYPE		++	—	+	—	context-dep	liver, disease
	CATEGORY		+	—	—	+	context-dep	activity, object
	REIFIED PROPER -TY	SUBSTANTIV -ATE	—	—	—	—	—	integral-structure
		ROLE	—	—	—	—	+	aetiologic agent
PROPERTY			+	+	—	+	not applied	integral, red
RELATION			+	+	—	+	not applied	part, at right of

Tab. 2: The (cognitive) ontological commitment of meta-level categories in ON9 representation ontology.

Thus, a dependent role is called in this perspective a *role* tout court, which also corresponds to common sense, while an independent role is called a *substantivate*, to stress that it actually is the sortal (nominal) counterpart of a relational (adjectival, property-like) application.*Tab. 2* summarizes the current ON9 representation ontology (formal definitions are retrievable at http://saussure.irmkant.rm.cnr.it/HOME/ON9/metaontology/index.html).

Conclusions

As a result of our experience in developing medical terminological ontologies through ONIONS, we can conclude that:

(a) as far as validity is concerned, ONIONS methodology appears to be suitable in creating as well as in integrating, updating, extending and maintaining ontologies; however, we need more feedbacks from other users. We hope to get it from current cooperative modeling experiments.

At present, use and integration of ON9 are negotiated or customized on the WWW (through some dedicated tools, cf. [Gangemi et al., 97]).

(b) as far as conceptual integration of terminologies is concerned, ONIONS may support:
• conceptual explicitness and formal upgrading of terminology systems: term classification and definitions are available in a common, expressive formal language;
• mappings to other terminology systems: local term definitions are constructable, even though the source does not include them explicitly;
• conceptual upgrading of terminology systems: term classification and definitions are translated such that they can be included in an ontology library which has a subset constituted of motivated generic ontologies.

(c) as far as reuse and maintenance are concerned, ONIONS may support:
• a motivated generic ontology library, from the integration of generic and domain sources;
• specialized domain ontologies which use some subset of ontologies from the ontology library;
• a refinement of the ontology library through the integration of other generic and domain sources: an integrated medical ontology.

(d) as far as implementation is concerned: representing and situating a terminological ontology requires complex formal specifications involving first-order sentences, some second-order sentences about situation and contextual change, pervasive existential quantification, definition of meta-level categories of the representation language, etc. Our experience suggests that Ontolingua, OCML, and Loom are fitting to these purposes.

(e) as far as representation ontology is concerned, our medical ontology has been built and modeled without any a-priori formal constraint on ontological commitment, through a methodology finalized to knowledge integration. A-posteriori we analyzed it through the ontological commitment costraints proposed by Guarino; the analysis showed that to a great extent those requirements are satisfied in our medical ontology. As the requirements were not widely fulfilled in the sources, this outcome suggests as plausible that one could find out a theory of equivalence between methodological assumptions on integration and a settlement of costraints on MLC commitment.

The necessity of extensive off-line human intervention in the search, choice, and formalization of generic ontologies seems to be an unavoidable bottleneck in ONIONS ontology construction. An appealing alternative would be to adopt a systemic approach in the generic library, which is widely shared and formally available. Our analysis evidentiates that system theory, widely used in engineering domains (the usual configuration of component-state-event-process), does not fit well enough to the medical domain. The basic principles motivating the conceptualization of terminology in medical domains seem to refer also to other fields, often non formalized, such as linguistics, philosophy, and cognitive science.

Acknowledgements

We thank the anonymous referees and Nicola Guarino for their useful suggestions. This work has been partly funded by the Italian National Research Council project SOLMC (Ontologic and Linguistic Tools for Conceptual Modeling).

References

Bateman JA. The Theoretical Status of Ontologies in Natural Language Processing. Report cmg-lg/9704010

Borgo S, Guarino N, Masolo C. Stratified Ontologies: The Case of Physical Objects. in Vet (ed.) *Proceedings of ECAI96 Workshop: Ontological Engineering* (1996).

Borst P, Akkermans H, Top J. Engineering Ontologies. *Int. Journal of Human-Computer Studies*, 46 (1997).

Brachman R, McGuinness DL, Patel-Schneider PF, et al. Living with Classic. in JF Sowa (ed.): Principles of Semantic Networks, San Mateo, CA, M Kaufmann (1991).

CEN prENV 12264:1995. Medical Informatics - Categorial structure of systems of concepts - Model for representation of semantics. Brussels: CEN (1995).

Cohn AG, Randell DA, Cui Z. Taxonomies of Logically Defined Qualitative Spatial Relations. *International Journal of Human-Computer Studies*, 43 (1996).

Coté RA, Rothwell DJ, Brochu L (eds). SNOMED International, 3rd ed., 4 vols. Northfield, Ill: College of American Pathologists (1994).

Davidson D. A Nice Derangement of Epitaphs. in R Grandy, R Warner (edd): Philosophical Grounds of Rationality: Intentions, Categories, Ends. Oxford, Clarendon Press (1986).

Eco U. Semiotica e filosofia del linguaggio. Torino, Einaudi (1984).

EPISTOL Core Group. Knowledge Processing for Decision Support in the Health Sector. in Barahona P & Christensen JP (eds.): Knowledge and Decisions in Health Telematics, IOS Press (1994).

Evans DA, Cimino JJ, Huff SM, Bell DS for the CANON Group. Toward a Medical-Concept Representation Language. *Journal of the American Medical Informatics Association* 1:207-17 (1994).

Falasconi S, Stefanelli M. A Library of Medical Ontologies. in Workshop on Comparison of Implemented Ontologies, ECAI 94 (1994).

Falasconi S, Lanzola G, Stefanelli M. Using Ontologies in Multi-Agent Systems. in B Gaines, M Musen (eds), *Proceedings of KAW96* (1996).

Fankhauser P, Kracker M, Neuhold E. Semantic vs. Structural Resemblance of Classes. Special issue: Semantic Issues in Multidatabase Systems, SIGMOD RECORD, Vol. 20, No. 4, December, pp. 59-63 (1991).

Fillmore CJ. Types of Lexical Information. DD Steinberg, LA Jakobovits (eds): Semantics: an Interdisciplinary Reader in Philosophy, Linguistics and Psychology, Cambridge UP (1971).

Gabrieli E. A New Electronic Medical Nomenclature. *Journal of Medical Systems*; 3 (1989).

GALEN Project. Documentation available from the main contractor Rector AL, Medical Informatics Group, Dept. Computer Science, Univ. Manchester, Manchester M13 9 PL, UK, (1992-1994).

Gangemi A, Steve G, Giacomelli F. ONIONS: An Ontological Methodology for Taxonomic Knowledge Integration. in Vet (ed.) *Proceedings of ECAI96 Workshop: Ontological Engineering* (1996).

Gangemi A, Steve G, Pisanelli DM, Giacomelli F. WWW Tools for Ontology Negotiation. CNR-ITBM-RIM Technical Report 0497B (1997).

Genesereth MR, Nilsson NJ. Logical Foundations of Artificial Intelligence. Kauffman, Los Altos (1987).

Gennari JH, Tu SW, Rothenfluh TE, Musen M. Mapping Domains to Methods in Support of Reuse. *International Journalm of Human-Computer Studies*, 41, 399-424 (1994).

Gerstl P, Pribbenow S. Midwinters, Endgames, and Body Parts: A Classification of Part-Whole Relations. *International Journal of Human-Computer Studies*, 43 (1996).

Gruber T. A Translation Approach to Portable Ontology Specifications. *Knowledge Acquisition*; 5 (1993).

Guarino, N. Concepts, Attributes and Arbitrary Relations: Some Linguistic and Ontological Criteria for Structuring Knowledge Bases. *Data & Knowledge Engineering*, 8: 249-261 (1992).

Guarino N, Boldrin L - Concepts and Relations - in Guarino N, Poli R: *Pre-Proceedings of the International Workshop on Formal Ontology*, Ladseb, Padova 1-17 (1993).

Guarino, N., Carrara, M., and Giaretta, P. An Ontology of Meta-Level Categories. In J. Doyle, E. Sandewall and P. Torasso (eds.), *Principles of Knowledge Representation and Reasoning: Proceedings of the Fourth International Conference (KR94)*. Kaufmann, San Mateo (1994).

Guarino N. Formal Ontology, Conceptual Analysis and Knowledge Representation. In N Guarino & R Poli (eds.) Formal Ontology in Conceptual Analysis and Knowledge Representation, special issue of *International Journal of Human-Computer Studies*, 43 (1995).

Haimowitz IJ, Patil RS, Szolovits P. Representing Medical Knowledge in a Terminological Language is Difficult. in Greenes RA (ed.): Proc. of the Twelfth SCAMC. Los Angeles, IEEE Computer Society (1988).

Harnad S. The Symbol Grounding Problem. *Physica D*, 42 (1990).

Hartmann N. Zur Grundlegung der Ontologie. Berlin, de Gruyter, (1966).

Humphreys BL, Lindberg DA.The Unified Medical Language System Project. in Lun KC et al. (eds.) MEDINFO 92. Amsterdam: Elsevier Science Publishers (1992).

Kuhn, T. The Structure of Scientific Revolutions. Cambridge Press (1962).

Lakoff, G. The Invariance Hypothesis: is Abstract Reason Based on Image Schemas? *Cognitive Linguistics*, 1 (1990).

Langacker, RW. Concept, Image, and Symbol. The Cognitive Basis of Grammar - Berlin, De Gruyter (1991).

Laresgoiti I, Anjewierden A, Bernaras A, et al. Ontologies as Vehicles for Reuse: a mini-experiment. in B Gaines, M Musen (eds), *Proceedings of KAW96* (1996)

Lenat DB, Guha RV. Building Large Knowledge-based Systems: Representation and Inference in the CYC Project. Menlo Park, Addison-Wesley (1990).

Mac Gregor RM. A Description Classifier for the Predicate Calculus. in *Proceedings of the Twelfth National Conference on Artificial Intelligence, (AAAI 94)* (1994).

Marjomaa E. Different Senses of 'Relevance' in Information Modelling. in H Kangassalo et al. (edd.): Information Modelling and Knowledge Bases, IV. Amsterdam, IOS Press (1993).

Martil R, Turner T, Terpstra P. Knowledge Reuse in Technical Domains: The KACTUS Project. in *Proc. of The Impact of Ontologies on Reuse, Interoperability and Distributed Processing*, Unicom Seminar London (1995)

McCarthy J, Buvac S. Formalizing Context. Stanford Un. Tech. Note STAN-CS-TN-94-13 (1994).

McGuire JG, Kuokka DR, Weber JC et al. SHADE: Technology for Knowledge-Based Collaborative Engineering. *Journal of Concurrent Engineering*, 1 (1993).

Menzies T. Assessing Responses to Situated Cognition. In B. Gaines, M Musen (eds.): *Proceedings of the Conference KAW96, Track on Sharable and Reusable Ontologies* (1996).

Miller GA, Johnson-Laird PN. Language and Perception. Cambridge UP (1976).

Motta E. KBS Modeling in OCML. Modeling Languages for KBS, VU Amsterdam (1995).

Musen M. Dimensions of Knowledge Sharing and Reuse. *Computers and Biomedical Research*; 25 (1992).

Neches R et al. Enabling Technology for Knowledge Sharing. *AI Magazine*; fall:35-56 (1991).

National Library of Medicine. MeSH Medical Subject Headings. Bethesda Maryland: NLM (1996 edition)

Owsnicki-Klewe B. A General Characterization of Term Description Languages. in Bläsius KH & al. (eds.): Sorts and Types in Artificial Intelligence, Springer Verlag, (1989).

Patel-Schneider PF, Swartout B. Draft of the Description Logic Specification from the KRSS group of the DARPA Knowledge Sharing Effort (1993).

Peirce, Charles Saunders. On Signs and the Categories. In I fondamenti della semiotica cognitiva. Torino (1980).

Petitot, J, Smith, B, New Foundations for Qualitative Physics - in JE Tiles, GJ McKee, GC Dean (eds): Evolving Knowledge in Natural Science and Artificial Intelligence, London, Pitman (1991).

Prince G. Narratology. De Gruyter, Berlin (1982).

Rector A, Gangemi A, Galeazzi E, Glowinski A, et al. The GALEN CORE Model Schemata for Anatomy: Towards a Re-Usable Application-Independent Model of Medical Concepts. in Proc. of MIE94 (1994).

Rosch, E, Mervis CB , Gray WD, Johnson DM, Boyes-Braem P. Basic Objects in Natural Categories, *Cognitive Psychology* 8, pp 382-439 (1976).

Rossi Mori A, Gangemi A, Steve G, et al. An Ontological Analysis of Surgical Deeds. in *Proc. of Artificial Intelligence in Europe, AIME97*, (1997).

de Saussure, F. Cours de linguistique générale. Payot, Lausanne (1906/11) Italian Tr., Bari, Laterza (1970).

Simons, P. Parts: a Study in Ontology. Clarendon Press, Oxford (1987).

Sowa JF. Top-Level Ontological Categories. In N Guarino & R Poli (eds.) Formal Ontology in Conceptual Analysis and Knowledge Representation, *International Journal of Human-Computer Studies*, 43 (1995).

Stedman DL. Stedman's Medical Dictionary. Baltimore, Williams & Wilkins (1995).

Steve G, Gangemi A. Ontological Commitment for Medical Ontologies Reuse in the ONIONS Methodology. In B. Gaines, M Musen (eds.): *Proceedings of KAW96, Track on Sharable and Reusable Ontologies* (1996).

Steve G, Gangemi A. Some Theses on Ontological Engineering in the Context of ONIONS Methodology. in A Farquhar (ed.) *AAAI97 Spring Symposium on Ontological Engineering* (1997).

Sujansky W, Altman R. Bridging the Representational Heterogeneity of Clinical Databases. Stanford University Knowledge Systems Laboratory Report KSL-94-07 (1994).

Swartout B, Patil R, Knight K, Russ T. Toward Distributed Use of Large-Scale Ontologies. in B Gaines, M Musen (eds), *Proceedings of KAW96 (Knowledge Acquisition Workshop)* (1996).

Talmy L. The Cognitive Culture System. *The Monist*, 78 (1995).

Tate A. Towards a Plan Ontology. *Journal of the Italian AI Association* (1996)

Uschold M, King M. Towards a Methodology for Building Ontologies. *IJCAI95 Workshop on Basic Ontological Issues in Knowledge Sharing* (1995).

Valente A, Breuker J. Towards Principled Core Ontologies. in Gaines, Musen (eds), *Proc. of KAW96* (1996)

van Heijst G, Schreiber ATh, Wielinga BG. Using Explicit Ontologies in KBS Development. *International Journal of Human-Computer Studies*, (1997)

Varzi A. Le strutture dell'ordinario. in Logos, teorie dell'essere, teorie della norma, Milano, Giuffre' (1996).

WHO. International Classification of Diseases 10th revision. Geneva: WHO (1994).

Information Modelling and Knowledge Bases IX
P.-J. Charrel et al. (Eds.)
1998, IOS Press

Querying Heterogeneous and Distributed Data Repositories Using Ontologies

Alfredo Goñi[1]   Eduardo Mena[2,*]   Arantza Illarramendi[2]

[1]*Departamento de Informática e Ingeniería de Sistemas. Universidad de Zaragoza.*
María de Luna, 3. 50015 Zaragoza, Spain.
[2]*Facultad de Informática. Universidad del País Vasco (UPV/EHU)*
Apdo. 649, 20080 Donostia-San Sebastián. Spain.
http://siul02.si.ehu.es/~jirgbdat

Abstract. The facility that allows users to query heterogeneous and distributed data repositories the majority of users. Moreover, that facility should hide all the intrinsic problems related to the context such as location, organization/structure, query language and semantics of the data in various repositories. In this paper a query processing strategy that focuses on information content is presented. For that, domain specific ontologies that capture the information content of data repositories are used. Those ontologies are described using a system based on Description Logics. It is also explained the different steps followed to provide incremental answers to user queries navigating across ontologies, using pre-defined semantic interontology relationships. Description Logics systems capabilities are exploited to optimize queries and guide the query processing.

1. Introduction

On the global information infrastructure, the great expansion of the communication networks has made available to the users a huge number of heterogeneous and autonomous data repositories. However, these repositories present different structures/organizations, query languages and data semantics, making very difficult for the users to access the data stored on them.

A possible solution to lighten the problem of lack of uniformity when dealing with the available repositories consists on defining new information retrieval techniques with a strategy that focuses on information content and semantics. We propose to describe the content of the repositories by ontologies [14]. We make available to users several domain specific ontologies from which they can construct queries. Ontologies give a concise and declarative description of semantic information independent of the underlying syntactic representation of the data. This information can be used to determine the relevance of the underlying data without actually accessing the data, thus enabling scalable query processing. Domain ontologies can also be used to capture new and different world views, thus enabling wider accessibility of data.

---

*This work was supported by a grant of the Basque Country Government.

In our proposal, ontologies are described using a system based on Description Logics (DL). Moreover, terms from those ontologies are linked to the underlying repositories through mapping informations that are expressed using the extended relational algebra. Reasoning mechanisms from DL are useful to perform query optimization and, in particular, semantic and caching optimization. DL systems are also appropriated to offer intensional answers to the users [12]. Mapping descriptions play a key role in encapsulating the heterogeneity due to different formats and organization of the data in the various repositories. They act as an intermediary language between the DL expressions and the query languages of the local repositories.

In the proposed framework of loosely-coupled ontologies, the query processor takes as input a user query expressed in Description Logics, using terms from a chosen ontology, and tries to find the answer in the underlying data repositories. When a full answer cannot be obtained because the data are spread over several repositories under different ontologies, then the system navigates other component ontologies (until the user is satisfied with the answer) of the global information infrastructure translating terms in the user query into the "language" of component ontologies. This determines the relevant data repositories under the component ontologies providing a solution for the resource discovery problem [20].

In the literature different approaches for query processing in global information systems can be found. However, they mainly can be classified into three groups: syntactic keyword-based approaches (e.g. [2, 15, 16]), operational approaches based on Mediators (e.g. [8]), and approaches that use semantically rich views (expressed using Object Oriented models or Knowledge Representation Systems) describing data sources, either a global view (e.g. Carnot project [9], Information Manifold project [17], Cooperative Information System [10]) or several views (e.g. [3, 22]).

Our approach is representative of the works that use several views; in particular we deal with several domain specific ontologies. Our contribution is that we tackle the vocabulary sharing problem by using translations of a user query constructed from concepts in one domain ontology to other domain ontologies in the system. We also consider the cases where there is loss of information and use well established metrics like *precision* and *recall* to measure this loss. However we do not study the problem of building the ontologies as they do in [21].

The main goal of this paper is the presentation of the defined query processing strategy that:

1. allows one querying heterogeneous and distributed data repositories in a smart way focusing on information content,

2. provides incremental answers in two different ways: extensional and intensional,

3. gives a measure of a loss of information for extensional answers when it corresponds, and

4. takes advantage of the capabilities provided by DL systems.

In the rest of the paper we present first the global framework, then the main steps followed when accessing data underlying an ontology. Next, the process of enriching the answer by managing other ontologies, and last we conclude with some details about the prototype that has been implemented.

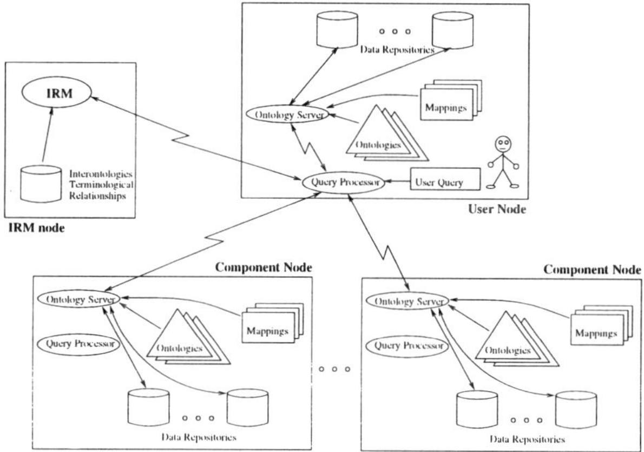

Figure 1: OBSERVER Global Architecture

2. Framework

The architecture of the OBSERVER[1] system that provides incremental answers to user formulated queries in a Global Information System has the following main components: Query Processor, Ontology Server, Interontology Relationships Manager (IRM) and the ontologies (see Figure 1). That architecture was explained in detail in [20] so we present it here briefly.

- *Query Processor.* It takes as input a user query expressed in DLs using terms from a chosen *user ontology*. The Query Processor communicates to the corresponding ontology Server which accesses the underlying data stored in the repositories under the user ontology. If the user is not satisfied with the answer, the Query Processor will translate the user query into the "language" of another (target) ontology by utilizing predefined terminological relationships (synonyms, hyponyms and hypernyms) between the user and the target ontology. The result is, in general, a list of translations or *plans* with an associated measure of the loss of information (that can be zero in the case of translating using only synonyms). The translation with less loss is chosen to access new data and the remaining plans are stored because they can be used later to upgrade the answer. Finally, the new answer (with or without loss of information) is correlated and presented to the user. This process is repeated until the answer satisfies the user.

- *Ontology Server.* The Ontology Server provides term definitions in the ontology and retrieves data underlying the ontology for the Query Processor. *Mappings* that link each term in an ontology with structures in data repositories are combined by the Ontology Server in order to access and retrieve data from the repositories with the help of wrappers. This addresses the *structure/format heterogeneity* problem. We describe in detail the access to underlying data sources in Section .

---

[1]OBSERVER (*Ontology Based System Enhanced with Relationships for Vocabulary hEterogeneity Resolution*) is our approach of using multiple pre-existing ontologies to access heterogeneous, distributed and independently developed data repositories [20].

- *Interontology Relationships Manager (IRM).* Terminological relationships relating the terms in various ontologies are represented in a declarative manner in an independent repository. This enables a solution to the *vocabulary sharing problem.*

- *Ontologies.* Each ontology is a set of terms of interest in a particular information domain; in our work, such terms are expressed using DLs. They are organized as a lattice and may be considered as semantically rich metadata capturing the information content of the underlying data repositories. These semantically rich descriptions can be used to query the Global Information System.

Description Logics

Systems based on DLs, also known as Terminological Systems, are descendants of *KL-ONE* [7] and allow us to define ontologies by using terminological descriptions. Some systems based on DLs are *CLASSIC* [6] (used in our prototype), *BACK* [24], *LOOM* [18] and *KRIS* [1]. The main features of the DL systems are described below:

- The language contains unary relations called *concepts* which represent classes of objects in the domain and binary relations called *roles* which describe relationships between objects. Concepts and roles are created via *terminological descriptions* built from preexisting concepts, roles and a set of operators (ALL, ATLEAST, ATMOST, etc.).

  Queries, that are also concept descriptions have the following format:

  $$[<projections>] \; for \; < concept\text{-}description >$$

  where < concept-description > defines the necessary and sufficient conditions that objects that form the answer verify. < Projections > contains the roles which values have to be projected.

- *Primitive and defined terms.* Terms (concepts and roles) are *primitive* if their descriptions specify only the necessary conditions and are *defined* if their descriptions specify both the necessary and sufficient conditions.

- *Subsumption of terms* allows to determinate whether a term is more general than another. The *subsumption* relationship is used by the DL system to maintain a classification hierarchy/lattice of terms (which is useful in dealing with large collections of definitions) and to *classify* new terms as well as queries. This classification mechanism allows the system to detect *incoherent* and *disjoint* descriptions.

  There exist two distinguished concepts, *Anything* and *Nothing*, in every ontology; the first one subsumes all the concepts in the ontology and the second one is subsumed by the rest of the concepts of the ontology (they are the top and the bottom of the ontology). Analogously, roles *Anyrole* and *Norole* are the top and bottom, respectively, of any role hierarchy.

3. Query Processing in OBSERVER

In the strategy proposed for query processing in Global Information Systems the following steps are remarkable (see Figure 2): *Query Construction, Access to Underlying*

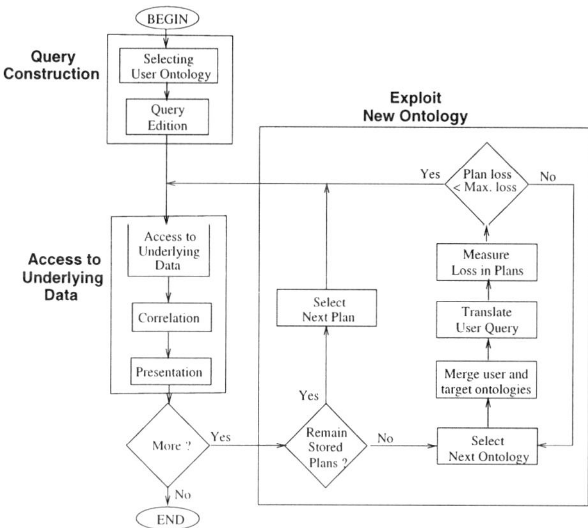

Figure 2: Detailed Query Processing in OBSERVER

Data and, if the user wants to enrich the answer, *Exploitation of a New Ontology*. Last two tasks are explained in detail in Sections and , respectively. All the process will be illustrated with an example in which the user wants to get an answer to the next query:

'Get the number of pages of documents which are periodical technical manuals written by only one author which is some kind of organization'

Query Construction

In this step two main tasks take place:

1. Selecting the User Ontology. The user browses the ontologies available in the Global Information System looking for an ontology that contains all the terms needed to express the exact semantics of her/his information needs. The chosen ontology will be called the *user ontology*. In the example, the Stanford-I ontology is selected (see Appendix), to express the query since it contains all the terms needed to express the semantics of the query.

2. Query Edition. By using a graphical tool, the user chooses terms from the user ontology to build the constraints and projections that compound the query:

*[number-of-pages] for (**AND** document periodical-publication technical-manual
(**ATLEAST** 1 doc-author-name) (**ATMOST** 1 doc-author-name) (**ALL**
doc-author-name organization))*

Moreover, a *defined term* (see Section) Q corresponding to the query is created in the user ontology.

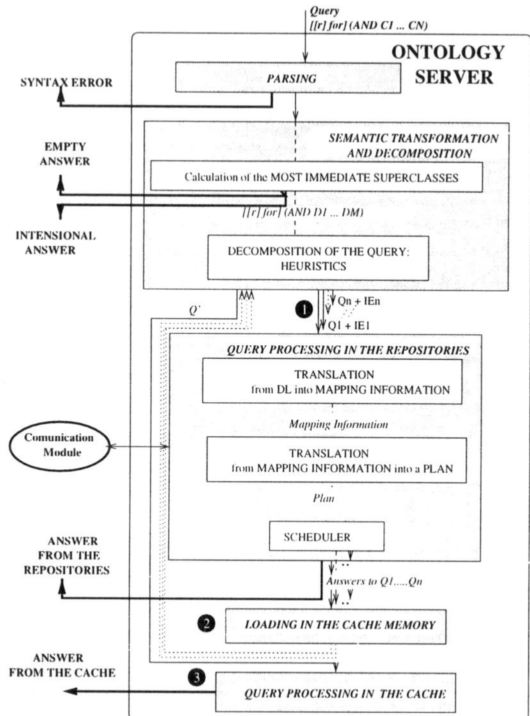

Figure 3: Steps for accessing data underlying an ontology.

4. Access to Data Underlying an Ontology

In this section we explain the way in which the Ontology Server accesses underlying data repositories. Five main stages are followed by the Ontology Server: parsing of the query, semantic transformation and decomposition, query processing in the underlying repositories, loading of the answers brought from the repositories in the cache memory and query processing in the cache memory. In Figure 3, those steps and the relationships among them are showed.

During the parsing, lexical and syntactical errors are detected. In our case this is achieved by using the parser of the DL system.

4.1. Semantic Transformation and Decomposition

The semantic transformation consists on finding a semantically equivalent query to the user query. For that, the set of *Most Immediate Superconcepts* ($\mathcal{MIS}$) is calculated (see [13]).

Theorem: The concept description of the query $\mathcal{C}$, is semantically equivalent to the intersection of all the immediate superconcepts in the set $\mathcal{MIS}$. The demonstration appears in [13].

In the semantic transformation and decomposition stage, different situations may happen: a) the query is detected as inconsistent (the empty answer is shown to the user) and therefore the process ends, b) the query is answered from the cache memory (number 3 in Figure 3) but first, if needed some subqueries are asked in the underlying repositories (numbers 1 and 2) or c) the query is answered directly from the underlying repositories and nothing is loaded in the cache memory (number 1 in the Figure 3).

When working with DL systems, it is also possible to give intensional answers, that is, answers in terms of the descriptions that the objects that form the extensional answer satisfy. Two different types of intensional answers are possible: *Most Specific Formulation* (MSF) of the query and *Extended Formulation* (EF) of the query. The first one is formed by the elements of the $\mathcal{MIS}$ set corresponding to the query and the second one is formed by recursively substituting the concepts in the initial query by their definitions. Both types of intensional answers (MSF and EF) are offered to the user by request but, in particular, the EF is also offered when the initial query is inconsistent, because it becomes more explicit where the inconsistency is.

Cache optimization

Dealing with ontologies connected to several data repositories, it is worth having some data cached within the ontologies in order to avoid accessing the underlying repositories each time a user formulates a query. There is a cache memory for each node where an ontology exists. This cache memory only stores objects and role values for terms existing in its corresponding ontology. Communications costs involved in transferring intermediate results and the final reconstruction of the answer can thus be avoided. So, if some data are cached, during the query processing it is necessary to detect if the query can be answered with the data stored in the cache, that is, if the query *is contained* in the cache (query completeness).

Luckily, when working with a DL system, the subsumption mechanism of concepts can be used to verify if queries are cached.

The test for query completeness is the next one:

A query is cached if all the concepts whose names appear in the set $\mathcal{MIS}$ corresponding to the query are explicitly or implicitly cached and all the roles that appear in the set $\mathcal{MIS}$ and the roles to be projected in the query are also cached.

The definitions of the notions of explicit and implicit caching that appear in the previous test are:

- *A concept C that belongs to the ontology, is explicitly cached by storing in the cache memory the objects that such a concept represents.*

- *A role is explicitly cached for a concept by storing their corresponding values in the cache memory. A role can be explicitly cached only for concepts that are explicitly cached.*

- *A query is implicitly cached, if all the concepts whose names appear in the set $\mathcal{MIS}$ corresponding to the query are explicitly or implicitly cached and all the roles that appear in the set $\mathcal{MIS}$ and the roles to be projected in the query are also cached.*

Query Decomposition

If a query cannot be completely answered with the contents of the cache memory then it must be decomposed. Query decomposition implies to obtain and analyze all the possible combinations of subqueries that can be made on the underlying repositories in order to get the query answer. However, in general the previous process is very complex because there can be many different ways of decomposing a query in subqueries[2] and statistic information and access paths in the local systems are not available. For that reason we have defined a set of heuristics that try to reduce such number of possibilities. These heuristics take into account if some parts of the semantically equivalent query to the initial one are cached, domain semantics and statistics about queries previously formulated. The goals of these heuristics are:

- Goal 1: To avoid that the answer sent from each repository is too large.

- Goal 2: To try that the computation cost in each repository is small, unless it is needed to reach the goal 1.

- Goal 3: To try not to bring parts that are already cached, unless it is needed to reach the previous goals.

- Goal 4: To try to send subqueries that are executed in parallel in different repositories, if these subqueries satisfy the two first goals, in order to avoid communication cost among the repositories and a greater computation cost in them.

The heuristics are presented in table 1.

Table 1: Heuristics used during Query Decomposition step.

H.	Goals	Description
H1	1,2,3	Substitute a non-cached defined concept without alternative[3] mapping information by its most specific definition
H2	1,2	Maintain a non-cached defined concept with alternative mapping
H3	1,3	Substitute a non-cached concept by one of its non-cached subconcepts only if the rest of the subconcepts are all cached
H4	1,3	Not to send a subquery with projection of a role that is already cached
H5	1	Reduce the size of the answer for a subquery within a repository
H6	4	Merge subqueries made over different repositories in order to reduce the size of the answer
H7	2	Transform a subquery with several restrictions over the same role by a subquery with the projection of that role

A more detailed explanation of these heuristics goes out of the scope of this paper.

---

[2]If the query is composed by n terms, there are as much possible decompositions as the number of possible partitions in a set of cardinality n. Moreover, the possibilities are greater because a term can appear in more than one subquery and a defined term can be substituted by its definition.

[3]Concepts and roles may have more than one mapping information to which we call alternative mapping informations.

4.2. Query Processing in the repositories

The set of subqueries that have been selected in the previous stage have to be asked in the underlying repositories. Before generating the database queries or application programs that retrieve the data, it is convenient to optimize the mapping information that has been expressed in a language independent of the access languages of the underlying repositories: the multidatabase extended relational algebra. The idea of the mapping information is *to view a data repository as a set of relations and attributes, independently of the concrete organization of the data in the repository.* Therefore, in this stage, for each DL subquery its corresponding optimal mapping information is generated. This optimization appears completely detailed in [11].

4.3. Loading and Query Processing in the Cache Memory

This stage is only performed when it is decided in the semantic transformation and decomposition stage. If it is needed, some subqueries are asked in the repositories under the ontology and then, the objects and role values that form the answer are loaded in the cache memory as objects (or role values) of new concepts added to the ontology (but that are not visible to users).

For example, the objects that form the answer for next subquery:

(**AND** *magazine* (**ATLEAST** *1 doc-author-name*) (**ATMOST** *1 doc-author-name*))

can be loaded in a new defined concept *magazine#1* whose description is exactly the previous subquery.

Once all the answers to the subqueries are loaded in the cache memory then, the semantically equivalent query to the initial one is asked in the cache memory and the answers for that query are the answers for the initial query. As it can be seen the correlation of the answers coming from the different data repositories is performed in the cache memory.

4.4. Example

In figure 4 we show briefly the different query processing steps for the query presented in section :

[number-of-pages] for (**AND** *document periodical-publication technical-manual* (**ATLEAST** *1 doc-author-name*) (**ATMOST** *1 doc-author-name*) (**ALL** *doc-author-name organization*))

5. Exploit a New Ontology

If the user is not satisfied with the answer, the Query Processor will retrieve more data from another ontology to "enrich" the answer. Notice that the answer is given in an incremental way. Therefore, the first task consists on selecting a component ontology, that we call *target ontology.* Once a target ontology is selected, the remaining task is to rewrite the user query in terms of that target ontology. Three main tasks take place: *Integration of user and target ontologies, Translation of the user query* and *Measure of Loss of Information.*

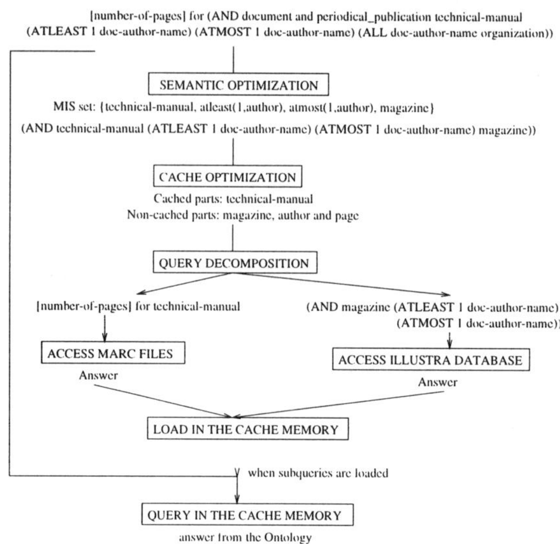

Figure 4: Example of query processing performed by the Ontology Server.

5.1. Integration of user and target ontologies

Rewriting user query terms implies to deal with terminological relationships, stored in the IRM, between terms of different ontologies. However, DL systems provide functions that calculate terminological relationships between term descriptions in an ontology. In fact, we would need a DL system dealing with distributed ontologies and there does not exist any DL system with that feature.

The solution seems to be the integration of the user and the target ontology taking advantage of the deductive power of the DL system [4]. Properties between terms in both ontologies are exactly the interontology relationships stored in the IRM[4], so no intervention of the user is needed. Although some of the previous relationships can be redundant the DL system will classify the terms in the right place of the integrated ontology. To know if the resulting terms are *primitive* or *defined* we apply the rules described in [5].

Following with the example, and taking as target ontology WN (see Appendix), the result of the integration of the user and the target ontology by applying the relationships defined between them is shown in Appendix . Any term without any parent in the figure is really a subconcept of *Anything*. Terms from the ontology WN are in uppercase and terms from Stanford-I are shown in lowercase; you can see that the user query, Q, has been also classified by the DL system in the right place.

5.2. Translation of the user query

Once the integrated ontology is built, the only task that the system has to perform is to fully translate Q (already simplified semantically) into terms labeled as terms from the target ontology (in the example, those in lowercase). Hereafter, the Query Processor will only deal with the integrated ontology since it contains all the needed information.

---

[4]There can exist semantic relationships among ontologies describing different domains.

Any conflicting term in the user query (those with no synonym in the target ontology) is substituted by the intersection of its immediate parents/hypernyms or by the union of its immediate children/hyponyms. This method is applied recursively until a full translation of the conflicting term is obtained. Moreover, every expression obtained is simplified (using DL systems capabilities) in order to eliminate redundant subexpressions. Notice that it is always possible to get at least one full translation of any conflicting term in both directions since terms *Anything* and *Nothing* (see Section) are terms from the target ontology (they always exist in any ontology).

Traversing hyponym and hypernym relationships can result in several possible translations. All the possibilities are explored and the result is a list of tuples in the format $< Plan, Loss >$, where *Plan* is an expression in Description Logics using only terms from the target ontology, and *Loss* is a number between 0 and 100 representing the percentage of loss of information of *Plan* with respect to Q. The loss of information of a plan is calculated after obtaining all the possible plans (see Section). At the end, that plan with less loss of information is chosen to enrich the answer to the user.

After all the possible plans are generated, they are optimized by removing the redundant plans following this rule:

$$< Plan1, Loss1 > \subset < Plan2, Loss2 > \Leftrightarrow Plan1 \subset Plan2 \wedge Loss1 > Loss2$$

In such a case, $< Plan1, Loss1 >$ will be eliminated. If the first condition if not satisfied, Plan1 could bring new relevant objects; if the second one is not satisfied, Plan1 will be chosen before Plan2 before it has less loss. After optimizing plans, the one with less loss is chosen to access new relevant data. The rest of the plans are stored and could be used if the user still wants more data.

Let us see now the resulting plans that are obtained in our example. Remember that the target ontology is WN and the query built using terms of Stanford-I, after semantic transformation, is the following:

$$Q = [number\text{-}of\text{-}pages] \; for \; (\mathtt{AND} \; magazine \; periodical\text{-}publication \; technical\text{-}manual$$
$$(\mathtt{ATLEAST} \; 1 \; doc\text{-}author\text{-}name) \; (\mathtt{ATMOST} \; 1 \; doc\text{-}author\text{-}name)$$

After integrating Stanford-I and WN ontologies Q is rewritten in the following way:

$$Q = [PAGES] \; for \; (\mathtt{AND} \; MAGAZINE \; technical\text{-}manual \; (\mathtt{ATLEAST} \; 1 \; CREATOR)$$
$$(\mathtt{ATMOST} \; 1 \; CREATOR)$$

We can observe that the only term without translation is 'technical-manual' due to the non-existence of a synonym in WN of such a term. Then, the only way to obtain a full translation of Q is to substitute the conflicting term by a combination of term parents either a combination of term children. As 'technical-manual' has no children the only way is upwards, i.e., to substitute 'technical-manual' by the intersection of its parents. In this case, the only parent is 'MANUAL' which is a term of WN, the target ontology. Therefore, the only plan to translate Q completely into terms of WN ontology is the following:

$$< [PAGES] \; for \; (\mathtt{tt} \; MAGAZINE \; MANUAL \; (\mathtt{ATLEAST} \; 1 \; CREATOR)$$
$$(\mathtt{ATMOST} \; 1 \; CREATOR), ? >$$

5.3. Measure of Loss of Information

The change in semantics caused by the use of hyponym and hypernym relationships must be measured not only in order to decide which substitution minimizes the loss of information but also to present to the user some kind of "level of confidence" in the new answer. The loss of information can be measured in an extensional manner and in an intensional manner.

We use measures based on the underlying extensions of the terms in the ontologies in order to measure the extensional loss of information. That information can be obtained and updated by batch processes so that it is available when needed for answering queries. We propose an adaptation of well established measures like *precision* and *recall* to measure the information loss when a term is translated by its hyponyms or hypernyms. A composite measure combining precision and recall [23] is used to choose a translation with the least information loss. See [19] for more details about this measures.

Moreover, using the DL systems capabilities an intensional loss based on the terminological difference can also be calculated.

Following with the example, the loss of information of the plan obtained in the previous subsection is calculated based on the extensions of the terms 'technical-manual' from Stanford-I and 'MANUAL' from WN ontology. We use a parameter called 'user-precision' which is a percentage describing the relevance for the user of precision over recall; we assume in the example that it is 50%.

$$Ext(technical - manual) = 19, Ext(MANUAL)^5 = 1$$

$$\text{Precision.low} = \frac{Ext(technical-manual)}{Ext(technical-manual)+Ext(MANUAL)} = 0.95$$

$$\text{Precision.high} = \frac{Ext(technical-manual)}{max[Ext(technical-manual),Ext(MANUAL)]} = 1$$

$$\text{Recall} = 1$$

$$\text{Loss.low} = 1 - \frac{1}{\frac{user-precision}{Precision.high} + \frac{user-recall}{Recall.high}} = 0$$

$$\text{Loss.high} = 1 - \frac{1}{\frac{user-precision}{Precision.low} + \frac{user-recall}{Recall.low}} = 0.025$$

Finally, the data underlying the previously presented plan is accessed. The information retrieved must be correlated with the previously presented to the user, in order to remove redundant information. After correlation, the new answer is presented to the user with the following explanation:

"The answer has been updated with information underlying WN ontology. The new answer is composed of magazines which are manuals with exactly one author. They are technical manuals (as the user requested) with a probability between 97.5% and 100%"

6. Conclusions and Future Work

We have presented in this paper a new strategy based on information content for querying heterogeneous and distributed data repositories. All the followed steps for the query processing have been explained briefly. Moreover we want to mention the existance of a prototype that allows accessing different heterogeneous data sources in the domain

---

[5]Although 'MANUAL' subsumes semantically 'technical-manual' as they belong to different ontologies/data repositories their extensions can not satisfy the property but our measures take this into account.

of bibliographic references, which is only an example application domain. Both data repositories and ontologies describing them have been designed by other working groups and organizations. A complete description of ontologies and data repositories can be found in [20]. It is important to notice the heterogeneity among the ontologies (semantic heterogeneity) as well as in the data repositories (structural heterogeneity, different data structures: plain files, databases, WWW documents, etc,) and operational heterogeneity (some data repositories are accessed using SQL commands, others by WWW browsers, and some of them they do not even have a defined query language or access method) because they have been developed by different organizations. In this way we want to capture a real case and deal with problems that never arise when ontologies and data repositories are designed under the same point of view.

The prototype has been developed using last technology in programming techniques: fully implemented in Java (*applets* and *servlets*), CORBA is the communication protocol and VRML has been used to provide a 3D representation of ontologies. It is accessible for WWW browsers at http://siul02.si.ehu.es/ jirgbdat/OBSERVER. We are developing several graphical interfaces to help users and administrators of ontologies, data sources and IRM.

References

[1] E. Achilles, B. Hollunder, A. Laux, and J. Mohren. KRIS: Knowledge Representation and Inference System. Technical Report D-91-14, DFKI Kaiserslautern-Saarbrucken, 1991.

[2] Altavista. http://www.altavista.digital.com.

[3] Y. Arens, C.A. Knoblock, and W. Shen. Query reformulation for dynamic information integration. *Journal of Intelligent Information Systems*, 6(2-3):99–130, 1996.

[4] J. M. Blanco, A. Illarramendi, A. Goñi, and J. M. Pérez. Using a terminological system to integrate relational databases. In *Information Systems Design and Hypermedia*. Cepadues-Editions, 1994.

[5] J.M. Blanco, A. Illarramendi, and A. Goñi. Building a Federated Database System: An approach using a Knowledge Based System. *International Journal on Intelligent and Cooperative Information Systems*, 3(4):415–455, December 1994.

[6] A. Borgida, R. Brachman, D. McGuinness, and L. Resnick. CLASSIC: A structural data model for objects. In *Proceedings of ACM SIGMOD-89*, 1989.

[7] R. Brachman and J. Scmolze. An overview of the KL-ONE knowledge representation system. *Cognitive Science*, 9(2), February 1985.

[8] S. Chawathe, H. Garcia-Molina, J. Hammer, K. Ireland, Y. Papakonstantinou, J. Ullman, and J. Widom. The TSIMMIS project: Integration of heterogeneous information sources. In *Proc. of the 10th IPSJ, Tokyo, Japan*, 1994.

[9] C. Collet, M. N. Huhns, and W. Shen. Resource integration using a large knowledge base in CARNOT. *IEEE Computer*, pages 55–62, December 1991.

[10] D. Florescu, L. Raschid, and P. Valduriez. A methodology for query reformulation in CIS using semantic knowledge. *International Journal of Cooperative Information Systems*, 5(4):431–467, 1996.

[11] A. Goñi, J.M. Blanco, and A. Illarramendi. Connecting knowledge bases with databases: a complete mapping relation. In *Proc. of the 8th ERCIM Workshop. Trondheim, Norway*, 1995.

[12] A. Goñi, A. Illarramendi, and E. Mena. Semantic query optimization and data caching for a multidatabase system. In *Proceedings of the Basque International Workshop on Information Technology*. IEEE Computer Society Press, July 1995.

[13] A. Goñi, A. Illarramendi, E. Mena, and J.M. Blanco. An optimal cache for a federated database system. *Journal of Intelligent Information Systems*, 9(2), 1997.

[14] T. Gruber. A translation approach to portable ontology specifications. *Knowledge Acquisition, An International Journal of Knowledge Acquisition for Knowledge-Based Systems*, 5(2), June 1993.

[15] Infoseek. http://www.infoseek.com.

[16] B. Kahle and A. Medlar. An Information System for Corporate Users : Wide Area Information Servers. *Connexions - The Interoperability Report*, 5(11), November 1991.

[17] A.Y. Levy, D. Srivastava, and T. Kirk. Data model and query evaluation in global information systems. *Journal of Intelligent Information Systems*, 5(2):121–143, September 1995.

[18] R. MacGregor. A deductive pattern matcher. In *Proceedings AAAI-87*, 1987.

[19] E. Mena, V. Kashyap, A. Illarramendi, and A. Sheth. Scalable query processing in dynamic and open environments: An approach based on information brokering across domain ontologies. Submitted for publication, 1997.

[20] E. Mena, V. Kashyap, A. Sheth, and A. Illarramendi. OBSERVER: An Approach for Query Processing in Global Information Systems based on Interoperation across Pre-existing Ontologies. In *Proc. of the First IFCIS International Conference on Cooperative Information Systems (CoopIS'96), Brussels (Belgium), June*. IEEE Computer Society Press, 1996.

[21] S. Milliner and M. Papazoglou. Scalable information elicitation in large heterogeneous database networks. To be published in IEEE Internet Journal, 1997.

[22] R. Bayardo, W. Bohrer, R. Brice, A. Cichocki, G. Fowler, A. Helai, V. Kashyap, T. Ksiezyk, G. Martin, M. Nodine, M. Rashid, M. Rusinkiewicz, R. Shea, C. Unnikrishnan, A. Unruh, and D. Woelk. Infosleuth: Semantic integration of information in open and dynamic environments. In *Proceedings of the 1997 ACM International Conference on the Management of Data (SIGMOD), Tucson, Arizona.*, May 1997.

[23] C. J. van Rijsbergern. *Information Retrieval*, chapter 7. http://dcs.glasgow.ac.uk/Keith/Chapter.7/Ch.7.html.

[24] K. von Luck, B. Nebel, C. Peltason, and A. Schmiedel. The anatomy of the BACK system. Technical Report KIT Report 41, Technical University of Berlin, Berlin, F.R.G., 1987.

Appendix A. Ontologies

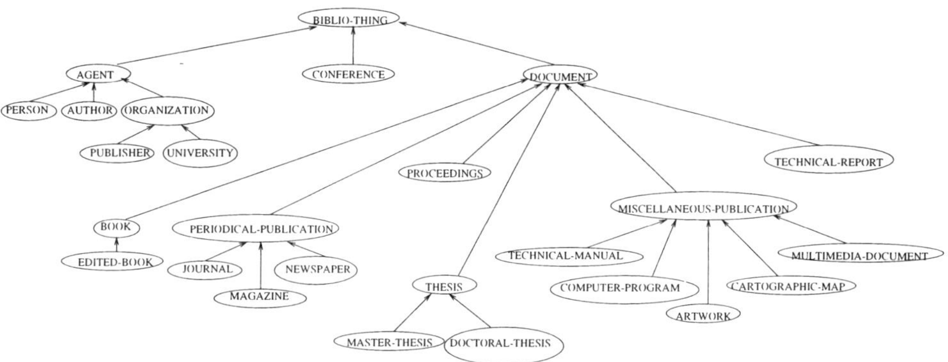

Figure 5: Stanford-I: A subset of the Bibliographic-data ontology

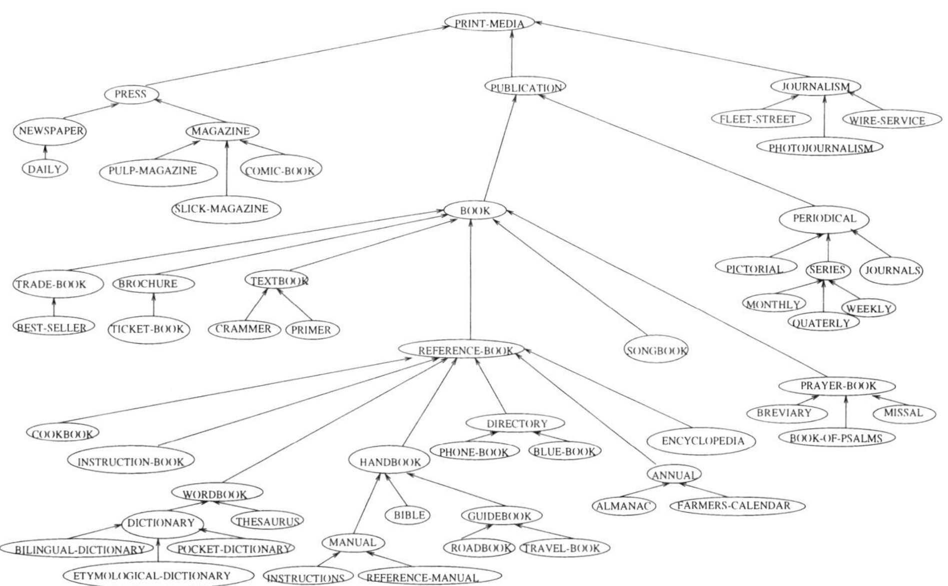

Figure 6: WN: A subset of the WordNet ontology

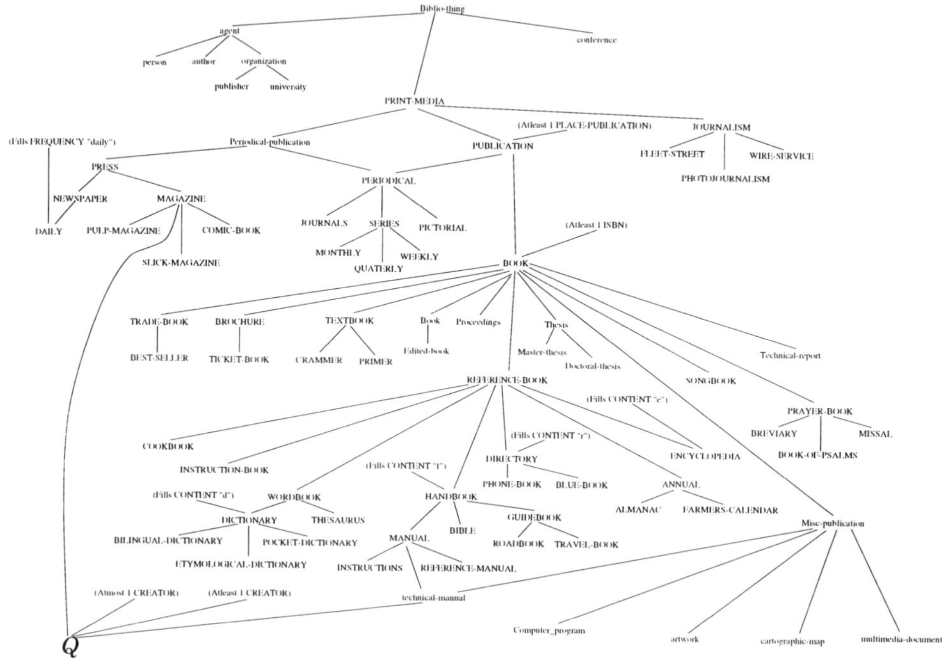

Figure 7: Integration of Stanford-I and WN ontologies

A Support to Domain Knowledge Modelling: A Case Study

C. Reynaud* - N. Aussenac-Gilles** - F. Tort*
LRI, Univ. de Paris Sud, Bât 490, F-91405 Orsay Cedex, {cr,tortfr}@lri.lri.fr
**IRIT, Univ. P. Sabatier, 118 rte de Narbonne, F-31062 Toulouse Cedex,
aussenac@irit.fr*

Abstract. Current knowledge engineering research works agree in describing the structure of knowledge based systems through highly structured models. More and more, knowledge acquisition combines problem-solving and domain knowledge modelling in an iterative process. Modelling domain knowledge involves two activities: constructing domain models which describe collections of statements about the domain (or domain theories) and constructing domain ontologies which provide the vocabulary for expressing domain models. In this article, we introduce an extended E/R Model that we defined. We show that the constructs it offers fulfil the requirements for domain knowledge modelling. Indeed, we explain how it can help to identify concepts, to structure a domain model and to elicit additional domain knowledge. Then, we focus on a case study extracted from an operational project. Through this case, we explain how the language helps in analysing the information acquired during interviews, we report the consequences on the model and in a last section, we list four structuring criteria which guided us in the ontology design.

1. Introduction

Current knowledge engineering research works agree in describing the structure of knowledge based systems (KBS) through highly structured models. Such models contain several components, each of them corresponding to a specific characterisation of the system knowledge used to solve problems. Today, the concepts of domain model, task model and problem-solving method seem to gain wide acceptance. Domain models describe the specific knowledge of the domain. Task models describe the application goals and the problems to be solved. A problem-solving method represents the means and the control knowledge to achieve these goals.

This analysis turns a KBS into a system composed of interrelated sub-systems. What may vary from one approach to another is not only the nature and contents of each model. In each one, the interactions between the different models are more or less strong. This choice depends on the approach requirements. For instance, the interaction must be made explicit in order to identify and select as soon as possible adequate reusable problem solving models. The interaction also is crucial if the domain model is explored to refine the problem solving model. In the first case, the domain model is built up afterwards, according to the roles that knowledge plays during problem solving. In the second one, the domain is modelled a priori, and may reveal information to define or select a problem solving method.

More and more, however, the knowledge acquisition process is viewed as an iterative one, combining problem-solving and domain knowledge modelling. Modelling domain knowledge involves two activities [17]: construct domain models which describe collections of statements about the domain (or domain theories) and construct the ontological framework (vocabulary and structure) or domain ontologies for expressing domain models. Thus domain models gather domain ontologies and domain theories.

A significant goal of a domain ontology is the elicitation of the structure of domain knowledge [13]. Ontologies may serve various purposes in the knowledge engineering process. In PROTEGE, the application ontology is the basis of a tool used to "populate" the application knowledge base [19]. In Cue, ontologies are used to direct domain knowledge acquisition, to integrate various representation formalisms and also to update an ontology library [22]. Our approach aims at automatically suggesting the description of problem-solving methods that perform user-specified tasks, and makes these proposals by analysing the domain ontology. Our hypothesis is that the domain ontology should be formal so that it could contain structured information to help select abstract methods. From a methodological point of view, we assume that in some cases, it is easier to first acquire and describe domain knowledge, from which a domain ontology can be built and then problem-solving methods can be identified.

To experiment these ideas, we developed ASTREE [15]. This system enables domain knowledge modelling with a formal language, built on the extended Entity/Relationship (E/R) Model [5] with is-a links [3]. These models are domain ontologies. In ASTREE, user-specific tasks can be described with a task-method language adapted from LISA [7]. ASTREE is able to analyse the syntactical and semantical properties of a domain ontology to suggest relevant methods that perform the tasks and apply on domain entities. ASTREE is supposed to be used mainly within a bottom-up process, such as the one proposed in the MACAO methodology [1] [2], in which it is supposed to be integrated.

The benefits brought by the E/R Model have been largely recognised for the development of information systems and, in particular, database modelling. Not only this model provides a basis for communicating and thinking about information systems. It also results very effective as a technique for database design. Yet, in knowledge engineering, such a model is either not used, or, when used, altered by additional constructs. In our mind, the E/R Model, with its standard constructs, can be an excellent tool for designing domain ontologies. When no new construct is added, all the modelling rules still offer the advantages they bring to develop information systems. Morover, we do not aim at enriching the representation from the data modeller's point of view because it could make it less easy to understand for non technical people. Thus, in this article, we insist on the gains brought by the use of the E/R Model in knowledge engineering. Our objective is not to contribute to database design at all but to show that data modelling techniques are attractive for knowledge modelling.

In the next section, we argue that the E/R formalism offers constructs that fulfil the requirements in domain knowledge modelling. Then, we show how it can help to identify concepts, to structure the domain model and to elicit additional domain knowledge. In the following section, we focus on a case study whose context is the design of a document consultation system in the domain of electric network planning, the Hyperplan project. With examples taken in this project, we explain how the language may guide in analysing the information elicited during interviews. We also report on the consequences on the model. In the last section, we list four structuring criteria that emerged from our experience. They stress that this language helps to represent a domain ontology.

2. A language to represent domain ontologies

A domain ontology is a model which defines and characterises classes of objects and relationships between these classes [9]. The objects and relationships are those used by an expert in the field when speaking about the application task from a static point of view. In an ontology, individual domain objects (detailed knowledge) are not explicitly represented.

Current domain modelling approaches distinguish the domain ontology from the domain models too [21], [17]. Yet, in all these approaches, building ontologies remains difficult. Given an application, the knowledge engineer can generally build a domain ontology in different ways. For example, a concept may be represented as a class in one domain ontology, as an attribute in another one as well as a relationship in a third one.

In this article, we focus on the E/R language used to represent domain ontologies in our approach. The E/R language is widely used in conventional software development. It is like a standard in the design field. Although this model is currently said not to be considered as intuitive, natural and easily understandable by non-specialists [18], we avoided to propose yet another model which would be totally unknown to users. Furthermore, research works in data modelling currently propose a number of modifications to the model that make it more understandable to business users [14]. The evolution can be integrated.

In our mind, the E/R Model is interesting for several reasons. Firstly, it is a simple language with a clear formal semantics. The main characteristics of this language are described in section 2.2 when stressing its benefits to support modelling in knowledge engineering. We mainly emphasise its formal semantics and especially its modelling rules which are a good means of organising and structuring knowledge. The modelling rules are, in particular, very useful to choose between different modelling possibilities as those illustrated above. The gains brought by applying these rules have been largely recognised for the semantic database modelling. Yet, as far as we know, the domain modelling approaches in knowledge engineering never evoke their application. We argue in this article that applying these rules is a good support for domain modelling because it leads to a better domain ontology. Nevertheless, we can take advantage of all these modelling rules only if we use the language with respect to its constructs. Thus, beforehand, in section 2.1, we show that the E/R Model offers constructs that fulfil the requirements in domain knowledge modelling.

2.1. An extension of the E/R language for domain modelling

The E/R language offers constructs developed in semantic database modelling. These constructs could be considered as too weak to model domain knowledge because more complex structures may be encountered in a KBS. Thus, some works (such as CML) have defined extensions to model expressions, heuristic rules or constraints, introducing new primitives and new types of relationships [16]. On the contrary, we propose to model such expressions without adding new constructs so as to take advantage of the definition rules of the E/R model. As a consequence, basic elements are entities, relationships and attributes. Domain objects are not represented. We illustrate below some of these expressions, and justify that their representation does not require any additional structure.

A first expression given in [16] is the following (example 1):
‖ "If temperature (patient) > 38 then fever (patient) = true".
This rule can be analysed as a means to obtain a property (fever) value of an object class (patient) from another property (temperature). So, we propose to define an entity PATIENT with two attributes "temperature" and "fever" of a different nature. Let "Temperature" be a non-calculated attribute. Its value must be given by the knowledge engineer when collecting

detailed expert knowledge. Let "Fever" be a calculated attribute. Its value is obtained by applying the following calculus formula: fever = true when temperature > 38. Indeed the modelling language proposes calculated attributes defined by a formula that makes it possible to calculate their value, and a high-structured language to write these formulas.

A second requirement in domain knowledge modelling can be illustrated by this other rule (example 2):

> Signal(input-port) = present, state(power-system) = on, state(volume-system) =on
> CAUSE
> signal(output-port) = present.

This second rule differs from the previous one because it refers to specific domain objects (input-port, power-system, etc.). The first one is much more general: it can be applied whoever the patient is. Yet, our model should reflect information about classes (entitites) but not about specific objects. As a consequence, "state" cannot be viewed as a calculated attribute of an entity labelled COMPONENT. In fact, calculus formula of calculated attributes must refer to entity attributes and not to object attributes.

Then we propose another model in which a component state is represented as an entity (STATE OF COMPONENT) so as to represent relationships with other entitites. In particular, we represent that the state of a component is an instance of STATE in relation with a given instance of COMPONENT. Moreover, in the rule, the cause is a set of states of components. So we also define another entity the instances of which are sets of instances of the entity STATE OF COMPONENT, as shown in figure 1. This entity is labelled GROUP OF STATES OF COMPONENTS. It is related to STATES OF COMPONENTS by the relationships "belongs-to". An alternative would be to represent GROUP OF STATES OF COMPONENTS as a system state: it would be a kind of STATE. This interpretation could also be represented in the extension of the E/R Model we consider. Yet, we favour a model where the names of the entities give information on their instance structure (element or set).

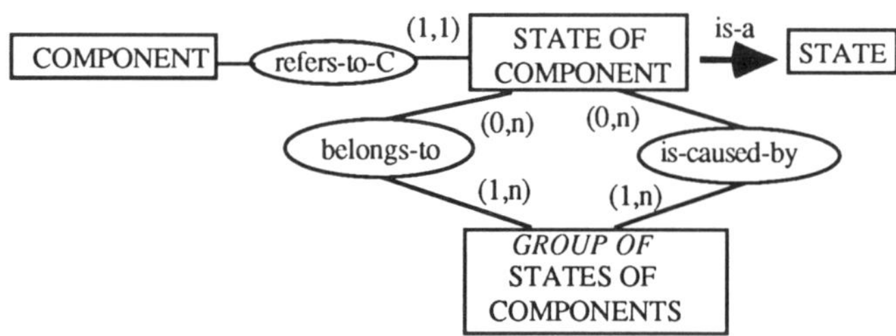

Figure 1 : The entity STATE OF COMPONENT

Let us suppose now that we want to represent the following expression (example 3):

> If the employees are heads of groups, they prefer large rooms with a central location,
> if they are secretaries, they prefer large rooms,
> if they are managers, they prefer small rooms with a central location, ...

In example 3, general rules connect, on the one hand, functions played by employees and, on the other hand, room characteristics. Any relationship between particular employees and rooms can be deduced from these general rules. In the E/R model, we represent such an expression with a relationship: "prefers" between the two entities FUNCTION and ROOM, each entity being described with its own attributes (such as *size* and *location* for ROOM). This representation is absolutely conventional. Moreover, to explicitly store the general rule which defines the relationship, we indicate that the relationship is "defined". Its definition contains the necessary conditions that instances must meet before being associated. To this end, we use a language which extends the standard E/R model. Then, the rules given in example 3 are formalised in the following way :

> Definition (prefer) ::
> (name of function = head of group AND size = large AND location = central)
> OR
> (name of function = secretary AND size = large)
> OR
> (name of function = manager AND size = small AND location = central)
> OR ...

Similar statements represented with rules are used in deductive databases to define relations. However, the semantics of our language is based on the canonical relational data model, it is a declarative semantics. We do not aim at deducing new facts as we could do it with Datalog rules, for example.

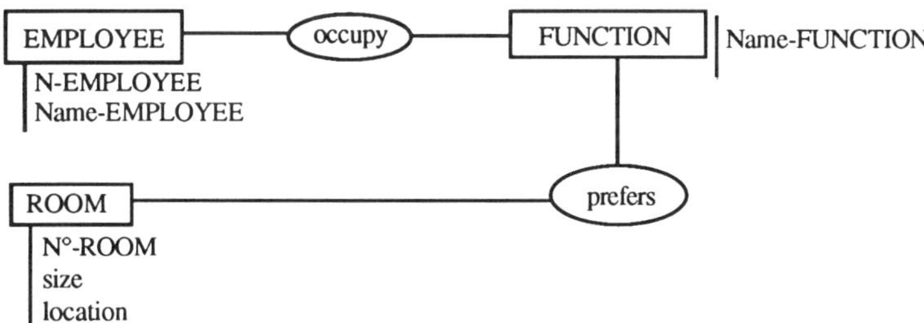

Figure 2: The entity and relationships model representing the expression in example 2

Note that the terms "defined" and "primitive" are also used in KL-ONE [4] to differentiate concepts. In KL-ONE, each concept has a definition. However defined concepts are fully described with necessary and sufficient conditions whereas only necessary conditions are specified for primitive ones. It is assumed that it is not possible to completely define primitive concepts. In our approach, a definition which corresponds to necessary conditions is given only for defined relations. It is assumed that it is not possible to define primitive relations.

The previous examples show that we use the E/R constructs just the same way as we would for data modelling. All the extensions illustrated just above must be viewed as additional information which do not absolutely modify the constructs of the E/R Model.

(1) For each relationship, we propose to specify whether it is defined or primitive. A relationship Ri is defined if the set of instances tconnected by this relationship do not need to be asserted (listed). In that case, it can be defined by a description of its features, called Definition (Ri), as a list of formal necessary conditions. When no definition can be written, the relationship is said to be primitive.

(2) We add descriptions of calculus formula to evaluate attributes when required. Thus, for each attribute, it is possible to specify whether it is calculated or not. Each value of a non-calculated attribute must be given by the developer when collecting the detailed knowledge of an application. This is not necessary when the attribute is calculated.

(3) We give a special label to entities the instances of which are sets of instances of other entities.

As a major advantage of these options, it is still possible to apply all the modelling rules of the E/R Model. We develop this point in the next section.

2.2.　*A support for domain knowledge modelling*

The E/R Model is a simple model, designed with very few basic primitives: entities, relationships, attributes. We adapted these primitives and, for each of them, we suggest a formal semantics detailed in [15].

In this section, we illustrate how the associated modelling rules and the language strong semantics, which are not available in other knowledge representations, guide domain knowledge modelling. Representing a domain ontology with the E/R language provides key advantages which are threefold: firstly, it guides to identify the main concepts thanks to the notion of entity; secondly, it provides a great help to structure the knowledge delivered by the expert; thirdly, it encourages the knowledge engineer to ask the expert for detailed knowledge so as to build a precise model. This model will be as complete as possible with respect to the expressive power of the language.

2.2.1. Identifying the main concepts

The E/R model allows to represent data at a conceptual level, where the canonical or semantical structure of data sets is described. The way data will later be implemented is not considered. The use of this language in knowledge engineering to model domain knowledge leads naturally to represent the concepts of a domain identified while analysing the expertise. They are supposed to be relevant from a conceptual point of view but not defined according to design or operational requirements. The concept names and attributes provide the vocabulary to describe collections of domain statements. Thus, they are part of what we have called a domain ontology.

2.2.2. Structuring the domain knowledge

The E/R language naturally helps to determine the classes, called entities, that can exist in a domain. An entity defines a class of objects (or instances) that share the same properties (or attributes). This principle is a first guide to structure a domain. It identifies the relationships allowed between objects of different classes (between instances of different entities). Entity attributes describe characteristics of their instances or characteristics of related instances. The validity of these definitions results from the application of two kinds of rules.

A first set of rules reflects the semantics of the primitives. Most of them concern the functional dependencies in the model, i.e. when an attribute value depends on another attribute value. Three main kinds of functional dependencies may occur in an E/R Model:
1.　　Attributes of an entity are functionally dependent on its identifier.
2.　　The identifier of an entity is functionally dependent on the identifier of another entity when the two entities are related by a relationship and when at the most one instance of the entity is associated with one instance of the other one.
3.　　Attributes of a relationship are functionally dependent on the identifiers of entities when all these entities are related by this relationship and when one instance of an entity participates in the relationship more than once.

Other applicable rules are borrowed from the relational data model [6]. One of their main objectives is to offer a strong basis to avoid data redundancy. To that end, normalisation rules have been defined. The benefits provided by the application of these rules have been largely acknowledged. Currently, some of these rules and especially those which allow a 3NF model to be represented, have to be applied when constructing a conceptual data model with the E/R language. Applying these rules is recognised as a good way to obtain entities which correspond to the main classes of objects, or to the main relevant concepts, of the real world. Moreover, the entity attributes fully characterise them. We recall below the rules, expressed in a textual form, which lead to a 3NF model:

1.　　An attribute must contain no internal structure;

2.　　When an entity has a compound identifier -made up of two or more attributes- any attribute that is not part of the identifier represents a characteristic of the "entire" entity, not a characteristic of something that would be identified by a part of the identifier;

3.　　Each attribute that is not part of an identifier represents a characteristic of the instance named by this entity identifier. It is not a characteristic of something named by other non-identifier attributes of this entity.

2.2.3. Eliciting additional domain knowledge

The expertise analysis in the early stages of knowledge acquisition is not always sufficient to build a domain ontology in the E/R language. Further questions may be required to better understand the knowledge and to describe the domain structure in respect to the language semantics and to the modelling rules. For instance, questions to determine whether a given functional dependency is true or false may be necessary. Other questions may be useful to precise the multiplicity constraints on the relationships. These constraints describe restrictions on the minimum and maximum number of instances of one entity that may be associated with any instance of a related entity. They are usually represented in an E/R Model. The aim of other questions may be to identify particular links as the "is-a" or "subtype" link or to precise particular constraints. For example, recently, extensions have been added to the E/R model to compare sets of instances associated by relationships as well as to compare subtypes.

In our approach, we required an extension of the E/R language because we model knowledge, not only data, for specific uses. In the context of knowledge base modelling, various knowledge structures may be encountered. Taxonomical relations are handled with *is-a* relations as used in data modelling. We have shown in section 1.1 the way rules can be represented. We have also described that knowledge about concepts can be represented in the definition part of relationships. That way, the E/R model in ASTREE is not just a template to record statements about instances of concepts as it is for data bases. The extensions of the E/R Model have to satisfy ASTREE requirements too. ASTREE identifies relevant methods from the knowledge structure in the domain ontology (the E/R model). Thus, in ASTREE, no piece of domain knowledge is modelled just as it is expressed. Beforehand, it is analysed. Then either it may be represented with relations, entities or attributes, or it may correspond to the definition of relations or to the calculus formula of an attribute (section 1.1). In these last cases, it is represented with a structured language that combine entities, attributes and relations. Thus, in ASTREE, whatever the way knowledge is considered, its structure is always explicitly defined with respect to basic elements in the model.

Such an approach is interesting because it guides knowledge elicitation. It leads the knowledge engineer to ask a lot of detailed questions to the expert so as to find the way knowledge must be considered and represented.

3. A case study

3.1. The Hyperplan Project

3.1.1. General purposes

The Hyperplan project aims at testing the concept of Hypertextual Technical Document Consulting System (TDCS). The originality of this system is to anticipate the possible requests during on-line consultation by taking into account the task for which the document is useful. We also validated the relevance of task modelling in this unusual context. Practically, we implemented a prototype of a hypertext-based system of the " Guide for Regional Networks Planning ".

Regional planners forecast the short and middle term evolution of electrical networks. They try to anticipate the electricity consuming and production rates in the next five years. According to these estimates, they evaluate the incident risk. Then, to prevent incidents, they schedule line extensions or strengthening, they plan the building of new transformers or any other kind of structure that compose the network.

In order to know the norms and rules to apply, the convenient calculation methods or procedure, planners consult the Guide, a 500 pages long technical document. However, the paper-based consultation is not flexible enough to allow them to easily reach all the information they need. In fact, the corresponding access modes, a table of contents and a reduced man-made index, do not provide sufficient guidance. To cope with this problem, the concept of TDCS was defined by the project partners. In a TDCS, the text is available on-line and it can be reached by three different means : (1) the traditional structure-based access, a table of contents ; (2) an extended terminological index ; (3) a model of the user's task enabling task-dependent contextual access. The user interface, a hypertext system, allows convenient text browsing through these three components.

The task model provides a contextual access to the document. It should help answer a reader's question such as " I am currently at this step of the planning process ; how can I produce the output xxx at this step ? ". So the task model needs to be closely connected to the text. Designing this model and setting relevant connections to the text has resulted a difficult and time-consuming task in the project. We have experimented the gain brought by the use of the MACAO knowledge acquisition methodology to build this task model [1]. Of course, the detailed task modelling has required the identification and description of domain concepts. Then, we had to connect each concept to some paragraphs of the Guide. For each use of a concept in the task model, we have selected the most relevant textual units that bring useful information about this concept when trying to perform this task [8]. The main knowledge sources to design this model were the Guide and interviews of domain experts.

3.1.2. The initial model

Because the objective was not the one for which MACAO is defined (building a model for a problem-solving system), we have adapted the modelling methodology. We first have read the document and met domain experts who explained us how they worked. From this information, we structured a first task model, that was validated and modified. The task decomposition granularity reflected to the degree of details about the task description in the text. Then, we have tried to fill this task model by describing the tasks inputs, outputs and methods, as well as the domain knowledge used to apply the methods. This is how concepts have emerged. This way of designing the model leads to a task-driven concept definition. Concepts are identified and described according to the needs of the task description.

Moreover, the connection to the document imposes an additional constraint : concepts are selected only when they can be used as an access to the text, and their description is related to the information read in the text.

At the end of this first analysis, two models were available : a problem solving model and a list of domain concepts. We have felt the need to organise all the domain concept and their task dependant description in a unifying domain model. By this mean, we wanted to describe each concept in a unique and coherent manner. Using the domain knowledge representation in MACAO, we have first drawn several graphs, one for each reasoning step. But we had many difficulties in merging the concepts and relations appearing in several graphs.

This first model was unsatisfactory for several reasons. It was a paper model because not all the functionalities of the MACAO software were available. It appeared as a huge network of concepts, very difficult to read. Both generic concepts and individual objects were represented. Some concepts were represented in various parts of the model, sometimes with different names. Furthermore, the model represented in the same graph both the structure of domain knowledge and task specific relationships between concepts. As a consequence, the model mixed domain concept and their roles in the reasoning process. For all these reasons, this first model was not only difficult to understand but also hard to build. The knowledge engineer had missed modelling rules which could have guided him. The only available guidance had been the semantics of the modelling primitives (concept and relationship).

To remedy to these drawbacks, we have decided to use ASTREE domain modelling framework. In the next section, we report the main steps of our work. Then, we detail the gains brought by language driven interviews in section 3.2 and the major modelling criteria in section 3.3.

3.1.3. Working steps

Our goal was to use the modelling techniques in ASTREE, and mainly the E/R language proposed to represent the domain knowledge. The clear formal semantics of this language as well as the well-defined modelling rules have motivated this choice. Another advantage of ASTREE was its suitability with MACAO: modelling primitives in ASTREE are compatible with MACAO, and the bottom-up process that it suggests corresponds to the one promoted by MACAO. Thus, we have decided to take advantage of the modelling approach in ASTREE and tried to build another more appropriate domain model. We have started from the first paper expertise model. The two knowledge engineers who had built this model have worked together with the ASTREE designers. They had a lot of documents in hands, borrowed from the expert, so that they were able to answer most of the questions asked by the ASTREE designers. Applying E/R modelling rules led us to ask additional questions to the experts. We illustrate below the benefits of these interviews.

3.2   The benefits of the interviews

Because the modelling constructs have a more precise semantics in the E/R Model, additional explanation was required to build an ASTREE model from the MACAO one. Our questions aimed at understanding better the domain knowledge, in particular the meaning of terms, so that it could be described with the convenient primitives. We report here on some of the explained assertions and the consequences on the model. In short, implicit knowledge has been put to light, new concepts have been added and the degree of knowledge generality has resulted much more accurate. Moreover, we could become aware of the semantical equivalence of several concepts. We illustrate all these consequences through several statements, extracted from the first model. For a better understanding of the initial model, we recall that, in MACAO domain models, concepts may refer either to generic classes or to instances. They have neither a formal description nor attributes. Relationships between concepts are labelled, with labels such as *are properties of*, *is an attribute of*, *is a*, *causes*, *influences*, *disturbs*, etc. But they have no formal semantics.

Statement 1: "electrical measurements are attributes of structures".

In fact, this means that the values of electrical measurements characterise the structures of the network. As the notion of value was implicit in the texts, it had not been considered in the first model. Moreover, the expert's domain analysis shows that some electrical measurements are characteristics of any structure of some kind whereas other measurements characterise any structure of another kind. Thus, "having measurements" is a general knowledge which concerns structure types but not specific structures.

Statement 2: "exploitation is an attribute of structures".

The formulation of this statement is very close to the previous one. Yet, according to the expert's comments, it means that each structure has proper exploitation values. So exploitation values are attributes of structures in particular, each one of them being used in reasoning. Thus, although statements 1 and 2 used to correspond to the same representation in the first model, their meaning is different and the difference must be stated.

Statement 3: "UCC is a nominal characteristic" - "Voltage is an attribute of a structure"

Analysing these two statements leads to make a connection between them. UCC means in fact short-circuit voltage, it is an electrical characteristic of structures. Moreover, the two terms UCC and voltage are equivalent for problem solving. So a single concept must replace the previous two.

Statement 4: "Increasing the PCC leads to a strong PCC".

According to the acquired explanations, increasing the PCC is an event linked to network operating. Other events may occur and are considered in the model. We have decided then to create an entity to group all these events together, labelled "kinds of event during network operating". This entity represents a new concept discovered when analysing the expertise.

Thanks to the answers we obtained during the interviews, the knowledge represented in the first model could be better understood and organised in a new model. We describe in section 3.3. some useful organising criteria derived from the modelling rules of the E/R language.

3.3.   *Some Criteria for Representing a Domain Ontology*

In the examples, we reorganise the representations in the first domain model to get a two-fold valid model : a domain ontology in the E/R language and a domain theory.

3.3.1. *Aggregation*

Given a term delivered by the expert, is there a set of instances corresponding to this term, mentionned by the expert in his reasoning, all characterised by the same properties and all associated the same way to the same entities ? An entity will be created in the model only if the answer to this question is yes.

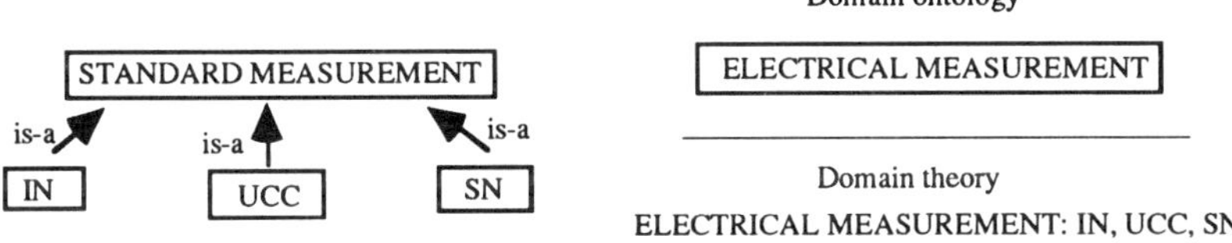

Figures 3 and 4 : The first and second models representing the Measurement concept

Applying this first criteria has led to modify the representation in the first model (figure 3) into the model shown in figure 4. Indeed, IN (standard intensity), UCC (short-circuit voltage), synonymous with voltage, and SN (standard power) had been modelled as sub-types of electrical measurement. These three electrical characteristics have no distinctive property a priori. At first sight, they do neither seem to have specific roles to play in the reasoning. In that case, all these objects can be aggregated in a unique entity, called ELECTRICAL MEASUREMENT.

Such an analysis may eliminate specialised entities, as in the example above, either because the specialised entities are in fact instances of a general one, or because differentiation is not justified in the application context. The expert makes no distinctions between these entities: they have the same properties and they play the same role in the reasoning.

3.3.2. Link between entities

If an information is an aggregation of data and corresponds to a link between two entities without any relation with other entities, then it must be represented as a relation and not as an entity. This is illustrated in figures 5 and 6.

Analysing the model has led to explicitly represent the structure hidden in expressions such as "line IMAP" and "electrical measurement of a line". In the new model, the concept of STRUCTURE TYPE is explicitly described. The electrical measurements of a line and of a cable are represented by an relation between STRUCTURE TYPE (whose instances are line, cable, etc.) and ELECTRICAL MEASUREMENT (with IMAP as an instance). The cardinality (.,n) means that a same electrical measurement can be used to characterise various structure types (IMAP characterises both lines and cables). "Characterises" is here a standard relationship whose semantics is denoted by its name.

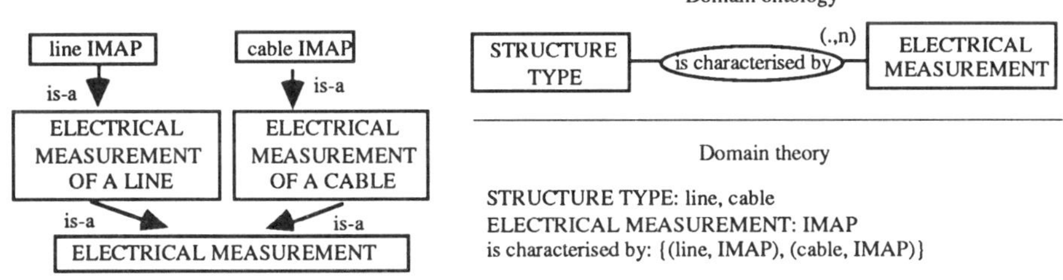

Figures 5 and 6 : The relationship between ELECTRICAL MEASUREMENT and STRUCTURE TYPES before and after applying the modelling rules

3.3.3. Identification

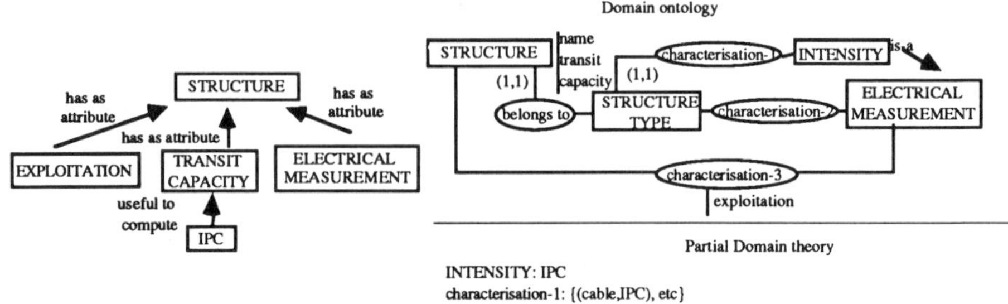

Figure 7 and 8 : The entities related to STRUCTURE before and after applying the identification rules

If a concept only refers to particular instances of an entity, if it has no identifier and if it does not play any role in regard to other entities, then this concept must be represented as an attribute. Furthermore, if its value is calculated, the formula to be applied is given in its definition in a textual form. The model indicates how to get to the arguments of the formula from a given calculated attribute.

Figure 7 is specific to cables. It means that their transit capacity is determined from IPC, an intensity value which characterises all the cables. More generally, we learn from the domain analysis that the transit capacity of a structure is determined from the exploitation value of the corresponding intensity. In the model, we add "transit capacity" as a calculated attribute of STRUCTURE (which will characterise cables in particular). A text describes the arguments of the corresponding calculation formula. The model requires the elicitation of its arguments. One of them is the "exploitation value" of a structure intensity to. In figure 8, the "exploitation value" is represented as an attribute of the relation "characterisation-3" because it is a property of the structure intensity and more generally a property of electrical measurement of structures. The intensity of cables is for example IPC. It is an instance of the entity INTENSITY, INTENSITY being a kind of ELECTRICAL MEASUREMENT. The structures which are studied are instances of the entity STRUCTURE. The intensity which must be considered to get the exploitation value is the intensity which characterises the STRUCTURE TYPE of the studied STRUCTURE (association "characterisation-1"), IPC for example for structures of a cable type. The cardinality (1,1) represents that there is only one intensity characterising a given structure type.

3.3.4. Personal Characterisation

The objective is to characterise an entity or a relation only with its own necessary attributes. We illustrate the application of this criteria on the following examples.

RATE is represented in figure 9 as an attribute of FLICKER which is a kind of disturbance. But, in fact, a particular rate characterises the flicker of a given structure. A lot of rates may correspond to a flicker, as many rates as structures concerned with this kind of disturbance. The functional dependency : Name of disturbance --> rate, is false. So rate can not be an attribute of KIND OF DISTURBANCE. We propose to represent it as an attribute of a relation which relates STRUCTURE and KIND OF DISTURBANCE. This way, the functional dependency : Name of disturbance, Code-S --fd--> rate will be valid.

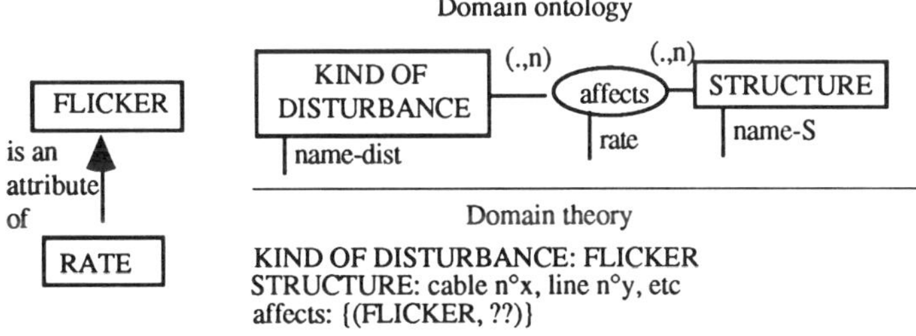

Figure 9 and 10: How specific objetcs are re-organised into classes

In figure 11, the identifier of STRUCTURE is first composed of the name of the structure type to which it belongs (Name-ST) and second of a number of structure (Number-S). Then, the entity STRUCTURE has the following properties: a type of intensity, a transit capacity. This model is not a 2NF model because the type of intensity is functionally dependent on Name-ST. For example, all the cables are characterised by the intensity IPC and only by this intensity. Such a rule is true for all structure types. Figure 12 represents in a different way the same reality: the identifier attribute of STRUCTURE is here Code-S. This model is not a 3NF because the type of intensity is functionally dependent on Name-ST which is not identifier attribute of STRUCTURE.

The modifications that we have proposed are illustrated in figure 13. The type of intensity will be represented as an attribute of a new entity : STRUCTURE TYPE. Indeed, the type of intensity does not vary from one structure to another but from one structure type to another. It is a model both in 2NF and 3NF. The attributes are characteristics of "entire" entities, not of something that would be identified by a part of their identifier, neither of something referred by other-non-identifier attributes of the entity. Furthermore, the functional dependency : Code-S --fd--> Name-ST is verified thanks to the cardinality (1,1). Then, as a structure belongs to only one structure type, STRUCTURE is also characterised by the attributes of the related STRUCTURE TYPE.

Using these criteria is a guide to elicit and represent the structure of domain knowledge. The two kinds of modelling rules described in section 2.2 are valid. That way, as for database modelling, the main domain concepts can be identified and described.

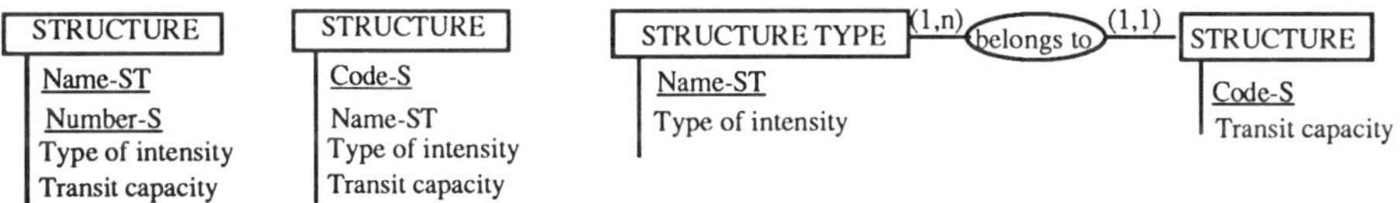

Figures 11, 12 and 13 : The evolution of the attributes associated to STRUCTURE along the characterization process

3.4. Consequences on the initial model

If we compare the new model to the initial one, the advantages brought by ASTREE are obvious and quite significant :
– the model is much more synthetic and dense : a reduced set of a dozen concepts and about ten relationships remained instead of several pages of graphs ;
– the model can be checked and seems to cover all the required domain knowledge ;

– the domain is more compact : information is gathered in the concepts, as their attributes or related instances ; only the attributed relevant for the task model were recalled ;
– the model is described at a better abstraction level : the major object classes appear at first sight, there is no confusion between concepts and instances any longer.

With this new model, the task description is more concise and precise. It is easier to set links towards the text. A natural following step of this project would be to apply ASTREE on this domain model and to compare the task model built with the help of ASTREE and the one hand-made in the early stages of the project.

4. Discussion and conclusion

Today, the crucial task in knowledge engineering still remains to define guidelines on how to build ontologies. Even with a good formalism, ontologies will not be useful unless their content is relevant and adequately organised. In particular, the structure of the domain knowledge must have been elicited and represented. Using a language with a clear formal semantics as the E/R Model is one of the solutions. Not only does it lead to better define concepts, relationships and attributes. It also urges to investigate the dependency relationships holding for a particular concept. Such relationships are fundamental to obtain a well-structured ontology [11]. We discuss some characteristics of this language in the following.

First, we want to recall that *is-a* links are not absent from our language. They are useful to separate what is in common with several entities and to isolate what is specific to an entity. A specialised entity has attributes or links in common with other entities while having its own specificity too. It must have its own attributes or it must be related to entities and, in both cases, more general entities must not be concerned with these attributes or relationships. Then, *is-a* links can be used. Yet, we think that the notion of relationship is fundamental too, because it allows additional information to be represented. One can model that some attributes are functionally dependent on two or more entities and not only once. Multiplicity constraints can be added. The application of rules borrowed from the relational data model leads to build entities with attributes which fully characterise them. Thus, even if the semantics of the relationships is only denoted by their name, the use of relationships in respect to the modelling rules described in this paper is very rich.

Now are domain ontologies built with this language reusable ? We cannot answer very precisely to this question because no experiments of reuse has been done until then. Yet, the domain ontologies that we build are task-dependent. In our approach, we assume that a domain ontology depends a lot on the way knowledge will be used in reasoning. Experts deliver knowledge in a way appropriate to their reasoning. Our idea, in ASTREE, is to exploit the structure of the domain ontology so as to find appropriate methods to achieve the application task. Our objective is then structure-oriented. It is not to design ontologies usable for classification, for example.

The model that we built in the Hyperplan project is abstract because only domain concepts are represented. It is a synthetic view on a whole domain. It cannot be compared only with the initial model in which both generic and individual objects were represented. The initial model must be compared with the whole domain model i.e. the domain ontology *and* the domain theory. The domain theory contains instances and tuples of entities and relationships in the domain ontology. This can be considered as a way to explain the vocabulary in the domain ontology.

The simplicity of the domain ontology is not the result of a compilation process. Instead, all pieces of knowledge are analysed. Their structure is either represented or defined in the definition part of relations or in the calculus formula of attributes. Yet the model is simple because it is an abstract model.

To conclude, let us note that, in the knowledge acquisition community, many research works are concerned with problem solving methods, their analysis and modelling. But only few studies stress the importance of domain model building. This trend may change. Indeed, Guarino recently claimed that a greater emphasis should be given to domain analysis [12]. He proposes to exploit (1) linguistic resources such as thesauri and (2) analysis techniques based on formal ontological principles. In [10], he made proposals to clarify the nature of a concept based on formal properties like rigidity, countability, dependence. Four main principles to build ontologies containing elements as generic and method-independent as possible are proposed in [20]: parsimony, clear theoretical basis, categories versus terms and coherence.

In this paper, we also addressed the problem of building a domain ontology. We have shown the advantages of using the E/R language in the scope of knowledge modelling. We have asserted four structuring criteria whose application can be a good guide to design an ontology in respect to modelling rules. Perspectives of this work will be now to validate other possible uses of ontologies built with this formalism. For instance, we would like to test whether these ontologies are reusable for a different task in the same domain or not. Another prospect could be to exploit the language syntax and semantics to anticipate automatic generation of detailed knowledge elicitation tools for a given ontology.

Acknowledgements

The work reported in this article owes a lot to all the people involved in the Hyperplan project: H. Assadi, D. Bourigault and C. Gros from the DER of EDF-GDF. A special thank to A. Courcelle from IRIT who worked as a knowledge engineer on this project and collected the domain knowledge.

References

[1] Aussenac-Gilles N., "Matta N., Making a method of problem solving explicit with MACAO". *International Journal of Human-Computer Studies*. 40, 193-219. 1994

[2] Aussenac-Gilles N., " How to combine data abstraction and model refinement: a methodological contribution in Macao ". In *A future for Knowledge Acquisition*, Proc. of EKAW94. Berlin: Springer Verlag. Lecture notes in AI 867, pp. 262-282. 1994.

[3] Battini, C., Santucci, G., "Top-down Design in the Entity-Relationship Model", in Chen P.P. ed, *E-R Approach to systems Analysis and Design*, proc. of the 1st Intern. Conf. on Entity-Relationship Approach, NorthHolland, Dec. 1979.

[4] Brachman, R. J., Schmolze, J. G."An Overview of the KL-ONE Knowledge Representation System". *Cognitive Science*. 9. pp. 171-216. 1985.

[5] Chen P. S., "The Entity-Relationship Model". *ACM Transactions on Database Systems*. 1:1. 1976.

[6] Codd, E. F. "A Relational Model for large Shared Data Banks". *Communications of the ACM*. 1970.

[7] Delouis-Jacob I., Krivine J.P., "Lisa, un langage réflexif pour opérationnaliser les modèles dexpertise". *Revue dIntelligence Artificielle*. 9 (1). Paris : Hermès. 1996.

[8] Gros C., Assadi H., Aussenac-Gilles N., Courcelle A. "Task models for technical documentation accessing". Position paper in Proceedings of the 9th European Knowledge Acquisition Workshop (EKAW96). Nottingham (UK). May 1996.

[9] Gruber, T.R. "A translation approach to portable ontology specifications". *Knowledge Acquisition*. London : Academic Press. 5:199-220. 1993

[10] Guarino N. "Concepts, attributes and arbitrary relations - Some linguistic and ontological criteria for structuring knowledge bases". *Data & Knowledge Engineering.* 8. p.249-261. 1992

[11] Guarino N. "Formal ontology, conceptual analysis and knowledge representation". *International Journal of Human Computer Studies.* 43 (5/6). Special issue on formal ontologies. 1995. 625-640.

[12] Guarino N. "Understanding, Building, And Using Ontologies". *International Journal of Human Computer Studies.* 46, pp 293-310. March 1997.

[13] Guarino N., Giaretta P., "Ontologies and Knowledge Bases : towards a Terminological Clarification".*Towards Very Large Scale Knowledge Based Systems: Knowledge Building and Knowledge Sharing.* N. Mars (ed.) Amsterdam : IOS Press. 25-32. 1995.

[14] Moody D., "Graphical Entity Relationship Models: Towards a more User Understandable Representation of Data", In B. Thalheim (Ed), 15th Int. Conf. on Conceptual Modelling, Cottbus, Germany, October 1996, Proceedings. Lecture Notes in Computer Science, Vol. 1157, Springer Verlag, 1996, 402-419.

[15] Reynaud C., Tort F., "Using Explicit Ontologies to Create Problem Solving Methods", *International Journal of Human Computer Studies*, 46, 339-364. 1997.

[16] Schreiber G., "A KADS Domain Description Language", in Schreiber G., Wielinga, B., Breuker, J., (eds), *KADS: A principled Approach to Knowledge-Based System development.* Academic Press. 71-91. 1993

[17] Schreiber, A. T., Wielinga, B. J., De Hoog, R., Akkermans, J.M., Van De Velde, W. "CommonKADS: A comprehensive methodology for KBS development". *IEEE Expert.* 9(6). 28:37. 1994

[18] Siau K., Wand Y., Benbasat I., "When Parents need not have children -- Cognitive biases in information modelling", In P. Constantopoulos, J. Mylopoulos, Y. Vassiliou (Eds): *Advances Information System Engineering, 8th International Conference, CAiSE'96*, Heraklion, Crete (Gr), May 20-24, 1996, Proceedings. Lecture Notes in Computer Science, Vol. 1080, Springer Verlag, 1996, 402-420.

[19] Tu, S.W., Eriksson, H., Gennari, J. H., Shahar, Y., Musen, M.A., "Ontology-based configuration of problem-solving methods and generation of knowledge acquisition tools: The application of PROTEGE II to protocol-based decision support". *Artificial intelligence in Medicine.* 1995

[20] Valente, A., Breuker, J., "Towards Principled Core Ontologies", *in Proceedings of KAW'96.* Banff (CAN). Oct 1996.

[21] Van Heijst G., Schreiber G., "CUE : Ontology Based Knowledge Acquisition", in L. Steels, A. Th. Schreiber and W. Van de Velde (eds.), *A future for Knowledge Acquisition* - Proc. of the 8th European Knowledge Acquisition Workshop EKAW'94, Lecture Notes in Artificial Intelligence, vol 867. Berlin : Springer-Verlag. 178-199. 1994.

[22] Van Heijst G., Schreiber A. Th., Wielinga B. J., "Using Explicit Ontologies in KBS Development". *International Journal of Human Computer Studies.* 46. 183-292. 1997.

An Engineering Framework for Domain Knowledge Modelling

Ernesto COMPATANGELO
Istituto di Informatica della Facoltà di Ingegneria, Università di Ancona
via Brecce Bianche, 30 – 60131 Ancona, Italy — compatan@inform.unian.it

Giovanni RUMOLO
Dipartimento di Informatica ed Automazione, Università di Roma TRE
via della Vasca Navale, 84 – 00146 Roma, Italy — rumolo@inf.uniroma3.it

Abstract. This paper describes a framework for modelling and analysing domain knowledge at a conceptual abstraction level. It addresses the ontological problems of concept modelling, as well as the methodological and operational problems of conceptual modelling. The framework supports distinct categories of information concepts endowed with a minimalist knowledge content and a formal semantics, which is based on description logics as a unifying knowledge representation. It introduces a distinct taxonomic relation for each category of information concepts, giving rise to different taxonomic hierarchies. This framework was introduced to evaluate the role and the extent of different concept models as well as of distinct approaches to conceptual modelling and analysis. It is being used for the development of a new generation of intelligent tools endowed with automated deductive capabilities.

1 Introduction

One of the most critical problems faced by analysts prior to system development is investigating the *application domain* and making discoveries about it [22, 35, 30, 14, 18, 7, 4]. An application domain, i.e. the universe of discourse (UoD) of a problem, is characterised by a set of properties about some relevant environmental aspects. These properties, called *information elements*, must not depend on the features of any kind of system (to be eventually) embedded in that domain [29]. Information elements are the components of a *domain model*, which is a (possibly suitable, complete and consistent) representation of the application domain. The term *domain knowledge element* is used to denote an information element which is described in terms of a *disciplined representation scheme* based on some set of *atomic constructors* and *composition rules*. Correspondingly, the term *domain knowledge* is used to denote information represented by some cluster of domain knowledge elements. The choice of a particular set of constructors and rules implicitly defines a *domain knowledge model*, as well as the syntactical and semantical *deductive services*, if any, which can be used to analyse a domain model. Although domain knowledge can be considered at different abstraction levels, focus in this paper will be limited to the *conceptual level*, where procedural and extensional features are not taken into account. At this level, a domain model and a domain knowledge model are currently denoted as a *conceptual model* and a *concept model* respectively.

Different kinds of conceptual errors, arising from incompleteness, inconsistency and ambiguity of information elements, can be introduced in a conceptual model. They strongly influence system requirements as well as its overall quality. Their propagation introduces major differences between the observed characteristics of the final product and the desired characteristics of the initial specification [3]. In many real-world situations, the large number of information elements prevents human search of conceptual errors from being appreciably successful. In order to be of more effective use, the so-called *knowledge content* of every information element [1] should be captured in such a formal way that it can be represented and processed inside computers [1]. In fact, automated reasoning services such as the detection of conceptual errors and the explicitation of hidden properties can make conceptual modelling and analysis much easier and powerful. This means that a formal knowledge representation scheme, supporting some kind of non-trivial automated deductive service, should be adopted in conceptual modelling. In dealing with any kind of domain modelling approach at the conceptual level, analysts are always faced by three fundamental problems:

1. what kind of information elements are captured and modelled;

2. what kind of language(s) is employed for this task;

3. what reasoning processes run on these languages.

These problems, which are bound to the *ontological* nature of *concept modelling*, are respectively denoted as *abstraction, representation* and *deduction*. Besides them, three engineering problems deeply linked to the preceding ones must be also considered:

4. how to develop a domain model using a disciplined approach;

5. how to share or merge different models of the same application domain;

6. how to assist domain modelling by means of automated deductive services.

These additional problems, which are bound to the *methodological* and *operational* nature of *conceptual modelling*, are respectively denoted as *construction, integration* and *support*. Together with the previous ones, they must be taken into account during the development of a conceptual model. All these problems characterise the different *dimensions* of the domain description ($\mathcal{DD}$) framework introduced and discussed in this paper. Making this engineering framework explicit is a fundamental step towards a general evaluation and classification of different concept models and conceptual modelling approaches. The $\mathcal{DD}$ framework emphasizes both (i) the role of domain-dependent abstractions whose representation is based on a formal semantics in concept modelling and (ii) the role of automated deduction in conceptual modelling. Its dimensions define an engineering background for the development of intelligent knowledge management environments to be used in modelling application domains with UoD elements [18].

The presentation is organised as follows. Section 2 surveys both different concept models and different approaches to conceptual modelling. Section 3 describes the three dimensions of the $\mathcal{DD}$ framework. Section 4 discusses ontological aspects of concept modelling. Section 5 outlines methodological and operational aspects of conceptual modelling. Finally, section 6 summarizes some major results and open problems.

---

[1] An information element is said to be endowed with a knowledge content if and only if it is described using a disciplined representation scheme. In this case, the information element is a domain knowledge element, so its knowledge content is given by the corresponding description of its structure.

2 Background and survey

The introduction of explicit knowledge representation and reasoning techniques in the early, conceptual stage of the engineering of computer-based systems in general, is not a new idea. At the beginning of the eighties, research work on requirement specifications [40, 2] first pointed out the importance of a formal representation of knowledge elicited during the phase preceding information systems development. Since then, several languages and systems have been proposed to model this knowledge [23, 22, 16, 30, 51, 1, 18, 47]. However, extensive field studies and critical surveys in this area show that an overall approach to concept modelling, which may provide at the same time a set of guidelines for conceptual modelling, is still missing [5, 33, 7, 37].

2.1 Fundamental features of concept modelling

At the conceptual level, where the extension vs. intension distinction is explicitly considered [50, 18], most modelling approaches deal with intensional UoD abstractions called *domain concepts*. They can be grouped into homogeneous sets which represent the extensions of more general *epistemological categories* called *meta-concepts* (see Sec. 4.1). Each homogeneous set shares the same *skeleton* of *epistemological properties*, such as the interpretation of information elements as data structures, enterprise processes, software objects, and so on. Here and in the following, the term *concept modelling* is thus used to denote the definition of domain concepts, i.e. sets of information elements considered as intensional descriptions of UoD properties. Correspondingly, the term *concept meta-modelling* is used to denote the definition of concept categories, each in terms of its own domain-specific skeleton of epistemological properties.

Each domain concept is characterised by its own description, which depends on the adopted *concept modelling scheme*. The latter includes both an *abstraction scheme* and a *representation scheme* (see Table 1). Current concept modelling schemes were developed following two different approaches, respectively based on *closed* and *open* ontologies [2] [48]. In closed ontologies, the view of the world is *fixed*, i.e. meta-concepts are predefined in the modelling scheme. Analysts are not allowed to change them and only those concepts which fit within an existing meta-concept can be captured and represented. Conversely, in open ontologies the view of the world is *variable*, i.e. meta-concepts are not predefined in the modelling scheme. In this case, analysts can define new categories of concepts, tailoring the modelling scheme to a particular domain. However, an ontology composed of zero meta-concepts is meaningless.

Under an abstraction-oriented viewpoint, modelling schemes based on closed ontologies use a *fixed set of abstractions*. Each of them corresponds to a specific meta-concept characterised by a predefined skeleton [11]. Data and process-oriented schemes (ER [39, 25], EER [41], SDF [12], IE [22]), as well as object-oriented schemes (OOA [35], OMT [27]) are typical examples of this first kind. Conversely, modelling schemes based on open ontologies use a *fixed set of concept constructors*, each corresponding to an atomic constructor. Different meta-concepts can be defined assembling these constructors in a disciplined way, according to the corresponding meta-concept syntax. Conceptual modelling schemes used in disciplined information construction (COMIC [18]) as well as object-centred schemes used in formal knowledge representation languages, such as the KL-ONE family [44, 50] or the RML - Telos family [2, 23, 48], are typical examples of this second kind of schemes.

---

[2]See sec. 3 for a definition of the term *ontology* in the above context.

Table 1: A framework for concept modelling schemes

Abstraction Scheme		Representation Scheme		
Closed Ontology	Open Ontology	Informal	Disciplined	
			Semiformal	Formal
(Fixed Abstractions)	(Fixed Constructors)	(No Deduction)	(Syntactical Deductions)	(Semantical Deductions)

Under a representation-oriented viewpoint, concept modelling schemes are classified as either *informal* or *disciplined*. Disciplined schemes can be further classified as either *semiformal* (*rigorous*) or *formal*. The following interpretation holds. Informal schemes are neither endowed with a well-defined syntax, expressed according to a predefined set of production rules, nor with a semantics. Disciplined schemes are endowed with a formal syntax and with an informal semantics expressed in terms of natural language. Formal schemes are endowed with a formal syntax and with a formal semantics expressed in terms of a logical, algebraic or analytical formalism. Schemes based on natural language are informal ones. Disciplined schemes such as ER, SDF, OOA and OMT are rigorous ones. Schemes based on knowledge representation languages such as RML, Telos and the KL-ONE family are formal ones. They extend rigorous schemes by means of a semantics which supports some kind of temporal or class-centered reasoning.

Under a deduction-oriented viewpoint, informal, semiformal and formal schemes are endowed with different automated reasoning capabilities. No kind of automated reasoning at all is possible with informal schemes, as in the case of natural languages. No automated reasoning capability, other than syntactical name conflict detection, is possible with semiformal schemes, as in the case of ER, SDF and OOA-OMT schemes. However, recent data-oriented [47] and object-oriented [9] formal schemes, endowed with both a well-founded semantics and a logical inference system, overcome these limitations. In the general case, automated deductive services can operate on domain models based on a formal semantics. In fact, the availability of a particular service explicitly depends on the decidability and on the computational complexity of the corresponding deduction problem, which depends on the adopted semantics. For example, proper fragments of first-order predicate logic (FOL) allow decidable and tractable concept classification based on subsumption, while FOL in its entirety does not [17].

2.2   *Fundamental features of conceptual modelling*

Under a construction-oriented viewpoint, conceptual modelling rules and techniques must be considered. In semiformal approaches based on closed ontologies, the adoption of a fixed set of abstractions leads to the introduction of general modelling principles explicitly depending on the detailed characteristics of each approach. In ER-like approaches, entities are typically captured and modelled before relationships linking them; the resulting model is quite flat, with all concepts at the same level. In SDF-like approaches, the domain model is built up in a top-down way starting from the so-called context level. These approaches introduce a multilevel abstraction mechanism based on clusterisation, which hides the cluster structure and its skeleton. In object-oriented approaches, structural object components (attributes) are defined before behavioural ones (methods); specifical structuring rules define the detailed construction sequence [35]. Objects captured in the UoD are clustered into few general "subject" classes using *is-a* and *part-of* hierarchies. Conversely, in formal approaches based on open ontologies, which focus more on general knowledge representation than on domain-dependent abstractions, a conceptual model can be built in a free way [45, 23]. However, the lack of an overall disciplined approach to conceptual modelling may be a source of additional methodological and operational complexity, preventing information integration or the availability of automated deductive supports. Little attention has been payed until now to all these aspects, which are the essence of the conceptual modelling process [8].

Under an integration-oriented viewpoint, different approaches were proposed to deal with the critical problem of merging different conceptual database models of the same information system. This problem, denoted as *schema integration* [6], is being tackled using object-centered, logic-based approaches [32, 38, 52]. All these approaches use a knowledge representation based on a formal semantics, which is needed to capture concepts (i.e. classes of information elements) defined according to distinct modelling schemes. However, a global approach coping with the more general problem of merging different concept and conceptual models, leading to the development of a shareable domain repository, is still missing. In fact, current approaches are mainly based on some enhanced version of the ER schema supporting the database kernel of information systems. Conversely, the integration of other domain concepts such as processes or objects is quite always not taken into account. When dealing with conceptual modelling schemes encompassing several domain-dependent concepts, things become even more complex than in the case of data-oriented schema integration. Different conceptual views of the same domain model may use distinct abstraction and representation schemes. Therefore, the integration problem is no more limited to knowledge representation, but involves concept dependencies and relations too. The introduction of different domain meta-concepts can lead to a more effective integration of modelling schemes by way of *information sharing*. The latter implies that each meta-concept subsumes a set of similar domain abstractions, capturing the meaning of information elements described according to distinct modelling schemes.

Under a support-oriented viewpoint, computer-based systems such as CASE tools are endowed with automated deductive services of two different kinds. The first kind includes systems endowed with control services operating on a syntactical basis. The second kind includes systems endowed with a full range of deductive services operating on a semantical basis. The CLASSIC [36] and CONCEPTBASE [31] intelligent knowledge management environments (IKMEs) are typical examples of this second kind. Notably CLASSIC, which belong to the KL-ONE family if knowledge representation languages and systems, allow automated concept classification, consistency check, contradiction detection, hidden property deduction and answers to complex queries. While syntactical tools cannot offer any of the above services, semantical tools suffer from a different kind of limitation. In fact, they were designed to operate on concepts belonging to generic domain knowledge elements, in which a single rule for the construction of concept hierarchies is used. This rule, which is based on set containment, is the same one used in the construction of a hierarchy of structural concepts in semi-formal approaches. However, it may be different from the one used in the construction of hierarchies of behavioural concepts, which is based on functional typing [28]. The need for different category-dependent rules in conceptual modelling was already pointed out in [19, 24].

3   The $\mathcal{DD}$ framework and its dimensions

Although domain modelling is currently regarded as a major conceptual topic in its own, there is still no complete agreement on the term *domain* [21]. There are at least two main interpretations which depend on the considered abstraction level; the choice of this level depends on the intended goal. If reuse-oriented goals are pursued, a higher abstraction level is considered and the modelling process gives rise to *generic* domain models. Conversely, if system-oriented goals are pursued, a lower abstraction level is considered and the modelling process gives rise to *application* domain models.

Generic domain models make use of information elements shared by a whole family of different environments [21], while application domain models describe the relevant characteristics and properties of specific environments [29]. In both cases, the conceptual modelling process leads to the description of general properties and rules captured in an application area. However, generic domain models focus on general abstractions which are specialised in application domain models. In the first case, domain concepts describe generic components which can be reused in similar contexts at a higher abstraction level (i.e. as shown in [14]). Conversely, application domain models focus on the specific properties of a given environment. In this second case, domain concepts describe specific components which can be used in a particular context at a lower abstraction level (i.e. as discusses in this paper). Here and in the following, the term domain is thus used as a synonym of application domain at the conceptual level.

Whatever the assumed interpretation, abstraction, representation and deduction problems can be classified as *ontological* aspects, model construction and integration problems as *methodological* aspects, support problems as *operational* aspects. These different aspects characterise the three dimensions of the $\mathcal{DD}$ framework for domain knowledge modelling. This framework is explicitly based on a formal representation scheme, i.e. it is endowed with a *formal ontology*. The latter is also necessary to cope with methodological and operational aspects such as the feasibility of information sharing and non-trivial automated deductive services. The adoption of a formal ontology implies that an application domain is represented using a language endowed with a non-ambiguous syntax and semantics. As opposed to domain knowledge, information about the methodological and operational aspects of domain modelling give rise to the so-called *framework knowledge*. The latter is part of *domain meta-knowledge* [3], i.e. knowledge about the whole domain modelling process. It includes rules for information construction, model integration and automated deduction.

Explicit *ontologies* were recently introduced in knowledge engineering to describe the structure and the vocabulary of domain knowledge [15]. An ontology can be defined as an explicit, partial account of a conceptualisation or, in other terms, as an agreement about a shared conceptualisation [34]. Among other things, it includes a conceptual framework for modelling domain knowledge and an agreement about the representation of a particular domain theory. A very simple case of ontology would be a type hierarchy, specifying classes and subsumption relationships, or a relational database scheme. An ontology is thus part of domain meta-knowledge, as considered in the above signification. In this paper, the term ontology encompasses the conceptualisation in terms of domain, generic *and* representation ontologies defined in [15]. Generic and domain ontologies are used in modelling knowledge about generic and application domains respectively.

---

[3]The semantics of these domain terms is not univocal. For example, in [4] the term *domain knowledge* has the same interpretation as the term *framework knowledge* introduced in this section. Moreover, the term *domain analysis* has the same interpretation as the term *domain modelling* used in this paper.

However, the borderline between these ontological kinds, as well as between generic and application domains is rather vague. The term *abstraction ontology* is thus used in this paper to denote both generic and application ontologies. Conversely, the term *representation ontology* is used to denote ontological aspects dealing with knowledge representation, as stated in [15]. Here and in the following, two distinct ontological representation levels are explicitly recognised; they are denoted as *epistemological* and *terminological* ontologies respectively (see sec. 4.2). Moreover, methodological aspects as defined in this paper correspond to method ontology as defined in [34].

Ontological, methodological and operational aspects are the essence of any framework addressing the domain knowledge modelling process and product. At the same time, they represent the conceptual dimensions which can be used to classify different modelling approaches. These dimensions are characterised as follows:

- the *ontological dimension* defines the different categories of concepts introduced to describe domain abstractions as well as the representation, the meaning (interpretation) and the available deductive services bound to each category;

- the *methodological dimension* defines a collection of guidelines used in the disciplined construction and integration of domain knowledge bases (DKBs) composed of concepts belonging to some specific categories.

- the *operational dimension* defines the support techniques used in the analysis of a DKB composed of concepts belonging to a given group of categories.

Although methodological and operational aspects fall within ontological ones in theory, things go differently in application contexts such as the ones upon which the $\mathcal{DD}$ framework is based. In these latter cases, even if ontological aspects are the most significant ones, the organisational effort should provide analysts with practical methods and tools of immediate use. In fact, an engineering framework must explicitly deal with those aspects which are closer to the real-world, multi-faceted situation. Moreover, the authors believe that analysts should be neither involved in the detailed definition of an ontology nor in its subsequent reification in the application context. In other words, analysts should work with predefined ontologies (i.e. with predefined meta-concepts) allowing a limited degree of expressive freedom in the definition of the skeleton of each domain concept. Therefore, different *framework levels* exist. The highest one is the *conceptual level*, where abstraction and representation schemes are defined. Below it, there is an *engineering level* whose methodological and operational aspects implicitly depend on ontological choices. The lowest one is the *application level*, where specific approaches and tools, which depend on the engineering level, are defined. At the ontological and engineering levels, the $\mathcal{DD}$ framework introduces the following major features:

- a *minimalist ontology* which uses the minimum number of abstractions with the minimum number of atomic model constructor to characterise a domain knowledge model in a non-ambiguous and non-trivial way. Knowledge about minimalist domain models is represented using the $\mathcal{EDDL}$ and $\mathcal{TDDL}$ languages (see [11]);

- a *disciplined methodology* for the development and the integration of $\mathcal{EDDL}$ DKBs. Automated support is performed in both cases by the $\mathcal{JANUS}$ intelligent knowledge management environment (IKME) [10];

- a set of *categorial operations* which use distinct rules for the construction of hierarchies composed of concepts belonging to different ontological categories.

Table 2: Levels and aspects in the $\mathcal{DD}$ framework

	Framework Aspect		
Framework Level	Ontological	Methodological	Operational
Conceptual	Abstraction, Representation, Deduction		
Engineering		Construction, Integration	Support
Application			Approach, Tool

Each of these features contributes to the definition of a new generation of intelligent support tools for conceptual modelling . The development of the $\mathcal{JANUS}$ IKME is among the main long-term goals of the approach based on the $\mathcal{DD}$ framework.

4 Ontological aspects

The $\mathcal{DD}$ framework is based on the idea that a *minimalist ontology* is necessary and sufficient to capture and describe an application domain. It extends and specialises the minimalist phenomenology introduced in [29] to allow a multi-paradigm domain description. In fact, a wide number of concepts can be elicited during a first investigation of a real-world application domain. However, a minimum number of meta-concepts is sufficient to characterise it in a non-trivial way. Moreover, for each meta-concept, there is a minimum number of atomic model constructors which is sufficient to characterise the corresponding domain abstraction in a non trivial-way.

The abstraction ontology defines the different domain meta-concepts introduced to capture abstractions identified in the UoD. Conversely, the representation ontology defines the representation schemes introduced to describe the skeleton as well as the semantics of each of the above meta-concepts. It is worth noting that the choice of a representation ontology deeply influences the related deduction problem.

In order to match the need for a user-oriented view of the UoD with the need for automated deductive services in domain modelling analysis, two different ontological levels were introduced in the $\mathcal{DD}$ framework. They are respectively denoted as *epistemological* and *terminological* level; each of them encompasses both ontological abstraction and representation issues. These two ontological levels are based on distinct abstraction and representation schemes. The epistemological level is mainly user-oriented; it emphasizes the role of a user-friendly syntax allowing the explicit description of domain concepts belonging to different categories. The terminological level is mainly machine-oriented; it emphasizes the role of formal semantics in automated reasoning.

4.1 Abstraction ontology

At the epistemological level, the $\mathcal{DD}$ framework introduces a minimalist abstraction ontology which considers data and process concepts as the sole essential components of a domain knowledge model. Objects are considered as composite concepts including one data concept together with all process concepts that use it. Data and processes are regarded as instances of two different concept categories, called *meta-data* and *meta-processes* respectively. These *meta-concepts* generalise two main structural and behavioural abstractions captured in the UoD and currently used in conceptual modelling. The term *concept* is used in this paper as a synonym of the term *class* used in object-oriented modelling [35, 27, 9], where it denotes a set of individuals (i.e. the set of all instances of a given concept). At the terminological level, more than one intermediate *pseudo meta-concept* can give rise to a single epistemological meta-concept [10].

In the $\mathcal{DD}$ framework, meta-data and meta-processes, which represent the result of a critical analysis of the conceptual content of domain knowledge, are called *epistemological meta-concepts*. Their introduction represents a fundamental trade-off between expressive power adequacy and automated reasoning capabilities. Meta-concepts accommodate *expressiveness* and *compositionality* within the same modelling scheme. Expressiveness depends on how well meta-concepts describe knowledge about the UoD, while compositionality is a semantical mechanism to link single concepts one another.

The abstraction ontology is considered as an *UoD meta-level*. Several concepts belonging to the same meta-concept can be defined at the *intensional UoD level*; each one is characterised by its specific class skeleton. Moreover, several information elements belonging to the same concept can be defined at the *extensional UoD level*; each one is characterised by its belonging to a specific class.

4.2 Representation ontology

The $\mathcal{DD}$ framework introduces a minimalist representation ontology derived from an ubiquitous rule of conceptual modelling. This rule states that concepts must not contain any reference to their internal structure or behaviour [3, 8, 18]. Concept descriptions must thus give rise to a coherent image of *what* composes the domain, but not of *how* each domain component is organised or behaves internally. More precisely, they are endowed with a purely *intensional* knowledge representation. Therefore, data are described as sets with no ordering structure, while processes are described as black boxes with no transfer function. Structural concepts must not represent individuals (i.e. instance specification). Correspondingly, behavioural concepts must not represent procedurality (i.e. time- or event-based control, sequence, iteration, selection).

The adoption of a representation scheme for domain knowledge modelling is an ontological choice which influences methodological and operational aspects as well. In the $\mathcal{DD}$ framework, domains are modelled using two different representation levels, namely an *epistemological* one and a *terminological* one. The epistemological level defines an external, user-oriented knowledge representation based on the $\mathcal{EDDL}$ language. The latter describes concept categories which generalise the main abstractions identified in the UoD of computer-based information systems. Each epistemological concept is built by way of an analyst-oriented syntax which can be easily understood by users as well. The terminological level defines an internal, machine-oriented knowledge representation based on the $\mathcal{TDDL}$ language. This concept language [4] allows automated reasoning about domain knowledge within the framework of terminological knowledge representation systems [44, 42, 49, 46, 26, 13, 36]. The $\mathcal{TDDL}$ language is a decidable member of the KL-ONE family [50]. It is endowed with a *set-theoretic* semantics which is independent of epistemological categories of real-world domain concepts.

---

[4] *Concept languages* are also called *frame-based [description] languages, term subsumption languages, KL-ONE-like languages, terminological languages, taxonomic logics, description logics.*

Each syntactical declaration of a given epistemological concept is mapped into a set of terminological expressions by way of a specific collection of rewrite rules [11]. These rules define the biunivocal mapping between $\mathcal{TDDL}$ and $\mathcal{EDDL}$. In this way, the syntax of the latter is formalised and indirectly endowed with a set-theoretic semantics. The epistemological representation can be used to investigate domain-dependent properties as well as the effectiveness of the overall expressive power of the $\mathcal{EDDL}$ language with respect to these properties. Conversely, the terminological representation can be used to investigate decidability, computational complexity and tractability problems with respect to the automated reasoning capabilities bound to the $\mathcal{TDDL}$ language. The introduction of these two intertwined knowledge representation schemes is an innovative feature of the $\mathcal{DD}$ framework. It avoids direct user interaction with machine-oriented details and it let analysts model the domain using a simple, almost natural language.

The epistemological representation implies the existence of a *closed* ontology, which defines the characteristics of real-world meta-concepts endowed with different description and hierarchy-forming rules. This means that (i) only predefined meta-concepts are allowed at the epistemological abstraction level and that (ii) the corresponding expressive power is constrained by the skeletal knowledge structure of each meta-concept. Conversely, the terminological representation implies the existence of an *open* ontology. The latter is necessary as a representation algebra in order to describe basic concept constructors. Terminological expressions are manipulated by automated reasoners without any reference to their epistemological meaning. This implies that (i) any kind of meta-concept can be described at the terminological abstraction level and that (ii) the expressive power at this level is only constrained by the trade-off between expressiveness and computational complexity of automated reasoning.

Automatic deductive services at the epistemological level implicitly depend on the corresponding knowledge representation at the underlying terminological level. These services are extremely useful in domain modelling and analysis, avoiding semantical inconsistencies, ambiguities and redundancies and thus enhancing the quality of the conceptual model. Moreover, they can be of great help in information sharing and knowledge integration. All these services, in which logical consequences of assertions about concepts can be calculated, are based on different *epistemological subsumption* rules for the allocation of concepts into hierarchies. The existence of distinct hierarchy-forming rules is an ontological consequence of the different interpretations of domain meta-concepts. For instance, while the interpretation of data inheritance is based on classification, the interpretation of process replacement is based on functional typing.

5   Methodological and operational aspects

As previously stated, methodological and operational aspects could be considered as part of ontological ones, at least in a broad sense. However, an explicit distinction among them was introduced in the $\mathcal{DD}$ framework. In fact, any true engineering approach to the development of domain models in real-world applications includes many features which do not depend on ontological choices. For instance, the top-down, bottom-up or middle-out model development strategies are absolutely independent from the adopted ontology of concepts. This means that the same ontology could be used both in the construction of a domain model starting from scratch and in the integration of two existing domain models. Of course, even if meta-concepts used in the two situations remain the same, the corresponding engineering problems are quite different.

5.1 Methodological aspects

Methodological aspects can be further divided into model construction and integration ones. Model construction is performed following a disciplined approach involving *categorial precedence* and *increasing definition level*. Categorial precedence means that structural domain concepts (i.e. data) must be defined before those behavioural domain concepts (i.e. processes) which use them. Moreover, composite units (i.e. objects) must be defined after the structural and behavioural concepts they incorporate, and so on. Increasing definition level means that the atomic domain concepts must be introduced first. They must be followed by partially defined concepts, totally defined concepts, concept constraints in this sequential order. This rule leads to the introduction of domain concepts characterised by a more structurally complex skeleton. In fact, atomic concepts carry no knowledge other than their name, while concept constraints add mutual limits to already existing concepts. Furthermore, circular definitions are allowed but syntactically disciplined. While it is not possible to have still undefined concepts as ancestors, concept properties whose attribute domains will be subsequently defined are tolerated. This limited usage of circular definitions was explicitly introduced in structural meta-concepts to capture the essence of ER modelling. In this way, descriptions such as "a STUDENT attends at least 2 and at most 4 COURSEs", where COURSE is subsequently defined as "attended by at least 2 and at most 30 STUDENTs" can be captured and modelled. As a consequence of categorial precedence, behavioural concepts must be declared in terms of already existing structural concepts representing their input and output context components, avoiding declarations in terms of undefined inputs or outputs. All the above construction constraints are embedded in the representation ontology of the $\mathcal{DD}$ framework, which implicitly characterises them.

Model integration is supported by the minimalist ontology. The possibility of modelling structural and behavioural concepts, as well as composite units encapsulating them, favours the integration of domain modelling approaches based on semi-formal schemes. The existence of a formal semantics based on description logics and the possibility of implementing non-trivial automatic deductive services greatly enhance integration capabilities. The integration problem is twofold. The first step towards integration deals with the problem of sharing information captured using different models of an application domains. In this phase, the shared ontology is the intersection of the original ontologies. The subsequent step towards integration deals with the problem of merging information provided by different sources, recognising similarities and variations among information elements which represent the same state of affairs or domain structure. In this phase, the resulting ontology is the union of the original ontologies.

The $\mathcal{DD}$ framework mainly addresses *information sharing*, i.e. the definition of a minimalist ontology which can be shared by different modelling approaches. In this way, domain analysts can use a semi-formal modelling approach so that it can be straightforwardly captured and interpreted. The reification of a shared domain knowledge model should conform to the above methodological rules for categorial precedence and increasing definition level in the construction of a domain model.

The epistemological representation ontology based on the $\mathcal{EDDL}$ language is endowed with several concept constructor options which support scheme integration. Multiple inheritance and concept name equality respectively allow the declaration of concept dependencies and aliases, while local attribute chaining allows the declaration of attribute dependencies and aliases. Moreover, dependencies and aliases on both concepts and attributes can be detected using automatic deductive services.

5.2   Operational aspects

The importance of operational aspects is bound to the need of support tools for conceptual modelling and analysis endowed with automated reasoning capabilities on a semantical basis. Knowledge management environments and support tools must be considered as intelligent agents which monitor analysts' actions and help them to detect contradictions, redundancies, incompleteness as well as semantical errors. Tools of this kind can be either regarded as analyst's assistants organising his work or as autonomous reasoners over the considered modelling scheme. The $\mathcal{DD}$ framework considers and supports the implementation of these tools as follows. First, they must help the analyst during the continuous revision process ending with the completion of the domain model. Second, they must decouple the user-oriented epistemological abstraction and representation ontology from the machine-oriented terminological counterpart. At first sight, modelling concepts explicitly offered by the $\mathcal{DD}$ framework might seem limited (and limiting) if compared with other current modelling approaches in information systems engineering. However, this kind of approach is explicitly intended to support automatic reasoning over conceptual schemes, emphasizing the role of deductive services offered by terminological knowledge representation and reasoning systems.

6   Conclusions

The $\mathcal{DD}$ framework was created to evaluate the role and the extent of both concept models and conceptual modelling approaches currently adopted in domain knowledge modelling and analysis. It is being used as an engineering background for the development of a new generation of intelligent knowledge management environments and tools endowed with automated deductive capabilities. It emphasizes the role of domain-dependent abstractions, knowledge representation and formal semantics in concept modelling, as well as the role of automated deduction in conceptual modelling. The $\mathcal{DD}$ framework is characterised by three ontological, methodological and operational dimensions which cope with some fundamental problems of both concept modelling and conceptual modelling. The ontological dimension, which is by far the most important and critical, is based on three main assumptions. First, the universe of discourse should be divided in two parts: the structural one and the behavioural one. It is worth noting that the behavioural part must be described only after the structural one. Second, the definition of indicative assertions about the UoD should be considered as the main goal of any domain knowledge modelling activity. In other words, the analyst should deal with the intensional outlook of reality. This approach constrains the analyst to make a definite distinction between what must be done and how it can be done. Third, any domain knowledge modelling activity should be focused on the description of UoD concepts as well as on assertions about them. Research work about the methodological and operational dimensions of the $\mathcal{DD}$ framework are not as much advanced as in the ontological case. More specifically, the integration and support problems need a much more detailed effort in order to reach more complete and general results.

Acknowledgements

The authors thank Francesco M. Donini (Università di Roma "La Sapienza") for his review of an early version of this paper and Nicola Guarino (LADSEB-CNR, Padova) for his remark on the attribution of the cited definition of the term ontology.

References

[1] A. Borgida and M. Jarke. Special Issue on Knowledge Representation and Reasoning in Software Engineering. *IEEE Transactions on Software Engineering*, 18(6), Jun. 1992.

[2] A. Borgida and S. Greenspan and J. Mylopoulos. Knowledge Representation as the basis for Requirements Specification. *IEEE Computer*, pages 82–91, Apr. 1985.

[3] A. M. Davis. *Software Requirements Analysis and Specification*. Prentice-Hall, 1990.

[4] A. T. Berztiss. Domains, patterns, reuse and the software process. In A. Sutcliffe and D. Benyon and F. van Assche, editor, *Proc. of the IFIP Joint Working Conference on Domain Knowledge for Interactive System Design (DKISD'96)*, pages 78–89. Chapman & Hall, 1996.

[5] B. Curtis and H. Krasner and N. Iscoe. A Field Study of the Software Design Process for Large Systems. *Communications of the ACM*, pages 1268–1287, Nov. 1988.

[6] C. Batini and M. Lenzerini and S. Navathe. A Comparative Analysis of Methodologies for Database Schema Integration. *ACM Computing Surveys*, 18:323–364, Dec. 1986.

[7] C. Potts. Software Engineering Research Revised. *IEEE Software*, pages 19–28, Sep. 1993.

[8] C. Rolland and C. Cauvet. Trends and Perspectives in Conceptual Modelling. In P. Loucopoulos and R. Zicari, editor, *Conceptual Modelling, DBs and CASE: an Integrated View of Information Systems Development*. John Wiley, 1992.

[9] C. Sernadas and J. Fiadeiro. Towards object-oriented conceptual modeling. *Data & Knowledge Engineering*, 6:479–508, 1991.

[10] E. Compatangelo. *A concept-based approach to domain knowledge modelling and analysis in information systems engineering (in italian)*. PhD thesis, Facoltà di Ingegneria, Università di Ancona, Italy, 1996.

[11] E. Compatangelo and G. Rumolo. $\mathcal{EDDL}_{DP} + \mathcal{TDDL}_{DP} =$ a double-level approach to Domain Knowledge Modelling. In H. Kangassalo and J. F. Nilsson [20].

[12] E. Yourdon. *Modern Structured Analysis*. Prentice-Hall, 1989.

[13] F. Baader and B. Hollunder. $\mathcal{KRIS}$: Knowledge Representation and Inference System. *ACM SIGART Bulletin*, 2(3), 1991.

[14] G. Grosz. Building Information Systems Using Generic Structures. In *Intl. Computer Software and Applications Conf. (ICSAC-92), Chicago (USA)*, 1992.

[15] G. van Heijst and B. Wielinga and A. T. Schreiber. Using Explicit Ontologies in KBS Development. *International Journal of Human and Computer Studies*, 46(2/3), 1997.

[16] H. B. Reubenstein and R. C. Waters. The Requirements Apprentice: Automated Assistance for Requirements Definition. *IEEE Transactions on Software Engineering*, 17(3), Mar. 1991.

[17] H. J. Levesque and R. J. Brachman. A Fundamental Tradeoff in Knowledge Representation and Reasoning. In R. J. Brachman and H. J. Levesque [43], pages 41–70.

[18] H. Kangassalo. COMIC: A system and methodology for conceptual modelling and information construction. *Data & Knowledge Engineering*, 9:287–319, 1992/93.

[19] H. Kangassalo. Conceptual Description for Information Modelling Based on Intensional Containment Relation. In *ECAI'96 workshop KRDB'96*, 1996.

[20] H. Kangassalo and J. F. Nilsson, editor. *Information Modelling and Knowledge Bases VIII*. IOS Press, 1997.

[21] J. Kramer. "Generalisations are False" ? In *Proc. of the 1st IEEE Int. Sym. on Requirements Engineering (RE'93)*, page 79. IEEE Computer Society Press, 1993.

[22] J. Martin. *Information Engineering*. Prentice-Hall, 1990.

[23] J. Mylopoulos and others. Telos: Representing Knowledge About Information Systems. *ACM Transactions on Information Systems*, 8(4):325–362, Oct. 1990.

[24] J. Palomäki. Three Kinds of Containment Relations of Concepts. In H. Kangassalo and J. F. Nilsson [20].

[25] J. Peckam and F. Maryanski. Semantic Data Models. *ACM Computing Surveys*, 20(3):153–189, Sep. 1988.

[26] J. Quantz and C. Kindermann. Implementation of the BACK System Version 4. Technical Report KIT-Report 78, FB Informatik, Technische Universität Berlin, Berlin, Germany, 1990.

[27] J. Rumbaugh and others. *Object-Oriented Modelling and Design*. Prentice-Hall, 1991.

[28] L. Cardelli. A Semantics of Multiple Inheritance. In G. Kahn and others, editor, *Semantics of Data Types*, volume 173 of *Lecture Notes in Computer Science*, pages 52–67, 1984.

[29] M. A. Jackson and P. Zave. Domain Descriptions. In *Proc. of the 1st IEEE Int. Sym. on Requirements Engineering (RE'93)*, pages 56–64. IEEE Computer Society Press, 1993.

[30] M. Jarke and others. DAIDA: An Environment for Evolving Information Systems. *ACM Transactions on Information Systems*, 10(1):1–50, Jan. 1992.

[31] M. Jarke and others. ConceptBase – A Deductive Object Manager for MetaData Bases. *Journal of Intelligent Information Systems*, 1994.

[32] M. Lenzerini and T. Catarci. Representing and Using Interschema Knowledge in Cooperative Information Systems. *International Journal of Intelligent and Cooperative Information Systems*, 2(4):353–398, Dec. 1993.

[33] M. Lubars and C. Potts and C. Richter. A Review of the State of the Practice in Requirements Modeling. In *Proc. of the 1st IEEE Int. Sym. on Requirements Engineering (RE'93)*, pages 2–14, 1993.

[34] N. Guarino. Understanding, Building and Using Ontologies. *International Journal of Human and Computer Studies*, 46(2/3):293–310, 1997.

[35] P. Coad and E. Yourdon. *Object Oriented Analysis*. Prentice-Hall, 2nd edition, 1991.

[36] P. F. Patel-Schneider and others. The CLASSIC Knowledge Representation System: Guiding Principles and Implementation Rationale. *ACM SIGART Bulletin*, 2(3):108–113, 1991.

[37] P. Hsia and A. M. Davis and D. Kung. Status Report: Requirements Engineering. *IEEE Software*, pages 75–79, Nov. 1993.

[38] P. Johannesson. Schema Standardisation as an Aid in View Integration. *Information Systems*, 19(3):275–290, 1994.

[39] P. P. Chen. The Entity-Relationship Model: Toward a Unified View of Data. *ACM Transactions on Database Systems*, 1(1):9–36, Mar. 1976.

[40] R. Balzer and N. Goldman and D. Wile. Operational Specifications as the Basis for Rapid Prototyping. *ACM Software Engineering Notes*, 5:3–16, Dec. 1982.

[41] R. Elmasri and S. Navathe. *Fundamentals of Database Systems, 2nd ed.* Benjamin-Cummings, 1994.

[42] R. J. Brachman and H. J. Levesque. KRIPTON: A Functional Approach to Knowledge Representation. In KR'85 [43], pages 412–429.

[43] R. J. Brachman and H. J. Levesque, editor. *Readings in Knowledge Representation.* Morgan Kaufmann, 1985.

[44] R. J. Brachman and J. G. Schmolze. An Overview of the KL-ONE Knowledge Representation System. *Cognitive Science*, 9(2):171–216, 1985.

[45] R. J. Brachman and others. Living with CLASSIC: when and how to use a KL-ONE-like Language. In J.F. Sowa, editor, *Principles of Semantic Networks*, pages 401–456. Morgan Kaufmann, 1991.

[46] R. MacGregor and R. Bates. The Loom Knowledge Representation Language. Technical Report ISI/RS-87-188, University of Southern California, Information Science Institute, Marina del Rey, Cal., 1987.

[47] S. Bergamaschi and S. Lodi and C. Sartori. The E/S Knowledge Representation System. *Data & Knowledge Engineering*, 14:81–115, 1994.

[48] S. Greenspan and J. Mylopoulos and A. Borgida. On Formal Requirements Modelling Languages: RML Revisited. In *Proc. of the 16th Int. Conf. on Software Engineering (ICSE'16)*, 1994.

[49] T. S. Kaczmarek and R. Bates and G. Robins. Recent Developments in NIKL. In *Proc. of the 5th Nat. Conf. on Artificial Intelligence (AAAI'86)*, pages 978–985, 1986.

[50] W. A. Woods and J. G. Schmolze. The KL-ONE Family. *Computers and Mathematics with Applications*, 23(2-9):1–50, 1992.

[51] W. L. Johnson and M. S. Feather and D. R. Harris. Representation and Presentation of Requirements Knowledge. *IEEE Transactions on Software Engineering*, 18(10):853–869, Oct. 1992.

[52] W.W. Song. Semantic Knowledge Acquisition and Computation in Conceptual Schema Integration. In H. Kangassalo and J. F. Nilsson [20].

Information Modelling and Knowledge Bases IX
P.-J. Charrel et al. (Eds.)
1998, IOS Press

A Multi-Agent Model for Co-Operative Communications in Crisis Management Systems:The Act of Communication

Alain CARDON

PSI & LIP6 Paris VI, INSA de Rouen BP 08, 76131 Mont-Saint-Aignan, France

Abstract We present a model of Communication and Information Systems dedicated to the management of crisis and emergency situations. This model allows the representation of the intentions and judgments expressed by decisional actors when they exchange information, introducing the notion of act of communication. The model is used for the development of a prototype of system founded on the use of dynamic multiagent systems. This multiagent systems present variable morphologies when the management system is running, according to the qualifications applied to the exchanged information. The system prototype produces synthetic and interactive descriptions of the different subjective characters provided by users, leaning on the representation of the morphology of multiagent systems.

1. Introduction

Nowadays, occidental societies are interested in Communication and Information Systems (CIS) which have to manage complex situations such as industrial disasters or military crisis [4]. These new systems use the most sophisticated ways of communication via computers, in order to access to various databases and to allow information exchanges generating tactical and strategic decisions. They have to co-ordinate numerous professionals and very large technical resources: they are complex systems, in the organizational way. So, many points of view are expressed about the evoluting situation, representing the perceptions of the different actors. The tremendous amount of messages no longer make us satisfied with centralized systems based on a given hierarchical structure [22].

In crisis management, the initial situation is not structured. The incoming data, considered as inaccurate and fuzzy, issued by potentially unreliable sources, will lead to a certain structuration of the problem domain. But since the actors that provided data, belong to different institutions, are geographically widespread, are in emergency situations and have a very partial view of the situation, the information they exchange on the network concerning the situation are very dependent on the emitting context, that is, they are encapsulated in their necessary pragmatic [11].

In CIS, actors must be able to generate no rational decision, but with spreading information about this kind of act, in indicating the situational context of its generation. They have to take into account what actors think about situations and also their intentions and engagements before decision. These systems aggregate in the action non homogeneous active parts, including distant and non professional spectators. The structure of these variable parts are modified in space and time. Finally, it is difficult to build their variable structure using a rigid and hierarchical order, based on the perfect quality of exchanged information.

Thus, we can consider that CIS are well-built systems in a systemic way [19]. They are organizationally complex, with many ways to divide them into well-identified parts. Their functioning takes into account the social complexity of the phenomenon they express and reacts on their structure. They are very reactive systems, distinguish themselves of the classical Information Systems ones.

The professionals that manage emergency or crisis situations have explicitly asked for a new kind of Information System, in European research projects [23]. Their analyses clearly emphasis that the effective knowledge of the *decision processes* and of the mental representations of actors about situations are essential in the knowledge of phenomenon and that if they are left aside, the management will be badly handled. We may imagine, using new ontological models and taking into consideration the most recent powerful ways of communication, a new approach for CIS. This approach is based on the representation of the decision process itself and of the variation of actors' behavior during phenomenon. It preserves encapsulation of a classical Information System by a reactive level. Moreover, the pragmatic of all statement is to be taken into account, since during crisis situations, actors' mental representations significantly alter their perception of the situation. Thus, the system that is in charge of communications must have an interpreting function of exchanged messages and allows a cognitive fusion of knowledge [9].

Successively, we present the limits of classical IS in crisis management field, the new model at the ontological level with its specific characters, and the architecture and specification of implemented prototype.

2. The classical functional IS Approach

In the field of complex situations, Information Systems (IS) use huge sophisticated computerized communication networks. The large bandwidth allows the transmission of multimedia information and lots of data, and so helps in the management of great amount of human and material resources. Such systems are modeled from the consideration of many physical entities classified into categories (institutions, structures, technical means...). The functional links between this categories are represented with graph models. So, the IS represents many characters of the physical world to provide information and plans about different situations.

In order to represent these physical objects, the IS need large data servers to provide the asking user with the right information at the right moment [3]. The Figure 1 below shows the three levels of organization in such IS.

3.   Movement, Organisations, Planning
2.   Space of development of the entities
1.   Physical world, Objective entities

Figure 1. Organizational levels of IS.

These three levels are descriptive of an objective situation. They describe respectively the studied physical field, the relations between its entities and the expected movements of the entities in space and time. Such information can be used to manage predictively well-informed situations. This information can allow the management of phenomenon only when its evolution is well-predictable.

But in emergency situations, we need to make fast co-operative decisions between actors belonging to different institutions (the Police, Firemen, Emergency Doctors, Officials...). Each decisional actor has its own vision of the phenomenon, his own mental representation about the situation including himself, built according to his formation and habits and which are eventually not consistent with any other. This gap of mental representation discloses for example contradictions with other actors and lack of structuring in the stated point of view. This default of coherence may create strong local oppositions between actors and therefore disrupt the previous plans. Then, this confrontations may interfere with the development of the global phenomenon, speed up dysfunction's. This inadequate interference, which may generate and propagate many others, may lead to real catastrophes: crisis on crisis [23].

In classical IS, such mental representations, such process of development of situation analysis are not expressed, because those elements do not appear in any levels of the organization (C.f. Fig. 1). So, IS can provide many information but don't express nor prevent dysfunction caused by non-adapted human estimations. As we show in Figure 2, the exchanged information between the different entities only takes into account the results of analyses (the named *Reference state*) but never its process of development (the generation of the *current situation*), and this would disclose actors' thoughts.

Such IS have a permanent exchanged information structure and they do not really change when the meaning of situation changes for users [7]. They adapt the information they provide to the different actors with difficulty, not according to their frame of mind. Indeed, the most important information according to the current situation should not be the same for different actors. In the present case, the system should adapt rather itself to the actor's step of reasoning, to the perception of the actor's situation, in order to help him and to leave him master of his decisions. So, we propose additional layers which allow the actors to express a part of their personal opinions and judgments about the phenomenon. Adding such a layer introduces the so-named phenomenological approach.

3. An Approach centred on the perceived phenomenon

A phenomenon based approach is different from the previous one. This approach takes into account the actors' behavior and how the reference states (C.f. Fig. 2) were explicitly generated in mind by different actors. It continually structures the collective representations of the situation and, after the obtaining of some knowledge about subjective characters of negotiations, it will be possible to plan co-operative actions and to make opportune decisions. In this way, the system must adapt itself to the actors' current perceptions of phenomenon. It must take into account, at the same time, the characters of mental representation the actors express through speech acts [21] and the generation itself of their decision process. It is an adaptive system.

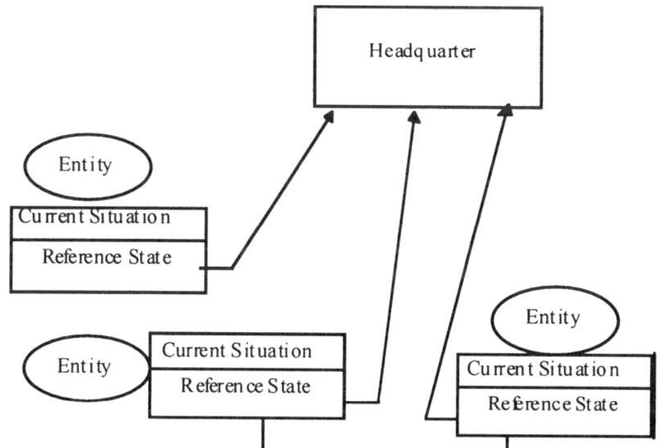

Figure 2. Communication of factual information in classical CIS.

In order to create such a system, we have to take into account the pragmatic of the statement of messages [12] like subjective characters, opinions, judgments, context, cultural background. We qualify as *Complex Systems* [8] the systems having such qualities of reaction and adaptation. They are mainly founded on the expression of human point of view about the current situation and not only on a pre-defined schema of a foreseen situation.

3.1 Communicational Complex Systems: the CCS

We represent, in the Figure 3 below, the six levels of modeling of such Communicational Complex System (CCS), which follow the organizational levels of complex systems [18]:

6. Rules of the social game, power relation, emergence of the global meaning of the phenomenon
5. Values, Symbols, meaning of the phenomenon, intentions

4. Information Communication

3. Movements, Organizations, Planning
2. Space of development of the entities
1. Physical world, Objective entities

Figure 3. The six levels of organization in CCS.

The levels 1 to 3 belong to the field of the classical IS (C.f. Fig. 1), the fourth allows the dynamic organization of this levels as in the classical CIS. The levels five and six belong to the social, psychological and cultural field. The importance and kind of psychological and social categories this levels represent, depend on the current situation itself and of their estimations by actors. This is for this reason that they can not be decomposed into fixed functional subsystems. Like this, these levels belong to a deep complexity domain [8]. We are interested, in these last levels, to take into account intentions, opinions and judgments of actors in the communication process, in order to represent the development of decision making.

3.2 The general architecture of CCS

The phenomenological approach consists in the grasp of the whole phenomenon, that is to say the observed facts of real situation and also the mental representations of this facts by the actors themselves. So, this approach includes the factual information and the development of the process of decision, the opinions and judgments of actors about the different situations and about themselves [1]. The actors' intentionality in the act of information exchange takes precedence over the transmission of neutral information.

In complex phenomena, the managed situation, particularly at the beginning, is vague, changing with a lot of contradictory aspects. The CCS ought to change its own internal structure in order to deal with the situation, thus reflecting in its internal organization the meaning of the phenomenon felt by the different actors. This is a structurally variable system, particularly reactive to the actors' feeling. So, to take into account the intentions and judgments of the actors and to make the system to be reactive, we elaborate some hypothesis and choice of architecture.

Therefore, the general structure of CCS is based on a distributed structuring system aggregating the communication nodes (C.f. Fig. 4). The communication nodes are entities representing the headquarters of each different institution managing crisis. They are made up of communication modules with two main functions. The first function allows many classical access to Geographical Information System or Data Bases, providing factual information to headquarters. The second function allows the representation of the various opinions about situations, development of the mental representations of actors and also the *development* of the decision process.

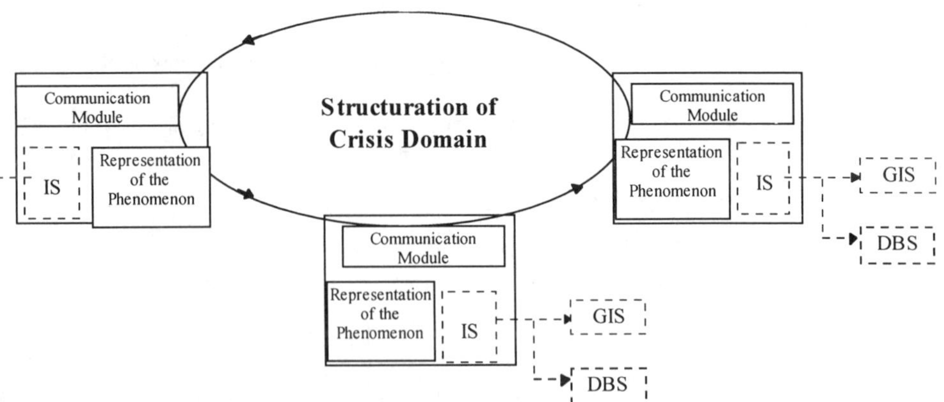

Figure 4. Organization of the CCS of crisis management.

4. The hypothesis at ontological level : self-reference, act of communication and emergence

We saw in 3.2, that the three first levels describe the characters of the objective situation. These levels are processed by the communicating information level (so named Level four). We make the hypothesis that the levels five and six can be represented by some system's inner entities. These levels constitute a very specific domain, expressing subjective, social and cultural aspects of the organization in progress. They are above the four previous ones and they garble their structure. This is the first hypothesis of self-reference in the system. This two last levels can not be represented, in the computational system, by functional pre-defined categories. Each message between decisional actors has a standard form. It is composed of standards words, icons and images belonging to some pre-defined semantic field. But each message expresses the actor's tendency to structure the collective representation of the situation: it has a potentiality to expresses a part of the situation but according to the mental representation of the actor. This is the *Communicational Data*. We represent this character of potentiality of meaning in exchanged messages with computational virtual entities in the system. The whole of this virtual entities, acting on a communication between actors, is the expression for the computational system of its *act of communication,* as a process of interpretation of the communicational data by the system. This set of virtual entities *qualifies* the communication and modifies structurally a part of the system itself: they are effective software actions (Cf. Fig. 5).

So we express in the system meaning categories in the two last levels with acts of communication. The perception of the phenomenon according to the different actors is very relative, including perceptions like opinions, judgments, points of view, context. The representation of this characters will be organizational modifications in space and time, wrapping communications. The main hypothesis is that plastic model and plastic architecture software are better to represent variable phenomena.

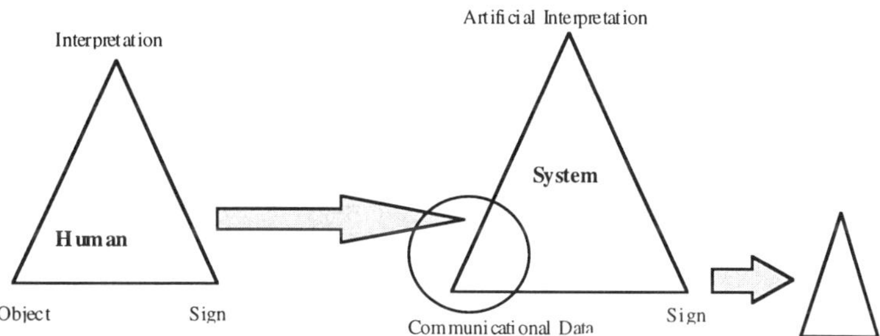

Figure 5. The process of adaptive interpretation between actors and system.

The only model which allows such a plastic representation is a dynamic and hybrid multiagent system [17] [9]. The global characters which can be found in the organization of the multiagent system (MAS) are *emerging characters* [13]. Thus, those agents, with their own particular behavior, may disturb the organization of the system and lead its self-reorganization, in order to exhibit new emerging characters [20]. In MAS, expected or unexpected structures may appear. We make the hypothesis that emerging structures will express the meaning of the communications in the system, as an act of artificial interpretation. This emerging structure represents the accurate views about the different perceptions of the phenomenon elaborated during communication acts. Because the system is dynamic, the whole emerging structures change, according to the evolution of the actor's perceived phenomenon. So, the agent structures and their evolution reflect the organization and the evolution of the phenomenon itself.

5. The ontological specification of CCS

A communication between actors is composed of the message (text, display sounds ..) and of some qualifications about the message, specifying the pragmatic context. Objects and relations allowing to characterize the qualification of communications between actors are constituted of different categories. In the system, we can consider than the actor is wrapped in a set of cognitive entities representing the modalities of meaning he takes about the situation and its evolution, when he exchanges information.

The categories specifying the meaning of the communications, look like the named fundamental categories of the cognitive systems, that we express as semantically unvarying [15]. This categories define the fundamental cognitive elements of the system, representing the meaning of the whole situation for the actors, and where used to built the software architecture.

5.1 Categorisation of the exchanged knowledge: the Communicational Data

We have to study an evolutionary situation, where the organizational characters are generated when required. This organizational characters will be specified in the communication acts. The general categorization of action in the communication act of an actor, as in the speech act [21], is represented with three fundamental categories, forming the Communicational Data:
1. the *object* of the communication, its topic for the transmitter actor, with the precision of a denototional signifier,
2. the *qualification* of the communication, in fact the quality in the meaning of value judgment, linked to the object of the message, expressing the pragmatic of the object,
3. the *intensity* of the qualification, the importance shown by the actor on the qualification of the communication.

In fact, we have three general categories. The transmitter actor of a communication expresses, by his act, an intention. This intention's actor, of course, is not directly accessible, because it take place at the level of the subject itself. But the qualifying action of the communication, clarified by the actor itself, will permit the regular representation of his intention in Communicational Data. And this qualification has three facets: the three general categories of the communication act.

Like this, each communication specifies, relatively to the actor, one ore more objects, qualified with one or more judgments, this last characters appreciated with one ore more intensities. The list of basic triplets of the communicational data is then :

(object,(qualities, values ....)), (object,(qualities, values ....)) ....

This cognitive preciseness, we will represent with symbolic entities, will modify the representation of the local knowledge environment of the actor. In the local system wrapping the actor, the cognitive entities will be categorized with regard to the quality, characterized with:

categories of quality, object or fact introducing the quality, state, strength, velocity

The three last characters are relative to the effective representation of quality and value. The state is the indication of development of the specified quality, the strength is its possible action on other quality categories and the velocity indicates the speed of changing of state, on the quality category.

There is no direct correspondence between the qualification of a message produced by the explicit act of an actor and the state of the cognitive system wrapped the communication. The actor specifies the object of the message setting the text of the message with characters of his intention and, at the time, the system holds the variation of the qualification and its modalities in a communicational data. By this, the current state of the cognitive system will be emerging upon the different qualifications wrapping the communications, at the level of the meaning of the perceived situation, rather than the only level of the objective facts.

5.2 Declination of the fundamental categories in the Communicational Data

In the Communicational Data, the object of the communication is the prime general category, specifying, for the actor, the objective reason of the communication. This category specifies the act of communication. It is explicitly denoted by speakers, using different list of pre-defined icons or symbols and is represented by sub-categories, a priori defined.

There is five kind of sub-categories of object type. The more general specifies the organization to manage, the setting problem. The following sub-categories are one relative to the space of the phenomenon and the temporality. This categories specify the meaning of the first category, making "to be aware of something".

The last category specify the kind of relation existing between the perceived situation and the actor: this is the sub-category of value or qualification, because actor is acting on and by the perceived situation. This sub-category is relative to the obligation of actor in the running situation: it specifies his project, what does he wants, according to his own intention.

In Communicational Data, each object, space and time sub-categories are linked with sub-category of qualification, allowing to precise its characters. The value affected to this qualification is always represented using a numeric and subjective scale.

5.2.1. Sub-category of organizational aspect of the situation

This category specifies the characters of the current observed situation. We distinguish what is relative to the general aspect of the situation of what is relative to a specific aspect. The four characters of this category are the identification of actors, the structure of the situation (plan, sub-structure ..) , the intelligence (command, action) and operating function of an actor.

For example, the sentence « The Mayor orders to take into account an ice risk, because there is ice on the south of the state. He precises this is very important » is interpreted, on Communicational Data as :

text: the text
sender: mayor
receiver: all public services
object : ice risk
intelligence: command
space: the city and its neighbor
time: in the next hours
operative function: clear because this is in the function of a mayor
qualification: judgment = importance, intensity = strength.

5.2.2. Sub-category about time

Each object can be appreciated as temporal, according to the appreciation of the actor. He can specifies a temporal aspect about any object already characterizing a situation, an action or a fact. Like that, this sub-category is subjugated the previous. This is for example:

- date, duration, instant, in the present, in the past, in the future ...

5.2.3. Sub-category about space

In the same way the previous, this category specifies the point of view of the actor about some space characters such point, zone, area, domain. Numerous sub-categories are used.

5.2.4. Sub-category about qualification.

This last category, which is fundamental, specifies the appreciation of the sentence stated by the actor. It is explicit, following the text of the message, or implicit, located in the meaning of the message. The qualifications are the possible judgments specified about any statement expressed by the actors:

The categories of judgment of strength or judgment of value are, for example:
- judgment of strength: important, fundamental, neutral ...
- judgment of value: credible, impossible, unprofitable, absurd, valid, pertinent ...
- judgment about persons: doubt, mistrust, fear ...

The categories of precision about a fact are, for example:
- valuation, precision, imprecision, prediction...

The intensity of a qualification is represented on a subjective scale, expressed the importance of the judgment.

Like that, each communication is expressed in a Communicational Data in the environment of the sender and, following, of the receiver actor. The form of such structure is, in the system, a kind of semantic pattern created with syntactic analysis of the text, using a set of matrix of semantical closeness. This choice is justified by the technical character of the domain we study. But the internal representation of the different qualifications will be no static and will be plastic, with a changing morphology, as are the states of mind.

6. The use of dynamic multiagent systems for the implementation of CCS

The structuring system ought to filter communications and express the communication acts between the actors. It is represented by multiagent systems. The different agents constitute an organizational wrapping around the communicating system of each actor. Such wrapping is named an *agents landscape*. This agents landscape is able to self-modify its morphology for its self-adaptation to the qualifications supplied by the actor during each communication, according to the fundamental categories (C.f. Fig 7). This character of self-modification allows to express the evolution of the meaning produced by each actor about some facts in an organizational way and not only on a structural way.

During the communication, a first static structure is created, according to the qualifications provided by the actor in the communicational data. This structure is a pattern created from the different categories and sub-categories expressing the qualifications of the message. This pattern set in motion the agents landscape, with creation of news agents and modification of others. The action of the communicational data on the agents landscape is as a closure in autopoietic system [25]. This is not the creation of a corresponding cognitive pattern according to the communicational data but *self-adaptation* on the agents landscape. The communicational system of each actor, representing the evolution of his own mental representations, has strong character of autonomy.

The structuring system wrapping communication is represented by different MAS. The general architecture is divided in three parts.

1. The first part represents the communicational network between decisional actors (headquarters of the institutions). The term actor means different entities like individuals, groups of professional institutions (the Police, Firemen, Emergency doctors,...). Each entity is a node of the communicational network [9]. These entities dialogue with others through a personalized interface, according to specific protocols. This part corresponds to the three classical IS levels of Fig. 3.

2. The second part describes the statements and intentions the actors may explicitly express during communication. At this level, we are trying to describe the actors' intentions and opinions about personal and co-operative situations and also the generation of decisions making about situations. This part is the representation of levels 4 and 5 in the Fig. 3 by named *aspectual* agents.

3. The third one draws the expressed judgments' complex shape on the interactive interface of actors, using representational graphics. This part corresponds to the sixth level in Fig. 3. An agent systems will, by operating on the aspectual agents' landscape, exhibit the pertinent organizational characteristics, the possible lectures, the possible causal and temporal structures. Theses agents, called *organizational agents*, that operate according to rational goals, try to exhibit the pertinent forms in the whole set of semantic traits, by constituting "chreods", aggregating aspectual agents into significant structures. Thus, the aspectual agents' landscape is made of different lectures, explicitly represented. A third

agent systems will consider all the local (relatively to each actor) organizational agents and will aggregate them for all sites, in order to form a synthesis of the perception of the situation, using their own messages on the network. These agents, called *morphological agents*, will not provide a global view of what has been expressed by the communicational data but rather a global view proper to each actor, one that will be in appropriate with his own views, that will take into account his own morphologies, a view that he will be able to understand. Each actor will have the representation of his own view about the phenomenon (the state of the multi-agent systems) enriched with that of the others, without showing a general, objective representation that would be *the* whole meaning of the phenomenon. Theses agents achieve decision making actions by choosing knowledge and local pragmatics' augmentation strategies. This decision is a emergence phenomenon that uses the aspectual and organizational agents systems' morphologies as decisional patterns. Decision is typically made of multiple points of view

These three parts are in a loop (C.f. Fig. 6) and are modeled with specific MAS we describe below.

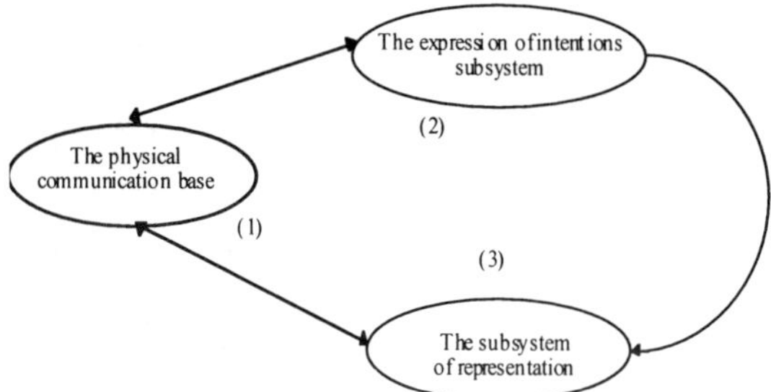

Figure 6. The three CCS subsystems.

6.1 The CCS Component for communication

At this level, we model the physical actors, the communication medium and the usual interfaces [16]. Each physical actor will be described by an agent called *concrete agent*. This agent is structured, taking into account its functions such as, for example, the expected behavior in its mission. The interfaces at this level must allow a clear and synthetic vision of objective facts about the situation. It must allow the making of data requests to information servers and to exchange multimedia information with the other actors [5]. The actors' communication network is modeled by a MAS with classical cognitive agents [13].

6.2 The CCS Component for the expresions of the actor's intentions

This subsystem allows the expression of the statements and judgments explicitly expressed by the concrete agent about the current situation during communications. It expresses all the ontological categories of the domain. Through the interface, each actor has to tell facts and opinions or judgments about the characters of the current situation or about other actors coming with communication. These qualifications express actor's vision of the situation.

Each point of view or judgment is taken into account from each communicational data, which we call *aspectual agents*. The aspectual agents represent the different categories and sub-categories, defined at the ontological level. Indeed, these aspectual agents bind themselves to an actor, develop and try to alter the actor's neighbors, with a strong character of autonomy, as shown in the Figure 6. This aspectual agents describe some categories of sense and meaning about the state of mind of the physical concrete agent (doubt, distrust, incomprehension, trust,...) at the communication time.

6.2.1. The behavior of aspectual agents.

The aspectual agents have, in the developed prototype, rational behavior. Their flexibility, variable number and actions capacities form a set in adequate relation with the structuration process of crisis management domain. They have goals: surviving and developing, according to the communication characteristics. These characters express justifications and reasons of the decision or lack of decision, or opinions about many facts in the evolution of situations. This is a *dynamic* world of agents. They have their own conquests and confrontations against the other parasites' strategies. These parasites are able to recuperate the concrete agent's judgments in order to impose their own vision of the world to the other parasites. This attempt of conviction is made by increasing the importance of the parasite or by increasing the number of its representatives.

If a parasite put forward in relative importance, it means that its importance is locally growing. The reason is that its corresponding concrete agent reinforces its action in the qualification of some message (for example, a concrete agent may *strongly* doubt). If the parasite increases the number of its representatives by generating some clones, it means that its subjective character is widespread. (a lot of concrete agents doubt about decision or an agent doubts about many things). Both methods of the parasite's development are not independents. We can reasonably think that if a doubt is spread; it will become locally important. Similarly, if a doubt is locally important, it will have tendencies to spread among concrete agents.

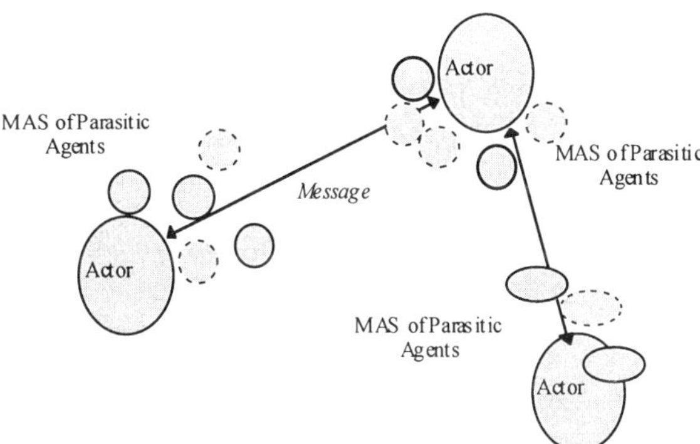

Figure 7. Aspectual agents enveloping the communication system.

A parasite agent has several ways of increasing the number of its representatives. It may generate clone, it means a exactly similar parasite of itself. It may also generate a richer parasite by grasping some characteristics and functions from other parasites (generalization by partial mutation) or a less rich one (specialization). It may, at least, merge with one or several other parasites (global mutation), adapting its behavior to the characters of the communication.

6.2.2. The MAS of aspectual agents

Each parasite is modeled by a cognitive agent [6]. Therefore, the whole set of parasite around the concrete agent form a dynamic MAS in which the quality and the quantity of its agent are changing. To stabilize such a set of agents, we generate for each parasite a dual parasite, according to the represented categories (for example trust and defiance). The development of one of them leads more or less quickly to the weakening or the death of the other. Both have the same goals (surviving and developing) and the same means, so they constantly fight with each other.

The reconfiguration of the landscape of agents directly affects the concrete agent's interface, with the inclusion of a specific graphic and by some effective alterations of this interface. Thus, the system modifies its interfaces according to the opinions given by the concrete agents about different situations. Each of the concrete agents, seeing in his interface the representation of intentions and judgments of others, then justifies its acts and therefore modifies the structure of the agents systems. The CCS operates in a loop including the actors.

6.3 Structure of aspectual agents

According to the plasticity of aspectual agents which ought to reflect the fineness of actor's mental representations, we use a double structure of transition networks for their modeling. The aspectual agents are modeled by a general transition network which has four steps: the named *macro-network* (Cf. Fig. 8). In the macro-network, the first step represents the initialization of the agent. During the second step, the agent tries to get information on its context, in order to know if it is viable. In such a case, it reaches the third step. There, the agent tries to impose its point of view. If it succeeds, it reaches the fourth step, which is the action state. Each step behavior is also modeled by a transition network called in the following lines graph or network. This complex structure must allow the fine representation of the subjective opinions.

A macro network has four nodes: the Initialization, the Deliberation, the Decision and the Action. That composing corresponds to the schema of the linear decision [24].

1. In the first step node, the agent wakes up. It tries to determine if the amount and the strength of the messages provided by its host is worth the process to be initiated.
2. In the second step, the agent tries to determine if its context is good for it. So, it will ask other aspectual agents some information about their state. According to these information, the agent will reach the third step or go back to the initialization step.
3. In the third step, the agent will try to impose its point of view at other aspectual agents. It will try to infect the other agents. It will act on the graph of other agents and send some clones to neighboring hosts. Those clones have the same role in the neighboring MAS. The aspectual agent may kill some of the weak agents of the MAS, and strengthen some other, in order to reach its goal: win and have the fourth step.
4. When an agent has won Decision, it enters the fourth step. There, it will act on the macro-graph itself of the other agents. At this step, we can say that the category it represents characterizes a significant and pertinent point of view of host.

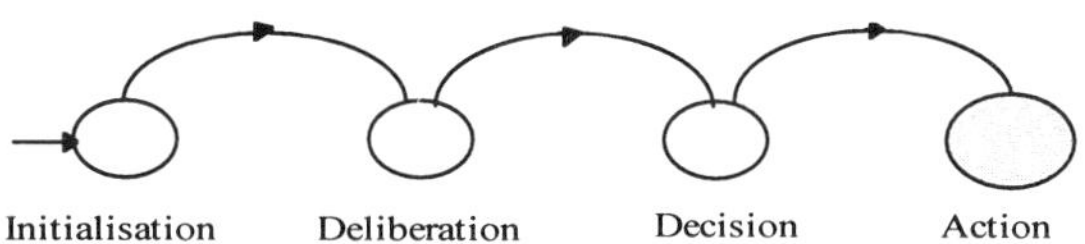

Figure 8 The Macro Transition Network

The different states of the Macro Transition Network are expressed with different automata and augmented transition networks, according to the characters of evolution and stability in the different SMA [10].

7. The emerging meaning of the phenomenon

The previously defined aspectual agents allow the expression of the local meaning for each communication, interpreting it as an act of communication. The set of the MAS bound to each concrete agent, allows the expression of the meaning of the phenomenon for him. This meaning is generated by an *emerging* structure on the morphology of MAS. For this, we have defined the notion of *algebra of agents*. They are the operations on MAS allowing the emergence of new general agents, characterizing the MAS morphology : breaking between some group of agents, dense set of agents, disjunction of groups, fast variation of aggregations. This is a very important point in our work, where we study the coherence and stability of MAS, expressing the global sense of the situation by the study of the agents landscape morphology.

Our goal is to have a structural and immediate connection between the set of concrete agents' ideas about the situation and the landscape of aspectual agents. This notion is central in the model and understood as a new form of meaning, expressing the synthesis of particular forms (the aspectual agents) around the different concrete agents.

The morphologic characters of the MAS, the characters of aspectual agents and their evolution identify the situation in the system among three possible states: Initialization of a global meaning, Deliberation towards a global meaning and Decision for this meaning category. So, the structure of emerging agents on morphology is of the same kind that the parasite ones.

7.1 The global representation of the phenomenon subsystem

The modification of the interface of concrete agents by aspectual agents expresses a local perception of the phenomenon, according to the advises given by concrete agent. The subsystem of representation of the phenomenon analyses the landscape of aspectual agents to exhibit a representation of its *morphology* using organizational and morphological agents. The landscape describe the whole set of concrete agents' opinions, judgments and intentions about the perception of some facts or characters of the phenomenon. We assume that the representation (thanks to an interactive geometrical shape) can express the global meaning of the phenomenon for the concrete agent.

The representation subsystem is, also, modeled with MAS, but using cognitive agents [13]. Each agents try to gather communicating concrete agents into *semantically connected components*. These components are aggregated set of concrete agents, according to a semantic proximity given by the characters of the MAS morphology.

Thus, we have a new topological reading of the meaning exchanged in the communicational network. These components gather concrete agents that have some matching characters, some nearby meanings and judgments. They express the notion of group of *common meaning* about the appreciation of the phenomenon. To produce these gatherings, agents monitor actors' judgments and gather those which often exchange some similar significant opinions. We link these gatherings to semantic values depending of the nature of these judgments. These values may be for instance, confrontation, uniformity, rupture...

In the prototype currently in use, this new topological reading linked to semantic values is represented on an interactive 3D surface in order to express the emergence of the global meaning of the phenomenon.

7.2 The simulation prototype

We have developed, in Smalltalk language, a prototype for simulation of communications between actors, according to the characters of the model. In this prototype (Cf. Fig. 9), each actor has a message window with a communicating box. The actors may send or receive different kinds of messages. When a concrete actor communicates (send or read a message), he may express his different opinions about the message, taking into account the different categories and sub-categories, on the exchange, or on other facts or actors. This opinions encompass the message and are represented by different aspectual agents in the MAS, linked to the local actor, developing themselves in the multiagent landscape in real time. The same operation of generation of aspectual agents is realized by the receiver of the message, but with his local conditions. In the MAS receiving the opinions as an act of communication, the aspectual agents interpret this opinions and act according to them. The expression of the multiagent landscape is describe using interactive graphics.

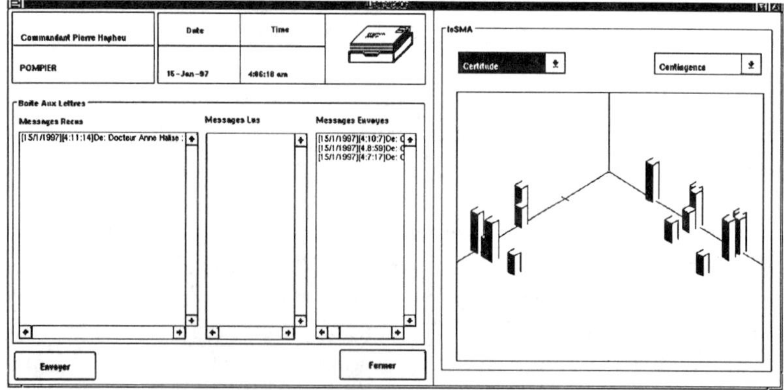

Figure. 9. Two actors in communication.

8. Conclusion

A CCS is defined as a plastic system, encompassing an usual communication system, strongly interacting with its environment. It manages situations that we call complex, in which all the actions are taken by actors out of their usual practices. The exhibition of mental representations is the key of reasonable management of phenomenon. As the actors' mental representations are not totally predictable and principally variable, we have to make the structure of the system strongly variable itself. So, we are prevailed to use model with dynamic hybrid multiagent. Therefore, we represent an *organizational memory* of the process of actors' reflection, leading fuzzy and subjective appreciation about situations to a well-structured and well-managed one, and without reduction.

The simulator we have developed, linking agents and Smalltalk objects, allows the validation of the model about categories of meaning, pertinence of visual representations of this categories, and allows the study of stability of MAS during the acts of communication.

This simulator of CCS is actually extended for effective use on the industrial area of Le Havre (France) using Distributed Smalltalk on Corba. In this system, actors will exchange subjective opinions about a complex and fluctuating phenomenon to make real co-operative decisions. By doing this, some propagation of uproars, useless confrontations, incomprehension and personal conflicts could be prevented. So, some crisis in the crisis, which are the worst events to occur in an emergency situation, could be also prevented. Such a model may be used in every social organizations which have a computerized communication network and where we want to express human actors' intentions to improve the general management.

References

[1] Balkanski C., *Action, belief and Intentions in rationale clauses and means clauses*, Proceeding of the 10th NCAI, p. 296-301, San-Jose, CA, 1992.

[2] Bares M., *Systèmes de commandement, Eléments pour une prospective*, Polytechnica, 1996.

[3] Bond A. H., Gasser L., *Readings in Distributed Artificial Intelligence*, Morgan Kaufman, 1988.

[4] Borodzicz E., Aragones J., Pidgeon N., *Risk communication in crisis: meaning and culture in emergency response organisations*, European conference on Technology & Experience in Safety Analysis and Risk management, Rome, 1993

[5] Brodie M., Ceri S., *On Intelligent and Co-operative Information Systems: a workshop summary*, Int. Journal of Intelligent and Co-operative Information Systems, Vol. 1, No 2., p. 249-289,1992.

[6] Bussmann S., Demazeau Y., *An agent model combining reactive and cognitive capabilities*, Proc of IEEE International Conference on Intelligent Robots and Systems, IROS'94, München, 1994.

[7] Cardon A., Rousseaux F., *A model for Communication and Information Systems (C3I) to assist crisis management, considered from the viewpoint of co-operation: an attempt to go beyond the Cartesian schema*, International Workshop on the Design of Co-operative Systems, Antibes, 1995.

[8] Cardon A., *Le caractère fondamental des systèmes finalisés : la complexité profonde*, Actes du Troisième Congrès Européen de Systémique, p. 951-956, Rome, 1-4 Octobre 1996.

[9] Cardon A., Blot E., Durand S., *Self-reactive servers on Internet*, WWW5 AI Workshop, Paris 6-10 May 1996, document http://www.info.unicaen.fr/-serge/3wia/workshop/papers/paper9.html.

[10] Cardon A., Durand S., *A Model of Crisis Management System Including Mental Representations*, AAAI Spring Symposium, Stanford University, CA, USA, 23-26 mars 1997.

[11] Cordier F., *Représentations cognitives et langage*, Armand Colin,1994.

[12] Eco H., *Sémiotique et philosophie du langage*, PUF, 1993.

[13] Ferber J., *Reactive Distributed Artificial Intelligence: Principles and Applications*, in Foundation of Distributed Artificial Intelligence, N. Jennings Ed., Wiley, 1995

[14] Guessoum Z., Dojat M., *A Real Time Agent Model in a Asynchronous-Object Environment*. Lectures notes in Artificial Intelligence 1038, Agent Breaking Away, W. Van de Valde and J. Param (Eds), Netherlands, pp 1990-1993, January 1996.

[15] Jackendoff R., *Semantics and Cognition*, Cambridge, M.I.T. Press, 1983.

[16] Kieras D., Polson P.G., *An approach to the formal analysis of user complexity*, Int. J. of Man-Machine Studies, 22, p. 365-394, 1985.

[17] Koriche F., *A method to model Cooperative Information Systems*, Ingenierie des Systemes d'Informations, Vol 4, N°2, 1996.

[18] Lapierre J.W., *L'Analyse des Systemes*, Syros, 1992

[19] Le Moigne J.-L, *La Modélisation des systèmes Complexes*, Dunod, Paris, 1990.

[20] Maturana H., Varela F., *Autopoiesis and Cognition: the realisation of the living*, Boston, D. Reidel, 1980.

[21] Searle J. R., *Speechs Acts*, Cambridge University Press, 1969.

[22] Shrivastava P., *Technological and organisational roots of industrial crisis: lessons from Exxon Valdez and Bhopal*, Technological Forecasting and Social Change, n°45, p. 237-253, 1994.

[23] STEP, *Can the processes of mental representation and decision-making in a major emergency or crisis situation be modified ?*, Final report, Contract CEE STEP CT 90-94.

[24] Sfez L., *Critique de la décision*, Presse de la fondation nationale des Sciences Politiques, 1992.

[25] Varela F., *Organism, a meshwork of selfelss selves*, East-West Symposium on the Origins of Language, Paris, 1996.

Multi-Strata Model and Its Applications
Particularly to Automatic Programming

Setsuo Ohsuga
Department of Information and Computer Science
School of Science and Engineering
Waseda University
3-4-1 Ohkubo Shinjyuku-ku Tokyo 169, JAPAN

Abstract. A goal of this paper is a new, general purpose intelligent computer system that behaves like a person at problem solving for a wide range of problems. The author has presented the way of designing a general purpose problem solving system and also made an introductory discussion on multi-strata modelling scheme. In this paper the author is presenting the further discussion on the multi-strata model and, especially its applications. Among these applications, automatic programming is a very important one. This paper discusses the possibility and a method of automatic programming by using the multi-strata modelling concept.

1. Introduction

The objective of this research is to propose a new, intelligent computer system which behaves like a person at problem solving, e.g., makes computer programs by itself. Here the term problem solving is used in a very wide sense to mean every activity to derive answer meeting given conditions in a given environment. To have high level intelligence means to have generality to accept different types of problems in the real world to include the wide range of activities in the actual scope and autonomy in solving real (not toy-level) problems. Key problems which must necessarily be considered in order to achieve the goal are as follows:
(1) How to aid persons for externalizing their ideas?
(2) How to assure the generality and autonomy for solving large and complex real problems?
(3) How to meet the time requirement as well?

Some parts of these issues has been discussed in [OHS95a, OHS96]. This paper is an extension of these discussions and presents a possibility and a method of automatic programming. Since this method needs a general purpose problem solving system that has been discussed in the previous papers, it is shown here very briefly in Chapter 2. In Chapter 3, a new modelling method named multi-strata modelling is discussed and automatic programming is discussed in Chapter 4.

2. General Purpose Problem Solving System (GPPSS)

The condition of a problem solving system being a general purpose system is that it should be able to deal with different types of complex problems in the same system. Since a complex problem extends over different problem domains and each problem requires domain specific knowledge, the system must be provided with a lot of knowledge covering the different domains and also with the capability to extract only the necessary knowledge therefrom for the problem in hand which the system is actually required to solve. For this purpose knowledge must be well structured so that only the necessary parts for solving problem in hand can be identified. Some parts of these ideas have already been implemented by the author's group and applied to various problems. The system named KAUS (Knowledge Acquisition and Utilization System) has been developed for the purpose [YAM93]. This chapter is a very short summary of the researches which have already been published. Refer [OHS94, OHS95a, OHS95b, OHS96] for the details.

2.1. Exploratory Problem Solving

Problem solving system must be able to solve different types of problem. Persons use a general method of problem solving as shown in Figure 1. Intelligent system must be provided with the same problem solving method. In Figure 1 the different blocks represent the different operations. Every operation is realized as a common deductive operation applied on a specific knowledge chunk.

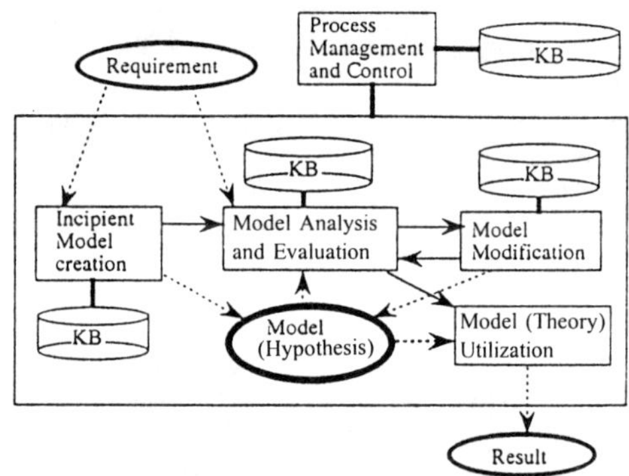

Figure 1 Exploratory problem solving method

2.2. Object Model

Object model plays an important role here. Generally speaking, an object model has structural information to represent a structural organization of the object from its components as well as a set of formal representations of functionality in relation with the object structure. Here the term "functionality" represents all the attributes, properties, functions, behavioral characteristics under the specific environment of the object, each of which is represented by a predicate. Furthermore, relations among the functionalities represent the activities of the object.

2.3. Externalization and Exploration

Problem solving starts when somebody creates a problem in one's brain. It is divided into two parts; externalization and exploration. Every problem must be represented in the way computers can accept it. Externalization is an activity to represent human ideas or problems explicitly, in the form of model. This externalization stage is common to all problem solving though there are various ways of making an object model by externalization, as depending on the cases [HOR94]. Then the exploration stage starts. The problem is solved in the system by exploratory problem solving such as shown in Figure 1.

2.4. Structures of Intelligent Functions and Knowledge Bases

A complex problem can be solved by using different intelligent functions. The exploratory problem solving method of Figure 1 is one of them. Other than this there are various intelligent functions such as model creating, problem decomposition, various mathematical methods of model analysis, learning, etc. These functions are related each other and each function is, in reality, represented as a structured knowledge base. Therefore the global function structure can be defined and be formed as a structure of knowledge bases (Figure 2). This structure, in combination with the inference engine, forms a general purpose problem solving system.

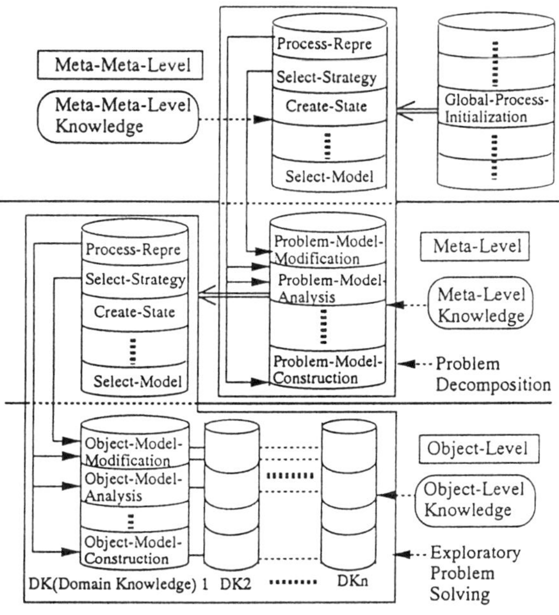

Figure 2 Structure of global knowledge base

2.5. Meta-Operation for Defining and Controlling Problem Solving

The search space at exploration is vast and, in the usual case, unforeseen. Guiding the process is very important. As the model-based operation is an application of knowledge to a model through the inference mechanism, its control is to select proper knowledge. This is a meta-level operation contrasting to the model manipulating operations. Thus the concept of meta-level representation is indispensable for developing intelligent systems. A special management system named the level manager is provided. It switches the operations across the boundaries of representation levels (object-level, meta-level and so on).

3. Multi-Strata Model

There are the more complex types of problems than considered, e.g. the ones including human activity. The modelling scheme defined in section 2.2 can not represent all of them. An extension of this modelling concept in such a way that a model is defined in the context of a relation between subject and object has been introduced and named Multi-Strata Model in [OHS95b].

With this model the more sophisticated problem solving becomes possible. When a problem is brought in through the externalization stage, the relevant knowledge chunks to this problem is identified and retrieved from the global knowledge structure and a specific structure is formed. It defines a special purpose problem solving system dedicated to the problem. The problem is solved with this special purpose system.

3.1. Multi-Strata Structure of Object

Everything in the world can be an object of human thinking. It can be a physical object or an abstract concept. It can even be a problem solving process by others. A new method of model building is necessary. The human way of building a model is studied and stated explicitly. This study is itself another problem composed of a subject and an object in which the object is a human mental activity of a person (S1) building a model and the subject is the other person (S2) who studies the activity (Figure 3). This forms a nested structure in which the inside process is for obtaining a solution directly on the lowest level object and the outside process is for obtaining a way of obtaining the solution in the inside process. This double process represents a process of computerizing problem solving. Let it be called a multi-strata object. Sometimes an object with a more number of strata must be considered.

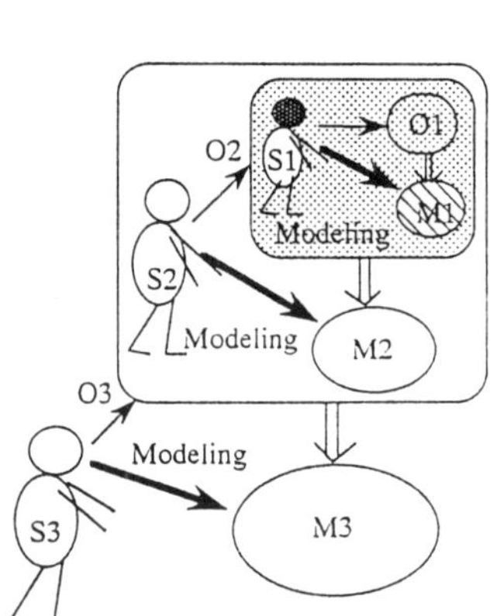

Figure 3 Multi-strata object

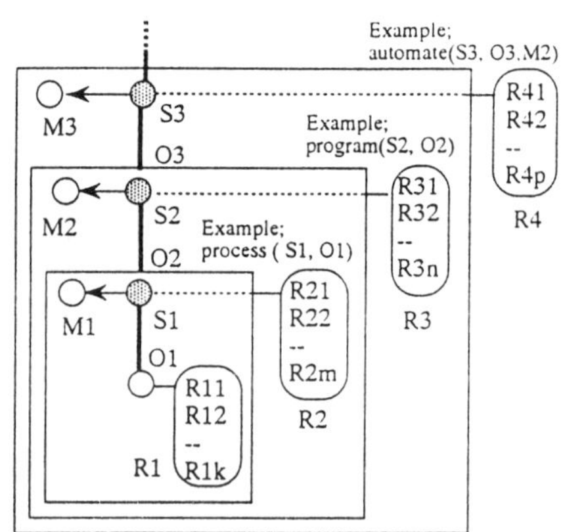

Figure 4 Multi-strata model

3.2. Multi-Strata Modelling Scheme

A multi-strata model is a formal model of a multi-strata object. It is made whenever an outside process is considered to an existing problem solving. It means to model the human activity when the subject of the inside process is a person. A scheme including a subject node for modelling multi-strata object is shown by an example in Figure 4. In a multi-strata object shown in Figure 3, a base level problem arises from some lowest level object (O1). Requirements given to O1 define a problem in this level. In the ordinary problem solving, a person (S1) makes its model (M1). This is the basic model as was discussed in 3.2. In the next level this problem solving itself is an object (O2) and another subject (S2) has a problem of making its model. The requirement given to S1 defines the task the person should do. For example, it may be a command given to S1 such as "design an object to satisfy the given object-level requirements". These specify the activities of Sl which are formalized in the next stratum and are considered as the requirement to define the model M2 of O2. Similarly some command is given to S2 to specify the task the S2 should do. For example, "automate the activity of lower stratum subjec" is given. If there is still an outer process, then this command becomes the requirement to define the model of the higher stratum object. These stratified requirements define a multi-strata object and are used to make a multi-strata model. The upper stratum requirement includes very often the lower stratum requirement. In order to represent it, a higher (meta) level representation scheme is necessary.

Even if the object is the same, the way of problem solving is different depending on the requirements given to the subjects in a multi-strata model. With the ordinary way of describing only the lowest object model, its representation is only in the brain of the person and the computer cannot know it nor can be an autonomous system. For example, the problems are completely different even with the same enterprise by the requirements given to the higher stratum subject. The requirement may be to restructure the whole enterprise or to automate the activities of persons working in a lower stratum in the enterprise. The multi-strata modelling method expands considerably the scope in which computers can work. Among a number of different problems in this scope, attention has to be paid to designing automatic systems. It is formalized as a process of making a multi-strata model and then generating a system to replace persons as subjects in the lower strata. This leads us to idea of automatic programming.

3.3. System Generation Based on Multi-Strata Model

Problem solving including a multi-strata object begins with making a multi-strata model as shown in Figure 4. Then the requirements distributed in this model are processed from the top. These are interpreted and processed. The specific operations to deal with them are activated. Here is the problem of deciding what operations are necessary. To specify an operation is to assign the related knowledge chunks in an intelligent system and to retrieve a substructure of them from the global knowledge base. As an example, let a requirement "automate the activity of lower stratum subjec" be given to a highest level subject (S2) in the simple two-strata model. Let it be represented as automateActivity (subject, (l), system) where subject, (l), and system denote the subject to which this requirement is given, the lower stratum subject to this subject and a system to be generated in order to replace the lower stratum subject, respectively. () represents the object of the given subject in the multi-strata model. This is a special symbol reserved for using multi-strata model. It is composed of a pair of the lowerstratum subject and its object. $l in () refers to the first item of the pair, i.e. (lower stratum) subject in the object. The objective is to retrieve the substructure of knowledge chunks to define a system to replace the lower stratum subject.

Knowledge is necessary to interpret this requirement and to resolve it into a set of operations. Let the requirement given to the lower subject (S1) be a design problem. A set of requirements which should be satisfied by an lower object (O1) is given but the object structure is not known. The role of Sl is to find such an object model that satisfies these requirements. In this case the requirement given to S2 is satisfied by generating a system which can do every operation which has to be done by S1. As has been discussed in Chapter 3, a general scheme of solving this problem is the one as shown in Figure 1. Therefore the requirement given to S2 can be satisfied by retrieving a knowledge structure to represent this scheme. The following rule can be used to fulfill the requirement.

automateActivity*(subject, ($1), system):-*
      identifySubject*(subject, ($1), subject1)*   ---*1*
      getSubjectRequirement*(subject1, requirement1)*   ---*2*
      generateSystem*(subject, requirement1, system)*   ---*3*
      evokeSubject*(subject, requirement1, system)*   ---*4*

This is a general rule and the terms in Italic represent variables to be bound at the evaluation of the rule. Every variable is universally quantified but it is abbreviated here. In the case of above example, *subject* and *subject1* corresponds to S2 and S1, respectively. *system* denotes a system to be generated. *requirement1* is the requirement of *subject1* (S1). This rule says that a *system* which replaces the lower stratum *subject1* is obtained by taking out the lower stratum subject (*1), taking out the requirement given to the lower stratum subject (*2), and generating a system to satisfy the requirement (*3). This operation (*3) is defined by another rule as shown below. After the *requirement1* is substituted by the requirement to S1 in the multi-strata model, the predicate generateSystem is evaluated. Since the system to be generated is different for various problem types, different rules must be provided for generating the system, as corresponding to possible types. In case of the above example, this is the type of problem given to S1, i.e. solveProblem(subject, object, domain) to which a rule is prepared as shown below. It is assumed that the name of problem domain is included in the requirement. Finally the system thus generated replaces the *subject1*. S2 evokes the system to replace S1 for operation and gives it the requirement (*4).

```
generateSystem(subject, solveProblem(subject1, object, domain), system):-
identifyObject(subject, subject1, object)                                 ---*1
getObjectRequirement(subject, object, objectReqirement)                   ---*2
problemType(subject, solveProblem(subject1, object, domain), type)        ---*3
identifyDomain(subject, solveProblem(subject1, object, domain), domain    ---*4
retrieveKnowledge(subject, type, domain, knowledgeChunk)                  ---*5
makeSystem(subject, system, knowledgeChunk)                               ---*6
```

This is also a general rule for the case when the requirement to *subject1* is represented quite generally such as 'solve a problem'. *Subject1, object,* are substituted again by S1 and O1 respectively. In many cases the requirement to S1 may be given more specifically such as design, diagnosis, control, programming etc. In these cases the problem type is included explicitly in the requirement. Otherwise the type of problem must be identified from the representation of the requirement on *object.* by the predicate *(*3).* Different problem types need the different rules and decides the knowledge chunk to define the problem solving scheme for this problem. The domain to which the problem belongs is obtained at (*4). This is necessary to select the domain specific knowledge chunks for analyzing and modifying the object model at the object-level. Then the necessary knowledge chunks are retrieved by (*5).

The predicate *(*6)* arranges these knowledge chunks in the basic framework to define a system and makes links to each other and also with the other part of the system such as human interface. Thus a problem specific problem solving system can be generated and substituted into *system.* This system is a knowledge based system to solve the problem by exploration. The knowledge chunks can be identified by the following rule.

```
retrieveKnowledge(subject, design, domain, knowledgeChunk):-
    getTaskKnowledge(subject, design, taskKnowledge)                      ---*1
    getDomainKnowledge(subject, domain, domainKnowledge)                  ---*2
    integrateKnowledge(subject, knowledgeChunk, taskKnowledge, domainKnowledge)
                                                                          ---*3
```

The first predicate takes out the knowledge to define design task from the global knowledge base. Since the design scheme is common to many domains, this task knowledge includes knowledge chunks that relate to different domains. The second predicate selects only the necessary domain knowledge. Finally, these knowledge chunks are integrated to form the knowledge chunks as required for the given domain.

3.4. Some Examples of Multi-Strata Model

A few examples which need multi-strata modelling are presented.

3.4.1. Education System

Education system is a typical example that needs the multi-strata scheme for making a model. This has been discussed in [OHS96] and omitted here.

3.4.2. Enterprise Model and Enterprise Design

Enterprises are becoming the objects of scientific/technological consideration [BUB93]. An enterprise is composed of many persons and, in most cases, they are organized to form a hierarchical structure. Each person is assigned a specific role depending on the position in this structure. A persons at the highest level, say a president, has the role to make a vision of the enterprise as a whole. This is either given from the beginning (made by a founder of the enterprise) or made by the president. To make a corporate strategy may also be his/her role. These are the highest level requirements given to this model. To make business strategy may be the role of senior executives at the next level. On the other hand, the actual operation tasks are assigned to the persons at the lower levels. These tasks are represented as functionalities and relations among them define the activities of the enterprise. Let us assume, as an example, a case of bank. In an old style bank system, for example, a teller at the counter (a subject) cooperates (is related with) the other persons (subjects) for an operation to respond to the request by a client to draw money by the following rule,

drawMoney*(subjTeller, clientName, date, time, accountNumber, drawAmount)*:-
   checkDeposit*(subjTeller, subjDB, client1d, date, time, accountNo, drawAmount)*,   ---*1
   payMoney*(subITeller, clientName, drawAmount)*,   ---*2
   sendReport*(subjTeller, subjReport, date, time, clientName,*
                                    accountNumber, drawAmount). ---*3

This is made only for the purpose of explanation and is very much simplified. *subjTeller, subjDB* and *subjReport* denote the subjects having the roles of telling at the counter desk, operating database and accumulating information in order to make a report. This relation and further ones including checkDeposit and sendReport define the activities of the bank. Usually this kind of rule has been made and exist in every bank to define the activities of banks. Nowadays, some special machines like ATM are introduced in many banks as a special human interface. The enterprise model must be changed slightly to include them.

Even if many persons are included in the enterprise, if these tasks are determined as parts of all task which are necessary to accomplish the objective of the enterprise and are fixed, then the enterprise is modelled by the ordinary object modelling scheme. It clarifies the activity of the enterprise and of the persons working there, and accordingly is used for making the specification of programs to be developed to this enterprise. For example, a job is defined as a flow of transactions in the structure. Tasks are defined as the way to deal with this information at the related nodes along this flow (Figure 5). This process is shown explicitly in the model and is displayed. Activities such as drawMoney shown above can be made in this way. This is an example of Externalization.

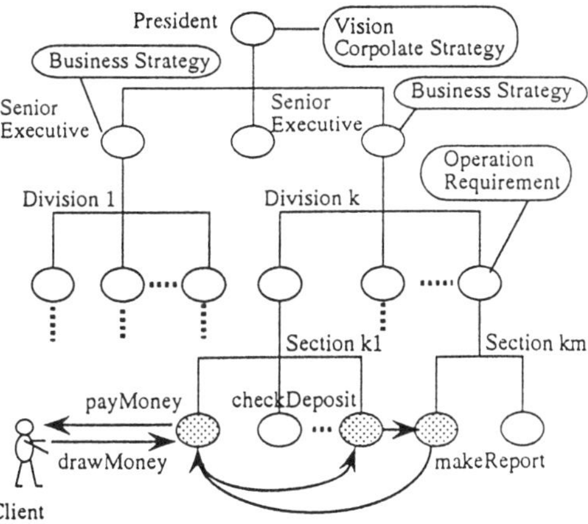

Figure 5 Enterprise modelling

If it is judged that this enterprise is not fitting to the changing social environment, then it must be restructured. The proper organization that adapts to the environment has to be found. It is investigated through analysis of its model whether it is well adapted to the environment or not, and if it is judged inappropriate, then it is restructured. This is the process of model building, model evaluation and model modification. This is quite similar to engineering design and is called enterprise design here.

There must be a (or more) designer who deals with the enterprise as a design object. In this case a multi-strata model becomes necessary, in which the designer is a subject and the enterprise is the object. Simulation may be only method to analyze the enterprise to achieve this design. If the functionalities and their relations are represented in detail in the enterprise model and knowledge is provided in the system for finding the required quantities, then the enterprise model as shown above can be used as a simulation model. Such a simulation has been performed for a part of a hypothetical bank organization by Ushijima [USH95].

He simulated the behavior of a team of employees who sell and buy money according to the variation of the money price in the market. Different behavioral conditions were given to senior and junior staff in this team. The simulation was performed using real economic data in past and balance sheet was made for 80 units of period.

It is possible to take the different approach for restructuring from this one. In some companies persons at the higher rank are required to evaluate the other persons at the lower rank and this result is used for the purpose of restructuring. This is the additional task different from those which are the parts of the activity to accomplish the objective of the enterprise. In this case, a multi-strata model must be created in which the persons at the higher rank and at the lower rank in the hierarchical organization are located in the different strata in the multi-strata model. Thus a concept of multi-strata model is introduced there.

This kind of restructuring was included in the above experiment by Ushijima. According to the balance sheet obtained, the organization of this team was restructured by the manager by removing/adding some persons from/to this team. In this experiment the decision rule of removing/adding some member was very simple. It was based only on the average amount of money earned or lost by the team. If it went over (below) the pre-defined upper (lower) level, a member was added (removed). It is possible to make a more sophisticated model in which the manager makes a mental model for each member and judge the member his/her suitability for the job.

3.4.3. Automatic Programming

A computer program is an automatic system that generates a solution to a given input and replaces a person who has been taking charge of this task. Programmer makes a program after analyzing the way which this person does his/her task. Automatic programming is therefore to automate the generation of automatic system. This scheme needs being represented by a multi-strata model in which the lowest stratum object O1 is a task which is processed by the person, a subject S1. For example, O1 is a transaction in an office information processing system and S1 is a teller at the counter in a bank. Object-level requirements R1 are made by manager to define tasks performed there. The requirement R2 given to subject S1 may be "to process this task". A programmer is the next stratum subject S2 with a next stratum object O2 composed of S1 and O1. S2 is given a requirement R3 "make a program for O2". A subject S3 studies the activity of S2 and generates a system to replace it. The requirement R4 to S3 is "automate the activity of S2".

Automatic programming is realized in two steps. The first step is to generate a system to satisfy the requirement of producing required output for the given input. This is to generate a problem specific, autonomous problem solving system as discussed in 3.3. With this system the given problem can be solved by exploration in principle. The second step is to convert the exploration based problem solving to a deterministic, procedural form.

The way of automatic programming is different case by case, especially driven by the characteristics of the lowest stratum object and by the tasks allotted to S1.

4. Automatic Programming

4.1. Problems Which Can Be Represented in the Procedural Form

Not for all problems procedural program can be made. The possibility of a problem being represented in the procedural form depends on the characteristics of the lowest stratum object. In the case of the office program in an enterprise in which the task of S1 is specified to the detail in relation with object O1, it is possible to state the task of the workers explicitly before programming by the nature of the problem, even though many efforts are needed for stating the task clearly by system engineers (SE). This type of problem requires no change to the model during problem solving, neither with respect to the object structure (enterprise organization) nor the functionalities, nor their relations. The program obtained as a solution can be fixed once determined and does not need any exploratory operation. This is the condition of representing problem solving in the form of procedural program though an exploratory operation may be necessary by the subject S2 in finding the solution before programming.

Even if the object-level problem needs exploratory operation, its programming is still possible if the alternatives are finite and can be fixed. Then it is possible to make a procedure for selecting one from among the alternatives, interpreting knowledge and backtracking, i.e. to include an inference operation in the program. But such a program is usually inefficient and a faster program can be made by interpreting and compiling knowledge in advance and including only its result in the program. A table driven program is an example. Every case for decision making can be enumerated in advance by interpreting knowledge off-line and representing the result in the form of decision table, consisting of pairs of a value of a control variable (index) and the corresponding operation. Then an exploration is replaced by a table look-up. A program can execute table look-up and call for the corresponding operation.

Before making such a program the definition of the decision table must be made. Let an operation be selected from a set of operations rl(y), r2(y), ---, rn(y), in which y represents a (set of) variable defined in these operations. Let these operations be represented inclusively by z(y) of which z is a variable with values any of rl or r2 or --- or rn. This is a meta-level representation. In general, an item of decision table is a pair(i, z(y)) in which i is an index and z is a corresponding operation name (one of rl or r2 or --- or rn). Then the definition of the decision table could be given as decisionTable *(tableName, index, z(y))*. The index is obtained by an operation to classify a control variable x of the other predicate p(x) into a set of finite discrete classes, i.e. classify(x, i).

In this case, control knowledge is included in the program in the form of decision table with the table look-up operation to take out an index for the given value of x and to select the corresponding operation. In order to effect this operation the following form is used together with the decision table.

index*(x, index)*:- *p(x)*, classify*(x, index)*.

selectRoutine*(x, z(y))*:- index*(x, index)*, decisionTable*(tableName, index, z(y))*,

　　　　　callRoutine*(x, z(y))*

z(y) is substituted by one of rl(v), r2(y), --, rn(y) depending on the index value obtained through the classification of the value *x* to the classes. The predicate decisionTable is a high level (meta-level) expression and a specific procedural program is provided to replace it at the time of translation into a procedural program. The predicates index and decisionTable belong to the problem specific knowledge. Therefore these are included in the object model. A special program structure (such as branching/conditional/case-of statement) is generated by using this knowledge, according to the special syntax of the ordinary programming language. When n=2 in selectRoutine, this represents an if-statement. Finally callRoutine*(x, z(y))* is a predicate for transferring operation control to *z(y)*.

callRoutine*(x, z(y))*:- *z(y)*

These predicates cause the same effect as control knowledge in the meta-level in exploratory operation after being translated into program. Sometimes a decision tree is made instead of decision table. In this case tree search operation is used instead of table look-up operation. One may think that the table look-up or the tree search can be represented by a set of the separate first order predicates as follows:

rl(y):- p(x), index$(x, 1)$, r2(y):- p(x), index$(x, 2)$, ---, rn(y):- p(x), index(x, n).

This is a way of representing the execution of an exploratory operation. But this is not proper for generating a procedural program because, with this representation, it is not possible to represent the procedure to select one out of possible alternatives in the program. This is discussed in section 4.3.2.[1].

In the other cases for which the alternatives cannot be fixed nor finite, the representation of problem solving in the form of procedural program is difficult because it implies to interpret unknown knowledge in the execution of the program. In this case it is better to use a declarative form of expression with an inference engine directly. This is the reason why knowledge representation may often be an alternative to ordinary programming language.

Thus problems are classified into two classes; one which can be translated into procedural programs and the other for which exploration is indispensable at problem solving. In principle, every problem needs exploratory operation for being solved. Among them those for which prior interpretation of knowledge, and therefore run time exploration in a previously known search space is possible, are classified into the first class and can be the object of the automatic programming. The basis for classifying a problem into one of these classes is not always clear when the problem needs exploratory operation to a certain but limited extent. It must be decided by the person as depending on the actual problem.

If an object-level problem is classified to the second class, i. e. the problem includes many exploratory operations, then the requirement for S1 is "solve problem" and those of S2 and S3 become "automate the activity of S1" and "automate the activity of S2" respectively. In this case the role of S2 is to extract the necessary and sufficient knowledge chunks based on the model of the object O1. Since the operation of S3 is the same as S2 and every necessary operation can be performed by S2, S3 becomes of no use and no more necessary. To use the three-strata model for this case is not necessary any more and it could be reduced to the two-strata model. This means that making a procedural program needs an additional operation to exploratory problem solving, and accordingly the more strata. In general, the procedural way of problem solving is more efficient than exploratory way. But it holds true only when the program is used repeatedly. Even if a problem meets the condition of being classified to the first class, an exploration based method may be better if one needs only its one shot operation.

Let the times for generating an exploratory problem solving system, for executing exploratory problem solving, for converting to procedural form and for executing the procedural program be t1, t2, t3 and t4 respectively. Then the total time required to satisfy the person's requirement is tl+n*t2 for the case of using exploratory problem solving directly, and tl+t2+t3+n*t4 for the case of using procedural program, in which n is the number of times the problem is solved repeatedly. In general t2 > t4. If and only if tl+ n*t2 $\geq$ tl+t2+t3+n*t4, i.e., (n*-1)t2- n*t4 $\geq$ t3, converting to procedural program is more effective than to use exploratory method directly.

---

[1] One may think these expressions somewhat strange because the variable y appears only in the head. y is a set of variable defined in the selected operation. It may or may not be included in p(x) and index(x, i) in the body. Or, ri(y) may or may not include x. In the case as shown above, ri(y) behaves as a proposition to the predicates including only the variable x. There is no substantial difference between these cases. For making the expression rather simple, the above expression is used.

4.2. The Operations of the Second/Third- Level Subjects

When a problem belongs to the first class, a procedural program is made by the second-level subject, S2. The role of the programmer in this case is mostly to find an efficient method to satisfy the given requirement based on the model representation, then to translate it into the computer executable form. The requirement to S2 is then "make a program for O2". This is different from the problem being in the second class in which "automate the activity of S1" was given to S2. The requirement to S3 is "automate the activity of S2". The role of S3 is to generate an automatic programming system and replaces the human programmer S2 by the system. S3 generates an exploratory problem solving system as has been discussed in 3.3 and a code conversion system as well. The exploratory problem solving system is given some example problems and it solves the problem of finding a path to reach the given goal (to satisfy the requirement given to the object O1). In general, this requires an exploratory operation. This specific path is generalized to cover all queries which can be given to the system. The generalized path is translated into a procedural program. Thus the following predicate is used to expand the predicate generateSystem in automateActivity.

generateSystem*(subject,* makeProgram*(subjec1, object, domain), system)*:-
    generateSystem*(subject,* solveProblem*(subject1, object, domain), system1),*   ---*1*
    generateSystem*(subject,* convertToProg*(subject1, object, domain), system1),*   ---*2*
    integrate*(system1, system2, system)*   ---*3*

The predicate *1 is for generating a system to solve problems as depending on the object-level problem. Following to the problem solving, the chain of the predicates which led to the goal is translated into a program code. The predicate *2 in the above rule is to generate a system which is used for translating the chain to a procedural code. Finally the predicate *3 is for integrating these extracted systems into a system.

Usually a solution path is found by backtracking at exploratory problem solving. The exploratory problem solving system not only solves problem but traces the operations and records the path which could succeed in reaching the goal. In order for the system to trace the problem solving procedure and to record the succeeded path, a special type of inference engine becomes necessary. Since the inference operation is implemented as a special program, it is possible to include this tracing function in the inference engine and allow users to specify the mode; normal mode and trace mode.

The predicate evokeSubject included in the predicate automateActivity (refer 3.3) is a special one to give control to the lower level subject. In reality, it is to urge the system to start the specified operation. The problem solving system interprets the predicate as follows.

evokeSubject*(subject,* makeProgram*(subject1, object, domain), system)*:-
                           makeProgram*(subject1, object, domain)*

The predicate makeProgram is composed of problem solving in the trace mode and then of the conversion of the obtained chain to program code.

makeProgram*(subject1, object, domain)*:- solveProblemT*(subject1, object, domain,chain),*
                          convertToProg*(subject1, object, chain, code)*

The predicate solveProblemT is the same as the ordinary exploration based problem solving except that it leaves only the proper path, i.e., a sequence of predicates leading to the goal behind by tracing. It includes problem decomposition when the object problem is large. The predicate convertToProg needs a further consideration which is discussed in the next section.

4.3. Generating a Program Code

4.3.1. Structural Components of Program

In general, a complex program can be synthesized as a structure composed from the less complex programs each of which is, in turn, composed from the structure of the still simpler programs. At the end of the structure are the primitive programs to do the primitive operations. The primitive programs are the components of making a large program. Developing a large program therefore is to make a structure of these component programs.

In any procedural programming language, every program structure is composed of a limited choice of structural components such as sequence, branch, loop and so on. In addition, the concepts of main-program and subroutine are important from the practical point of view. Hence the system must be able to represent these structural components and to generate any complex program structure by means of them. In this section the expressions in logic that correspond to the program structural components are discussed briefly (because of the lack of the space).

[1] Subroutine call

A subroutine is a separated part of a program and the reasons to take this structure are the convenience of program development for the first place and saving memory for those parts of program that are repeatedly used. In a logical sense whether to separate a program into a main program and subroutine(s) or not is insignificant. It is therefore no way to represent this program structure by first order logic, but a higher order logic expression is necessary. We can use subRoutine*(z(y))* similar to callRoutine*(x, z(y))* used in the definition of decision table for this purpose. subRoutine*(z(y))* generates a subroutine call procedure for the predicate *z(y)*. Let us assume, for example, in generating the sequence of predicates, solveProblemT counts the number of the same predicate being included in the succeeded path. If a predicate P is included more than two times, then the predicate is replaced by subRoutine(P) and generate the program for P independently. Binding variables in P may be different in every call. The program P must be defined to include the definition of variables.

[2] Branch

A way of realizing branch is to use a decision table. However it is rather a special way. Alternatively it is realized by a set of rules each of which has the same conclusion.

    predicate*(x, y)*:- p*(x)*, condition-1*(x)*, predicate-1*(x, y)*

    predicate*(x, y)*:- p*(x)*, condition-2*(x)*, predicate-2*(x, y)*

    -

    predicate*(x, y)*:- p*(x)*, condition-n*(x)*, predicate-n*(x, y)*

A special way of representation is necessary to combine them in a single predicate (see 4.3.2.).

[3] Loop

A loop is a way of repeating operations. The operation in every cycle of a loop may be different but it must be represented in the same form including a parameter which differentiate the content of each operation. Let i denotes i-th operation cycle. Then there are two cases depending on the way in which (A) i-th operation is defined based only on the index i and (B) the other which includes operation including parameters other than i.

(A) This is the case in which i-th operation includes only the index i. For example an operation to obtain a sum of n values, $v1$, $v2$, --, vn is represented by a loop operation to include sum = sum + vi and i+1 = i in which 'sum' is a variable to represent a partial sum. The loop is repeated until i becomes equal to n.

The 'sum' is not a variable in mathematical sense but is a place holder in programming. It plays an important role to represent every cycle in the same form and allow a repeated operation as a loop. On the other hand, every variable in predicate logic must be defined mathematically and there is no concept of place holder An alternative method is necessary therefore to represent operations in the same form for all cycles. A concept of set can be used instead of the place holder. Let summing up vi to 'sum' be replaced adding an entity vi to a set s. Thus the set s contains $v1$, $v2$, --, vn when the loop ends. Then an additional operation to sum up all the elements in the set s (addSet) produces the required result. Because of the lack of space, the further detail is abbreviated.

(B) In the other case, in which i-th operation is not closed with respect to i but include some value relating with i-1, i+1 or so, such an operation as addSet cannot be defined because, in this case, the quantity to be added to the set may not yet be evaluated. A typical example is a recursive function which needs function value with another index than i which may not yet be evaluated. The detail is abbreviated.

[4] Database access

Use of database is becoming more and more important. Since the database is an independent system from application programs, a method of accessing to databases must be provided. Actually the database, especially relational database, and logic are very close conceptually and it is possible to generate the database access procedure, by SQL for example, automatically. There were a number of research projects on this issue and the author and his colleague discussed the way in [YAM90]. Further detail is abbreviated here.

4.3.2. A Special Way of Knowledge Representation

A special way of knowledge representation becomes necessary in order to generate a procedural program from the sequence of predicates to reach the goal from the given problem. For example we saw, in the discussion of a decision table before, that the ordinary way of representation of the way of selecting the alternatives by the given index value in logic was,

r1*(y)*:- p*(x)*, index*(x, 1)*, r2*(y)*:- p*(x)*, index*(x, 2)*, --- rn*(y)*:- p*(x)*, index(x, n).

In this case, by tracing, only the path is recorded as determined by the specific index which a problem generates for a specific input but the others are discarded. In order to generate a program to cover all the cases that can occur with the required inputs, the set of above selection rules themselves must be included in a program. A special way of representation is necessary. For example, a simple branch operation represented by a set of separate rules are integrated to,

predicate*(x, y)*:- p*(x)*, condition-1*(x)*, predicate-1*(x, y)*+ p*(x)*, condition-2*(x)*,

predicate-2*(x, y)* + -- + p*(x)*, condition-n*(x)*, predicate-n*(x, y)*

The decision table operation and recursive function as discussed above are also represented in the integrated form as follows.

selectRoutine*(x, z(x))*:- p*(x)*, classify(x, i), decisionTable(#tableName, i, z*(x)*)),

callRoutine*(x, z(x))*

recursiveFunc*(x, i, x)* recursiveFunc(x, 0, a) +

recursiveFunc*(x, i-1, z)*, knownFunc*(x, y, i, x)*.

This means that a predicate including disjunction should be allowed. In order to avoid a difficulty expected to arise in dealing with the disjunctive expression, it may be better to restrict it only to the exclusive disjunction, i.e. one and only one in the disjunction is true at a time. It is not necessary nor desirable to assume order-sensitivity. If a set of rules are given in which the condition parts are not mutually exclusive, a special treaty is necessary. Let they be,

predicate*(x, y)*:- p*(x)*, condition-1*(x)*, predicate-1*(x, y)*

predicate*(x, y)*:- p*(x)*, condition-2*(x)*, predicate-2*(x, y)*

-

predicate*(x y)*:- p*(x)*, condition-n*(x)*, predicate-n*(x, y)*.

The rules are then classified into the different sets such that the rules in each of the sets are mutually exclusive. There may be the different ways of classification. It is desirable that the number of the sets be the least. The rules in a set are merged in a disjunctive rule. A separate rule is made corresponding to the different sets:

predicate*(x y)*:- p*(x)*, condition-a1*(x)*, predicate-a1*(x, y)* + --

+ p*(y)*, condition- ak*(x)*, predicate-ak*(x, y)*

predicate*(x y)*:- p*(x)*, condition-b1*(x)*, predicate-b1*(x, y)* + --

+ p*(x)*, condition-bm*(x)*, predicate-bm*(x, y)*

-

predicate*(x y)*:-p*(x)*, condition- a1*(x)*, predicate-p1*(x, y)* + --

+ p*(x)*, condition-pn*(x)*, predicate-pn*(x, y)*

It is desirable that the disjunction in each rule is not only exclusive but exhaustive, i.e., every value *x* of p*(x)* meets exactly one and only one condition in a disjunctive rule. In this case everything can be done with a single disjunctive rule. All the other rules are redundant and can be discarded. Or, if there are the other rules meeting this condition, the best one is remained. Since the disjunctive rule is converted to a branch operation in the procedural program, the rule with the least disjunction is the best. But usually this condition is not met unless the rules are made intentionally to be so. In this case more than one disjunctive rule are remained. This is the matter of rule design.

Among all predicates in a knowledge base some predicates are called terminal and are marked accordingly. Predicates accompanied with some specific procedure, so-called procedural predicate, are the terminal predicates. The predicates representing the program structures such as 'branch' and 'loop' and those concerning with the database access as discussed before are also dealt with as the terminal predicates tentatively for the convenience of transformation.

4.3.3. Generation of a Sequence of Predicates as a Source of Programming

In order to generate a procedural program the second stratum subject S2 studies first a way of satisfying the given requirement, for example, drawMoney in an office system. In case of automatic programming system, this is to solve the problem using domain knowledge by exploration. The result is a deduction tree composed of the predicates. By tracing the problem solving, only the predicates to generate the succeeding path are included in the tree.

For example, a problem drawMoney is made when an input format is defined in the office application. It includes variables and each variable has its domain. Its internal form is

(A*x*/person)(A*y*/person)(A*z*/day)(A*u*/time)(A*v*/integer)(A*w*/integer)

$$\text{drawMoney}(x, y, z, u, v, w)$$

where *x*; subjTeller, *y*; clientName, *z*; date, *u*; time, *v*; accountNumber, *w*; drawAmount. It encompasses various instances. The scope of the cases it covers depends on the sets given as the domains of the variables in the expression, this affects the scope of the generated program as well. Since each variable domain is given independently to each other, it is possible that some combination of the instances which does not occur in the real world are included in this form. If the input format is made carefully to exclude these cases, the program does not need to consider them. But it makes the requirement expressions difficult and may bring some inconvenience to users. The program is required to include the capability of checking the legality of the user's requirement. Thus the generation of the program and the design of input format are related.

In order that the program is able to accept every instance in the scope of the input representation including variables as well, the program should have scope of variables that corresponds to the input. One way to assure this is to try to solve this problem including variables (simply the general problem hereafter) by exploration. If a solution is found, then the generated path encompasses all the required cases. This is not possible in general because different instances may require different processing. For example, it is not possible to make a solution for a general problem including database access. The program must be made to discriminate the cases in the problem.

Another way is to solve an instance problem and generalize its solution instead to solve general problem directly. The system generates an instance problem from the general problem by tentatively specifying constant values for variables, then solves it. The deduction tree produced for this instance problem can be used to create the tree for the general case.

When making the instance problem, variables in the predicates are substituted by constants. In generating the deduction tree for the general problem (general tree for short), the predicates in the deduction tree of instance problem (instance tree) are replaced by predicates including the variables. Starting from the top node of the instance tree, each predicate is replaced by the original predicate with variables to represent a general problem. Let the selected predicate be called the problem predicate. In general a subtree is being made from this problem predicate by the deduction with respect to a rule. When the rule of the form A:- B1, B2, ---, Bn is used to which A is unified with this problem predicate, then an AND tree composed from B1, B2, ---, Bn is generated below the predicate. This tree might have already been made by the instance problem. Then the predicates in this subtree are generalized. It is performed by the following procedure. For ease of explanation the case of single variable is shown here.

Let the problem predicate, the rule, and the result of deduction be represented $(Qsx/S)F(x)$, $(Otx/T)[F(x) :- G(x)]$, and $(Qrx/R)G(x)$ respectively in which (Qs, S), (Qt, T), and (Qr, R) are (the quantifiers, the domains of the variable x) of the problem predicate, the rule and the result respectively. Then the (Qr, R) is obtained as is shown in Table 1. For the more general case refer to [OHS85].

Table 1. Inference rule of MLL

(Qs, S)	(Qt, T)	Unifiability Condition	(Qr, R)
(A, S)	(A, T)	$S \subseteq T$	(A , S)
(E, S)	(A, T)	$S \cap T \, (= Z) \neq empty$	(E, Z)
(E, S)	(E, T)	$S \supseteq T$	(A. T)
(A, S)	(E, T)	None	(--, --)

According to this rule the new quantifier and the variable domain for the general case are determined for all predicates in the instance tree. This operation proceeds from the top to the bottom. The predicate including the disjunction is also generalized. Let us see now the case when a predicate in the instance tree cannot be generalized according to the above rule. Since the predicate itself has worked for the instance program, it may happen when the domain of the variable does not meet the condition of Table 1. Another predicate is looked for such that the set-theoretical union of the domains of the variables meet properly the condition and it will be added to the tree to form an OR subtree. It is not assured that the new predicate selected here is the right one. It must be checked later. A new subtree must be generated for this predicate. It is considered to be a new problem starting from here. It is to be solved and a deduction tree is generated. It is possible that a new problem generated includes another loop. Thus multiple loops can occur. Database access also forms a special subtree. Its content depends on the database schema and the requirement. This is repeated to generate a new deduction tree.

While solving the instance problem by exploration, procedural predicates may be reached. The deduction path leading to the predicate ends here and the predicate forms the leaf nodes of the tree. The mark is given to the predicate to show that it is the terminal predicate and it can be replaced by the accompanying procedure later. The branch, loop and database access are also given the mark to show that these are the tentative terminal expressions.

4.3.4. Data Structure

Data structure is important as well as program structure. Different from the program structure which concerns problem solving procedure, a data structure concerns an object to which the problem is created. That is, data structure is a computerized representation of object model structure. It should be included in the predicate as a term, and consequently in the programs. Knowledge representation language must be so designed.

There is no reason to differentiate the definition of data structure used in knowledge and model representation from that used in the procedural program. The same data structure can be used. Then predicates are transformed into procedural program without changing the definition of the data structure.

There must be two types of predicates with respect to data structure; one for evaluating or describing data structure and the other for manipulating it. The latter one can be a procedural predicates of which procedures behind them execute the operations specified by the predicates.

4.3.5. Transformation into a Procedural Program

In this way the general tree is formed. This tree is transformed into the procedural code. Processing some of AND and OR nodes may be executed in parallel. But if it is to be processed sequentially, the predicates with the mark (at the terminal in the tree) is threaded in the order from the top to the bottom and from the left to the right. The subtrees starting from a branch are also processed in the same way but separately from the main tree. Thus a set of subsequences are made and merged finally. This threading generates a sequence of the predicates. This is the source code of the procedural program [LI93].

Every variable in every predicate is specified a domain with the quantifier in the prefix. These domain and quantifier are determined in the deductive operation according to the rule as shown in Table 1. In translating the sequence of predicates into procedural program, the type and the scope of every variable can be specified based on the domain of the variable. For example, a procedural predicate $(Ax/\text{integer})(Ey/\text{real})\text{inverse}(x, y)$ is translated into

int x; real y; y = 1/ x ;

Every predicate is processed one by one from the top as follows.

(0) For every predicate, if a new domain is specified for a variable in the rule as shown in Table 1, then the variable type and scope are declared for the procedure for the predicate,

(1) identify the type of predicate either procedural predicate or loop or branch or database access (or the access to other, independent systems),

(2) the procedural predicate is replaced by the accompanied program,

(3) for a loop type predicate, the loop type is analyzed, a loop structure provided for each type is introduced with the additional operation if necessary, and the subsequence generated from the subtree is embedded in the loop,

(4) for a branch type predicate, a branch structure is provided with switching by condition, and the subsequences generated from the subtrees are embedded in each branch,

(5) for database access, an access sequence is generated and it replaces the predicate.

5. Conclusion

Many things are remained to be discussed in this approach but abbreviated here. Only thing that must be emphasized is the necessity for a new language that enables us to take this approach. Its required characteristics are as follows.

(1) It must be a completely modular language;

(2) It must be able to represent any kinds of data structures which are needed to represent theobjects to be considered;

(3) It must be able to represent meta-knowledge;

(4) It must be able to define procedural predicates.

Such a language has been developed by the author's group and named Multi-Layer Logic (MLL). An intelligent system named KAUS (Knowledge Acquisition and Utilization System) has been developed based on MLL. The system has been used in a number of design type problems[GUA88, SUZ93]. Now the author is preparing to start an experiment of automatic programming.

References

[BUB93] Bubenko,J.A., Jr, and Wangler, B. Objectives Driven Capture of Business Rules and of Information System Requirements, IEEE Systems Man and Cybernetics '93 Conference. 1993

[GUA88] J. Guan, J. and S. Ohsuga, An Intelligent Man-Machine Systems Based on KAUS for Designing Feed-back Control Systems, Artificial Intelligence in Engineering Design, Elesevier Science Pub. Co., 1988

[HOR94] K. Hori, A system for aiding creative concept formation, IEEE Transactions on Systems, Man and Cybernetics, Vol.24, No.6, 1994

[LI93] C.Y. Li, and S. Ohsuga, A Meta Knowledge Structure for Program Development Support, Pro. 5th Intn'l Con. on Software Engineering and Knowledge Engineering (SAKE), 1993

[OHS85] S. Ohsuga and H. Yamauchi, Multi -Layer Logic - A Predicate Logic Including Data Structure As Knowledge Representation Language, New Generation Computing, 1985

[OHS94] S. Ohsuga, How Can Knowledge Based Systems Can Solve Large Scale Problems - Model Based Decomposition and Problem Solving, Knowledge Based Systems, Vol. 5, No. 3, 1994

[OHS95a] S. Ohsuga, A Way of Designing Knowledge Based Systems, Knowledge Based Systems, Vol. 6, No. 1, 1995

[OHS95b] S. Ohsuga, Aspects of Conceptual Modeling - As Kernel of New Information Technology, Proc. Fifth European-Japanese Seminar on Information Modelling and Knowledge Bases, 1995

[OHS96] S. Ohsuga, Multi-Strata Modeling to Automate Problem Solving Including Human Activity, Proc. Sixth European-Japanese Seminar on Information Modelling and Knowledge Bases, 1996

[SUZ93] E. Suzuki, T. Akutsu, and S. Ohsuga, Knowledge Based System for Computer-Aided Drug Design, Knowledge Based Systems, Vol. 6, No. 2, 1993

[USH95] M. Ushijima, Ph.D. Thesis in University of Tokyo, 1995

[YAM90] H. Yamauchi, and S. Ohsuga, Loose Coupling of KAUS with Existing RDBMSs, Data and Knowledge Engineering, Vol. 5, No. 3, 1990

[YAM93] H. Yamauchi, KAUS6 User's Manual, RCAST, Univ. of Tokyo, 1993

Information Modelling and Knowledge Bases IX
P.-J. Charrel et al. (Eds.)
1998, IOS Press

Towards Computing with Extensions and Intensions of Concepts

Jørgen Fischer Nilsson
Department of Information
Technology
Technical University of Denmark

Jari Palomäki
Department of Mathematical
Sciences/Philosophy
University of Tampere

Abstract: Conventional logical knowledge representation systems tend to focus on extensions of concepts, such as derivations of sets of instances falling under the concepts. Taking as point of departure net oriented knowledge representation systems, the paper discusses how to handle intensional aspects of concepts, having in mind also computational concerns. To this end a meta-logical system is proposed in the form of a restricted binary relational algebraic logic embedded in predicate logical clauses.

Keywords: Concept representation, conceptual models, intensionality, relational algebra, concept logics, computing with concepts.

1. Introduction

Concepts are distinct from sets, and it is our contention that the distinction is crucial to computational concept representation and reasoning. Concepts have an extension consisting of the instances of the concept, i.e. the set of all entities falling under the concept. However, concepts in contrast to sets possess also *intensions*, which consist informally of the properties attributed to all instances of the concept, see also e.g. [14] for an introductory discussion of concepts.

It is principled approaches to reasoning with intensional aspects of concepts which are in focus in this paper.

A diversity of knowledge representation formalisms and systems has been proposed for conceptual modelling and for representing and reasoning with concepts. As point of departure we consider net or graph oriented concept representations (knowledge representation nets). Common to these formalisms is the representation of concepts as nodes in a graph, with the arcs stating binary relationships between concepts. The concepts may be individual concepts as well as general ones (universals).

A number of theoretical approaches to formalization of intensionality, mostly based on possible world semantics, has been put forward, for instance the so called Transparent Intensional Logic, see e.g. [16]. However, we are concerned here also with computational aspects of the logics, and therefore we want to stick to first-order predicate logic and preferably even the more restricted logical clauses in logic programming.

In first-order predicate logic, terms denote individuals according to model theory, so that predicate logic admits reasoning with concept instances, only. For instance in a logic program dealing with kinships one can infer relationships between individuals, but one cannot directly reason with relationships between the kinship predicates, such as inferring, say, that grandparenthood implies parenthood. Therefore treatment of concept extensions as well as intensions in a logically principled manner in predicate logic (and more specifically in logic programs) calls for elaboration of a suitable representation scheme for general concepts.

This is a continuation of our studies of logical knowledge representation in [9, 15] and categorial modelling of concepts in [11].

Starting with a brief review of net oriented representations in sect. 2, and following an introduction to concept lattices in sect. 3, we reformulate net representations as binary relation algebras in sect. 4 and 5. Then in sect. 6 we formulate properties and relationships of concepts by embedding the relational algebraic representations in predicate logic. Finally in sect. 7 we formalize the introduced concepts of concepts in predicate logical clauses.

2. Concept net representations

Let us recall net or graph oriented symbolic knowledge representation models or systems [7, 17], of which prominent examples are:
– semantic nets
– conceptual graphs
– entity-relationship models (ER -models).

In these representations, jointly referred to here as concept nets, individual and general concepts form nodes in a graph whose labelled arcs or links are binary relationships. Common to these representations is thus the insistence on binary in favour of n-ary relationships, in contrast to relational data base models.

A sample binary relationship between individual concepts is

$$birthplace(Plato, Athens)$$

Sample binary relationships between general concepts are

$$isa(philosopher, human) \quad \text{and} \quad father(human, male)$$

There are also mixed forms such as

$$isa(Plato, philosopher).$$

The *isa* relationship enjoys a special status as a universal relationship common to all domains. The multiple interpretations of the *isa* relation tends to create confusion: On one hand there is the set-theoretical inclusion relation $\subseteq$ and the accompanying set-theoretical membership relation $\in$. These set-theoretical relations yield the *extensional* inclusion relation $\subseteq$ in contrast to the concept-theoretical *intensional* inclusion relation $\succeq$, (cf. [13, 15, 11]). The latter is in accord with our view of concept intensions as being rather independent of the underlying extension sets.

In order to develop a principled approach to intensionality the concept net formalisms are here reformulated in relational algebra, which is next embedded in predicate logic, and to the extent possible even within definite clauses of logic programming for the purpose of computerised reasoning with concepts. As a first step towards relational algebras in the next section is considered lattice algebras.

3. Taxonomic concept structures

The fundamental, pervasive concept relationship is the *isa* relationship, giving rise to a distinction between extension and intension. These companion notions, having roots in the philosophy of language dating back to Leibniz, arise also in conceptual modelling, cf. [12].

3.1 Intension and extension of a concept

The intension and extension of a concept can be defined as follows:

> The *intension* of a concept is the information content inherent in the concept, which enables us to recognise the individuals falling under the concept.

> The *extension* of a concept is the set of all those individuals which fall under the concept. An individual *falls under* the concept in question if the concept applies to it.

For example, if the concept of philosopher applies to a particular individual (e.g. Aristotle), then he falls under the concept of philosopher. He also belongs to the set of all philosophers, which is the extension of the concept of philosopher. However, basically it is decided by the intension of the concept of philosopher that he falls under the concept of philosopher and belongs to the set of philosophers.

Generally speaking, given a concept its extension set is determined (uniquely) by its intension. On the other hand, given a set we are not able to infer (uniquely) to which of several possible concepts it refers, i.e. whose extension the given set is. That is, there are many (perhaps infinitely many) non-identical but co-extensional concepts. This is why, among other reasons, cf. [15], we should not identify sets with concepts.

The intension of a concept may also be characterized as comprising all those properties which the individuals falling under the concepts must have. Thus, to understand a concept is to grasp the meaning of the predicates applying to it. This is the view adopted in this paper. For instance the intension of the concept of bachelor can be given by enumerating the predicates applicable to a particular class of individuals each of who is e.g. male, unmarried, human, etc.

3.2 Concept lattices

The *isa* relation applies to concepts viewed intensionally: $isa(p, q)$ holds whenever p possesses (inherits) all the properties which q has. We can say that the concept p contains intensionally the concept q, the concept q being a generalisation of the concept p, and the concept p being a specialization of the concept q.

It is easy to see that *isa* is a weak partial ordering (i.e. reflexive, antisymmetric, and transitive), cf. [13, 15, 11].

As additional mathematical properties we posit existence of least upper bounds (*lub*) and greatest lower bounds (*glb*) for each pair of concepts:

$$isa(X, Y) \wedge isa(X, Z) \ \leftrightarrow \ isa(X, glb(Y, Z))$$

$$isa(Y, X) \wedge isa(Z, X) \ \leftrightarrow \ isa(lub(Y, Z), X)$$

where X, Y, and Z are universally quantified.

Accordingly, the *isa*-relationship forms the ordering relation $\preceq$ in a lattice:

$$isa(p, q) \quad iff \quad p \preceq q$$

The ordering relation of a lattice induces operators *meet* ($\cong$ *glb*) and *join* ($\cong$ *lub*) in the concomitant algebraic conception of lattice through the mutual definitions:

$$X \preceq Y \quad iff \quad X = meet(X, Y) \quad iff \quad Y = join(Y, X)$$

according to lattice theory, cf. e.g. [6].

If a concept is conceived and formalised as a monadic predicate so that the extension of the concept is the set of individuals fulfilling the predicate, then for *isa* (and for two given general concepts p and q) it holds:

$$isa(p, q) \ \rightarrow \ \forall X (p(X) \rightarrow q(X)).$$

That is, if the concept p contains intensionally the concept q, then the set of individuals fulfilling the predicate p is extensionally contained in the set of individuals fulfilling the predicate q. From the intensional *isa* relation one can thus infer the set-theoretical containment relation; however, from the set-theoretical containment relation one cannot infer (uniquely) the intensional *isa* relation. Thus the inverse implication does not hold.

3.3 Concept nets as lattice Hasse diagrams

When concept structures are conceived as lattices they can be depicted as Hasse diagrams. This means that those *isa*-relationships which are implied by reflexivity or transitivity are left implicit as arcs. Those *isa* relationships explicitly represented here are also called *ako*-relationships (a-kind-of relationships).

Thus concept nets in this view reappear as Hasse diagrams, which are later to be appropriately extended with labelled arcs representing other relationships than the *isa* relationships. This means that a concept net has a *skeleton subnet* (formed solely by the containment ordering relationships) which is to constitute a lattice.

An example concept lattice:

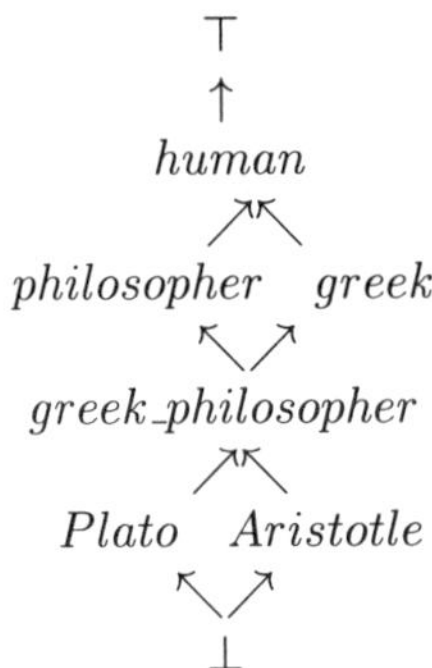

There is the convention that there are no other *isa* relationships than those given by the reflexive and transitive closure of the explicit links. The concept lattice thus arises as formalization of the well-known generalization/specialization hierarchies.

We assume that the concept lattice be bound: That is to say, there exists formally a universal concept top $\top$, also written *univ* below. And dually there exists formalistically a bottom concept $\bot$, also called *null*. We do not epistemologically claim existence of these boundary concepts, but introduce them as convenient auxiliaries in the logical formalization.

3.4 Lattice axioms

In the algebraic conception of the lattice the two lattice operations, $+$ for join (*lub*) and $\times$ for meet (*glb*), are axiomatized, cf. [6], by the equations:

Idempotency	$X + X \ = \ X$	$X \times X \ = \ X$
Associativity	$X + (Y + Z) \ = \ (X + Y) + Z$	$X \times (Y \times Z) \ = \ (X \times Y) \times Z$
Commutativity	$X + Y \ = \ Y + X$	$X \times Y \ = \ Y \times X$
Absorption	$X + (Y \times X) \ = \ X$	$X \times (Y + X) \ = \ X$
Boundaries	$\bot + X \ = \ X$	$\bot \times X \ = \ \bot$
	$\top + X \ = \ \top$	$\top \times X \ = \ X.$

The equality is the both way ordering relationship:

$$X = Y \quad \text{iff} \quad X \preceq Y \wedge Y \preceq X.$$

We assume that concept lattices are *distributive*, since distributive lattices are isomorphic to a field of sets, and these sets are conceived as the extensions of the concepts. That is to say, models of distributive lattices associate a set with each element of the lattice, with $+$ becoming set union and $\times$ becoming set intersection.

$$\textit{Distributivity} \quad X + (Y \times Z) \ = \ (X + Y) \times (X + Z)$$

Distributive lattices can be extended with a unary operator, the negation (complement)operator, to obtain Heyting lattice or Boolean lattice depending on the choice of axioms for the negation operator.

As such, distributive lattices are algebraic counterparts of a monadic predicate logic, where $+$ is logical disjunction and $\times$ is logical conjunction, and $\top$ is the universal predicate, and $\bot$ is "absurdity".

Thus the sample predicate logical expression forms

$$\forall X (\textit{philosopher}(X) \to \textit{human}(X)) \quad \text{and} \quad \textit{philosopher}(\textit{Aristotle})$$

becomes respectively in the algebraic setting

$$\textit{isa}(\textit{philosopher}, \textit{human}) \quad \text{and} \quad \textit{isa}(\textit{Aristotle}, \textit{philosopher})$$

which are devoid of variables.

As suggested by these examples replacement of the common calculus forms by algebraic forms form in the present setting by its absence of quantified variables simplifies the subsequent computing with intensions of concepts to be discussed in sect. 6-7.

4. Binary relational algebras

Distributive lattices are naturally conceived as basic algebraic logics of sets. They can be extended to handle general binary relations in addition to the distinguished extensional *isa* containment relation between sets. This leads to the binary relational algebras originally proposed by the 19th century philosopher C. S. Peirce and revived and further examined logically by A. Tarski [20].

There are basically two ways of treating relations algebraically [1], see e.g. [18]:

---

[1]In category theory allegories, cf. [8], provides an alternative formalism for dealing with relation algebra, allegories being to binary relations between sets what categories are to functions between

1. *Algebra of relations*, where relations are considered as ordered pairs of sets, thus allowing us to consider their intersections, unions, complements, and inclusions. With respect to these four operations the set of all relations on the given set V is a complete Boolean lattice.

There are the following definitions and notations for relations S and R on V:

$$\begin{aligned}
\textit{union} \quad\quad R \sqcup S &= \{(x,y)|(x,y) \in R \vee (x,y) \in S\}. \\
\textit{intersection} \ R \sqcap S &= \{(x,y)|(x,y) \in R \wedge (x,y) \in S\}. \\
\textit{complement} \ \bar{R} &= \{(x,y)|(x,y) \notin R\}. \\
\textit{inclusion} \quad R \subseteq S &\Leftrightarrow \forall x,y : [(x,y) \in R \to (x,y) \in S\}. \\
\textit{identity} \quad\quad I &= \{(x,y)|(x=y)\}. \\
\textit{converse} \quad R^{\top} &= \{(x,y)|(y,x) \in R\}. \\
\textit{product} \quad R \circ S &= \{(x,z)|\exists y \in V : (x,y) \in R \wedge (y,z) \in S\}.
\end{aligned}$$

Let the *empty relation* $\emptyset \subseteq V \times V$ be denoted by O. The entire Cartesian product $V \times V$, denoted by L, is called the *universal relation*. A relation A is called an *atom*, if $A \neq O$ and if $O \neq X \subseteq A \Rightarrow X = A$.

2. *Relation algebra*, which is a universal algebra in which all the identities and rules in effect for relations are made valid by appropriate axioms.

An axiomatic definition of a relation algebra $\mathbf{R} = \langle \mathcal{R}, \sqcup, \sqcap, \bar{\ }, \circ, {}^{\top} \rangle$ on the given set V is as follows:

$\langle \mathcal{R}, \sqcup, \sqcap, \bar{\ }, \circ, {}^{\top} \rangle$ consists of a nonempty collection $\mathcal{R}$ of relations on V such that

i) $\langle \mathcal{R}, \sqcup, \sqcap, \bar{\ } \rangle$ is a complete, atomic, Boolean algebra with
    zero element O, universal element L, and ordering $\subseteq$;

ii) $\langle \mathcal{R}, \circ, I \rangle$ is a semigroup with the unit element I, i.e.
    $Q \circ (R \circ S) = (Q \circ R) \circ S$, and $I \circ R = R = R \circ I$;

iii) the Schröder rule holds, i.e.
    $Q \circ R \subseteq S \Leftrightarrow Q^{\top} \circ \bar{S} \subseteq \bar{R} \Leftrightarrow \bar{S} \circ R^{\top} \subseteq \bar{Q}$; and

iv) the Tarski rule holds, i.e. $R \neq O \Rightarrow L \circ R \circ L = L$.

In many cases is also needed an algebra of relations interacting with sets, i.e. two-sorted algebras, e.g. Boolean modules, dynamic algebras, and even the so called Peirce algebra, cf. [4] [2] .

A *Boolean module* is a two sorted algebra $\mathbf{M} = \langle \mathbf{B}, \mathbf{R}, : \rangle$, where $\mathbf{B}$ is a Boolean algebra, $\mathbf{R}$ is a relation algebra, and : is the set forming operation on sets called *Peirce product* and defined as follows in the meta-language:

---

sets. However, we refrain from further categorical considerations in this paper.

  [2]Dynamic algebra is based on Kleene algebra, which is a relation algebra having a *star* operation $\star$, which is a reflexive transitive closure operation, but lacking the converse and complement operations. On the other hand, Boolean modules have both the converse and complement operations, but not the star operation. Both Boolean modules and dynamic algebras characterise the set forming operator algebraically. Peirce algebra is a Boolean module enriched with a relation forming operator called "right cylindrification", cf. [4].

$$\text{\textit{Peirce product}} \qquad R : X \;=\; \{x | \exists y [(x,y) \in R \wedge y \in X\},$$

Thus the Peirce product : is a mapping $\mathbf{R} \times \mathbf{B} \to \mathbf{B}$, written $R : X$ such that for any $R, S \in \mathcal{R}$ and any $X, Y \in \mathcal{B}$, the following equations hold, [4]:

M1) $R : (X \cup Y) \;=\; R : X \cup R : Y$;

M2) $(R \sqcup S) : X \;=\; R : X \cup S : X$;

M3) $R : (S : X) \;=\; (R \circ S) : X$;

M4) $I : X \;=\; X$;

M5) $O : X \;=\; \emptyset$;

M6) $R^\top : \overline{(R : X)} \cup \bar{X} = \bar{X}$; and

M7) $X \neq \emptyset \;\Rightarrow\; L : X = V$.

As it appears in the next section the Peirce product is instrumental in ascribing properties to concepts.

5. Algebraization of concept nets

The lattice of concepts from sect. 3 with *isa* relationships constituting the partial ordering relation is now extended to handle other forms of relationships than *isa* arcs. To this end the relational algebras offer themselves, cf. [3], but as a characteristic of the present approach we refrain from encorporating the full relational algebra by considering binary relations as features of concepts. Formally, this means replacing Peirce product terms $R : \varphi$ with terms $a_R(\varphi)$, where φ is a term, and where the 1-argument function a_R associated with R is conceived as an attribute whose value is denoted by term φ. Thus binary relations R are dispensed with in favour of attributes a, yielding the so called concept algebra [9], which is a 1-sorted (unsorted) universal algebra.

The operators a_i come with joint algebraic axioms

$$\begin{aligned}
a_i(\perp) &= \perp \\
a_i(X + Y) &= a_i(X) + a_i(Y) \\
a_i(X \times Y) &= a_i(X) \times a_i(Y)
\end{aligned}$$

as explained in [9], as amendment to the above lattice axioms. These axioms are proposed as the counterpart to the relational algebraic axioms. They provide multiple inheritance in the concept lattice. A property of the form $a_i(\varphi)$ is called a property concept.

5.1 Relations as attributed properties in concept algebra

Binary relations are thus reconceived as attributed properties. For instance the relationship *birthplace (Plato, Athens)* may be reformulated as assignment of the property of having the birthplace Athens, viz.

$$isa(Plato, birthplace(Athens))$$

where *birthplace* is a unary algebraic operator, an attribute (feature or role). Thus there is a unary attribute operator for each applied binary relation, *isa* being the only remaining relation, enjoying a special status as the lattice ordering relation.

This means that the sample lattice from sect. 3 can be extended with properties e.g. as follows:

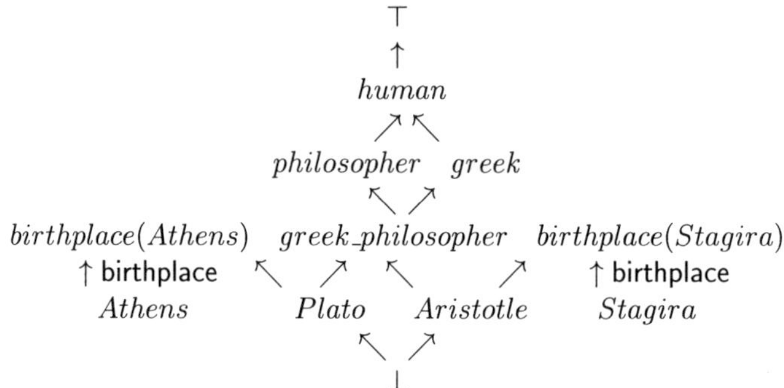

Notice the two arcs adorned with the **birthplace** attribute. An attribute a is now conceived as a function mapping its argument concept into the concept of being a value of a. For instance *Athens* is mapped into **birthplace**(*Athens*), that is the concept of having *Athens* as *birthplace* – a concept which is possessed by *Plato* among others properties ascribed to *Plato* according to the lattice diagram.

This concept algebra has ties to the so called description logics, see e.g. [5], which are variable-free combinatory fragments of predicate logic geared to expressing taxonomic knowledge. They may be conceived as combinator-logical variants of relational algebras. Usually they are applied extensionally like first-order predicate logic (and relational algebra); however see [5] for an extended description logic which similarly to ours endeavours to capture intensionality.

The representation of concept nets as algebras rather than as predicate logical formulae, cf. [7] facilitates the encoding into an embracing predicate logic as to be discussed next.

6. Embedding algebraic concept terms in logic

Having introduced an algebraic logic form of concept nets, we now return to the issue of intensionality. As they stand the above relational algebraic representations are extensional: They deal with concepts conceived extensionally as sets (of individuals) and with interactions between sets and binary relations (attributes) over members of the sets.

To achieve an intensional model of concepts we propose that the concept algebra be embedded in first-order predicate logic, following up on ideas in [9, 10].

6.1 A concept logic

Our intensional concept logic arises as a two-level logic where the outermost logic is first-order predicate logic whose terms t_i in logical atomic formulae

$$p(t_1, ..., t_n)$$

are terms of the applied concept algebra, including variables.

Thus in this *concept logic* there are two logical levels:
1) An inner algebraic logic, the concept algebra, providing the lattice- and attribute closed operations <u>on</u> concepts.
2) An outer logic (first-order predicate calculus) for expressing properties <u>of</u> concepts and relationships <u>between</u> concepts (including the distinguished *isa*-relationship).

The link between these two levels is the *isa* predicate constituting the partial ordering relation of the concept lattice.

From a strictly formal point of view this concept logic is an ordinary first-order logical theory with equality, where the inner algebra is established by including the algebraic axioms as equational axioms. Thus formally the predicates express relationships between individuals, only. They are however made to represent also general concepts by way of appropriate definitions and axioms as to be discussed next.

Let us consider a repertoire of predicates for expressing properties of concepts and binary relationships between concepts.

6.2 Relations between concepts

The following binary predicates are proposed and discussed below:

ako	The *ako* predicate serves to establish a concept structure in the first place by stating the explicitly given containment relationships (arcs in the Hasse diagram) in a lattice.
isa	The *isa* is the lattice partial ordering derived from *ako* by adding the properties of reflexivity and transitivity.
identco	Two concepts are considered identical if the *isa* as well as the inverse *isa* holds.
distco	Distinct concepts are concepts which are not identical.
inext	Expresses membership of an individual concept in the extension of the second argument general concept.

coext Co-extensionality, *coext*, expresses that the argument concepts have identical extensions.

extinc Extensional inclusion expresses that the extension of the first argument is a subset of the second argument extension.

inint Expresses membership of a concept in the intension of the second argument concept.

coint Co-intensionality *coint* expresses that the argument concepts have identical intensions.

This list is inspired by the characterizations in [22].

6.3 Properties of concepts

We suggest the following properties as unary predicates in the concept logic:

atomco An atomic (i.e. lattice atomic) concept *atomco* is a concept, just above $\perp$ (i.e., no intervening concepts.)

indiv An individual concept *indiv* is an atomic concept, which is furthermore declared as individual.

nullco The concept of null concept.

univco The concept of universal concept.

boundco A boundary concept is either the null concept or the universal concept.

properco A proper concept is a concept which is not a boundary concept.

genco A general concept is a concept, which is neither an individual nor the null concept.

These characterisations of concepts are meant as proposals specific to our concept logic and are not meant to be of universal validity. The above list is put forward as an open-ended list, where further aspects of concepts can be handled by appropriate augmentation.

The example from sect. 5.1 is now specified as follows:

indiv(*Plato*)
indiv(*Aristotle*)
indiv(*Athens*)
indiv(*Stagira*)

ako(*Plato, greek_philosopher*)
ako(*Aristotle, greek_philosopher*)
ako(*Plato, birthplace*(*Athens*))
ako(*Aristotle, birthplace*(*Stagira*))

$$ako(greek\_philosopher, philosopher)$$
$$ako(greek\_philosopher, greek)$$
$$ako(philosopher, human)$$
$$ako(greek, human)$$

Observe that the notion of individual concept is not a notion which can be specified in general, but has to be specified pointwise.

7. Towards computing with concepts

The general predicates in the concept logic introduced above are to be defined logically by appropriate predicate logical definitions.

In order to prepare for a subsequent elaboration of the definitions as logic programs (say, in PROLOG), the definitions are phrased to the extent possible as definite logical clauses:as definite logical clauses:

$$p_0(t_{01}, ..., t_{0n_0}) \leftarrow p_1(t_{11}, ..., t_{1n_1}) \wedge ... \wedge p_m(t_{m1}, ..., t_{mn_m})$$

well-known from logic programming. Variables are implicitly universally quantified.

The clausal definitions below are intended as specifications for logic programs. Rewriting and further elaboration are needed in order to ensure procedurally correct (terminating) programs.

The following clauses reflect the lists in the previous section:

The *isa* predicate is here established as the reflexive and transitive closure of the *ako* binary predicate constituting the given arcs in the concept lattice as Hasse diagram:

$$isa(X, Y) \leftarrow ako(X, Y)$$

$$isa(X, X)$$
$$isa(X, Z) \leftarrow isa(X, Y) \wedge isa(Y, Z)$$

$$isa(\bot, X)$$
$$isa(X, \top)$$

$$isa(X, Y \times Z) \leftarrow isa(X, Y) \wedge isa(X, Z)$$
$$isa(X, Y) \leftarrow isa(X, Y \times Z)$$
$$isa(X, Z) \leftarrow isa(X, Y \times Z)$$

$$isa(Y + Z, X) \leftarrow isa(Y, X) \wedge isa(Z, X)$$
$$isa(Y, X) \leftarrow isa(Y + Z, X)$$
$$isa(Z, X) \leftarrow isa(Y + Z, X)$$

$$boundco(X) \leftarrow nullco(X) \vee univco(X)$$

$$nullco(null)$$

$$univco(univ)$$

$$atomco(X) \leftarrow \neg \exists Y (distco(X,Y) \wedge properco(Y) \wedge isa(Y,X))$$

$indiv(i)$ for designated individuals i.

Additional clauses for *isa* directly obtainable from the algebraic lattice properties contribute to avoid making our notion of intensionality too fine-grained. For instance the laws of commutativity ensure that the concept *greek* × *philosopher* be identical to *philosopher* × *greek*.

$$identco(X,Y) \leftarrow isa(X,Y) \wedge isa(Y,X)$$
$$distco(X,Y) \leftarrow \neg identco(X,Y)$$
$$inext(X,Y) \leftarrow atomco(X) \wedge isa(X,Y)$$
$$coext(Y,Z) \leftarrow \forall X(inext(X,Y) \leftrightarrow inext(X,Z))$$
$$coint(Y,Z) \leftarrow \forall X(isa(Y,X) \leftrightarrow isa(Z,X))$$
$$extinc(Y,Z) \leftarrow \forall X(inext(X,Y) \rightarrow isa(X,Z))$$

Whether these definitions constitute complete inference rules for the concept logic is a matter of the intended notion (granularity) of intensionality.

These predicate logical formalizations lend themself to reformulation as logic programs. To this end (classical) negation in clauses is to be replaced with negation as (finite) nonprovability, *not*, recognised as the form of negation offered in PROLOG and contemporary logic programming systems under the name of negation-as-failure.

For instance the above definition of atomicity and distinctness may be re-expressed as

$$atomco(X) \leftarrow not(properco(Y) \wedge distco(X,Y) \wedge isa(Y,X))$$
$$distco(X,Y) \leftarrow not\ identco(X,Y)$$

Use of this form of negation rests on the precondition that the applied concept structure is already fully specified (completed), cf. the closed world assumption.

Use of negation-as-failure is not just a programming device for obtaining computational tractability as replacement for proper classical negation: The concept logic may exploit this non-monotonic form of negation in order to accomodate inheritance exceptions and defeasible reasoning (retraction of previous consequences in case of additions to the given concept structure) along the lines in [21, 19].

An interesting aspect to be analysed further is the interaction of classical/intuitionistic negation (*non*) in the concept algebra with negation-as-failure (*not*),

$$isa(X,(nonY)) \quad vis\text{-}à\text{-}vis \quad not\ isa(X,Y).$$

8. Concluding remarks about intensionality

The notion of intensionality is an evasive concept: There are grades of intensionality ranging from a course grained understanding with a high degree of identification of concepts to a fine-grained notion taking into account even the linguistic form of the concept phrases.

The traditional notion of intensionality based on possible worlds (as applied in Montague semantics) tends to be too coarse grained: For instance the concepts of equilateral triangle and equiangular triangle are identified since they happen to have the same extension (infinite set of triangles) in all possible worlds (which recognise mathematical truths). In a more fine-grained understanding, like the one we are aiming at as well as in [16, 1, 2], these two concepts are considered different concepts.

In [1, 2] Bealer advances a logical theory of properties, relationships, and propositions (dubbed PRP-logic) which is meant "simultaneously a foundation for philosophy, psychology, theory of language, and mathematics" (*opera cit.* p. 2). This theory, which has served us as a source of inspiration, similarly to the present proposal for a concept logic is a meta-logical construction in which predicate logical formulae are encoded as terms in first-order predicate logic.

The PRP-logic is comprehensive in accepting full predicate logic as inner language, and in offering a sophisticated mechanism for free and abstracted variables in the encoded formulae. However the present concept logic with its restricted relational algebra as inner language should be seen as an attempt to obtain a balance between the needs in typical conceptual modelling and knowledge base cases and concerns to computational tractability.

In [10] it is sketched how the concept logic properly restricted to definite clauses constitute an object oriented logic programming language in which the concept hierarchy (lattice) is taken advantage of as an object class inheritance structure.

References

[1] G. Bealer: *Quality and Concept.* Clarendon Press, 1982.

[2] G. Bealer: Fine-Grained Type-Free Intensionality, *Properties, Types and Meaning: Volume I: Foundational Issues.* Eds. G. Chierchia, B. H. Bartee, and R. Turner. Kluwer Academic Publishers, 1989, pp. 177-230.

[3] C. Brink and R. A. Schmidt: Subsumption Computed Algebraically, *Computers Math. Applic.*, Vol. 23, 1992, pp. 329-342.

[4] C. Brink, K. Britz, and R. A. Schmidt: Peirce Algebras, *Formal Aspects of Computing*, Vol. 6, 1994, pp. 339-358.

[5] A. Cappelli & D. Mazzeranghi: An intensional semantics for a hybrid language, *Data & Knowledge Engineering*, Vol. 12, 1994, pp. 31-62.

[6] B.A. Davey & H.A. Priestley: *Introduction to Lattices and Order.* Cambridge University Press, 1990.

[7] A. Deliyanni and R. A. Kowalski: Logic and Semantic Networks, *Communications of the ACM*, Vol. 22, 1979, pp. 184-192.

[8] P. J. Freyd and A. Ščedrov: *Categories, Allegories.* North-Holland, 1990.

[9] J. Fischer Nilsson: An Algebraic Logic for Concept Structures, *Information Modelling and Knowledge Bases V.* IOS Press, 1994, pp. 75-84.

[10] J. Fischer Nilsson: Object Logic for Conceptual Modelling with a Medical Domain as Case Study, *Information Modelling and Knowledge Bases VII.* IOS Press, 1996, pp. 330-343.

[11] J. Fischer Nilsson & J. Palomäki: A Categorial View on Concept Structures, *Information Modelling and Knowledge Bases VI.* IOS Press, 1995, pp. 239-256.

[12] H. Kangassalo: COMIC: A System and Methodology for Conceptual Modelling and Information Construction, *Data & Knowledge Engineering*, Vol. 9, 1992/3, pp. 287-319.

[13] R. Kauppi: *Einführung in die Theorie der Begriffssysteme.* Acta Universitatis Tamperensis, Ser. A Vol. 15, University of Tampere, 1967.

[14] P. Materna: How Many Concepts are There ?, *LOGICA '96* Proceedings of the 10th International Symposium, T. Childers *et al.* (eds.),Filosofia, Praha, 1997.

[15] J. Palomäki: *From Concepts to Concept Theory: Discoveries, Connections, and Results.* Acta Universitatis Tamperensis, Ser. A Vol. 416, University of Tampere, 1994.

[16] J. Palomäki: Three Kinds of Containment Relations between Concepts, *Information Modelling and Knowledge Bases VIII* H. Kangassalo, J. Fischer Nilsson, H. Jaakkola, S. Ohsuga (eds.): *Information Modelling and Knowledge Bases VIII*, IOS Press, 1997.

[17] J. F. Sowa: *Principles of Semantic Networks: Explorations in the Representation of Knowledge.* Morgan Kaufmann Publishers, 1991.

[18] G. Schmidt & T. Ströhlein: *Relations and Graphs: Discrete Mathematics for Computer Scientists.* Springer-Verlag, 1993.

[19] G. Simonet: On Sandewall's paper: Nonmonotonic inference rules for multiple inheritance with exceptions, *Artificial Intelligence* 86, 1996. pp. 359-374.

[20] A. Tarski: On the Calculus of Relations, *Journal of Symbolic Logic*, Vol. 6, 1941, pp. 73-89.

[21] R. H. Thomason & D.S. Touretsky: Inheritance Theory and Networks with Roles, in [17], pp. 231-266.

[22] P. Weingartner: On the Characterization of Entities by means of Individuals and Properties, *Journal of Philosophical Logic*, Vol. 3, 1974, pp. 323-336.

Information Modelling and Knowledge Bases IX
P.-J. Charrel et al. (Eds.)
1998, IOS Press

Semantics of General Data Structures

Marie DUŽÍ
FPF ÚMI, Silesian University, Bezručovo nám. 13, 746 01 Opava, Czech Republic

Jaroslav POKORNÝ
Department of Software Engineering, Faculty of Mathematics and Physics,
Charles University, Malostranské nám. 25, 118 00 Praha 1, Czech Republic

Abstract: An approach to data semantics based on transparent intensional logic is presented. The functional type system gives a possibility to use functional data objects, among them the notion of attribute plays a fundamental role. Here, an attribute is a function dependent on possible worlds and time moments. Attributes serve as an information container. Particularly, propositions denoted by sentences of a natural language are possible to generate from an attribute. To measure „information content" of attributes, the notions such as information capability, distinguishing capability, and comparison based on cardinality are defined and some theorems are presented. We discuss the use of attributes in conceptual modeling, too. Since attributes are attached to language expressions, we obtain in consequence a new view on database semantics that integrates the abstract level of attributes and propositions with the more usual conceptual level.
The rest of paper offers a taxonomy of data models and provides some notions necessary for measuring the expressiveness of conceptual models.

1. Introduction

A study of data semantics is an important topic of today's research. Let S_1 and S_2 denote two (conceptual/database) schemes. Semantics must be captured to support solutions of at least the following tasks:

- *accessing problem*: querying through S_1 database stored under S_2 (and vice-versa),
- *viewing problem*: viewing through S_1 databases stored under S_2,
- *data exchange problem*: transforming data stored under S_1 into a database stored under S_2,
- *design problem:* transforming schema S_1 into S_2.

On the other hand, we are far from adequately capturing the semantics that could be derived using all the senses, cognition, perception, and interaction between multiple agents [SHET95].

Unlike the classical results of database theory that concern problems such as schema equivalence, a formal work on conceptual models has been largely ignored. Practitioners have felt that theoretical approaches to conceptual modeling are not applied in usual CASE tools they use. So their work is driven by intuition. However, above problems need something more. They require a deeper understanding data semantics because a potential heterogeneity of schemes could be the cause of a partial usability of the given databases in a heterogenous environment.

The objective of the paper is to introduce and use rigorous theoretical tools for studying data semantics in the context of conceptual modeling. We show an approach that is based on formal fundamentals of transparent intensional logic (Section 2). We highlight the notion of attribute and use it as a basic construct for conceptual modeling (Section 3). Informally, our attributes generalize usual functional constructs used in the conceptual modeling. They are conceived as basic constructs bearing information. In comparing to analytical functions (e.g. count, sin, etc), attributes explicitly depend on state-of-the world.

As a formal language supporting manipulation of functions we briefly present a version of the typed lambda calculus with tuples (Section 4). Sections 5-6 present some definitions and basic results concerning information capability of attributes, their definability and some other measures of attribute quality. In Section 8 the general theory is applied to database environment. Notions such as a conceptual schema and a conceptual model are formalized here. A new classification of conceptual models and a view on data semantics are given here as well. In Section 9 the expressiveness of conceptual models is discussed. Finally, we conclude with a comparison of our approach to some relevant approaches and outline some further possibilities of research.

2. Basic Notions of Transparent Intensional Logic

When developing a solid theory of data semantics, we are confronted with the problem of semantically analysing natural language expressions because data items stem from these expressions. Our hypothesis is that information „hidden" in data is connected with sentences in some sense. The most promising approach to dealing with natural language expressions can be found in Transparent Intensional Logic (TIL) [TICH88], a fragment of which is applied in this paper. TIL is based on *possible-world semantics* which enables us to distinguish between *intensions* and *extensions*.

Possible world in TIL is an exactly defined abstract entity. To explain this notion we need some preliminaries. First, there is a collection of *a priori* given abstract features assigned to objects of our interest. The distribution of the features among the objects is unpredictable and can change in time. Hence *possible world* is the chronology of logically possible (consistent) distributions of basic traits among the objects of our interest.

2.1 Type System

In our type system, we need functions as arguments of other functions, functions that give other functions as a result, etc. Therefore the classical ADT approach is not sufficient. A slightly modified version [ZLAT86] of the simple theory of types [CHUR40] meets this demand. We define the type system **T** as follows:

Definition 1. The existence of a *base B* is assumed. The base is a collection symbols.

i) Every member of the base B is an *(elementary) type* over B.

ii) If T_1, T_2 are types over B, then $(T_1 \rightarrow T_2)$ is a *(functional) type* over B.

iii) If T_1, ..., T_n ($n > 1$) are types, then $(T_1,...,T_n)$ is a *tuple type*.

The *type system* **T** *over B* is the least set containing types given by (i)-(iii).

◊

If the members of B are interpreted as mutually disjoint non-empty sets, then $(T_1 \rightarrow T_2)$ denotes the set of all (total or partial) functions from T_1 into T_2, $(T_1,...,T_n)$ denotes the Cartesian product $T_1 \times ... \times T_n$. An element O of a type T is called an object of the type T or a T-object, denoted O/T.

2.2 Intensions & extensions

The base in TIL (called *epistemic* base) is a collection of four elementary types o, ι, τ, ω. Type o is the set of truth values {True, False}, type ι is the universe of discourse and its members are individuals, τ is the set of time points or real numbers also playing the role of their surrogates, ω is the set of possible worlds. Intensions and extensions are inductively defined over this epistemic base as follows.

Definition 2.

i) A T-object, where $T \neq (\omega \to T')$ for any T', is an intension of the 0th order or an *extension*.

ii) Let a T-object be an intension of the nth order. Then $(\omega \to T)$-object is an *intension* of the $(n+1)^{st}$ order.

Further we shall use the term intension only for intensions of the nth order, where $n > 0$.

$\Diamond$

Natural language expressions usually denote objects (intensions) of a type $(\omega \to (\tau \to T))$. For example, „the capital of France" is $(\omega \to (\tau \to \iota)$-object, „the capital of France is Paris" is $(\omega \to (\tau \to o)$-object. Whenever we shall not need to work separately with parameters of the type ω, τ, time dependent intensions will be handled as if they were of type $((\omega,\tau) \to T)$ which will be abbreviated by $(\omega\tau \to T)$. Members of the couple (ω,τ) will be called *states of affairs*. We shall denote them shortly as W.

Examples of intensions and extensions:

extension	intension
class of T-objects	property of a T-object
$(T \to o)$	$(\omega\tau \to (T \to o))$
n-ary relation-in-extension	n-ary relation-in-intension
$((T_1,..., T_n) \to o)$	$(\omega\tau \to ((T_1,..., T_n) \to o))$
{True, False}	proposition
o	$(\omega\tau \to o)$
analytical function	empirical function
$(T_1 \to T_2)$	$(\omega\tau \to (T_1 \to T_2))$

Note that we represent sets (classes) and relations (-in-extension) by their characteristic functions.

3. Attributes

Some natural language expressions denote very natural 'object structures' usable in building a database, the so-called *attributes* (see, e.g., [MAPO81]). In our HIT data model (HIT is an acronym for Homogeneous, Integrated, Type-oriented, see [DKMS86]) attributes play the role of a basic modeling construct. 'The address of a given person', 'the salary of a given person' are examples of attributes. That attributes are empirical functions (intensions) is obvious. Thus, e.g., 'the address of ...' associates each person with its address. But a person can move - the address of a person can change with time, and it is not logically necessary that a person have an address, say A. He/she could live anywhere else. Hence a type of an attribute must be $(\omega\tau \to (T_1 \to T_2))$.

Similarly to other data models, in the HIT data model the role of elementary types is played by 'sorts'. So instead of the epistemic base we use a base {E, D, o, τ, ω}, where E are entity sorts and D descriptive sorts. An *entity sort* (which is essentially the same as an 'abstract' type of [HUKI87]) is given solely by a property. Since property is an intension, it is not representable (printable) [MATE87]. *Descriptive sorts* ('printable' types - [HUKI87]) are usual recursive sets.

Thus attributes (of a database schema) are objects of the two following types:

a) singular attribute: $(\omega\tau \to (T_1 \to T_2)$

b) multivalued attribute: $(\omega\tau \to (T_1 \to (T_2 \to o)))$

where T1, T2 are types of sorts or tuples of sorts. Hence an attribute selects in every state of affairs a function mapping a sort or a tuple of sorts to a sort or a tuple of sorts (singular case), or to their power set (multivalued case). The above mentioned function will be from now on called an *extension of an attribute.* Note that our notion of attribute is a broader one than traditional ones. It covers a *tuple construct* as well as a *set construct*, and, moreover, it also covers *relationships between entity sorts.*

Example: MATERIAL, SUPPLIER entity sorts, NAME, MONTH, QUANTITY descriptive sorts:

A. 'Name of a material' / $(\omega\tau \to (MATERIAL \to NAME))$
   - singular 'descriptive' attribute

B. 'Suppliers who deliver a material' / $(\omega\tau \to (MATERIAL \to (SUPPLIER \to o)))$
   - multivalued attribute ('a nested relation')

C. 'Accepted quantity of a material from a supplier per a month'/
   $(\omega\tau \to ((MATERIAL, SUPPLIER, MONTH) \to QUANTITY))$
   - singular attribute with tuple ('relationship')

$\Diamond$

Essentially, our HIT data model is an *object-function-model* (cf. [SCSC90]), the manipulation tool of which is not an object algebra but the typed lambda calculus (see below) with tuples. It can be also considered as a generalization of *functional models* (e.g. Daplex [SHIP81], Iris data model [FISH89]). Using just one modeling construct - attribute - enables us to formalise and exactly handle all the operations on general data structures, i.e. derived data, views, integrity constraints, ISA relationships as well as multiple inheritance (with a semilattice of types) [ZLAT86, DKMS86]. We are able to formally describe and manipulate general data structures which can be constructed in a more complicated way. Thus generally empirical functions which are taken into account here are not restricted to the above form. For instance, 'the departments in a company' can be viewed as an attribute of type

   $(\omega\tau \to (COMPANY \to ((EMPLOYEE \to o) \to o)))$,

where COMPANY and EMPLOYEE are entity sorts, i.e. departments are classes of employees (not separate entity sorts). In the paper we show that it is possible to formally compare informational capability of different data structures, e.g. of a flat relation and a nested relation, etc.

4. Manipulating Functions

A version of the typed lambda calculus with tuples [ZLAT86] is used here as a manipulation tool which directly supports manipulating objects typed by our type system **T**. Starting with a collection **Func** of constants, each of a fixed type, and denumerably many variables for each type, the *language of lambda terms* (LT) is inductively defined as follows:

Definition 3. Let types $T, T_1, ..., T_n (n \geq 1)$ are elements of **T**.

i) Every variable of type T is a *term of type* T.

ii) Every constant (a member of **Func**) of type T is a *term of type* T.

iii)If M is a term of type $(T_1,...,T_n \rightarrow T)$ and $N_1,...,N_n$ are terms of type $T_1,...,T_n$, respectively, then $[M \, N_1,...,N_n]$ is a *term of type* T - *application.*

iv)If $x_1,...,x_n$ are distinct variables of types $T_1,...,T_n$, respectively, and M is a term of type T, then $\lambda x_1,...,x_n \, (M)$ is a *term of type* $(T_1,...,T_n \rightarrow T)$ - *lambda abstraction.*

v) If $N_1,...,N_n$ are terms of types $T_1,...,T_n$, respectively, then $(N_1,...,N_n)$ is a *term of type* $(T_1,...,T_n)$ - *tuple.*

vi)If M is a term of type $(T_1,...,T_n)$, then $M_{(1)},...,M_{(n)}$ are *terms* of types $T_1,...,T_n$ - *projections.*

◊

Terms can be interpreted in a standard way by means of an interpretation assigning to each constant symbol from **Func** an object of the same type, and by a semantic mapping from LT into all functions given by the type system **T**. In short, we assume a standard 'fixed' interpretation in which an application is evaluated as the application of the associated function to given arguments, a lambda abstraction 'constructs' a new function of the respective type, etc.

Logical connectives, less then and equal tests, quantifiers, etc. are interpreted as (analytical) functions, i.e. objects of the respective functional types. As for our notational convention, we use an infix notation for logical connectives (not as applications according to point iii) of our definition). Quantifiers for a type T, i.e. Π^T, Σ^T, types $((T \rightarrow o) \rightarrow o)$, will be written as usual - for '$[\Pi^T \lambda x \, ...]$' we simply write '$\forall x \, ...$', similarly for Σ^T ('$\exists x \, ...$'). The singularizer I^T (Russell's *iota inversum*) of the type $((T \rightarrow o) \rightarrow T)$ is interpreted as a function which on a singleton of T-objects produces the single member of the singleton and is undefined on the other classes. Again, instead of '$[I^T \lambda x \, ...]$' we simply write '$\downarrow x \, ...$' (the only x such that ...).

5. Informational Capability of Attributes

In this section we compare some specific general data structures, i.e. sets of attributes, for their 'informational content'. Informational content of a set A of attributes in a state of affairs W is given by the set of natural language statements 'stemming' from A in W. But some statements of natural language are less informative than others. We adopt here Carnap's idea that the fewer possible worlds a proposition admits, the more informative it is [CARN52]. But there are two flaws to this explanation. First, following this idea thoroughly, we would arrive at the conclusion that the proposition FALSE which admits no possible worlds bears the greatest information! Moreover, there is the question of whether a proposition which is not true in the actual world is informative. For instance, is the proposition that the Earth is flat informative? Second, comparison based on cardinality is rather peculiar in the case of infinite sets.

To solve the first problem, we assume that the set of possible worlds and time-points in which our propositions (arising from attributes) are true includes the actual possible world and a reasonable time interval. In other words, we take into account only correct data. The second problem is hereby solved by means of logical implication, which makes comparing informational capability of attributes feasible on the basis of the set theoretical inclusion of 'generated information'.

To precisely define informational capability of a set of attributes, i.e. to determine the semantics of a general data structure, we need some preliminary notions. We first define the set of basic propositions generated by an attribute A in a state of affairs W. Then by means of the notion of logical implication we define informational capability of an attribute A as the set of all the logical consequences of basic propositions, which enables us to compare various sets of attributes as for their 'informational content'.

Preliminary definition 1. Let A be an attribute of a type $(\omega\tau \to (T \to S))$, where T is a sort or a tuple of sorts, S is a sort or a tuple of sorts (singular attribute), or $S = (S' \to o)$ where S' is a sort or a tuple of sorts (multivalued attribute). Then the set of basic propositions $B(A)^W$ generated by A in a state of affairs W is defined as follows:

$$B(A)^W = \lambda p \; \exists x \exists y \; ([[AW]x] = y \wedge p = (\lambda w \; [[Aw]x] = y)),$$

where variables $w, p \; x, y$ are of the respective types:

    $p \, / \, (\omega,\tau \to o)$ - proposition

    $w \, / \, (\omega,\tau)$ - state of affairs

    $x \, / \, T, \; y \, / \, S$

◊

Example: An attribute A the extension of which in a state of affairs W is given by the table 1. It generates in W the set of propositions:

$\{\lambda w([[Aw]t_1] = s_1), \lambda w([[Aw]t_2] = s_2), \lambda w([[Aw]t_3] = s_3), ...\}.$

T	S
t_1	s_1
t_2	s_2
t_3	s_3
etc.	

Table 1 - Extension of A

The set of basic propositions does not bear all the information we can obtain from an extension of an attribute. We can obtain all the logical consequences of these basic propositions as well.

Preliminary definition 2. Let π be the type of propositions $(\omega\tau \to o)$, $P \, / \, (\pi \to o)$, $Q \, / \, (\pi \to o)$ sets of propositions.

Logical implication $\Rightarrow$ of the type $(((\pi \to o), (\pi \to o)) \to o)$ is defined as follows:

P implies Q ($P \Rightarrow Q$ - infix notation will be used) iff, in all the states of affairs in which all the members of *P* are true, the members of *Q* are true as well.

◊

The relation $\Rightarrow$ is reflexive and transitive. It is not antisymmetric because if $P \Rightarrow Q$ and $Q \Rightarrow P$ then *P, Q* are true in the same states of affairs but they do not have to be necessarily false or undefined in the same states of affairs.

Preliminary definition 3. Cn - *entailment* of the type $((\pi \to o) \to (\pi \to o))$ is a function which associates any set of propositions *P* with the set of all the logical consequences of *P*: $Cn = \lambda p \, [\cup \lambda q \, (p \Rightarrow q)]$, where *p, q* are variables of the type $(\pi \to o)$, $\cup$ is the set theoretical union of sets of propositions, i.e. a $(((\pi \to o) \to o) \to (\pi \to o))$ - object.

Note: Obviously, the operation Cn is idempotent - $[Cn[Cn \, P]] = [Cn \, P]$, and $P \Rightarrow Q$ iff ,$[Cn \, Q] \subset [Cn \, P]$.

Summarising these considerations we can claim that a set of propositions *P* is more informative that a set *Q* iff *P* implies *Q*, or iff the set of all the logical consequences of *Q* is a subset of all the logical consequences of *P*.

Definition 4. Informational capability of an attribute A in a state of affairs W is the set of propositions $P(A)^W$ generated by A in W, i.e., the set of all the logical consequences of basic propositions generated by A in W:

$$P(A)^W = [Cn \, B(A)^W]$$

◊

Definition 5. A set of attributes $\{A_1, ..., A_m\}$ is *informationally redundant* with respect to a set of attributes $\{B_1, ..., B_n\}$ iff, for every state of affair W it holds that

$$[Cn \cup_{i=1}^{m} P(A_i)^W] \subset [Cn \cup_{j=1}^{n} P(B_j)^W].$$

Sets of attributes $\{A_1, ..., A_m\}$, $\{B_1, ..., B_n\}$ are *informationally equivalent* iff, for every state of affairs W, it holds that $[Cn \cup_{i=1}^{m} P(A_i)^W] = [Cn \cup_{j=1}^{n} P(B_j)^W]$.

$$\lozenge$$

6. The Definability Relation

In this section, we define the relation of definability and show that this relation induces informational redundancy of attribute sets, which is one of the main contributions of this paper. Intuitively, an attribute A is definable over an attribute B if there is an algorithm enabling us to compute in every state of affairs W the extension of A from the extension of B.

From now on, we will abbreviate the application $[Aw]$ as A_w for any attribute A.

Definition 6. An attribute A is *definable over* a set of attributes $\{B_1,...,B_n\}$ (denoted $A \leftarrow_D \{B_1,...,B_n\}$) iff $\exists f \forall w\ (A_w = [f(B_{1w},...,B_{nw})])$, where f ranges over surjections. A set of attributes A *is definable from* a set of attributes B ($A \leftarrow_D B$) iff every member of A is definable over a subset of B. Finally, sets of attributes A, B are *mutually definable* ($A \leftrightarrow_D B$) iff $A \leftarrow_D B$ and $B \leftarrow_D A$. An attribute A is said to be definable from an attribute B if $\{A\} \leftarrow_D \{B\}$.

$$\lozenge$$

Example: Let PERSON be an entity sort of persons.

a) Attribute A = 'parents of a person', B = 'age of a person', C = 'average age of parents of a person'; $C \leftarrow_D \{A, B\}$: $\exists f \forall w\ (C_w = [f(A_w, B_w)])$, where the respective function F is defined as follows (variables a/PERSON $\rightarrow$ (PERSON $\rightarrow$ o), b/PERSON $\rightarrow$ τ, p/PERSON, q /PERSON, n/τ, Ave is the function 'average'):
   $F = \lambda ab\ \lambda p\ [Ave\ \lambda n\ \exists q\ (n=[bq] \wedge [[ap]q])].$

b) Attributes A = 'superior of a person', B = 'subordinates of a person';
   $A \leftrightarrow_D B$: $\exists f \forall w\ (A_w = [f\ B_w])$ and $\exists g \forall w\ (B_w = [g\ A_w])$, the respective functions F, G are defined as follows (variables a/PERSON $\rightarrow$ PERSON, p/PERSON, q/PERSON) , b/PERSON $\rightarrow$ (PERSON $\rightarrow$ o):
   $F = \lambda b\ \lambda p\ \rceil q\ ([[bq]p]),\ G = \lambda a\ \lambda p\ \lambda q\ ([aq]=p).$

$$\lozenge$$

Now we will prove that a set of attributes A is informationally redundant with respect to a set of attributes B iff $A \leftarrow_D B$.

Lemma. An attribute A is definable over a set of attributes $B_1,..,B_n$ ($A \leftarrow_D \{B_1,...,B_n\}$) iff, in all the states-of-affairs W it holds that $P(A)^W \subset [Cn \cup_{i=1}^{n} P(B_i)^W]$, i.e. iff

$$\cup_{i=1}^{n} P(B_i)^W \Rightarrow B(A_i)^W.$$

Proof:

if) Let for every w $\cup_{i=1}^{n} P(B_i)^W \Rightarrow B(A)^W$. If there were no analytical function F such that $A_w = [F(B_{1w},...,B_{nw})]$ then A and $B_1,...,B_n$ would be logically independent. This means that there would have to be a pair W_1, W_2 such that all the members of $\cup_{i=1}^{n} P(B_i)^W$ as well as $B(A)^W$ would be true in W_1, whereas the members of $\cup_{i=1}^{n} P(B_i)^W$ would be true in W_2 and some members of $B(A)^W$ would be false in W_2, which contradicts the assumption.

(only if) Let there be a function F such that $A_w = [F(B_{1w},...,B_{nw})]$ for each w. Let every member of $\cup_{i=1}^{n} P(B_i)^W$ be true in a state W. If there were a proposition generated by A in

this W which were not true then it would mean that the function F defining A from $B_1,...,B_n$ would have to depend on w, which contradicts the assumption.

Theorem 1: Let $A = \{A_1,..,A_n\}$, $B = \{B_1,..,B_n\}$ be sets of attributes. Then A is informationally redundant with respect to B iff $A \leftarrow_D B$, and A, B are informationally equivalent iff A $\leftrightarrow_D$ B.

Proof: Follows from the previous lemma and the idempotency of the operation Cn.

This theorem explicates the intuition introduced at the beginning of this section. Informational comparability of attribute sets is based on the definability relation. Since our notion of attribute is a general one, this result makes it possible to compare informational capability of different data structures.

7. Relations of Distinguishing Capability and Comparison Based on Cardinality

If the intensional character of attributes were not taken into account, the definability relation could be confused with the relation of distinguishing capability. In this section we show that the distinguishing capability has nothing to do with the informational capability. Intuitively, the greater the number of discernible classes of an attribute A, the greater the 'force' of A. Imagine now two attributes A, B 'sharing their domain', i.e. of types $(\omega\tau \rightarrow (T \rightarrow S_1)$ and $(\omega\tau \rightarrow (T \rightarrow S_2)$, respectively, such that A and B distinguish in every state of affairs exactly the same subsets of T. A question arises: „Is the information connected with A the same as the information connected with B"? Or a weaker question: „Is the amount of information connected with A the same as the amount of information connected with B"? In this section we prove negative answers to both questions.

From now on attributes A, B are of the above types, where T is a sort or a tuple of sorts, S_1, S_2 are sorts or tuples of sorts, or power sets of (tuples) of sorts, variables *w, x, y* are of types (ω, τ), T, T, respectively.

Definition 7. An attribute A has *greater distinguishing capability* than B $(A \geq_{dc} B)$ if
$\forall w\, x\, y\, (\, ([A_w\, x] = [A_w\, y]) \supset ([B_w\, x] = [B_w\, y])\,)$.
$(A =_{dc} B)$ if $A \leq_{dc} B$ and $B \leq_{dc} A$.

◊

To be able to compare the $\leq_{dc}$ relation with the informational capability of attributes, we have to be able to compare it with the $\leftarrow_D$ relation. The following assertions make it possible.

Theorem 2: $A \leq_{dc} B$ iff $\forall w \exists f \forall x ([A_w\, x] = [f\, [B_w\, x]])$, where $f / (S_2 \rightarrow S_1)$ ranges over surjections.

Note that the theorem does not claim that there is a 'universal' function for all the states of affairs *w*. Particular functions can differ in distinct states of affairs.

Corollary. $A =_{dc} B$ iff $\forall w \exists f \forall x ([A_w\, x] = [f\, [B_w\, x]])$, where $f / (S_2 \rightarrow S_1)$ ranges over bijections.

For attributes A, B of the above types a stronger notion of definability can be defined which can be compared with the relation of distinguishing capability.

Definition 8. An attribute A is *strongly definable* from an attribute B $(A \Leftarrow_D B)$ if $\exists f \forall w \forall x ([A_w\, x] = [f\, [B_w\, x]])$, where $f / (S_2 \rightarrow S_1)$ ranges over surjections. Attributes A, B are said to be strongly mutually definable $(A \Leftrightarrow_D B)$ if $A \Leftarrow_D B$ and $B \Leftarrow_D A$.

◊

Theorem 3: Strong definability implies definability, and, consequently, strong mutual definability implies mutual definability.

It is obvious that the reversal of this theorem does not hold. In other words, definability does not imply strong definability.

Example. Let PERSON be an entity sort of persons. Attributes A = 'superior of a person', B = 'subordinates of a person' are mutually definable (informationally equivalent) $(A \leftrightarrow_D B)$, but they are not strongly mutually definable. Knowing a person $[A_w\ p]$ - a boss, we cannot compute the set of his/her subordinates. We need the whole table $[A_w]$ to compute the table $[B_w]$ and vice versa.

◊

Now we can compare distinguishing capability of attributes with their informational capability.

Theorem 4: If $A \Leftarrow_D B$ then $A \leq_{dc} B$ but not vice versa.

Proof: $\exists f \forall w \forall x\ ([A_w\ x] = [f\,[B_w\,x]])$ obviously implies

$\qquad \forall w \exists f \forall x\ ([A_w\ x] = [f\,[B_w\,x]])$, but not vice versa.

Example. Let attributes A, B be as follows: A = 'town of an address', B = 'ZIP code of an address', i.e. A_w/ADDRESS $\rightarrow$ TOWN, B_w/ADDRESS $\rightarrow$ ZIP. Then $A \leq_{dc} B$:

$\forall w\ x\ y\ (\ ([B_w\ x] = [B_w\ y]) \supset ([A_w\ x] = [A_w\ y])\ )$. But A is not (strongly) definable from B because there is not a universal function which would enables us to compute a town name from the ZIP code. The assignment of ZIP codes to towns is empirical, not analytical.

◊

Corollary. If $A \Leftrightarrow_D B$ then $A =_{dc} B$ (in this case the respective function F is a bijection), but not vice versa.

Now we can answer the question on the connection between distinguishing capability of attributes and their informational content. We have proved that informational comparability of attributes is based on the $\leftarrow_D$ relation, whereas distinguishing comparability is determined by the $\leq_{dc}$ relation. These two relations contain $\Leftarrow_D$ relation as their common intersection. The $\leq_{dc}$ relation is based on the existence of a function mapping a range of the extension of an attribute to a range of the extension of another one. If this function is a universal one (i.e. the same in all the states of affairs) then it establishes the strong definability, otherwise the two attributes are not informationally comparable.

Our disconnecting the $\leq_{dc}$ relation and information might meet an intuitive objection. Imagine two witnesses X and Y informing the police in the following situations:

a) Witness X knows the name of the wanted person (attribute A), whereas witness Y reproduces the identity card number of the wanted person (attribute B).

b) Witness X states the identity card number of the wanted person, witness Y the birth date identity number of the wanted person (birth date identity number is the unique number assigned to a person of the form YYMMDDSSS, where YY is the year of the birth, MM the month or the month + 50 in case of a female person, DD the date, and SSS is the sequential number within the given date).

ad a) It holds that $A \leq_{dc} B$ and it might seem that the witness Y were more informative that X. We could claim such a fact if $A \leftarrow_D B$, which is not the case. However, are we able to compare 'the amount of information' connected with these two attributes? Bearing in mind Carnap's idea of comparing informativeness of our assertions, we could try to compare cardinalities of possible ranges of the two attributes. But this comparison is not based on the $\leq_{dc}$ relation.

ad b) It might seem that two attributes of the same distinguishing capability provide us with the same amount of information. But this example illustrates the falseness of such an assumption. Indeed, the date of birth and sex of a given person can be deduced from the birth date identity but not from the identity card number, though the two attributes have the same distinguishing capability.

To be able to grasp such a situation as well, we define:

Definition 9. A $\leq_{bc}$ B *(comparison based on cardinality)* iff
[Card $\lambda y \, \exists wx \, ([A_w \, x] = y)] \leq$ [Card $\lambda z \, \exists wx \, ([B_w \, x] = z)]$.
A $=_{bc}$ B iff A $\leq_{bc}$ B and B $\leq_{bc}$ A.

◊

Example. Compare attributes N_1 = 'first name of a person', N_2 = 'surname of a person'. We are again tempted to claim that the former gives less information than the latter. In this case this assertion is justified: the greater informativeness of N_2 can be explained by the fact that the cardinality of the set of all the usable surnames is greater than the cardinality of the set of all the usable first names, hence $N_1 \leq_{bc} N_2$. (To ensure the correctness we can restrict our considerations to European first names and surnames.) This does not, of course, mean that the less than relation is valid between the cardinalities of the ranges of the extensions of these attributes in all the states of affairs. In an apocalyptic state of affairs where only the Smith family has survived and its members have different first names the proposition λw (Card $\lambda y \, \exists x \, ([N_{1w} \, x] = y) \geq$ Card $\lambda z \, \exists x \, ([N_{2w} \, x] = z))$ takes the value True.

◊

Comparing (the amount of) informational content of attributes is sometimes confused with comparing '*the value*' of information provided. It is highly probable that the information obtained from the identity card number will be more valuable to the policeman than the information obtained from the name. But being on an island where our policeman knows the names of all the inhabitants, and where he does not have a file of identity card numbers, we would agree that the name is a more valuable piece of information for him, which, of course, does not contradict the fact that logically it provides less information.

It might seem that if A $\leq_{dc}$ B then A $\leq_{bc}$ B. But this does not hold. These two notions are not comparable. The only fact that can be stated is the following: If A $\leq_{dc}$ B then $\forall w$ ([Card $\lambda y \, \exists x \, ([B_w \, x] = y)] \geq$ [Card $\lambda z \, \exists x \, ([A_w \, x] = z)])$, from which it does not follow that A $\leq_{bc}$ B. (This is a correction of [DUMA90].)

In summary, speaking about informational redundant attributes is justified only in case of the definability relation ($\leftarrow_D$). This relation is also defined for sets of attributes, which enables us to compare informational capabilities of general data structures. The distinguishing capability relation ($\leq_{dc}$) is not connected with informational capability of attributes. Only a subset of this relation - the strong definability ($\Leftarrow_D$) - specifies informational redundancy. The relation based on cardinality ($\leq_{bc}$) can only be connected with the amount of information generated from attributes, and is not comparable with the $\leq_{bc}$ relation.

8. Modeling Databases

Well-known database notions can be redefined on the base of attributes. Following [POKO96c] we suppose LT with **Func** containing appropriate functions such as quantifiers, set constructs etc. This (generic) language LT is called *database-applicable language* here.

Attributes exactly model an application realm. They include all necessary information for generating so called information base. We could imagine it as set of basic propositions. On the conceptual schema level it is mostly appropriate to add usual ICs that provide a guide for an implementation of an associate database. Their patterns on the abstract level of attributes are propositions called often *consistency constraints* (CCs) [ZLAT86].

Definition 10. A *conceptual schema* (with respect to LT) is a couple S_{LT} = (**A**, **I**) where **A** is a tuple $(A_1,...,A_n)$ of typed variables of LT called *attribute identifiers* and **I** is a tuple of other terms of LT representing CCs. They are called *integrity constraints* (ICs). For a given state of affairs W (usually the actual one) the set of basic propositions $B(\mathbf{A})^W$ determines the *information base* of $\mathbf{S}_{LT}$.

◊

Obviously, each conceptual schema $\mathbf{S}_{LT}$ is a term of LT. It is reasonable to restrict ICs to terms with attribute identifiers as the only ones free variables.

When is $\mathbf{A}_W$ representable in a database? For example, while its type is built from user defined sorts from B. The database level is dependent on the database model chosen. Usually, we can easily omit parametrizing by W in typing $\mathbf{A}$ in most of cases. The conceptual ICs are transformed to sentences of a formal language (usually they are expressed as closed formulas of the predicate calculus). Possibly, other ICs will appear. They correspond to so called inherent ICs (e.g. the functionality of LT may cause generating functional dependencies in RDM). The resulted schema of database semantics is depicted in figure 1.

The importance of the notion of attribute as a universal modeling construct has been emphasised in many previous works ([DKMS86], [POKO93], [POKO96c]). We can easily use our type system $\mathbf{T}$ for characterization of conceptual or database models.

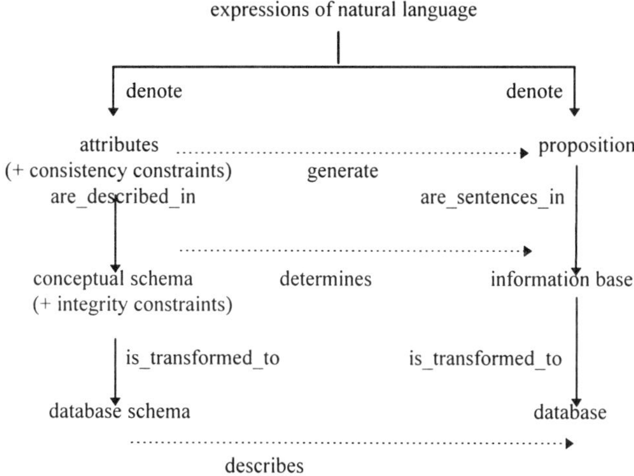

Fig. 1. Schema of database semantics

Definition 11. Let **Sorts** be a countable set of *sort variables* ranging possible (entity and descriptive) sorts. Replacing the base B by the set of sort variables in the definition of type system $\mathbf{T}$, we obtain *parametrized types* $\mathbf{T}_{Par}$. Then any subset of $\mathbf{T}_{Par}$ is said to be a *modeling tool*. Its members are called *modeling constructs*.

◊

Definition 12. If the only types allowed as valuations of sort variables are descriptive sorts, then each defined modeling tool is called a *value-oriented* (or *database*) *model*. If a modeling tool is not value-oriented model, then it is called a *conceptual model* (alternatively *entity-* or *object-oriented model*).

◊

Remark:
◊ Today, the notion object-oriented is rather applied in object-oriented approach, where objects own methods etc.

Now we illustrate the above notions by examples. By E we will denote variables valuated by entity sorts, D will be used for descriptive sorts, C denotes either E or D, states of affairs are omitted. The following modeling tools cover some well-known database and conceptual models:

- $E_1,...,E_n,D_1,...,D_m$ $(m,n \geq 1)$ *sortalization*
- $((D_1,...,D_m) \rightarrow o))$ $(m \geq 1)$ *relational data model*
- $((E_1,...,E_m) \rightarrow o)$, $(m \geq 2)$ *Chen's E-R model*
  $((E_1,...,E_m) \rightarrow D)$ $(m \geq 1)$
- $((E_1,E_2) \rightarrow o)$, $((E,D) \rightarrow o)$,   *Binary E-R model without functionality*
  $((D,E) \rightarrow o)$,
- $(D \rightarrow E)$, $(E \rightarrow D)$, $(E_1 \rightarrow E_2)$ $((E_1,E_2) \rightarrow o)$ *Binary E-R model with functionality*
- $((E_1,...,E_m) \rightarrow o)$ $(m \geq 1)$ *Chen's E-R model with class construct*
  $((E_1,...,E_m) \rightarrow D)$
- $((E_1,...,E_m) \rightarrow D)$ $(m \geq 2)$ *Chen's E-R model with*
  $((E_1,...,E_m) \rightarrow D)$ $(m \geq 1)$ *multivalued attributes*
  $((E_1,...,E_m) \rightarrow (D \rightarrow o))$
- $((E_1,...,E_m) \rightarrow o)$ $(m \geq 1)$ *Chen's E-R model with class construct and*
  $((E_1,...,E_m) \rightarrow D)$ *class attribute*
  $((E \rightarrow o) \rightarrow D)$

Remarks:

◊ Other higher-level modeling construct may be specified. For example, relationships of classes are usable in modeling statistical data [POKO96b]. Subtyping (ISA-hierarchies) is also possible [POKO96a].

◊ Allowing E variables among parametrized simple types results in construct that are supported in modeling tools known as *complex objects*.

9. Expressiveness of Modeling Tools

Recent conceptual models are based on the classical E-R approach. Many new constructs and symbols to provide additional semantics have been studied in their particular versions. There is a belief that a variety of different construct enables a more comprehensive representation of the real world. On the other hand, due to so called semantic relativism (e.g. [POKO93]) the expressive power of the such models does not increase. This fact is intuitively reflected in an observation that we are always able to „reconstruct" our modelled world and to map it with a given set of conceptual constructs into a conceptual schema which fits our requirements.

A natural question appears: how to compare various approaches to the conceptual modeling with respect to their expressive power. In [POKO93] we focused on a formalization of expressiveness of modeling tools. The main goal of these ideas is to support a schema integration in a heterogeneous environment where e.g. two different conceptual models are used in two different but similar applications in that should be integrated. It is shown there that this integrability depends on basic objects given in the respective conceptual realms (on a certain "similarity" of elementary types) and on basic constructs allowing to construct conceptual bridges between notions used in these realms.

9.1 Unification of Bases

Ensuring a bidirectional "compatibility" of two different applications can be partly achieved by a *unification* of bases of elementary types and via so called *integration attributes*. To be of the same expressive power, two conceptual models have to guarantee that every conceptual schema in the former model must be expressible in the latter model and vice versa.

First, we extend the notion of informationally equivalent attribute sets to schemes built on two, in general, different bases B_1 and B_2. To do two sets of attributes mutually „compatible", the types in B_1 that are not in B_2 must be expressible by means of substitution as types of B_2 and vice versa. We could remind the attribute „departments in a company (see Section 3). Departments could be not classes of employees but elements of a basic sort. Obviously, employees would be in a relationship to these departments.

Formally, a *type substitution*, Θ_{ij}, is a finite mapping from B_i to $\mathbf{T}_j$ ($i \neq j$). $B_i\Theta_{ij}$ stands for the result of applying Θ_{ij} to B_i. Thus, we can assign a new base of elementary types, B_i', to B_i. Each substitution can be written as a set of bindings enclosed in curly braces. A particular case is adding elementary types allowed by type substitutions of the form $\{\leftarrow S\}$, where $S \in B_j$.

Example: Let $B_1 = \{o,S_1,S_2,S_3\}$, $B_2 = \{o,R_1,R_2\}$, and $\Theta_{12} = \{S_3 \leftarrow ((R_1{\rightarrow}o){\rightarrow}o)\}$, $\Theta_{21}=\{R_2 \leftarrow (S_1,S_2)\}$. After applying these substitutions we obtain bases B_1' and B_2'. It is easy to verify that $B_1' = B_2'$.

◊

If there are substitutions Θ_{12} and Θ_{21} such that $B_1'= B_2'$, then B_1 and B_2 are said to be *unifiable*. According to unifiability, B_1' and B_2' are said to be *unified*. Results of particular substitutions results in B-unifiability. We say that B_i' is B_j-*unified* ($i{\neq}j$). Obviously, two identical bases are unifiable. Further we must to modify the notion of information equivalence. Let A and B are defined as in Theorem 1, but over unifiable bases B_1 and B_2, respectively. In general, the sets $[Cn \cup_{i=1}^{m} P(A_i)^W]$ and $[Cn \cup_{j=1}^{n} P(B_j)^W]$ will be different. A sufficient condition for meaningful notion of information equivalency in this case is the logical equivalence of both proposition sets. We denote this information equivalence *implicational* (shortly *I- informational equivalence*).

In the case of $B_1 = B_2$ two equal sets of propositions are obviously logically equivalent. Thus, the following theorem holds:

Theorem 5. Let A and B be two sets of attributes over base B. Then information equivalence of A and B implies their I-information equivalence.

Definition 13. Let $\mathbf{A}_i$ ($i=1,2$) be two sets of attributes defined over the respective unifiable bases B_i. Let $\mathbf{I}_i$ ($i=1,2$) be respective sets of ICs. Schemes $\mathbf{S}_i = (\mathbf{A}_i,\mathbf{I}_i)$ ($i=1,2$) are said to be *informationally equivalent* iff $\mathbf{A}_1$ and $\mathbf{A}_2$ are I- informationally equivalent and $\mathbf{I}_1$ may be converted into $\mathbf{I}_2$ by appropriate substitutions of attributes and vice versa.

◊

Remark:
◊ The substitutions among ICs are made in accordance with mutual definability of the respective attribute sets.

In practice, we specify the substitution by a set of bindings. For example, bases specified in example are unifiable. Thus, a notion denoting an object of type R_2 is expressible by a couple of notions of type (S_1,S_2).

The substitution Θ_{ij} is not only a formal construction as should be to seem from the above considerations. Let us to consider, for a moment, the base

$$B_3 = \{o,S_1,S_2,S_3,R_1,R_2\},$$

i.e. $B_3 = B_1 \cup B_2$. Then, e.g., S_3 given by the binding $S_3 \leftarrow ((R_1{\rightarrow}o){\rightarrow}o)$ has one possible interpretation expressing an association (a bijection) of objects o/S_3 to objects $o'/((R_1{\rightarrow}o){\rightarrow}o)$. On an intuitive level, the base B_3 makes an integration environment for "miniworlds" given by bases B_1, B_2. In other words, there is a so called *integration attribute* Is-explained-as of type $(S_3{\rightarrow} ((R_1{\rightarrow} o){\rightarrow}o))$. The reversed attribute to it can be called Is-covered-by/ $(((R_1{\rightarrow}o){\rightarrow} o){\rightarrow} S_3)$. Notice that Is-explained-as and Is-covered-by are rather generic names for expressing these semantic connections. Thus, a unification of bases is designer-oriented (empirical) process. The above integration attributes are in a good accordance with our intuition. They express a deepness of our notions used in modeling the object system.

9.2 Expressiveness of Conceptual Models

Comparability of two conceptual models is based on the following idea: what is conceptually expressible in the first modeling tool must be expressible in the second and, possibly, vice verse. However, the unifiability of base is not enough for obtaining sufficiently general results. First, a connection of conceptual models to LTs must be specified. We say that a conceptual model Γ is *applied w.r.t. a language* LT, if sort variables of Γ are valuated by sorts of LT.

We propose the following definition (a modification of the definition in [POKO96c]):
Definition 14. Let Γ_1 and Γ_2 be two conceptual models applied w.r.t. LT_1 and LT_2, respectively, that differ mutually in B_1 and B_2 only. Then Γ_2 *dominates* Γ_1, if for each conceptual schema $\mathbf{S}_1$ in Γ_1 there is B_2' and a conceptual schema $\mathbf{S}_2$ in Γ_2 applied w.r.t LT_2' (i.e. LT_2 with the base B_2') such that $\mathbf{S}_1$ and $\mathbf{S}_2$ are I-informationally equivalent. We say that Γ_1 and Γ_2 have the *same expressive power* if each of them dominates the other.

$\Diamond$

In previous works we proved for different conceptual models their same expressive power. Note that the proofs of these facts use transformations of attributes from $\mathbf{S}_1$ into $\mathbf{S}_2$ and vice versa with the help of type substitutions. Clearly, the notion of definability must be replaced here by *T-definability* (transformation definability). Defining terms for attributes over B_i will use variable substitutions according to type substitutions needed to unifying both bases. Then T-definability will be equivalent to I-information equivalence.

An important (but not unexpected) result is that the Binary E-R model without functionality play a role of „assembler" among conceptual models. It seems to be sufficiently powerful for conceptual modeling. Any higher construct does not increase its expressive power. Typical examples are offered in conceptual modeling of statistical data [POKO96b] On the other hand, HIT data model gives us a meaningful compromise for modeling, i.e. we use a sufficiently small amount of constructs with a close relationship to the natural language.

10. Related Works and Conclusions

Results concerning information capability (level of attributes) are often confronted with information capacity in the sense of [HULL86] on the database level. Databases in our approach are only approximations of information bases. This fact follows from impossibility to design all ICs explicitly. However, nobody knows them in general. With the assumption of correct data it is possible to find schema transformations from the conceptual level into the database level that induce correct mapping between sets of instances of the schemes (definition in the sense of [MILL94]). Various transformations of the E-R model have been successfully studied in the past (e.g. [MAMA90], [HAIN96]). They result in correct implementations on the database level. In such cases, information equivalence at the level of attributes in our sense can imply the information equivalence at the database level (in the sense [HULL86]).

Our approach emphasises a role of the natural language with respect to the conceptual modeling. An interesting approach is offered in [ORSC96]. The authors see the conceptual modeling of an application system as a process of linguistic (re-)construction in so called normative language. In the first phase of reconstruction expert terms are examined and in the following phase these language constructions are used for the specification in a formal (conceptual) language. Our approach mixes both phases into one based on typed expressions of the natural language.

In [POKO94], the functional approach is extended to three-level description of behaviour is described. Due to a very close relationship between conceptual modeling and object-oriented technology, the strategy used in [POKO96a] to specify typed objects, and data functions (attributes) in object-oriented environment, follows the above database philosophy. Further work could be devoted to the study of attributes in these environments.

References

[CARN52] Carnap, R., Bar-Hillel, Y.: An Outline of the Theory of Semantic Information. TR No. 247, MIT Research Laboratory in Electronics, 1952.

[CHUR40] Church, A.: A Formulation of the Simple Theory of Types. J. Symb. Logic, 5, 1, 1940, pp. 337-387.

[DKMS86] Duží, M., Krejčí, F., Materna, P., Staníček, Z.: HIT Method of Data Base Design (a Functional Approach to Information Representation). Res. Rep., Technical Univ. Brno, 1986.

[DUMA90] Duží, M., Materna, P.: Attributes: Distinguishing Capability versus Information Capability. Computers and AI, Vol. 9., 1990, No. 2, pp. 169-185.

[FISH89] Fishman, D.G.: Overview of the Iris DBMS. In W. Kim, F.H. Lochovsky (eds), Object-Oriented Concepts, Databases and Applications. ACM Press New York, 1989.

[HAIN96] Hainaut, J.-L.: Specification Presevation in Schema Transformations - Application to Semantics and Statistics. Data and Knowledge Engineering, Vol. 15, Elsevier, 1996, pp. 251-288.

[HUKI87] Hull, R., King, R.: Semantic database modellling: Survey, applications and research issues. ACM Trans. on Database Systems, 6, 1981, pp. 351-386.

[HULL86] Hull, R.: Relative information capacity of simple relational database schemata. SIAM J. of Comput., 15,3,1986, pp. 856-886.

[MAMA90] Markowitz, V.M., Makowsky, J.A.: Identifying Extended Entity-Relational Object Structures in Relational Schemas. IEEE Transactions on Software Engineering, Vol. 16, No. 8, 1990.

[MATE87] Materna, P.: Entity Sorts: What are They ?. Computers and AI, 6, 4, 1987.

[MAPO81] Materna, P., Pokorný, J.: Applying Simple Theory of Types to Databases. Information Systems,6,4,1981, pp.283-300.

[MILL94] Miller, R.J., et al: Schema Equivalence in Heterogeneous Systems: Bridging Theory and Practice. Proc. of 4th Int. Conf. on Extending Database Technology, M. Jarke, J. Bubenko, K. Jeffery (Eds.), Springer-Verlag, 1994.

[ORSC96] Ortner, E., Schienmann, B.: Normative Language Approach: A Framework for Understanding. Proc. Of 15th Int. Conference on Conceptual Modeling, Cottbus, LNCS 1157, Springer Verlag, 1996, pp. 261-275.

[POKO93] Pokorný, J.: Semantic relativism in conceptual modeling. Proc. of Int. Conf. DEXA' 93, Springer-Verlag, 1993, pp. 48-55.

[POKO94] Pokorný, J.: On Behaviour Modeling Using a Functional Approach. Proc. of the 4th Int. Conf. ISD' 94, Bled, 1994, pp. 73-82.

[POKO96a] Pokorný, J.: Functional information modeling in an object-oriented environment. Proc. of the Fifth International Conference Information Systems Development - ISD' 96, Gdansk, 1996, pp. 437-449.

[POKO96b] Pokorný, J.: Conceptual modeling of statistical data. Proc. of Int. Conf. DEXA' 96, Zurich, 1996, pp. 377-382.

[POKO96c] Pokorný, J.: Database semantics in heterogeneous environment. Proc. Int. Conferfence SOFSEM' 96. Milovy, Czech Republic, 1996, pp. 125-142.

[SCSC90] Scholl, M.H., Scheck, H.-J.: A Relational Object Model. Proc. 4th Int. Conf. on Database Theory ICDT' 90, Paris, 1990.

[SHIP81] Shipman, D.: The functional Data Model and the Data Language DAPLEX. ACM Trans. Database System, Vol. 7, No. 1, 1981.

[SHET95] Sheth, A.: Data Semantics: what, where and how? Summary of the Panel discussion of DS-6 Conference, 1995

[SHKA93] Sheth, A., Kashyap. V.: So far (schematically) yet So Near (Semantically). Proc. of the DS-5 Conf. on Semantics of Interoperable Database Systems, Hsiao, D., Neuhold, E., Sacks-Davis R. (eds.), IFIP Transactions A-25, North-Holland, 1993.
[TICH88] Tichý, P.: The foundations of Freges Logic. de Gruyter, Berlin - New York, 1988.
[ZLAT86] Zlatuška, J.: Data Bases and the Lambda Calculus. Proc. IFIP86, World Comp. Congress, Dublin, 1986, pp. 97-104.

Information Modelling and Knowledge Bases IX
P.-J. Charrel et al. (Eds.)
1998, IOS Press

An Interactive-Graphic Environment for Discovering and Using Conceptual Knowledge

Tu Bao Ho, Trong Dung Nguyen, Hiroshi Shimodaira, Masayuki Kimura

Japan Advanced Institute of Science and Technology
Tatsunokuchi, Ishikawa, 923-12 JAPAN

Abstract. In this paper we describe our ongoing project whose objective is to develop an interactive-graphic environment of related tools for discovering and using conceptual knowledge in relation to influential aspects of the environment and representation. These aspects include the amount of supervision, the manner of data presentation, the regularity of the domain, the representation of data and knowledge. The core of this project is two supervised and unsupervised learning methods that induce knowledge in the form of concept hierarchies. The project aims at improving the performance of these methods and at integrating their implementation in the X Window with the direct manipulation style of interaction. The ultimate goal of the project is to provide an environment in which the user can find and use knowledge from data with low-cost and high-quality.

1. Motivation and background

How to acquire knowledge for knowledge-based systems (KBS) remains as the main difficult and crucial problem of KBS technology. In addition to this difficulty, the explosive growth in the quantity of data stored in databases leads to a common situation of "data rich and knowledge poor". This situation creates a need of techniques and tools for understanding and extracting useful knowledge from data. Knowledge discovery in databases (KDD), the rapidly growing interdisciplinary field of computing which merges together databases, statistics and machine learning techniques, aims at achieving these goals [7]. Thus, the goals of KDD are essentially similar to those of traditional knowledge acquisition (KA) for the KBS development.

In this paper we describe our ongoing project whose objective is to develop an interactive-graphic environment of related tools for discovering and using conceptual knowledge in relation to influential aspects of the environment and representation. The core of our project is the supervised learning method CABRO [12] and the unsupervised learning method OSHAM [14], [15], [16] which induce effectively knowledge in the form of concept hierarchies. The project aims at improving the performance of these methods and integrating their implementation in the X Window with the direct manipulation style of interaction [11], that allows the user to find and use knowledge from data with low-cost and high-quality.

In this section we discuss the three main motivations of our project: "Why do we choose the hierarchical model of conceptual knowledge", "Why do we need to deal with different aspects of the environment and representation?", and "Why do we need to build an interactive-graphic system for modelling?". In sections 2 and 3 we will present the basic ideas and the evaluation of CABRO and OSHAM. Sections 4 and 5 address some issues in the project implementation and conclusions.

1.1 Hierarchical models of conceptual knowledge

Conceptual modelling is a process of forming and collecting conceptual knowledge about the universe of discourse, and documenting the results in the form of a conceptual schema [20]. Conceptual modelling is a widely recognized activity in the process of KBS development. It is important to notice that in the knowledge acquisition community "expertise transfer" paradigms have been replaced in recent years by "knowledge modelling" paradigms [8]. Clancey, the defender of the *modelling view* of knowledge acquisition, argues that "the primary concern of knowledge engineering is modelling systems in the world, not replicating how people think" [4].

The process of forming conceptual knowledge relates closely to the *organization* of knowledge. Among three main alternative schemes of decision lists, inference networks, and concept hierarchies for organizing knowledge descriptions, we are particularly interested in the last ones which are fundamental for the basic modeling scheme of information processing [26] and are widely used in AI products such as KBS tools KEE, Kappa, Nexpert Object, etc. The hierarchical model for conceptual modelling also shares the common structured models on Object-Oriented Modelling [29].

A *concept hierarchy* is a structure composed of nodes and links. Each node represents a concept with its associated intensional description. The links connecting a node to its children specify an "IS-A" or "subset" relation, indicating that the parent's extension is a superset of each child's extension. Typically, a node covers all of the instances covered by the union of its descendents, making the concept hierarchy a subgraph of the partial ordering by generality. More abstract or general nodes occur higher in the hierarchy, whereas more specific ones occur at lower levels [23].

The most widely used forms of concept hierarchies are decision trees and discrimination networks. A *decision tree* is a classifier in the form of a tree structure whose node is either a leaf (a class of instances) or a decision node that specifies some test to be carried out, with one branch for each possible outcome of the test. A *discrimination network* has a similar structure of trees but concepts at a branch do not have to be mutually exclusive, so multiple father nodes can arise. A decision tree/discrimination network can be easily converted into a set of decision rules [27].

Being modelled as a concept hierarchy, the exploitation of knowledge for a classification process involves sorting instances downward through the hierarchy. In general, the modelling task with this structure can be stated as follows:

- *Given:* A set of instances with/without class information;
- *Find:* A concept hierarchy that, to the extent possible, makes accurate predictions about unknown instances.

1.2 Influential aspects of environment and representation

Techniques for acquiring conceptual knowledge are deeply influenced by different aspects of the environment and of the representation of data and knowledge. Similarly to those in [23], one can distinguish the following influential aspects:

- The conceptual knowledge involves *one-step* classification and prediction or *multistep* inference or problem solving;

- The application domain is *supervised* or *unsupervised*. The degree of supervision concerns whether the class information in data or a domain expert is available. In case of a supervised domain, there is a feedback about the appropriateness of the discovered results and the discovering process is essentially error-driven. Without this feedback in case of unsupervised domain, the discovering process is essentially the search for regularities in data. In our opinion, the degree of supervision is the most important aspect based on it we can choose techniques.

- The manner in which data are provided. One distinguishes a *nonincremental* task when data are presented simultaneously (offline) and an *incremental* task when data are presented serially (online).

- The *regularity* of the environment (e.g., complexity of the target knowledge, number of irrelevant attributes, the amount of noise and missing values, etc.).

- The representation nature of data and knowledge affects the discovering process. One distinguishes data which contain *symbolic attributes* that are nominal or ordinal ones, *numeric attributes* that take on real values, and *relational literals*.

- The three alternative schemes for *organizing the knowledge* descriptions of decision lists, inference networks, and concept hierarchies [23]. As mentioned in subsection 1.1, we are particularly interested in the concept hierarchy structure that is widely used in KBS.

All of these aspects may occur in realistic situations and influence the conceptual modelling process. Often, each discovering method can deal with one or some mentioned aspects but not all. For example, most data analysis or optimization systems are developed for numeric data and most machine learning systems are developed for symbolic data. In the practical use of a discovery system, it is expected that it can function in different situations.

For more complex data, our project shares some common tasks with the ESPRIT European project SODAS [10] of 18 partners on a software for *symbolic data analysis*. Symbolic data analysis [5] is a new attempt that aims at extending problems, methods and algorithms used in standard data analysis to more complex data such as a set of values, intervals of values, or a probabilistic distribution, etc.

1.3 An interactive-graphic environment for discovering

We perceive that conceptual modelling is an iterative cycle of knowledge refinement in which the system provides and receives interactively feedback to and from the user.

Current discovery systems do not always equal the human ability in identifying useful concepts, and as the search problem in such a complex process requires much background knowledge and heuristics, the human factor in discovery process is always necessary [13].

A strong interaction between the discovery system and the user is expected to be a common feature of discovery systems as the discovery systems cannot produce maximally useful results when operating alone. Recently, there are much efforts in the development of *interactive-graphic environments* in order to improve the performance of discovery systems. In [22] the authors develop an interactive-graphic environment for constructing decision trees. In [24] the author develop system WinViz that integrates multidimensional visualization with the program C4.5 for learning decision trees [27].

To support the knowledge acquisition modelling process, we use a Visual Interactive Model through a rich graphical environment. A Visual Interactive Model (VIM) aims at combining "meaningful pictures and easy interactions to stimulate creativity and insight; promoting a process of 'generate and test', it facilitates a rapid cycle of learning" [1]. Concretely, in our environment VIM offers the user two main benefits: (1) better understanding the induction process and generated decision trees/concept hierarchies, especially by the Tree Visualizer; and (2) a more active role in the modelling process with a interactive mode of operation.

2. Supervised discovery of knowledge

2.1 R-measure

The basic task of supervised discovery of conceptual knowledge is from a given set of labelled instances to find a classifier that correctly predicts classes of unseen instances. Among approaches to this problem the *decision tree induction* is probably the most active and applicable one.

Table 1 gives a brief description of the common scheme for decision tree induction. Decision tree induction systems differ from each other in their way to deal with two crucial problems of *attribute selection* (choosing the "best" attribute to split a decision node in terms of a measure for "goodness of split") and *pruning* (avoiding overfitting and obtaining statistical reliability). We have developed a decision tree induction method called CABRO which uses R-measure for the attribute selection, a new measure stemmed from the theory of rough sets [28].

Table 1. Framework of decision tree induction

---

1. Choose the "best" attribute by an attribute selection measure.
2. Extend tree by adding new branch for each attribute value.
3. Sort training examples to leaf nodes.
4. If examples unambiguously classified then stop else repeat steps 1–4 for leaf nodes.
5. Prune the obtained tree.

Rough set theory is a mathematical tool to deal with vagueness and uncertainty. The basic idea in this theory is to "view" approximately each subset X of an object set O by its *lower* and *upper* approximations w.r.t. an equivalence relation $E \subseteq O \times O$. These approximations of X are defined, respectively, by $E_*(X) = \{o \in O : [o]_E \subseteq X\}$ and $E^*(X) = \{o \in O : [o]_E \cap X \neq \emptyset\}$, where $[o]_E$ denotes the equivalence class of an object o in E. A key concept in the rough set theory is the *degree of dependency* of a set of attributes Q on a set of attributes P, denoted by $\mu_P(Q)$ $(0 \leq \mu_P(Q) \leq 1)$, defined as

$$\mu_P(Q) = \frac{card(\bigcup_{[o]_Q} P_*([o]_Q))}{card(O)} = \frac{card(\{o \in O : [o]_P \subseteq [o]_Q\})}{card(O)} \tag{1}$$

If $\mu_P(Q) = 1$ then Q totally depends on P; if $0 < \mu_P(Q) < 1$ then Q partially depends on P; if $\mu_P(Q) = 0$ then Q is independent of P.

The measure $\mu_P(Q)$ can be used directly in decision tree induction for the attribute selection with Q stands for the class attribute and P stands for a descriptive attribute. In [12], our analysis and experiments have shown that $\mu_Q(P)$ is not robust with noisy data and not enough sensitive when partitions of O generated by P and Q are nearly identified. From this analysis, we have generalized and formulated a measure for degree of dependency of an attribute set Q on an attribute set P

$$\mu'_P(Q) = \frac{1}{card(O)} \sum_{[o]_P} max_{[o]_Q} card([o]_Q \cap [o]_P) \tag{2}$$

The main difference between $\mu_P(Q)$ and $\mu'_P(Q)$ is the latter measures the dependency of Q on P in maximizing the predicted membership of an instance in the family of equivalence classes generated by Q given its membership in the family of equivalence classes generated by P.

Theorem. *For every attribute set P and Q we have*

$$\frac{max_{[o]_Q} card([o]_Q)}{card(O)} \leq \mu'_P(Q) \leq 1$$

This property allows us to define that Q totally depends on P iff $\mu'_P(Q) = 1$, Q partially depends on P iff $max_{[o]_Q} card([o]_Q)/card(O) < \mu'_P(Q) < 1$, and Q is independent of P iff $\mu'_P(Q) = max_{[o]_Q} card([o]_Q)/card(O)$. In practice, to emphasize rules those have the higher generalities we use the following formula, and call it R-measure

$$\tilde{\mu}_P(Q) = \frac{1}{card(O)} \sum_{[o]_P} max_{[o]_Q} \frac{card([o]_Q \cap [o]_P)^2}{card([o]_P)} \tag{3}$$

2.2 Evaluation

Three criteria on the size, prediction accuracy and understandability mentioned in [25] for evaluating decision trees are common used, among them the prediction accuracy of pruned trees is widely considered to be of fundamental importance.

We have carried out carefully experimental comparative studies of R-measure with some widely used measures as gain-ratio in C4.5 [27], gini-index in CART [2], χ^2 in statistics [25], by k-fold stratified cross validation.

In k-fold stratified cross validation, the dataset is randomly stratified and divided into k mutually exclusive subsets (folds) of approximately equal size and the same proportions of labels as in the original dataset. One subset is used as testing data and the union of the rest ones is used as training data. One run of k-fold cross validation is the repeat k times of this process each with a new testing subset, and the accuracy is estimated as the average of the accuracies of k runs. The experiments were designed as follows

- use a large number of datasets;
- use 10-fold stratified cross-validation with a random shuffle of data;
- implement studied techniques in a system based on the scheme of CLS;
- to evaluate selection measures we run the system with different attribute selection measures while fixing a pruning and a discretization technique.

Eighteen datasets from the UCI repository of machine learning databases were used. Experimental results are reported in Table 2 in which included the following information
- the letters c, g, χ and R stand for gain-ratio, gini-index, χ^2 and R-measure, respectively (first column).
- datasets features: name, number of attributes $\times$ number of instances, numeric, symbolic or mix data;
- the size of trees before and after pruning (even columns);
- the error rates on testing data before and after pruning (odd columns);

Table 2. Experimental results on attribute selection measures

	unpruned		pruned		unpruned		pruned	
	size	errors	size	errors	size	errors	size	errors
Vote, 16x300, symbolic					**Cancer, 9x700, symbolic**			
c	22.6 ± 2.5	7.3 ± 3.6	4.0 ± 0.0	5.0 ± 2.8	87.9 ± 23.1	7.3 ± 2.2	46.1 ± 19.1	7.4 ± 2.9
g	24.7 ± 2.8	7.0 ± 3.0	7.0 ± 4.2	5.9 ± 2.7	92.3 ± 26.0	6.9 ± 2.3	36.2 ± 11.9	7.4 ± 3.5
χ	24.7 ± 2.8	7.0 ± 3.0	7.0 ± 4.2	5.9 ± 2.7	92.3 ± 26.0	6.9 ± 2.0	36.2 ± 11.9	7.4 ± 3.5
R	25.0 ± 3.0	7.5 ± 3.4	5.8 ± 2.9	5.7 ± 2.7	94.5 ± 26.4	7.0 ± 2.2	37.3 ± 11.2	7.1 ± 3.4
Shuttle, 9x956, symbolic					**Promoters, 45x105, symbolic**			
c	88.4 ± 10.9	0.2 ± 0.1	53.4 ± 15.8	0.2 ± 0.1	18.2 ± 3.3	25.5 ± 9.8	9.8 ± 4.3	24.5 ± 7.5
g	144.8 ± 6.6	0.2 ± 0.1	114.2 ± 12.2	0.2 ± 0.1	19.0 ± 4.0	23.6 ± 12.7	9.4 ± 3.7	22.7 ± 10.0
χ	199.0 ± 17.2	0.3 ± 0.1	162.7 ± 30.4	0.3 ± 0.1	19.0 ± 4.0	23.6 ± 10.9	9.4 ± 3.7	22.7 ± 10.0
R	165.3 ± 15.6	0.2 ± 0.1	135.3 ± 18.3	0.3 ± 0.1	19.0 ± 4.0	23.6 ± 12.7	9.4 ± 3.7	22.7 ± 10.0
Solar Flare, 12x1286, symbolic					**Diabetes, 8x768, numeric**			
c	104.0 ± 11.6	26.8 ± 2.5	26.8 ± 7.8	25.3 ± 1.5	41.2 ± 2.2	24.4 ± 3.1	18.2 ± 9.4	25.3 ± 2.6
g	150.8 ± 15.0	28.4 ± 2.9	54.4 ± 15.0	27.8 ± 1.3	53.0 ± 4.4	25.3 ± 2.7	22.0 ± 4.8	25.6 ± 2.5
χ	168.6 ± 24.6	28.3 ± 2.2	45.8 ± 18.1	26.6 ± 2.0	47.6 ± 5.1	25.3 ± 2.7	13.6 ± 6.2	25.5 ± 2.5
R	155.0 ± 19.4	26.9 ± 1.8	44.6 ± 31.1	25.5 ± 1.0	74.2 ± 8.6	24.7 ± 2.6	27.8 ± 19.8	25.3 ± 2.6
Splice, 45x3189, numeric					**Glass, 9x214, numeric**			
c	529.8 ± 68.0	10.2 ± 1.5	245.8 ± 36.8	8.0 ± 1.7	21.0 ± 3.2	33.2 ± 8.6	17.3 ± 5.5	34.5 ± 8.2
g	565.8 ± 72.0	10.4 ± 2.4	214.6 ± 39.8	8.4 ± 1.8	35.2 ± 4.4	33.2 ± 7.7	22.3 ± 6.9	36.8 ± 6.8
χ	585.8 ± 76.0	10.5 ± 2.4	253.0 ± 56.8	8.8 ± 1.7	29.6 ± 2.8	35.0 ± 5.6	19.1 ± 7.5	37.3 ± 6.4
R	569.8 ± 77.4	11.0 ± 2.5	207.4 ± 30.4	8.6 ± 1.9	32.2 ± 5.8	34.1 ± 7.3	18.7 ± 6.8	35.9 ± 6.9
Waveform, 36x3195, symbolic					**Heart Disease, 13x270, mixed**			
c	1148.3 ± 179.5	28.9 ± 1.7	223.9 ± 72.9	25.7 ± 1.1	13.8 ± 5.4	25.6 ± 4.1	8.8 ± 3.8	25.6 ± 4.1
g	1320.5 ± 193.9	27.8 ± 1.3	244.5 ± 69.5	24.4 ± 1.6	33.0 ± 4.0	27.4 ± 4.7	25.8 ± 2.6	25.6 ± 5.6
χ	1355.7 ± 185.0	28.4 ± 1.6	340.6 ± 191.6	26.8 ± 1.3	26.6 ± 9.7	27.4 ± 4.7	9.0 ± 3.2	26.3 ± 4.9
R	1432.3 ± 193.5	29.3 ± 1.5	249.6 ± 78.4	25.1 ± 1.1	38.0 ± 13.4	27.4 ± 4.7	8.2 ± 5.1	25.2 ± 4.6
Vehicle, 18x846, numeric					**Hypothyroid, 25x3163, numeric**			
c	174.5 ± 35.9	32.4 ± 5.2	131.9 ± 40.7	32.7 ± 5.1	22.6 ± 2.5	1.1 ± 0.4	11.8 ± 1.5	0.9 ± 0.4
g	222.8 ± 38.4	31.9 ± 3.2	111.4 ± 37.8	32.0 ± 3.7	49.2 ± 5.4	1.3 ± 0.5	16.8 ± 3.7	0.9 ± 0.4
χ	216.2 ± 40.4	30.2 ± 3.9	111.4 ± 47.4	31.9 ± 3.2	54.8 ± 5.0	1.3 ± 0.5	10.6 ± 0.6	0.9 ± 0.4
R	218.2 ± 39.6	31.6 ± 3.2	101.5 ± 28.7	31.8 ± 3.5	57.8 ± 6.0	1.4 ± 0.4	18.2 ± 4.9	0.9 ± 0.4
Audiology, 70x226, symbolic					**Cars, 8x392, numeric**			
c	49.8 ± 9.0	29.6 ± 13.7	28.4 ± 13.3	30.9 ± 11.0	32.3 ± 2.0	24.8 ± 4.8	17.1 ± 9.5	26.0 ± 2.0
g	68.2 ± 12.4	29.6 ± 11.5	37.0 ± 16.0	30.9 ± 11.9	44.7 ± 10.3	24.0 ± 4.8	21.4 ± 8.5	26.8 ± 5.2
χ	93.9 ± 22.3	44.3 ± 8.9	66.9 ± 14.9	45.2 ± 8.7	41.8 ± 8.8	23.8 ± 5.0	17.4 ± 9.1	26.5 ± 5.2
R	72.1 ± 10.3	28.3 ± 10.9	41.3 ± 13.4	29.1 ± 11.7	44.6 ± 12.5	24.2 ± 5.1	21.8 ± 12.8	25.2 ± 4.8
Horse-colic, 28x368, numeric					**Pima-diabetes, 8x768, numeric**			
c	48.9 ± 9.1	16.2 ± 3.8	8.2 ± 4.1	14.3 ± 5.1	34.3 ± 6.7	24.9 ± 4.5	17.6 ± 5.8	23.4 ± 3.6
g	86.4 ± 19.1	17.8 ± 1.9	30.9 ± 20.3	16.8 ± 3.5	45.4 ± 3.5	24.7 ± 4.2	25.4 ± 8.3	23.5 ± 3.5
χ	92.0 ± 25.8	18.1 ± 2.3	22.0 ± 22.4	17.0 ± 3.3	40.0 ± 4.2	24.7 ± 4.2	18.5 ± 9.0	23.5 ± 3.5
R	115.6 ± 22.7	17.0 ± 1.7	15.8 ± 13.7	15.9 ± 4.2	65.1 ± 8.5	24.7 ± 4.2	30.6 ± 17.4	23.9 ± 3.2
Segmentation, 19x2310, numeric					**Iris, 4x150, numeric**			
c	327.4 ± 48.2	6.3 ± 1.5	236.4 ± 46.5	6.2 ± 1.6	4.3 ± 0.5	4.0 ± 3.2	4.0 ± 0.0	3.3 ± 3.3
g	341.3 ± 30.9	5.9 ± 1.7	257.5 ± 81.2	6.1 ± 2.0	4.3 ± 0.5	3.3 ± 3.3	4.0 ± 0.0	2.7 ± 3.2
χ	373.2 ± 25.2	7.3 ± 1.6	310.7 ± 48.3	7.6 ± 2.0	4.3 ± 0.5	4.7 ± 3.7	4.0 ± 0.0	4.0 ± 4.0
R	342.5 ± 33.6	6.1 ± 1.8	272.0 ± 90.4	6.1 ± 2.1	4.3 ± 0.5	4.7 ± 3.7	4.0 ± 0.0	4.0 ± 4.0

As error rates of pruned trees are of most importance, we indicate the lowest error rate of pruned trees for each dataset among four measures by bold numbers. The error rates of four measures on eighteen datasets are summarized in Table 3 and Figure 1.

Table 3. Error rates of pruned trees for four measures

datasets	Gain-Ratio	Gini-Index	χ^2	R-measure
Shuttle	**0.2 ± 0.1**	**0.2 ± 0.1**	0.3 ± 0.1	0.3 ± 0.1
Hypothyroid	**0.9 ± 0.4**	**0.9 ± 0.4**	**0.9 ± 0.4**	**0.9 ± 0.4**
Iris	3.3 ± 3.3	**2.7 ± 3.2**	4.0 ± 4.0	4.0 ± 4.0
Vote	**5.0 ± 2.8**	5.9 ± 2.7	5.9 ± 2.7	5.7 ± 2.7
Breast cancer	7.4 ± 2.9	7.4 ± 3.5	7.4 ± 3.5	**7.1 ± 3.4**
Segmentation	6.2 ± 1.6	**6.1 ± 2.0**	7.6 ± 2.0	**6.1 ± 2.1**
Splice	**8.0 ± 1.7**	8.4 ± 1.8	8.8 ± 1.7	8.6 ± 1.9
Horse-colic	**14.3 ± 5.1**	16.8 ± 3.5	17.0 ± 3.3	15.9 ± 4.2
Waveform	25.7 ± 1.1	**24.4 ± 1.6**	26.8 ± 1.3	25.1 ± 1.1
Solar Flare	**25.3 ± 1.5**	27.8 ± 1.3	26.6 ± 2.0	25.5 ± 1.0
Heart-disease	25.6 ± 4.1	25.6 ± 5.6	26.3 ± 4.9	**25.2 ± 4.6**
Diabetes	**25.3 ± 2.6**	25.6 ± 2.5	25.5 ± 2.57	**25.3 ± 2.6**
Promoters	24.5 ± 7.5	**22.7 ± 10.0**	**22.7 ± 10.0**	**22.7 ± 10.0**
Pima-Diabetes	**23.4 ± 3.6**	23.5 ± 3.5	23.5 ± 3.5	23.9 ± 3.2
Vehicle	32.7 ± 5.1	32.0 ± 3.7	31.9 ± 3.2 7	**31.8 ± 3.5**
Audiology	30.9 ± 11.0	30.9 ± 11.9	45.2 ± 8.7	**29.1 ± 11.7**
Glass	**34.5 ± 8.2**	36.8 ± 6.8	37.3 ± 6.4	35.9 ± 6.9
Cars	26.0 ± 2.0	26.8 ± 5.2	26.8 ± 5.2	**25.2 ± 4.8**

Other information as the tree sizes, error rates before pruning in Table 2 can be viewed as additional factors for evaluating methods. Some conclusions can be drawn from our various experimental results reported in Table 2, Table 3.

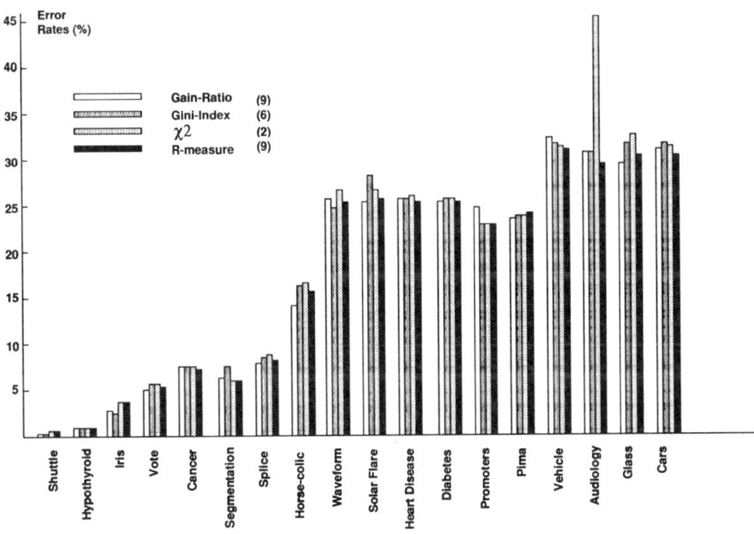

Figure 1. Graphical representation of error rates of pruned trees

- For pruned trees, the numbers of datasets on which each measure attains the lowest error rate are 9 (gain-ratio), 6 (gini-index), 2 (χ^2) and 9 (R-measure), and the smallest size are 11 (gain-ratio), 2 (gini-index), 5 (χ^2) and 5 (R-measure). These results verified that though certain methods are very good but they are not always the best, and it may be necessary to select the most suitable technique in certain applications of decision tree induction. Our easy-to-use system described in next section aims at supporting this selection.

- Careful experimental results show that R-measure is a good one. Evaluating together with the most widely used and stable measures, R-measure attains reasonably comparable error rates in various datasets. This allow us to believe in the high performance of R-measure and its application potential.

3. Unsupervised discovery of Knowledge

3.1 Concept representation and clustering

The basic task of acquiring knowledge in this situation is that from a given set of unlabelled instances to find simultaneously a hierarchical clustering that determines useful object subsets and intensional definitions for these subsets of objects. Essentially, unsupervised concept learning methods differ from each other in two factors of *views on concepts* and *constraints of categorization*. Among views on concepts, the classical, prototype and exemplar ones are widely known and used. Among categorization constraints, the similarity, feature correlation, and structure of the concept hierarchy are widely known and used. The learning system OSHAM proposed in [14], which employs the classical view on concepts, and is able to form effectively a concept hierarchy from unlabelled data. Essentially, OSHAM searches to extract a good concept hierarchy by exploiting the structure of Galois lattice of concepts as the hypothesis space. OSHAM has been extended to a hybrid system that allows obtaining a higher performance by combining its original view on concepts with the prototype and exemplar views [15].

Instead of characterizing a concept only by its intent and extent, OSHAM represents each concept C_k in a concept hierarchy $\mathcal{H}$ by a 10-tuple

$$< l(C_k), f(C_k), s(C_k), i(C_k), e(C_k), d(C_k), p(C_k), d(C_k^r), p(C_k^r|C_k), q(C_k) > \qquad (4)$$

where

- $l(C_k)$ is the level of C_k in $\mathcal{H}$;
- $f(C_k)$ is the list of direct superconcepts of C_k;
- $s(C_k)$ is the list of direct subconcepts of C_k;
- $i(C_k)$ is the intent of C_k (set of all common properties of instances of C_k);
- $e(C_k)$ is the extent of C_k (set of all instances satisfying properties of $i(C_k)$);
- $d(C_k)$ is the dispersion between instances of C_k;
- $p(C_k)$ is the occurrence probability of C_k;
- $d(C_k^r)$ is the dispersion of local instances of C_k which are not classified into subconcepts of C_k;
- $p(C_k^r|C_k)$ is the conditional probability of these unclassified instances of C_k;
- $q(C_k)$ is the quality estimation of splitting C_k into subconcepts C_{k_i}.

Explanation and analysis of this hybrid representation can be found in [15]. Below is an example of concepts discovered by OSHAM

```
CONCEPT 43
Level = 5, Super_Concepts = {29}, Sub_Concepts = {52, 53}
Features = (Uniformity of Cell Size, 1) ∧ (Bare Nuclei, 1) ∧ (Bland Chromatin, 1) ∧
(Uniformity of Cell Shape, 2)
Local_instances/Covered_instances = 6/25
Local_instances = {8, 127, 221, 236, 415, 661}
Concept_probability = 0.041666
Local_instance_conditional_probability = 0.240000
Concept_dispersion = 0.258848
Local_instance_dispersion = 0.055556
Subconcept_partition_quality = 0.519719
```

Table 5 presents the essential ideas of the main algorithm in OSHAM which allows to discovering both disjoint and overlapping concepts depending on the user's interests by refining the condition 1.(a) and the intersection operation. In [16] we corrected and improved the interpretation procedure for OSHAM introduced in [15] that combines the concept intent, hierarchical structure information, probabilistic estimations and the nearest neighbors of unknown instances.

Table 4. Framework for unsupervised induction

---

1. While C_k is still splittable, find a new subconcept of it that corresponds to the hypothesis minimizing the quality function $q(C_k)$ among η hypotheses generated by the following steps

   (a) Find a "good" attribute-value pair concerning the best cover of C_k.

   (b) Find a closed attribute-value subset S containing this attribute-value pair.

   (c) Form a subconcept C_{k_i} with the intent is S.

   (d) Evaluate the quality function with the new hypothesized subconcept.

   Form intersecting concepts corresponding to intersections of the extent of the new concept with the extent of existing concepts excluding its superconcepts.

2. If one of the following conditions holds then C_k is considered as unsplittable

   (a) There exist not any closed proper feature subset.

   (b) The local instances set C_k^r is too small.

   (c) The local instances set C_k^r is homogeneous enough.

3. Apply recursively the procedure to concepts generated in step 1.

3.2 Evaluation

A way to evaluate unsupervised learning system is to employ supervised data but hide the class information in the whole learning and interpreting phases and use the class information only to estimate the predictive accuracy. We employ this way to evaluate unsupervised learning systems where the predicted name of each learned concept C_k

is determined by the most frequently occurring name of instances in $e(C_k)$. With this predicted name of learned concepts, the error rate of an unsupervised learning system can be estimated as the ratio of the number of testing instances correctly predicted regarding the predicted name over the total number of testing instances [18].

Table 5. Predictive accuracies of AUTOCLASS and OSHAM

datasets	attributes		inst.	class	AUTO-CLASS	OSHAM
	disc	cont				
Wisconsin breast cancer	9	–	699	2	**96.6**	92.6
Congressional voting	17	–	435	2	91.2	**93.7**
Mushroom	23	–	8125	2	86.5	**88.2**
Tic-tac-toe	9	–	862	9	82.3	**92.6**
Glass identification	–	9	214	6	55.7	**65.3**
Ionosphere	–	35	351	2	**91.5**	84.6
Waveform	–	21	300	3	59.2	**73.0**
Pima diabetes	–	8	768	2	68.2	**72.7**
Thyroid (new) disease	–	6	215	3	**89.3**	84.6
Heart disease cleveland	8	5	303	2	49.2	**60.8**

Table 5 report the predictive accuracies of AUTOCLASS [3] and OSHAM, estimating on ten datasets from the UCI repository of machine learning databases. The numbers of attributes (discrete and continuous), instances and "natural" classes of these datasets are given in columns 2–5.

All experiments on these datasets are carried out with 10-fold cross validation. For AUTOCLASS, we use the public version AUTOCLASS-C implemented in C and run three steps of *search, report* and *predict* with the default parameters. The predicted name and predictive accuracy of AUTOCLASS and OSHAM are obtained as mentioned above. Some conclusions can be drawn from these experiments.

- The predicted name obtained in OSHAM and AUTOCLASS by the majority of occurring name of instances in concepts is different from the concept name obtained in supervised learning (e.g., C4.5) using the pruning threshold based on the class information. An unsupervised concept in the worse case may contain nearly equal numbers of instances belonging to different natural classes, and an unsupervised classification may be failed in distinguishing very similar instances. It explains that while the predictive accuracies between these supervised and unsupervised methods look not so different, they are slightly different in nature.

- The predictive accuracies of OSHAM and AUTOCLASS in these experiments are only slightly different. In these first trials, each system is better in several datasets and these two systems can be considered having comparable performance.

- One advantage of OSHAM is its concept hierarchies can be easily understood by its extended classical view on concepts and the graphical support.

4. An interactive-graphic environment

We address the improvement and implementation of CABRO and OSHAM in order to deal with different situations of the practical use mentioned in section 1.

CABRO and OSHAM are originally designed for discrete attributes with unordered nominal values. We choose the discretization of continuous attributes into discrete ones before learning process. For continuous attributes in supervised data, we employ the recursive entropy minimization based on *Minimum Description Length* according to the experimental analysis in [6]. For continuous attributes in unsupervised data, we use the well-known *k-means clustering* [9]. In fact, for each continuous attribute the k-means algorithm is applied to cluster its values into k groups ($k = 1, 2, ..., K$). A criterion based on within-class and between-class similarities with the Euclidean distance is used to choose a value of k that corresponds to the best partition according to this criterion.

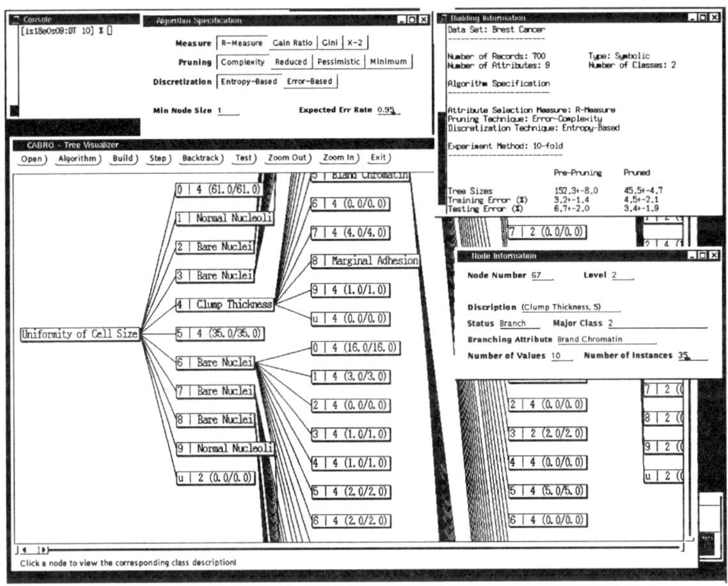

Figure 2. Generating decision trees by CABRO

CABRO and OSHAM are originally designed for a nonincremental environment. As the execution cost of CABRO is low even with large datasets, this program can be applied effectively in an incremental environment by reapplying it for the whole updated dataset. As the execution cost of OSHAM is relatively high, we have started to develop INCOSHAM – an incremental algorithm derived from OSHAM – that extracts a concept hierarchy from the hypothesis space with the Galois lattice structure. INCOSHAM preserves the nonexhaustive search strategy of OSHAM and exploits only the relevant part of the hypothesis space [17].

Recently, by combining common features between the rough set theory and formal concept analysis, a theory of rough concept analysis with the slogan "rough set + formal concept = rough formal concept" was introduced [21]. The rough concept analysis provides a framework for representing and learning *approximate concepts*. In this framework we developed unsupervised conceptual clustering method A-OSHAM, inspired by OSHAM, for inducing concept hierarchies with their approximations [19]. Concept approximations allow us to refine the common outcomes of predicting unknown instances.

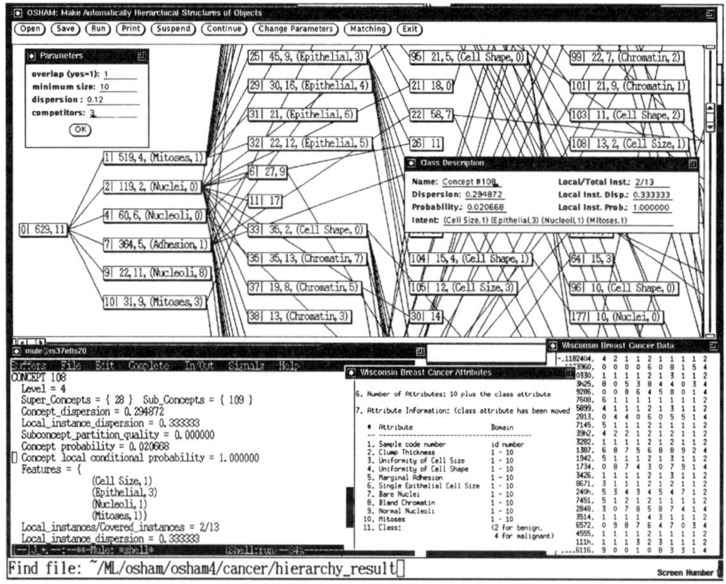

Figure 3. Generating hierarchies with overlapping concepts

Figure 2 shows a generated decision tree by CABRO and Figure 3 shows a main screen of the interactive OSHAM with an overlapping concept hierarchy learned from the Wisconsin breast cancer dataset.

We are investigating feature selection techniques to deal with irrelevant attributes, or techniques to mitigate the noise effect, the missing data in a pre-treatment process before using CABRO and OSHAM.

We are now integrating programs CABRO and OSHAM in a common system implemented in the X Window on the workstation with the direct manipulation style of interaction [11]. The conceptual architecture of the system is shown in Figure 4. This system accepts input in various situations of application domains (e.g., Boolean, symbolic, numeric attributes, nonincremental or incremental data, supervised or unsupervised data) and results as output decision knowledge that can be used for KBSs.

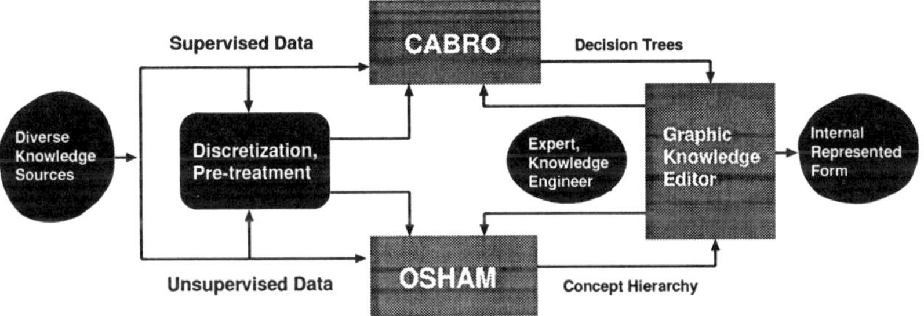

Figure 4. Conceptual architecture of the system

As introduced in subsection 1.3, the Tree Visualizer gives the users a graphical view of both decision tree/concept hierarchy structure and the detail information of each node, in spite of the size of the tree/hierarchy. To gain a full comprehension of the tree/hierarchy, the user can navigate through tree/hierarchy structure, switch among several view modes, or choose alternatively which parts of the tree/hierarchy to be displayed.

In the interactive mode of operation, the users can easily make a concrete decision tree/concept hierarchy building algorithm just by selecting a combination among various techniques for attribute selection, pruning and discretization problems, etc. The cycle of changing parameters, generating tree/hierarchy, testing and comparing can also be faster and more effective. Moreover, the users can take more control in the building process by run it step by step, examine intermediate tree/hierarchy, backtrack or go-forward in order to find a high potential trees/hierarchies with respect to the categorization scheme.

5. Conclusion

We have briefly presented the main ideas of our current project for knowledge discovering in databases which is based on two methods CABRO and OSHAM. The relevant domains for CABRO and OSHAM probably are those with one-step classification and prediction tasks, or with some form of multi-step inference or problem solving. With the high prediction accuracy of CABRO and OSHAM and the effectiveness of the interactive-graphic environment as illustrated in this paper, we expect that the project will achieve its ultimate goals and provide an environment for discovering high-quality knowledge in data with low-cost.

Acknowledgements

This work is supported by Kokusai Electric Co., Ltd., Monbusho (Ministry of Education, Science, Sports and Culture) and JAIST (Japan Advanced Institute of Science and Technology, Hokuriku). Thanks are also given to the donors and maintainers of the UCI Repository for providing access to the databases.

References

[1] Belton, V. and Elder, M.D., "Decision Support Systems: Learning from Visual Interactive Modelling", *Decision Support Systems*, Vol. 12, 1994, 355–364.

[2] Breiman, L., Friedman, J., Olshen, R., Stone, C., *Classification and Regression Trees*, Belmont, CA: Wadsworth, 1984.

[3] Cheeseman, P., Stutz, J., "Bayesian classification (AutoClass): Theory and results ", *Advances in Knowledge Discovery and Data Mining*, U.M. Fayyad *et al.* (Eds.). AAAI Press/MIT Press, 1996, 153–180.

[4] Clancey, W.J., "The knowledge level reinterpreted: Modeling Socio-technical systems", *International Journal of Intelligent Systems*, Vol. 8 (1), 1993, 33–49.

[5] Diday, E., "Des objets de l'analyse de données à ceux de l'analyse de connaissance", in *Induction Symbolique et Numérique à partir de Données*, Y. Kodratoff and E. Diday (Eds.), Cepadue Editions, 1991, 9–75.

[6] Dougherty, J., Kohavi, R., Sahami, M., "Supervised and unsupervised discretization of continuous features", in *Proceedings 12th International Conference on Machine Learning*, San Francisco, 1995, 194–202.

[7] Fayyad, U.M., Piatetsky-Shapiro G., Smyth P., Uthurusamy R., "From data mining to knowledge discovery: An overview", in *Advances in Knowledge Discovery and Data Mining*, U.M. Fayyad et al. (Eds.), AAAI Press/MIT Press, 1996, 1–36.

[8] Gaines, B.R., "Transforming rules and trees into comprehensible knowledge structures", in *Advances in Knowledge Discovery and Data Mining*, U.M. Fayyad et al. (Eds.), AAAI Press/MIT Press, 1996, 205–226.

[9] Hartigan, J.A., *Clustering Algorithms*, Wiley, New York, 1975.

[10] Hebral, G., "The SODAS project: A software for symbolic data analysis", *Proceedings Data Science, Classification and Related Methods*, 1996, 175–178.

[11] Helander, M., *Handbook of Human-Computer Interaction* (Ed.), Elsevier Science Publisher, 1991.

[12] Ho, T.B., Nguyen, T.D., Kimura, M., "Induction of Decision Trees Based on the Rough Set Theory", in *Data Science, Classification and Related Methods*, C. Hayashi et al. (Eds.), Springer-Verlag Tokyo, June 1997 (in press).

[13] Ho, T.B., Nguyen, T.D., "Integrating Human Factors With An Concept Formation Process", *6th International Conference on Human-Computer Interaction*, Yokohama, July 1995, 74.

[14] Ho, T.B., "An Approach to Concept Formation Based on Formal Concept Analysis ", *Journal IEICE Trans. Information and Systems*, E78-D, 1995, 553–559.

[15] Ho, T.B., "A Hybrid Model for Concept Formation", in *Information Modelling and Knowledge Bases VII*, Y. Tanaka et al. (Eds.), IOS Press, 1996, 22-35.

[16] Ho, T.B., "Discovering and Using Knowledge From Unsupervised Data", to appear in *Decision Support Systems*, Elsevier Science, June 1997.

[17] Ho, T.B., "Incremental Conceptual Clustering in the Framework of Galois Lattice", in *KDD: Techniques and Applications*, H. Lu, H. Motoda and H. Luu (Eds.), World Scientific, 1997, 49–64.

[18] Ho, T.B., Luong, C.M., "Using Case-Based Reasoning in Interpreting Unsupervised Inductive Learning Results", *International Joint Conference on Artificial Intelligence IJCAI'97*, Nagoya, August 1997, 258-263.

[19] Ho, T.B., "Acquiring Concept Approximations in the Framework of Rough Concept Analysis", *7th European-Japanese Conference on Information Modelling and Knowledge Bases*, Toulouse, May 1997, 186–195.

[20] Kangassalo, H., "On the concept of concept for conceptual modelling and concept detection", in *Information Modelling and Knowledge Bases III*, S. Ohsuga et al. (Eds.), IOS Press, 1992, 17–58.

[21] Kent, R.E., "Rough concept analysis", in *Rough Sets, Fuzzy Sets and Knowledge Discovery*, Springer-Verlag, 1994, 248–255.

[22] Kervahut, T. and Potvin, J.Y., "An interactive-graphic environment for automatic generation of decision trees", *Decision Support Systems*, Vol. 18, 1996, 117–134.

[23] Langley, P., *Elements of Machine Learning*, Morgan Kaufmann, 1996.

[24] Lee, H.Y., Ong, H.L., Quek, L.H., "Exploiting visualization in knowledge discovery ", *Proceedings of First International Conference on Knowledge Discovery and Data Mining*, Montreal, 1995, 198–203.

[25] Mingers, J., "An Empirical Comparison of Selection Measures for Decision Tree Induction", *Machine Learning*, 3, 1989, pp. 319–342.

[26] Ohsuga, S., "Aspects of conceptual modelling - As kernel of new information technology", in *Information Modelling and Knowledge Bases VII*, Y. Tanaka et al. (Eds.), IOS Press, 1996, 1-21.

[27] Quinlan, J.R., *C4.5: Programs for Machine Learning*, Morgan Kaufmann, 1993.

[28] Pawlak, Z. (1991) *Rough Sets – Theoretical Aspects of Reasoning About Data*, Kluwer, 1991.

[29] Rumbaugh,J., Blaha, M., Premerlani, W., Eddy, F., Lorensen, W., *Object-Oriented Modelling and Design*, Prentice Hall, 1991.

Object-Oriented Conceptual Modeling of Databases for Macromolecular Structures

David Massart
Université catholique de Louvain,
IAG-QANT, Place des Doyens 1,
B - 1348 Louvain-la-Neuve, Belgium,
e-mail: massart@qant.ucl.ac.be.

Jean Richelle
Université Libre de Bruxelles,
UCMB, Av. Héger P2 - CP160/16,
B - 1050 Bruxelles, Belgium,
e-mail: jean@ucmb.ulb.ac.be.

Abstract

Conceptual design is an important phase of the database design process. This paper introduces an expressive object-oriented model and proposes a conceptual schema suitable for biological macromolecule structures.

The proposed schema enhances existing schemas, taking into account information that usually is disseminated on separate databases. It is suited for all types of biological macromolecules. It can represent experimental results (of any experimental techniques) as well as references, and integrates them using a new data abstraction called materialization.

1. Introduction

Designing a database involves describing the relevant aspects of an application domain in terms of data structures that can be processed by a *DataBase Management System* (DBMS). Unfortunately, it is somewhat complicated to describe complex objects (e.g., proteins) in terms of files, records, strings or integers.

Conceptual design is an early phase of the database design process. It permits to reduce the intellectual distance between the application domain (e.g., molecular biology) as naturally perceived by domain specialists (e.g., molecular biologists) and its first computer formalization. This phase consists in producing a description of the information content of a database. This description, called *conceptual schema*, enables designers to understand the structural properties of data independently of any DBMS.

Most often, conceptual design is reduced or absent during the design of molecular biology databases. In most cases, data are directly described in terms of storage structures used by an *a priori* chosen DBMS.

The lack of expressiveness of these storage structures causes many problems (e.g., waste of time and resources, inadequacy or inefficiency in meeting application demands, limited documentation, and difficult maintenance). These problems can be avoided by representing the complex nature of information at a conceptual level. This is particularly true for complex domains like molecular biology.

This paper presents an object-oriented conceptual schema suitable for biological macromolecule structures. Advantages of this conceptual schema are discussed. This work follows up the EU BRIDGE Database Project [GKR+96].

The rest of the paper is structured as follows. Section 2 presents an object-oriented conceptual model. Section 3 proposes a conceptual schema using this model and shows its adequacy to represent biological macromolecules. Section 4 briefly presents some examples of the object-oriented models of actual molecular biology databases and applications.

2. Object Model

The model used in this paper has been composed from object-oriented concepts, which seem best suited to our objectives. Most of our notation comes from the Object Modeling Technique [RBP+91].

2.1 Objects and classes

An *object* is an abstract description of an application domain concept, i.e., a description limited to the aspects of the concept that are relevant in the context of the application domain. Each object has an *identity* independent of its characteristics, its name, and its history.

A *class* describes the characteristics shared by a set of objects. These characteristics are static properties called *attributes* and behaviors called *methods*. A link, called *is-of relationship*, relates each object to its class.

A class (Figure 1a) is pictured as a box with three parts. The name of the class (Atom[1]) appears in the upper part of the box. Attributes, i.e., properties shared by all the objects of the class (e.g., name, weight and valence), are written in the middle part of the box. Methods, i.e., functions or transformations that can be applied to objects of the class (e.g., distance: calculates the distance between two atoms), stand in the lower part of the box.

An object is pictured as a rounded box containing values for each attribute of the object class (name = carbon, valence = 4, weight = 12). The arrow from object Carbon to class Atom depicts the is-of relationship.

2.2 Links and relationships

A *link* is a connection between two or more objects. A *relationship* describes a set of links sharing the same structure and semantics. A relationship can be regarded as a class of links, and each link is related to its relationship by an is-of relationship.

For example, a relationship (Figure 1b) is depicted as a line between the related classes SuperStructMotif and Sheet[2]. The relationship name "Contains" is written above the relationship line. The arrowhead indicates the preferred reading direction of the relationship (e.g., sheet contains super-structure motif).

Multiplicity constrains the number of objects related by the links of a relationship. The ● at the Sheet end of relationship Contains denotes that a sheet can contain 'zero to many' super-structure motifs. A ○ stands for 'zero to one', no indication denotes '1 to 1', and other multiplicities, e.g., '3 to 5', are indicated between parentheses (3-5).

The relationship Ladder between Strand (Figure 1c) is modeled as a class and hence can contain attributes and methods. Moreover, this relationship is recursive, both ends

---

[1]In the text, class and relationship names are underlined.

[2]For short, classes are only depicted by their upper part. Attributes and methods are hidden.

are connected to the same class. The names 'first' and 'second' enable to distinguish between the roles that can be played in the relationship by the objects of class <u>Strand</u>.

2.3 Special relationships

Our model supports 3 kinds of special relationships: generalization-specialization, aggregation. and materialization.

2.3.1 Generalization-specialization

Generalization-specialization (Figure 1d) enables to represent the relationship between a class (superclass) and one or more specialized versions of it (subclasses). In a generalization, every object of a subclass is also an object of the superclass. In our example, <u>Chain</u> specializes into two subclasses: <u>NucleicChain</u> and <u>PeptidicChain</u>.

Generalization can be **t**otal or **p**artial, *exclusive* or **o**verlapping. A generalization is total if an object of the superclass belongs to at least one of the subclasses. A generalization is exclusive if an object of the superclass belongs to at most one of the subclasses. In Figure 1d, the generalization is total and exclusive.

Since the properties described at the superclass level (attributes, methods. and relationships) are valid for its subclasses, it is not necessary to repeat their descriptions at the level of each subclass. These properties are inherited by each subclass as if they were explicitly defined for this subclass.

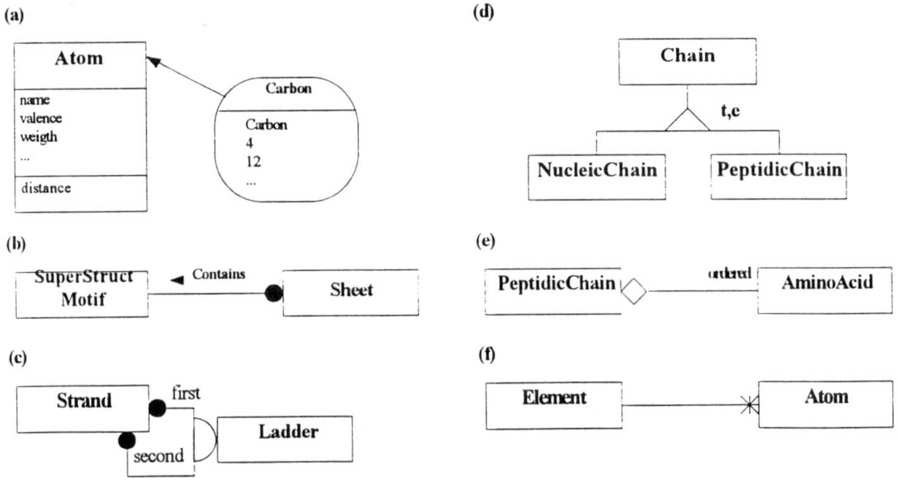

Figure 1: Notations for the conceptual model. (a) Class and object. (b) & (c) Relationships. (d) Generalization-specialization. (e) Aggregation: the ◇ shows the composite class. When meaningful, the "ordered" at the component end says that components are ordered in a defined sequence. (f) Materialization: the ⋆ shows the concrete class.

2.3.2 Aggregation

Aggregation (Figure 1e) models the relationship between a composite (e.g., a peptidic chain) and its components (e.g., the residues of this peptidic chain).

Values can be propagated from the composite to the components or from the components to the composite [HGP92]. There exist 3 types of propagation mechanism: the value of an attribute can be propagated without modification; the propagated value can be transformed (e.g., molecular weight of a molecule is the sum of the atomic weights of the atoms part of the molecule); and values of a composite attribute can be constituted by the collection of the values of component attributes (e.g., the color of a composite is constituted by the colors of its components).

2.3.3 Materialization

Materialization (Figure 1f) models the relationship between a class describing an abstract concept (e.g., chemical element) and a class standing for a more concrete concept (e.g., atoms) [PZMY94]. In short, we talk about abstract and concrete classes.

There exist 3 mechanisms of value propagation associated with materialization, all based on the same principle: an abstract object owns properties valid for all the concrete objects that are its materialization. For example, the atomic weight of the sulfur element is inherited by all the sulfur atoms.

2.4 Constraints

The expressiveness of our object-oriented model is rich, but not enough to express all the rules of the application domain. We need integrity constraints to protect domain semantics by forcing schemas to obey the rules. They are part of the schema.

Constraints specify dependencies between objects. They can show relationships between two or more objects at the same moment or relationships between different values of the same object at different moments.

3. Conceptual Schema

A complete description of biological macromolecules comprises structural information and also experimental considerations.

Atoms are the basic elements of all molecules. They are linked to form groups (e.g., amino acids). These groups are linked into polymeric molecules of high molecular weight (e.g., polypeptides). In turn, molecules can aggregate to form complex (e.g., proteins).

Information about a macromolecule differs according to the experimental method used to determine its structures. For example, data obtained by NMR do not share the same structure as those obtained by crystallography.

Other aspects have to do with the geometric structures of macromolecules. It is necessary to be able to represent spatial motifs such as secondary structures of polypeptides or active sites of enzymes.

For brevity, only the general structure of classes are presented. The attributes and methods of classes as well as integrity constraints are not discussed in this paper. Their description can be found in [Mas95].

3.1 Aspects related to the nature of macromolecules

This section presents the schema describing macromolecules from a *bottom-up* point of view, i.e., from atoms to complexes.

3.1.1 Atoms

A biological macromolecule can be regarded as a set of atoms connected by different kinds of chemical links. The schema of Figure 2 models this view.

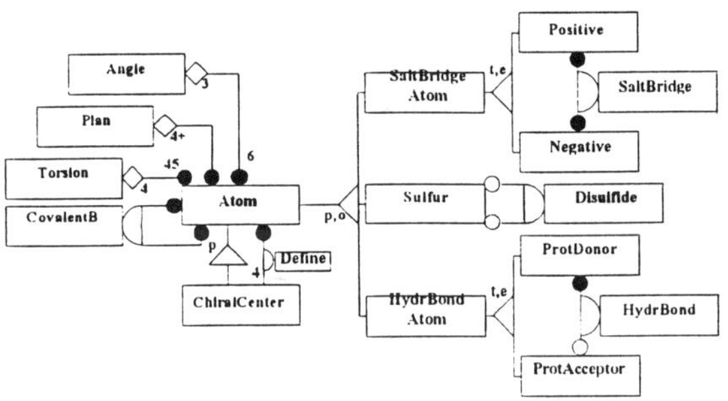

Figure 2: Atoms and links.

Covalent bonds are essential for keeping atoms together in a molecule. They are modeled by the recursive relationship <u>CovalentB</u>. Atoms connected by covalent bonds present different characteristics: angles, torsions, plans and chiral centers. <u>ChiralCenter</u> is modeled as a partial atom specialization defined by its four substitutes. <u>Angle</u>, <u>Torsion</u> and <u>Plan</u> are modeled as aggregations of their constituent atoms.

Atoms also specialize along a partial and overlapping hierarchy based on the kind of links in which they participate: salt bridge, hydrogen bond, and disulfide. These links are modeled by relationships between the concerned subclasses of <u>Atom</u>.

3.1.2 Atom groups

Biopolymers consist of repeated linked monomers, each being a relatively light and simple *atom group*. As shown by the schema of Figure 3, <u>AtomGroup</u> is a composite of class <u>Atom</u>. AtomGroup specializes through a total and exclusive hierarchy, into chain units (monomers: nucleotides or amino acids), solvent units (e.g., a molecule of water), and ligand units (e.g., a molecule of heme).

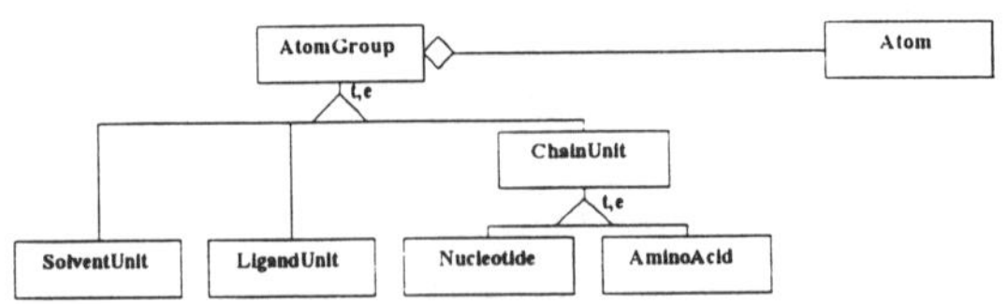

Figure 3: Atom groups.

The number of atom group types being limited (e.g., there are only 20 kinds of natural amino acids), it is interesting to store as a reference the information common to the atom groups of each type. We call *libraries* such references.

Figure 4 shows the schema of the atom group library. It is very similar to the schemas of Figures 2 and 3. Atom groups, now modeled by class AtomGroupLib, are composed of atoms (AtomInGrp) bound by different kinds of links. The main difference comes from the relationships <u>has</u> between AtomGroupLib and other classes. Accompanied by the adequate constraints, they model covalent bonds, angles, chiral centers, torsions, plans, salt bridges, disulfides, and hydrogen bonds as atom group characteristics.

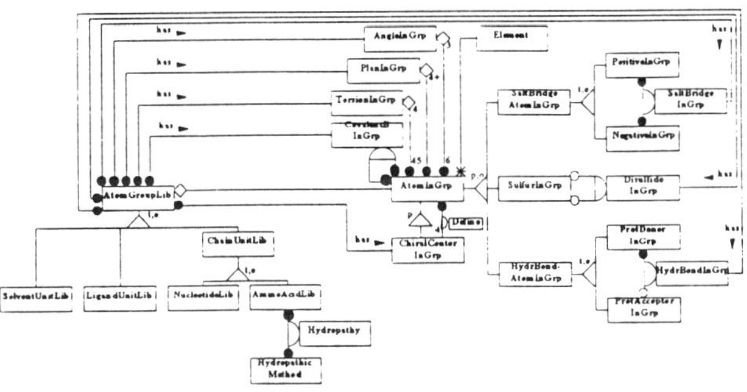

Figure 4: Atom group library.

Another difference consists in considering class AtomInGrp as a materialization of class <u>Element</u>. Some information (e.g., atomic number, weight, valence) is identical for all atoms of the same element. Materialization enables atoms to inherit this information from elements and thus to avoid repeating it at the atom level. In other words, class <u>Element</u> is also a library.

Since schemas, as the former one, are complex, we propose to cluster their classes and relationships into a *high-level class* in order to produce high-level schemas that are easier to handle. The clustering operation is heuristic. A class, which is intuitively perceived as dominant, is chosen as the basis of the clustering operation. For example, in the schema of Figure 4, class AtomGroupLib is a good candidate since other classes of the schema are its subclasses or components (or related to its subclasses or components).

Figure 5 shows an intermediate view of the clustering operation. The future high-level class is symbolized by a two-part box. Its name is in the upper part of the box. It is derived from the name of the class used as basis for the clustering AtomGroupLib. The * appended to the class name indicates that it is a high-level class. The schema in the lower part of the box shows classes involved by the clustering operation.

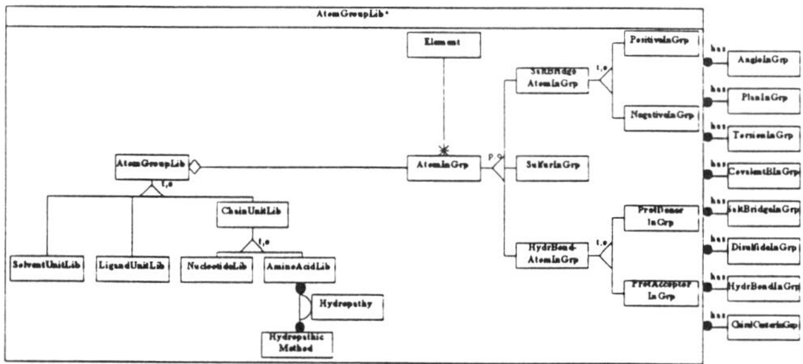

Figure 5: Intermediate view of the 'atom group library' clustering operation.

Classes. that were related by relationships <u>has</u> to class AtomGroupLib (Figure 4), are now related to box AtomGroupLib*.

Finally, Figure 6 shows high-level class AtomGroupLib* after the clustering operation.

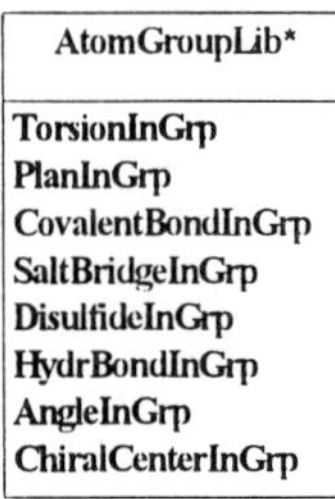

Figure 6: AtomGroupLib*: the high-level view of the atom group library.

Classes that, in Figure 5, are related to AtomGroupLib* by relationships <u>has</u> are turned into attributes. These attributes can be involved in inheritance and value propagation mechanisms between high-level objects. It is also possible to materialize AtomGroupLib* into another high-level class used to represent atom groups in a molecule.

See [Mas97a, Mas97b] for further details on the clustering mechanism.

3.1.3 Molecules

The schema of Figure 7 shows classes (<u>SolventUnit</u>, <u>LigandUnit</u>, <u>Nucleotide</u> and <u>AminoAcid</u>) examined in previous sections.

Like polymers. nucleic chains and peptidic chains are modeled by classes <u>NucleicChain</u> and <u>PeptidicChain</u>. respectively, as ordered composites of <u>Nucleotide</u> and <u>AminoAcid</u>. They generalized into class <u>Chain</u>.

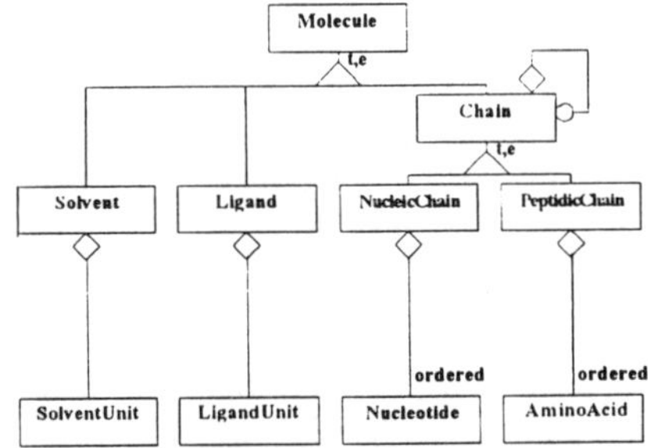

Figure 7: Molecules. Note that the recursive aggregation of <u>Chain</u> enables to indicate that formerly, some chains (e.g., chimotrypsine) formed one.

We call ligand, or solvent, the set of ligand units (e.g., molecule of heme), or solvent units (e.g., molecule of water), associated with a macromolecular structure. <u>Ligand</u> is modeled by aggregation as a composite of <u>LigandUnit</u> and <u>Solvent</u> as a composite of <u>SolventUnit</u>.

<u>Ligand</u>, <u>Solvent</u> and <u>Chain</u> generalize into class <u>Molecule</u>.

A library of molecules (<u>MoleculeLib*</u>: not shown) has a structure similar to that of <u>AtomGroupLib*</u>.

3.1.4 Complexes

A complex is a set of associated molecules. Thus, e.g., hemoglobin is constituted of 2 α chains, 2 β chains, 4 hemes, and molecules of water. Class Complex represents information about experimental protocols used to determine the conformation of the different components (molecules) of a complex. As shown in Figure 8, in order to describe specific techniques, Complex specializes into 4 subclasses: Crystallography, NMR, Model and Other.

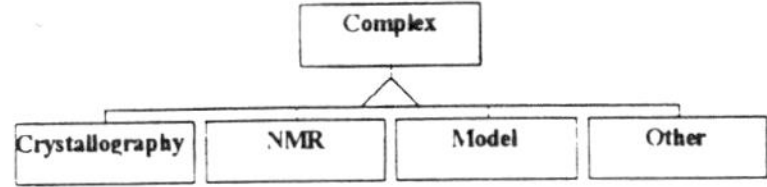

Figure 8: Complexes.

3.2 Experimental considerations

When determining the conformation of a complex, one observes structure variations: alternative positions of an atom, an atom group or a molecule can exist in the complex. Such variations can be independent of each other or not.

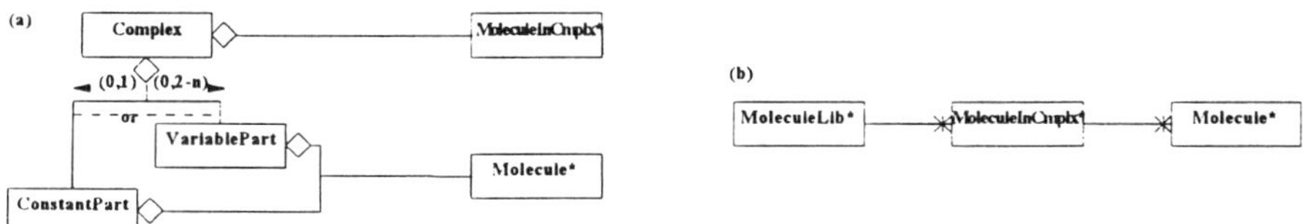

Figure 9: Variation of complex.

The schema of Figure 9a models this situation. Class Complex is a composite of 2 classes: ConstantPart and VariablePart. The former is a composite of all constant parts of a complex, the latter is a composite of each variable part of the complex. Each variation is characterized by an *apparition frequency* represented by an attribute occupancy of class VariablePart.

Complex is a composite of high-level class MoleculeInCmplx* (low-level classes involved in this aggregation are shown in Figure 10). MoleculeInCmplx* models information that is true for every complex variations.

Molecule* is obtained by clustering the class Molecule and classes depending on it. It models information specific to each complex variation.

For a better understanding, imagine a complex made of only two atoms A and B bound by a covalent link. A varies: in 70% of the cases, it is in position a_1, in the remaining 30%, it is in position a_2. B does not vary: it is in position b. The fact that A and B are bound by a covalent link in the complex is described at the MoleculeInCmplx* level. The fact that B is in position b is described by an object of Molecule* which is a component of the class ConstantPart. The fact that A can be in position a_1 or a_2 is described by two objects of Molecule*. A in position a_1 is described as the component of an object of VariablePart and A in position a_2 is described as the component of another object of VariablePart.

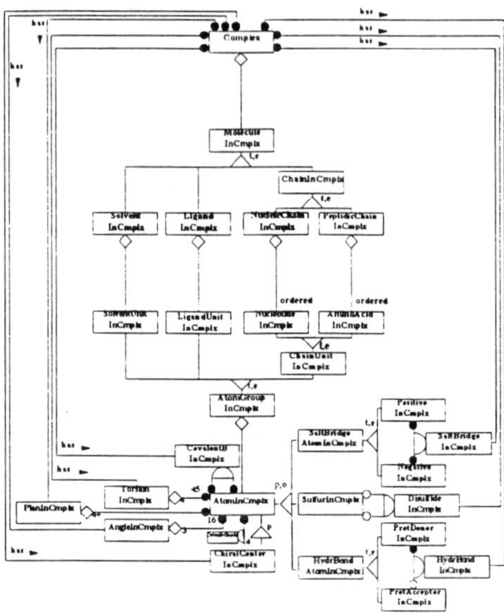

Figure 10: Complex.

The schema of Figure 9b shows that <u>Molecule*</u> is a materialization of <u>MoleculeInCmplx*</u> that is, in turn, a materialization of <u>MoleculeLib*</u>. At each level, from the more abstract to the more concrete, information is added to information inherited from the previous level. <u>MoleculeLib*</u> describes each molecule of the complex, information specific to the complex (e.g., links between molecules) are added at the <u>MoleculeInCmplx*</u> level. Finally, spatial coordinates of atoms are added at the <u>Molecule*</u> level.

3.3 Aspects related to geometric structures

Macromolecular structures exhibit spatial patterns. The description of these geometric structures is based on the more concrete layer of the schema. The objects (atoms, atom groups or molecules) involved in the spatial motif of a complex have to belong to the same structure variation of this complex.

3.3.1 Segments and secondary structures

A segment is a piece of a peptidic or nucleic chain. Figure 11 shows a schema for segments.

Segments themselves are modeled by class <u>Segment</u>. They can be grouped into categories represented by class <u>FoldingClass</u>. <u>Segment</u> is the materialization of <u>FoldingClass</u>. It specializes, totally and exclusively, into 3 subclasses: <u>UserDefined</u>, <u>Chain</u> and <u>Structure</u>.

<u>UserDefined</u> enables users to define any piece of chain as a segment. It is an ordered composite of <u>ChainUnit</u>.

<u>Chain</u> is a <u>Segment</u> since a segment, being a piece of chain, can cover a whole chain. In general, this is not the case and <u>Chain</u> is also viewed as a composite of <u>Segment</u>.

<u>Structure</u> is an ordered composite of <u>AminoAcid</u>. Algorithmic methods that examine peptides, each amino acid in turn, are used to assign a structure category (e.g., helix, strand, etc.) to each amino acid and to each segment of contiguous amino acids of the

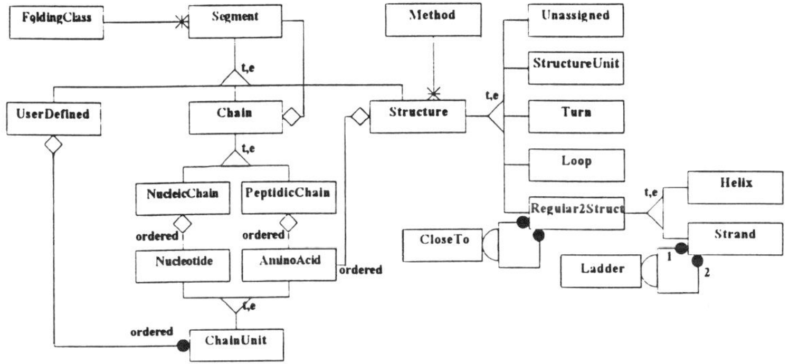

Figure 11: Secondary structures.

same category.

The easy way for a computer scientist to model this situation consists in building a subclass of <u>Structure</u> for each category. Unfortunately, biologists disagree with this view of the problem. For them, the number and the type of categories are not fixed, they depend on the method used. Biologists are only interested in categories known by the method they use and only when they decide to use this method.

The adopted solution is a compromise. Class <u>Structure</u> specializes into 5 predefined subclasses corresponding to 5 general categories of structures: <u>Turn</u>, <u>Loop</u>, and <u>Regular2Struct</u> (<u>Helix</u> or <u>Strand</u>) for segments that are identified by methods, as belonging to one of these categories of secondary structures; <u>StructureUnit</u> for segment categories derived from other categories; <u>Unassigned</u> for segments to which methods are not able to assign a category. These classes own an attribute type to specify subcategories, e.g., attribute type of class <u>Turn</u> enables to specify the type (β, γ, etc.) of a given turn.

Class <u>Method</u> represents methods used to assign categories to segments. It is related to class <u>Segment</u> by a materialization. Five of its attributes, structure_unit, turn, loop, helix and strand, enable to enumerate the subcategories of structure units, turns, loops, helix and strand that the method is able to recognize. This implies that the values allowed[3] for the attribute type of a <u>Segment</u> subclass (e.g., subclass <u>Turn</u>) are limited to the values of the corresponding attribute (here, turn) of the method used to determine the segments. This constraint is captured by the second mechanism of value propagation associated to materialization (for further details see [PZMY94]).

3.3.2 Biological units, super-structures and functional sites

Biological units of a complex (i.e., units playing a biological role) are represented by class <u>BiologicalUnit</u>. They are composed of molecules and can include super-structures. Super-structures are made of structures organized in space. Figure 12 shows the schemas used to describe biological units. Class <u>Structure</u> and its specialization tree come from Figure 11. Class <u>SuperStruct</u> represents super-structures. It can be seen either as an ordered composite of <u>Structure</u> or as a composite of Regular2Struct or both. To enable a more precise description of sheets, <u>SuperStruct</u> specializes partially and exclusively into <u>SuperStructMotif</u> and <u>Sheet</u>.

---

[3]The domain of the attribute.

Class <u>Sheet</u> is a composite of class <u>Strand</u>. Relationship <u>IsContainedIn</u> indicates super-structure motifs (e.g., Greek key motif) contained by sheets.

Super-structures can be grouped into categories. Class <u>PatternDescr</u> enables to represent these categories. It materializes into class <u>SuperStruct</u>.

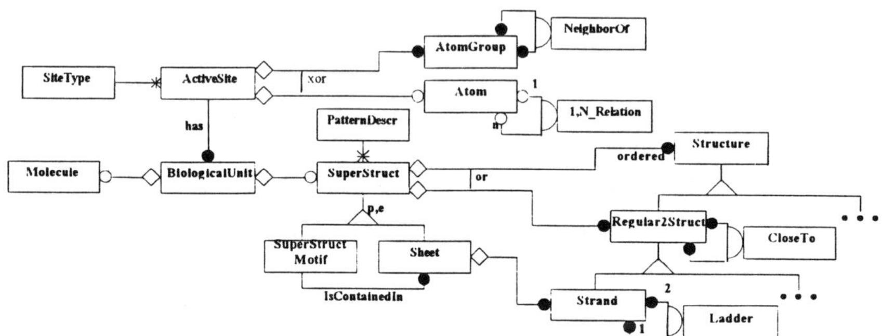

Figure 12: Biological units, super-structures and functional sites.

Biological units may have active sites which are represented by class <u>ActiveSite</u>. Relationship <u>has</u> enables to relate active sites to their biological units. Types of active sites are described in class <u>SiteType</u> that materializes into class <u>ActiveSite</u>.

Depending on the power of the experimental tools, it is possible to obtain either a precise description of an active site, atom by atom, or a less precise one limited to the atom groups involved in the site. Class <u>ActiveSite</u> is thus either a composite of <u>Atom</u> or a composite of <u>AtomGroup</u>.

4. Other object-oriented models for macromolecule modeling

Since the different macromolecular databases share an important part of their application domain, the information represented in their schemas is globally equivalent. All the protein databases, for example, have to express information about primary, secondary, tertiary, and quaternary structures[4].

This common information is expressed more or less directly and naturally in the different schemas according to the expressiveness of the data model used.

This section presents some object-oriented models that have been developed for modeling biological databases.

Models can be characterized by the set of primitive concepts available for modeling a domain (e.g., class, relationship) and the set of abstraction mechanisms for structuring an information based along different dimensions (e.g., generalization, aggregation) [Myl95]. The following presentation is based on these two criteria.

---

[4]Of course, these representations can be more or less complete and important details can vary from a database to an other according to the role this database is intended to play.

4.1 C++ like data model

Persistent object-oriented programming languages (POOPLs) permit that objects created during a program execution be saved and referred to during a future execution[5]. These POOPLs have been used to implement databases of biological interest (e.g., MapBase [GRS94]).

Beyond the fact that persistent C++ systems are not DBMSs[6] [KDD95], their data model is poor. It is limited to the primitive concepts of object, class, and attributes; moreover it is limited to the abstraction mechanisms of instanciation and generalization. Relationships, aggregation, and materialization are not supported by the model. These mechanisms must be simulated by supplementary code [Zim96], [KP97].

4.2 The Object Protocol Model

Object Protocol Model (OPM) is a data model that allows to express database schemas in terms of objects and *protocols* specific to molecular biology applications [CM95].

OPM's primitive concepts and abstraction mechanisms are object, object class, attribute, protocol, protocol class, input and output attribute, and generalization.

Protocol is an original concept introduced in OPM. Protocol classes can be recursively specified to model experiments. In addition to regular attributes, protocol classes are related to special attributes that permit to model input and output data regarding an experiment.

The absence of a relationship concept in the model is partially balanced by the intensive use of attributes. An attribute can be either a simple attribute, a tuple of simple attributes, or an object, and it can be either single valued, set valued, or list valued.

4.3 ReLiBase

ReLiBase is an object-oriented database schema[7] whose purpose is to integrate data from the different databases of protein structures and the tools for the analysis of receptor-ligand-docking [Abe95]. It has been implemented using VODAK, an object-oriented DBMS with an original metaclass system that permits to enrich the model with new abstractions.

The conceptual model of ReLiBase supports object, class, attributes, and generalization. Its main difference with the models presented previously consists in providing relationship and aggregation (hasSetOf and hasListOf relationship) as primitive concepts. These relationships cannot own attributes.

4.4 BRIDGE

A standard schema of object class and relationship describing protein structures and sequences has been proposed by the EU BRIDGE Database Project Consortium. It is destinated to develop an integrated environment for protein study and engineering[GKR+96].

---

[5]ObjectStore, for example, is an object storage manager based on C++.

[6]A good presentation of the problems of managing biological data with C++ can be found in [Goo95].

[7]http://este.darmstadt.gmd.de:5000/dimsys/docking-d/schema.ps

The conceptual model used by BRIDGE owns the primitive concepts of object class, attribute and relationship and the abstraction mechanism of generalization. There is no possibility for a relationship to own attributes.

4.5 General note on object-oriented models

Allowing to express complex structures directly and providing powerful data types are two advantages of the object-oriented databases that are well-recognized in the field of macromolecular databases. However, as shown by these examples, the object models used so far for designing macromolecule databases are generally far from exploiting all the modeling facilities provided by the object paradigm.

5. Conclusion

Conceptual modeling is an important phase of the database design process that, most often, is reduced or absent for molecular biology databases. This paper has introduced an expressive object-oriented model and proposed a conceptual schema suitable for biological macromolecule structures.

The proposed schema is a description of the macromolecular structure domain. It is at the same time a formalization and a description of the domain that is close to the perception of domain specialists and free of implementation considerations. The schema takes into account all types of biological macromolecules. It can represent experimental results (of any experimental techniques) as well as references (libraries). Although both layers (experimental data and libraries) can exist independently, materialization provides a powerful mechanism for integrating them. Moreover, the schema provides structures to enable users to work on data and to integrate the result of their work.

This schema can be used in many applications: from integrating old applications to designing new ones. Its independence from implementation and its generality make it a good *global schema* for database integration. It can be used in the definition of data structures of programs that handle information on macromolecules. Applied to database design, it provides good criteria to choose a target DBMS.

References

[Abe95]   K. Aberer. The used of object-oriented datamodels for biomolecular databases. In *Proceedings of Object-Oriented Computing in the Natural Science*, Heidelberg, Germany, 1995.

[BJZ94]   J. Bocca, M. Jarke, and C. Zaniolo, editors. *Proc. of the 20th Int. Conf. on Very Large Databases, VLDB'94*, Santiago, Chile, 1994. Morgan Kaufmann.

[CM95]   I.A. Chen and V.M. Markowitz. An overview of the object-protocol model (OPM) and OPM data management tools. *Information Systems*, 20(5):393–418, 1995.

[GKR+96]   P. Gray, G. Kemp, C. Rawlings, N. Brown, C. Sander, J. Thornton, C. Orengo, S. Wodak, and J. Richelle. Macromolecular Structure Informmation and Databases: The EU BRIDGE Database Project Consortium. *Trend in Biochemical Science*, (21):251–256, 1996.

[Goo95]   N. Goodman. An object-oriented DBMS war story: Developing a genome mapping database in C++. In Kim [Kim95], pages 216–237.

[GRS94]   N. Goodman, S. Rozen, and L. Stein. Building a laboratory information system around a C++-based object-oriented DBMS. In Bocca et al. [BJZ94], pages 722–729.

[HGP92]   M. Halper, J. Geller, and Y. Perl. An OODB part relationship model. In Y. Yesha, editor, *Proc. of the 1st Int. Conf. on Information and Knowledge Management, CIKM'92*, Baltimore, USA, November 1992.

[KDD95]   A. Kotz-Dittrich and K. Dittrich. Where object-oriented DBMS should do better: a critique based on early experiences. In Kim [Kim95], pages 238–254.

[Kim95]   W. Kim, editor. *Modern Database System - The Object Model, Interoperability, and Beyond.* Addison-Wesley, 1995.

[KP97]   M. Kolp and A. Pirotte. An aggregation model and its C++ implementation. Technical Report YEROOS TR-97/02, IAG-QANT, Université catholique de Louvain, Belgium, January 1997. Submitted for publication.

[Mas95]   D. Massart. Modélisation orientée-objet des macro-molécules biologiques. Mémoire de Licence Spéciale en Sciences de l'Information et de la Documentation, INFODOC, Université Libre de Bruxelles, September 1995.

[Mas97a]   D. Massart. Complexity management of object schemas. Technical Report YEROOS TR-97/07, IAG-QANT, Université catholique de Louvain, Belgium, March 1997. Submitted for publication.

[Mas97b]   D. Massart. On the status of high-level relationships in complexity management of conceptual schemas. Technical Report YEROOS TR-97/08, IAG-QANT, Université catholique de Louvain, Belgium, April 1997. Submitted for publication.

[Myl95]   J. Mylopoulos. Conceptual modeling for information systems engineering. Lecture Series presented at the University of Namur (Belgium), April 24 - May 4, 1995.

[PZMY94]   A. Pirotte, E. Zimányi, D. Massart, and T. Yakusheva. Materialization: a powerful and ubiquitous abstraction pattern. In Bocca et al. [BJZ94], pages 630–641.

[RBP+91]   J. Rumbaugh, M. Blaha, W. Premerlani, F. Eddy, and W. Lorensen. *Object-Oriented Modeling and Design.* Prentice Hall, 1991.

[Zim96]   E. Zimányi. Implementing materialization in C++. Technical Report YEROOS TR-96/08, INFODOC, Université Libre de Bruxelles, Belgium, 1996.

Information Modelling and Knowledge Bases IX
P.-J. Charrel et al. (Eds.)
1998, IOS Press

Visual Rule Language for Active Database Modelling

MIHHAIL MATSKIN

Department of Computer Science

Norges Teknisk-Naturvitenskapelige Universitet

7034 Trondheim, Norway

misha@idt.unit.no

DANILO MONTESI

Department of Computer Science

University of Milano

Via Comelico 39/41

20135 Milano, Italy

montesi@dsi.unimi.it

School of Information Systems

University of East Anglia

Norwich NR4 7TJ, UK

dm@sys.uea.ac.uk

Abstract

This paper introduces a visual language for active database systems. We present a new approach to database programming based on visual active language that allows us to describe active rules in a graphical way. The resulting visual language can be transformed into a textual one. In addition, an active system can be represented with several different graphs showing the interactions of rules and transactions. These graphs can be used by a database designer for programming, analysis, debugging and maintenance of the system. Indeed, they can be used to visualise the dynamic behaviour of an active database under either immediate or deferred semantics. In order to test our approach we have implemented a prototype of the resulting visual programming tool that is briefly discussed.

1. Introduction

The motivation for building visual systems is considered quite in detail in cognitive literature (e. g. [17] about "dual brain"). The benefit of any visual language is that it uses the synthesis power of the eye. Visual programming has been used to program a system using a predefined set of graphical symbols and relationships that are converted into a textual program and then executed. The visual representation makes the programming task and the debugging easier [9]. Visual languages are very useful in the context of databases to define queries and visualise the results [6]. Visual formalisms have also been used to express data models (i.e. ER graph [18]). However, little attention has been devoted to represent the behaviour of the database. In the past few years active databases have emerged as an important technology promising to extend the relational database framework including rule processing and the active behaviour [14, 10]. Active behaviour allows the database to engage into actions that are not defined into the user defined transaction. Therefore the active behaviour extends the behaviour of passive databases where the behaviour is mainly defined through the user defined transaction. Active databases provide a uniform mechanism for a number of features including integrity constraint enforcement, derived data maintenance, triggers, alerts, protection, version control, and others [20].

Active databases are made of active rules that have the form $E, C \Rightarrow A$. They are expressed through an *event* part (E), a *condition* part (C) and an *action* part (A). The informal meaning is that when an event arises if the condition holds then the action is performed. An important feature of active rules is that a rule is triggered when an action matches with the event part of that rule. This matching is similar to the "goto" of imperative programming languages. Even worst there is no label where to jump. Indeed, you have to scan the whole set of rules and look for those that have the event part that matches with the action. Then if the condition holds the action of the triggered rule(s) is performed. There are two important points to note here. A single action can trigger several rules. Some active database systems consider priority among rules to have only one triggered rule [21]. We do not consider priority to have a simple model, but the framework can be easily extended to priority. The second point is that matching is more complex than goto. Indeed, there is also a parameter passing between action and event. It should be clear that even considering just few active rules the traditional textual programming became quickly very difficult to understand and its execution complex to follow. Moreover, active rules perform actions on databases that are related to user transactions. This complicates the execution and the debugging process even more.

In this paper we propose a solution to the above problem based on visual programming. Visual programming allows structuring and relating rules in a graphical way. In textual programming it would be difficult to follow the triggering relationships among rules. Thus the main feature of visual language is the graphical representation of such relationships. Moreover, it is easy to program with a visual language that allow to express the active database concepts. Then we can transform the visual program into a textual one and execute it in a particular system. Since it is very difficult to follow active rule execution in the textual form, we visualise the execution in the visual environment. In this case graphical representation can serve for visual debugging and to follow rule triggering. In addition, the visual language that we propose allows to define the program in several steps refining the description and hiding details that are not relevant. Therefore it is amenable to modular programming and to the development of an active database design methodology. In the following we consider active databases over the relational model that have a clear foundation [18] and allow to take advantage of formal techniques developed in [15].

Our approach is based on three steps visual programming. The first step defines an active program through a set of graphs. Each graph, corresponding to a rule, defines a specific functionality. For instance how to repair the violation of integrity constraints or how to react to a specific operation. The second step defines the control (or triggering) of rules. For instance which rule triggers which. These step should allow a designer to describe a desired or obligatory order of triggering as well as types of executions: sequential, concurrent etc. In the third step a user defined transaction is expressed through a transaction graph. Then these graphs are combined to produce a graph that will express the combined reaction of user defined transaction and the active program. This allows to express the active program and the transaction independently and then to combine and visually execute the transaction with the active program. The advantages of this approach are related to the uniformity and modularity of the graphical representation of transactions and active programs. Uniformity is due to the fact that transactions, rules and control are represented within the same visual language. Modularity allows to define in different steps concepts like functionalities, the relationship among them and transactions [4]. The resulting visual environment turns out to be very useful for debugging as well for generating the corresponding textual active program.

To the best of our knowledge there are very few graphical approaches to active rule programming. The main approaches are based on visualisation of active rules described in a textual form. For example, in [3] visual form of active rules (activation graph) is generated from textual description and in [5] from event and rule repositories. A larger number of work is done in the area of visualisation in expert systems (production rules), however they differ from active rules, in treating dynamical aspects. Moreover, our approach can be seen as a first step towards integration of visual representation for data and behaviour models [13].

In this paper we do not consider particular methods for rule analysis, e.g. checking termination and confluence properties of rule system. These aspects are investigated in a number of papers [1, 2] which propose different types of graphs (activation, triggering and other graphs) for such analysis. We would like to underline that these graphs are intended for analysis of rules but not for their description. Our purpose was to consider visual expressiveness of active rule systems and our set of graphs is primarily intended to support expressiveness of rule description. In order to relate our work with the above-mentioned ones we should say that activation, triggering and other graphs can be generated from our visual representations and would provide a designer with additional powerful means for debugging and analysis as well as any other debugging techniques and methods. We consider our approach as a construction of visual interface to active rule system and its implementation as a kind of shell to existent active rule systems.

The paper is organised as follow. Section 2 introduces the active databases and a simple textual active language. Section 3 defines visual active language and Section

4 describes the implemented visual environment and its features. Finally in Section 5, we draw some conclusions and sketch further research issues.

2. Active databases and a simple example

An active database is made of a database instance (or state) s and an active program P. A user interacts with the active database through transactions. A transaction t is a finite sequence of operations $u_1; \ldots; u_n$ in which either all the operations are executed or none of them must be performed. An operation has the form $\pm r[c]$ where r is a relation, c is a condition and $+$ denotes insertion (and $-$ deletion). A condition is a set of literals [18]. Updates are not considered to have a simple language. However, they can be easily included. We consider the case of relational databases where the scheme S is a collection of relational schemes. An active program P is a set of (active) rules of the form

$$u^e, c \Rightarrow u^a$$

where u^e is an event specification, c is a condition and u^a is either an insertion or a deletion such that each variable occurring in u^a also occurs in u^e. In the left hand side of the rule there are the *event part* and the *condition part* and in the right hand side of the rule there is the *action part*. Note that the above simple language can be equivalently expressed as **WHEN** u^e **IF** c **THEN** u^a. We consider two different types of semantics: either immediate or deferred semantics. Under immediate semantics the user defined transaction $t = u_1; \ldots; u_n$ induces the transaction

$$t_I = u_1; \bar{u}_1^P; \ldots; u_n; \bar{u}_n^P$$

where $\bar{u}_i^P$ denotes the sequence of operations computed as *immediate reaction* of the operation u_i with respect to a set of active rules in P. This reaction can be derived by matching[1] the operation u_i with the event part of the active rules. Clearly the obtained action can themselves trigger other rules, hence this reaction is computed recursively. As noted above, several transactions can be obtained in this way. We do not consider the issue in this paper. Note that under the immediate modality the induced transaction is an interleaving of user defined operations with rule actions. Under the deferred semantics, the induced transaction has the form:

$$t_D = u_1; \ldots; u_n; \bar{u}_1^P; \ldots; \bar{u}_n^P.$$

Hence the *reaction is deferred* (or postponed) until the end of the user transaction. Here again the induced operations can themselves trigger other rules, and so the reactions of the original operations are recursively computed, but using the immediate semantics. Formal results of the above simple language on semantics, confluence,

---

[1] The operation u_i matches with u^e iff $\sigma(u_i) = \sigma(u^e)$.

equivalence and optimisation are in [15]. In the following we denote an *active system* as an active program and optionally a transaction. Let us consider a personnel database composed by two relations: emp(name,dname,sal) and dep(dname,mgr). The former defines the employee name, the department name and the salary. The latter defines a department with the name of the manager. We want to define a set of rules expressing the following functionalities:

- When a department is deleted then all the employees working in such a department must be removed (cascading delete).

- If an inserted employee has a salary greater than 50k then he/she is a manager of the department in which he/she works and so, according to that, a tuple is inserted in the relation dep.

- When all the employees of a department are deleted, assign as manager tom (the CEO).

Then the active program describing these functionalities is $P = \{R_1, R_2, R_3\}$ where:

R_1 $-\text{dep}[\text{dname} = \text{D}] \Rightarrow -\text{emp}[\text{dname} = \text{D}]$

R_2 $+\text{emp}[\text{name} = \text{N}, \text{dname} = \text{D}], \text{sal} > 50\text{k} \Rightarrow +\text{dep}[\text{dname} = \text{D}, \text{mgr} = \text{N}].$

R_3 $-\text{emp}[\text{dname} = \text{D}] \Rightarrow +\text{dep}[\text{dname} = \text{D}, \text{mgr} = \text{tom}].$

In the next sections we assign to rule textual names. We call the rule R_1 "no department - no employees", rule R_2 "employee with salary 50K is a manager" and rule R_3 "tom is manager of an empty department". Note that rules R_1 and R_3 have empty conditions (i.e. they are equivalent to *true*). Now consider the user defined transaction

$$t1 = + \text{emp}[\text{name} = \text{bill}, \text{dname} = \text{toy}, \text{sal} = 60\text{k}]; -\text{dep}[\text{dname} = \text{toy}].$$

The first operation triggers rule R_2 and thus bill becames a manager. The second operation triggers rule R_1 deleting all the employees working in the toy department and then R_3 inserting tom as manager of the toy department. Thus the resulting induced transaction (under immediate semantics) is

$$
\begin{aligned}
t1I = \quad &+\text{emp}[\text{name} = \text{bill}, \text{dname} = \text{toy}, \text{sal} = 60\text{k}]; \\
&+\text{dep}[\text{dname} = \text{toy}, \text{mgr} = \text{bill}]^*; \\
&-\text{dep}[\text{dname} = \text{toy}]; \\
&-\text{emp}[\text{dname} = \text{toy}]^* \\
&+\text{dep}[\text{dname} = \text{toy}, \text{mgr} = \text{tom}]^*
\end{aligned}
$$

where * denotes an induced operation. Under the deferred semantics the induced transaction is

$$\begin{aligned}
\texttt{t1D} = \quad &+\texttt{emp}[\texttt{name} = \texttt{bill}, \texttt{dname} = \texttt{toy}, \texttt{sal} = \texttt{60k}]; \\
&-\texttt{dep}[\texttt{dname} = \texttt{toy}]; \\
&+\texttt{dep}[\texttt{dname} = \texttt{toy}, \texttt{mgr} = \texttt{bill}]^*; \\
&-\texttt{emp}[\texttt{dname} = \texttt{toy}]^* \\
&+\texttt{dep}[\texttt{dname} = \texttt{toy}, \texttt{mgr} = \texttt{tom}]^*.
\end{aligned}$$

It is clear from the above example that even three rules and a simple user defined transaction can lead to complex active rule processing due to the nature of active rules. This makes the textual programming and debugging very difficult. Therefore we turn our attention to visual programming.

The above example is used to illustrate our approach in the next sections. It is a very small example, however, our approach is scalable and can be extended to more practical cases.

3. Visual active language

3.1 Preliminaries

The visual active language that we propose relies on a Statechart-like approach [8]. We do not consider the issue of schema design that we consider addressed with other conceptual tools like the ER graph. Thus we concentrate on the active part of the database. The designer has to draw three different graphs using a set of predefined visual symbols and annotations. The visual symbols consist of nodes and edges for each type of graph. The annotations define the events, queries and actions of interest for the database designer. A rule graph defines a single rule, thus the event, condition and action parts of the rule and it has quite simple straightforward form. We expect to have several rule graphs. The control graph defines the triggering among a set of rules. Thus it defines the control of rules. There can be several control graphs corresponding to several sets of interconnected rules. The number of control graphs depends on designers choice and reflects the conceptual modelling approach used. The transaction graph defines a single transaction. These are the graphs that specify an active system: rule graph G^r, control graph G^c and transaction graph G^t.

The choice of two different types of graphs (G^c and G^r) for program description is motivated by requirement to support granularity and visual simplicity of descriptions. It also provides some methodological discipline for representation of active systems. For example, in case of control graph we ask a system designer to describe knowledge which will not be used for generating a textual rule but which helps to understand how rules cooperate. This implies that the visual language forces the designer to think about the problem in more details. The transaction graph allows to express with the same visual language the user defined transaction that contributes to define the behaviour of the active system. The next three graphs are generated automatically by the system starting from G^c, G^r and G^t to visualise

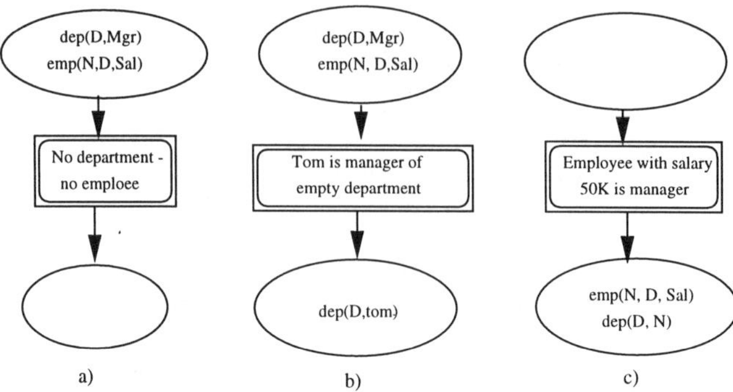

Figure 1: Control graphs.

the behaviour: combined graph G^{cm}, rule interaction graph G^i and specialised rule interaction graph G^{ic}.

The purpose of these graphs is to provide user with additional graphical sources for analysis, debugging and visualisation of behaviour of an active system. The graphs are constructed by transformations τ_1, τ_2 and τ_3 as follow: $G^{cm} = \tau_1(G^c, G^r)$, $G^i = \tau_2(G^{cm})$ and $G^{ic} = \tau_3(G^i, G^t)$.

The transformation τ_1 is a substitution of $G^r s$ into G^c (some nodes in G^c refer to $G^r s$). If there are several control graphs then after the application of τ_1 there will be several combined graphs. The transformation τ_2 is joining several combined graphs into a rule interaction graph and τ_3 is joining G^i and G^t graphs. Particular algorithms for the transformations are described in [11]. Informally, the purpose of G^{cm} and G^i is to visualise triggering relationships among rules (G^{cm} for a particular control graph and G^i for all control graphs). The purpose of G^{ic} is to have a graphical pattern to visualise the active rule processing taking into account a transaction. The derived graphs can not be modified by the user.

In the following each graph is represented by two sets: the nodes (N) and the edges (E). In order to distinguish nodes and edges in different graph we use upper index. For example, $G^r = (N^r, E^r)$, for a rule graph. An edge $E^j \in E$ is a pair where the left element of the pair is a node where the edge begins and the right element is a node where the edge ends. All edges in all graphs follow the above mentioned pattern. Nodes can have labels but edges are without labels. Different graphs may have different types of nodes (e.g. different numbers of subsets of N) and different types of edges (e.g. different numbers of subsets of E). Now we consider the above mentioned graphs in more details starting with the control graph.

3.2 Control graph

The control graph represents an abstract level to express active rule systems. Its purpose is to allow a user to describe triggering of rules (if any) and the states of

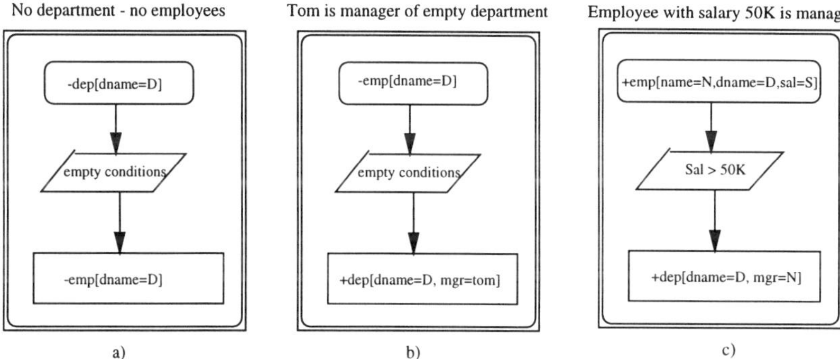

Figure 2: Rule graphs.

active systems before and after triggering rules. The control graph (G^c) contains two types of nodes N_s^c and N_t^c such that $N_s^c \cap N_t^c = \emptyset$. A node denoting a *state* (N_s^c) represents a particular database state. A node denoting *transition* (N_t^c) is an active rule which presents a movement between states within the active system.

An edge from a state to a transition node describes the state of database which may cause a rule triggering, and an edge from a transition to a state node describes a state of the database which is the result of the action performed by the rule. Under this approach, a graph $G^c = (N_s^c \cup N_t^c, E^c)$ represents the triggering of a set of active rules. Thus the transition nodes in a control graph are labeled by names of active rules and state nodes are labeled with the description of particular relations of a database or by some meaningful name corresponding to the state.

Figure 1 shows control graphs corresponding to the example from Section 2. Only data relevant to the rules are described explicitly in state nodes. In this example each control graph corresponds to one active rule (no interaction between rules is defined by the designer).

However a designer can prescribe a desired or obligatory order of triggering rules if he knows or requires it. For example, if a rule R1 should be triggered always before a rule R2 then it should be expressed as a directed edge from transition node R1 to transition node R2 in a control graph. Absence of such edge between transition nodes assumes arbitrary or unknown (by the designer) order of triggering. There are other types of control between rules that can be presented in the control graph. However we do not consider them in this paper.

An important point about a control graph is that it may contain more information about the rule system than it is usually described in a textual form (more detailed contents of state nodes or an order of rule triggering). This may provide a designer with a valuable source for analysis of a system.

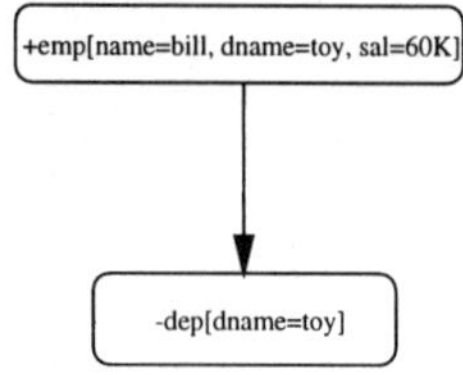

Figure 3: Transaction graph.

3.3 Rule graph

A rule graph represents a particular active rule and it has three types of nodes (three subsets of N^r): event nodes (N_e^r), condition node (N_c^r) and action nodes (N_a^r). They are pairwise disjoint. Event nodes correspond to events which switch on active rules. Condition nodes correspond to conditions to be checked in order to trigger rules and action nodes represent actions performed by rules. Directed edges on rule graph connect event node with condition node and condition node with action node. Thus $G^r = (N_e^r \cup N_c^r \cup N_a^r, E^r)$. The whole rule graph is labeled by name of the active rule and it is represented by a transition node with corresponding label in a control graph. Nodes of the rule graph are labeled following the syntax introduced in Section 2. An event node is labeled by the corresponding event specification (u^e). Similarly, for condition and action (with c and u^a respectively). Figure 2 shows the rule graphs corresponding to the example from Section 2.

3.4 Transaction graph

The purpose of the transaction graph is to represent a sequence of operations forming a transaction. A user transaction is represented as a transaction graph containing sequence of *update* nodes (N_u^t) and directed edges between them. Thus a transaction graph is defined as $G^t = (N_u^t, E^t)$. Figure 3 shows a transaction graph corresponding to the example from Section 2.

3.5 Combined graph

The idea of combined graph G^{cm} is to visualise triggering relationships among rules of an active system for a particular control graph. Thus G^{cm} can be seen as an instantiation of a G^c by G^rs (transformation τ_1). We recall that the transition nodes of G^c refer to rule graphs (i.e. $G^r = N_t^c$). The combined graph $G^{cm} = (N_s^{cm} \cup N_c^{cm} \cup N_o^{cm}, E^{cm})$ has three types of nodes: state nodes (N_s^{cm}), condition nodes (N_c^{cm}) and operation nodes (N_o^{cm}). These sets of nodes are pairwise disjoint. The combined graph is a transformation (τ_1) of G^c and G^rs as follows.

First, the set N_o^{cm} is constructed as union of N_e^r and N_a^r of rule graphs. We apply this transformation because at this level we are not anymore interested in

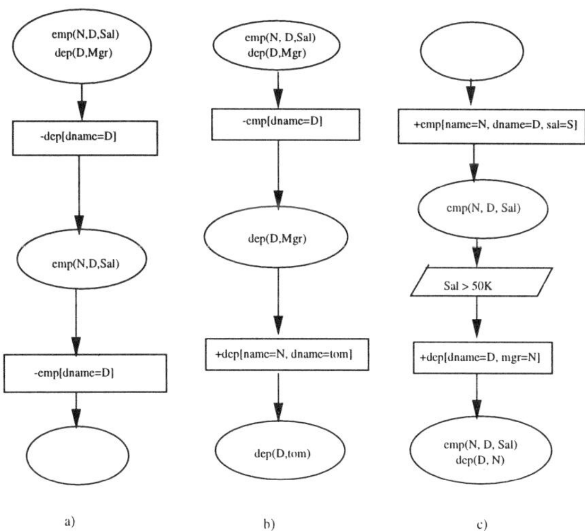

Figure 4: Combined graphs.

distinguishing the triggering process. Indeed, an event and the corresponding action generating such event represent the same faces of the concept of operation. Second, $N_s^{cm} = N_s^c$. However operations described in the event of a rule are applied to a corresponding incoming state of the rule graph G^r. This application may cause the creation of new states in N_s^{cm}. If states in control graph G^c are labeled by a meaningful name (not by name of relation) then additional transformations are not performed. Third, we would like to keep track of a particular rule in the combined graph G^{cm}. In order to do so, the set E^{cm} is decomposed into subsets $E^{cm1}, \ldots, E^{cm(n+1)}$ where n is the number of active rules in G^{cm}. Therefore $E^{cm1} = E^c$ and each set $E^{cmj}, j = 2, \ldots, n + 1$ corresponds to a particular rule and contains its set of edges E^r. Since N_e^rs and N_a^rs of different rule graphs are not disjoint sets and they may have equal elements which are glued together after the union operation, the edges of a combined graph (E^{cm}) will be updated in order to reflect the glueing. Finally, N_c^{cm} is a disjoint union of N_c^rs of different rule graphs and empty condition nodes are removed. We would like to notice that we do not glue together equal elements of N_c^rs and keep duplicates. Figure 4 shows combined graphs obtained from rule and control graphs from Figure 2 and Figure 1.

Actually it could be possible to allow a user to specify directly G^{cm} and consider it as a visual description of active rules. However we think that such task requires thinking on two different levels of abstraction (operational level and description level) at the same time and could be confusing for database designers. This is the reason why we separate these abstraction levels into two visual representations: G^c and G^r. Note that if there are several control graphs, then several combined graphs will be generated.

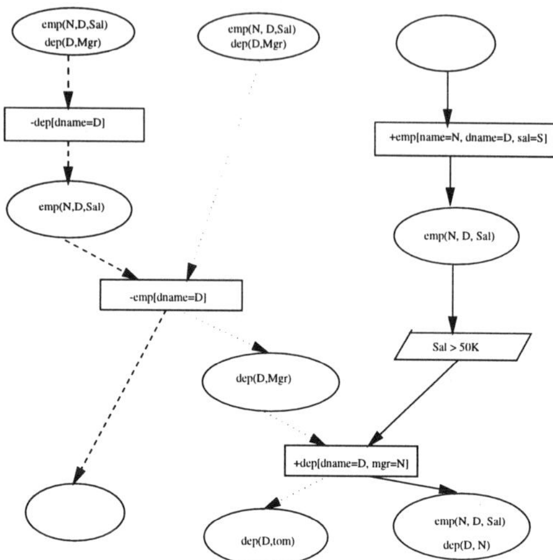

Figure 5: Rule interaction graph.

3.6 Rule interaction graph

The purpose of rule interaction graph is to visualise triggering relationships among all active rules. To achieve this task we join together all generated combined graphs. Rule interaction graph $G^i = (N_s^i \cup N_c^i \cup N_o^i, E^i)$ has three types of nodes: state nodes (N_s^i), condition nodes (N_c^i) and operation nodes (N_o^i). These sets of nodes are pairwise disjoint. The rule interaction graph is a transformation (τ_2) of G^{cm}s as follows. First, the set N_o^i is the union of N_o^{cm}s of combined graphs. Second, the set E^i is constructed as union of E^{cm}s. Since N_o^{cm}s of different combined graphs are not disjoint and they may have equal elements which are glued together after the union operation, the edges of rule interaction graph (E^i) are modified in order to reflect the glueing. Third, the set N_s^i is constructed as a disjoint union of the sets N_s^{cm}s of combined graphs. Finally, N_c^i is the disjoint union of N_c^{cm}s of combined graphs. We do not glue together equal elements of N_c^{cm}s and N_s^{cm}s and keep duplicates. Figure 5 shows a rule interaction graph obtained as transformation of combined graphs from Figure 4. Different rules in G^i (different subsets of E^i) are marked by lines of different style. It is important to note that the rule interaction graph discloses interaction between rules even when they are described independently by the designer.

3.7 Specialised rule interaction graph

Both combined and rule interaction graphs represent active rule systems without considering transactions. In order to visualise the behaviour of a set of active rules

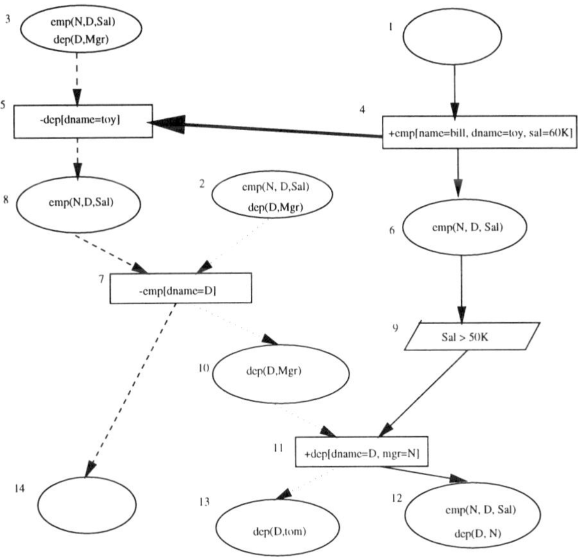

Figure 6: Specialised rule interaction graph.

during execution of a transaction we have to embody a particular user defined transaction into a rule interaction graph. This is done by generating specialised rule interaction graph.

The specialised rule interaction graph $G^{ic} = (N_s{}^{ic} \cup N_c{}^{ic} \cup N_o{}^{ic}, E^i)$ has three types of nodes: state nodes ($N_s{}^{ic}$), condition nodes ($N_c{}^{ic}$) and operation nodes ($N_o{}^{ic}$). These sets of nodes are pairwise disjoint. G^{ic} is generated by transformation τ_3 of G^i and G^t. The only difference between G^i and G^{ic} is that $N_o{}^{ic}$ in addition to elements $N_o{}^i$ from G^i will contain elements from $N_u{}^t$ connected by edges.

The resulting G^{ic} describes the abstract behaviour of an active system (without knowing the database state). In addition it provides a visual tool to describe step by step the behaviour of the active system. Assuming that there exists a symbolic interpreter for the system (see [16]) the step by step execution is visualised by tracing (highlighting) operation nodes and instantiation of other types of nodes of the specialised rule interaction graph. In this case a particular trace (i.e. sequence of operations) and instantiation of nodes will depend on the active rule semantics (see Section 2).

Consider our example and its corresponding specialised rule interaction graph of Figure 6. The behaviour is visualised by highlighting the operation nodes of the specialised rule interaction graph. For example, in case of immediate semantics the order of operation nodes is 4, 11, 5, 7, 11 and in case of deferred semantics it is 4, 5, 11, 7, 11, which corresponds to induced transactions of Section 2. For both semantics the final state is node number 13.

4. Visual Environment

The environment we propose has four components: a visual editor, the transformations τ_1, τ_2 and τ_3 (see [11]), a symbolic interpreter and the animation tool. As visual editor we have chosen the NUT system [12, 19]. It is a graphical tool which allows the designer to describe his/her own graphical objects and connect them via ports in order to describe corresponding relations. A graphical object contains several views. First, it is represented as an icon in a graphical menu. Second, it is represented with a graphical image which is drawn in a graphical window when corresponding icon is selected. In general the idea is similar to traditional graphical editors where graphical menus contain elements to be drawn (lines, rectangles, ovals, text etc.). However the main difference of the NUT editor is that in addition to standard graphical elements the designer can define its own graphical objects and use them as in a traditional graphical editors. This feature makes easier the definition of complex visual symbols and their manipulation. In addition there is a non-traditional way for manipulating graphical objects: they can be connected by links via defined ports and therefore constitute a graph which can be interpreted by the system.

The visual editor has been designed in an incremental bottom-up fashion. Thus the first step is to define the primitive graphical objects like state, rule, event, action and condition. Each of them has two views: icon (bitmap) and image.

Once these graphical objects are defined they are included into graphical menus and can be used for description of a particular rule graph (see Figure 7a). Texts into event, condition and action nodes are inserted by "zooming in" corresponding graphical object. Then primitive graphical objects for a control graph (considering states and rules) are defined in a similar way. At the end of this process a graphical menu for description of a control graph will have the elements shown in Figure 7b.

Another possibility for describing control graph is as follows. Instead of defining one primitive rule node different rule nodes are constructed from corresponding rule graphs and inserted into control graph menus as different icons (see for example Figure 7c). In this case we have a library of rule graphs which can be reused for constructing different control graphs. The opening of a rule node in a control graph will open the corresponding rule graph in a separate window. Similar approach can be implemented for state nodes. The other graphs are visualised as described in Section 3. The advantage of this approach is to combine a great flexibility and a pre-defined library of objects. Together they allow to have a short learning curve for the database designer as well as an open visual environment.

The transformations allow to produce the different types of graphs to define the active system. Then the symbolic interpreter allows to define the call pattern of the rules (without considering the database state) producing the trace modelling the active system behaviour according to the chosen rule semantic. At this point the trace is passed to the animation tool visualising the resulting behaviour. Note that the transformation producing the textual representation can be executed at

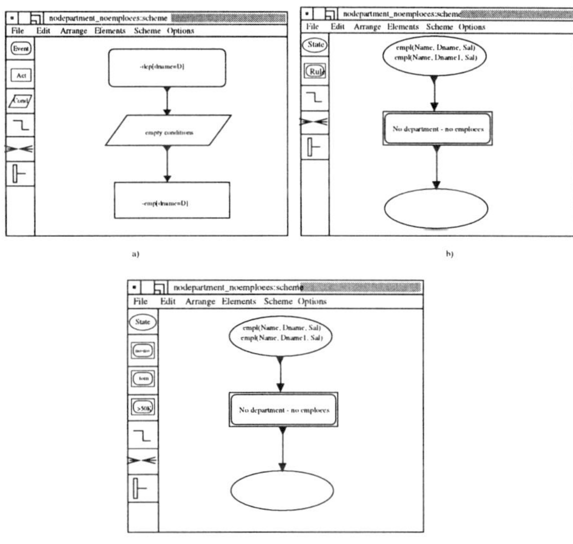

Figure 7: Description of a graph.

any time after the rule graph is defined.

5. Conclusions and future works

We have presented a new approach to database programming based on a visual active language that allows us to describe active rules in a graphical way and to transform the graphical representation of rules into textual and visual forms. The resulting visual representation facilitates the programming, debugging and maintenance phases and allows to visualise the dynamic behaviour under different active rule semantics through graph animation. In addition, we would like to underline the following points:

- We consider a visual language for active rules description rather than visualisation of textually described active rules. This is the main difference of our work with other works on active rule visualisation (for example, [3, 5]).

- The visual language allows to describe knowledge which are not usually presented in textual active rule language. We can refer to such knowledge as to graphical comments, however, they may force a designer to think about the problem in more detail.

- The usual graphical structures for active rule analysis, such as activation or triggering graphs can be easily extracted from our visual representation of active rules. This allows to consider our approach as a construction of visual interface to an active rule system and its implementation as a kind of shell to existent active rule systems.

In order to test our approach we have implemented a prototype version of the resulting visual environment (symbolic interpreter and animation tool are under construction now).

References

[1] A. Aiken, J. M. Hellerstein, and J. Widom. Static Analysis Techniques for Predicting the Behavior of Active Database Rules. ACM Transactions on Database Systems, TODS 20(1), 1995, pages 3–41.

[2] E. Baralis, S. Ceri and S. Paraboschi Improved Rule Analysis by Means of Triggering and Activation Graphs In *Proc. of RIDS'95*, LNCS 985, Springer-Verlag, 1995, pages 165–181.

[3] E. Benazet, H. Guehl, M. Bouzeghoub. VITAL: A Visual Tool for Analysis of Rules Behavior in Active Databases In *Proc. of RIDS'95*, LNCS 985, Springer-Verlag, 1995, pages 182–197.

[4] J. Blakeley. Component database systems. In *Proc. Fifth International Workshop on Database Programming Languages*, Gubbio, 1995.

[5] S. Chakravarthy, Z. Tamizudding and J. Zhou. A Visualisation and Explanation Tool for Debugging ECA Rules in Active Databases n *Proc. of RIDS'95*, LNCS 985, Springer-Verlag, 1995, pages 197–212.

[6] M. P. Consens and A. O. Mendelzon. Graphlog: a Visual Formalism for Real Life Recursion. In *Proc. of the ACM Symposium on Principles of Database Systems*, pages 404–416, 1990.

[7] O. Diaz, A. Jaime, N. W. Paton. DEAR: a DEbugger for Active Rules in an object-oriented context. In RIDS'93, Workshops in Computing, Springer 1994, pages 180-193

[8] D. Harel. Statecharts: a visual formalism for complex systems. *Science of Computer Programming*, (8):231–274, 1987.

[9] W. Kim. *Modern Database Systems: The Object Model, Interoperability, and Beyond.* ACM Press and Addison-Wesley, 1995.

[10] N. W. Paton et al. Formal specification of active database functionality: A survey. In *Rules in Database Systems, Second International Workshop*, 1995.

[11] M. Matskin and D. Montesi. Visual Active Rule Language. NTNU, Institutt for Datateknikk, Teknisk notat 6/96, ISSN-nr. 0802-6394, Trondheim, Norway, December 1996, 29 p.

[12] M. Matskin and E. Tuygu. The NUT Language. Royal Institute of Technology (KTH), Stockholm, Sweden, TRITA-TCS-SE-9212-TR, 1992.

[13] D. Montesi, K. G. Jeffcry and J. Kalmus. Towards a Visual Formalism for Business Modelling. In *Proc. International Conference of the Information Resources Management Association*, Vancouver, 1997, To appear.

[14] D.R. McCarthy and U. Dayal. The architecture of an Active Data Base Management System. In *Proc. Int'l Conf. ACM on Management of Data*, pages 215–223, 1989.

[15] D. Montesi and R. Torlone. A Rewriting Technique for the analysis and the Optimisation of Active Databases. In G. Gottlob and M. Y. Vardi, editors, *Proc. Fifth Int'l Conf. on Database Theory*, volume 893 of *Lecture Notes in Computer Science*, pages 238–251. Springer-Verlag, 1995.

[16] D. Montesi and R. Torlone. A Transaction Transformation Approach to Active Rule Processing. In *Proc. IEEE International Conference on Data Engineering*, pages 109–116. IEEE Computer Society Press, 1995.

[17] N. C. Shu. *Visual Programming*. New York: Van Nostrand Reinhold, 1988.

[18] J. D. Ullman. *Database and Knowledge-Base Systems*. Computer Science Press, 1989.

[19] B. Volozh, M. Kopp, and E. Tyugu. NUT Graphics, TRITA-IT-9305, Dep. of Teleinformatics, KTH, 1993.

[20] J. Widom and S. Ceri. *Active Database Systems: Triggers and Rules for Advanced Database Processing*. Morgan-Kaufmann, 1995.

[21] J. Widom and S. J. Finkelstein. Set-Oriented Production Rule in Relational Databases Systems. In H. Garcia-Molina and H.V. Jagadish, editors, *Proc. Int'l Conf. ACM on Management of Data*, pages 259–270, 1990.

Information Modelling and Knowledge Bases IX
P.-J. Charrel et al. (Eds.)
1998, IOS Press

An Efficient Search Method for Context-Based Queries in the Meme Media System

Mina AKAISHI and Yuzuru TANAKA
Meme Media Laboratory,
Graduate School of Engineering, Hokkaido University, Sapporo, 060 Japan
{mina, tanaka}@meme.hokudai.ac.jp

Abstract. This paper presents an efficient search method for processing context-based queries. This method allows us to develop a new type of database capable of handling large amounts of arbitrarily composed object instances. In our system, new media objects are defined by combining existing object instances and have no corresponding classes, while current object-oriented database (OODB) systems use class definitions as database schemes. Most queries in our system partially specify composition structures of target object instances. Such queries, called context-based queries, show extremely poor performance when processed by current OODB systems. This paper proposes the use of a special signature file as a filtering mechanism to reduce the number of media objects that need to be searched when processing a query. It also gives the results of an analytical performance study to the proposed algorithms.

1. Introduction

Computers and networks are now rapidly spreading through many fields all over the world. People can share and reuse knowledge resources to produce new items, using new types of media objects. Called meme media [1], they can carry a variety of knowledge resources, replicate and recombine themselves, and adapt to their environments. The IntelligentPad system [2,3] is based on the meme media architecture. The wide coverage of this system and the ease of object construction allow a user, or a society of users sharing its resources, to rapidly accumulate composed media objects. That forms a large meme pool that includes multimedia documents, desktop tools, application services and even junk objects [4,5]. Meme pools requires their management by database systems.

It was first thought that these media objects could be efficiently managed by an OODB system [6,7]. This was found not to be the case for two reasons. Current OODBs use class definitions as database schemes, while in our system, new media objects are defined by combining existing object instances, and therefore have no corresponding class definitions. In addition, most queries in our system partially specify composition structures of the target object instances. Such queries show extremely poor performance when processed by current OODB systems. This paper presents an efficient search method for the processing of context-based queries in OODBs. This method will allow us to develop a new type of OODBs capable of handling large amounts of arbitrarily composed object instances.

2 Management of Meme Media

2.1. *IntelligentPad system*

The IntelligentPad system is based on the meme media architecture [1]. It provides its users with a toolkit for the construction of various interactive media objects including multimedia documents, desktop tools, and application systems. Any component is presented as a meme media object, called a pad. People can easily replicate composite pads, exchange copies among themselves, reedit them by paste and peel operations and distribute their new creations. The basic pad provided in such a system is called a primitive pad, while a pad constructed by the combination of primitive pads is called a compound pad or a composite pad.

In an IntelligentPad system, users can easily compose any document or any tool by directly pasting some pads on top of another. Such a paste operation simultaneously defines both the layouts of its components in the composed pad and the functional linkage among component pads. Users can easily replicate any pads, paste a pad on another, and peel a pad off a composite pad. These operations can be equally applied to both primitive pads and any composite pads.

In the IntelligentPad architecture, container media is separated from their contents, and standardizing the logical structure and the interface of the container media. Figure 1 shows the logical structure of a pad. Each primitive pad consists of its shell and its contents. Its shell defines its standard media structure and interface. It is up to the developer of each pad how the contents are implemented in the standard shell.

A pad in the IntelligentPad consists of a display object and a model object. Its display object defines its GUI, while its model object defines its internal state and behavior. Each display object further consists of a controller object and a view object. Its view object defines its view on the display screen, while its controller object defines its reaction to user events. A pad may define some of its slots in its model object, and some others in its view object (Figure 2).

The application-linkage interface of each pad is defined as a list of slots. Each slot can be accessed either by a 'set' message 'set <slot_name>' or by a 'gimme' message 'gimme <slot_name>'. Each of these tow messages invokes the respective procedure attached to the slot. Each slot S_i may have two attached procedures, $proc_{i,set}$ for the 'set' message and $proc_{i,gimme}$ for the 'gimme' message. The default for $proc_{i,se}$ stores the parameter value into

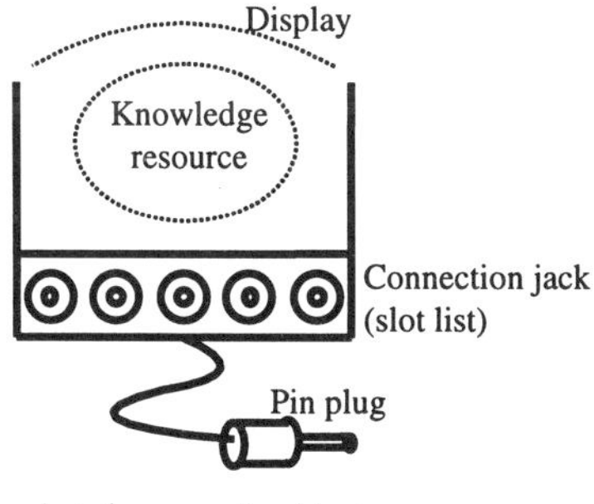

A pad as a media object

Fig. 1 The logical structure of a pad that allows its generic definition.

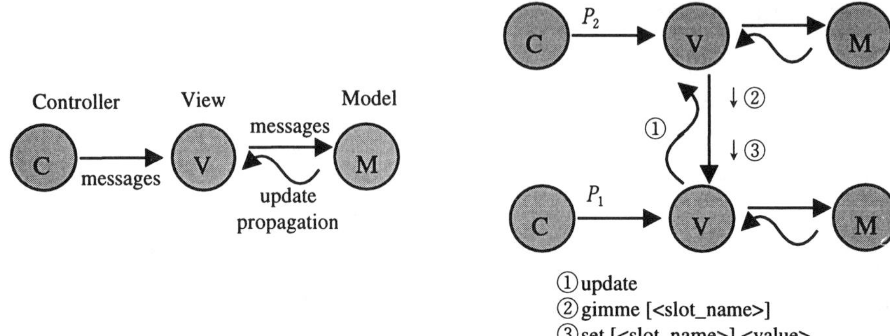

Fig. 2   The architecture of each primitive pad.   Fig. 3   The standard message interface between pads.

the slot register, while the default for $proc_{i,gimme}$ returns the slot register value.   A slot with default procedures for the two messages is called a data slot.   Its slots and attached procedures define the internal mechanism of each pad.   They are defined by its developer.

When a pad P_2 is pasted on another pad P_1, the IntelligentPad constructs a linkage between their view parts (Figure 3).   This defines a dependency from P_1 to P_2.   If P_1 has more than one slot, we have to select one of them to associate it with P_2.   The selected slot name is stored in a standard slot of the subpad P_2 named connectslot.   A subpad can send either 'set' message or 'gimme' message to its master, while the master pad, when its state is changed, can send some of its subpads an 'update' message without any parameter to propagate an update event.   The interpretation of the update message again depends on the implementation of the sender and the receiver pads.   It is usually used to inform the subpads of a master's state change.   The two messages 'set s v' and 'gimme s' sent to a pad P are forwarded to its masterpad if P does not have the slot s.

2.2.   *Management for pads*

There are three means of managing pads in IntelligentPad: the browsing, the navigation, and the conditional retrieval.   The browsing uses catalogs where all types of pads are listed and can browse through when searching for a particular pad.   A pad in the image of a book, called a binder pad, has been prepared for this purpose.   The navigation uses links and processing techniques adopted by hypermedia.   IntelligentPad offers two types of pads to perform this link function: link pads and anchor pads.   The conditional retrieval is classified into the form-base and the pad-base functions.   A form-base groups together and processes pads of the same format, while a pad-base processes pads of different formats together.   A form-base can be easily constructed by combining primitive pads.   The specification of retrieval requests in a form-base is carried out using QBE methods [10, 11].

A pad-base groups together and processes various primitive and composite pads, and offers the ability to retrieve specific pads.   Every pad has a given set of characteristics including a nickname, record number and slot values.   These attributes can be used in conditional retrieval.

A pad-base can be easily constructed by combining basic pads.   Figure 4 shows the display hardcopy of a pad-base.   IntelligentPad uses GemStone [11] (Object-oriented Database Management System) to establish a pad-base.   Pad-base pad has a proxy of a pad-base manager to connect IntelligentPad and GemStone.   Through a pad-base pad, the

IntelligentPad system users can use a set of database functions as a pad. A pad-base manager has connection with the database to send the messages and to return the results as pads. The query pad is showed in the left upper area of pad-base pad. The query pad is constructed with a pulley pad and a spring pad. The pad-base retrieves all composite pads, which contain all of the primitive pads in the query pad. One of the results is shown in the right area. The specification of retrieval requests in a pad-base is carried out using QBP (Query By Pad) method as same as QBE. The results are also provided as pads.

2.3. An overview of the context-based query processing

Retrieval methods are classified into content-based retrieval and context-based retrieval. A query in the former class specifies a part of the information stored in the target objects, while in the latter one uses context information concerning the target objects' environments. A pad-base should provide both methods, each one being more efficient in certain cases. In the sequel, we will focus on the context-based retrieval in a pad-base.

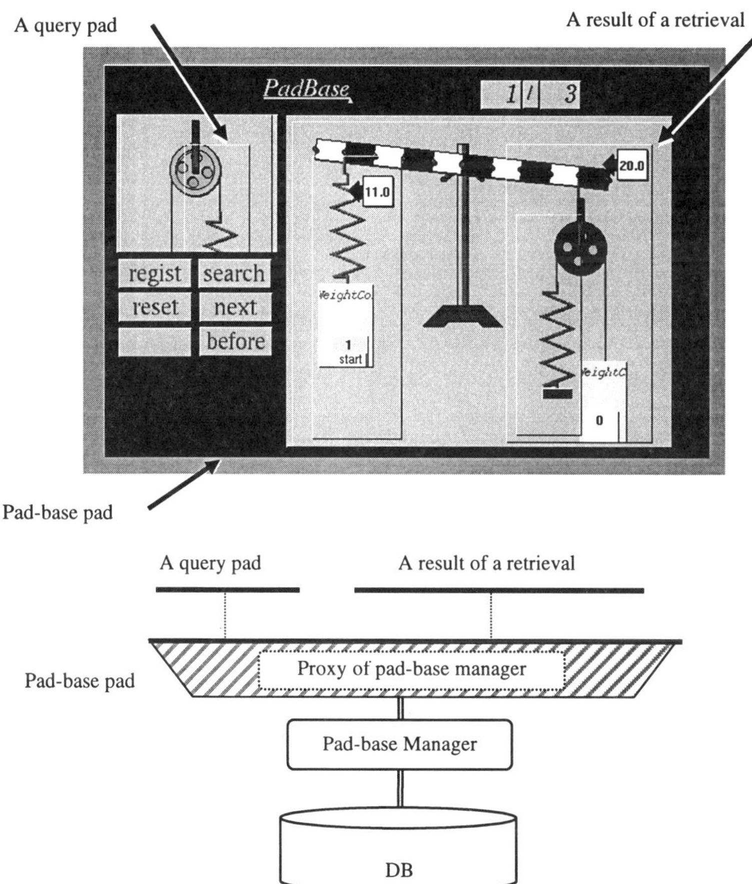

Fig. 4   Display hardcopy of the pad-base showing a spring in the query pad and a complex pad
containing a spring in the result pad and architecture of pad-base.

In IntelligentPad, a compound pad's function is defined by its primitive pads and their combinations. The same pad may play different roles in different composite pads. The primitive pad's function is defined by its position in the compound pad and its combination with other pads, that is to say that a primitive pad's function depends on the context. For users wishing to retrieve compound pads by specifying their functions, it is most efficient to retrieve compound pads that have specified structures. This is one aspect of context-based retrievals. For example, a user searching a calculator could retrieve a target pad by specifying its substructure, which represents a part of its function, without specifying names or product companies. In figure 5 a query pad specifies a substructure of calculators. The pads included the structure of query pad are searched. They are a simple calculator, a complex calculator and a timer. The timer is not a calculator but also satisfies the query. Figure 5 shows a search for pads with specified composition structures as their substructures.

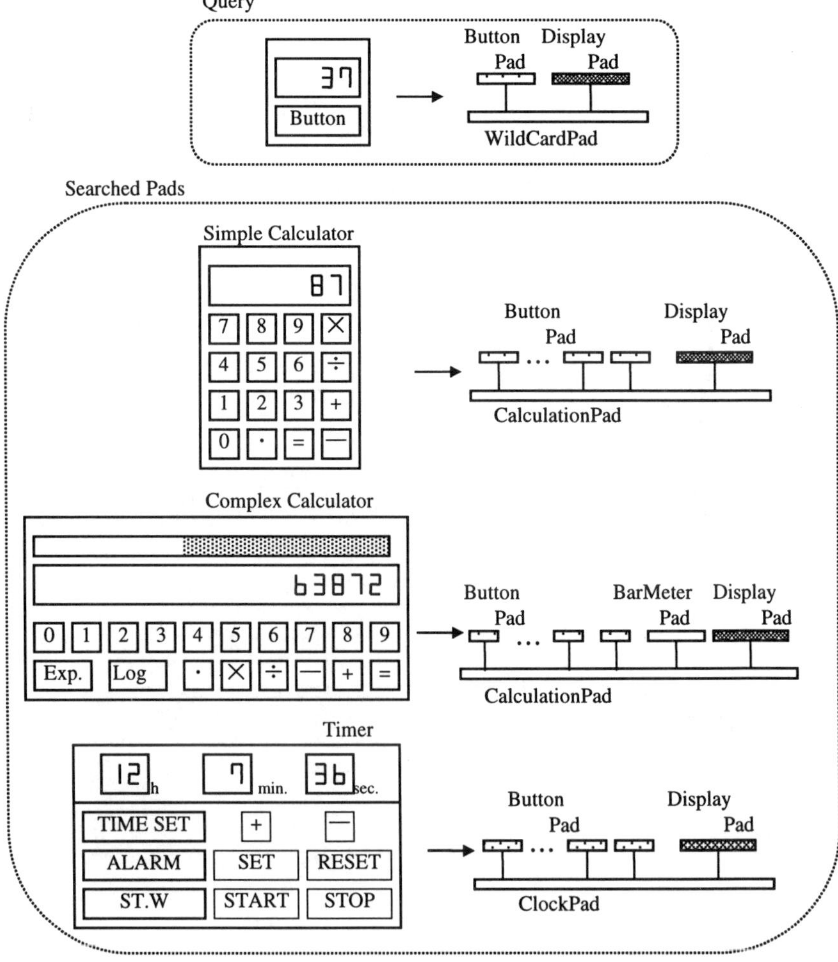

Fig. 5   Search for pads with the specified composition structure as their substructures.

Compound pad structures are defined dynamically. Users can dynamically and freely paste or peel pads to create composite pads. However, indexing techniques of OODBs are not designed for dynamic structures of compound objects. The indexing techniques surveyed in [11] are based on statically defined structures of nested objects. Techniques include nested index, path index and multi-index. All of them suppose the static structures of objects defined in advance by the class definition. As a result, OODB indexing techniques do not provide enough performance for the retrieval of junk objects. We need a new efficient retrieval method based on dynamically defined structures of pad instances.

3. Search methods for a Context-based Retrieval

3.1. *Access method using a signature file*

This section describes an access method using a signature file [12] for processing context-based queries. Figure 6 shows a retrieval process. The structures of compound pad are represented as trees. When a pad is stored in the database, a pad signature is yielded by encoding its structure. Details of the encoding method for the pad structures will be provided later. At the time of query processing, the query signature is yielded from the query pad composition structure. Next, qualifying signatures are extracted from the signature file, and a list of object identifiers (OIDs) corresponding to the extracted signatures is obtained. For a pad signature to satisfy a query signature, every bit position

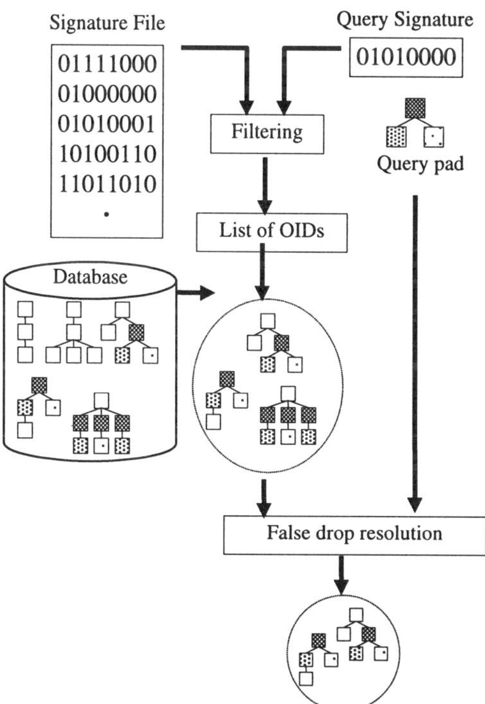

Fig. 6   Our access method using a signature file.

that is set to '1' in the query signature must also be set to '1' in the pad signature.   It is possible that a pad signature may match a query signature, but the corresponding pad does not satisfy the query.   Such an occurrence is referred to as a false drop.   After false drops are excluded, all pads that satisfy the query will be obtained.

3.2.   Encoding pad composition structures

In this section, an encoding method for a compound pad structure is described.   This method is based on the superimposed coding [13].   Each compound pad yields a bit pattern of size f.   The method works as follows:

[Step 1: class signature]

Let each primitive pad P_i in the compound pad have a record number $C(P_i)$ that identifies its class, where $i \in [1,\ldots,n]$ and n is the number of primitive pads in the compound pad. Each component pad P_i sets one of the bits in the signature to '1'.   This bit position is determined by the class of this pad, using the following hash function $h_1(C(P_i))$:

$$h_1(C(P_i)) = a\, C(P_i) \bmod f: \quad a \text{ is a coefficient.} \tag{1}$$

This is called a class signature.

[Step 2: combination signature]

Let each pad combination pair $(P_i\text{-}P_j)$ in the compound pad denote that a primitive pad P_j is pasted on a primitive pad P_i.   Each pad combination pair $(P_i\text{-}P_j)$ sets one bit in the signature to '1'.   Let the record number of P_i be $C_p = C(P_i)$ and the record number of P_j be $C_c = C(P_j)$. The bit position is given by the following hash function $h_2(C_p, C_c)$:

$$h_2(C_p, C_c) = (\beta C_p + \gamma C_c) \bmod f: \quad \beta \text{ and } \gamma \text{ are coefficents.} \tag{2}$$

This is called a combination signature

[Step 3: pad signature]

The bit patterns of a class signature and a combination signature are OR-ed together to define the pad signature.

Figure 7 shows an example of the superimposed coding of pads, where $a=1$, $\beta=3$ and $\gamma=5$. The first example pad P_1 was encoded to '0000001000001100' and the second P_2 was encoded to '1111011000001110'.   Such a signature, called a pad signature, encodes the classes and the composition structures of components in a compound pad.   The signatures of P_1 and P_2 were extracted by the query signature '0000001000001100'.

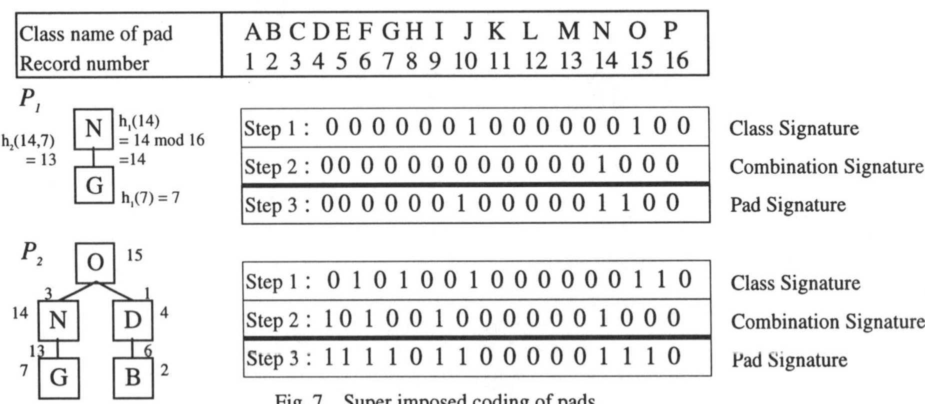

Fig. 7   Super imposed coding of pads.

Class name of pad	A B C D E F G H I J K L M N O P
Record number	1 2 3 4 5 6 7 8 9 10 11 12 13 14 15 16

Step 1 : 0 0 0 0 0 0 0 0 0 0 1 0 1 0 0 1	Class Signature
Step 2 : 0 0 0 0 0 0 1 0 0 0 0 0 0 1 0 0	Combination Signature
Step 3 : 0 0 0 0 0 0 1 0 0 0 1 0 1 1 0 1	Pad Signature

Fig. 8   Super imposed coding of pads.

Suppose the pad P_3 that structure is illustrated in figure 8.   The pad signature for the pad P_3 is '0000001000101101'.   Although the signature of P_3 is also extracted by the query signature '0000001000001100', the pad P_3 does not include the structure of pad P_1.   In that case, the pad P_3 is called a false drop.

4.   Analysis of retrieval costs

An analytical study of the performance is described in this section.   All symbols are shown in Table 1.

4.1.   *Retrieval cost model*

A simple model for retrieval cost (response time) has the following form:

$$\text{cost} = a_1 t_1 + a_2 fn + a_3 F_d, \tag{3}$$

where $a_1 t_1$ is the time to yield a query signature, $a_2 fn$ the time to filter the signature file and $a_3 F_d$ accounts for process of false drop resolution.   Because of $a_1 t_1 + a_2 fn \ll a_3 F_d$, it is possible to suppose that the cost is directly proportional to the value of F_d.   Accordingly, F_d was used in this paper as the retrieval cost of our method.   In the following section, we will discuss how to make F_d small.

Table 1   List of symbols used in the text.

Symbol	Definition
f	Number of bits for a pad signature
W	Number of 1s (weight) in the pad signature
W_q	Number of 1s (weight) in the query signature
k	Number of bits set for each pad class
s	Number of bits set for each pad pair
n	Number of component pads for a compound pad
K	Number of all pad classes
$W(k,s,n)$	Number of 1s (weight) in the pad signature
$Ps(W,W_q)$	Probability that a pad signature is extracted
P_q	Probability that a pad is actually qualify
$P_q(n)\text{min}$	Probability that a pad constructed with n components actually qualifies a query pad consisting of two components
F_d	False drop probability

4.2.   Analysis of false drop probability

As discussed in the previous section, the number of false drops affects the retrieval performance.   In this section we clarify the necessary condition to keep false drop probability small.

False drop probability F_d is the proportion of the number of those pads that are falsely qualified by a given query signature to the number of all the pads that do not satisfy this query.   Mathematically, this is expressed as follows,

$$F_d = \text{Prob.}\left\{ \frac{\text{Pad is falsely qualified by the query signature}}{\text{Pad does not satisfy the given query}} \right\}. \qquad (4)$$

To estimate F_d, we suppose the following data model and an improved encoding method for pad signatures.   Then, we calculate a weight of a pad signature, the probability that an arbitrarily selected pad is actually qualified and the probability that an arbitrarily selected pad signature matches the given query signature.

4.2.1. Data model

To simplify the analysis, the rest of this paper discusses only the following cases.   All of the compound pads in the database are constructed with n primitive pads.   The numbers of primitive pads belonging to every class are equal in a database.   Every pad might randomly connect another pad.

That data model is the general model.   Actually, the numbers of primitive pads of every class are partially in a database.   Although we have to analyze false drop probability according to an actual data model, we first discuss the basic analysis based on the general data model in this paper.

4.2.2. Encoding method

Encoding method is improved by the following.   In order to change the weight for the same signature size, our method of encoding pad signatures is improved as follows.
[Step 1]   Each component pad's record number is hashed to k bit positions.
[Step 2]   Each pad combination pair is hashed to s bit positions.
[Step 3]   The bit patterns thus obtained are OR-ed together to define the pad signature.
For example, the pad P_1 in the fig. 7 is encoded to '1100101000001100' and the pad P_3 in the fig.8 is encoded to '0000001000101111' with $(\alpha, \beta, \gamma) = (1, 3, 5)$ and $(7, 11, 13)$, when $k=2$ and $s=2$.   In this case, because the signature of P_3 is not matched the signature of P_1 as query signature, the pad P_3 is not a false drop.

4.2.3. Weight of a pad signature

A weight of signature is the number of bits set to '1' in the signature.   The weight depends on the parameters k, s and f, where k is the number of bits set for a class of primitive pad, s is the number of bits set for a pad pair and f is the size (length) of signature.

If we set one bit per a compound pad, the probability that an arbitrarily selected bit is set to '1' is $1/f$.   Then the probability that a bit is not set to '1' is $(1-1/f)$.   If we set m bits per

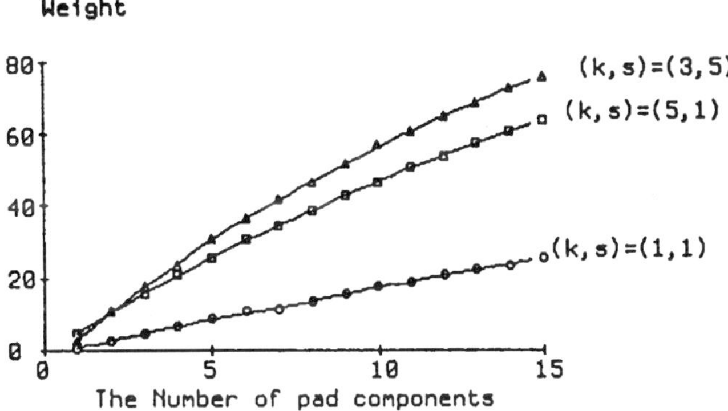

Fig. 9   Signature weight as a function of the number of pad components.

a compound pad, the probability that an arbitrarily selected bit is not set to '1' is $(1-1/f)^m$. So the expected number of the bits that are not set to '1' is $f(1-1/f)^m$.   Then the expected number of weight is $W = f-f(1-1/f)^m$.   An approximation to W is $W = f(1-\exp(-m/f))$ [11]. The expected weight of a pad signature is then given by

$$W(k, s, n) = f(1-\exp(-((nk+(n-1)s)/f))),\tag{5}$$

where $m = nk+(n-1)s$.

The results are plotted in figure 9.   It shows the signature weight as a function of the number of pad components, while (k, s) is assigned $(3, 5)$, $(5, 1)$ and $(1, 1)$.   The weight depends on the parameters k, s and f.   In the later, we clarify the necessary condition of k and s to keep false drop probability small.

4.2.4. *The probability that pad is actually qualified*

Let us suppose that a query pad is constructed with two primitive pads.   Because the worst false drop probability is obviously observed when the number of query pad components is smallest ($=2$).   The looser conditions make false drop probability the worse.

The probability that an arbitrarily selected pad is actually qualified is given by the following,

$$P_q(n)\min = 1 - ((K^2-1)/K^2)^{n-1},\tag{6}$$

where the number of query pad components is assumed to be two (see Appendix A).

4.2.5. *The probability that a pad signature is matched a query signature*

The probability that an arbitrarily selected pad signature matches the query signature is given by the following function,

$$Ps(W, Wq) = \prod_{i=0}^{Wq-1}(W-i)/(f-i),\tag{7}$$

where W and W_q are the weight of the pad signature and the weight of the query signature (see Appendix B).   The results are plotted in figure 10, where $W=72, 64$ and 56.   When

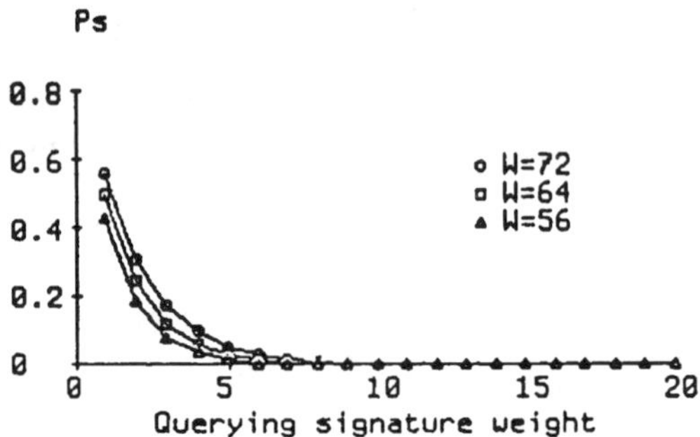

Fig. 10   Qualifying signature probability as a function of the querying signature weight.

the pad signature weight is smaller and the query signature weight is bigger, the probability P_s is smaller.

4.2.6. *False drop probability*

False drop probability F_d is the proportion of the number of those pads that are falsely qualified by a given query signature to the number of all the pads that do not satisfy this query.   False drop probability F_d is expressed as follows,

$$F_d = \text{Prob.}\left\{ \frac{\text{Pad is falsely qualified by the query signature}}{\text{Pad does not satisfy the given query}} \right\} = (P_s - P_q)/(1 - P_q), \qquad (8)$$

where P_s is the ratio of the number of the matched pad signatures to the size of the signature file, and P_q is the ratio of the number of actually qualified pads to the total number of pads.

4.2.7. *The necessary condition*

To reduce the false drop probability, the probability P_s should be small.   So the expected weight of a query signature should be increased and the expected weight of a pad signature in the database should be decrease.   By solving these problems, the necessary conditions of k and s are clarified as follows.

(i) $k >= 1$ and $s >= 1$

(ii) The increase rate of W should be smaller.   The increasing of W depends on k and s for the same f.   The increase rate of W is larger when k is increased than when s is increased, because it holds that $\partial W / \partial k - \partial W / \partial s = \exp(-((nk+(n-1)s) / f)) > 0$. Therefore, the increase of k is given a higher priority, which leads to satisfy $k \geq s$.

(iii) The weight W of a pad signature should be smaller.   If $W(k, s, N) < W(k', s', N)$ where $W(k, s, n_0) = W(k', s', n_0)$ and $n_0 < N$, then it holds that $k+s < k'+s'$.   The formula $W(k, s, N) < W(k', s', N)$ is transformed to $(k+s)N - s < (k'+s')N - s'$ by using the formula (5).   In the same way, the formula $W(k, s, n_0) = W(k', s', n_0)$ is transformed to $(k+s) n_0 - s = (k'+s')n_0 - s'$.   Therefore it holds that $(k+s) (N - n_0) < (k'+s') (N - n_0)$, which leads to $k+s < k'+s'$.

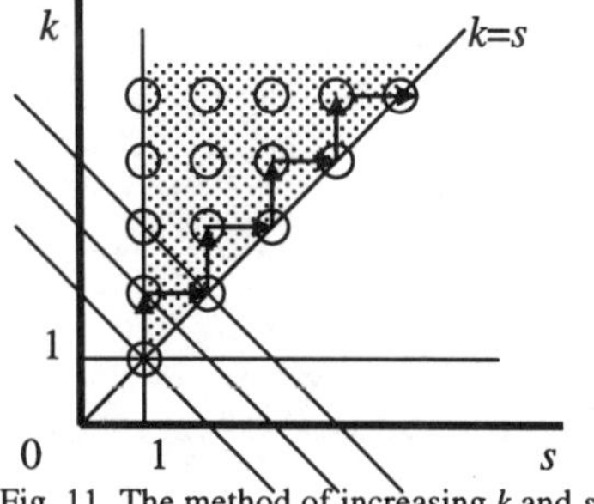

Fig. 11 The method of increasing k and s.

These conditions (i)~(iii) restrict the values of k and s to the shaded area in Fig. 11. If there still exist alternative combinations of k and s, it is better to increase s first, because the number K of all primitive pad classes is smaller than its square K^2 that is equal to the number of all the pad combination pairs.

The probability of a false drop remains small due to the appropriate choice of the parameters k and s satisfying $k=s$ or $k=s+1$.

4.3.　result of an analysis for retrieval costs

Figure 12 shows the false drop probability as a function of the number of pad components. For $n>33$, F_d takes its smallest value at $(k, s)=(1, 1)$. For $33>n>20$, F_d has its smallest value at $(k, s)=(2, 2)$. For $n<20$, F_d takes its smallest value at $(k, s)=(3, 3)$. It can be seen that when k and s are appropriately adjusted for different number of pad components, the false drop probability can be kept small.

It was proposed in [10,11] that the signature size f directly affects the number of false drops, whereas approximately half the number of bits should be '1' in a signature. The number of components in a compound pad has no upper limit. It would be impossible in our system for all of a pad signature's weight to be kept half the signature size, when the parameter k, s and f are constant. The probability of a false drop can be arbitrarily reduced by the appropriate choice of parameters.

The false drop probability is now analyzed as a function of the size of the pad signature. Figure 13 shows the false drop probability as a function of the number of components for some different parameters as shown in the figure. The optimum length of a pad signature depends on the number of pad components. It is impossible to determine its size beforehand, because the number of pad components has no upper limit. The optimum length of a pad signature should be calculated from the number of pad components. Figures 14 and 15 show the false drop probability that is always kept less than maxF_d by optimally changing the values of k, s and f for the different ranges of the number of pad components. Table 2 (a) shows the details of these optimum parameter values concerning

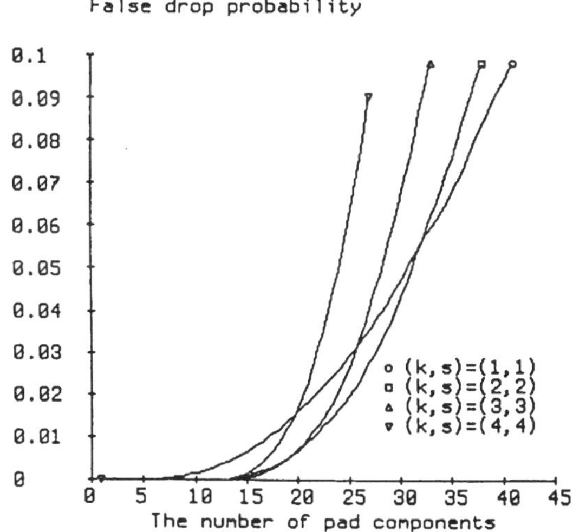

Fig. 12　False drop probability as a function of the number of pad components.

Fig. 14, and (b) shows the details of these optimum parameter values concerning Fig. 15.

The probability of a false drop can be made small by appropriately choosing the parameters k, s and f. The search schemes are shown in Fig. 16. During the query processing, several query signatures are obtained for different parameters, and each signature file is searched for the query signature that is obtained for the same parameter values. The time to obtain query signatures can be ignored, since it is negligible compared to the time necessary for false drop resolution.

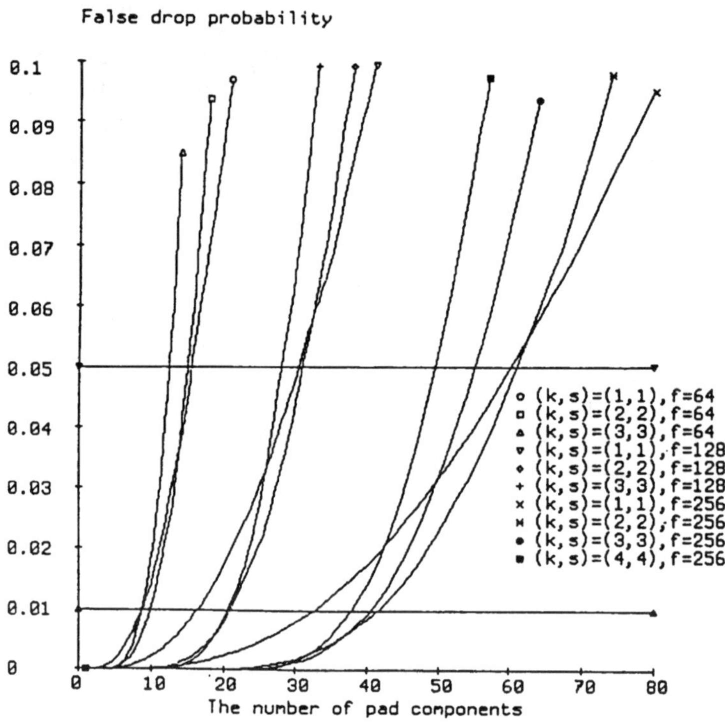

Fig. 13   False drop probability as a function of the number of pad components.

Table 2   Relationships among the number of primitive pads, the signature size and the different coding rule.

(a) maxFd = 0.01			(b) maxFd = 0.05		
n	f	(k, s)	n	f	(k, s)
0~6	64(f_0)	(3,3)	0~6	64(f_0)	(3,3)
~11	64(f_0)	(2,2)	~15	64(f_0)	(2,2)
~19	128(f_1)	(3,3)	~19	128(f_1)	(3,3)
~21	128(f_1)	(2,2)	~30	128(f_1)	(2,2)
~25	256(f_2)	(4,4)	~37	256(f_2)	(3,3)
~37	256(f_2)	(3,3)	~60	256(f_2)	(2,2)
~41	256(f_2)	(2,2)	...	...	...
...	...	...	...	...	...

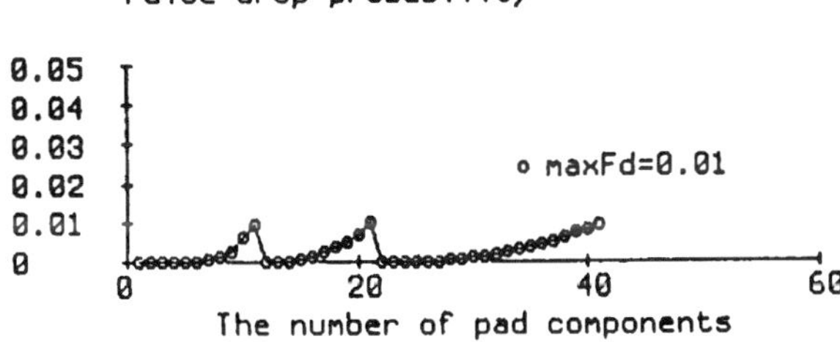

Fig. 14   False drop probability as a function of the number of pad components.

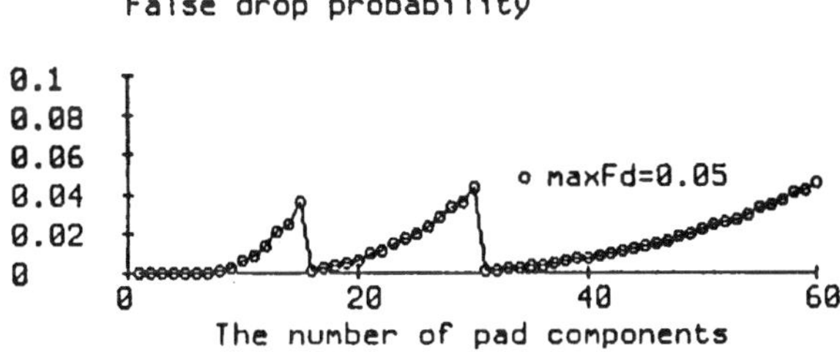

Fig. 15   False drop probability as a function of the number of pad components.

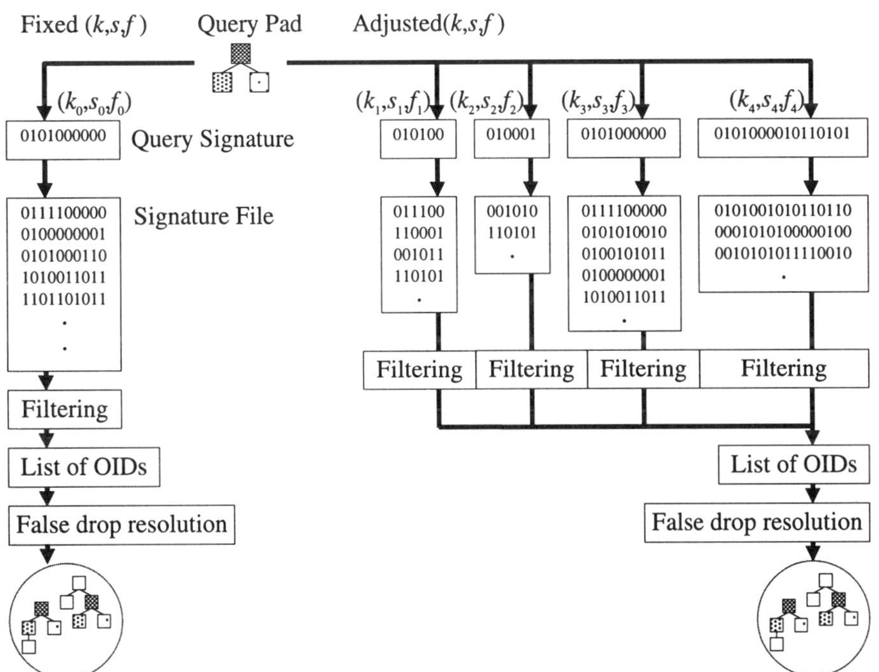

Fig. 16   Two different search schemes for the two different coding schemes.

5. Conclusion

The purpose of a pad-base is to manage a large variety of media objects.   It provides functions to retrieve specified media objects.   Those functions are classified in the content-based retrieval and the context-based retrieval.   This paper has shown that the context-based retrieval can be performed efficiently for the IntelligentPad system.   The context-based query specifies a common substructure of the pads to be searched.   Our search method uses the superimposed coding and signature files to evaluate the context-based queries.   We have analyzed the performance of our method to select the optimum design parameters that minimize the false drop probability.

A pad-base provides users with the pad management functions as a pad called pad-base pad.   Users can arbitrarily paste or peel the pad-base pad and the other existing pads to create new composite pads.   Moreover, a pad-base pad can be published world wide through the Internet by embedding it in arbitrary web page, which provides its functions to our society.

References

[1] Tanaka, Y.: Meme media and a World-Wide meme pool, Proc. The Fourth ACM International Multimedia Conference, MULTIMEDIA '96, pp.175-186 (1996)

[2] Tanaka, Y.: A Synthetic Dynamic-Media System, Proc. International Conference on Multimedia Information Systems, Singapore, pp.299-310 (1991)

[3] Tanaka, Y., Nagasaki, A., Akaishi, M. and Noguchi, T.: A Synthetic Media Architecture for an Object-Oriented Open Platform, Proc. IFIP 12th World Computer Congress Madrid, Spain, pp.194-110 (1992)

[4] Tsichiritzis, D.: Object-Oriented Development for Open Systems, Proc. IFIP Congress '89, San Francisco, pp. 1033-1040 (1989)

[5] Tanaka, Y. : A Toolkit System for the Synthesis and the Management of Active Media Objects, Proc. 1st International Conference on Deductive and Object-Oriented Databases, Kyoto, pp.269-277 (1989)

[6] Cattell, R. G.G.: Object Data Management: Object-Oriented and Extended Relational Database Systems, Addison-wesley, Reading, Massachusetts (1991)

[7] Bancilhon, F., Delobel, C. and Kanellakis, P.: Building an Object-Oriented Database System, Morgan Kaufmann, San Mateo, California (1992)

[8] Zloof, M. M.: Query-by-Example: A Database Language, IBM Systems Journal, Vol. 16, No. 4, pp.324-343, (1977)

[9] Zloof, M. M.: QBE/OBE: A Language for Office and Business Automation, IEEE Computer, Vol. 14, No. 5, pp.13-22, (1981)

[10] Copeland, G. and Maier, D.: Making Smalltalk a Database System, Proc. ACM SIGMOD International Conference on Management of Data, pp. 316-482 (1986)

[11] Bertino, E. and Kim, W. : Indexing Techniques for Queries on Nested Object, IEEE trans. Knowledge and Data Engineering, Vol. 1, No.2, pp.196-214, (1989)

[12] Faloutsos, C. and Christodoulakis, S. : Signature Files : An Access Method for Documents and Its Analytical Performance Evaluation, ACM Trans. On Office Information Systems, Vol.2, No.4, pp.267-288 (1984)

[13] Stiassny, S.: Mathematical Analysis of Various Superimposed Coding Methos, American Documentation, Vol.6, pp.155-169 (1960)

[Appendix A]

The proportion of the number of actually qualified pads to the total number of pads is given by the following,

$Pq(n)\min = 1 - ((K^2-1)/K^2)^{n-1}$,

where the number of query pad components is assumed to be two.

Let K denotes the number of all primitive pads' classes, Q a query pad and P an arbitrarily selected pad from the database. Suppose that the query pad Q is constructed with two primitive pads Q_1 and Q_2. We represent this pair as $(Q_1\text{-}Q_2)$, which means that the primitive pad Q_2 is directly pasted on the primitive pad Q_1. The proportion Pq turns out to be the probability that the pad composition structure has this pair $(Q_1\text{-}Q_2)$ as its substructure. Let us assume that the pad P is constructed with n primitive pads. Let P_1 and P_2 be two pads in an arbitrary pair in the composite pad. We represent this pair as $(P_1\text{-}P_2)$. If the class of P_1 and the class of Q_1 are the same, and if the class of P_2 and the class of Q_2 are the same, then the pair $(P_1\text{-}P_2)$ matches with the pair $(Q_1\text{-}Q_2)$. The probability that the class of P_1 and the class of Q_1 are different is given by $(K\text{-}1)/K$, while the probability that the class of P_1 and the class of Q_1 are the same and that the class of P_2 and the class of Q_2 are different is given by $(1/K)((K\text{-}1)/K)$. Then the probability that the pair $(P_1\text{-}P_2)$ does not match the query is given by $(K^2\text{-}1)/K^2$. The number of all the pairs in the pad P is obviously $n\text{-}1$. The probability that P does not include the query pair is now given by $((K^2\text{-}1)/K^2)^{n-1}$. Therefore, the probability that an arbitrarily selected pad is actually qualified is given by
$Pq(n)\min = 1 - ((K^2-1)/K^2)^{n-1}$.

[Appendix B]

The ratio of the number of the matched pad signatures to the size of the signature file is given by

$$Ps(W, Wq) = \prod_{i=0}^{Wq-1} (W-i)/(f-i),$$

where W is the weight of a pad signature and W_q is the weight of a query signature.

Let the bits that are set to '1' in the query signature be b_0, b_1, b_2, b_3, $\cdots$, b_{wq-1}, and the bits in the pad signature corresponding to b_0, b_1, b_2, b_3, $\cdots$, b_{wq-1} be s_0, s_1, s_2, s_3, $\cdots$, s_{wq-1}. The bit positions of b_i and s_i are the same. First, the probability that the two pad signatures' bits b_0 and s_0 are both set to '1' is given by W/f. Secondly, the probability that the two pad signatures' bits b_1 and s_1 are both set to '1' is given by $(W\text{-}1)/(f\text{-}1)$. In the same way, the probability that the two pad signatures' bits b_i and s_i both set to '1' is given by $(W-i)/(f-i))$. Then the probability that all are all set to '1' is given by $(W/f)\cdot((W\text{-}1)/(f\text{-}1))\cdots((W\text{-}(W_q\text{-}1))/(f\text{-}(W_q\text{-}1)))$.
Therefore, it holds that

$$Ps(W, Wq) = \prod_{i=0}^{Wq-1} (W-i)/(f-i).$$

Information Modelling and Knowledge Bases IX
P.-J. Charrel et al. (Eds.)
1998, IOS Press

Consistency of Information in Requirements Engineering

Marite Kirikova

Department of Systems Theory and Design, Riga Technical University, 1 Kalku, Riga, LV-1658 LATVIA, e-mail: marite@itl.rtu.lv

Consistency of information in requirements engineering does not guarantee that stated requirements will be correct and complete. However, it is a precondition for successful analysis of the application system and finding right requirements. Therefore possible sources of inconsistencies must be taken into consideration with the purpose to avoid a propagation of inconsistent information during requirements engineering.

1. Introduction

Consistency has been recognised to be a necessary quality of requirements specifications [1]. Nevertheless, few requirements engineering methodologies provide the possibility of computer aided consistency checking. Lack of interest in consistency can be argumented by scientifically proved impossibility to acquire completely correct information. As only formally incomplete information is at the disposal of a systems developer during requirements engineering, he never knows for certain whether it is correct or not, because incomplete information can be incorrect even if it is consistent. On the other hand, an attempt to examine consistency of information can require additional time for information acquisition and analysis, and this may threaten the possibility of doing the project in time.

It is true that consistency of information does imply its correctness if and only if the information is complete. Entirely complete information as well as entirely correct information is not available to human beings due to the limitations of their knowledge. However, there is a reason to consider consistency of information in requirements engineering even under the circumstances where fully correct and complete information is not available.

Requirements engineering is an enterprise that is intended for making changes in the application organisation with the purpose of improving its behaviour, functionality or competitiveness. For making changes in the organisation it is necessary to find basic causes of current problems, as well as to propose changes that eliminate current and do not cause new serious problems. However, it is recognised in organisational theory that in many cases, when the attempt to improve organisation is made, "the players involved are not getting to the basic causes of the problems. They are solving problems in superficial ways, and they are unrealisingly kidding themselves that this is not so" [2]. This organisational problem inherently becomes a requirements engineering problem because of the following reasons:

- problem may be present in the application organisation;
- requirements engineering team (with its goals and resources) itself is an organisation.

One of the reasons why problems are solved superficially can be the presence of defensive routines in an organisation. "Organisational defensive routines are actions or policies that prevent individuals or segments of the organisation from experiencing embarrassment and threat. Simultaneously, they prevent people from identifying and getting rid of the causes of embarrassment and threat. Organisational defensive routines are antilearning, overprotective and self sealing" [2]. A necessary condition for starting defensive routines is *the presence of inconsistent information* in decision making processes. The result of defensive routines is the propagation of inconsistent information. Defensive routines in an organisation are like positive feedback in a technical system, i.e. they gradually can cause unmanageability of an organisation. Therefore it is reasonable to detect these routines (if present) in the application organisation (old system), avoid them in the process of requirements engineering, and do not introduce them by the requirements into the new system. This, in turn, leads to the hypothesis that requirements engineering methodologies and tools have to be equipped with proper means for consistency support and checking.

The second section of the paper discusses sources of inconsistencies and its relationships with other qualities of information, such as completeness and correctness. The third section discusses the role of consistent information in requirements engineering. The fourth section analyses possibilities of consistency support and checking concerning present methodological state of art in requirements engineering. The fifth section consists of brief conclusions and shows the areas of further research.

2. Inconsistency of information, where does it come from?

While listening to somebody's presentation our brain is usually doing a consistency check and we are putting a question mark in each place where inconsistency is noticed. However, we are not always aware of inconsistency, because we also automatically add our own additions or replacements to the information to make the message logically sound, i.e. consistent [3]. Therefore, because of possible misunderstandings, not only the provider of information, but also the elicitor of knowledge can become a source of inconsistent information.

Inconsistencies are transferred by the language. In the context of the language we can consider three types of inconsistencies: syntactic, semantic and pragmatic [3, 4]. Syntactic inconsistency can be caused either by the use of two different systems of syntax, or by the violation of laws of syntax. For example, considering the concept "hill", the syntactic notions "kalns" and "hile" can be recognised as inconsistent. The former notion correctly expresses the concept "hill" in Latvian, but the latter one has originated from the incorrect spelling of the same concept in English. Semantic inconsistency arises from speaking about two different concepts, but pragmatic inconsistency, in turn, from considering the same concept in different contexts.

Consistency means that two or more "pieces" of information do not contradict in a given context. Requirements engineering is a process where information comes from many different natural knowledge systems. The interpretation of knowledge depends on the contents and functionality of a particular knowledge system. Language is just a mean of expressing knowledge, therefore basic causes of inconsistencies have to be searched in knowledge discrepancies and goals of participants involved in common activities [5, 6, 7].

2.1 Sources of inconsistent information in organisations

Two different sources of inconsistencies will be discussed in this subsection. Different background knowledge of participants in organisational activities is the first source of inconsistencies [6]. A defensive behaviour of one or more members of an organisation is the second one [2]. There is also the third possible source of inconsistencies, namely, the inconsistent knowledge of a particular individual. This kind of inconsistency can be checked only if the inconsistency is represented in an externalisation of the individual's knowledge.

Human knowledge is a dynamic system that gradually develops on the basis of its own contents and capabilities by using data and information available [8]. Although there is knowledge common to all people or particular groups of individuals, each individual possesses a unique knowledge system. In the organisational context, individual knowledge, as well as ways of knowledge development, may differ in a variety of ways and for different reasons (figure 1). The driving forces of knowledge development are the goals or purposes of an individual [9]. The process of knowledge development is influenced by different communication means available to the individual. Background knowledge differs also according to the actual work experience and education.

It is necessary to take into consideration that each individual understands organisation from its own viewpoint [10]. The viewpoint of the individual, in turn, is situated in a particular point in the space of possible organisational knowledge. The "location" of the point depends on the level of abstraction, the level of aggregation and the particular aspect or combinations of aspects of an organisation. Those three characteristics are not intended as an alternative definition of a viewpoint [10, 11], but are chosen pragmatically on the basis of research in organisational theory and information systems development. The relationships between different kinds of abstraction, generalisation, aggregation and partitioning possibilities [7, 12, 13] is a topic of further research and will not be discussed in this paper.

Inconsistent information, if detected, can be further analysed and, if possible, eliminated. However, organisational theory and practice show that the decision makers do not always seek for consistent information. They often base their decisions on inconsistent information. In that way the decision making process itself becomes an additional source of inconsistent information. If the use of inconsistent information is covered up, the defensive routines in organisation are enforced. These routines, in turn, are propagators of existing inconsistencies and generators of new inconsistencies. An embarrassment and threat perceived or anticipated by members of organisation can be a reason for the use of inconsistent information and involvement in the resulting organisational defenses [2].

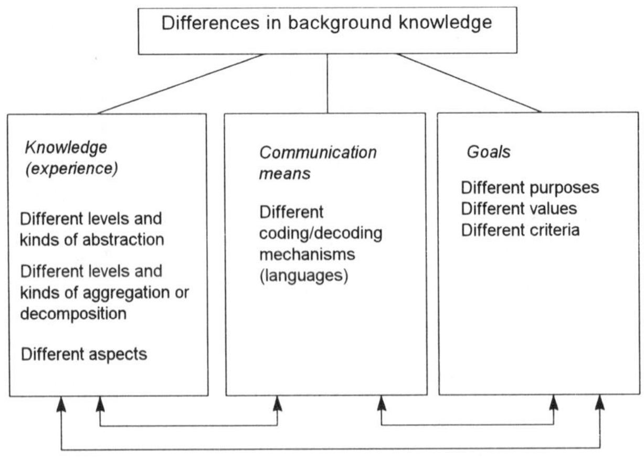

Fig. 1 Interrelated causes of differences in background knowledge

The mechanism of propagation and generation of inconsistent information by defensive routines is shown in figure 2. Making decisions on the basis of inconsistent information (the first bubble in figure 2) is a violation of managerial stewardship, that causes some threat to the decision maker concerning the error. To avoid the threat, it is covered up as regards to how and why the decision has been made (the second bubble). In that way inconsistency involved in the first decision is propagated further and new inconsistency introduced. Covering up also is a violation of managerial stewardship, therefore covering up is covered up, too (bubble 3). So, again previous inconsistencies are propagated and new ones introduced. Such decision making activities create inconsistent feedback in the organisation and gradually can crush managerial processes [2].

Organisational defensive routines are barriers that do not permit to find root causes of malfunctioning of organisations and consequently to state right requirements. Several organisational puzzles help to illustrate the barrier. The puzzles are the following [2]:

- The activities that produce success produce also failure.
- How the success is framed covers up the failure.
- The criteria of success in activities are not tough enough to deal with problems that plague managers in all levels in many different kinds of organisations.
- Players involved are not getting to the basic causes of the problems.

Figure 3 graphically depicts relationships between the puzzles. Business activities usually bring some failure together with the success. The activities are evaluated with respect to their goals. If the goals are reached, the activities are considered successful and framed in a way that the failure is not seen. In that way failure is covered, "put under the ground". However, it can not be taken out of an organisation and sooner or later manifests itself in different symptoms of malfunctioning of the organisation [2].

2.2 Relationships between inconsistency, incorrectness and incompleteness of information

According to A. Aamodt and M. Nygard [8] information is interpreted data. Knowledge, in turn, is information incorporated in an agent's reasoning resources and made ready for active use within a decision process. Neither an individual, nor humankind as a whole possesses entirely correct and entirely complete knowledge and information. So here we can discuss only relatively complete and relatively correct information. Information will be considered as complete if it comprises all the information relevant to particular decision making activity. Information will be considered correct if it corresponds to the laws and facts of nature and the society. Similarly, we can speak about complete and correct knowledge.

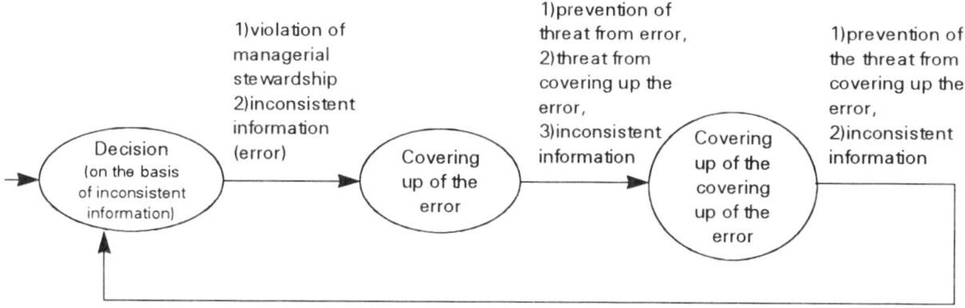

Fig. 2 Mechanism of organisational defenses

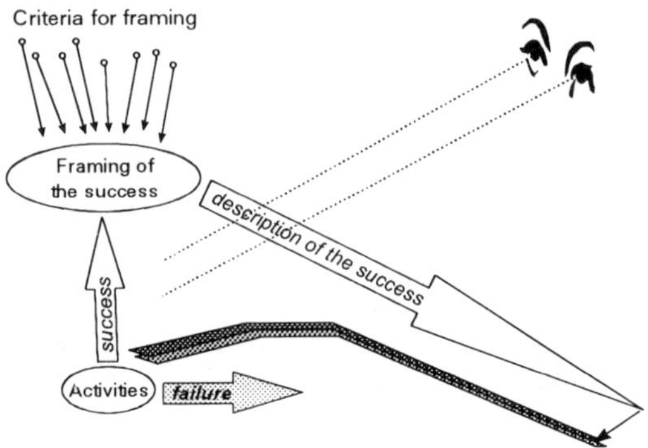

Fig. 3 Relationships between organisational puzzles: Cover up of failures by organisational defenses

Relationships between different qualities of knowledge are amalgamated in table 1. This table is arranged as follows. If information has a quality, depicted by the particular row of the table, then it also has (+) or has not (-) a particular quality depicted by the column. For example, if information is complete it is also correct and consistent and can not be incomplete, incorrect and inconsistent.

Table 1 clearly shows why the consistency of information may not be very interesting to researchers and practitioners in the field of information systems development. The reason is that the consistency of information does not imply its completeness or correctness. May be more notable is the fact that inconsistent information is necessarily incomplete. The relationship between inconsistency and correctness is interesting. Strictly speaking, inconsistent information is incorrect, however, if information is presented in different frames of reference it can be inconsistent (e.g. syntactically), but still correct. Correctness can be proved by translation from one frame of reference to another. If the frames of reference are appropriate, then inconsistency of information becomes quite an important quality to be investigated. In such situations it is a signal or symptom of incorrectness and incompleteness of information. In other words, consistency itself does not guarantee a good quality of information, but it is a precondition of such quality.

Table 1
Relationships between qualities of information

	Complete	Correct	Consistent	Incomplete	Incorrect	Inconsistent
Complete		+	+	-	-	-
Correct	+, -		+ (+, -)	+, -	-	- (+, -)
Consistent	+, -	+, -		+, -	+, -	-
Incomplete	-	+, -	+, -		+, -	+, -
Incorrect	-	-	+, -	+		+, -
Inconsistent	-	- (+, -)	-	+	+ (-, +)	

Decision making, an inherent organisational activity, uses information as its input and produces information as its output. However, the decisions are made not only on the basis of information but also on the basis of decision maker's knowledge [8]. Relationships between the quality of information and the quality of decision maker's knowledge are illustrated in table 2. The table is organised as follows. Rows show qualities of information. Columns depict qualities of knowledge. The "+" mark in cells means that, if information with a particular quality is processed by knowledge with a particular quality, then information still keeps its quality. In turn, "-" means, that information loses its quality. The mark "*" is used only for incomplete, inconsistent and incorrect information. This mark means that knowledge with a particular quality can identify a particular quality of information. Table 1 and Table 2 do not consider occasionalities, e.g., situations where incorrect information processed by incorrect knowledge produces correct information.

Table 2 shows two opportunities. The first is the opportunity of having complete, correct and consistent information. Information with such qualities may successfully pass (if there are necessary preconditions) processing by knowledge of different quality. The second is the opportunity of having complete, correct and consistent knowledge. Such knowledge can identify undesirable qualities of information.

There are several sources of inconsistent information in organisations (figure 4). Consistent information may not be available, because complete and correct, i.e., qualitative, information is not available at all. Qualitative information may not be known by individuals participating in an enterprise. It may also not be popular or not serving goals of particular individuals and groups and therefore not considered. Qualitative information can be misunderstood due to different background knowledge, frames of representation and communication modes of individuals (see also figure 1).

From the point of view of requirements engineering inconsistency of information is worth considering. The detection of inconsistencies can be helpful in finding effective ways of organisational analysis. Being a functioning system, organisation can introduce new inconsistencies, as well as propagate the existing ones. Investigation of propagation routes probably can also give additional material for finding the right requirements. According to section 2.1, two modes of propagation are to be considered: *open* propagation and *defensive* (covered up) propagation.

Another hypothesis suggested in this section is the importance of qualitative information with respect to decision makers' knowledge. A requirements engineering team, using appropriate methods, is able not only to identify inconsistent information, but it can also propagate consistent information for each individual participating in requirements engineering activities [14].

Table 2
Relationships between qualities of information and knowledge

	Complete	Correct	Consistent	Incomplete	Incorrect	Inconsistent
Complete	+	+, -	+, -	+, -	+, -	+, -
Correct	+	+, -	+, -	+, -	+, -	+, -
Consistent	+	+, -	+, -	+, -	+, -	+, -
Incomplete	*	+, *	+, *	+	+	+
Incorrect	*	+, *	+, *	+	+	+
Inconsistent	*	+, *	+, *	+	+	+

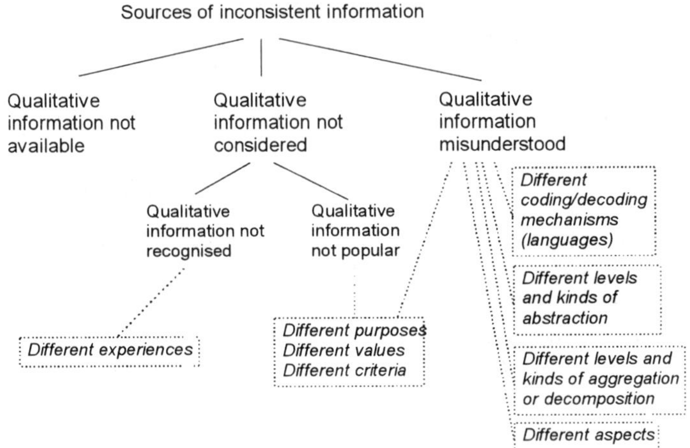

Fig. 4 Sources of inconsistent information in organisations

3. Role of consistent information in requirements engineering

Consistency of information in requirements engineering does not guarantee that stated requirements are correct and complete. However, non-contradictoriness of gathered information is a precondition for successful analysis of the application system and stating right requirements. Consistency of information is also necessary in order to avoid, detect and overcome organisational defenses during requirements engineering.

There are several reasons why organisational defenses are relevant for requirements engineering (figure 5):

1. Uncovered organisational defenses may be incorporated in requirements.
2. It may not be recognised that overcoming of defensive routines will take time and therefore the process of application organisation's development will be temporary slowed down.
3. Organisational defenses may slow down the process of requirements engineering.
4. Organisational defenses in the application (user) organisation may create organisational defenses in the development organisation.
5. Organisational defenses may be introduced by the development organisation.

If organisational defensive routines remain covered and are incorporated in the requirements, the new application system may function even worse than the old one. The reason for this is that the inconsistent feedback created by organisational defenses is supported by better means of propagation. More potent feedback may rush the processes in organisation more quickly.

When organisational defenses are uncovered, requirements evidently have to incorporate a system for overcoming organisational defenses. However, as the overcoming is based on application organisation's learning [2], the recovering from defensive behaviour can take quite a long time and requirements should be stated taking into consideration temporary slowdown of the application organisation.

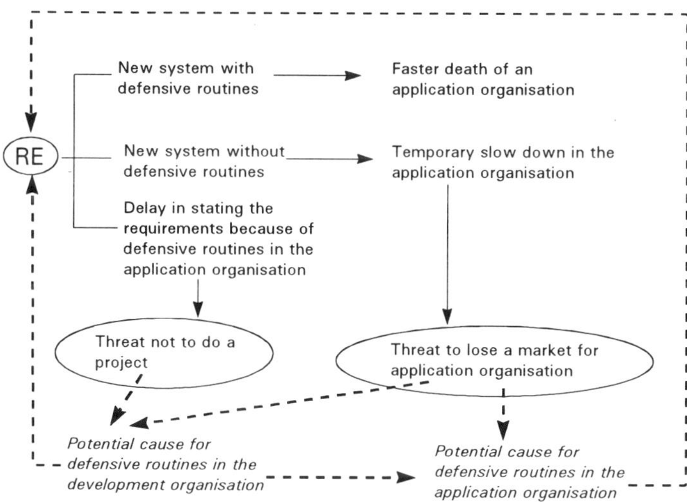

Fig. 5 Requirements engineering (RE) in an organisation with defensive routines

Other consequences of organisational defenses are problems with prompt decision making [2]. Requirements engineering requires lots of decision making activities on the part of application organisation's management. If the decision making is slowed down, then the stating of requirements is delayed, too. It, in turn, threatens the possibility to do the systems reengineering project in time.

The recognition of defensive routines, as well as the recognition of the necessity to slow down processes in organisation due to overcoming organisational defenses, may threaten the application organisation and introduce one more defensive feedback that influences the application organisation as well as the process of requirements engineering. Moreover, the threat of the application organisation may cause a threat to the development organisation concerning the threat of the application organisation's threat to accept the proposed project.

The threat of development organisation to do not do or stop the project can become a cause for the establishment of defensive routines by the development organisation. If that happens, the double defensive feedback influences the process of requirements engineering (RE) and hinders its success. Defensive feedback is maintained by inconsistent information. It seems that its presence is not a very rare event in a systems development practice. Inconsistent information may even be introduced by development organisation, e.g. by separately built functional and data oriented representations that do not fit together [15].

Another reason to seek for consistency of information is the necessity to facilitate organisational learning. During requirements engineering organisation learns not only by sharing information among the individuals, but also by becoming acquainted with artificial knowledge [14], i.e. information amalgamated in repositories. Therefore it is essential to have means for consistency check of artificial knowledge offered to individuals.

4. Eliminating inconsistencies during requirements engineering

This section will focus on possibilities of eliminating inconsistencies during the process of requirements engineering. The possibilities will be discussed from three different perspectives. The first perspective is the identification of inconsistent information. The

second perspective is the identification of propagation of inconsistencies and, the third one -
the facilitation of consistency by supporting organisational learning.

4.1 Identification of inconsistencies

In requirements engineering we can distinguish between the following two introducers of
inconsistent information:
- an application organisation - the provider of information;
- a requirements engineering team - the elicitor and amalgamator of information.

With respect to an application organisation, two kinds of inconsistencies must be
considered; namely, inconsistency provided by one particular individual and inconsistency of
information provided by different individuals. The latter has caused a problem in information
systems development, that is known as view or scheme integration and has been approached
in different ways by different researchers [11, 12, 16, 17]. Methods of view or scheme
integration may be useful in eliminating inconsistencies.

This paper proposes a hypothesis that a high quality of modelling capabilities can be
very helpful in the identification and elimination of inconsistencies. At the present state of art
different families of models are used in requirements engineering. They differ in
representation capabilities and architecture. There is no one general system of models and it
is argued that there is no need for such a system, as different methods are needed for
different situations [18]. However, complete, correct and consistent knowledge is helpful in
the detection of inconsistencies (table 2 in section 2.2). A system of models used in
requirements engineering, actually, may be considered as knowledge (artificial knowledge
[4]) that, if *satisfactory complete*, can be used for detecting inconsistency of information.
Further research is necessary to state explicit 'satisfactory completeness' criteria. Therefore
only two frameworks, that probably can be considered as complete, will be discussed in this
section, namely, the systematic framework for cognitive systems engineering [19] and the
theoretical framework for information systems development [20].

The systematic framework, that makes it possible to relate material and conceptual
characteristics of work environment to the cognitive characteristics and subjective
preferences of the staff, is suggested by the research work in cognitive systems engineering
[19]. This framework includes the following perspectives:
1. Work domain analysis in terms of means - ends structure.
2. Activity analysis in
    - work domain terms;
    - decision making terms;
    - terms of mental strategies that can be used.
3. Cognitive resources analysis in terms of actors competency, criteria and values.

The richest theoretical framework of models for information systems development
suggested by J.F. Sowa and J.A. Zachman offers the following perspectives:
1. Scope (planners perspective).
2. Enterprise model (owners perspective).
3. System model (designers perspective).
4. Technology (builders perspective).
5. Components (sub-contractors perspective).
This framework prescribes the following abstractions: data, functions, network (space),
people, time and motivation.

Actually, each diagram used in a family of models is a kind of abstraction. Several
abstractions from different perspectives or aspects can be made on the basis of the same
information. The particular level of completeness of artificial knowledge is necessary to
generate new abstractions from the information amalgamated in the repository. The

possibility to generate new information from the existing one is exemplified in figure 6. Diagrams D1 and D2 represent a combination of functional and time perspectives. Diagram D3 represents people's perspective. On the basis of these three diagrams the diagram D4 can be generated. It represents network perspective.

The possibility to generate new information on the basis of the information already amalgamated in the repository may be called a continuity of models. The continuity of models can be used as the means of checking inconsistencies. It gives the possibility to reframe information I^x, elicited and amalgamated in terms of perspective or abstraction X, in a way this information could be compared with information I^y that reflects the same phenomenon, but has been acquired from another perspective or level of abstraction Y. Modelling environment GRADE [21] is an example of family of models that partly exploits the continuity of models. Potentially, architecture of many other methodologies also has this capability, but continuity of models usually is not exploited [22].

Activity analysis in decision making terms [19] is a quite rare quality of requirements engineering methodologies [6, 23, 24]. However, this kind of modelling formality is essential for considering inconsistencies with respect to organisational defenses (figure 2 in section 2.1). If consistency check is impossible, then defensive routine cannot be recognised. Therefore models that support analysis of decision making processes seem to be a necessary constituent of requirements engineering frameworks. This kind of analysis is useful not only in decision making processes in application organisations, but also in decision making processes performed by the requirements engineering team.

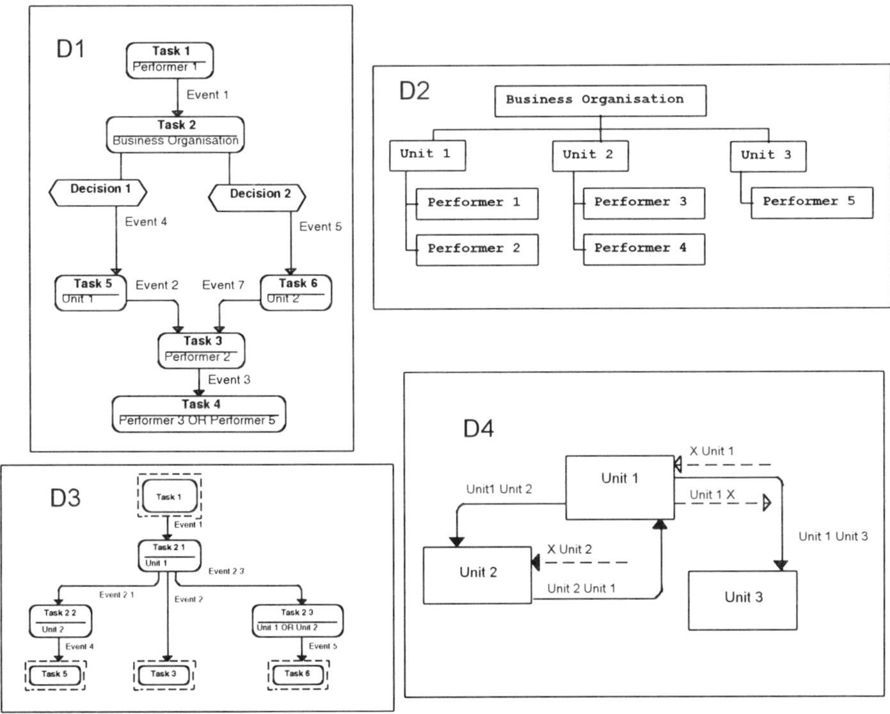

Fig 6 Continuity of models in modelling environment GRADE

4.2 Analysis of inconsistencies propagation

There are two possible modes of propagation of inconsistencies in organisation: open propagation and defensive propagation. Open propagation of inconsistencies can be analysed by investigation of information paths in process models of an enterprise. A more complicated problem is the analysis of defensive propagation of inconsistencies. In this case an inconsistency of information is covered up and usually cannot be directly recognised. Possibilities of analysing defensive propagation of inconsistencies will be discussed in the remainder of this subsection.

Existence of defensive routines in organisations can show up as several symptoms of malfunctioning of organisation [2]. Some of these symptoms are presented in figure 7. Identification of symptoms could be the first step in the analysis of defensive propagation of inconsistencies. Computer aided means for symptoms detection may be useful, although not all symptoms can be identified in a formal way.

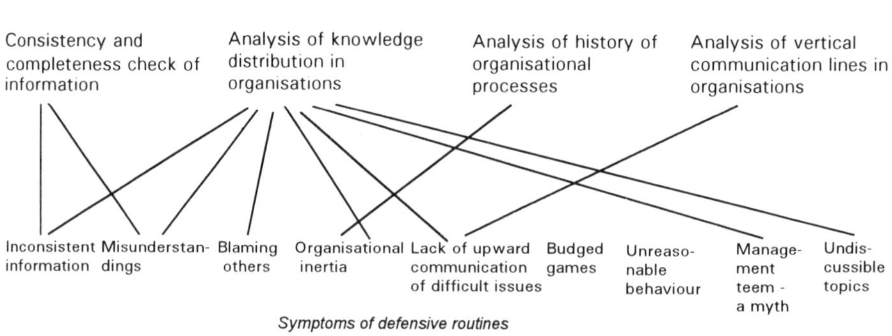

Fig. 7 Some possible computer aided means for the identification of a number of symptoms

The following computer aided means of symptoms detection can be used during requirements engineering:
- consistency and completeness check of information (described in section 4.1);
- analysis of knowledge distribution in organisations [14];
- analysis of history of organisational processes;
- analysis of vertical communication lines in organisation.

After the detection of symptoms some kind of failure analysis can be applied. However, the application of fault analysis in the setting of organisations analysis differs from the fault analysis in technical systems and is not yet properly researched.

Defensive propagation of inconsistent information could be analysed also by framing the success *and* failure, not success alone (figure 3). Business activities usually bring some failure besides success. The activities are evaluated with respect to their goals. If goals have been reached, the activities are considered as successful and framed in a way that the failure is not seen. However, experienced systems analysts suggest to consider positive, as well as negative, aspects of intended innovations [25, 26]. The hypothesis concerning dilemmas of IS development [26] is one more argument regarding reasonability to frame both, success *and* failure. The hypothesis states that to be successful one must often address the opposite and contradictory alternatives of the dilemma simultaneously, even though one can not pursue them at the same time. The hypothesis can be supported by application of Kelly's Personal Constructs Theory in requirements engineering. The theory has been introduced in psychology and is applied also by business consultants and supported by appropriate tools [27].

4.3. Facilitating organisational learning

In an organisation the process of learning takes place during requirements engineering. From the point of view of organisational theory [2] it is essential to acquire consistent information. Decision making on the basis of consistent and valid information, supported by necessity to monitor responsibility for decisions made, in turn, stimulates organisation to seek valid and consistent information (figure 8).

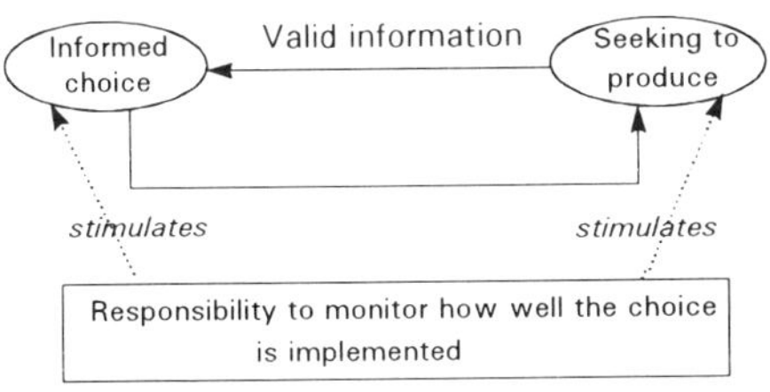

Fig. 8 Overcoming organisational defenses by organisational learning [2]

Requirements engineering team should be able to offer valid and consistent information concerning the current state of the systems development activities in order to avoid, not to introduce, and overcome organisational defensive routines. This requirement can be met if there are means for consistency checking of the information amalgamated in the repository. To facilitate organisational learning, information concerning individual knowledge used in requirements engineering process, i.e. maintenance of knowledge distribution, can be helpful. The analysis of knowledge distribution opens the possibility of the following improvements in knowledge exchange and communications [14], which are relevant in organisational learning:

1. Selection of people for group sessions may be based on taking into the consideration cognitive aspects of communication [3]
   - people with different understanding of the same concepts may be invited to clarify their understanding, as well as models reflecting the concepts under discussion;
   - before interviews and group sessions potential participants may be assisted by materials presented in a form that stimulates their thinking about the topic under discussion (concepts provided are directly or associatively related to the concepts used by the particular individual) .
2. Partners for non-formal communications may be chosen on the basis of knowledge distribution.

One more conclusion to be drawn here is the necessity to model responsibility patterns of individuals to facilitate seeking for consistent information. Analysis of responsibilities is a well known means for total quality management [28], but it is not always included in the toolbox of requirements engineering.

Only some of the means for eliminating inconsistencies in requirements engineering are discussed in this section. Actually, all sources of inconsistencies should be considered (figures 1, 2 and 3) for the development of the means that promote consistency of information. The paper presents only first findings on consistency support and does not claim to completeness of suggestions.

5. Conclusions

Consistency of information in requirements engineering sometimes is not considered as an essential quality of knowledge amalgamated in repositories. However, the usage of inconsistent information can cause many problems in systems development, e.g., such as incorporation of organisational defensive routines in requirements. Therefore means for consistency checking and support can be helpful for eliminating errors in requirements engineering and stating the right requirements.

The following means for checking, maintenance, and support of information consistency are suggested:

- consistency check of externalised individuals knowledge;
- completeness of modelling frameworks;
- usage of continuity of models;
- investigation of information paths in process models of an enterprise;
- modelling activities in decision making terms;
- framing the success and failure simultaneously;
- maintenance of consistency in a repository;
- analysis of responsibility patterns.

The paper presents initial research results concerning maintenance of reasonable consistency of models developed during requirements engineering. Further research is envisaged concerning representation frameworks and analysis procedures supporting consistency checking and maintenance.

Acknowledgement

I acknowledge Professor Janis Grundspenkis (Riga Technical University, Latvia) for valuable comments on the draft of the paper.

References

[1] Davis A.M. *Software Requirements: Analysis and Specifications.* Englewood Cliffs, N.J.: Prentice Hall, Inc., 1990.

[2] Argyris C. *Overcoming Organisational Defenses: Facilitating Organisational Learning.* Prentice-Hall, Inc., 1990.

[3] Anderson J.R. *Cognitive Psychology and Its Implications.* Freeman and Company, 1990.

[4] Beaurgrande R. General Constraints on Process Models of Language Comprehension. *Issues in Cognitive Modelling.* A.M. Aithenhead and J.M. Slock (Eds.), Lawrence Erlbaum, Ltd., 1990.

[5] McGraw K.L. and Harbison-Briggs K. *Knowledge Acquisition: Principles and Guidelines,* Prentice Hall, Inc., 1989.

[6] Zuurbier J., et al. Towards a Design Methodology for Decision Support Systems. *Proceedings of the Twenty Seventh Annual Havaii International Conference of Systems Sciences (HICSS-27).* J. Nunamaher and R. Sprogue (Eds.), IEEE Computer Science Press, Vol. III, 1994, P. 25 - 32.

[7] Marjomaa E. Categories and Mutual Relevance: A semiotic point of view. *Information Modelling and Knowledge Bases.* Y.Tanaka et al. (Eds.), IOS Press, 1996, P. 139 - 153.

[8] Aamodt A. and Nygard M. Different roles and mutual dependencies of data, information, and knowledge - An AI perspective on their integration. *Data and Knowledge Engineering* 16 (1995) P. 191-222.

[9] Newell A. The Knowledge Level. *Artificial Intelligence,* 18, 1982, P. 87 - 127.

[10] Charrel P-J., et al. Multiple Viewpoints for the Design of Complex Space Systems. *Proceedings of the 4th Workshop on Artificial Intelligence and Knowledge-Based Systems for Space* 17-19 May, 1993. ESTEC, Noordwijk, The Netherlands, 1993. P. 251 - 272.

[11] Batini C., et al. Views Integration. *Methodology and Tools for database design.* S. Ceri (Ed.), North-Holland, 1983. P. 57 - 84.

[12] Kangassalo H. COMIC: A system and methodology for conceptual modelling and information construction. *Data &Knowledge Engineering,* 9, North Holland, 1992/93. P. 287 - 319.

[13] Motschning R. and Kaasboll J. Part-Whole Relationship categories and Their Application in Object-Oriented Analysis. *Proceedings of the 5th International Conference on Information Systems Development.* S. Wrycza and J. Zupancic (Eds.), Gdansk, Poland, September 24 -26, 1996.

[14] Kirikova M. Knowledge Distribution During Requirements Engineering. *Information Modelling and Knowledge Bases VIII.* H. Kangassalo et al. (Eds.), 1997, P. 167 - 180.

[15] Coad P. and Yordon E. *Object Oriented Analysis,* Object International, Inc., 1991.

[16] Song W. *Schema Integration - Principles, Methods, and Applications.* Doctoral Thesis. Department of Computer and Systems Sciences, Stockholm University, The Royal Institute of technology, Sweden, 1995.

[17] Hakkarainen S. Analysing and Evaluating Heuristic Support for Scheme Comparison. *Information Modelling and Knowledge Bases.* Y. Tanaka et al. (Eds.), IOS Press, 1996, P. 105 - 119.

[18] Brinkkemper S. Method Engineering: Engineering of Information Systems Development Methods and Tools. *Proceedings of the 5th International Conference on Information Systems Development.* S. Wrycza and J. Zupancic (Eds.), Gdansk, Poland, September 24 -26, 1996, P. 227 - 286.

[19] Rasmussen J., et al. *Cognitive Systems Engineering.* John Willey & Sons, Inc., 1994.

[20] Sowa J.F. and Zachman J.A. Extending and Formalising the Framework for Information Systems Architecture. *IBM Systems Journal.* Vol. 31. No 3, 1992, P. 590 - 616.

[21] Barzdins J., et al. *Business Modelling Language GRAPES BM - 3.0 and Its Use,* Riga, RITI, 1996, (in Latvian).

[22] Kirikova M., et al. Acquiring Additional Information from Repositories. *Proceedings of the 5th International Conference on Information Systems Development.* S. Wrycza and J. Zupancic (Eds.), Gdansk, Poland, September 24 -26, 1996, P. 227 - 286.

[23] Ramackers G.J. *Integrated Object Modelling: An Executable Specification Framework for Business Analysis and Information Systems Design.* Dissertation. Amsterdam. Thesis Publishers, 1994.

[24] Joosten S. and Brinkkemper S. Fundamental Concepts for Workflow in Practice. . *Proceedings of the 5th International Conference on Information Systems Development.* S. Wrycza and J. Zupancic (Eds.), Gdansk, Poland, September 24 -26, 1996, P. 311 -322.

[25] Kendall, K.E. and Kendall, J.E. *Systems Analysis and Design,* 3rd edition, Prentice Hall International, Inc., 1995.

[26] Iivari J. Dilemmas of IS Development. *Proceedings of the 5th International Conference on Information Systems Development.* S. Wrycza and J. Zupancic (Eds.), Gdansk, Poland, September 24 -26, 1996, P. 35 - 54.

[27] Cropper S., et al. Keeping Sense of Accounts Using Computer Based Cognitive Maps. *Social Science Computer Review 8:3. Fall 1990.* Duce University Press., 1990.

[28] Sage A.P. *Systems Engineering.* John Willey & Sons, Inc. , 1992.

Information Modelling and Knowledge Bases IX
P.-J. Charrel et al. (Eds.)
1998, IOS Press

Mutual Redundancy in Conceptual Schemas

Peter Eden
Centre for Information Systems Research
School of Information Technology
Swinburne University of Technology
Hawthorn, Victoria 3122
AUSTRALIA
Email: peden@swin.edu.au

Abstract: It is desirable to incorporate different user's views into a conceptual schema, but inclusion of redundant information structures can complicate the schema. Where there are mutually redundant fact types to be modelled in a conceptual schema, we show the *commuting loop* constraint is adequate for practical situations. Even if the constraint is not immediately evident, it can be admitted by introducing a new semantically meaningful concept to the schema.

1. Introduction

Conceptual modelling aims to represent users' understandings of information in their own organisational context. Each user has their special view of the organisation, parts of which will be shared with other users. The full extent of information about the real world which any user views is known as the Universe of Discourse (UoD) [24]. Semantic and object oriented data models have been used to model UoD information structures. The task of conceptual schema design is to integrate all user views of UoD facts in a single schema. Where mutual redundancy exists, that is there are views that are mutually related by logical implication, it is important that this data structure is fully specified.

There are certain principles we recognise as influencing the quality of the conceptual schema. [24][30][1]. A conceptual schema should not contain any information that was not implicit in any user view (Conceptualisation principle); specifically there should be no bias towards any particular storage implementation. Distinct UoD concepts should be modelled by distinct and unique constructs in the conceptual schema (Separation of concepts). Any concept not directly represented should be inferable from the schema (Inferential completeness); rather than represent every user view directly, the schema should be sufficiently complete to derive all views by transformation [20][30]. UoD concepts should be represented in the simplest possible way to facilitate communication and reasoning (Minimum complexity).

In practice there is a tradeoff among these desirable properties. Not all user views can be directly represented without requiring complex constraints. A single integrated schema that supports multiple perceptions is the best compromise.

This paper addresses the problem of how best to represent mutually redundant fact types in conceptual schemas. We find that by assuming some apparently reasonable limits on the complexity of natural information structures, a single structure called a *commuting loop* is sufficient to model mutually redundant fact types.

The problem of multiple representations of a UoD has been addressed in different ways by authors of data and conceptual modelling, specifically in respect of the relational data model, NIAM and view integration. In the relational data model, two alternative equivalent lossless join database designs imply the existence of a pair of mutually redundant sets of base relations, each derivable from the other by projection and join. The problem of nonunique lossless join 4NF database designs [13] stimulated the search for a design method that would generate all alternatives for situations encountered in practice. The richness of functional and multivalued dependencies seemed to allow a complexity not met in practice [29]. The Simplified Universal Relation Assumption (SURA) states that constraints that are likely to be encountered in the real world are limited to a single join dependency with embodied functional dependencies [18]. Even under SURA, nonunique designs are possible, but by extending the database schema by adding attributes, it is possible to restrict any nonuniqueness to decomposition of the components of the join dependency by the Integrated Approach [4]. Even though semantic and object oriented models deal with more complex data than the relational data model, this result is relevant in limiting the complexity of natural information.

In conceptual modelling by NIAM [21], the semantics of the conceptual schema is based on the notion of valid schema populations. A population is a relational database where each row is a deep structured representation of a natural language fact. Although the problem of nonunique representation has been mitigated by the use of schema transformations [20] in conceptual modelling, none of these transformations permit the recovery of the alternative database designs allowed by the Integrated Approach. This suggests that NIAM may not always deliver a conceptual schema that is sufficiently redundant to contain the views of all alternative database designs and therefore all users.

View integration is concerned with resolving alternative view of shared information [6]. When modelling users' concepts of the UoD, based on their verbalisation, it is not uncommon for users to describe shared views in different ways. This may result in conflicts between the conceptual schemas representing the different views. The literature on view integration has been concerned with merging conceptual schemas by resolving conflicts between component schemas. They compare structural features in the schemas themselves, rather than the semantics in underlying populations. Merging views on the basis of structural similarity would be validated by expert users. Conflicts arising from naming are primary because users can only communicate in a shared view if they share a vocabulary. Thereafter, structure conflicts arise from different ways of representing shared concepts in the component views. Thus a relationship in one schema could be derived by a join of relationships in another [25]. Arbitrary equivalent join paths in component schemas result in inter-schema loops in ERC+ view integration [28]. Generally mutually derivable relationships have not been treated in view integration.

The commuting loop constraint [12] was recognised as significant in semantic data modelling and recently for mutual redundancy [16]. It was originally identified as the *repeating dependency* [8] in the relational data model. Independently, an equivalent notion, *path equation* constraint, was formulated for an object-oriented data model [10]. The implications of this constraint for mutual redundancy in semantic and object-oriented data models has not otherwise been observed.

The organisation of the paper is as follows. In the next section we review the data model used in the paper, the Predicator Set Model (PSM). All schemas are based on PSM. In the following section, mutual redundancy is defined with examples to illustrate how it is modelled by the commuting loop constraint. The commuting loop theorem generalises the examples. In the next section, we generalise mutual redundancy and show that with the addition of a new object type, it can still be reduced to a commuting loop. This construction is illustrated with an example. In the last section, we observe that further generalisation of mutual redundancy is unlikely to be of practical value. We conclude with a summary, a conjecture about the complexity of natural information and possible further work.

2. PSM Conceptual Schema

As we are concerned here only with conceptual views of information, we take a traditional semantic data modelling approach to the conceptual modelling process as shown in NIAM [21] based as it is on natural language. NIAM is one of the earliest [31] and most comprehensive information modelling processes. In this approach, concepts are validated by populations of natural language sentences. However NIAM is suitable for modelling only flat data and cannot directly model complex structured objects. An extension, the Predicator Set Model (PSM) [22] [23], allows sets and lists of objects. The NIAM conceptual modelling process can be extended to PSM [11]. We briefly describe the PSM conceptual data model.

The Universe of Discourse (UoD) is defined as the set $\mathcal{U}$ of all possible valid populations of linguistic utterances or sentences about the world. A population is a snapshot which describes a possible legal state of reality. The conceptual modelling task is to find a well formed schema Σ such that every valid population $\mathbf{P} \in \mathcal{U}$ is a true interpretation of the schema Σ, $\mathbf{P} \models \Sigma$.

The conceptual modelling language used in PSM is based on many sorted predicate logic [2] [19]. A PSM [22] schema Σ consists of a set of predicators p (attributes) each of which is attached to an object type $Base(p)$. An object type is either atomic or complex. An atomic object type is either lexical or nonlexical, associated with a domains of values that are lexical or abstract, respectively. A complex object is either a fact type or a power type. A fact type f is constructed from a set f of predicators. Each predicator p belongs to a unique fact type $Fact(p)$. A power type g is constructed from an object type $Elt(g)$. Binary fact types whose two predicators have lexical and an atomic nonlexical domain are called reference types. The semantics of a PSM schema is given by populations. The population $Pop(x)$ of an atomic object type x is a set of values from its domain. The population of a fact type f is a set of tuples t over f such that $t(p) \in Pop(Base(p))$. The population of a power type g is a set of subsets of $Pop(Elt(g))$. PSM supports a number of constraint types, particularly uniqueness and mandatory role constraints. A legal population $\mathbf{P}$ of a schema Σ is a collection of populations of object types of the schema that satisfy the constraints, $\mathbf{P} \models \Sigma$.

A fact *t* in a population of the fact type $f \in \Sigma$ can be understood as a deep structure tree-diagram [9] whose constituents are abstract values *t(p) for p* $\in$ *f*. For example, the tuple LIKES(*john, {icecream, chocolate}*) represents the deep structure in Fig. 1.

By replacing the surrogate object identifiers by references, for example, *john* by *Person with PersonName "John"*, the fact is transformable to the surface structure sentence *John likes icecream with chocolate*. By using different references or different linguistic transformations the same fact can have different surface expressions. Thus a population of facts can be validated with the user in natural language. The graphical notation used to draw PSM schemas is shown in Fig.2.

To standardise and simplify schema specification, it is convenient to borrow notation from the relational model. Wherever possible, name predicators *p* by their base object type names and so a fact type *L* will be written LIKES(Person, SetofFood). The schema in Fig. 2 is then Σ = ({LIKES(Person, SetofFood), MADE-OF(Food, SetofFood)}, Δ}, where Δ is the set of constraints.

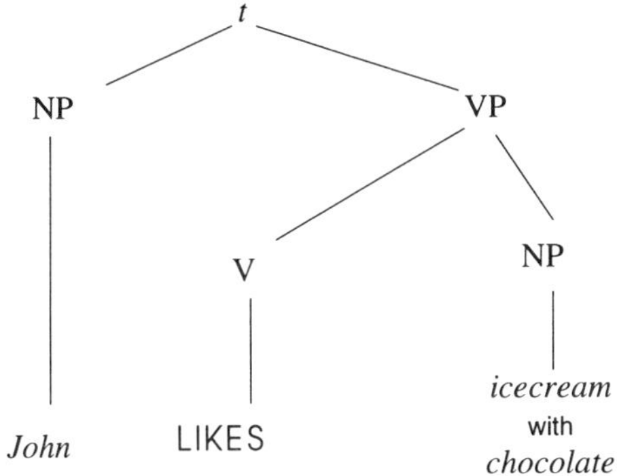

Fig. 1 Deep Structure

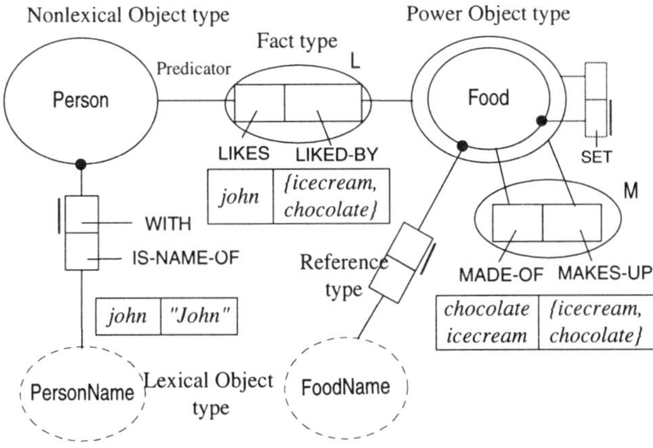

Fig. 2 PSM Schema

In PSM, a relational algebra that includes projection [], selection and join $\bowtie$ allows new fact types to be derived. If a set of predicators is "joinable by common object types" [3], the fact types along the path formed by the predicators and common object types can be joined "naturally". For example in Fig. 2, predicators **LIKES** and **MAKES-UP** are joinable by common object type **Food**. With an abuse of notation, the join looks like a relational natural join:

LIKES$\bowtie$ MADE-OF(Person, Food) = LIKES(Person, SetofFood) $\bowtie$ MADE-OF(Food, SetofFood)[Person, Food]

with Pop(LIKES$\bowtie$ MADE-OF) = {*<john, chocolate icecream>*}

NIAM provides a rich set of constraints which are used to limit the sets of allowable populations to those observable in the UoD. Uniqueness and mandatory role constraints are illustrated in Fig. 2 where a **Person** can have only one **PersonName** and must have a **PersonName**. Subset (inclusion) constraints are also supported; for example the constraint that *"A person likes a food made from any combination foods he likes"* is notated as:

LIKES(Person, SetofFood) $\bowtie$ MADE-OF(Food, SetofFood) $\bowtie$ SET (Food, SetofFood') [Person, SetofFood'] $\subseteq$ LIKES[Person, SetofFood'].

In summary, PSM is structurally object oriented in having a record (fact) and set (power) type constructors and object identifiers (abstract values).

3. Mutual Redundancy

By mutual redundancy in a (PSM) schema Σ, we understand there are at least two subcollections of fact types $\mathcal{B}_1$, $\mathcal{B}_2$ of (base) fact types such that any fact type $f \in \mathcal{B}_1\backslash\mathcal{B}_2$ and any $g \in \mathcal{B}_2\backslash\mathcal{B}_1$ can be derived (by the relational algebra) from fact types in $\mathcal{B}_2$. and $\mathcal{B}_1$, respectively. Specifically, the redundancy is between $\mathcal{B}_1\backslash\mathcal{B}_2$ and $\mathcal{B}_2\backslash\mathcal{B}_1$. If the derivation of any fact type in $\mathcal{B}_1\backslash\mathcal{B}_2$ requires more than one fact type in $\mathcal{B}_2\backslash\mathcal{B}_1$ (or vice versa), there is *multiple* mutual redundancy, otherwise it is *single*. We will be investigating derivations of the form $(\bowtie F)[X] \subseteq g$ where $F\subseteq \mathcal{B}_1$, and $g \in \mathcal{B}_2\backslash\mathcal{B}_1$.

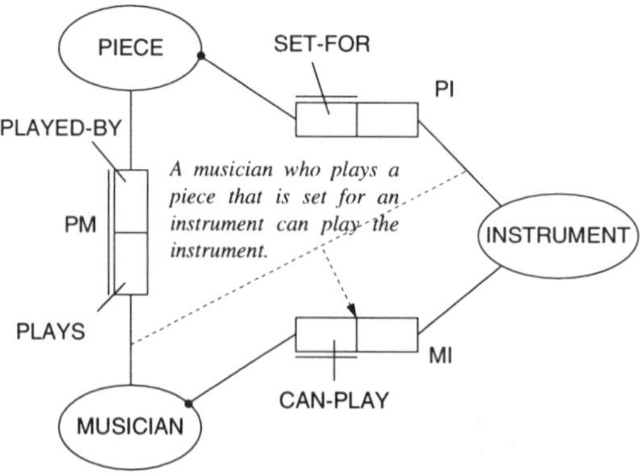

Fig. 3 PMI with Join Subset Constraint

For example, consider the situation where in one view, musical pieces are set for instruments and are played by musicians and in another view, musicians play pieces and can play instruments. Let us assume that pieces are set for only one instrument and that a musician can play only one instrument. The two views can be combined in the schema in Fig.3. As a musician who plays a piece must be able the instrument for which the piece is set, the two views are compatible only with the addition of a join subset constraint [21]: PM▷◁PI [MI] ⊆ MI[MI], shown graphically in Fig.3.

Observe also that musicians play only the pieces set for the instrument they can play. We add another "mirror image" join subset constraint, as shown in Fig. 4. This example is a simple, but yet essential illustration of a pair of mutually redundant fact types, viz PI and MI. If the subset constraints are strengthened to equality constraints, we generate three lossless join database designs; {PI,PM}, {PM,MI}, {PI,PM,MI}. This is an example of *single* mutual redundancy. The mutually redundant fact types PI and MI have functional uniqueness constraints with a common object type INSTRUMENT, called the *intersecting attribute*.

This situation is the most common one involving mutual redundancy that is likely to occur in practice. It has been argued that this situation should be modelled by a single constraint , the *commuting loop* constraint [16] in the conceptual schema. It has also been shown [15] that pairs of partially redundant fact types with functional uniqueness constraints are always characterised by the commuting loop constraint. The semantics are best understood by equality of evaluation of queries along alternative paths concluding at the intersecting attribute, INSTRUMENT. The notation is illustrated in Fig. 5.

In this example, mutual redundancy seems to depend critically on the functional uniqueness constraints. If we allow a musician to play multiple instruments or a piece to be set for many instruments, the join subset constraints fails, along with the redundancy.

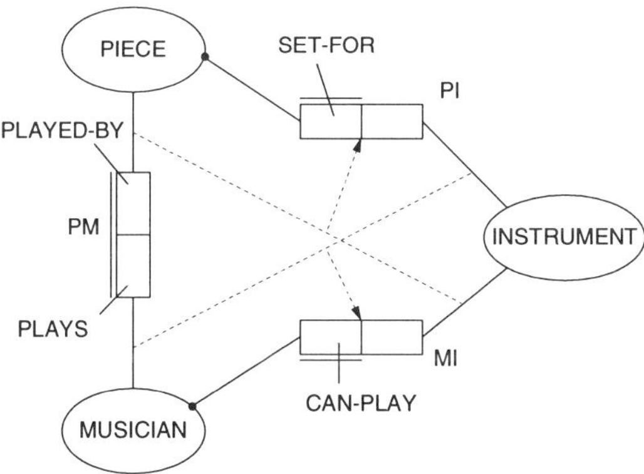

Fig. 4 PMI Join Subset Constraint Pair

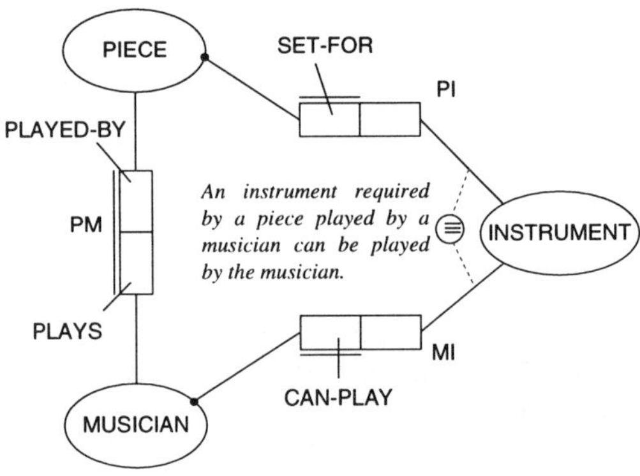

Fig. 5   PMI Commuting Loop Constraint

4. Commuting Loop Constraint

Simple mutual redundancy with functional fact types determining a common intersecting attribute has a number of equivalent formulations established by the commuting loop theorem.

4.1 Commuting Loop Theorem

Given a nonintersecting path of connected fact types R in a PSM schema, naming predicators by their base object types, define the join along the path by the natural join $J=\bowtie R(X)$ over the corresponding relations $R(X)$.

The commuting loop constraint captures the semantics that for any object type in a loop, if a value in the population of the object type is chosen, there is a unique corresponding value of another object type, called the *intersecting attribute*, which is the same, no matter what path of intermediate values is chosen. This is captured in the formal definition: a commuting loop constraint applies at intersecting attribute A if the join J around the loop from A and back to A results in identical columns ie. $J[A_p\ A_q\ ] \subseteq J[AA]$, written $J{:}A_p \equiv A_q$. See Fig.6.

The Commuting Loop Theorem states that the commuting loop constraint is fully characterised by certain combinations of uniqueness and join subset constraints.

Let predicators p and q with common base object type A, be in a loop such that the join $J(A_pXZYA_q) = P\bowtie R\bowtie Q$ along the loop is defined, where $P(A_pX)=Fact(p)$, $Q(YA_q)= Fact(q)$ and $R(XZY)$ is the (possibly derived) fact type which closes the loop. See Fig.6. There is no limit imposed on the size of the loop.

Suppose constraints
$P[X] \supseteq R[X],\ \ Q[Y] \supseteq R[Y]$ hold.
then
$R\bowtie Q[XA_q] \subseteq P[XA_p]^{①} \wedge\ P{:}\ X \to A_p$

$\Rightarrow$

$P\bowtie R\bowtie Q\ :\ A_p \equiv A_q$

$\Leftrightarrow$

$$P \bowtie R[A_p Y] \subseteq Q[A_q Y]^{\oslash} \wedge R \bowtie Q: Y \to A_q$$
and
$$P \bowtie R \bowtie Q : A_p \equiv A_q$$
$$\Leftrightarrow$$
$$R[XY] \subseteq P \bowtie_{p=q} Q[XY]^{\oslash} \wedge P \bowtie R: X \to A_p \wedge R \bowtie Q: Y \to A_q$$

For a proof of the theorem see [15]. The theorem tells us that a number of different combinations of uniqueness and join subset constraints are equivalent to the commuting loop.

The UoD is a theoretical construct used to found data modelling. In practice, it can never be known. The NIAM modelling process assumes that *significant* populations are known, ie. the population is a set of Armstrong relations [27]. NIAM directs that any facts that are derivable from other facts are eliminated. Only the user expert can decide if a fact is subsumed by other facts. There is no guarantee that a sample population is minimal with respect to logical implication. Choosing between whether sample facts should be modelled by a base fact type or a derived fact type may violate the conceptualisation principle. Alternatively, we could choose to retain derivable sample facts, especially if they originated from a valid user view and model them as base fact types. Consequently, populations will in general give rise to schemas whose component fact types are related by logical implication. To specify consistency between conjunctions, a subset constraint over a join is required [14]. It is particularly desirable to model alternative views if they are mutually derivable, so recognition of the commuting loop as a simple and comprehensive characterisation of mutual redundancy is a useful contribution to conceptual modelling. This strategy would seem to better promote inferential completeness and minimal complexity of the conceptual schema.

It is not immediately evident whether the commuting loop is sufficient to model all situations involving mutually redundancy, so we explore this next.

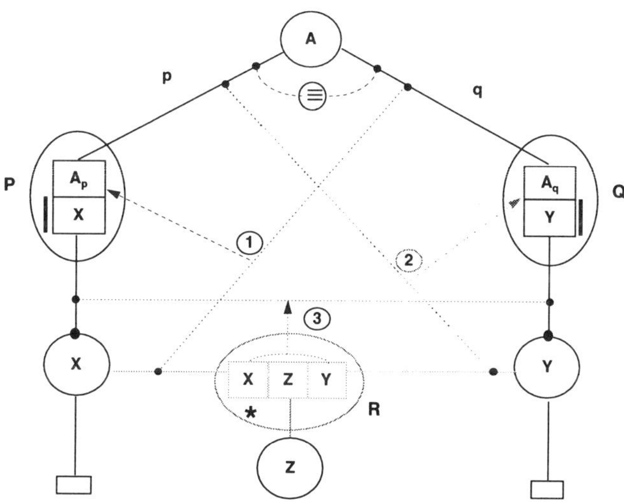

Fig. 6 Commuting Loop Theorem

5. Single Mutual Redundancy

The commuting loop fully characterises single, mutually redundant, functional fact types that determine a common object type. In this section, we show that a schema with general simple mutual redundancy can be extended in such a way that the mutual redundancy can be made equivalent to a commuting loop. That is, even if the mutually redundant single fact types are not functional, there is still an underlying commuting loop structure.

Proposition:

In any schema where there are single mutually derivable fact types, the schema can be transformed to an equivalent one by the addition of an intersecting attribute and a commuting loop.

Nonconstructive Proof:

Consider a schema in which two relationships R(XY), S(UV) are mutually derivable: ie. there exist relationships P(XU), Q(VY) with equality dependencies: R[XY] = P▷◁S▷◁Q[XY], S[UV] = P▷◁R▷◁Q[UV] as in

Fig. 7(a). As predicators are unique to fact types, attribute sets X,Y,U,V are disjoint. As P▷◁R▷◁Q▷◁S = P▷◁R▷◁Q = P▷◁S▷◁Q, MVDs U→→X|VY, V→→Y|UX, X→→U|VY, Y→→V|UX hold in the context of P▷◁R▷◁Q▷◁S. In [4], it is shown that where a pair of MVDs X→→*DEP*(X), U→→*DEP*(U) have an *intersection anomaly*, ie. X∩U→→*DEP*(X)∩*DEP*(U) does not hold, a transformation which introduces a new attribute A will remove the anomaly. The transformed schema becomes XA→→*DEP*(X), UA→→*DEP*(U), X∩UA→→*DEP*(X)∩*DEP*(U), X→A, U→A. Here A is an intersecting attribute. This extension when projected preserves all original FDs and MVDs. Applying this transformation (twice) to the schema, as shown in

Fig. 7(b), eliminates the complex equality dependencies and replaces them with simpler commuting loop constraints.

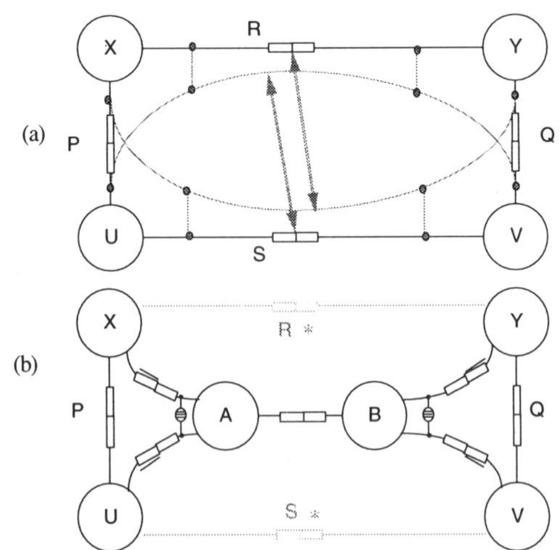

Fig. 7 Transforming Mutually Derivable Fact Types

The above proof is nonconstructive and does not provide semantics for the new attributes. If the uniqueness constraints in Fig. 6 are relaxed, simple mutual redundancy is shown in Fig. 8. Introduce an object type K, as in Fig. 9 whose instances are equivalence classes on R under the equivalence relation formed by the transitive closure of ~ where $\forall xzy,$ $x'z'y' \in Pop(R)$, $xzy \sim x'z'y'$ iff $x=x'$ or $y=y'$ [5] (see Fig. 10). This object type K is an intersecting attribute and is the strongest of any intersecting attribute L in the sense that X→L and Y→L can be factored through K: X→K→ L and Y→ K→L . So there may in fact be a choice of intersecting attributes to introduce. In practical situations, a concept meaningful in the UoD should be sought to play the role of the intersecting attribute.

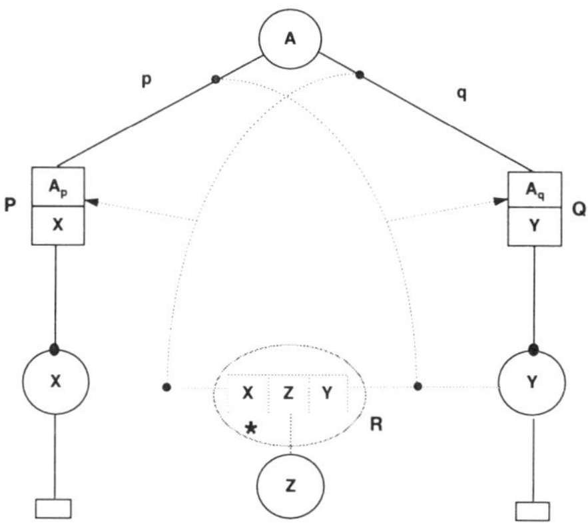

Fig. 8 Simple Nonfunctional Mutual Redundancy

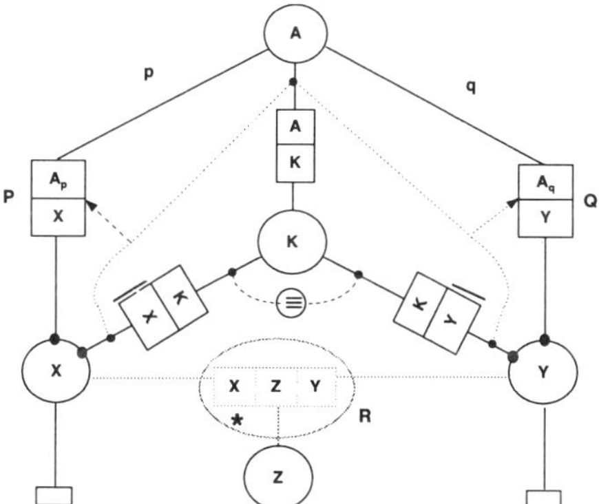

Fig. 9 Introducing an Intersecting Attribute

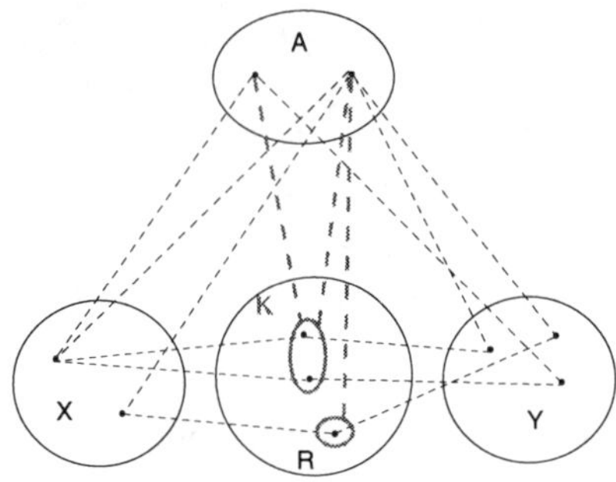

Fig. 10 Semantics of Strong Intersecting Attribute

5.1 Example

The proposition above suggests that schemas involving simple mutual redundancy might be improved by the recognition or introduction of intersecting attributes. Consider an example illustrated by the schema in Fig. 11 involving concerts of pieces of classical music requiring instruments. We consider concerts where pieces are all set for the same instruments.

Σ = ({SET-FOR(PIECE, INSTRUMENT), PERFORMED-AT(PIECE, CONCERT),
        PLAYED-AT(INSTRUMENT, CONCERT)}, Δ}

Δ = {SET-FOR $\bowtie$ PERFORMED-AT[INSTRUMENT,CONCERT] $\subseteq$ PLAYED-AT[INSTRUMENT, CONCERT][1],

PERFORMED-AT $\bowtie$ PLAYED-AT[PIECE, INSTRUMENT] $\subseteq$ SET-FOR[PIECE, INSTRUMENT][2]}

[1] *If an instrument is played at a concert at which a piece is performed, the piece set for the instrument.*

[2] *If a piece set for an instrument is performed at a concert, then the instrument was played at the concert.*

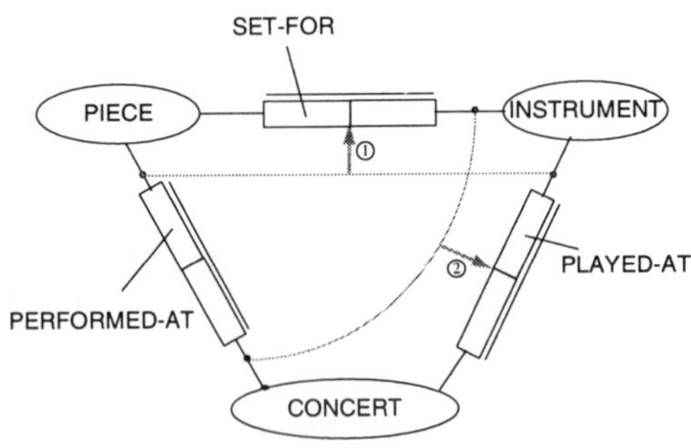

Fig. 11 Simple Nonfunctional Mutual Redundancy

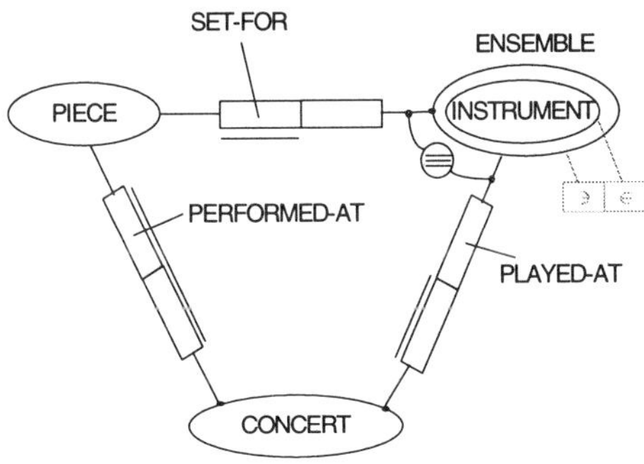

Fig. 12 Extended Schema with Introduced Object Type ENSEMBLE

Constraints ① and ② constitute single mutual redundancy, so introduce a new object type ENSEMBLE being a set (or more correctly a *bag*) of instruments. Fact types SET-FOR and PLAYED-AT are factored through ENSEMBLE, as shown in the schema in Fig. 12. The strong intersecting attribute is a common property of CONCERT and PIECE that has the same value if the piece is performed at the concert. This allows for the possibility there may be additional restrictions other than the ensemble eg. the acoustic of the hall.

6. Multiple Mutual Redundancy

The Proposition above cannot be generalised to schemas where there are sets of mutually derivable fact types. For example, BVP[BVP]=PCB▷◁PCV[BVP], BVC[BVC]=PCB▷◁PCV[BVC], PCB[PCB]=BVP▷◁BVC[PCB], PCV[PCV]=BVP▷◁BVC[PCV] is equivalent to MVDs BV→↠PIC, PC→↠BIV which have a *split-lhs anomaly* [4]. There is support for the conjecture that split-lhs anomalies never occur in real world data structures [29], [18], [4]. The schema depicting this example of multiple mutual redundancy graphically appears in Fig. 13. It is not really feasible to show this kind of constraint graphically.

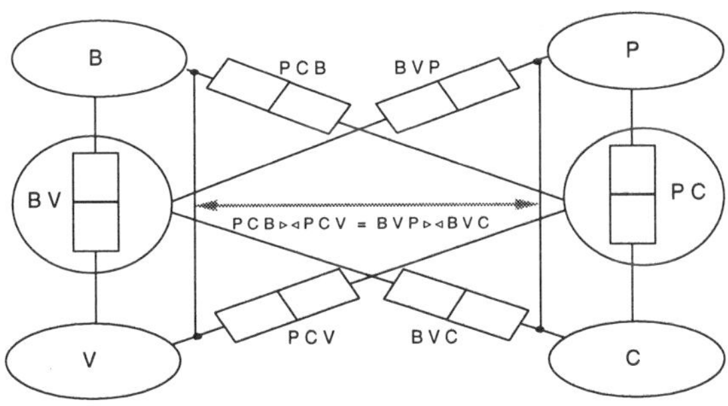

Fig. 13 Multiple Mutual Redundancy

The equality dependencies required in the case of split-lhs anomalies do not involve pure cycles [17]. We conjecture that only inclusion dependencies involving pure cycles are realistic. A cycle $(S_1,S_2,...,S_m,S_{m+1})$ where $S_{m+1}=S_1$ is a *pure cycle* if $S_i \cap S_j =\varnothing$ unless $j=i+1$ and if $m=3$, then $S_1 \cap S_2 \cap S_3 =\varnothing$. For example, the cycle (BVP, PCB, PCV) is not simple.

7. Conclusion

The quality of a conceptual, schema depends on how faithfully user views are integrated and can be reconstructed, and on how concisely and comprehensively constraints are modelled. In this paper, the commuting loop is presented as a solution to modelling practical situations where there are alternative user views of information, neither of which is subsumed by the other. It was found that for natural UoDs, the commuting loop was sufficient to enforce consistency among mutually derivable fact types. In some cases, the schema had to be extended to admit the constraint. So it is possible to maintain modelling alternatives in a single integrated schema.

Further it is possible that for all situations that occur in reality, the search for constraints involving multiple fact types may be restricted to commuting loops and subset constraints involving pure cycles. As NIAM conceptual modelling is based on user views expressed in natural language, this observation could be seen as a commentary on language and the structure of natural information. The success of graphic semantic models like the Entity-Relationship model [7] and its many successors may be partly attributable to the lack of complex logical derivations between different sets of base relationships. More complex structures that would be awkward graphically seem never to occur in practice.

We presume that where the schema needs to be extended to admit a commuting loop, the introduced object type corresponds to a natural concept. The object type may however be complex. It is not known what type constructors are sufficient to model any such introduced object type. The commuting loop constraint relies on equality of values the intersecting attribute and therefore on equality of types. In moving from relational to object-oriented information structures, there are more ways to associated values than by explicit relations. Paths involving coercion between complex object types may allow a more general formulation of the commuting loop as in Fig. 14.

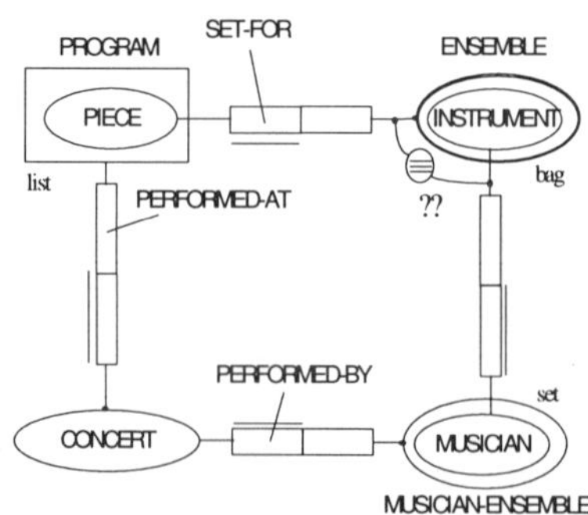

Fig. 14 A more General Commuting Loop

References

[1]   Biskup J. "Database Schema Design Theory: Achievements and Challenges", Information Systems and Data Management, 6th Int. Conf., CISMOD '95, LNCS 1006, Springer, 1995

[2]   Beeri C. "A formal approach to object-oriented databases", DKE 5 (1990) 353-382

[3]   Van Bommel P., ter Hofstede A.H.M & van der Weide Th.P. "Semantics and Verification of Object-Role Models" Inf. Sys. 16, 5 471-495 1991

[4]   Beeri C & Kifer M "An Integrated Approach to Logical Design of Relational Database Schemes" TODS 11, 2 (1986)

[5]   Beeri C & Kifer M "Elimination of Intersection Anomalies from Database Schemes", JACM, Vol.33, No. 3 July 1986, 423-450

[6]   Batini, C., Lenzerini M., Navathe S.B. "A Comparative Analysis of Methodologies for Database Schema Integration", ACM Computing Surveys, 18 (4), Dec. 1986.

[7]   Chen P.P., "The Entity-Relationship Model - Towards a Unified View of Data", ACM TODS, Vol 1, No 1, March 1976, 9-36

[8]   Casanova M.A., Fagin R. & Papadimitriou C.H. "Inclusion Dependencies and their interaction with Functional Depenedencies", Journal of Computer System Sciences 28, 29-59 (1984)

[9]   Crystal, D., "An encyclopedic dictionary of language and languages", Penguin, 1994

[10]   Coburn N. & Weddell G.E.: "Path Constraints for Graph-Based Data Models: Towards a Unified Theory of Typing Constraints, Equations, and Functional Dependencies", DOOD 1991: 312-331

[11]   Collignon M.A. & van der Weide T.P., "An Information Analysis Method Based on PSM", Proc. NIAM-ISDM Conference, 1993

[12]   Dampney, C.N.G., Johnson M., Dazeley P. & Reich V. (1994) "A higher order 'commuting loop' structure that supports information system data and process architecture", Proc. TC8AUS IFIP Information Systems International Working Conference: Business Process Re-Engineering: Information System Opportunities & Challenges.

[13]   Dutka, Alan F. & Howard H. Hanson., "Fundamentals of data normalization", Addison-Wesley, 1989

[14]   Eden, P. "Independent NIAM Schemas", Proc. First International Conference on Object Role Modelling, 1994

[15]   Eden, P., " Non-Local Constraints in Conceptual Data Models", WorkingPaper 95-8, CISR, Swinburne University of Technology, 1995

[16]   Eden P. & Ravalli G. "Commuting Loop Constraints in Object Role Modelling", Proc. 7th Australasian Conference on Information Systems

[17]   Fagin, R. "Degrees of Acyclicity for Hypergraphs and Relational Database Schemes" J. ACM 30, 3, 514-550 (1983)

[18]   Fagin, Mendelzon & Ullman "A Simplified Universal Relation Assumption and its Properties" TODS 7, 3 (1982)

[19]   Gogolla M. "An Extended Entity-Relationship Model", Springer-Verlag, 1994

[20]   Halpin T., "A Fact Oriented Approach to Schema Transformation" in MFDBS 91 : Proceedings 3rd Symposium on Mathematical Fundamentals of Database and Knowledge Base Systems, Rostock, Germany, May 6-9, 1991, B. Thalheim, J. Demetrovics, H.-D. Gerhardt (eds.), Springer-Verlag,, c1991

[21]   Halpin T.A. "Conceptual Schema and Relational Database Design" Prentice-Hall 1995

[22]   ter Hofstede A.H.M. & van der Weide T.P., "Expressiveness in conceptual data modelling", DKE 10 (1993), 65-100

[23]   ter Hofstede A.H.M., Proper H.A. & van der Weide T.P., "Formal Definition of a Conceptual Language for the Description and Manipulation of Information Models", Information Systems, 18(7), 1993

[24]   International Standards Organization, "Information Processing Systems - Concepts and terminology for the conceptual schema and the information base", TR 9007, ISO, 1987

[25]   Lee M.L & Ling T.W. "Resolving Structural Conflicts in the Integration of Entity-Relationship Schemas", OO'95, Object-Oriented and Entity-Relationship Modelling, LNCS 1021, Springer 1995

[26]   Loucopoulos P. & Zicari R. "Conceptual Modelling, Databases and CASE", Wiley, 1992

[27]   Mannila H. & Räihä K-J. "The Design of Relational Databases" Addison-Wesley 1992

[28]   Spaccapietra S., "View Integration: A step Forwatrd in Solving Structural Conflicts", IEEE TKDE, Vol. 6, No. 2, 1994, 258-274

[29]   Sciore E. "Real World MVDs" ACM PODS 1981

[30]   Spaccapietra S. & Parent C. "ERC+: An Object-Based Entity Relationship Approach", in [26]

[31]   Verheijen G.M.A. & van Bekkum "NIAM: An Information Analysis Method" in Information System Design Methodologies: A Comparative Review (Olle T.W. ed.) pp.537-590. North-Holland 1982

A Multiple View Mechanism with Semantic Learning for Multidatabase Environments

Yasushi Kiyoki*, Akiko Miyagawa* and Takashi Kitagawa**

* Faculty of Environmental Information
Keio University
Fujisawa, Kanagawa 252, Japan
phone: 81-466-47-5111, fax: 81-466-47-5041
e-mail: kiyoki@sfc.keio.ac.jp, miyagawa@sfc.keio.ac.jp

**Institute of Information Sciences and Electronics
University of Tsukuba
Tsukuba 305 Japan
phone: 81-298-53-5187, fax: 81-298-53-5206
e-mail: takashi@is.tsukuba.ac.jp

Abstract. In this paper, we present a multiple view mechanism for realizing personalized retrieval environments in multidatabase systems. In multidatabase systems, a multiple view mechanism is essentially required for individual users to have their own retrieval environments for extracting appropriate information from different databases.

For realizing the multiple view mechanism, we propose a new learning method for semantic associative search. This learning method is used for adapting retrieval results according to individual variation and for improving accuracy of the retrieval results. This method is applied to extract semantically related information to users' own keywords which are issued to a multidatabase system.

1 Introduction

A number of databases have spread in wide-area computer network environments, and we have opportunities to obtain significant information from those heterogeneous databases. It is difficult for individual users to extract appropriate information without knowledge on the concrete contents and structures of local databases. In multidatabase systems, the realization of semantic interoperability is one of the most important issues for resolving semantic heterogeneity among different databases[1, 2, 4, 11, 14]. Semantic interoperability is the essential foundation for extracting information from different and autonomous databases. We have proposed a fundamental framework for realizing semantic interoperability at the level of semantic relationships between data items (data contents) in multidatabase environments[3, 6]. We have designed a semantic associative search method to extract semantically related information according to user's requests in multidatabase environments[5, 7].

In this paper, we present a multiple view mechanism for providing personalized retrieval environments for multidatabase system users. In multidatabase systems, a multiple view mechanism is essentially required for individual users to have their own views for extracting appropriate information from different databases. By using the mechanism, each user can obtain his/her own view, that is, the personalized retrieval environment where he/she can request semantic associative search by using his/her own keywords.

We have prposed a semantic associative search method for extracting semantically related information by giving a keyword and a sequence of context words which explains the context of the keyword[5, 7]. This method can be used to translate a keyword, which is issued by a user, into local keywords for local databases. Those local keywords are semantically corresponding to the given keyword. Each translated local keyword is issued to corresponding local databases and the retrieval results are extracted from those local databases in the multidatabase system.

For realizing the multiple view mechanism for transforming a given keyword to the semantically corresponding data representation in each database, we propose a learning method for the semantic associative search. In the initial phase for retrieval, each user uses keywords which are commonly defined and shared among multidatabase users. The semantic associative search might not always select appropriate data items from databases because the judgement of accuracy is dependent on individual users. A multiple view mechanism is needed for adapting retrieval results according to individual variation and for improving accuracy of the retrieval results. In this case, the learning method is applied to adjust the retrieval results to the given keywords. Those keywords are stored as individual private keywords for each user, and those private keywords are used in subsequent retrieval. By using this method, users can issue their own keywords to a multidatabase system, and those keywords can be adapted to each local database automatically.

2   The Semantic Associative Search Method

In this section, we briefly review the semantic associative search method which we have presented in [5].

In this method, we assume that each data item includes various meanings. That is, the meaning of a data item is not fixed statically, but it is fixed only when the context for explaining its meaning is given. This method provides functions for performing the semantic interpretation and recognition of contexts and extracting semantically related information according to the given context.

In this method, a machinery for computing contexts is realized by creating an orthogonal knowledge space[5, 7]. Each data item is placed as a single coordinate point in the knowledge space and dynamically extracted by semantic associative search. In this knowledge space, each context corresponds to one of the subspaces. A subspace is named "semantic subspace." Given a context, a semantic subspace corresponding to the context is selected. This selection means the recognition of a context. Each data item is mapped into the semantic subspace selected according to a given context, and the relationships between data items are dynamically computed by using our metric in the selected semantic subspace reflecting the context. As a number of subspaces are included in this space, various semantic relationships between data items can be dynamically computed. In the selected subspace, the data item with the closest meaning to a keyword is extracted. By using this method, we can extract semantically related information to a given keyword from multidatabases.

2.1 *Definition of the Knowledge Space*

1. Assumption :

   To create an orthogonal knowledge space, a data matrix K is created. When m data items are given as the basic data items for creating the space, each data item is characterized by n features $(f_1, f_2, \cdots, f_n)$. For given $\mathbf{d}_i(i = 1, \cdots, m)$, the data matrix K is defined as the $m \times n$ matrix whose i-th row is $\mathbf{d}_i$. Then, each column of the matrix is normalized by the 2-norm to creat the matrix K.

2. Defining the knowledge space $\mathcal{KS}$:

   First we construct the correlation matrix $K^T K$ of K with respect to the features. Then, we execute the eigenvalue decomposition of the correlation matrix and we normalize the eigenvectors. We define the "knowledge space $\mathcal{KS}$" as the span of the eigenvectors which correspond to nonzero eigenvalues. We call such eigenvectors semantic elements. We note that since the correlation matrix is symmetric, the semantic elements form orthonormal bases for $\mathcal{KS}$. The dimension ν of the knowledge space $\mathcal{KS}$ is identical to the rank of the data matrix K. Since $\mathcal{KS}$ is ν dimensional Eucledian space, various norms can be defined and a metric is naturally introduced.

2.2 *The set of the semantic projections* Π_ν

We consider the set of all the projections from the knowledge space $\mathcal{KS}$ to the invariant subspaces (eigen spaces). We refer to the projection as the "semantic projection" and the corresponding projected space as the "semantic subspace." Since the number of i dimensional invariant subspaces is $(\nu(\nu - 1) \cdots (\nu - i + 1))/i!$, the total number of the semantic projections is 2^ν. That is, this model can express 2^ν different phases of the meaning.

The projection P_{λ_i} is defined as follows:

$P_{\lambda_i} \stackrel{d}{\Longleftrightarrow}$ Projection to the eigenspace corresponding to the eigenvalue λ_i,

i.e. $P_{\lambda_i} : \mathcal{KS} \rightarrow span(\mathbf{q}_i)$.

The set of the semantic projections Π_ν is defined as follows:

$$\Pi_\nu :=$$

$$\{\, 0\,,\ P_{\lambda_1}, P_{\lambda_2}, \cdots, P_{\lambda_\nu},$$

$$P_{\lambda_1} + P_{\lambda_2}, P_{\lambda_1} + P_{\lambda_3}, \cdots, P_{\lambda_{\nu-1}} + P_{\lambda_\nu},$$

$$\vdots$$

$$P_{\lambda_1} + P_{\lambda_2} + \cdots + P_{\lambda_\nu}\,\}.$$

2.3 *Constructing the Semantic Operator*

Suppose a sequence s_ℓ of ℓ words which determines the context is given. We construct an operator S_p to determine the semantic projection according to the context.

A sequence

$$s_\ell = (\mathbf{u}_1, \mathbf{u}_2, \cdots, \mathbf{u}_\ell)$$

of ℓ context words and a positive real number $0 < \varepsilon_s < 1$ are given, the semantic operator S_p constitutes a semantic projection $P_{\varepsilon_s}(s_\ell)$, according to the context. That is,

$$S_p : T_\ell \longmapsto \Pi_\nu$$

where T_ℓ is the set of sequences of ℓ words and $T_\ell \ni s_\ell, \Pi_\nu \ni P_{\varepsilon_s}(s_\ell)$.

This operator automatically selects the semantic subspace which is highly correlated with the sequence s_ℓ of the ℓ words which determines the context. This method makes the dynamic semantic computation of contexts possible. We emphasize that, in our model, the "meaning" is the selection of the semantic subspace, namely, the selection of the semantic projection and the "interpretation" is the best approximation in the selected subspace.

The semantic associative search procedure is summerized as follows:

1. Fourier expansion of $\mathbf{u}_i (i = 1, 2, \cdots, \ell)$.

   First we map the ℓ words in the sequence s_ℓ to the knowledge space $\mathcal{KS}$. This mathematically means that we execute the Fourier expansion of the sequence s_ℓ in $\mathcal{KS}$ and seek the Fourier coefficients of the words with respect to the semantic elements. This corresponds to seeking the correlation between each word of s_ℓ and each semantic element.

   The inner product u_{ij} of $\mathbf{u}_i$ and $\mathbf{q}_j$ is computed, i.e.

   $$u_{ij} := (\mathbf{u}_i, \mathbf{q}_j) , \ for \ j = 1, 2, \cdots, \nu.$$

   We define $\widehat{\mathbf{u}}_i \in \mathcal{I}$ as

   $$\widehat{\mathbf{u}}_i := (u_{i1}, u_{i2}, \cdots, u_{i\nu}).$$

   This is the mapping of the context word $\mathbf{u}_i$ to the knowledge space $\mathcal{KS}$.

2. Computing the semantic center $\mathbf{G}^+(s_\ell)$ of the sequence s_ℓ.

   We sum up the values of the Fourier coefficients for each semantic element. This corresponds to finding the correlation between the sequence s_ℓ and each semantic element. Since we have ν semantic elements, we can constitute a ν dimensional vector. We call the vector normalized in the infinity norm the semantic center of the sequence s_ℓ.

   $$\mathbf{G}^+(s_\ell) := \frac{\left(\sum_{i=1}^\ell u_{i1}, \cdots, \sum_{i=1}^\ell u_{i\nu}\right)}{\left\| \left(\sum_{i=1}^\ell u_{i1}, \cdots, \sum_{i=1}^\ell u_{i\nu}\right) \right\|_\infty},$$

   where $\| \cdot \|_\infty$ denotes infinity norm.

3. Determining the semantic projection $P_{\varepsilon_s}(s_\ell)$.

If the sum for a semantic element is greater than a given threshold ε_s, we employ the semantic element to form the projected semantic subspace. We define the semantic projection by the sum of such projections.

$$P_{\varepsilon_s}(s_\ell) := \sum_{i \in \Lambda \varepsilon_s} P_{\lambda_i} \quad \in \Pi_\nu,$$

where $\Lambda_{\varepsilon_s} := \{\, i \mid |(\mathbf{G}^+(s_\ell))_i| > \varepsilon_s \}$.

This operator automatically selects the semantic subspace which is highly correlated with the sequence s_ℓ of the ℓ words which determines the context.

2.4 Dynamic metric

A dynamic metric $\rho(\mathbf{x}, \mathbf{y}; s_\ell)$ for $\mathbf{x}, \mathbf{y} \in \mathcal{KS}$ is introduced to compute the semantic equivalence and similarity between data items. This metric dynamically changes depending on the context. This metric is designed in order that the model faithfully reflects the change of the context. The metric $\rho(\mathbf{x}, \mathbf{y}; s_\ell)$ is defined as follows:

$$\rho(\mathbf{x}, \mathbf{y}; s_\ell) = \sqrt{\sum_{j \in \Lambda_{\varepsilon_s}} \{c_j(s_\ell)(x_j - y_j)\}^2},$$

where the weight $c_j(s_\ell)$ is given by

$$c_j(s_\ell) := \frac{\sum_{i=1}^{\ell} u_{ij}}{\left\| \left(\sum_{i=1}^{\ell} u_{i1}, \cdots, \sum_{i=1}^{\ell} u_{i\nu} \right) \right\|_\infty},$$

$$j \in \Lambda_{\varepsilon_s}.$$

The weight c_j is proportional to the sum of Fourier coefficients $u_{ij}, i = 1, \cdots, \ell$ which represents the correlation between the sequence s_ℓ and the j-th semantic elements $\mathbf{q}_j$.

3   A New Learning Mechanism

In a multidatabase environment, individual users need to have their own retrieval environments for extracting appropriate information by using their own keywords.

Consider that retrieval candidate data items are located in the knowledge space $\mathcal{KS}$. If a user gives a keyword and its context words, the semantic subspace is selected by the semantic operator, and in this subspace, one of the retrieval candidate data items is selected as the semantically closest data item to the given keyword.

In this case, it might happen that the data item with the currently closest meaning to a keyword is not located in the closest location to the keyword in the selected semantic subspace. Although the user requires to extract the semantically closest data item, it is not currently selected. It is caused when the keyword or the data item is not appropriately located in the knowledge space. We introduce a new learning mechanism for semantic associative search where each user can obtain the appropriate, that is, the semantically closest data item.

It is important that the learning mechanism realizes the concept of adaptivity where each user's learning does not affect other users' retrieval. To realize this concept, the locations of the retrieval candidate data items must not move to the new locations in the knowledge space. As the retrieval candidate data items are shared among individual users, their locations must be invariant.

We propose a learning mechanism which can avoid side effects caused by learning for other users and realize appropriate semantic associative search according to individual users. The learning mechanism adjusts the locations of user's keywords in the knowledge space $\mathcal{KS}$.

Given the context words as a list of the ℓ words:

$$s_\ell = (\mathbf{w_{u1}}, \mathbf{w_{u2}}, \cdots, \mathbf{w_{u\ell}}),$$

the semantic subspace corresponding to this context is selected in the knowledge space $\mathcal{KS}$ by the semantic operator. In the semantic associative search, the closest retrieval candidate data item to the keyword $\mathbf{w}_k$ is extracted in the selected semantic subspace. Here, the data item $\mathbf{w}_r$ which must be the closest to the keyword $\mathbf{w}_k$ is specified by the user. In the computations of distances between the keyword $\mathbf{w}_k$ and each retrieval candidate data item, the learning mechanism is applied when the data item $\mathbf{w}_r$ is not extracted, that is, this data item is not located in the closest location to the keyword in the semantic subspace.

The keyword $\mathbf{w}_k$ and the target data item (retrieval candidate data items) $\mathbf{w}_r$ are located in the knowledge space $\mathcal{KS}$. Their locations in the knowledge space are represented as follows:

The coordinate of the keyword $\mathbf{w}_k$: $\mathbf{k} := (k_1, \cdots, k_\nu)$
The coordinate of the target data item $\mathbf{w}_r$: $\mathbf{r} := (r_1, \cdots, r_\nu)$

By the learning mechanism, the keyword $\mathbf{w}_k$ is moved toward the target data item $\mathbf{w}_r$ so as to make the data item $\mathbf{w}_r$ the closest to the keyword. As the constraint in this learning, the movement distance of $\mathbf{w}_k$ is minimized. This constraint is introduced to minimize the influence of learning in the knowledge space.

In the selected semantic subspace, the locations of $\mathbf{w}_k$ and $\mathbf{w}_r$ are represented as $\mathbf{K}$ and $\mathbf{R}$, respectively, as shown in Fig. 1.

The algorithm of the learning mechanism is described as follows:

Step-1: In the selected semantic subspace, the distance between the keyword $\mathbf{w}_k$ and the data item $\mathbf{w}_r$ is computed as follows:

$$\rho(\mathbf{k}, \mathbf{r}; s_\ell) = \sqrt{\sum_{i \in \Lambda_\varepsilon} \left\{ c_i(s_\ell)(k_i - r_i) \right\}^2} \tag{1}$$

where $\Lambda_\varepsilon := \{ i \mid c_i(s_\ell) > \varepsilon \}$.

Step-2: As the initial values, the current maximum distance ρ_{max} between the locations $\mathbf{K}$ and $\mathbf{R}$ is set to $\rho_{max} = \rho(\mathbf{k}, \mathbf{r}; s_\ell)$, and the current minmum distance ρ_{min} is set to $\rho_{min} = 0.0$.

Step-3: The termination condition for computing the dichotomy is specified as $(\rho_{max} - \rho_{min} \leq threshold)$.

If this condition is satisfied, the current location of the keyword $\mathbf{K}$ is fixed as the location of the keyword $\mathbf{w}_k$, and the learning process is terminated.

If $(\rho_{max} - \rho_{min} > threshold)$, the following steps are executed.

Step-4: The location $\mathbf{K}$ is moved so that the distance between the keyword $\mathbf{w}_k$ and the target data item $\mathbf{w}_r$ is changed to $\rho(\mathbf{k},\mathbf{r};s_\ell)' = (\rho_{max} + \rho_{min})/2$. As shown in Fig. 1, we consider a sphere with the center $\mathbf{R}$ and the radius $\rho(\mathbf{k},\mathbf{r};s_\ell)' = (\rho_{max} + \rho_{min})/2$. This movement means that the location of the keyword $\mathbf{w}_k$ is moved to the surface of the sphere. The new location of the keyword $\mathbf{w}_k$ after this movement is set to $\mathbf{X}$, and its coordinates in the knowledge space is represented as:

$$\mathbf{x} := (x_1, \cdots, x_\nu).$$

The new distance $\rho(\mathbf{k},\mathbf{r};s_\ell)'$ between the keyword $\mathbf{w}_k$ and the target data item $\mathbf{w}_r$ is represented as:

$$\rho(\mathbf{k},\mathbf{r};s_\ell)' = \sqrt{\sum_{i \in \Lambda_\varepsilon} \{c_i(s_\ell)(x_i - r_i)\}^2} \tag{2}$$

$$\text{where } \Lambda_\varepsilon := \{\, i \,|c_i(s_\ell) > \varepsilon\}.$$

This formula can be regarded as the ν-dimensional ellipse sphere as shown in Fig. 2, where the weight $c_i(s_\ell)$ is multiplied in each semantic element in the formula of the distance. This ν-dimensional ellipse represents the surface of the same distance between the target data item $\mathbf{w}_r$ and the keyword $\mathbf{w}_k$ in the metric ρ. The ν-dimensional ellipse is expressed as follows:

$$\sum_{i \in \Lambda_\varepsilon} \frac{(x_i - r_i)^2}{\left(\frac{\rho(\mathbf{k},\mathbf{r};s_\ell)'}{c_i(s_\ell)}\right)^2} = 1 \tag{3}$$

$$\text{where } \Lambda_\varepsilon := \{\, i \,|c_i(s_\ell) > \varepsilon\}.$$

Step-5: In the constraint that the movement distance of the keywird $\mathbf{w}_k$ is minimized, to move the keyword $\mathbf{w}_k$ toword the target data item $\mathbf{w}_r$, a perpendicular line which passes the point $\mathbf{K}$ to the ellipse is drawn as shown in Fig. 3. The intersection of this line and the ellipse is set to the location $\mathbf{X}$.

In Fig. 3, the expression of the perpendicular line which passes both the locations $\mathbf{X}$ and $\mathbf{K}$ is described as follows:

$$\left(\frac{\rho(\mathbf{k},\mathbf{r};s_\ell)'}{c_i(s_\ell)}\right)^2 \left(\frac{k_i}{x_i - r_i} - 1\right) = \left(\frac{\rho(\mathbf{k},\mathbf{r};s_\ell)'}{c_j(s_\ell)}\right)^2 \left(\frac{k_j}{x_j - r_j} - 1\right) \tag{4}$$

$$\text{where } i \neq j, (i,j \in \Lambda_\varepsilon).$$

Here, this expression can be represented as follows:

$$\left(\frac{\rho(\mathbf{k},\mathbf{r};s_\ell)'}{c_i(s_\ell)}\right)^2 \left(\frac{k_i}{x_i - r_i} - 1\right) = t, \tag{5}$$

$$\text{where } i \in \Lambda_\varepsilon.$$

By this expression, the following expression is obtained:

$$x_i = r_i - \frac{\rho\left(\mathbf{k},\mathbf{r};s_\ell\right)'^2 r_i}{c_i(s_\ell)^2 t + \rho\left(\mathbf{k},\mathbf{r};s_\ell\right)'^2} \tag{6}$$

where $i \in \Lambda_\varepsilon$.

The formula of ν-dimensional ellipse sphere is represented by assigning this expression as follows:

$$\sum_{i \in \Lambda_\varepsilon} \frac{\left(\frac{\rho(\mathbf{k},\mathbf{r};s_\ell)'}{c_i(s_\ell)}\right)^2 k_i^2}{\left(t + \left(\frac{\rho(\mathbf{k},\mathbf{r};s_\ell)'}{c_i(s_\ell)}\right)^2\right)^2} = 1, \tag{7}$$

where $i \in \Lambda_\varepsilon$.

This expression can be expressed as follows:

$$f(t) = \sum_{i \in \Lambda_\varepsilon} \frac{\left(\frac{\rho(\mathbf{k},\mathbf{r};s_\ell)'}{c_i(s_\ell)}\right)^2 k_i^2}{\left(t + \left(\frac{\rho(\mathbf{k},\mathbf{r};s_\ell)'}{c_i(s_\ell)}\right)^2\right)^2} - 1 = 0, where\ i \in \Lambda_\varepsilon\ and\ t > 0. \tag{8}$$

Step-6: In the condition of $t > 0$, the value t is computed by using the Newton method.

Step-7: By using the value of t, the crossing point $\mathbf{X}$ is computed.

Step-8: In the selected semantic subspace, the distance between the new location $\mathbf{X}$ and the location $\mathbf{R}$ of the target data item $\mathbf{w}_r$ is computed.

If the target data item $\mathbf{w}_r$ is the closest to the location $\mathbf{X}$, the location $\mathbf{X}$ is set to the new location $\mathbf{K}$ of the keyword $\mathbf{w}_k$. In this case, the current maximum distance ρ_{max} between the locations $\mathbf{K}$ and $\mathbf{R}$ is set to $\rho_{max} = \rho\left(\mathbf{k},\mathbf{r};s_\ell\right)$, and the current minmum distance ρ_{min} is set to $\rho_{min} = \rho\left(\mathbf{k},\mathbf{r};s_\ell\right)'$ as shown in Fig.4. Then, Steps 3 to 8 are repeated.

If the target data item $\mathbf{w}_r$ is not the closest to the location $\mathbf{X}$, the location $\mathbf{X}$ is set to the new location $\mathbf{K}$ of the keyword $\mathbf{w}_k$. In this case, the current maximum distance ρ_{max} between the locations $\mathbf{K}$ and $\mathbf{R}$ is set to $\rho_{max} = \rho\left(\mathbf{k},\mathbf{r};s_\ell\right)'$, and the current minmum distance is set to $\rho_{min} = 0.0$. Then, Steps 3 to 8 are repeatedly executed.

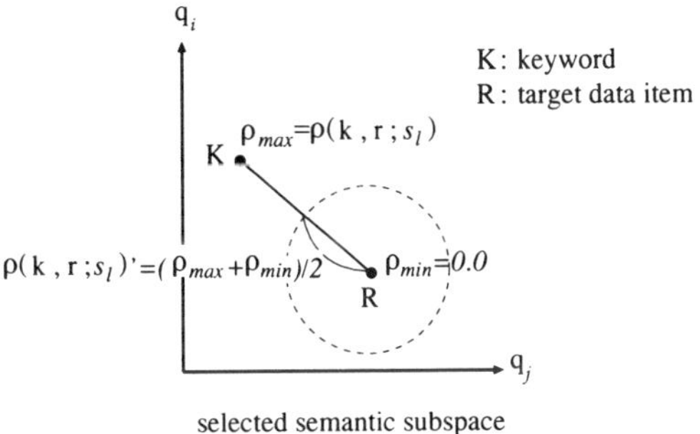

Figure 1: Sphere with center **R** and the radius $\rho(k, r; s_\ell)'$

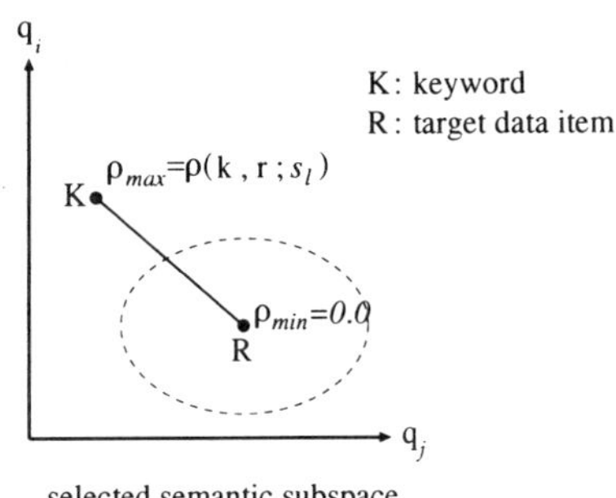

Figure 2: Ellipse sphere with center **R**.

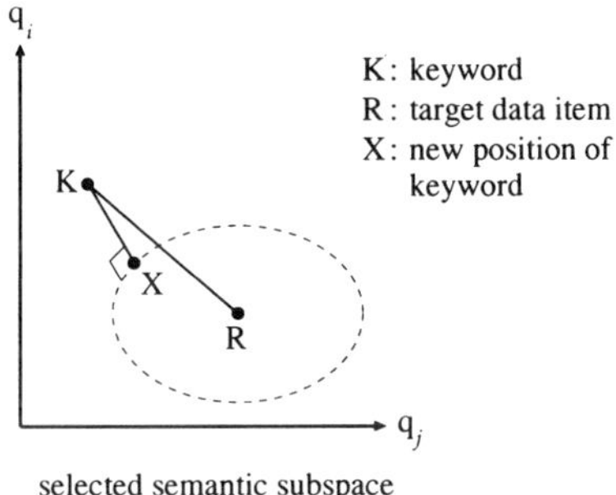

Figure 3: Perpendicular line to the ellipse sphere.

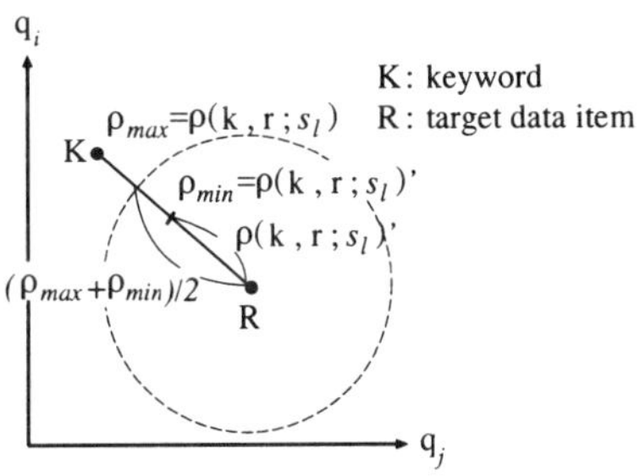

Figure 4: The case that target data item $\mathbf{w}_r$ is selected.

4   Application of the Learning Method to the Multiple View Mechanism

4.1   Application of the learning method to a multidatabase environment

To obtain the appropriate information from the multidatabase system, we apply our semantic associative search method to the multidatabase environment.

If appropriate retrieval results are not extracted from the multidatabase system, the learning mechanism is applied to transform the locations for keywords to the new locations in the knowledge space. After the learning, correct retrieval results can be extracted in the subsequent retrieval. The new locations for keywords are registered as the personalized metadata which reflects the user's intention correctly in semantic associative search. The users have their own views to the multidatabase system. By this multiple view mechanism, the users can issue their own keywords, and those keywords can be adapted to the multidatabase environment automatically.

The system structure for realizing the multiple view mechanism in a multidatabase environment is shown in Fig.5.

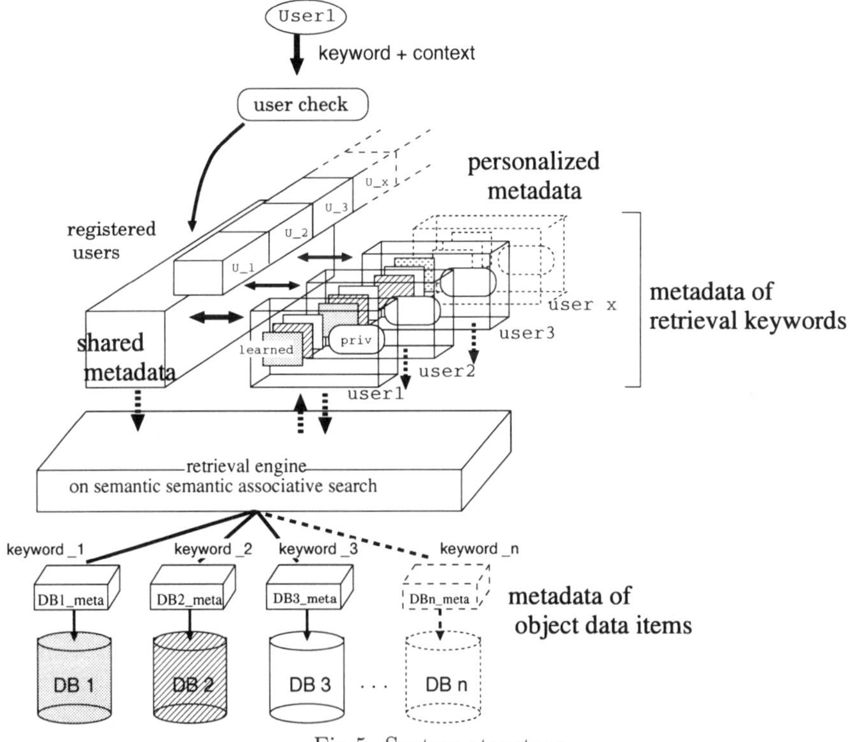

Fig.5: System structure

4.2   Creation of metadata items

Three types of metadata items are used in this system.

1. metadata items for creating the knowledge space
2. metadata items for retrieval candidates (retrieval objects)
3. metadata items for keywords and context words

All the metadata items are represented in vectors which are located in the knowledge space.

(1) metadata items for creating the knowledge space

The metadata items in this category are used for creating the orthonormal knowledge space $\mathcal{KS}$.

To create a data matrix K automatically, we have referred to the English dictionary named "General Basic English Dictionary [13]" in which only 874 basic words are used to explain every English vocabulary entry. Those basic words are used as features, that is, they are used as the features corresponding to the columns in the data matrix K. Namely, 874 features are provided to create the knowledge space. And, 2328 words are used to represent the words corresponding to the rows in the data matrix K. These 2328 words have been selected as the basic vocabulary entries. These entries are the same as the basic explanatory words used in the English dictionary named "Longman Dictionary of Contemporary English [12]." The 2328×874 data matrix is used to automatically create the knowledge space $\mathcal{KS}$.

The created knowledge space represents various semantic subspaces for computing distances between keywords and data items. A given keyword and data items are mapped into this space. Furthermore, basic words corresponding to vocabulary entries are mapped to the knowledge space by the Fourier expansion. The procedure for the creation of the knowledge space is as follows:

1. Each of 2328 vocabulary entries corresponds to a row of the matrix K. In the setting of a row of the matrix K, the columns corresponding to the explanatory words (features) which appear in each vocabulary entry are set to the value "1". If the explanatory word is used as the negative meaning, the column corresponding to the word is set to the value "-1". The other columns are set to the value "0". This process is performed for every vocabulary entry. And then, each column of the matrix is normalized by the 2-norm to creat the matrix K. To create the data matrix K from the dictionary automatically, we have implemented several filters which remove unnecessary words, such as articles and pronouns, and transform conjugations and inflections of words to the infinitives.

2. By using this matrix K, an knowledge space is created as described in Section 2. This space represents the semantic space for dynamically computing semantic relationships between keywords and data items.

(2) metadata items of retrieval candidates

The metadata items in this category are represented as vectors which correspond to retrieval candidate data items. For each local database, they are created in the same way as the creation of the row in the matrix in *(1)* by using the basic words in General Basic English Dictionary as features.

(3) metadata items of keywords and context words

The metadata items in this category are represented as vectors which correspond to keywords and context words used by users. Those vectors are also created in the same way as in *(1)*.

The system supports this category of shared metadata items of keywords and context words among users. The system also supports personalized metadata items of keywords and context words which are personally used by each user. Personalized metadata items are created by learning of keywords. These metadata items create multiple user views, as shown in Fig.5.

When appropriate retrieval results are not obtained in semantic associative search, the learning mechanism is applied to a keyword for each local database, as described in Section 3. Then, the metadata item corresponding to the keyword is registered as the personalized metadata item. That is, personalized metadata items are registered for each local database, and they are used as the personalized keywords in the multi-database environment.

4.3 Procedure for creation of personalized views

The overview of the multiple view mechanism is shown in Fig.5. The procedure for creating a personalized view is as follows:

1. A user inputs a user name, a keyword and context words.

   - If the personalized metadata item for the keyword is registered, it is used for semantic associative search.
   - Otherwise, the metadata item shared among users is used.

2. In the case that the appropriate retrieval result is not obtained, the learning mechanism is applied to the metadata item of the keyword and the learned metadata item is registered as the personalized metadata item.

Each user owns a personalized user view, so that the adaptive retrieval environment can be constructed dynamically. The procedure which applies the learning mechanism to a specified keyword is performed independently from other users' learning. The results of learning are reflected as the personalized view, and appropriate retrieval results can be obtained in the subsequent semantic associative search.

5 Experimental Study

5.1 Experimental environment

We have implemented an experimental system for the multiple view mechanism with the learning method.

In this experiment, we used two actual databases, ENVIRONLINE(for short ENV) and POLLUTION ABSTRACT(for short POL) as the simple multidatabase environment.

These databases include a lot of data items. As the example, we restricted the retrieval candidate data items whose subject is 'Nile river'. The 427 data items are extracted from ENV and the 310 data items from POL. Some examples of those data items are listed in Table 1 and Table 2. Similarly to the case of the basic data items, these data items are defined as ν-dimensional vectors through the filtering process by referring to "General Basic English Dictionary".

We selected the basic explanatory words in "Longman Dictionary of Contemporary English[12]" for the data items which were used as keywords and context words. These data items are not included in the database body. By the semantic associative search method, semantically related data items can be extracted by giving some of these data items as keywords and context words. These data items are also defined as ν-dimensional vectors.

In this experiment, the semantic relations between the keyword and the retrieval candidate data items are computed dynamically in the semantic subspace corresponding to the given context.

We have performed several experiments in which several patterns of contexts to a specific keyword are checked whether they can obtain appropriate data items(target data items) when the learning mechanism is applied.

Some combinations of a keyword and contexts are provided as a set. For each combination, we specify a target data item which should be the closest to the keyword. Every time the retrieval is performed, the learning mechanism is applied to the keyword so that the specified target data item is selected according to the context. The learning is applied to the retrieval for all the combinations. We call the learning process for all the combinations "1-cycle for the learning". The cycle for learning is repeated until the target data item is selected as the closest data item to the keyword in each combination.

As examples, three experimental results are shown in Tables 3 to 15. In the cases of three keywords, "farm", "sand", and "weather", the retrieval results of the data items adjusted after the learning in each semantic associative search are shown in Tables 4,5,8,9,12,13,14 and the order transition of the target data item (specified in the bold face in Tables) on the effect of learning cycles are shown in Table.6,10,15. In the column corresponding to a cycle, the left number of the arrow indicates the order of the target data item before learning in every cycle which is affected by learning to other contexts. The right one of the arrow is the rank of the target data item in the order after learning.

By the keyword learning, the location of the keyword is corrected on the semantic subspace according to the context. In the next step, when the same keyword learning to the new context is performed, the location of the keyword is corrected again on the new semantic subspace. The same query doesn't always lead to extracting the same metadata item as the result because of the side effect caused by other learning. Therefore, the learning mechanism must be applied repeatedly to the keyword.

Our experimental results show that the target data items are selected correctly in any contexts. When the keyword learning is repeated, the order of the target data items varies. And, finally the appropriate results are obtained in each semantic associative search. It is clarified that the data item with the closest meaning is selected flexibly by applying the learning mechanism to the semantic associative search in multidatabase environment.

Table 1: List of the data items stored in the database "ENV" and their explanatory words in General Basic English Dictionary

area	[n.]	stretch of land etc. :
areas	[n.]	stretch of land etc. :
beach	[n.]	stretch of sand, stones, at edge of sea :
cattle	[n.]	farm animals, sp. cows :
climate	[n.]	weather conditions of place :
desert	[n.]	stretch of dry or waste country, sp. sand :
environment	[n.]	persons and conditions among which one is placed :
farming	[v.i.t.]	keep a farm :
field	[n.]	marked-off stretch of land on farm etc. :
fields	[n.]	marked-off stretch of land on farm etc. :
marine	[a.]	of, in, produced by, the sea :
river	[n.]	body of moving water in naturally formed bed :
sand	[n.]	powder produced when different sorts of stone get rubbed down by motion of sea etc. :
seasonal	[a.]	any of the 4 divisions of the year based on weather :
sea	[n.]	stretch of salt water covering more than half the earth, sp. as opp. - land :
seasonal	[a.]	any of the 4 divisions of the year based on weather :
waterlogging	[a.]	(of boat etc.) so full of water that it is in danger of going down :

Table 2: List of the data items stored in the database "POL" and their explanatory words in General Basic English Dictionary

agricultural	[a.]	science or process of farming land :
area	[n.]	stretch of land etc. :
areas	[n.]	stretch of land etc. :
cattle	[n.]	farm animals, sp. cows :
climate	[n.]	weather conditions of place :
deposits	[n.]	put down (on, in) :
desert	[n.]	stretch of dry or waste country, sp. sand :
environment	[n.]	persons and conditions among which one is placed :
field	[n.]	marked-off stretch of land on farm etc. :
flood	[n.]	coming of water over land normally dry :
geology	[n.]	science of earth's history as recorded in beds of stone etc. :
lagoon	[n.]	stretch of salt water parted from sea by sand etc. :
plant	[n.]	living structure which is not an -animal, with leaves, getting its food from air, water, earth :
silicon	[n.]	substance formed, which is the chief part of sand and certain sorts of hard stone :
soil	[n.]	earth as substance, land :
spraying	[v.t.]	liquid sent into the air in very small drops by wind or apparatus:
storm	[n.]	violent weather conditions with thunder, strong wind, much rain or snow etc. :

Table 3 : The target data item to the keyword **"farm"**

	ENV	POL
context1 person	farming	agricultural
context2 land	field	field

Table.4 : Retrieval results of semantic associative search (1)

context : person, keyword : farm

ENV database

POL database

Before learning		After learning		Before learning		After learning	
data item	Distance	data item	Distance	data item	Distance	data item	Distance
areas	0.473280	areas	0.467954	area	0.473280	**agricultural**	0.342260
area	0.473280	area	0.467954	area	0.473280	area	0.388598
cattle	0.499341	**farming**	0.467954	cattle	0.499341	areas	0.388598
farming	0.511849	field	0.500248	field	0.515218	aerial	0.456571
field	0.515218	fields	0.500248	**agricultural**	0.539464	field	0.477474

Table.5 : Retrieval results of semantic associative search (2)

context : land, keyword : farm

ENV database

POL database

Before learning		After learning		Before learning		After learning	
data item	Distance	data item	Distance	data item	Distance	data item	Distance
area	0.657635	**field**	0.329497	area	0.657635	**field**	0.675133
areas	0.657635	fields	0.329497	areas	0.657635	areas	0.731995
field	0.690546	area	0.526053	**field**	0.690546	areas	0.731995
fields	0.690546	areas	0.526053	cattle	0.714295	agricultural	0.733600
cattle	0.714295	agriculture	0.613683	yield	0.742898	terrestrial	0.828969

Table.6 : The order of the target word item in learning cycles in keyword "farm"

ENV database

Context \ Order	Before learning	After 1cycle	After 2cycle
person	4	1	$7 \to 1$
land	3	$4 \to 1$	1

POL database

Context \ Order	Before learning	After 1cycle	After 2cycle
person	5	1	$3 \to 1$
land	3	$3 \to 1$	1

Table 7 : The target data item to the keyword "sand"

	ENV	POL
context1 land	desert	desert
context2 water	beach	silicon

Table.8 : Retrieval results of semantic associative search (3)

context : land, keyword : sand

ENV database | | | | POL database | | |

Before learning		after learning		Before learning		after learning	
data item	Distance	data item	Distance	data item	Distance	data item	Distance
sand	0.000000	**desert**	0.554964	fresh	1.005442	**desert**	1.057226
beach	0.875308	beach	0.642830	various	1.005845	fresh	1.108002
marine	0.969617	marine	0.692092	deposits	1.042071	various	1.113945
various	1.005845	progress	0.723810	deposited	1.042071	lagoon	1.124728
progress	1.026966	kingdom	0.724814	lagoon	1.044584	hydraulic	1.137431
desert	1.053691	coast	0.735044	hydraulic	1.048185	deposited	1.143916
insecticides	1.059450	applying	0.738266	**desert**	1.053691	deposits	1.143916

Table.9 : Retrieval results of semantic associative search (4)

context : land, keyword : sand

ENV database | | | | POL database | | |

Before learning		after learning		Before learning		after learning	
data item	Distance	data item	Distance	data item	Distance	data item	Distance
sand	0.000000	**beach**	0.163807	geology	0.316882	**silicon**	0.293836
beach	0.283455	desert	0.176779	soil	0.326703	accumulation	0.300584
marine	0.308490	mediterranean	0.202757	soils	0.326703	geology	0.311610
soil	0.326703	countries	0.207501	**silicon**	0.326893	uranium	0.314042
erosion	0.334434	marine	0.213925	insecticides	0.334714	yield	0.316220

Table.10 : The order of the target data item on learning cycles in keyword "sand"

ENV database

Context \ Order	Before learning	After 1cycle	After 2cycle
land	6	1	$2 \to 1$
water	2	$2 \to 1$	1

POL database

Context \ Order	Before learning	After 1cycle	After 2cycle
land	7	1	1
water	4	$10 \to 1$	1

Table.11: The target data item to the keyword "**weather**"

	ENV	POL
context1 water	waterlogging	flood
context2 land	climate	climate
context3 rain	seasonal	storm

Table.12 : Retrieval results of semantic associative search (5)

context : water, keyword : weather

ENV database				POL database			
Before learning		after learning		Before learning		after learning	
data item	Distance	data item	Distance	data item	Distance	data item	Distance
streams	0.517815	**waterlogging**	0.296945	storm	0.266480	**flood**	0.262440
screening	0.539958	discharge	0.296945	spraying	0.396243	jetting	0.262440
sea	0.568645	discharging	0.296945	streams	0.520589	river	0.264159
river	0.603242	outlet	0.305033	jetting	0.549849	streams	0.274369
waterlogging	0.616395	channel	0.313871	sea	0.571644	plant	0.275216

Table.13 : Retrieval results of semantic associative search (6)

context : land, keyword : weather

ENV database				POL database			
Before learning		after learning		Before learning		after learning	
data item	Distance	data item	Distance	data item	Distance	data item	Distance
climate	0.626553	**climate**	0.887402	**climate**	0.628752	**climate**	0.694697
environment	0.761472	intervention	0.918147	storm	0.762258	environment	0.794831
intervention	0.800116	equilibrium	0.949165	environment	0.763578	intervention	0.807889
v screening	0.803042	environment	0.965118	intervention	0.802384	storm	0.849173
equilibrium	0.806911	fauna	0.978453	raw	0.858782	raw	0.857559

Table.14 : Retrieval results of semantic associative search (7)

context : rain, keyword : weather

ENV database				POL database			
Before learning		After learning		Before learning		After learning	
data item	Distance	data item	Distance	data item	Distance	data item	Distance
streams	0.478355	**seasonal**	0.279927	**storm**	0.322533	**storm**	0.653738
sea	0.520151	waterlogging	0.336508	spraying	0.341863	sea	0.730162
screening	0.553937	climate	0.343195	jetting	0.477513	spraying	0.747084
river	0.559765	fluxes	0.347091	streams	0.489105	white	0.776582
waterlogging	0.561540	dam	0.353790	sea	0.530208	flow	0.782969

Table.15 : The order of the target data item on learning cycles in the keyword "weather"

ENV database

context \ order	Before learning	After 1cycle	After 2cycle	After 3cycle
water	5	1	371 → 2	141 → 1
land	1	1	1	1
rain	30	4 → 1	5 → 1	1

POL database

context \ order	Before learning	After 1cycle	After 2cycle	After 3cycle	After 4cycle
water	48	1	14 → 1	16 → 1	14 → 1
land	1	1	1	1	1
rain	1	306 → 1	119 → 1	2 → 1	1

6 Conclusion

In this paper, we have presented a multiple view mechanism for introducing personalized retrieval environments for multidatabase system users. For realizing the multiple view mechanism, we have proposed a new learning method for semantic associative search. The learning method is applied to adjust retrieval results to keywords issued by individual users. The multiple view mechanism makes it possible to extract appropriate and significant information by issuing users' own keywords in a multidatabase environment. We have implemented the experimental system to clarify the feasibility of the multiple view mechanism and the learning method. Several experimental results have shown that the multiple view mechanism and the learning method are appropriately applied to the multidatabase environment. In the future work, we will design a query processing system for multidatabases with the multiple view mechanism[4, 6]. Furthermore, we will extend the learning method to semantic associative search in multimedia database applications [9, 10].

References

[1] Batini, C.,Lenzelini, M. and Nabathe, S.B., "A comparative analysis of methodologies for database schema integration," *ACM Comp. Surveys*, Vol. 18, pp.323-364, 1986.

[2] Bright, M.W., Hurson, A.R., and Pakzad, S.H., "A Taxonomy and Current Issues in Multidatabase System," *IEEE Computer, Vol.25, No.3*, pp.50-59, 1992.

[3] Kitagawa, T. and Kiyoki, Y., *"The mathematical model of meaning and its application to multidatabase systems,"* Proceedings of 3rd IEEE International Workshop on Research Issues on Data Engineering: Interoperability in Multidatabase Systems, pp.130-135, April 1993.

[4] Kiyoki, Y. and Kitagawa, T., *"A metadatabase system for supporting semantic interoperability in multidatabases,"* Information Modeling and Knowledge Bases (IOS Press), Vol. V, pp.287-298, 1993.

[5] Kiyoki, Y. and Kitagawa, T., *"A semantic associative search method for knowledge acquisition,"* Information Modelling and Knowledge Bases, Vol. VI, pp.7.1-14, 1994.

[6] Kiyoki, Y., Kitagawa, T. and Hitomi, Y., *"A fundamental framework for realizing semantic interoperability in a multidatabase environment,"* Journal of Integrated Computer-Aided Engineering, Vol.2, No.1(Special Issue on Multidatabase and Interoperable Systems), pp.3-20, John Wiley & Sons, Jan. 1995.

[7] Kiyoki, Y., Kitagawa, T. and Miyahara, T., *"A fast algorithm of semantic associative search for databases and knowledge bases,"* Information Modelling and Knowledge Bases (IOS Press), Vol. VII, 4.1-4.16, 1995.

[8] Kiyoki, Y., Kitagawa, T. and Kurata, K., *"An Adaptive Learning Mechanism for Semantic Associative Search in Databases and Knowledge Bases,"* Information Modelling and Knowledge Bases (IOS Press), Vol. VIII, May 1996.

[9] Kiyoki, Y., Kitagawa, T. and Hayama, T., *"A metadatabase system for semantic image search by a mathematical model of meaning,"* ACM SIGMOD Record, Vol.23, No. 4, pp.34-41, Dec. 1994.

[10] Kiyoki, Y. and Hayama, T., *"The design and implementation of a distributed system architecture for multimedia databases,"* Proceedings of 47th Conference of International Federation for Information and Documentation, pp. 374-379, Oct. 1994.

[11] Litwin, W., Mark, M., and Roussopoulos, N., *"Interoperability of Multiple Autonomous Databases,"* ACM Computing Surveys, Vol.22, No.3, pp.267-293, 1990.

[12] *"Longman Dictionary of Contemporary English,"* Longman, 1987.

[13] Ogden, C.K., *"The General Basic English Dictionary,"* Evans Brothers Limited, 1940.

[14] Sheth, A. and Larson, J.A., "Federated database systems for managing distributed, heterogeneous, and autonomous databases," *ACM Computing Surveys*, Vol.22, No.3, pp.183-236, 1990.

Modelling a Natural Phenomenon for a Pictorial Computer-Based Simulation

Marjatta Kangassalo
University of Tampere, Department of Teacher Education
P.O. Box 607, FIN-33101 Tampere, Finland
Email: kamaka@uta.fi

Abstract: This article will describe the modelling process of a natural phenomenon for a pictorial computer-based simulation, PICCO. The computer simulation has been constructed for the research, where the aim has been to study the formation of a child's conceptual model of the selected natural phenomenon when a child is using the simulation program. In the article the ontological and epistemological starting points in the modelling situation have been examined. Especially, attention has been paid to the existence of the physical reality and the development of a child's mental constructs. The requirements for the modelling of the natural phenomenon for the simulation have been examined from the basis of ontological and epistemological starting points. After that the modelling procedure has been described. In this case the modelling method, the modelling process and the model of the phenomenon have been given. For the modelling of the natural phenomenon Newton's method of invention has been applied. At the end of the article, Newton's method for the modelling of natural phenomena for multimedia programs, has been discussed. A brief review concerning the results of the research project in question has been presented. In connection with this the formation of the children's conceptual models has been described in the situations when the children have used PICCO.

1. Introduction

This article will describe the modelling process of a selected natural phenomenon for a pictorial computer based simulation, PICCO. The pictorial computer based simulation has been constructed for the author's research. In the research the main idea was to study, whether a child's independent exploration by using PICCO could support a child's analysis and organization of the selected phenomenon and the shaping of the interconnections in the phenomenon. The research questions concerned the formation of a child's conceptual model of the selected natural phenomenon and the development of a child's strategies when a child was exploring the phenomenon by using the program. (See [9].) A conceptual model of the selected natural phenomenon is formed of concepts and their interconnections concerning the phenomenon in question. In this particular case concepts concern objects, properties, relations and their interconnections. The research is an educational research in which theoretical knowledge and research results, concerning cognition and cognitive growth, done within the cognitive science paradigm, are utilized. This article will concentrate on the modelling of the natural phenomenon for a computer simulation. The natural phenomenon was the variations of sunlight and heat of the sun, as experienced on the earth, related to the positions of the Earth and the Sun in space. Chapter 2 will examine the epistemological and ontological starting points in the modelling process. Chapter 3 will describe the modelling of the selected natural phenomenon for a computer simulation. In that connection a modelling method, a modelling process and a model of the phenomenon will be examined. Chapter 4 will give a brief account of the research results concerning the formation of children's conceptual models of the phenomenon when using PICCO. Finally, in chapter 5 conclusions will be made concerning the modelling and especially the modelling method which has been used.

2. Ontological and Epistemological Starting Points

Concerning the design of the computer simulation the ontological starting points are based on a conception about the existence of the physical reality, physical objects and physical states, which are existing independently of mental states. In an interaction with the physical reality, mental constructs concerning the physical reality are developing in the human mind. Further, the human mind can develop and construct material or abstract objects, for example, physical artifacts. These physical artifacts have not been constructed without the human mind. Physical artifacts are a part of products of a human culture, and they form their own realm belonging, at the same time, to the physical reality. (Cf. [19, 21].)

In this research, the purpose was to construct a pictorial computer simulation of the selected natural phenomenon, as a means of studying, whether a child's use of the simulation could support the organization of the phenomenon in a child's mind. When comparing the task with the above described entirety, the selected natural phenomenon belongs to the physical reality, the pictorial computer simulation is an artifact, and the aim is to study the formation of a child's conceptual model concerning the natural phenomenon when a child is using the simulation. In addition, in this case it is the human mind, that of the researcher, which constructs the artifact, and is the modeller of the phenomenon and the designer of the simulation. (See Figure 1.)

In the following parts, a natural phenomenon, a child's cognition, a pictorial computer simulation and a modeller will be examined as an aim to realize those starting points and requirements, which have to be taken into account in the modelling of the natural phenomenon for the simulation. In connection with this, the concept of "a phenomenon" has been defined as one of the objects of physics, the others being "entities", "space" and "time". "A phenomenon" refers to an event or events. The first phase in the modelling was to shape and identify the phenomenon which was the object of the modelling. The selected natural phenomenon for the simulation program is a part of the physical reality which exists as its own without a human being.

When the human interacts with the physical reality, mental constructs concerning the reality are developed and constructed. The physical reality consists of physical information which is a property of the universe. Physical information means the organization, organization level and complexity of physical systems. (See [17, 25].) Physical information creates a basis from

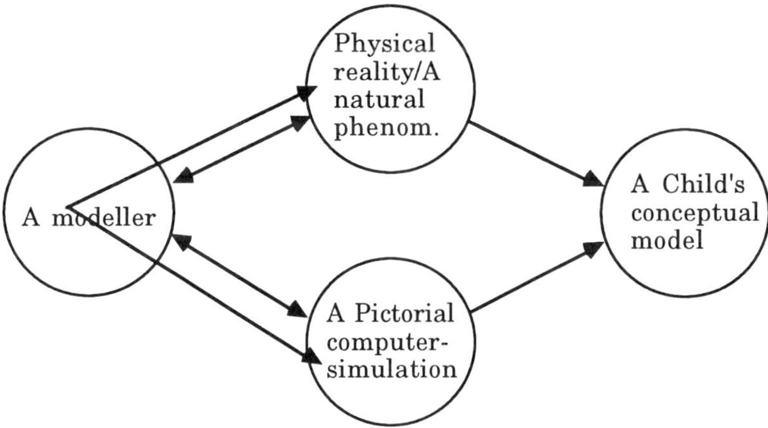

Figure 1. The starting points

which the shaping and organizing of the selected natural phenomenon in the human cognition begin to construct. According to research results concerning the shaping of the human brain, the organization of the brain occurs on the basis of self-organization, until a certain point where an active state exists in the interaction of the human brain and the surrounding environment (see e.g., [1, 15]). This means that epistemological starting points in this research are founded both on neural network theory and constructivism. The constructivist conception, to which this research is based on, emphasizes the interaction of the physical reality and the human. The physical reality exists without a person's existence, but when a person is in contact with the physical reality, mental constructs concerning the reality start to develop. The more complicated, for example, the physical phenomena are, the more a person's own mental activity is necessary, such that the understanding and the development of mental constructs concerning the phenomenon are possible. (Cf. [20].) When emphasizing both an environment and a person's own cognitive capacity in the shaping of the physical reality, both Vygotsky's and Piaget's views of a person's cognitive development have been integrated. Vygotsky emphasized especially, the part of the products of the human culture as being important for a child's cognitive development, while Piaget emphasized a child's cognitive process and its interactions with an environment in a child's cognitive growth. (See e.g., [27].)

When examining further the knowledge acquisition process of a person, the formation and definition of the concept of the concept becomes necessary. The conception of the concept forms one epistemological starting point in this research, which further imposes requirements for the modelling of the natural phenomenon for the simulation. Regarding a certain entity, a concept in this research is seen a potential set of representations activated from the memory, each of which has a high probability of being triggered by a given stimulus and of occurring together with the others (see [2]). A concept is an activated representation of the neural networks of the brain. It is a representation or the group of the representations by which a perceived or recalled entity is possible to be conceived and joined with a particular object. The activated representations give the features and dimensions embodied in the co-evoked representations from the basis of which conceiving, defining and naming the object are possible. The activated representations can represent information which is recorded in different sense modalities. Activated representations concerning a certain entity can change from time to time. This is, for example, because of recording new information in the memory or the changed situation where representations are activated. "Furthermore the range of representations that form the basis for a certain concept varies from individual to individual depending on the acquaintance with the object, the type of experience the perceiver has had in relation to the object, the value of the object to the perceiver, and so on" ([2, p. 26]). In this case the intension of a concept is emphasized. The intension of a concept refers to activated representations from the brain's neural networks concerning the entity in question. Activated representations are information structures in the brain's neural networks. In this case information means a certain organization of the brain's neural networks in relation to the entity in question (cf. [18]).

The above described approach to the concept of a concept gives a possibility to keep different definitions of the concept of a concept only as different ways to elicit stored information, concerning a certain entity, from the brain's neural networks. This concerns the classical view, the prototype view, the exemplar view, and concepts as theory dependent view of a concept (see [5]).

Vygotsky and also Piaget especially emphasize the importance of the context where the cognitive development by a child occurs (see e.g., [27]). In this research the aim has been to construct a multimedia environment where a child could explore the selected phenomenon using different approaches and strategies, from the basis of his or her own thoughts. This pictorial computer based simulation, PICCO, gives possibilities to progress further to more and more difficult and complicated phenomena in the simulation, according to a child's own interest. In order that the simulation could support the best way for a child to shape and organize the phenomenon and finally the formation of a developed conceptual model of the phenomenon in question, particularly in the modelling of the natural phenomenon for the simulation, the following has to be taken account: The knowledge which a child can obtain by exploring the phenomenon, with the help of the simulation, has to support a child's perceptions and experiences in reality. This is because children's concepts and conceptual structures, concerning the phenomenon in question, form mainly on the basis of physical information provided in the real world around them in relation to their own action and experiences. This means that the modelling has to take place from the basis of physical information from the real world concerning the natural phenomenon. In addition, physical information has to be represented visually in the form of events. This is because children's thinking at this age occurs mainly through visual images and events.

The selected natural phenomenon for the simulation is a dynamic, multi-level entirety containing other sub-phenomena. Central to the phenomenon are the changes which manifest in relations, objects, properties and their interconnections. Relations can be qualitative or quantitative, spatial and temporal. Of importance for the final model of the phenomenon, is that all forms and structures, for example the form of the trees, the texture of the trunks, correspond to the forms, structures and models in the 'real' world. This is important because the better children learn to recognize entities and their structures and regularities in the environment, the better the basis for remembering and thinking to take place (e.g. [4, p. 94]). The aim is to model the phenomenon, with its qualitative relations, in the way that occurs around us in reality on the earth level and according to the analogue model of the solar system at the space level. The modelling has to take place according to the scientific knowledge and theories concerning the phenomenon, such that the development of a child's conceptual model concerning the phenomenon could progress towards the scientific theories of the phenomenon in question.

From the modeller's point of view, of essential importance is that the modeller models physical information concerning the phenomenon in question. This means that the modeller has to recognize his or her own concepts and conceptions of the phenomenon and, if necessary, to abandon them such that the modelling of the phenomenon is possible in the way that it occurs in the physical reality, and according to the existing scientific knowledge and theories. This is important because of a child's concept formation. The phenomenon which is modelled on the computer simulation has to be parallel with the real-life phenomenon such that the exploration of the phenomenon, by using the simulation program, could support a child's concept formation according to the scientific knowledge of the phenomenon and not according to the modeller's concepts and conceptions of the reality. This is important because the modeller himself may have some misconceptions and/or undeveloped concepts and conceptions of the phenomenon. In this kind of modelling situation the recognition and, if necessary, abandonment the modeller's own conceptions is relatively easy when compared, for example, with phenomena in psychological or sociological subject areas.

3. Modelling a Natural Phenomenon for a Pictorial Computer Simulation

3.1. Modelling Method

In the modelling process it was necessary to find a modelling method or some kind of a frame in which the modelling of the natural phenomenon could occur. A selected method should be suitable for modelling the subject, which is the dynamic, to different science areas belonging phenomenon. In the modelling process it was important to keep the phenomenon as a whole whereby the relations, objects and properties of the phenomenon and changes in them were the subject of the modelling. Attention should also be paid to qualitative and quantitative, as well spatial and temporal, relations in the phenomenon and its sub-phenomena. Furthermore, a final simulation model for a computer should be pictorial and to proceed as events.

The basis for the method which directed the modelling was derived from Newton's method of invention (see [16, p. 156-165, 17, p. 308]). Newton's method of invention could give a frame within which the modelling could start. Newton has described his method, according to Hintikka [8, p. 278], as follows: it is an analysis that proceeds from "entireties to parts, from movements to forces that produce them, from effects to causes, from particular causes to more general causes". Through this method, an attempt is made to organize the phenomenon and dynamic relations prevailing in it, in order to find the interdependencies proceeding "...from results to causes and from specific causes to general causes until the process of deduction (argument) arrives at the most general causes. That is the method of analysis ...".

Newton's method of analysis provides a good starting point and direction for modelling the phenomena for simulations, since the approach is phenomenon-centred. The phenomenon being modelled and organized for simulation can be kept whole. Likewise, in modelling, attention can be paid to the changes occurring in the phenomenon as well as in their interrelations and interdependencies. The modelling, according to these guidelines, is like a theory construction at a more general level keeping inside the phenomena and aspects which belong to the different science areas. All existing theoretical knowledge of these subject areas, forms the basis for the modelling of the selected phenomenon.

Newton's method of invention is used in both planning and modelling the selected natural phenomenon for simulation. When modelling the phenomenon, suitable parts from Kurki-Suonio, Kervinen and Korpela's [12] organization of observing physical phenomena (see also [13]) have been used. The afore-mentioned methods are of help in constructing a model which illustrates the phenomenon for the pictorial computer-based simulation. The author is not aware of this type of method ever being used in modelling phenomena for multimedia environments.

3.2. Modelling Process

By applying Newton's method, the modelling process proceeded from the whole to the parts, from effects to causes and from particular causes to general causes. At this point, each modelling stage will be examined one by one, and it will be noted what was clarified and modelled at each stage. It was important to first model, limit and clearly recognize the chosen phenomenon, which includes phenomena of different, hierarchically organized levels. In the first stage, the core elements and factors forming the target phenomenon had to be recognized. The organising process started from the following question: What occurs in the phenomena? A particular event is always a change or a series of successive changes. In the analysis, attention was thus paid to the change in the phenomenon. After this, the following issues were considered: What is it that changes? How does the change occur? What is the direction of change and its relationship to other changing factors? What are the interrelations of the changing factors and changes occurring in them? It was essential at all times to examine the phenomenon as a whole, in other words, identify the relationship of an individual change in the phenomenon to other changing factors and their interconnections. The object of change can be, among other things, objects, qualities and relations, where temporal, spatial and qualitative relations are concerned. The change was examined from the phenomenon's viewpoint, proceeding from essential overall changes to more specific changes.

From the viewpoint of the selected phenomenon, the central changing factors are variations of sunlight and heat of the sun on the earth and changes resulting from these in nature. In the variations in the amount of sunlight and its heat on the earth, the central regularities alternate between light and dark and also between warmer and colder periods of time, as a result of which, changes in nature take place. From changes in nature, attention was paid especially to changes in the activities and interaction of living organisms. In modelling the phenomenon for simulation, the following things needed to be examined and clarified as far as changes occurring in nature are concerned: What is it that takes place in nature? What point in time does it take place? Is the phenomenon in question observed in the dark or only in daylight? How is the phenomenon or target related to the environment? When observing the relationship of the phenomenon or object to the environment, the following things need to be looked at: What does the occurrence of the phenomenon or target require of the conditions or environment? What is, for example, the habitat, nesting or feeding place like, and so on? Next, a list of targets about which the previously mentioned aspects have to be clarified: birds, mammals, insects, reptiles, larvae, trees, bushes, flowers, berries, mushrooms, etc. In addition, different traces left by living creatures are modelled: droppings, tracks, feathers, and when and where they were found. Likewise, it was of importance to note the state of water at different times of year, for example, when lakes are frozen. A bird's song has been taken account in some cases.

In addition to what has been previously stated, signs of human activity in nature are examined and clarified at different times. These are, for example, skiing tracks, boats, fishing rods, etc. When constructing the simulation model, attention was also paid to the terrain, the form of the terrain, soil, rock types and their shape, as well as different structures and possible buildings at the place of observation. Changes in the nature from one season to another can be seen, as an example, in Figure 2.

In the following stage of modelling it was proceeded by applying Newton's method, from effects to causes. At this phase, particular causes for the variations in the amount of sunlight and its heat on the earth and changes in nature have been modelled. For this the apparent orbit of the sun in the sky was modelled every day hour by hour. This requires exact knowledge of the time and place of sunrise and sunset, at what time the sun is at its highest in the sky, how high up it is then, and for how many hours daily the sun lies above the horizon. For the modelling of the sun's paths in the sky of the latitude 61° 31' Figure 3 shows an example of this phase of the modelling. The points in the picture refer to the sun and its position in the sky hour by hour every day of the year. The picture, in Figure 3, is only one part of the modelled entirety.

Figure 2. Changes in nature from one season to another

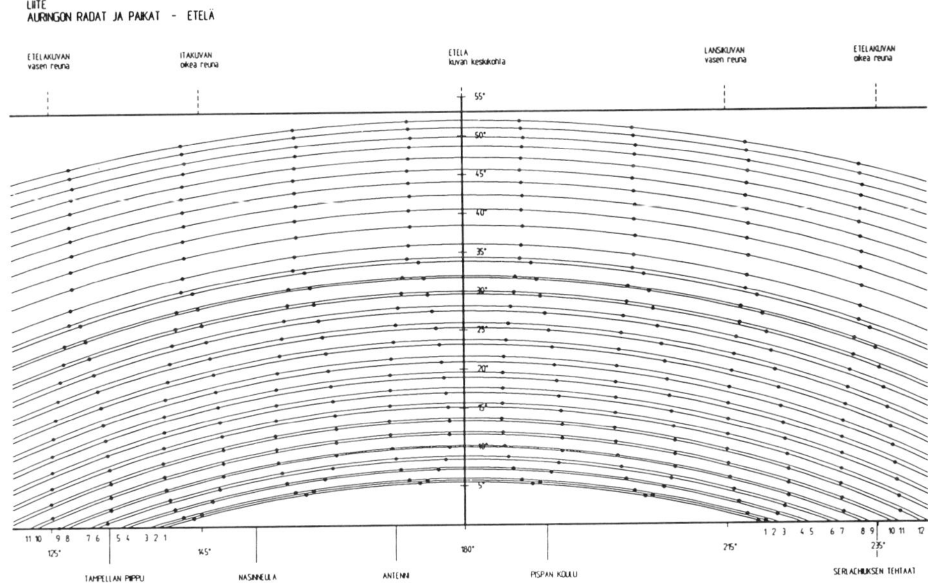

Figure 3. One part of the sun's paths and positions in the sky in a year
examined towards the south at the latitude 61° 31'

The last stage of modelling proceeded according to Newton's method
"from particular causes to more general causes", where the general factors
causing variations in the amount of sunlight and its heat on the earth were
modelled. This phase the examination of the phenomenon occurred at space
level, where attention was paid to the interconnections of the Sun and the
Earth. At this phase the Earth's motion, orbit and angle as it revolves
around its axis, on its orbit around the Sun was modelled. The location of the
Earth in relation to the Sun was modelled every day of the year with an
accuracy of one hour. Prior to this, it was necessary to decide the visual
angle of the phenomenon, to be examined at space level, and clarify the
universally accepted common agreements on measuring the Earth's
movements and time.

The phenomenon occurs in the solar system within the interrelations of
the Earth and the Sun. From the viewpoint of the phenomenon, the central
essential qualities are, the angle of the Earth that remains the same when it
revolves around its axis and the Sun on its orbit, the form of its orbit, its

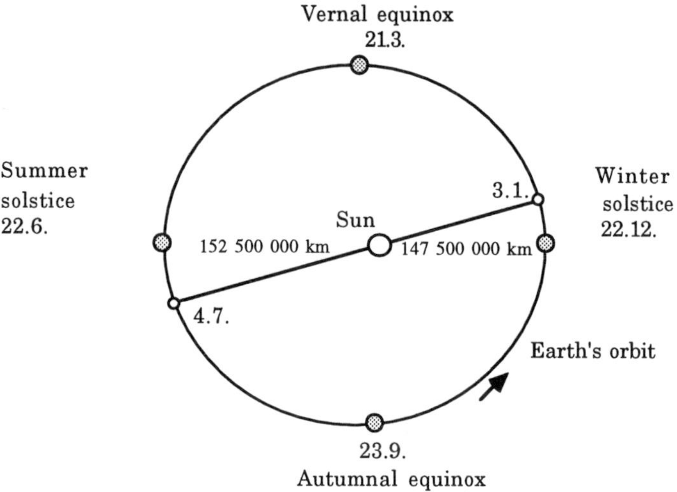

Figure 4. Earth's orbit and seasons (see [26, p. 27])

distance from the Sun at different times of the year, as well as the form and size of both the Sun and the Earth. In Figure 4 it is possible to see the Earth's orbit and the positions of the Earth in relation to the Sun during different seasons. Modelling continued from this to details which concerned the Earth's positions in relation to the Sun every hour a year.

As a result of the modelling process, the model which describes the phenomenon can be organized as follows:
1.   Phenomena which occur in nature on the earth.
2.   The apparent movement of the sun, examined from the earth level, hour by hour every day of the year.
3.   The interrelations of the Sun and the Earth observed at the space level.
The model describes the progress of the modelling process that took place by applying Newton's method of invention from the whole to parts, results to causes, and from specific causes to more general ones.

3.3. Model of the Natural Phenomenon

The selected natural phenomenon for the pictorial computer simulation, was the variations of sunlight and heat of the sun, as experienced on the earth, related to the positions of the Earth and the Sun in space. In the simulation it is possible to explore the variations of sunlight and heat of the sun and their effects on the earth in a natural environment as well as the origin of these phenomena from the basis of the interconnections and positions of the Earth and the Sun in space. The use of the simulation occurs by using the following icon pictures which add also important aspects to the model: a pictorial calendar, a clock, the pictures of a child sleeping and eating, pictures of binoculars, a telescope, a magnifying glass and a microscope, a space shuttle and a picture map with different points of the compass. The simulation concentrates on phenomena which are close to children's everyday experiences, such as day and night, seasons, changes in the life cycle of plants and birds, and so on. The exploration of the phenomenon by means of the simulation is possible, for example, hour by hour, day by day, month by month or season by season at different point of the compass on the earth level and in the same way at the space level. The selected place on the earth, from where the phenomenon has been modelled and simulated for the computer, is the suburb of Lentävänniemi in Tampere, in Finland. In Figure 5 and 6 some examples of views on the screen can be seen in April 1st at 7 o'clock in the morning toward the east and in January 1st at 12 o'clock at the space level. At the space level the enlarged picture of the Earth, the map of Finland and the aerial photo from Tampere are seen.

The modelling of the phenomenon is carried out by describing and presenting the core features and central events in the phenomenon, such as they are in the 'real life' phenomenon. By means of the model, created on the computer, the phenomenon is imitated and simulated. (Cf. [14, 23, 24, 7].) A simulated model of a phenomenon means that the phenomenon's events, objects, their characteristics, mutual time and space-related relations and changes in them are included in the model. The simulated model of the phenomenon is presented pictorially. Pictures depict realistic phenomena observed from the earth and are analogous to the solar system model examined from the space level. The imitation of the phenomenon by means of pictures is constructed to be used and manipulated by the computer. (Cf. e.g., [14, 23, 12, 28].)

This constructed pictorial simulation model of a phenomenon can be considered as a qualitative description of a phenomenon that belongs to Qualitative Physics. This is because the phenomenon, the changes in it and their interrelations are described in their qualitative relations, such as they can be observed in natural situations in nature and the environment. (See [22, 6, 3].) Information about the phenomenon can be obtained mainly in two ways: 1) By observing the phenomenon in natural conditions at the location, from which the phenomenon will be modelled for the computer simulation; and 2) through literature.

The simulated natural phenomenon forms a complex entirety containing interwoven and different levels of models. Models differ from each other concerning the level of the abstraction. They can be models of micro or macro levels. Further, models concern different entities, for example, objects and relations and their changes. The models differ from each other also concerning their explanatory power. The simulation model of the selected phenomenon, as a whole is descriptive, but there are, as part of the simulation, possibilities to find explanations for the phenomena and to infer what is occurring in the phenomenon. Thus it is possible to state that the simulated model has within in it an explanatory and predictive mechanism. The possibilities to explore the phenomenon by using the simulation contain many kinds of exploring methods, strategies and their combinations. For example, the exploration can move on inductively or deductively, from entireties to parts or vice versa. This is important because it supports a child's knowledge acquisition process effectively taking account the phase of the organization of the reality in a child's memory.

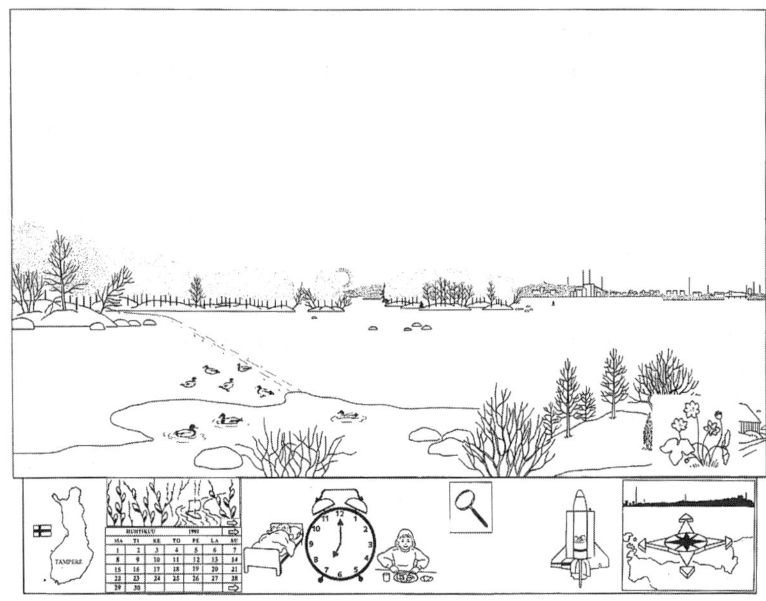

Figure 5. April 1st at 7 o'clock in the morning toward the east

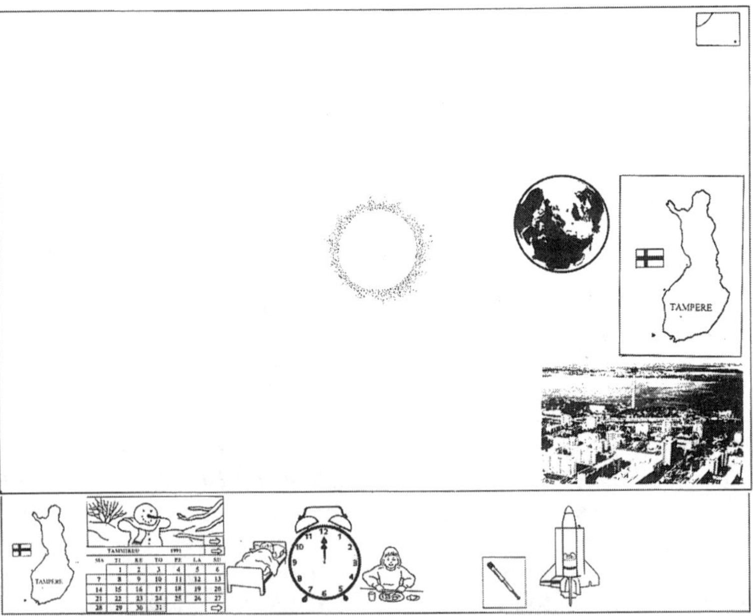

Figure 6. January 1st at 12 o'clock at the space level with the enlarged Earth,
the map of Finland and the aerial photo from Tampere

4. Formation of Children's Conceptual Models concerning the Particular Natural Phenomenon Using PICCO

The pictorial computer simulation, PICCO, has been used in research experiments in a day care centre and at school. The aim was to investigate, to what extent the independent use of the pictorial computer simulation of the selected natural phenomenon could be of help in the organization of the phenomenon and the forming of an integrated picture of that phenomenon. Attention was paid to the construction of a conceptual model of the phenomenon by children and children's exploring strategies during the use of the simulation. The children in the research groups were seven and eight years old. The research period both at the day care centre and at school was about four weeks. There was a total of 34 children who attended these experiments.

Children's conceptual models were elicited before and after their using of PICCO. Children's conceptual models of the phenomenon before the use of PICCO were at different levels. During the exploration processes the development and construction of the children's conceptual models varied to a certain extent but the main direction seemed to follow the currently accepted scientific knowledge. The children's different conceptual models, before the use of PICCO, formed a starting point from which the exploration of the phenomenon by children was activated. Children's exploration processes seemed to contain wandering, investigating and seeking for something and experimenting with an aim. The more developed and integrated the conceptual model was, the more the children's exploration contained goal-orientated investigation and experimentation. (See [10, 11].)

To summary it is possible to say that the children's exploration of the phenomenon by using PICCO could help children with the construction of the interconnections and the whole picture of the phenomenon in question. The construction occurred to a different extent with the children but the direction was mainly heading towards the current scientific knowledge of the phenomenon.

5. Conclusions

The application of Newton's method of invention has proved to be a very usable method when modelling the complicated natural phenomenon for a multimedia program. The method meets both the ontological and epistemological requirements in this research, the requirements concerning the modelling of the selected natural phenomenon and the requirements which have been imposed for the pictorial computer based simulation.

The modelling using Newton's method gives good possibilities to model physical information in the physical reality. The object of interest especially concerns the changes in the selected natural phenomenon, when there are changes in objects, properties, relations and their interconnections. In addition, changes can be qualitative and quantitative, and relations can be spatial and/or temporal. The method gives also possibilities to model both visual and auditive information. Thus the model of the phenomenon in the simulation can be represent visually by pictures, and the simulation of the phenomenon can take place by events. Modelling occurs from the entireties to parts, from effects to causes and from particular causes to general causes.

The modelling and the model in the simulation supports a child's exploration and knowledge acquisition of the phenomenon in reality. The simulation model places a child in an environment which gives possibilities for many kinds of exploration. By using the simulation program a child can, for example, make hypothesis and test them, experiment or only look at something interesting. According to the research results done at the school and in a day care centre, the exploration of the selected phenomenon by using the program supports children's knowledge acquisition and the formation of children's conceptual models of the phenomenon.

Acknowledgments

I express my great thanks artist Aila Penttilä for the drawing of the pictures and BA, Msc Gail Stankler for the linguistic examination of the article.

References

[1]   Arbib, Michael A. (Ed.) 1995. The Handbook of Brain Theory and Neural Networks. Cambridge, Mass.: The MIT Press.

[2]   Damasio, Antonio R. 1989. Forum: What is a Concept? 3. Concepts in the Brain. Mind & Language 4 (1 and 2), 24-27.

[3]   De Kleer, Johan and Brown, John Seely 1984. A Qualitative Physics Based on Confluences. Artificial Intelligence 24, 7-83.

[4]   Donaldson, Margaret 1982. Miten lapsi ajattelee. (Children's minds. Translated into Finnish by Marja-Leena Sakki.) Espoo: Weilin+Göös.

[5]   Eysenck, Michael W. (Ed.) 1990. The Blackwell Dictionary of Cognitive Psychology. Cambridge, Mass.: Basil Blackwell.

[6]   Forbus, Kenneth D. 1988. Qualitative Physics: Past, Present and Future. In Howard E. Shrobe (Ed.) Exploring Artificial Intelligence: Survey Talks from the National Conferences on Artificial Intelligence. San Mateo, CA: Morgan Kaufmann, 239-296.

[7]   van Gigch, John P. 1991. System Design Modeling and Metamodelling. New York: Plenum Press.

[8]   Hintikka, Jaakko 1969. Tieto on valtaa ja muita aatehistoriallisia esseitä. (Knowledge in power and other essays in intellectual history. Author's translation.) Porvoo: WSOY.

[9]   Kangassalo, Marjatta 1992. The Pictorial Computer-Based Simulation in Natural Sciences for Children's Use. In Setsuo Ohsuga, Hannu Kangassalo, Hannu Jaakkola, Koichi Hori and Naoki Yonezaki (Eds.) Information Modelling and Knowledge Bases III: Foundations, Theory and Applications (pp. 511-524). Amsterdam: IOS Press.

[10] Kangassalo, Marjatta 1996. PICCO as a Cognitive Tool. In Y. Tanaka, H. Kangassalo, H. Jaakkola and A. Yamamoto (Eds.) Information Modelling and Knowledge Bases VII. Amsterdam: IOS Press, 344-357.

[11] Kangassalo, Marjatta 1997. The Formation of Children's Conceptual Models concerning a Particular Natural Phenomenon Using PICCO, a Pictorial Computer Simulation. Acta Universitatis Tamperenses 559. University of Tampere. Tampere.

[12] Kurki-Suonio, Kaarle, Kervinen, Martti ja Korpela, Reino 1985. Kvantti 3b. Fysiikan laaja oppimäärä. (Extensive Course in Physics. Author's translation.) Tampere: Weilin+Göös.

[13] Kurki-Suonio, Kaarle ja Kurki-Suonio, Riitta 1988. Everybody Physics eli Fysiikan peruskurssi I. (Basic Course in Physics I. Author's translation.) Helsinki: Limes ry.

[14] Maddison, Alan 1982. Microcomputers in the Classroom. London: Hodder and Stoughton.

[15] Miller, Kenneth D. 1996. Receptive Fields and Maps in the Visual Cortex: Models of Ocular Dominance and Orientation Columns. In E. Domany, J.L. van Hemmen, K. Schulten (Eds.) Models of Neural Networks III. Association, Generalization and Representation. New York: Springer, 55-78.

[16] Niiniluoto, Ilkka 1983. Tieteellinen päättely ja selittäminen. (Scientific Deduction and Explanation. Author's translation.) Helsinki: Otava.

[17] Niiniluoto, Ilkka 1988. Tieteellisen tradition nousu ja tuho. Teoksessa Raimo Lehti, Tapio Markkanen ja Jan Rydman (toim.) Isaac Newton - jättiläisen hartioilla. (The Rise and Fall of Scientific Tradition. In Raimo Lehti, Tapio Markkanen and Jan Rydman (Eds.) Isaac Newton - on the Shoulders of a Giant. Author's translation.) Tähtitieteellinen yhdistys URSA. Helsinki, 297-312.

[18] Niiniluoto, Ilkka 1989. Informaatio, tieto ja yhteiskunta. Filosofinen käsiteanalyysi. (Information, knowledge and society. Philosophic concept analysis. Author's translation.) Valtionhallinnon kehittämiskeskus. Helsinki: Valtion painatuskeskus.

[19] Niiniluoto, Ilkka 1990. Maailma, Minä ja Kulttuuri. Emergentin materialismin näkökulma. (The World, I and The Culture. The Standpoint of Emergent Materialism. Author's translation.) Helsinki: Otava.

[20] Phillips, D.C. 1995. The Good, the Bad, and the Ugly: The Many Faces of Constructivism. Educational Researcher 24 (7), 5-12.

[21] Popper, Karl R. 1972. Objective Knowledge. An Evolutionary Approach. Oxford: University Press.

[22] Qualitative Physics: A Personal View. 1990. In Daniel S. Weld and Johan de Kleer (Eds.) Readings in Qualitative Reasoning about Physical Systems. San Mateo, CA: Morgan Kaufmann, 1-10.

[23] Roberts, Nancy, Andersen, David F., Deal, Ralph M., Garet, Michael S. and Shaffer, William A. (1983). Introduction to Computer Simulation: The System Dynamics Approach. Reading, Mass: Addison-Wesley.

[24] Rothenberg, Jeff 1989. The Nature of Modeling. In Lawrence E. Widman, Kenneth A. Loparo and Norman R. Nielsen (Eds.) Artificial Intelligence, Simulation, and Modeling. New York: John Wiley & Sons, 75-92.

[25] Stonier, Tom 1990. Information and the Internal Structure of the Universe. London: Springer-Verlag.

[26] Strahler, Arthur N. and Strahler, Alan H. 1987. Modern Physical Geography. Third Edition. New York: John Wiley&Sons.

[27] Tryphon, Anastasia and Vonèche, Jacques (Eds.) 1996. Piaget - Vygotsky The Social genesis of Thought. East Sussex: Psychology Press.

[28] Zeigler, Bernard P. 1976. Theory of Modelling and Simulation. New York: John Wiley& Sons.

Modeling Digital Image into Informative and Noise-Like Regions by a Complexity Measure

Eiji Kawaguchi and Michiharu Niimi
Kyushu Institute of Technology
1-1 Sensui-cho, Tobata, Kitakyushu
804 Japan
E-Mails : kawaguch@kawa.comp.kyutech.ac.jp
niimi@know.comp.kyutech.ac.jp

Abstract. In recent years image data are commonly used in information systems. The data size of an image is quite large. However, not every data in the image is informative for human. Rather, it includes a large amount of noise-like portions. All gray-scale and color images are decomposed into a set of bit-planes of binary (black-and white) pictures. In such pictures informative areas are simple in pattern, while, nose-like areas are complex. The authors give, first of all, a definition of a complexity measure for binary pictures, and demonstrate their assertion that informative and noise-like regions are separable by segmenting the region by such measure. Throughout the replacement experiments of noise-like regions with random patterns, the authors became convinced that human can not perceive any shape information on the 99.997% of all possible 8×8 binary patterns. In other word, human can recognize only on the 0.003% of all possible binary patterns.

1. Introduction

Image data are getting more and more important both in human-human and man-machine communications by computers. Almost all web contents today include image data of black-and-white, gray, and color pictures. Also, motion pictures are included. Those images are all digital; and they are stored in computers and transmitted through networks.

When designing an information system, which should be capable of automatic image perception and understanding, we face a big problem in handling huge data amounts. We know not all image data are always useful as informative information. There are a lot of unnecessary portions included. We need informative portions which human can perceive, and do not need the rest.

Traditional image processing researches, however, have been tackling this problem only as a data compression problem. They did not care about losing part of informative portion of the image if the compression ratio increases. But such approaches are not useful for image perception modeling.

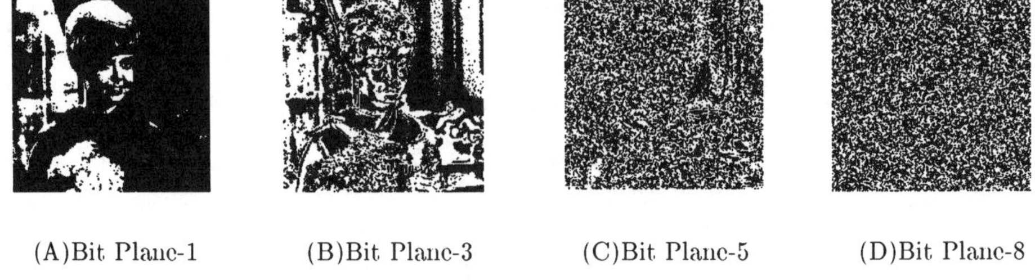

(A)Bit Plane-1	(B)Bit Plane-3	(C)Bit Plane-5	(D)Bit Plane-8

Figure 1: 1, 3, 5, 8-th bit-planes of GIRL in PBC system

Digital images are categorized in either black-and-white, or multi-valued pictures despite their actual color. We can decompose an n-bit image into a set of n binary images by bit-slicing operation[1, 2]. Therefore, binary image analysis is essential to all digital image analysis for perception modeling. Bit-slicing is not necessarily the best in the Pure-Binary Coding system (PBC), but in some case the Canonical Gray Coding system (CGC) is much better [3].

We can see a black-and-white image by "simple or complex" measure. For example, "all-white" and "all-black" patterns are the most simple images among all image patterns, while an "all-noise" pattern looks quite complex. We often see such a complicated image pattern in the least significant bit-plane of a gray image regardless of PBC or CGC system. We can not perceive any pattern information in there. Fig. 1 illustrates bit-planes of a gray image titled GIRL.

In Fig. 1, Plane-1 looks all informative, i.e., every area of this bit-plane gives us some pattern information. Even a white/black area carry shape information. While, in Plane-8 we can not see any significant pattern information. Every area looks nothing but noise. However, in Plane-5, we see partly informative and partly noise-like areas.

It is very obvious that significant (i.e., informative) area is relatively simple as binary pattern. In Fig. 1, Plane-1 and 3 are simpler than Plane-5 and 8. We will be safe to say that a too much complex image is too difficult for human to recognize it as informative. While, a simple image is easy to recognize it as a shape.

In this paper we will first introduce the definition of image complexity in two manners in Section 2, and apply them to natural images. We will see informative images are mostly simple, while noise-like images are complex. This leads to our fundamental proposition that "we can model image data into two regions,

(A) Informative region

(B) Noise-like region

in terms of image complexity."

In Section 3 we will give a theoretical discussion on the ratio of Informative and Noise-like image data among all possible binary patterns. We introduce a new notion "image conjugation" to formalize the discussion.

Section 4 describes the possible applications of our modeling to data compression technique and to some other purposes.

We give the summary and conclusion of our work in Section 5.

2. Complexity measure for binary image

The complexity of a binary image can be defined case by case [4]. There is no standard definition of image complexity. Kawaguchi discussed the problem in relation to image thresholding problem, and proposed three types of complexity measures[5, 6].

In this section we will review two types of complexity definitions after Kawaguchi's idea.

2.1. *Complexity measure by the length of black-and-white border*

The length of black-and-white border in a binary image looks a good measure for image complexity. Let us use the four-connectivity neighborhood method (both black and white regions) for our present discussion. In that case, the total length of black-and-white border equals to the summation of the number of color-changes along the rows and columns in the image. For example, a single black pixel surrounded by white background pixels has the boarder length of 4. We assume the image frame is always square having $2^N \times 2^N$ pixels. Practical image size is $N = 8 \sim 12$. Let us count the color-changes in the interior area of the image. Therefore, the minimum of the border length is 0 (either black or white pattern), while the maximum is $2 \times 2^N \times (2^N - 1)$ (checker board patterns). We will define the image complexity measure by the following.

$$\alpha = \frac{k}{2 \times 2^N \times (2^N - 1)} \tag{2.1}$$

Where, k is the total length of black-and-white border in the image. So, the value of α ranges over:

$$0 \leq \alpha \leq 1 \tag{2.2}$$

2.2. *Complexity measure by the number of connected areas*

Another definition of the complexity measure is the number of connected areas in the image. We also take the $2^N \times 2^N$ size image with the four-connectivity method. The simplest, and the most complex image in this case is the black/white, and the checker board patterns again. Let m be the number of connected areas in the image. Then the complexity measure is defined by:

$$\beta = \frac{m}{2^N \times 2^N} \tag{2.3}$$

The value range is:

$$1/(2^N \times 2^N) \leq \beta \leq 1 \tag{2.4}$$

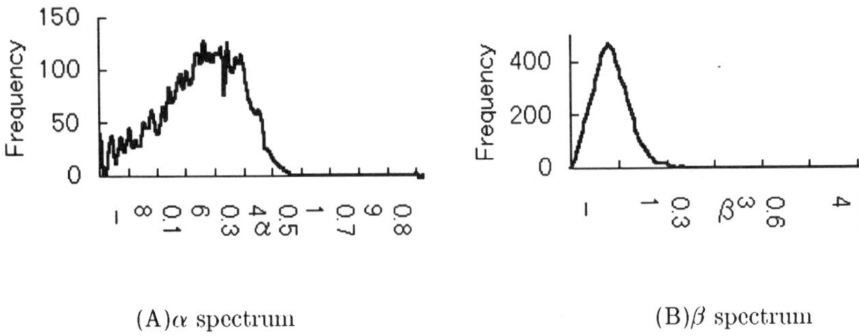

(A)α spectrum   (B)β spectrum

Figure 2: Complexity-spectrum of Plane-4 of GIRL

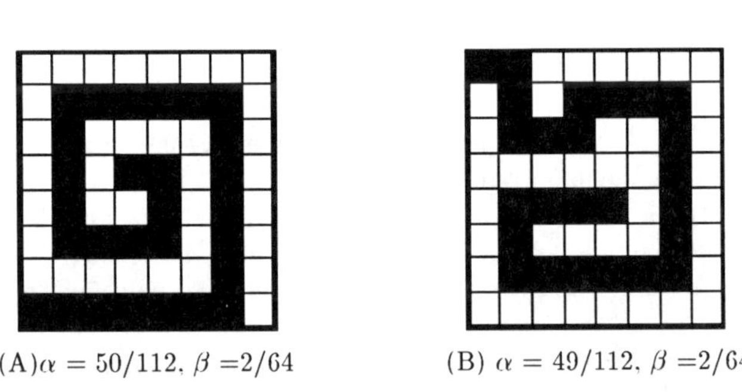

(A)$\alpha = 50/112,\ \beta = 2/64$ (B) $\alpha = 49/112,\ \beta = 2/64$

Figure 3: Image examples having a large α and a small β

2.3. Local complexity measure

(2.1) and (2.3) are defined globally, i.e., α and β are calculated over the whole image area. They give us an overall complexity measure. However, we can also apply those measures to local image analysis. A practical local image size is $N = 2 \sim 4$.

2.4. Relation between α and β

It is very interesting to see if α and β are similar or different in real images. We made some experiments to check this. Fig. 2 (A) and (B) illustrate the complexity spectrum of α and β of Plane-4 of GIRL. The horizontal axis shows the complexity measure for $N = 3$ local areas, while the vertical axis shows the number of local areas having each complexity value. The reason we have set $N = 3$ for the local area size is based on our experience. We used many test images. The result showed α and β are not similar in the sense that α and β's spectrum shapes are alike.

We concluded from this experiment that both α and β work as complexity measures, but they are not the same. In some case two measures show a big difference (cf. Fig. 3). It may be possible to set a better measure by combining them.

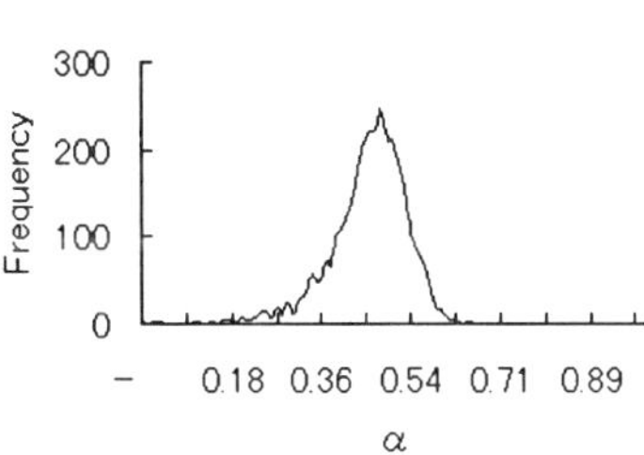

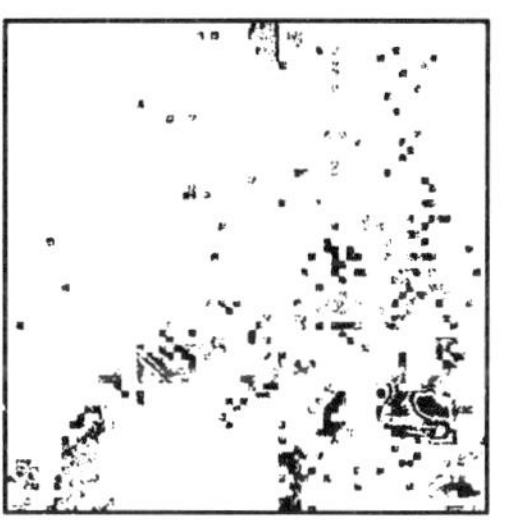

(A) Complexity spectrum of Plane-5 of GIRL   (B) Thresholding result(α=0.40)

Figure 4: Spectrum of local complexity α and thresholding result

2.5. *Informative area and noise-like area in a natural image*

Our fundamental view to model natural binary images is that the informative regions are simple, while the noise-like regions are complex. "Natural image" actually refers to a photo image taken by a camera. "Binary image" in practice is a "bit-sliced" bit-plane pattern of a gray or color picture.

In order to prove this view, we used the α complexity measure to segment images. The objective of this experiment was to know if we can segment informative regions from noise-like regions just by thresholding a binary image using the α value.

Fig. 4 illustrates the result. Fig. 4 (A) is the local complexity spectrum of Plane-5 of GIRL. This spectrum shows there are many local areas which have the complexity α at around 0.5. (B) is the thresholded bit-plane at $\alpha = 0.40$. Only informative areas (with the complexity value less than $\alpha = 0.40$) are shown in the figure. As a result of this experimental study, we became certain that,

(1) Natural binary images can be categorized into "Informative Region" and "Noise-like Region" in terms of the local complexity measure.

(2) α is a good measure for it.

We will use α as our complexity measure in the rest of this paper.

3. Analysis of Informative and Noise-Like region

Informative images are simple, while noise-like images are complex. However, this is true in case such binary images are part of a natural image. We can make a very complex binary image artificially, and we can still see some pattern information in it (See Fig. 5).

In this section we will discuss how many image patterns are informative and how many patterns are noise-like. We will first introduce "conjugation" operation of a binary image.

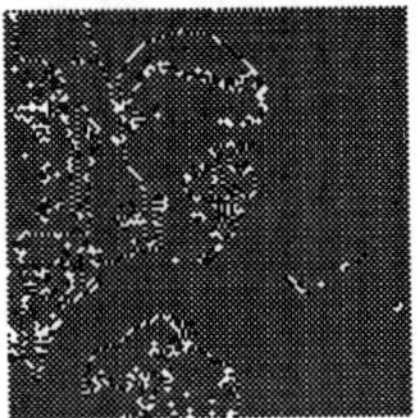

Figure 5: Example of a very complex pattern including perceivable information

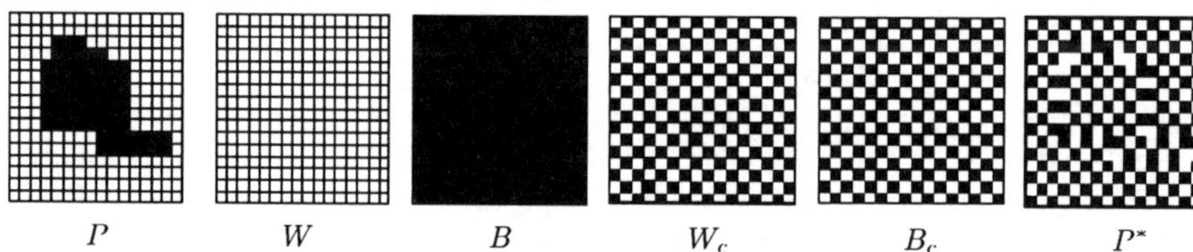

$$P \qquad W \qquad B \qquad W_c \qquad B_c \qquad P^*$$

Figure 6: Illustration of each binary pattern (N=4)

3.1. *Conjugation of binary image*

Let P be a $2^N \times 2^N$ size black-and-white image with black area as the foreground and white area as the background area. W and B denote all white and all black patterns, respectively. We introduce two checkerboard patterns W_c and B_c, where W_c has a white pixel at the most upper-left location, and B_c is its complement, i.e., the most upper-left pixel is black (See Fig. 6). We regard the black and white pixels have logical value "1" and "0", respectively.

P can be interpreted as the pixels in the foreground area have B pattern, while the pixels in the background area have W pattern. Now we define P^* as the conjugate of P which satisfies:

(1) The foreground shape is the same as P.

(2) The foreground area has the B_c pattern.

(3) The background area has the W_c pattern.

Correspondence between P and P^* is one-to-one, onto. The following properties hold true for such conjugation operation. "$\oplus$" designates the exclusive OR operation.

$$(a) \qquad\qquad P^* = P \oplus W_c \qquad\qquad (3.1)$$

$$(b) \qquad\qquad (P^*)^* = P \qquad\qquad (3.2)$$

$$(c) \qquad\qquad P^* \neq P \qquad\qquad (3.3)$$

We can easily prove these properties.

The most important property about conjugation is the following.

(d) Let $\alpha(P)$ be the complexity of a given image P, then we have,

$$\alpha(P^*) = 1 - \alpha(P) \qquad\qquad (3.4)$$

[Proof]

Each row/column color-change on P adds the boarder length by one. Therefore, if the number of total color-changes in P is k, then,

$$\alpha(P) = \frac{k}{2 \times 2^N \times (2^N - 1)}.$$

While, each foreground-background boarder on P^* reduces the number of color-changees on the boarder by one from the total number of the checkerboard color-changes (i.e., $2 \times 2^N \times (2^N - 1)$). Therefore,

$$\alpha(P^*) = \frac{2 \times 2^N \times (2^N - 1) - k}{2 \times 2^N \times (2^N - 1)} = 1 - \alpha(P)$$

QED.

It is evident that the combination of each local conjugation (e.g., $2^3 \times 2^3$ area) makes an overall conjugation (e.g., $2^9 \times 2^9$ area). (3.4) says that every binary image pattern P has its counterpart P^*. The complexity value is always symmetrical in reference to $\alpha = 0.5$. Fig. 5 was, in fact, the conjugate pattern of Plane-1 of GIRL.

3.2. Conjugate of multi-valued Image

Conjugation operation on binary image is applicable to a multi-valued image. Let

$$P = (P_1, P_2, \cdots, P_k, \cdots, P_K)$$

be a multi-valued image where $P_1, P_2, \cdots, P_k, \cdots, P_K$ are all their bit planes in either PBC or CGC system. The conjugate of P is defined as:

$$P^* = (P_1^*, P_2^*, \cdots, P_k^*, \cdots, P_K^*)$$

Fig. 7 (A) illustrates a P (a printed characters in 8 bits PBC). (B) is the conjugate of its first plane. (C) is an artificial 8 bit image P' made from respective bit-planes of GIRL=$(P_1, P_2, \cdots, P_8)$ which is composed by:

$$P' = (P_1^*, \bar{P}_2^*, P_3^*, \bar{P}_4^*, P_5^*, \bar{P}_6^*, P_7^*, P_8^*)$$

Most bit-planes in P' is very complex (more than 0.5 and less than 1.0), yet we can see some shape information. This fact ensures our claim that "both simple and very complex patterns, even if they are combined into a gray-scaled, can be perceptible by human."

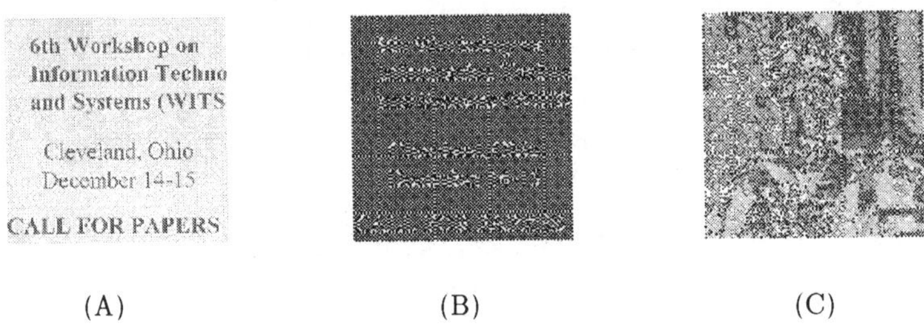

(A)   (B)   (C)

Figure 7: Example of conjugate images

3.3. *Image transformation between simple and complex patterns*

Property (d) in Section 3.1 provides us of a technique to transform an excessively complex image into a simple image, or vice versa, without losing any shape information. For example, if a given P has local areas, some of which have a complexity less than 0.5, then we can make the local conjugation operation to enlarge each complexity to a value more than 0.5.

Reducing image complexity is useful for image storing and transmission by using typical image compression technique. In that case, however, we must keep the local "conjugation-map" to recover the original image.

3.4. *Criterion for informative and noise-like image segmentation by α*

We are interested in how many binary image patterns are informative, and how many are noise-like regarding α. As we think $2^3 \times 2^3$ is a good size for local area, we need to know the total number of $2^3 \times 2^3$ binary patterns in relation to α value. This means we must check all 2^{64} of $2^3 \times 2^3$ patterns. However, 2^{64} is too huge to make an exhaustive check by any means.

Our practical approach is as follows. We first generate random $2^3 \times 2^3$ binary patterns as many as possible, where each pixel value is set random, but has equal black-and-white probability. Then we make a histogram of all generated patterns in terms of α. This simulates the distribution of 2^{64} binary patterns.

Fig. 8 shows the histogram for 4,096,000 of $2^3 \times 2^3$ size patterns generated by our computer. This histogram shape almost exactly fit the normal distribution as is shown in Fig. 8. The average value of the complexity in this histogram was very close to 0.5. The standard deviation was 0.047 in α. We denote this deviation by σ.

Our next question is how much image data we can discard without losing human perceivable image quality. To discard data means to replace local image areas with random noise patterns. If we replace all the local areas having complexity value $\alpha_0 \leq \alpha \leq 1 - \alpha_0$, yet it does not damage any quality, and if α_0 is the minimum value for such, then such α_0 is regarded as the complexity value for informative/noise-like segmentation threshold. We can determine that local image patterns less complex than α_0, and more complex than $1 - \alpha_0$ are all informative, while local patterns with $\alpha_0 \leq \alpha \leq 1 - \alpha_0$ are all noise-like.

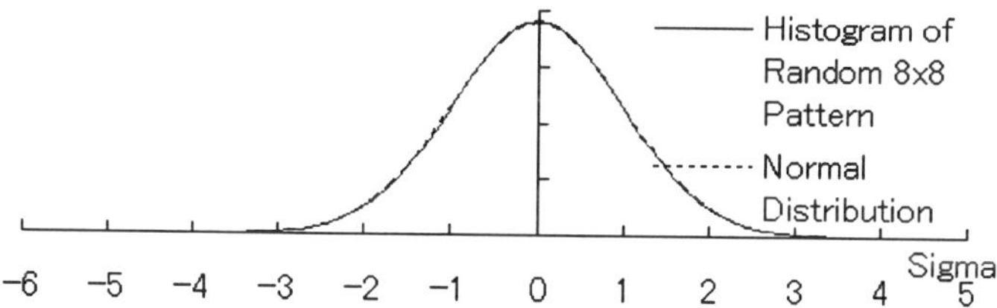

Figure 8: Histogram of randomly generated 8×8 binary patterns

Figure 9: Results of noise replacement

Of course this is probabilistically true for natural images. Some artificial images having $\alpha \cong 0.5$ may be informative (cf. Fig. 3).

As we have illustrated in Fig. 4, the complexity criterion for a plain black-and-white image seems to be around $0.5 - \sigma$. However, when we apply such thresholding operation to gray images (including color pictures), the complexity criterion must be smaller.

We have made a noise replacement experiment of each bit-plane (by CGC) about test images which were all 512×512 size gray scale images. We thresholded at $\alpha = 0.5 - \sigma$, $0.5 - 2\sigma, 0.5 - 3\sigma, \cdots$, and $0.5 - 9\sigma$, then replaced all noise-like areas with random patterns produced by a computer. Fig.9 illustrates some of the results with CGC GIRL image.

Some of the conclusions from those experiments are that the "informative" and "noise-like" criterion about 8×8 size area is around $\alpha = 0.5 - 4\sigma$ for 8 bit images. Even if we have thresholded at $0.5 - 7\sigma$, the image quality was still not very much damaged. If we threshold at a very small value, the resulting image highlights the feature points in the original image, because the informative area converges to the very informative portion of the image, that is the feature points such as line edges.

The reason we adopted the CGC coding system was the following[7].

(1) In PBC system black-and-white boarders at a higher bit are inherited down to lower planes.

(2) While, in CGC system, as long as in a continuous area, no upper bit boarders are inherited to lower planes.

This means each boarder on CGC planes is specific to the original image, while PBC boarders are redundant within continuous area.

3.5. The estimated number of informative/noise-like local image patterns

It is easy to estimate the number of informative/noise-like local image patterns by referring to normal distribution table. In this estimation we neglect the possibility that even a natural image include very complex patterns (that is, $0.5 < \alpha$).

As we found the complexity criterion is around $0.5 - 4\sigma$, the number of locally informative patterns is 0.0032% of all possible binary patterns (0.000032×2^{64} different patterns). The rest (99.9968%) are all noise-like patterns. If we can set $\alpha = 0.5 - 7\sigma$, informative patterns reduces to $1.3 \times 10^{-10}\%$. Even in that case, we still have 2.4×10^{7} different informative 8×8 patterns left.

We can generally say that natural image can be described by very limited patterns on the bit-planes, yet it is enough to represent a huge number of image patterns.

4. Possible application of this work

The fact that local areas with complexity $\alpha_0 \leq \alpha \leq 1 - \alpha$ is neglectable without losing pattern information allows us to discard such areas. When we need to restore the image, we can only insert "random noise" into discarded areas. This leads to a high image compression technique.

If we threshold at a very low α value such as $0.5 - 8\sigma$, we can focus the "feature points" only in the informative regions.

Another application will be a secret data transmission. Because a lot of local image areas are noise-like, and we can replace them by random patterns, why not we replace them with secret data which can disguise human eye just as noise areas. Maybe we can code ordinary text data as binary patterns having local complexity value around 0.5 (never less than α_0). Then, we can threshold "secret data" area from the "dummy image" area just by α_0 value. In this case, however, information compression technique is not available.

5. Conclusions and future study

The objective of this paper was to demonstrate our claim that digital image can be modeled as Informative part and Noise-like part. We can segment them only by thresholding local areas using complexity measure such as the α.

We have discussed the following topics and showed our experiments.

1. We can model a natural binary image as informative areas and noise-like local areas. It is applicable to multi-valued images by bit-slicing technique such as by CGC coding system.

2. We can only threshold the areas by a complexity value such as $\alpha = 0.5 - 4\sigma$.

3. This technique can be applied to data compression as well as secret data transmission.

We think those aspects should be taken into consideration in practical information system designs. Our next work is to make more intensive experiment using wider range of images including color pictures. Practical applications to secret data transmission sound very interesting.

References

[1] Hall, Ernest L., "Computer Image Processing and Recognition", Academic Press, New York, 1979.

[2] Jain, Anil K., "Fundamentals of Digital Image Processing", Prentice Hall, Englewood Cliffs, NJ, 1989.

[3] Kawaguchi, E., Endo, T. and Matsunaga, J., "Depth First picture expression viewed from digital picture processing", *IEEE Trans. on PAMI*, Vol.5, No.4, pp.373–384, 1988.

[4] Maragos, P., "Pattern spectrum and multiscale shape representation", *IEEE Trans. on PAMI*, Vol.11, No.7, pp.701–716, 1989.

[5] Kawaguchi, E. and Taniguchi, R., "Complexity of binary pictures and image thresholding - An application of DF-Expression to the thresholding problem", Proceedings of 8th ICPR, Vol.2, pp.1221–1225, 1986.

[6] Kawaguchi, E. and Taniguchi, R., "The DF-Expression as an image thresholding strategy", *IEEE Trans. on SMC*, Vol.19, No.5, pp.1321–1328, 1989.

[7] Kamata, S, Eason, R. O., and Kawaguchi, E., "Depth-First Coding for multi-valued pictures using bit-plane decomposition", *IEEE Trans. on Comm.*, Vol.43, No.5, pp.1961–1969, 1995.

Information Modelling and Knowledge Bases IX
P.-J. Charrel et al. (Eds.)
1998, IOS Press

A Completely Codeless Model for Algorithm Animations

Takehiro Tokuda, Chanchai Ritthongpitak, and Ken Kawai
Department of Computer Science, Tokyo Institute of Technology
Ohokayama, Meguro, Tokyo 152, Japan
{tokuda,chanchai,kawai}@cs.titech.ac.jp
Fax: +81-3-5734-2912

Abstract

A completely codeless model for algorithm animations is presented. This model enables us to quickly construct algorithm animations by giving three types of graphical definitions for already written algorithm programs.

1. Introduction

Algorithm animations are techniques to produce animations of the behavior of already written programs such as sorting, searching and binary tree construction as shown in Fig. 1 for the purpose of learning, analysis and debugging [1, 5, 12].

The goal of algorithm animations is to graphically show essential information about the behavior of the algorithm nicely with little additional effort. Namely we may insert additional event generation commands at appropriate points in the source codes of original algorithm programs, but we must construct everything else separately from the original algorithm programs.

Traditionally, however unlike the goal, we usually have to modify the source codes of the original algorithm programs globally or we have to write a large amount of additional codes by a programming language. This is because what we can use is essentially libraries of graphical routines.

So far, unlike models in other areas of animations, models we can use is at best path-transition model used in XTANGO system [12, 13].

A path-transition model clearly extracted concepts of paths and transitions from algorithm animations. A path is a line along which animation objects can move. A transition is a graphical change of animation objects which takes place along the path. However as shown in Fig. 2, path-transition model forces us to write everything in terms of programming codes. Fig. 2 shows an algorithm part and an animation part for a bubble sort animation.

In the domain of interactive animations, Director system [6, 7] uses a cast-score model. A cast is a graphical definition of animation objects. A score is a two-dimensional matrix of programs indexed by relative time called frame numbers and scenery-layer numbers called channels. Unfortunately Director system is not suitable for algorithm animations, because the score controls the entire animation process explicitly.

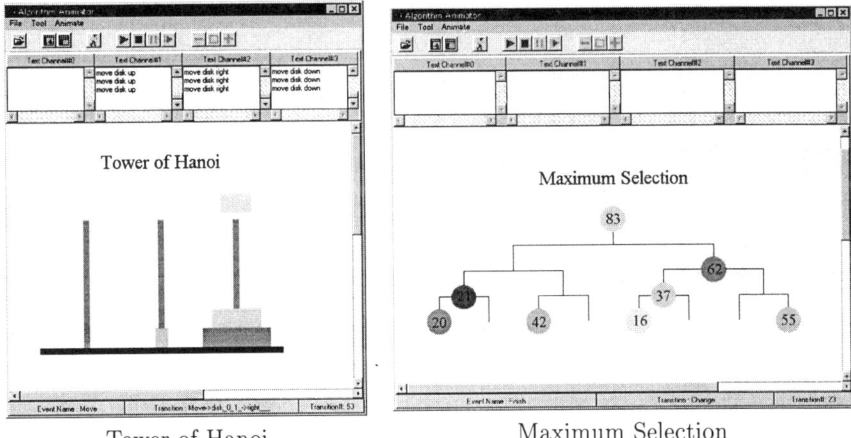

Tower of HanoiMaximum Selection

Fig. 1: Typical algorithm animations produced by our completely codeless model

In this paper we present a completely codeless model for algorithm animations. By codeless we mean that we do not have to write additional codes using a programming language for constructing the animation, except the insertion of event generation commands in the original algorithm program. Our model is expressive enough to deal with typical complicated algorithm animations using very small amount of graphical definitions.

We implemented two versions of algorithm animation systems based on our models. A Tcl/Tk version based on our first model of Section 2 is available now. A Java version based on our second model of Section 2 is also available.

The organization of the rest of this paper is as follows. In Section 2 we present our completely codeless model. In Section 3, we show five typical examples of algorithm animations. In Section 4, we give concluding remarks.

2. A completely codeless model

Historically we have reached a completely codeless model, which we call transition composition model, via an almost codeless model, which we call, path-activation model. Hence we explain an almost codeless model first and then a completely codeless model.

2.1 Path-activation model

Path-activation model has 4 components as shown in Fig. 3

1. Cast: A cast is a graphical definition of animation objects with possible parameters as attributes. The examples of casts are lines, rectangles, ellipses, polygons, texts and graphic images.

2. Path: A path is a graphical definition of line along which movement of an animation object takes place. A path also has possible parameters as attributes.

3. Location: Location is a graphical definition of position of animation objects.

4. Controller: A controller is a definition of correspondence of events to transitions by codes. Events are generated by original algorithm programs.

```
#include <stdio.h>
#include "xtango.h"

void ANIMInit(), ANIMInput(), ANIMDraw(),
     ANIMExchange();

static NAME_FUNCT fnc[] = { ("Init",     1, (VOID, (FPTR)ANIMInit)},
                            ("Input",    1, (VOID, (FPTR)ANIMInput)},
                            ("Draw",     1, (VOID, (FPTR)ANIMDraw)},
                            ("Exchange", 1, (VOID, (FPTR)ANIMExchange)}
                            (NULL,       0, NULL, NULL) };

main()
{
    int n,i,j;
    int temp;
    int a[300];

    int count;

    TANGOalgoOp(fnc, "BEGIN");

    printf("Input number of elts in array\n");
    scanf("%d",&n);

    TANGOalgoOp(fnc, "Init");

    printf("Enter the elements\n");
    for (count=0; count<n; ++count)
       { scanf("%d",&a[count]);
         TANGOalgoOp(fnc, "Input", a, count, a[count]);
       }

    TANGOalgoOp(fnc, "Draw", a, n);

    for (j=n-2; j>=0; --j)
       { for (i=0; i<=j; ++i)
            { if (a[i] > a[i+1])
                 { temp = a[i];
                   a[i] = a[i+1];
                   a[i+1] = temp;
                   TANGOalgoOp(fnc, "Exchange", a, i, a, i+1);
                 }
            }
       }
    TANGOalgoOp(fnc, "END");
}
```

Algorithm Part

```
#include <stdio.h>
#include <xtango.h>
int max = 0;
/*  Create an association */
void ANIMInit()
{
    ASSOCinit();
    ASSOCmake("DATA",2);
}
/* save the values in the array */
void ANIMInput(int id,int index,int val)
{
    ASSOCstore("DATA",id,index,val);   /* save the values in the array */
    if (val > max) max = val;
}
void ANIMDraw(int id,int n)
{
    int        i;
    double     vals[200],between,height,maxwidth,spacing;
    TANGO_PATH  path;
    TANGO_TRANS trans;

    for (i=0; i<n; ++i)
       { vals[i] = (double)((int)ASSOCretrieve("DATA",id,i)) / (double) max;}

    spacing = height = 0.8/ (double)(2*n-1);
    if (height < 0.0) {
      printf("Too many elements to display in window (not enough space)\n");
      exit(0);
    }

    maxwidth = 0.8;

    TWISTcreate_image_array(NULL,id,n,TANGO_IMAGE_TYPE_RECTANGLE,0,1,0.5,0.1,
               vals,maxwidth,NULL,height,spacing,1,TANGO_COLOR_BLACK,1.0);

    path = TANGOpath_null(3);
    trans = TANGOtrans_create(TANGO_TRANS_TYPE_DELAY,NULL,path);
    TANGOtrans_perform(trans);
    TANGOpath_free(1,path);
    TANGOtrans_free(1,trans);
}
void ANIMExchange(int p1,int p2,int p3,int p4)
{
    TANGO_LOC loc1, loc2;
    TANGO_IMAGE rect1, rect2;
    TANGO_PATH onepath, path1, path2;
    TANGO_TRANS move1, move2, flip;

    rect1 = (TANGO_IMAGE) ASSOCretrieve("ID", p1, p2);
    rect2 = (TANGO_IMAGE) ASSOCretrieve("ID", p3, p4);
    loc1 = TANGOimage_loc(rect1, TANGO_PART_TYPE_C );
    loc2 = TANGOimage_loc(rect2, TANGO_PART_TYPE_C );
    onepath = TANGOpath_null(1);
    path1 = TANGOpath_example(loc1, loc2, onepath);
    path2 = TANGOpath_example(loc2, loc1, onepath);
    move1 = TANGOtrans_create(TANGO_TRANS_TYPE_MOVE, rect1, path1);
    move2 = TANGOtrans_create(TANGO_TRANS_TYPE_MOVE, rect2, path2);
    flip = TANGOtrans_compose(2, move1, move2);
    TANGOtrans_perform(flip);
    ASSOCstore("ID", p3, p4, rect1);
    ASSOCstore("ID", p1, p2, rect2);
    TANGOpath_free(3, onepath, path1, path2);
    TANGOtrans_free(3, move1, move2, flip);
}
```

Animation Part

Fig. 2: A bubble-sort animation definition by XTANGO system.

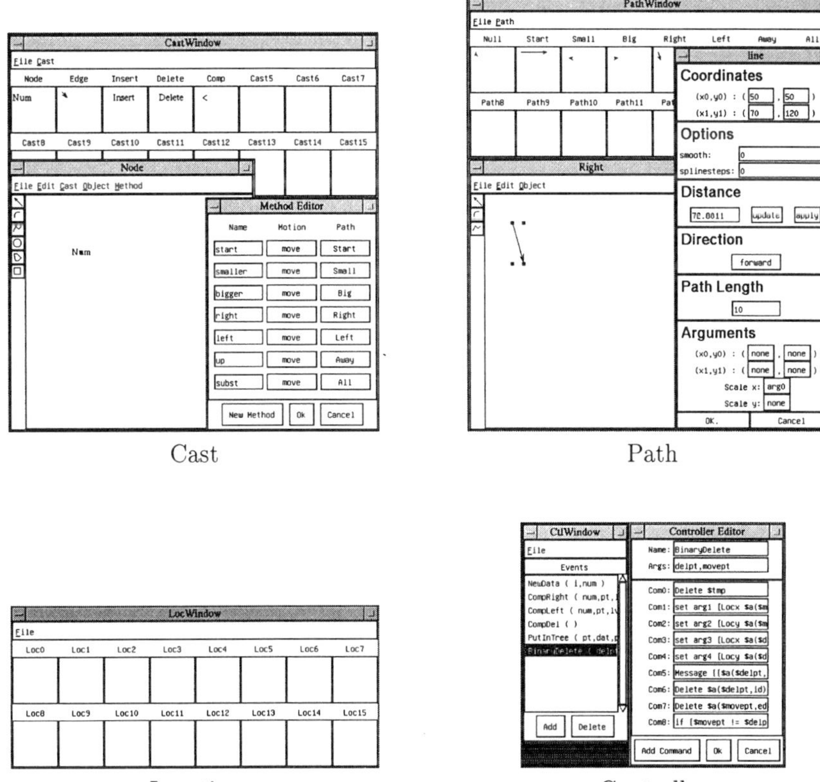

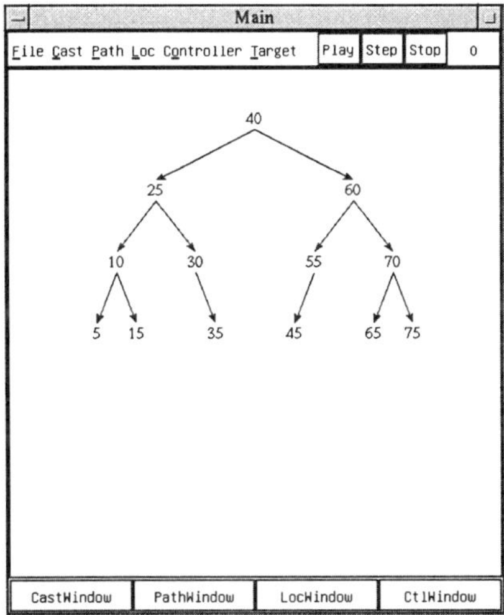

Fig. 3: A screen shot of path-activation model

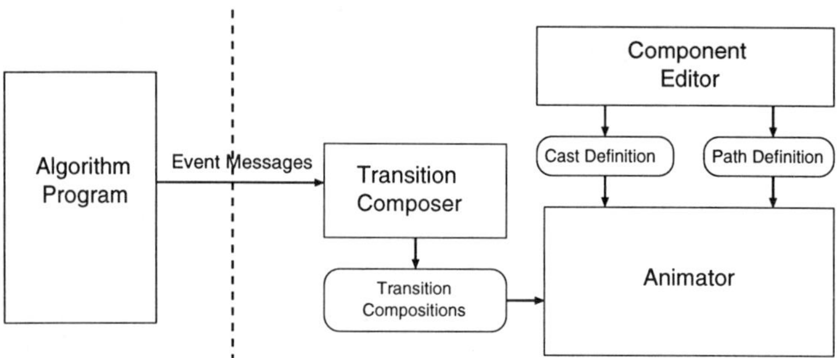

Fig. 4: A framework of transition composition model

2.2 Transition composition model

In the previous model, the controller part must be written as a program. For typical applications, we may safely define basic predefined transitions and methods for composing basic transitions. There are 3 components in transition composition model,

1. Cast: A cast is a graphical definition of animation objects with possible parameters as attributes.

2. Path: A path is a graphical definition of line along which movement of an animation object takes place.

3. Transition: A transition is a change of cast's states or cast's properties which defines how animation objects will be shown. We define 5 types of transitions which cover necessary actions used in most animations.

    (a) Move: Changing of cast's location along a predefined path.
    (b) Change: Changing of cast's properties such as scale, color, and dimension.
    (c) Create: Creation of a cast on the animation screen.
    (d) Remove: Removing of a cast from the animation screen.
    (e) Wait: Waiting for a certain amount of time.

Using these definitions, we can control the animation by composing various types of transitions instead of writing programming codes in the controller as in Path-Activation model. With the help of 2 composing tools, Iterator and Composer, our method is flexible enough to replace all the typical controller codes used to control animations. Hence we are able to produce animations without writing codes. The framework of our model is shown in Fig. 4. One example of transition composition is shown in Fig. 5.

3. Examples

To demonstrate the usefulness of our transition composition model, we show necessary graphical definitions used in the following five typical algorithm animations in Fig. 6. You may notice that various animations can be created with very small number of graphical definitions and composition of transitions.

- Maximum selection for finding the largest number.
- Merge Sort for sorting numbers using merging of sorted sequences of numbers

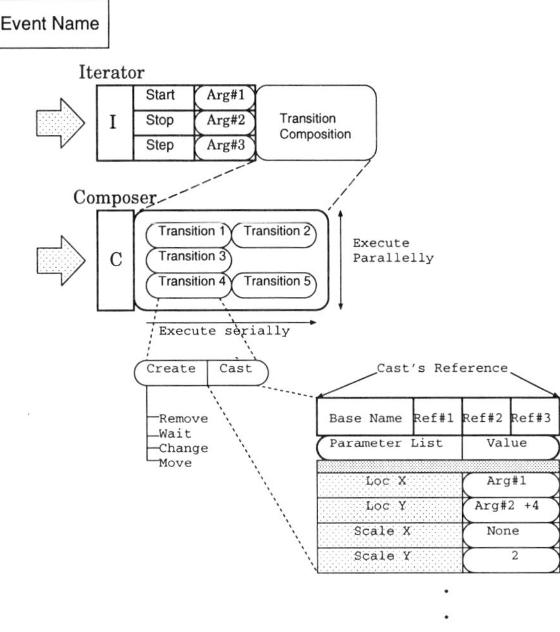

Fig. 5: An example of transition composition

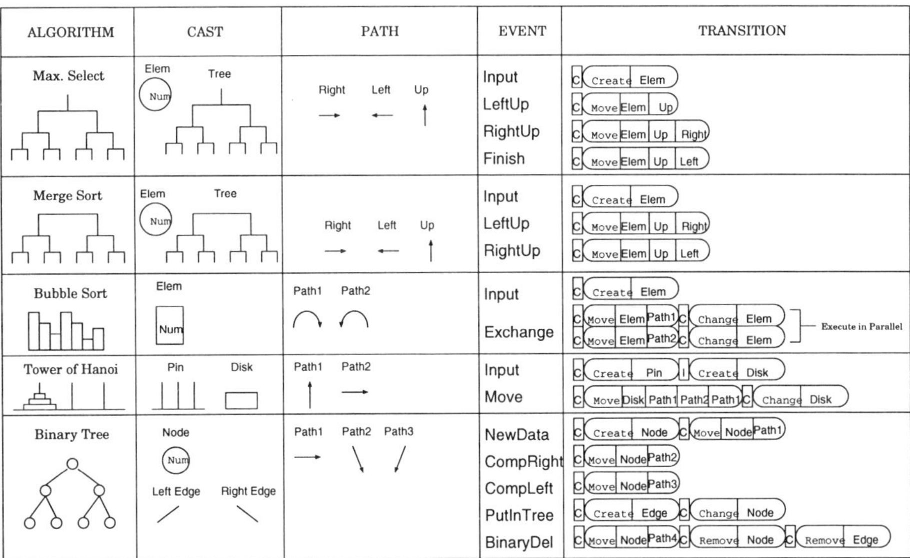

Fig. 6: Five examples of graphical definitions

- Bubble sort for sorting numbers using exchange of immediate neighbors
- Tower of Hanoi for moving sorted discs from one tower to another under constraints
- Binary tree construction for constructing a binary search tree

The outline of typical processes of making algorithm animations according to our approach is as follows.

(0) We define a number of animation events and insert event generation commands in the given algorithm program.

(1) We define necessary casts and paths graphically.

(2) We define transitions for events using given composition methods of predefined transitions.

Concrete and complete steps of making an algorithm animation of moving a ball using our MO disk are as follows.

(0) Make a directory "ex1" under the directory "data" of the directory "work" in the MO disk. Make two directories "ComponentList" and "EventList" under the directory "ex1". Create a text file "ex1.evm" consisting of two lines of "start", for example. Here start is an event name.

(1) Double click on a batch file "Aa.bat" in the top level of the MO disk.

(2) The Algorithm animator starts. Start Component editor from the Algorithm animator.

(3) Define one cast "ball" and three transitions "up", "down" and "back" by drawing a circle and three lines respectively. Change "name" properties to the above names and delete values of "reference1" properties. Save the result as a file "ex1.col".

(4) Start Transition composer from the Algorithm animator. Open component list "ex1.col". Add an event whose name is "start" and add transition composedness.

(5) Add sequentially three transitions, "move ball up", "move ball down", and "move ball back". Save the result as a file "ex1.evl".

(6) Generate a file "ex1.tcp" from a file "ex1.evm".

(7) Select "animate" from the Algorithm animator.

(8) The generated animation is shown in the Algorithm animator.

The summary of the comparison of path-transition model, path-activation model, and transition composition model is as follows. In path-transition model we must define everything in terms of programming codes. In path-activation model we still have to define the controller part in terms of programming codes. In transition composition model no definition in terms of programming code is necessary as shown in Fig. 7.

4. Conclusion

We have presented a completely codeless model for algorithm animations. Our model is powerful enough to express typical algorithm animations neatly. We can easily create algorithm animations by giving three types of graphical definitions for an already written algorithm programs.

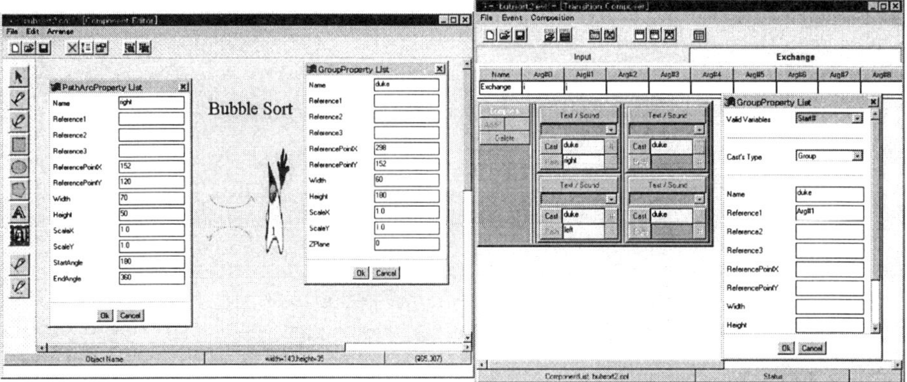

Cast and Paths   Transition composition

A produced animation

Fig. 7: A screen shot of transition composition model

References

[1] Brown, Marc H. and Hershberger, John, "Zeus: A System for Algorithm Animation", Proceedings of IEEE 1991 Workshop on Visual Languages, pp.4-9, IEEE CS Press, Los Alamitos, Calif., Order No.2330, 1991.

[2] Brown, Marc H. and Hershberger, John, "Color and Sound in Algorithm Animation", Computer, Vol.25, No.12, pp.52-63, December 1992.

[3] Brown, Marc H. and Najork, Marc A., "Algorithm Animation Using 3D Interactive Graphics", UIST'93 Conference Proceedings, pp.93-100, 1993.

[4] Kawai, Ken, "Algorithm Animation Based on Path-Activation Model", Master thesis of Computer Science Department, Tokyo Institute of Technology, 1995

[5] Lawrence, Andrea, Badre, Albert and Stasko, John, "Empirically Evaluating the Use of Animations to Teach Algorithms", Proceedings of the 1994 IEEE Symposium on Visual Languages, St. Louis, MO, October 1994, pp. 48-54.

[6] MacroMedia Inc., "Director Version 3.0 Interactivity Manual", 1991

[7] MacroMedia Inc., "Director Version 3.0 Studio Manual", 1991

[8] Muthukumarasamy, Jeyakumar and Stasko, John T., "Visualizing Program Executions on Large Data Sets Using Semantic Zooming", Graphics, Visualization, and Usability Center, Georgia Institute of Technology, Atlanta, GA, Technical Report GIT-GVU-95-02, January 1995.

[9] Ousterhout, John K., "Tcl and the Tk Toolkit", Addison-Wesley Publishing Company, 1994.

[10] Ritthongpitak, Chanchai, "Design and Implementation of A Completely Codeless Algorithm Animation System", Master thesis of Computer Science Department, Tokyo Institute of Technology, 1997

[11] Rosanna Lee and Patrick Chan, "The Java Class Libraries: An Annotated Reference", Addison-Wesley Publishing Company, 1996

[12] Stasko, John T., "The Path-Transition Paradigm: A Practical Methodology for Adding Animation to Program Interfaces", Journal of Visual Languages and Computing, Vol.1, No.3, September 1990, pp.213-236.

[13] Stasko, John T., "Animating Alogrithms with XTANGO", SIGACT News, Vol.23, No.2, Spring 1992, pp.67-71.

[14] Stasko, John T. and McCrickard, D. Scott, "Real Clock Time Animation Support for Developing Software Visualizations", Australian Computer Journal, Vol.27,No.3,Novembe 1995,pp.118-128

[15] Stasko, John T. and Turner, Carlton Reid, "Tidy Animations of Tree Algorithms", Proceedings of the 1992 IEEE Workshop on Visual Languages, Seattle, WA, September 1992, pp.216-218.

Information Modelling and Knowledge Bases IX
P.-J. Charrel et al. (Eds.)
1998, IOS Press

Acquisition of an Object Structural Model of a Class

Yoshiaki YASUMURA   Katsunori ORIMOTO

Noboru BABAGUCHI   Tadahiro KITAHASHI

I.S.I.R., Osaka University

8-1 Mihogaoka, Ibaraki, Osaka 567, Japan

abstract

In this paper, we propose a method of acquiring of an object structural model from range images of the objects in a class. This structural model is considered as a standard model for segmenting three dimensional objects in a class into parts with common constituents. First, we define an expression of an object structure as a graph based on the location of the connected parts. This expression allows us to define the structure of the shape that is represented with superquadrics. A structural model is acquired from the structures of the objects in a class. This model enables us to arrange all objects in the class with common constituents. Finally, we present experimental results of our method based on a set of actual objects.

1. Introduction

Model acquisition is one of the central issues in the field of AI, and has pushed forward the study on what can be symbolically represented. Also in the field of CV, model acquisition is regarded as a promising scheme in automatically constructing a model of an object. However, acquiring symbolically represented models of shapes of objects from image data have been discussed in only a few articles, because shapes are difficult to be represented by symbols. We have proposed a method for acquiring a model of three dimensional (3D for short) objects in a class[1].

We view the model acquisition of the objects as producing a typical shape and shape distribution of the object from some instances of the 3D objects in a class. In this method, 3D shapes are expressed with superquadrics [2] which can represent geometric features of 3D shape by some parameters. This expression enables acquisition of the object model by manipulating these parameters. However, a complicated shape must be segmented into parts, since superquadrics can represent only a primitive shape. Therefore, the first part of this paper is devoted to the discussion on a method of segmentation of a 3D object into parts.

As far as segmentation of a 3D object is concerned, the existing methods have mainly focused on segmenting an object into reasonable parts[3][4]. Since these methods scarcely take into account of the concept of the object class, the objects in a class might be segmented into parts in various manners even though they are similar in shape. This causes difficulty on object comparison that is needed for model acquisition and object recognition.

We cope with the problem by proposing a method of acquiring a common structural model of objects in a class from their cylindrical range data. This proposal is based on

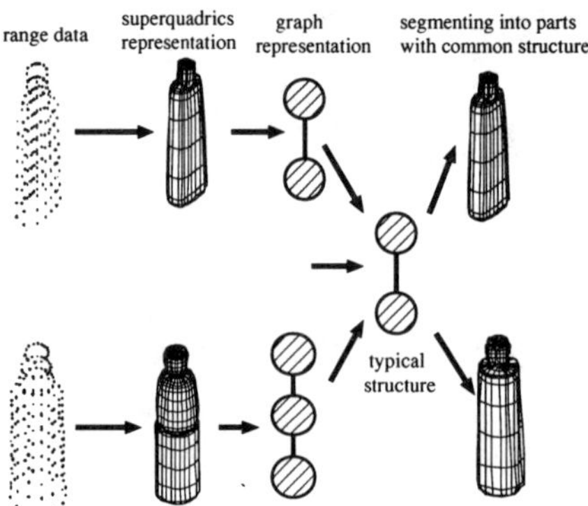

Figure 1: Procedures of the proposed method

the hypothesis that a representative structure of instances in an object class is shared by most of them in the class, if some are different from it.

Fig.1 shows the procedures of this method. Input data are cylindrical range images of 3D objects in a same class. First, the input objects are segmented into parts based on the surface curvature, and the parts are represented with superquadrics. Since the objects in a class might be segmented into parts with various structures, a structural model is acquired for segmenting 3D objects with common structure. Next, the structures of the objects are expressed by 3D graph based on the location of the connected parts. From the structures expressed by the graph, a structural model is acquired. This structural model enables us to arrange all objects in the class with common constituents.

2. Representation of a 3D object

A primitive convex shaped object can be described by superquadrics represented by the following parametric formula.

$$
\begin{cases}
x = f_1(z)\cos^{\varepsilon_1}\eta\cos^{\varepsilon_2}\omega \\
y = f_2(z)\cos^{\varepsilon_1}\eta\sin^{\varepsilon_2}\omega \\
z = a_3\sin^{\varepsilon_1}\eta
\end{cases}
$$

$$
f_i(z) = (1 - k_i\frac{z}{a_3})a_i, \quad i = 1, 2.
$$

Parameters η, ω correspond to latitude and longitude angles from the x-y plane and the x-z one, respectively. Parameters a_1, a_2, a_3 define the size of a superquadric body on x, y, z coordinates, respectively. ε_1 is the squareness parameter in the z-y plane and ε_2 is the one in the x-y plane. Function $f_i(z)$'s are the tapering functions of the shapes of the body in the z direction, and k_i's are the tapering parameters.

To represent a 3D shape by superquadrics, the approximate method based on least squares minimization is applied. Since the approximated shape depends on initial values of the parameters, the proper initial values are determined based on the axis orientation of the shape, because superquadrics can model only axis-symmetrical shapes.

A complicated object should be segmented into parts, each of which has a shape simple enough to be expressed by superquadrics. The precise expression of the structure

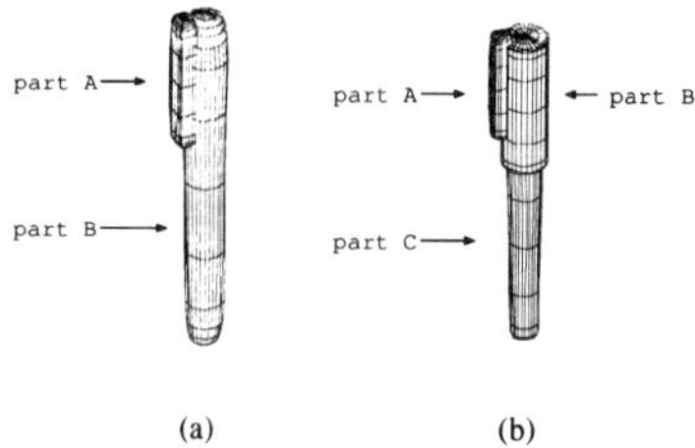

Figure 2: An example of the pens

of the object requires to include the coordinates of the positions of their connecting points and the mutual relationship of orientations of parts.

Humans usually understand the form of an object in qualitative way instead of the quantitative way such as determining each parameters of the superquadrics representing the object. For example, they understand a table as a piece of furniture consisting of a wide rectangular plate supported by upright four legs at the four corners, one by one. Such kinds of the shape description can be obtained by segmenting the surface of an object into several areas and orientations into several groups so that they can uniquely be associated with conceptual description such as a corner and a top surface, and can be determined independent of the actual size and the form in an allowable range.

For instance, the typical areas of the surface of superquadrics representing a cylinder can be determined as follows. The top surface, the side one and the bottom one of it are associated with the three parts of superquadrics having the latitude angles of $\theta > 45°$, $-45° < \theta < 45°$ and $\theta < -45°$, respectively. This expression allows us to define a location of a connected point of object parts in a quantitative manner in the form of qualitative description such as latitude and longitude angles like the following example.

3. Acquisition of a structural model

For the model acquisition of a compound shape, objects in a class are desired to share a structure with common constituents, because it is difficult to compare shapes having different structures with each other. For example, (a) and (b) in Fig.2 is viewed as objects belonging to the class of "pen". However, (a) is composed of two parts and (b) is of three parts, that is, (a) and (b) are segmented into parts with different structures. This segmentation causes difficulty on the comparison of them. Therefore, we propose a method of determining a common structured model for 3D objects in a class.

3.1 Segmentation of an object

First, the initial segmentation is applied to each object. The initial segmentation is based on the surface curvature of each data point that is determined by the maximal curvature calculated from the range data of the surrounding points. Since the procedure usually provides excessive segmentation by the effects of noise in the range data, the divided parts should be merged into reasonable areas. This integration is fulfilled on the base of the estimation by "Reasonable Parts Decomposition using AIC (Akaike's Information Criterion)"[3]. This method determines the best decomposition by selecting

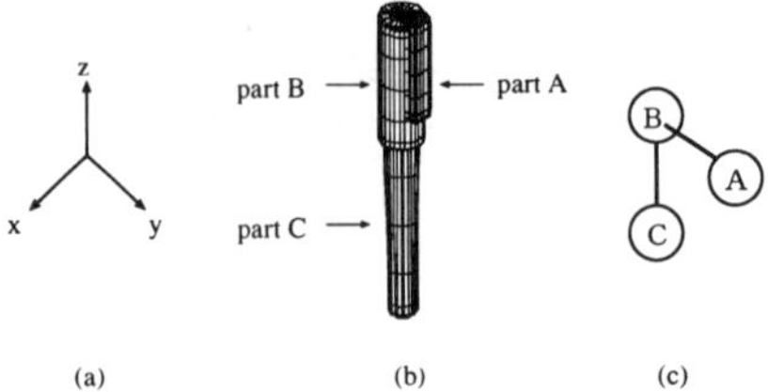

Figure 3: Object structure graph

the one with minimum errors between the object data and the superquadric model for all considerable combinations of parts. In other words, this method realizes a segmentation that an object is expressed with fewer parts and less error of approximation using AIC as the criterion.

3.2 Object structure graph

There can be a variety of structural models even for an object class, because they are abstract representation of the structures of them in various view points. We employ such an abstract one as expressed in the form of 3D graph, since we use the model only to show the three dimensional configuration of parts of an object. We name it as an object structure graph. It consists of nodes and oriented edges corresponding to the parts and the orientation of the connection between the parts as shown in Fig.3, respectively. An edge also represents a 3D orientation of a part at a connected point in local coordinates of one of the discrete part. The orientation of a part at a connected point is defined by the orientation of the surface normal at that point. It is expressed by a direction out of the six ones i.e. $\pm x, y, z$ axis direction of the coordinates of the part, intending compact representation of a complicate shape. Table1 shows the grouping of the direction of the connected point in terms of the normalized latitude and longitude angles. This expression makes it possible to represent the structure of a 3D object by superquadrics.

3.3 Acquisition of a typical structure

Let's move to discussion on a common structural model of objects in a class. One reasonable candidate of the common structure of objects in an object class is the maximal set of them grouped by the number of parts.

To acquire a more structural model, it is necessary to ensure the similarity of parts corresponding among the objects in the maximal set. Comparing the objects necessitates correspondence of parts of objects, although a primitive method causes numbers of possible combinations of part correspondence between objects with a common structure. We determine the part correspondence between objects by finding the minimum dissimilarity of the combination of the part correspondence. The dissimilarity between objects is defined by both shapes of the parts and ratios of the volume of connected parts. The rough shape of a part can be described by ratios of scale parameters, i.e., $a_1/a_2, a_2/a_3, a_3/a_1$. The volume of a part is defined as the product of scale parameters, $a_1 a_2 a_3$.

The final structural model of the objects in the class proposed in this paper is

Table 1: Classification of the direction

direction	latitude angle θ, longitude angle ϕ
z	$45° < \theta \leq 90°$
$-z$	$-90° \leq \theta \leq -45°$
x	$-45° < \theta \leq 45°, -45° < \phi \leq 45°$
y	$-45° < \theta \leq 45°, 45° < \phi \leq 135°$
$-x$	$-45° < \theta \leq 45°$ $-180° < \phi \leq -135°, 135° < \phi \leq 180°$
$-y$	$-45° < \theta \leq 45°, -135° < \phi \leq -45°$

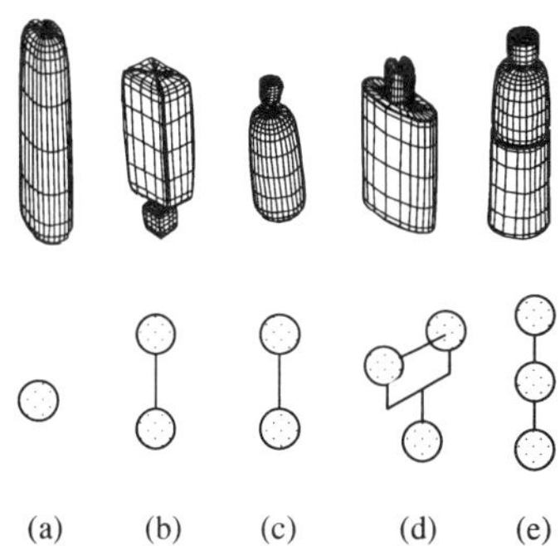

Figure 4: The shapes and structures of bottles

obtained by averaging the corresponding parameters of the objects in the maximal set. By using the dissimilarity from this model, all objects in the class are arranged to have the common structure by integrating after segmenting into parts.

4. Experimental results

Let us show experimental results by applying the proposed method to the segmentation of bottles. Input data are cylindrical range data of 40 bottles.

An initial segmentation into parts of each object is performed by grouping the points having similar maximal curvature. This often causes excessive partition effected by noise in the range data. After the all parts are approximated by superquadrics, they are reconstructed through integrating some parts into the best structure in the sense of AIC. Fig.4 shows some shapes represented with superquadrics and their structure graphs. Since 23 objects have the common object structure graph in Fig.5, this can be a representative structure of the class. Thus, a structural model of the class is acquired from the objects in the maximal set. Table 2 and Table 3 show the values of the parameters of the model. v_A, v_B are the volumes of part A, part B, respectively. We can get the features of the object shapes in the class by interpreting values of the model as follows.

- Since the average of v_A/v_B is big, Part A is much bigger than Part B.

- Part A's average of a_2/a_3 is small and that of a_3/a_1 is big, thus Part A is slender

Figure 5: Typical structure of the bottle

Table 2: The values of the model (1)

	Part A		Part B	
	average	variance	average	variance
a_1/a_2	0.730	0.036	1.033	0.029
a_2/a_3	0.483	0.032	0.875	0.066
a_3/a_1	3.234	0.881	1.238	0.019

shape.

- Since Part B's average of a_1/a_2 is nearly 1, the width is equal to the depth.

Next, the structures of all objects in the class are tuned to the structural model by merging the parts of great dissimilarity from the corresponding parts of the model. Fig.6 shows some results of the arrangement. As an experimental result, all objects in the class of bottles are segmented into a "body" and a "cap".

5. Conclusion

We summerize this paper as:

- The object structure graph can express 3D object compactly. This is convenient to compare the rough forms of objects.

- The typical structure is obtained as the most common structure of objects in a class. This allows us to segment objects in a class into common constituents.

- The experimental result indicates the validity of this method. The result of this method can be applied to comparison of objects in a class.

Acknowledgement We are grateful to Prof. N.Yokoya and H.Iwasa in Nara Institute of Science and Technology, who supported to get range data of objects.

References

[1] Y.Yasumura, K.Orimoto, N.Babaguchi, T.Kitahashi: "Inductive Learning of 3D Shapes with Superquadrics Representation", Proc. ACCV'95, Vol.3, pp.310-314(1995.12).

Table 3: The values of the model (2)

	average	variance
v_a/v_b	15.653	45.853
v_b/v_a	0.081	0.002

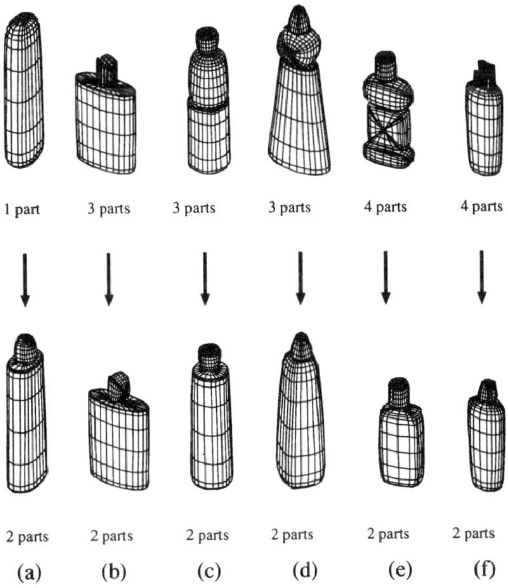

Figure 6: The results of arrangement

[2] F. Solina and R. Bajcsy : "Recovery of Parametric Models ¿from Range Images: The Case for Superquadrics with Global Deformations", IEEE Trans. Pattern Anal. & Mach. Intell.,PAMI-12,2,pp.131-147 (1990).

[3] T. Horikoshi and S. Suzuki: "3D parts Decomposition from Sparse Range Range Date using Information Criterion", Proc. CVPR, pp.168-173(1993).

[4] T. Darrel, S. Scalaroff, and A. Pentland : "Segmentation by Minimal Description", Proc. 3rd ICCV, ICCV, Osaka, pp.1691-1700(1994.9).

Information Modelling and Knowledge Bases IX
P.-J. Charrel et al. (Eds.)
1998, IOS Press

Guiding Design through Causal Reasoning

Keiichi Nakata
School of Computing & Mathematical Sciences
Oxford Brookes University
Headington, Oxford OX3 0BP
United Kingdom

Abstract

One of the most common events when designing an artefact is the introduction of a new functional requirement to the existing mechanisms. Focusing on the functional aspect of physical devices, we view the design task as the achievement of desired behaviours of a device and its environment. The idea put forward in this paper is the application of Shoham's temporal logic to represent and reason about physical systems in the design task. Devices and environmental knowledge such as laws of physics are described in terms of causal rules, and from these rules together with facts and assumptions we can construct a model of the most likely behaviour of the system. The design specification is provided as a behavioural specification, which consists of the desired sequence of events. The predicted behaviour of the system is compared with the behavioural specification for evaluation. The design modification is performed by modifying the set of causal rules which represent the device. The design problem we anticipate is of practical and medium-size domain, and we have so far worked on logic circuits. Although computationally complex, this method contributes to the formal treatment of temporal constraints and knowledge in the design task.

1. Introduction

One of the most common events when designing an artefact is the introduction of a new functional requirement to the existing mechanisms. This new requirement often serves as a motivation to design a physical device which would accomplish the task of achieving the desired function. Such view of a physical device concentrates on its functional aspect—each device has its own function as a part of the mechanism. From this point of view, it is reasonable to represent a physical device as functions which provide additional causal effects in the world. This new function is often desired by those who consider such function necessary, thus motivating design of a physical device which would bring about this effect. From such functional view of design, it is reasonable to represent physical devices, or the components of a device, as functions which provide new causal consequence to the existing environment.

One of the earliest works on such view of design is by Freeman and Newell [4] who maintained the validity of representing physical devices as functions and demonstrated the configuration task as the combination of various functions. Later, Barrow [1] suggested a formal method to verify the correctness of digital circuits based on the comparison of intended and desired behaviours. More recently, functional representation [10], which provides a formal representation for the functioning of a device in various levels of abstraction, is integrated with qualitative simulation for the design verification task [6]. There have been so far, however, a relatively small amount of research on the formal representation and reasoning about temporal constraints in design.

The idea put forward in this paper is the application of causal reasoning to guide design. Causal reasoning primarily provides the prediction of the behaviour of the device in a current design, and when the behaviour does not satisfy the requirements of design, suggest a plausible modification based on causal knowledge. The characteristics of the design problem we anticipate here is that there may be dynamic change both in the device itself and the interactions between the device and the environment. Moreover, at this point, we focus on the feasibility of a device in terms of its functions, and place less emphasis on optimisation. The framework for the causal reasoning is based on the temporal logic devised by Shoham [11]. Although suggested as a means to deal with the frame problems, the formal language of temporal logic with capability to deal with nonmonotonic reasoning is well suited to the representation and the computation of the design task we anticipate.

2. Logical description of behaviour-oriented design

One of the early approach to formalising design was that of design as a deductive process. This view was best described as "form follows function". If we have a strong theory about the design process then it follows that a specification will, quite naturally, deduce a design. However, as we have examined, design is not a well-structured task. If we borrow March's words, "when we are designing we do not have a clear picture of what the design is; if we did, our task is needless." [8, p.21]. Contrary to the deduction model of design, a design is not what we obtain through deduction, but is the thing about what we make deductions. If we have a design, then we can deduce its functionality, features and validity. This leads to the idea that design is a reverse process of deduction. This process is what is known as *abduction*—it is not a logically sound process, but can be seen in everyday human reasoning.

2.1. Abduction model of design

One of the systems which incorporated this abduction model of design is RESIDUE [3]. In this approach, the solution to a design problem is to find a *residue* for a design goal. More precisely, given the initial world model W and the design goal G, the solution is the *residue* R such that

$$W \cup R \vdash G$$

where $W \cup R$ is consistent and R can be made true. RESIDUE then applies a deductive procedure to derive R as the design solution, but it is essentially an abductive process since R is being derived as the realiser of G.

The design model we introduce is focused on the behavioural aspect of a device. The design goal is to provide a design that realises the desired behaviour in a designated environment. In this formulation, there are four elements involved for a device to exhibit its desired behaviour. There is an *environment* (E)—the world in which the device is meant to be placed and operate—which is governed and represented by a set of physical laws and unchangeable facts. There is also a set of isolated events, which we call a *scenario* (S), and this can be considered to be the events known or expected to occur independently from physical laws or the operation of the device. The scenario may change within the same environment depending on the various assumptions made about the world. *Design* (D) is the knowledge about functions and the configuration of the device which would initiate a sequence of events which would not have occurred without its presence. These elements together form a *system* in which the device operates and produce a sequence of events called *behaviour* (or *predicted* behaviour) (B).

In the design task there is an additional element, the *behavioural specification* (BS). Since design activity is motivated to produce a desired behaviour of a system, there should be a specification for such behaviour. The behavioural specification of a device is the sequence of events and states which are desirable and necessary to its performance.

Given these elements, a successful design task can formally be described as follows. The behaviour of the system can be derived from the environment, scenario and the artefact (design), i.e.,

$$E, S, D \models B$$

and the aim of design activity is to construct a design D which would result in the desired behaviour, $B = BS$. E and S are specified by the domain and setup of the design problem. In this abductive model of the design process, the analogy with the conventional iterative view of design method can be seen as follows; the evaluation process is the comparison of B and BS, the feedback is the abductive reasoning about D, which leads to the modification of design. Note that typically reasoning process to obtain B is nonmonotonic. It is easy to see that adding or removing an assumption in S or D may change the behaviour of the system. Additionally, since S and B consist of temporal sequences of events, the construction of the model B involves a form of temporal reasoning.

3. Formulation by causal theories in logic CI

The framework for the causal reasoning we have chosen is the logic CI [11]. Logic CI is a nonmonotonic temporal logic which provides a unique model for a causal theory. A *causal theory* Ψ is a set of *causal rules*, which depict the causal relations between events, *boundary conditions* which represent facts and events known, or assumed, to be true, and *inertial rules* which represent events that are potentially true over a duration of time. A causal rule is of the form

$$\Phi \wedge \Theta \supset \Box\varphi$$

where

φ: a formula TRUE(t_1, t_2, p), indicating that the proposition p holds between time points t_1 and t_2,

Φ: a (possibly empty) conjunction of the 'necessary' formulae $\Box\varphi$,

Θ: a (possibly empty) conjunction of the 'contingent' formulae $\Diamond\varphi$

and describes that the conditions Φ and Θ causes $\Box\varphi$. It is important to note that the latest time point in the antecedent always precedes the initial time point of the consequent.[1] A boundary condition is a causal rule with an empty Φ, which shows that its consequent is asserted as a fact instead of a causal consequence.

Inertial rules have the same form as the causal rules but the consequents are potential terms POTEN($t_1, t_2, \text{p}-q$), indicating that the proposition q *potentially* holds, i.e., if nothing that prevents or terminates q is known, between time points t_1 and t_2. Rules of the form PROJECT($t_1, \text{p}-q, t_2, t_3, q$) where $t_1 \leq t_2 \leq t_3$ projects the potential proposition q between time points t_1 and t_3. Causal rules and inertial rules with empty Φ are called *boundary conditions* since their consequents are asserted as facts instead of causal consequence.

The advantages of using this language are that 1) it is declarative, 2) it can represent default conditions, 3) a sound and consistent causal theory would have a single model which is the most likely outcome, and 4) it can treat processes in a qualitative manner similar to the approach in qualitative simulation [7]. Since it is declarative, it is easy to add and remove causal rules and boundary conditions without altering existing rules. In the domain such as design, there are a large number of conditions and parameters we must specify and it is more efficient to have default specifications. By extending the language from the propositional case to the first-order case (see for example [2]), we can introduce other useful reasoning methods such as qualitative reasoning. This capability is advantageous when considering the integration of the reasoning techniques.

Using this language, we can represent the elements of design described in Section 2. Environment E, which is a collection of physical laws in the domain, can be represented by a set of causal rules corresponding to each physical causality. Scenario S, which is a collection of assumptions, can be represented by a set of boundary conditions. Design D can be represented by a set of causal rules, each representing the function of a component or subcomponents of which it consists. Behavioural specification BS is a set of events represented by φ in temporal sequence. It is important to note that given a domain in which the system operates, the causal rules in E cannot be removed or altered, whereas S can be changed depending on the different setups of conditions.

All of the causal rules and boundary conditions in E,S and D are collected into a causal theory which represents the system as a whole. Owing to the "unique cmi model theorem"[2] [11], a sound and consistent causal theory has a cmi model which is the most likely behaviour. In this case, the cmi model is the behaviour B of the system.

3.1. Representation by logic CI

To summarise, each of the elements E,S,D,B and the behavioural specification BS are represented in the language CI as follows.

● *Environment*
The laws of physics and causal knowledge in the domain are represented as causal rules. An environment comprises of sets of causal theories each representing a set of knowledge for a particular aspect. For instance, a domain for a logic circuits comprises of causal theories for AND-gates, OR-gates, NAND-gates, etc. The relation between causal theory for environment Ψ_E and an environment E is $\Psi_E \in E$.

---

[1] Implying that the cause always precedes the effect.

[2] The abbreviation cmi stands for *chronologically maximally ignorant*.

- *Scenario*

A sequence of events which is assumed to occur is represented by base terms and potential terms. These comprise the boundary conditions for causal theories. This is described in detail in the next section. A scenario S a set of these terms, i.e., $\Box\varphi$, POTEN$\varphi \in S$.

- *Design*

Each component and the causal connexions as the results of certain configuration are represented as causal rules. The relation between causal theory for design Ψ_D and a design D is $\Psi_D \in D$.

- *Behaviour*

Once the causal theories for E,S and D are merged together to form a larger causal theory, it would have a unique cmi model for prediction. This model represents the behaviour of the combined causal theory which represents the current design under a particular scenario. In this case, the unique cmi model M is equivalent to the behaviour B, i.e., $M \equiv B$.

- *Behavioural specification*

Behavioural specification is a set of desired events in a total temporal order specifying their sequence. Each event is an atomic base formula, such that for a behavioural specification BS, $\varphi \in BS$. Given a behaviour B, the purpose of design is, ideally, to achieve $BS = B$.

4. Design process

4.1. Three phases of design

There are roughly three phases in each stage of design, which are simulation, verification and modification, and a design process can be seen as an iterative cycle of these phases. A design process terminates when, in the verification phase, the design is achieving what has been described in the specification. In our framework, these phases are performed as follows.

4.1.1. Simulation

The simulation of the behaviour of the system is given as the result of the prediction task, in this case the computation of the unique cmi model. This model provides the most likely outcome from the causal theory constructed from E,S and D described in the previous section. The characteristic point here is that because it computes the unique cmi model, there is always *one* prediction per system. The validity of this feature, as opposed to the multiple prediction, is discussed later in Section 5.

4.1.2. Design verification

Once the prediction of the behaviour is obtained through simulation, the next step is to see if it fulfills the behavioural specification. Given a set of events in the behavioural specification and the predicted behaviour which is the set of events in the cmi model, the design verification task is to detect the difference between the two sequences of events. If there is no discrepancy between the two, we can conclude that the current design in the provided scenario satisfies the specification. Otherwise, the design should be modified.

Discrepancies between two sequences of events arise when there exist incompatible transitions of events. There are basically three types of discrepancies: 1) insufficient (events missing), 2) redundant (have extra undesirable events), and 3) divergence (branching into incompatible sequence of events). These cases are illustrated in Table 1 and Figure 1. In the first two cases, the sequences of events are basically the same but there are some events being inconsistent. It should be noted that the time points (t_n) are not absolute, but relative; they merely describe the order in which these events occur. In the first-order case, the basic discrepancies are the same as in the propositional case, except that the comparison of the events involves unification. For instance, the next event occurring in the specification is $value(1)$ and the prediction gives $value(X)$, where X is a variable, these two events are consistent provided that the variable X has not been instantiated to another value throughout the scope of the sequence. Also, owing to the semantics of the first-order logic, two terms are inconsistent not only when they are contradictory by negation (e.g. $p(a)$ and $\neg p(a)$) but semantically (e.g. $value(output(+))$ and $value(output(-))$).

Table 1: Three basic cases of discrepancies.

MODEL	insufficient	redundant	divergence
(t_1,p_1)	(t_1,p_1)	(t_1,p_1)	(t_1,p_1)
(t_2,p_2)	(t_2,p_3)	(t_2,p_2)	(t_2,p_2)
(t_3,p_3)	(t_3,p_4)	(t_3,q)	(t_3,q_3)
(t_4,p_4)	(t_4,p_5)	(t_4,p_3)	(t_4,q_4)
(t_5,p_5)	—	(t_5,p_4)	(t_5,q_5)
—	—	(t_6,p_5)	—

As mentioned earlier, since the discrete time points attached to the events have no significance other than the definition of the ordering among the events, the sequence of events should be compared by their relative orderings. The basic strategy to detect the discrepancies is to start from the earliest time points of the two sequences of events and proceed chronologically until the first incompatibility is found. Since the behavioural specification consists of *necessary* events, all events in it should appear in the predicted behaviour. On the other hand, we can ignore some of the intermediate events in the predicted behaviour which do not appear in the behavioural specifications as irrelevant or unimportant events. If the predicted behaviour contains all the events, in chronological order, consisting the behavioural specification, we can judge that the specification has been fulfilled. Otherwise, the modification process is invoked to fix the discrepancies.

4.1.3. Modification

As the result of design verification, we can identify the point where modifications are necessary in order to obtain the desirable behaviour of the system. The idea is to 'cause' such events which are missing in the predicted behaviour by asserting a causal rule which does this job. Typically this rule is a very abstract rule which may exhibit no intuitive causality whatsoever, but has an effect of 'forcing' an event which is desirable to occur. To make this causal rule implementable, we need to rewrite the rule into a feasible rule whose causal relation is

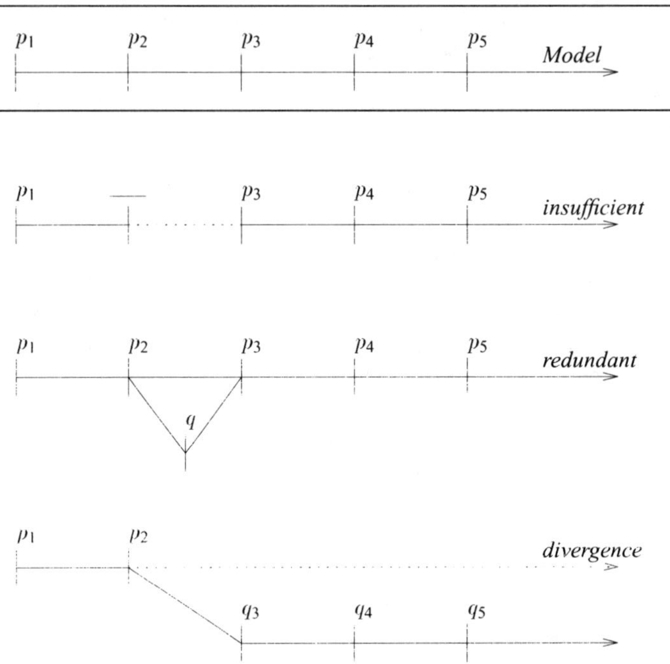

Figure 1: Three basic cases of discrepancies: *insufficient* — an event missing, *redundant* — an extra event, *divergence* — histories diverging.

more intuitive. There are two operations, one each for the antecedent and the consequent of the rule, we can apply in rewriting the rule. For its antecedent, we look for an existing causal rule which has the common events in its antecedent. For its consequent, we perform abduction, using existing causal rules. This process is described in Figure 2. The purpose of these operations is to bridge the gap between the causal relation depicted by the asserted rule, which is analogous to the task of problem decomposition. Since each rule in the causal theory for design D represents a function of a component, asserting a rule to the set is analogous to adding a new component to the configuration of design. More importantly, these operations preserve the temporal constraints among the events.

Similarly, the removal or the replacement of a component is performed by removing one or more rules from the theory. Retracting a causal rule is equivalent to removing a function from which an undesirable event was derived, and, as a result, detaching a component which was responsible for the behaviour. There are essentially two cases for this.

- The causal rule which concluded the event is retractable (i.e., design component rules).

- The causal rule which concluded the event is *not* retractable (i.e., environment causal rules such as laws of physics).

In the first case, removing the rule solves the problem.[3] It is equivalent to removing

---

[3]The implication of removing the rule can be more problematic. In some cases, the rule may have concluded

Asserted rule

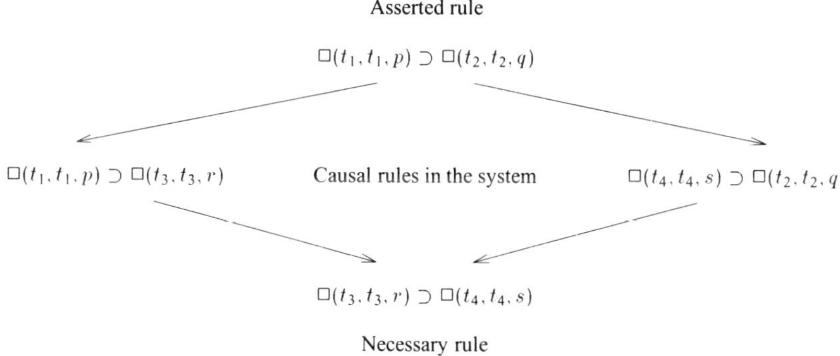

Figure 2: Proof operation of an asserted rule. $(t_1 < t_3 < t_4 < t_2)$

a component in the design. An alternative is to keep the rule but suppress it from firing by removing the events which satisfy the premise. We will take the first strategy and not the second since it is always possible to reconstruct the rules which would effectively have the same result.

In the second case, since it is not reasonable to remove the rule (unless we can alter the environment), the strategy will be the second of those mentioned in the previous paragraph. We first take a look at the causal rule and see what were the events that caused the rule to fire. The aim now is to choose an event among them and prevent that to take place. By checking which causal rule caused the event, we would have the same task we originally had, but with different events and rules, and at the preceding time point. This process continues until we find a retractable rule, or possibly a boundary condition. This process will always terminate since we always assume that there is an initial time point where the prediction initiates. The soundness and the consistency of the causal theory must be maintained by monitoring the changes in the rules.

4.2. Summary of the algorithm

We have so far described the three phases of a design stage in the context of behaviour based design. The overall process of the process can be summarised by the following algorithm. Assuming that there are n possible scenarios to consider. For scenario S_i $(i \leq n)$

1. Provide behavioural specification BS_i.

2. Construct the prediction model (cmi model) M_i incorporating S_i in the causal theory.

3. Compare M_i and BS_i; detect the earliest discrepancy.

4. If there is *no discrepancy* proceed to the next scenario S_{i+1} and continue from 1.
   Else if *insufficient*, add causal rules to provide necessary event to occur. Then repeat from 2.

---

a desirable event elsewhere, which no longer could be supported. It is, however, possible to reconstruct a causal rule which concludes the desirable event but with different premises.

Else *redundant*, add/remove causal rules to suppress the occurrence of the redundant. Then repeat from 2.

Here we assumed only two types of discrepancies for simplicity. The process terminates when no discrepancy is detected for all scenarios considered. Adding/retracting of causal rules is interactive although the suggestions are generated by the method outlined in the previous section.

4.3. Examples

We have so far tested this technique primarily in the circuit design domain. Here we present two examples, one for the static case, and the other for the dynamic case.

● *Set-Reset flip-flop circuit*

The behavioural requirement for the set-reset flip-flop circuit is described as follows (extracted from [5, p.44]):

1. S and R are normally held at 0 and the outputs remain constant in either one of the $Q = \overline{Q'}$ states.

2. An input sequence of 0 to 1 then back to 0 at the S input will ensure that $Q = 1$ and $Q' = 0$.

3. A similar $0 - 1 - 0$ input sequence at the R input ensures that $Q = 0$ and $Q' = 1$.

4. In normal circuit design the input condition $S = R = 1$ should not be allowed.

5. If power is connected to the circuit with $S = R = 0$, the circuit will take either one of the states $Q = \overline{Q'}$.

Among the five requirements listed above, we can construct four scenarios. (There will not be a scenario for requirement 4 since there is no temporal constraint to this specification.) For instance requirements 2 and 3 give the following two scenarios:

$$S_1 = \{\Box(1,2,s(0)), \Box(3,4,s(1)), \Box(5,6,s(0))\}$$
$$S_2 = \{\Box(1,2,r(0)), \Box(3,4,r(1)), \Box(5,6,r(0))\}$$

These describe the input sequence of $0 - 1 - 0$ for S and R respectively. From the behavioural requirements, behavioural specifications for each scenario are described as follows.

$$BS_1 = \{\Box(1,2,s(0)), \Box(3,4,s(1)), \Box(5,6,s(0)), \Box(7,\infty,q(1)), \Box(7,\infty,q'(0))\}$$
$$BS_2 = \{\Box(1,2,r(0)), \Box(3,4,r(1)), \Box(5,6,r(0)), \Box(7,\infty,q(0)), \Box(7,\infty,q'(1))\}$$

The environment rules include the causal rules for the logic gates. For example, a NAND gate is represented by the causal rules

$$\Box(t,t,input(X,a,1)) \wedge \Box(t,t,input(X,b,1)) \wedge \Diamond(t,t,powerSupply(on))$$
$$\supset \Box(t+1,t+1,output(X,0))$$
$$\Box(t,t,input(X,a,0)) \wedge \Diamond(t,t,powerSupply(on)) \supset \Box(t+1,t+1,output(X,1))$$

$$\Box(t, t, input(X, b, 0)) \land \Diamond(t, t, powerSuppply(on)) \supset \Box(t+1, t+1, output(X, 1))$$

where a and b represent the two inputs into the NAND gate X. There are also some rules for the connections between the terminals. There are other gates such as AND gates, OR gates, NOT gates etc.

In this example we assumed as a prototype design, NAND gates without any connection between them. The causal rules describing a NAND gate are

$$\Box(t, t, input(X, a, 1)) \land \Box(t, t, input(X, b, 1)) \supset \Box(t+1, t+1, output(X, 0))$$
$$\Box(t, t, input(X, a, 1)) \land \Box(t, t, input(X, b, 0)) \supset \Box(t+1, t+1, output(X, 1))$$
$$\Box(t, t, input(X, a, 0)) \land \Box(t, t, input(X, b, 1)) \supset \Box(t+1, t+1, output(X, 1))$$
$$\Box(t, t, input(X, a, 0)) \land \Box(t, t, input(X, b, 0)) \supset \Box(t+1, t+1, output(X, 1))$$

The causal theory of the system is then constructed by collecting the causal rules and the boundary conditions for the environment, scenario and design. The soundness and consistency of the causal theory is then checked and dealt with whenever these conditions are violated. For each corresponding scenario and the behavioural specification, we can compute the cmi model as the predicted behaviour [9] describes this procedure in detail). By comparing the predicted behaviour and the behavioural specification, all necessary connections between the terminals are found. Figure 3 shows the connections constructed under scenario S_1 and the behavioural specification BS_1. The broken line in the figure shows the connection which was not required by scenario S_1 but is produced by adaptation after S_2.

It is important to note that Figure 3 is one of several solutions. Some solutions involve multiple assertions of NOT gates (a sequential pair of these is equivalent to a mere connection), or redundant NAND gates. There is no valid optimisation procedure in the process at this moment, but there are some heuristics which prevent obviously unreasonable combinations. One plausible optimisation is to prefer those which introduce the least number of components. In this sense, the solution given above is optimal.

- *Verification of asynchronous circuits*

One of the problems in the domain of logic circuits, which involves more temporal constraints, is that it requires the representation of delays. An example is an asynchronous binary counter such as illustrated in Figure 4. In this device, the output value of each JK flip-flop is the input of the next one and the change in the outputs propagates from I to III. Since each JK flip-flop must wait for the change in the previous one, there is some delays between the changes in the outputs A,B,C which make it asynchronous.

In this example, the delay between the change of the value in each output and the input to the next flip-flop plays the important part in the behaviour of the system. For instance, the causal rule which describes the connection between the first and second JK flip-flop is described as

$$\Box(t, t, output(jkI, X)) \supset \Box(t+1, t+1, input(jkII, X))$$

The temporal ordering causes delays between the changes in the output of I and the input to II. Such representation of delays produces an accurate model for the behaviour of the counter. In this case, we can represent each JK flip-flop by the causal relation between its inputs

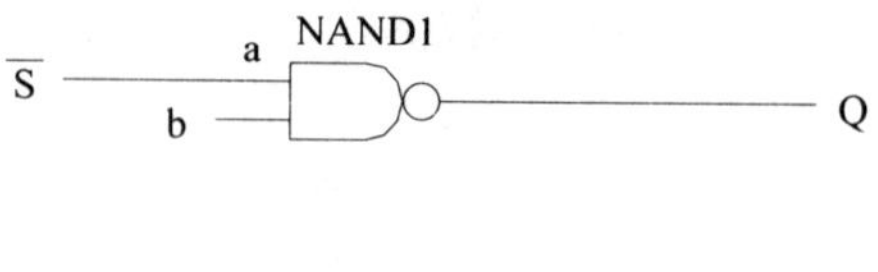

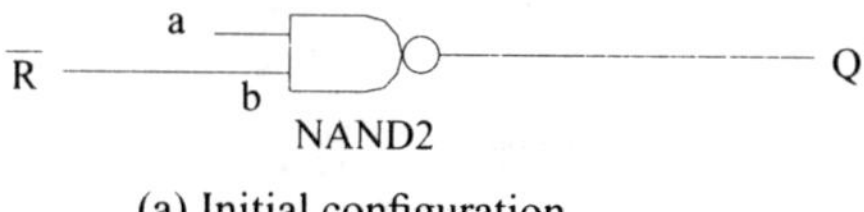

(a) Initial configuration

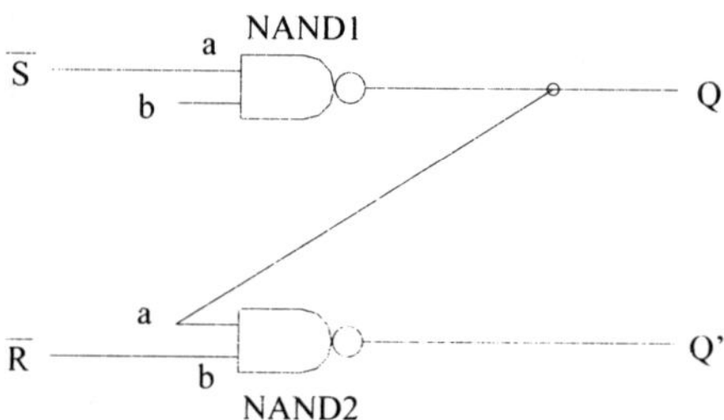

(b) Wiring after modification under Scenario1

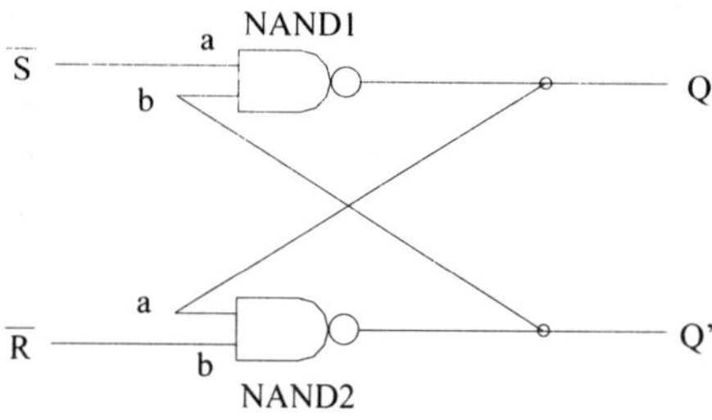

(c) Wiring after modification under Scenario2

Figure 3: Configuration of SR flip-flop circuit: solid lines after scenario S_1, broken line after scenario S_2

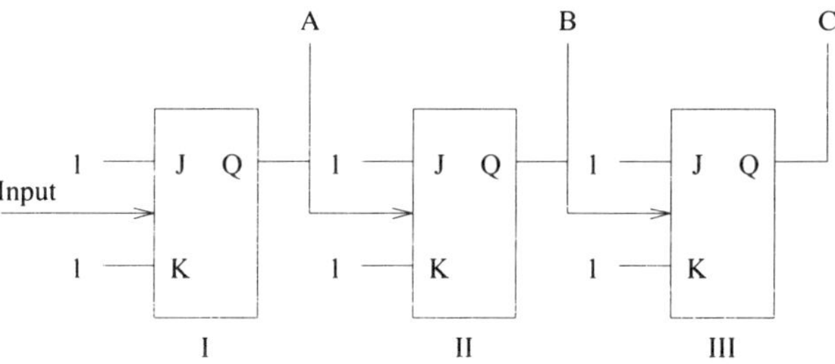

Figure 4: Asynchronous divide-by-eight counter: the rectangles (I,II,III) represent JK flip-flops, and A,B,C the output terminals.

and outputs; in other words, although it consists of an SR flip-flop and some NAND gates, it is not necessary to describe them in terms of subcomponents. Once a device is 'proved' to show a certain function, we can compile it as an available device in the environment. The output sequence of the circuit is given in Table 2 and it shows that there are transients between the upward changes in the value.

The significance of this example is that the representation with causal rules is capable of producing a precise simulation of the system. This feature becomes very important when we are concerned not only by 'what' is actually achieved, but 'how' it is achieved.

Table 2: The output sequence of Figure 4

t_1	C	B	A	
t_2	0	0	0	initial state
t_3	0	0	1	
t_4	0	0	0	transient state
t_5	0	1	0	
t_6	0	1	1	
t_7	0	1	0	transient state
t_8	0	0	0	transient state
t_9	1	0	0	
	...	...		

5. Discussion

5.1. The validity of cmi model as the prediction

The unique cmi model shows that there is only one most preferable model for a causal theory [11]. This might be too restrictive if we consider the possibility of having multiple possible behaviours from a design. To focus on the most likely outcome would raise the danger of overlooking a non-deterministic aspect of the design. It might be more informative if we could maintain all possible behaviours in order to evaluate the design.

Focusing on the unique model, however, does not exclude other possible behaviours.

It is merely suggested as 'the most likely behaviour' under 'given conditions and (default) assumptions'. Typically, a causal theory would split into different histories depending on whether the default is overridden, since there is no need to state the default conditions in a causal rule when they do not affect the causal outcomes. Whenever the predicted behaviour contradicts the expected behaviour, there is always a possibility that the default assumed is not right. We can check this by listing out the default conditions used in the modelling process, and if there is any 'wrong' default, it is easily overridden by adding a boundary condition. In most cases, multiple worlds occur due to lack of information about specific conditions that distinguish the worlds.

There is another case where there arises more than one behaviour. When a variable is universally quantified and there is no need to assign any value to it, there are as many possible worlds as the number of members in the set of individuals semantically assigned to the variable. A typical example of this case is the 'don't care' state in the logic gates. Since there are no restrictions to the value of the variable, assuming the 'most likely' value to it seems to be plausible.

The reason why we think unique model is appropriate is that it gives flavour of how a device would behave by default. If the designer is satisfied with the outcome, maybe using the default is good enough; if not, s/he can find out which default to override. In case of multiple worlds, we can see what 'can' happen, but sometimes the number is exceedingly high to manage. The process of choosing the 'right' one would nevertheless be the same.[4]

5.2. Conflicting specification

The evaluation-modification cycle of the design process does not always work, especially when there is a conflict in the initial specification. Although the proof process in the modification stage is aimed to make an abstract causal rule to be a feasible one, it is not always guaranteed to be the case. Since it is based on a mechanical application of operations, sometimes the 'feasible' rules may still be counterintuitive or simply impossible.

For example, the causal rule might give a description of a device which reads "when the power of the magnetic field increases, the mass decreases", or "when a given object is travelling at the speed of light, it accelerates."[5] When such impossible causation is derived as the most plausible among other alternatives, there is something wrong with the behavioural specification.

In such case, there will be no alternative but to modify the specification. Since there will be some index to the boundary conditions that are responsible for the undesirable events after the failure of the proof, it is possible to figure out the conditions under conflict. Automatic resolution of these conflicts is not in the scope of the current research, but it should be possible to support the designer by indicating the necessary conditions to obtain the desired behaviour.

---

[4]In this context, we are assuming that a device would behave uniquely under given condition. There are cases when a device should have multiple behaviour, but we think this happens only when the design is under-constrained.

[5]The former is the case when the causal connection is not obvious or non-empirical, but *may be* possible with additional knowledge about physics. The latter is simply impossible to have such an effect in real physics.

6. Conclusion

The essence of the approach illustrated in this paper is to treat the functionality of design components in terms of causality. Causal relations among events produce a chronological sequence of events (or causal chains), and along with the causal rules describing the design components, we can specify the behaviour of the device. The causal rules are manipulated according to Shoham's temporal logic which incorporates the nonmonotonic aspect of the prediction task. The formulation is based on a well-defined theory, with clearly defined theoretical justification.

The advantages of this approach are:

- the behavioural specification of devices allows more intuitive descriptions of the functionality of the system, especially in dynamic systems where the devices interact with the environment, and

- it utilises temporal constraints for design evaluation and modification, which enables the representation of delays and relative timings in the occurrence of the events. Without temporal logic, we must rely on the implicit ordering of events and it is difficult to represent the relative ordering of events.

On the other hand, the main drawback in the design stage of this approach is its complexity. There are typically a number of candidates for which rule to choose for the abduction process, and the combinatorics become more complex as the number of such rules and the number of conditions in their premise become greater. At the moment, some primitive heuristics are used to reduce the search space, and some choices are reserved for the human user to decide. This permits the users to incorporate their preference, but as the number of rules increase in more complex domain, it is necessary to introduce more elaborate optimisation procedure to guide search.

References

[1] H. G. Barrow. VERIFY: A Program for Proving Correctness of Digital Hardware Designs. *Artificial Intelligence*, 24:437–491, 1984.

[2] J. Bell. Extended causal theories. *Artificial Intelligence*, 48:211–224, 1991.

[3] J. J. Finger and M. R. Genesereth. Residue a deductive approach to design synthesis. Technical Report HPP-85-1, Dept of Computer Science, Stanford University, January 1985.

[4] P. Freeman and A. Newell. A model for functional reasoning in design. In *Proc. IJCAI-71*, pages 621–640, 1971.

[5] J. R. Gibson. *Electronic Logic Circuits (Second Edition)*. Edward Arnold, London, 1983.

[6] Y. Iwasaki and B. Chandrasekaran. Design verification through function- and behavior- oriented representations: bridging the gap between function and behavior. In J. S. Gero, editor, *Artificial Intelligence in Design '92, Pittsburgh*, pages 597–616. Kluwer Academic Publishers, Dordrecht, The Netherlands, 1992.

[7] B. Kuipers. Qualitative Simulation. *Artificial Intelligence*, 29:289–338, 1986.

[8] L. March. The logic of design and the question of value. In L. March, editor, *The Architecture of Form*, pages 1–40. Cambridge University Press, Cambridge, Massachusetts, 1976.

[9] K. Nakata. An application of temporal logic for representation and reasoning about design. In *Applied Logic Conference: Logic At Work, Amsterdam*, Dec 1992.

[10] V. Sembugamoorthy and B. Chandrasekaran. Functional Representation of Devices and Compilation of Diagnostic Problem-Solving Systems. In J. L. Kolodner and C. K. Riesbeck, editors, *Experience, Memory and Reasoning*, pages 47–73. Lawrence Erlbaum Associates, Hillsdale, NJ, 1986.

[11] Y. Shoham. *Reasoning about Change*. The MIT Press, Cambridge, Massachusetts, 1988.

Meta-Modelling for Cooperative Processes

Selmin NURCAN, Colette ROLLAND
Centre de Recherche en Informatique, Université Paris 1 - Panthéon - Sorbonne
17, rue de Tolbiac 75013 Paris, France

Abstract. Cooperative work techniques are becoming very important in organisations as well as in the information systems community. The Computer Supported Cooperative Work (CSCW) discipline makes the assumption that collaborative work can be supported by software tools. This requires among others to develop models able to represent cooperative work processes. This paper presents a meta-modeling framework to deal with a range variety of cooperative work models. A cooperative process meta-model from which models can be instantiated is introduced and exemplified. The meta-model is taylored to support the modeling of both well-structured and ill-defined work processes and their interactions.

1. Introduction

We are interested in Computer Supported Cooperative Work (CSCW) which examines the possibilities and effects of technological support for humans involved in collaborative group communication and work processes. Organizations are built on the principle that groups of people can carry out tasks which are not feasible individually. Therefore in most applications, well-structured, individually performed procedures coexist with ill-structured tasks which require cooperative work processes and both of them must be managed in the final solution. Cooperative work techniques become very important in organizations as well as in the information systems community. One can note the emergence of cooperative information systems. The development of information systems is itself becoming performed in a cooperative manner [26]. In the CREWS[1] project we are developing an approach for supporting cooperative requirements engineering based on scenarios. Therefore, it is necessary to understand the specificities of cooperative work processes in order to take them into account in models and software tools built for supporting their enactment.

Our purpose is to propose a process meta-model, which can deal with both well-defined and wickled work procedures and their interactions, so as to represent a wide range of cooperative work processes.

This paper is organised as follows: In section 2, we introduce computer supported cooperative work and situate workflow with respect to groupware. We shall notice that

---

[1] This work is partially supported by the european ESPRIT long term research project CREWS (Cooperative Requirements Engineering With Scenarios).

organizational reasons justify the joint use of these technologies. In section 3, we introduce our needs, in terms of models and ways of working, for modelling and guiding cooperative work processes. In section 4, we present a cooperative process meta-model which provides means to deal with secure and well-structured cooperative work processes and has the flexibility to handle ill-structured cooperative work processes.

2. Cooperative work

The cooperative work or group work is the object of a multidisciplinary research field called Computer Supported Cooperative Work. The growth of connectivity greatly expands opportunities for office workers to cooperate and work together. Most organizations acknowledge that process simplification and automation are key success factors in the present competitive environment where the watchwords are productivity and quality.

Groupware is defined in [6] as follows: "*Computer-based systems that support groups of people engaged in a common task (or goal) and that provide an interface to a shared environment*". A well-known categorization [6, 9] is the division into synchronous or asynchronous activity and co-located or distributed activity (see figure 1).

Workflow is mainly concerned by scheduling and coordinating work between actors [10, 18]. It is defined for instance in N. Naffah [13] as a «*cooperative work involving a number of actors which must realize tasks, in a given time span, according to a predefined procedure and having a global aim*». In workflow applications, cooperative work means that several persons are involved in reaching a common goal, but each of them acts individually in a specific step of the work.

Based on the Ellis' definition of group work (involves a common task (or goal) and a shared environment), one might argue that workflow does not fulfill the requirements of the CSCW community because only one person executes his/her own task with his/her own data at a given time. However, taking a general view of the procedure, there is a common goal to reach by a group of people which share the same information.

Workflow is classified by J.Grudin [8] in the distributed asynchronous area of the previous matrix as electronic mail systems. For many people, groupware supports unpredictable and ad-hoc interactions that occur in work group, whereas workflow automates strategies and predefined procedures. However, their global aims are the same: to increase the collective efficiency of groups of people engaged in fulfilling a common goal.

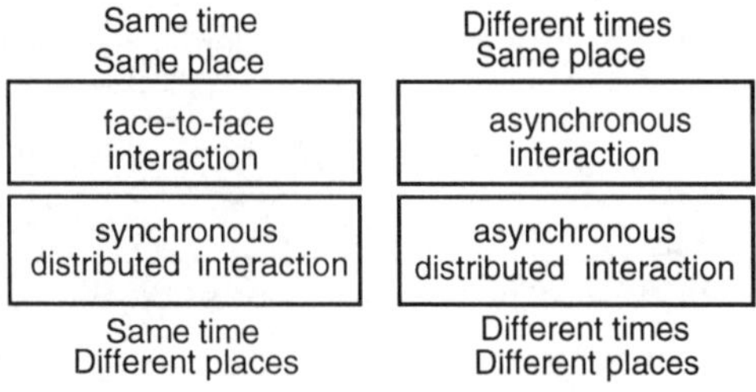

Figure 1. Johansen's Space/Time matrix

Workflow applications have been divided into two different categories depending on the nature of the supported processes [19]. The first concerns well-structured and repetitive processes having important coordination and automation needs [14]. In most current workflow software tools supporting well-structured processes, a procedure is a predefined set of partially ordered tasks. Each task has an assigned role corresponding to a group of actors, and the actor who actually executes the task is chosen from this group.

The second category of workflow applications deals with occasional and ill-structured (ad-hoc) work processes in organizations; a response to a call for tender in a commercial service or problem solving activities are examples of this class. The main characteristic of these applications is the information and knowledge-sharing within the work group more than the ordering of their tasks.

For many organizations, well-structured and ill-structured work processes coexist and must be managed in the final solution [15] [16] [17]. The integration aims to make the transition between the different types of group activities transparent. Current workflow products and their underlying control flow models require a strict respect of the predefined procedures. Therefore they cannot be used for ad-hoc workflow applications or deal with the dynamic modifiability of predefined scripts. More and more, users ask for adaptive workflow products and models which can provide the robustness and the security of the predefined scripts and the flexibility of ad-hoc applications.

Providing a single set of concepts to model both aspects of group work processes is our concern is this paper.

3. Models and way of working

Group work application development starts with the modeling of the process to implement. The implementation of this kind of application requires a preliminary analysis phase before the process may be modeled. For each stage of the work, one has to determine who does what within the task, when, after and before which other task. Information holders, types of handled documents, possible locking points,… etc, have also to be defined.

When the work process is well-structured, the corresponding procedure is a predefined set of partially ordered tasks. Partially ordered means that tasks are not necessarily executed sequentially: loops and parallelism can appear. Each task has an assigned role corresponding to a group of actors, and the actor which shall execute the task shall be chosen among this group.

Finally, the modelling of a procedure (see figure 2) requires the identification of:
- event(s) which trigger(s) the procedure,
- tasks which compose it and their relationships with the others: these relationships define sequential, parallel (with rendezvous points) and conditional transitions, and for each task:
    - events which trigger its execution,
    - resources (data+tools) which are necessary for its execution, and
    - the associated role.

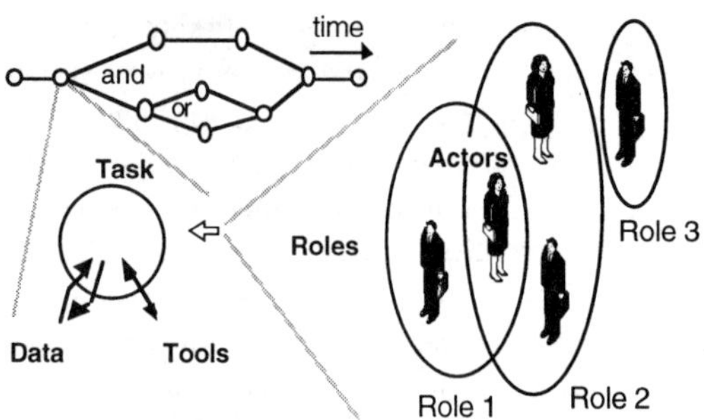

Figure 2. Procedure representation

We have considered seven models dealing with task-workflow-agent-role representations, respectively OSSAD [3] [4], ICN [5] [7], InConcert [12], VPL [27], I* [28], Enterprise Modelling [2, 11] and ITHACA [1]. This study showed a convergence on a set of concepts such as goal, procedure, task, role, actor, resource, decomposition of tasks, etc. However, an appropriate model for a large variety of cooperative work processes (going from well-structured to ill-structured) must also provide means to represent unstructured activities. We integrated these concepts in one single meta-model that we present in the following section.

4. A process meta-model for the representation of cooperative work

An approach to generate guidance centered process models has been initially proposed in [20] and further developed in [21, 22, 23]. Authors refer to these models as "ways-of-working" since they are intended to guide application engineers in their way of working to solve a design problem. We believe that the proposed approach is applicable to any process. However the problem of distributed process guidance has not be tackled in [23].

We have extended the process meta-model presented in [23] in order to obtain a *cooperative process meta-model* to be used for any cooperative process.

4.1. The cooperative process meta-model

We propose a *meta-model* as a basis for process model definition. Since a process meta-model carries information about the process model, an instantiation of it shall result in a process model. Our approach introduces three levels of process modelling:
-At the lowest level, process traces are recorded.
-At the second level, ways-of-working are defined. A way-of-working is a process model i.e. a description of process. It has a prescriptive purpose and is similar to the concept of plan. A process is then, an instantiation of a process model which is executed.
-The knowledge required to design such models is related to the third level of abstraction and takes the form of a process meta-model. A process meta-model provides a set of generic concepts for describing ways-of-working which are therefore, instances of the process meta-model.

The process meta-model allows us to deal with many different situations in a flexible, decision-oriented manner. Moreover the meta-model can support different levels of granularity in decision making as well as non determinism in process performance. It identifies a decision in context as the basic building block of ways-of-working and permits their grouping into meaningful modules. Parallelism of decisions and ordering constraints are also supported.

The output of a process is a *product*, it can be requirements specification or a conceptual schema or a loan offer to a client in a bank or messages exchanged between members of a group or a set of business goals.

In the presentation of the *cooperative process meta-model* we follow a bottom up approach starting with the concept of *context*, intoducing then the concepts of *role*, *action* and *product*, and ending with an overall view of the concepts progressively introduced.

4.2. The concept of context

The central concept of the process meta-model is the one of *context* which associates a situation with a decision made on it.

A *situation* is a part of the product it makes sense to take a decision on. Situations can be of various granularity levels; they can be either atomic like an attribute of an object class or they can be coarse-grained like the whole product.

A *decision* reflects a choice that a user can make at a given moment in the process. A *decision* refers to an *intention*. An *intention* expresses what the user wants to achieve, the goal.

A *context* is the association of a *situation* and a *decision* which can be taken in this situation. A decision is not sufficient in itself, it needs to be associated with the situation in which it applies. A situation can be associated with several decisions. Acting in a context corresponds to a step in the process: in a given situation, and in order to progress in the process, the user has to take a decision (figure 3).

4.3. The concept of role

A role is the definition of an organizational intention shared by a collection of users, all of whom have the same privileges and obligations to a set of work processes in an organization. For example, the role of a reservation service clerk, that of an accounts officer, etc.

In procedural workflow applications, tasks are individual and are performed by individual roles. Each task is assigned to a role corresponding to a group of actors (i.e. the collection of the role object).

According to the process meta-model, acting in a context should correspond to a step in the cooperative process. In a given situation, a user has an intention (because of his/her role in this process), and that makes him/her progress in the cooperative process.

To this end, we introduce the concept of *role*, and then specialise it into *individual role* and *group role* (figure 3). For example, the reservation service clerk is an individual role whereas public relations team is a group role. A group role *contains* several individual roles.

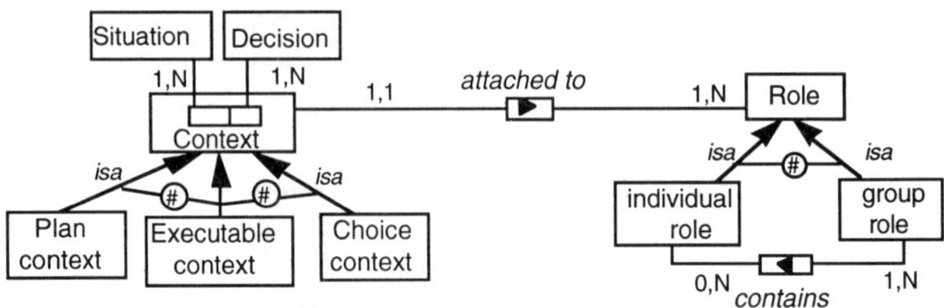

Figure 3. The context is attached to a role

We attach the context of the process meta-model to a role. This captures knowledge about which decision can be taken by which role. Therefore, the basic division of responsibility in cooperative processes is imposed on the set of decisions of the meta-model. This helps us in representing co-ordination of roles, providing access control, and in giving more appropriate guidance which is completely tailored to the role.

4.4. The different types of contexts

A situation exists at different levels of granularity. Further, decisions have consequences which differ from one granularity level to another. The different contexts are classified (figure 3) according to their consequences in the meta-model into *executable contexts*, *plan contexts*, and *choice contexts*.

4.4.1. Executable context

At the most detailed level, the execution of any process can be seen as a set of transformations performed on the product, each transformation resulting from the execution of a deterministic action. Such an action is a consequence of a decision made in a certain context. This leads to the introduction of the concept of an *executable context*.

An *executable context* implements a decision, its intention is realised by an action (figure 4). Therefore, in the meta-model (figure 5), an executable context is associated with an action. An *action* performs a transformation of the product, it is the implementation of a decision. Performing an action changes the product and may generate a new situation (figure 6) which is itself, subject to new decisions.

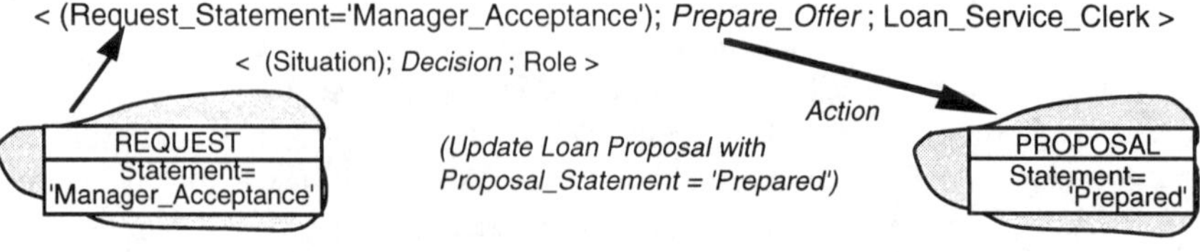

Figure 4. Example of an executable context

The concept of action

We classify actions into two types (figure 5) according to their characteristics: *individual action* and *conversation action*.

Performing an individual action or a conversation action does not change the same kind of product. Individual actions perform transformations of artefacts while conversation actions create messages.

Therefore, we classify the concept of *product* into *artefact* and *message* (figure 5). *Artefact* represents the information system.

We need to represent also the unstructured -conversational- activities of the group work. So, we must be able to keep track of these conversations. We introduce the *message* concept as the basic component of the conversational activity. A *message* may *concern* several *artefacts.*

The *individual action* can be complex or simple. A *complex individual action* is composed of *individual actions.* A *simple individual action* performs a tranformation of *(changes)* an artefact by creating, updating or deleting it. An *individual action* is performed by an *individual role* (figure 6). Figure 4 shows an executable context which is applied by an individual action.

We want also to deal with group activities, in the sense that several participants can synchronously act in the same conversational activity by exchanging messages. We represent this type of cooperation by the *conversation action.*

The *conversation action* is *performed by* a *group role*. It creates several messages, each message being *produced by* an individual role *contained by* the previous group role (figure 6).

From any *conversation action* may *emerge* new *contexts* (figure 6). These contexts can be executable and associated to actions, which might be conversational and then, triggers new contexts and so on. This feature enables the cooperative process meta-model to deal with ill-structured cooperative work processes as well-structured cooperative work processes. An example of conversation action is given in section 4.5.

Executable contexts establish situation-based links among contexts, namely *correlation links.* This is modelled in figure 6 by the loop among contexts through action and situation. The term *correlation link* refers to the composition of the three following relationships: *applied by, changes/creates,* and *built on.*

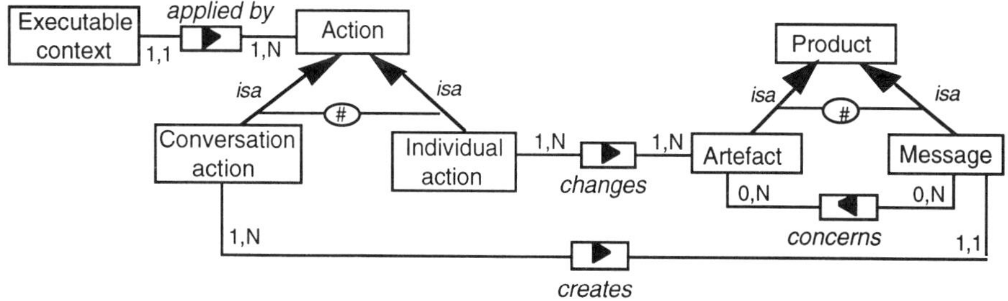

Figure 5. Actions and products that they transform

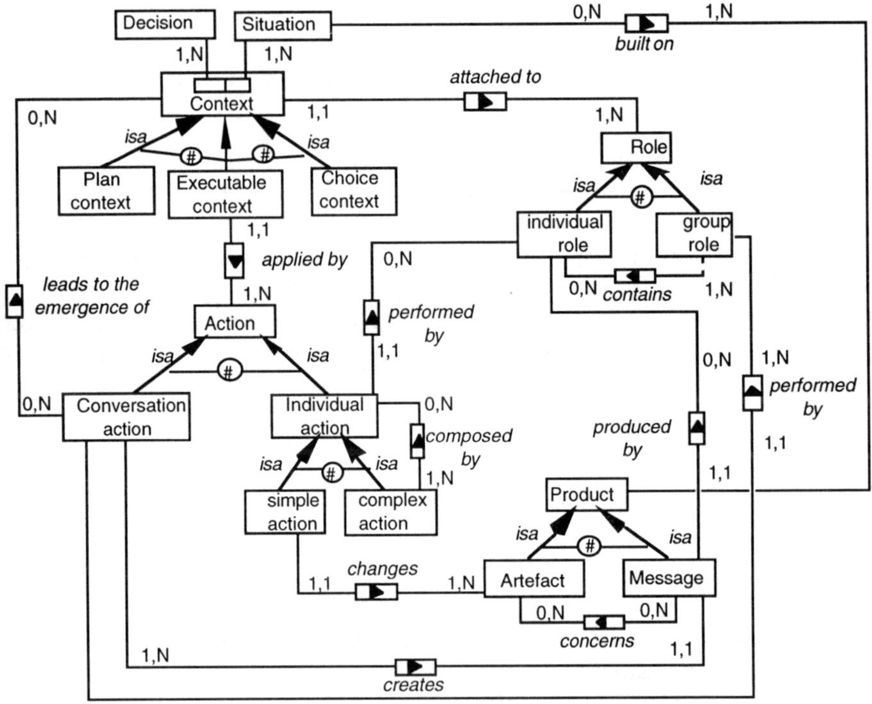

Figure 6. The cooperative process meta-model

4.4.2. *Choice context*

A user may have several alternative ways to fulfil a decision. Therefore, he/she has to select the most appropriate one among the set of possible choices. In order to model such a piece of process knowledge, we use a second specialisation of the concept of context, namely the *choice context* (figure 7).

A *choice context* corresponds to a situation which requires the exploration of alternatives in decision making. Each alternative is an approach or a strategy for the resolution of the issue being faced by the user in the current situation. By definition, a choice context offers a choice among a set of strategies, all of them achieving the same purpose. In this sense, one can look upon the choice context as being goal oriented.

There are two major differences between the *choice context* and the *executable context*: the first one lies in the absence of any alternatives in the latter and the second is that a choice context has no direct consequence on the product.

In the process meta-model, the various alternatives of a choice context are represented in the *alternative* relationship (figure 7). They are associated to choice criteria based on arguments.

A *choice criterion* is a combination of arguments which *supports* or *objects to* an alternative of a choice context. It may provide priority rules to select one alternative among several depending on the *arguments*.

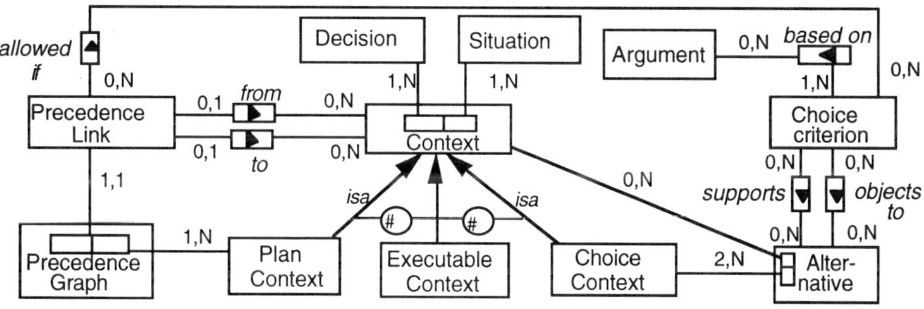

Figure 7. The representation of the concept of context

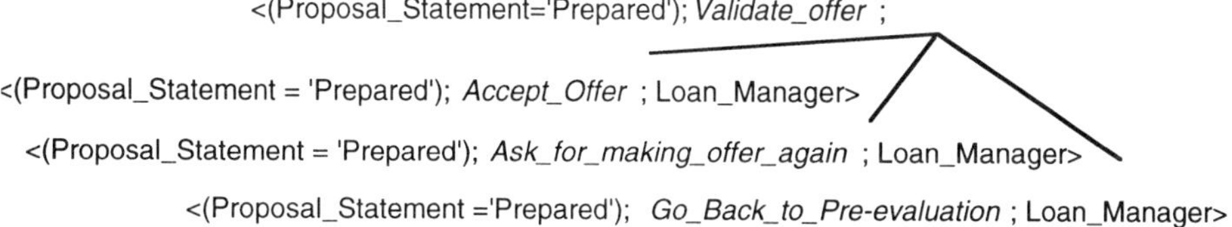

Figure 8. Example of a choice context

Since alternatives of a choice context are also contexts, contexts may share an *alternative* relationship (figure 7), leading to *alternative-based hierarchies of contexts*. The alternative-based relationship among contexts allows the refinement of large-grained decisions into more fine-grained ones. This is a means by which the process meta-model handles the granularity problem (figure 8).

The introduction in the process meta-model of *alternatives* and *choice criteria* will allow the way-of-working to support the user in exploring possible strategies to resolve an issue and in selecting the most appropriate one. This alternative-based guidance leaves freedom to the user who can make a choice which is not even one of the predefined alternatives proposed by the way-of-working. This feature enables the cooperative process meta-model to deal with exception handling in workflow applications.

4.4.3. Plan context

In order to fulfil an intention associated to a certain situation, a user may be required to take a set of decisions on corresponding situations; he/she has to follow a plan. To this end, a third specialisation of context, namely, *plan context* is introduced. A *plan context* is an abstraction mechanism by which a context viewed as a complex issue can be decomposed in a number of sub-issues. Each sub-issue corresponds to a sub-decision working on a sub-situation. The decomposition of context is another means provided by the meta-model to solve the granularity problem.

The component contexts can be of any type i.e. executable, choice or plan contexts. For example, for the intention named "Process_Loan_Request" to be fulfilled, the two intentions "Record_Request" and "Evaluate_Request" must be satisfied. This is modelled (figure 9) by a plan context called "<(Request_Message), Process_Loan_Request, Loan_Service_Clerk>" decomposed into two contexts:
"<(Request_Message), Record_Request, Loan_Service_Clerk>" executable context and "<(Request_Statement='Recorded'), Estimate_Request, Loan_Service_Clerk)>" choice context.

In the process meta-model the decomposition of a plan context into its more elementary contexts is represented (figure 7) by the relationship *precedence graph* between *context* and *plan context*. The ordering of the contexts, within a plan, is defined by the *precedence graph*. The nodes of this graph are contexts while the links -called *precedence links*- define either the possible *ordered transitions* between contexts or their possible *parallel enactment*. Based on arguments, a choice criterion may be assigned to a link. The choice criterion defines when the transition can be performed. Flexibility is introduced by allowing several sets of possible parallel or ordered transitions to be defined in the same graph. This feature enables the cooperative process meta-model to deal with well-structured workflow applications which require the use of a model in terms of ordered steps. The precedence graph corresponding to the previous plan context is shown by the figure 10.

Decomposition of contexts can be made iteratively leading to hierarchies of contexts. This hierarchical link is refered to as a *decomposition link*. Notice that this link corresponds in figure 7 to the composition of the precedence graph relationship with the *from* and *to* relationships.

Plan contexts provide a different type of guidance than executable and choice contexts do. They support users in performing long term transactions, providing advice on the ordering of component activities, whereas *choice contexts* help in making the appropriate choice in the situation in hand and *executable contexts* tell how to implement the decision taken.

Each type of context influences the on-going process in a different manner: an executable context affects the product and generates a new situation, which itself becomes the subject of decisions; a choice context does not change the product but helps to further the decision making process through the refinement of an intention; a plan context provides the means to manage the complexity of an intention by providing a decomposition mechanism. Performing *decomposition* and *refinement* iteratively allows the users to reach executable intentions and thus, to act on the product.

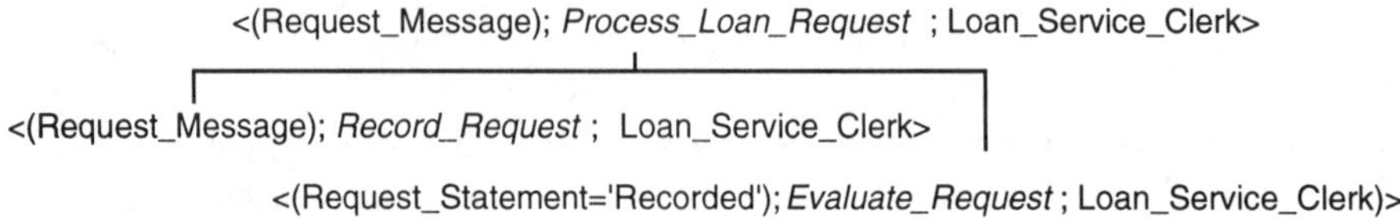

Figure 9. Example of a plan context

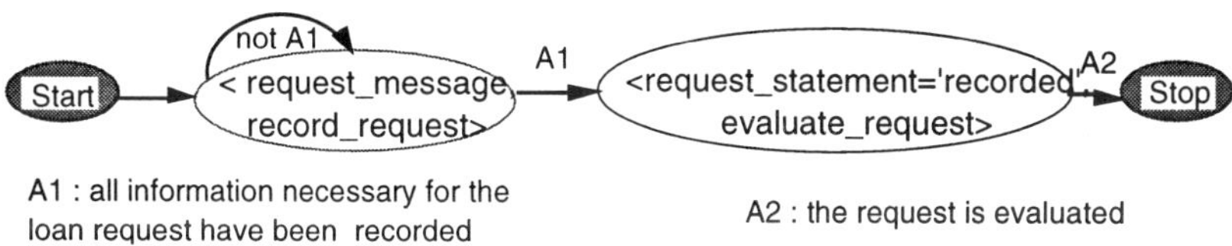

Figure 10. Example of a precedence graph

4.5. Conversation action

In this section, we examplify the use of the conversation action for a non structured group activity. Let us take an example from the Air Traffic Control case study and assume that the context C < G1 "minimize risks of accidents", Operationalise G1> requires to call a group of experts (we name it the "risk elucidation group") for a brainstorming session.

In other words, the strategy selected for context C is "brainstorm". The guidance provided by this strategy [24] suggests:

(1) to define the group role required for this cooperation,

(2) to execute a conversation action within the previously defined group role and having the initial input context as situation.

The *Risk elucidation group* is a group role which contains the following individual stakeholders: Airport manager, ATC center manager, a representative of airlines managers, a representative of pilots, and a local autority.

The executable context is applied by a conversation action leading to the creation of several messages (figure 11).

Let assume as an example that the flow of messages is the following:

Message 1:   (ATC center manager)
     Have we got a report about reasons of accidents happened during the five last years in the world ?

Message 2:   (Airport manager)
     No, we don't. But we have some informations about the last three major accidents.

Message 3:   (ATC center manager)
     So, what about the reasons ?

Message 4:   (Airport manager)
     In Strasbourg in France, it was a human error.
     At Delhi, the reason was twofold; the accident was partly due to the heavy air traffic and partly to a human error, due to his poor knowledge of the english language, the pilot misunderstood the message of the control tower.
     In the US, it was a confusion about the airport. The pilot made an error in typing the airport and the computer understood the airport code as Bogota in South America while the aircraft was to land in California.

Message 5:   (Representative of airline managers)
So if we want to minimize risks of accidents we have to *decrease risk of human error.*

Message 6:   (Pilots representative)
Sometimes what is called human error is not. How to decrease the human error in the accident occurred in US. You must rather review computer systems.

Message 7:   (ATC center manager)
It's more convenient to talk about Human-Computer interface for this accident. So, our goals are to *decrease risk of human error and to review all human-computer interactions.*

Message 8:   (Pilots representative)
And what about the accident in Delhi ? The human error was not the unique reason, isn't it ?

Message 9:   (ATC center manager)
The number of aircrafts allowed to cross the controlled airspace is too high in Delhi.

Message 10:   (Local autority)
Precisely, since 2 years local autorities argue that this number must decrease in our city too. People living near the airport are disturbed because of the noise and late/early take offs and landings. In order to minimize risks of accidents we must *limit the number of aircrafts allowed to cross the controlled airspace.*

As a conclusion of this message exchange, the conversation action generates three emerging contexts :

- < message 5, create G2 "decrease risk of human error">

- < message 7, create G3 :"review human-computer interactions">

- < message 10, create G4 :"limit the number of aircrafts allowed to cross the controlled airspace">. The new contexts are inserted in the contexts pile for further processing.

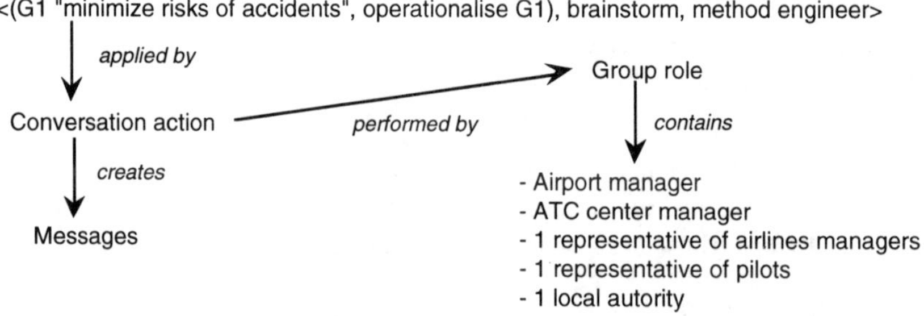

Figure 11. An executable context leading to the execution of a conversation action

4.6. The concept of way-of-working

It should be clear now that due to the meta-model concepts, the basic building block of a way-of working is an instance of context that we call also *context*. Contexts in the meta-model have hierarchical relationships of two different types, decomposition and refinement. In the way-of-working, we suggest a grouping of contexts based upon these links. The modules resulting from this grouping are hierarchies of contexts called *trees*. Finally, a way of working can be composed of several trees. This leads to the final vision of a way-of-working as a *forest* of trees (figure 12).

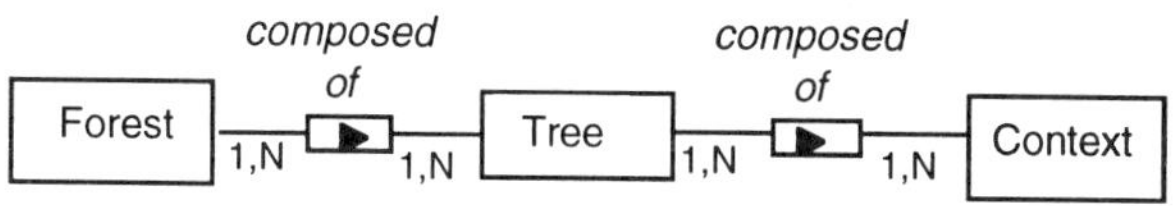

Figure 12. The way-of-working structure

4.7. An example of way of working as a forest of trees

We plan to model the loan process in a bank (figure 13). The working rules are given below:

When a customer applies for a loan, the bank clerk in charge of his banking account analyses the loan request according to its nature.

He/she can decide to accept or refuse the request himself/herself, or to ask for a deeper evaluation. In the third case, first a pre-evaluation is made by the financial department (ill-structured task carried out synchronously by a group of experts), then the request is examined by the loan manager in order to accept or to refuse it.

The study of the request by the loan service clerk must be validated by the loan manager who has the possibility to either :
. accept the loan offer prepared by the loan service clerk, or
. ask the loan service clerk to review it, or
. ask the financial department for a complete re-evaluation of the loan request.

When the decision is favourable, a proposal of loan is sent to the customer by the clerk's assistant. When the decision is unfavourable, a refusal letter is sent by the same person.

Four different roles are involved in the loan process :
- The loan service clerk which is in charge of the client account,
- The loan manager,
- The work group constitued by the financial manager and three experts in the financial departement,
- The clerk's assistant.

The information systems' objects that we defined are: REQUEST, PROPOSAL, CLIENT.

Request and *proposal* have noticeable states during their life cycle, respectively represented by *request_statement* and *proposal_statement*.

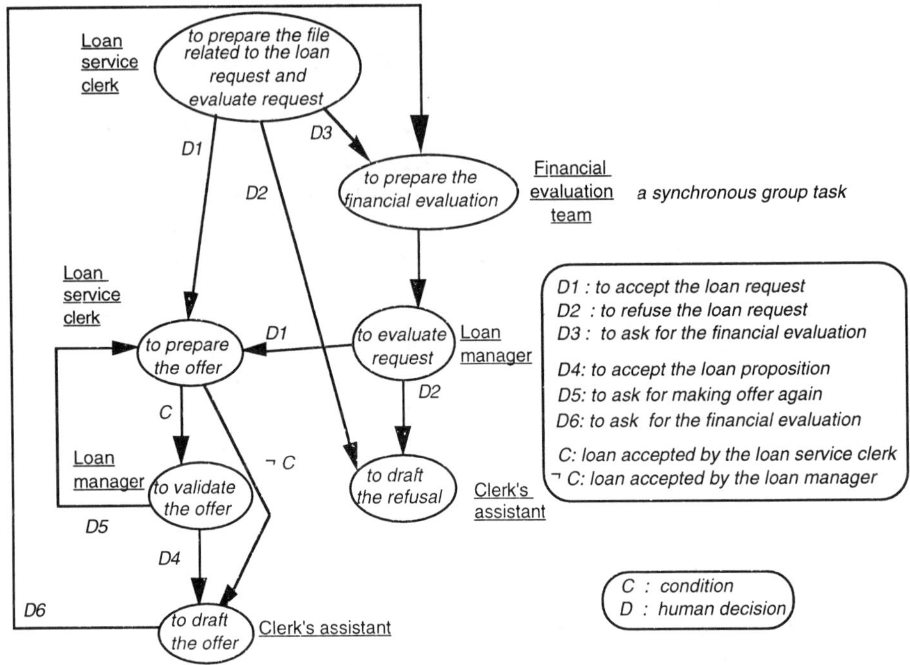

Figure 13. The graphical representation of the Loan Request case study

The approach consists of instantiating the concepts of the meta-model. We have to define the executable, choice and plan contexts, and their decomposition and refinement links.

The loan process is then represented by a forest composed of six trees.

Each tree describes a piece of knowledge about the process associated to a given role. The trees describe the process in a workflow style but, in addition, encapsulate guidance to support the participants performing their tasks.

The *first tree* (figure 14) describes the evaluation of the loan request by the loan service clerk. The first component context of this plan is an executable one associated to an individual action: Create Request. The second component of the plan is a choice context with three alternatives. It provides an alternative-based guidance to the clerk.

The *second tree* (figure 15) describes the way-of-working for the group work *processed by* the financial evaluation team and the loan manager. The root of the tree is a plan context which represents the risk evaluation by the financial evaluation team, then the request evaluation by the loan manager. The predefined decomposition of this group work is described in the corresponding precedence graph (figure 16).

The risk evaluation is a group work synchronously processed by a group of experts in the financial department. It is represented by an executable context associated to a conversation action. The evaluation of the request by the loan manager is defined by a choice context with two alternatives, to accept or to refuse the request, each of them being described by an executable context.

Process Tree 1

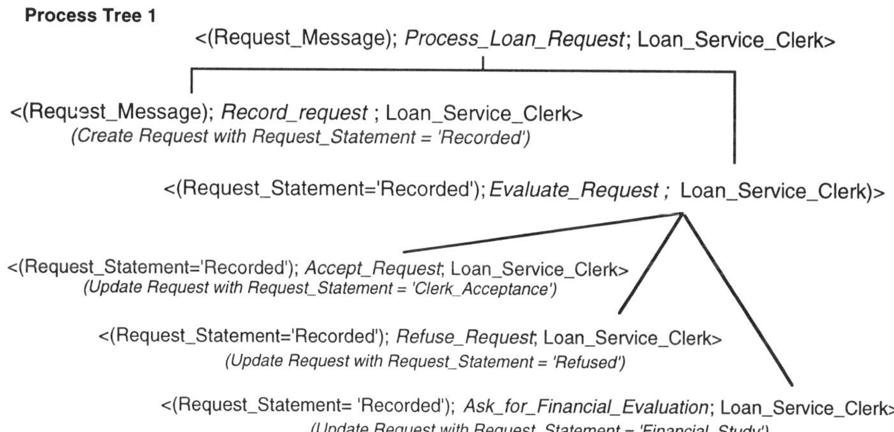

Figure 14. Way-of-working for *Process_Loan_Request*

Process Tree 2

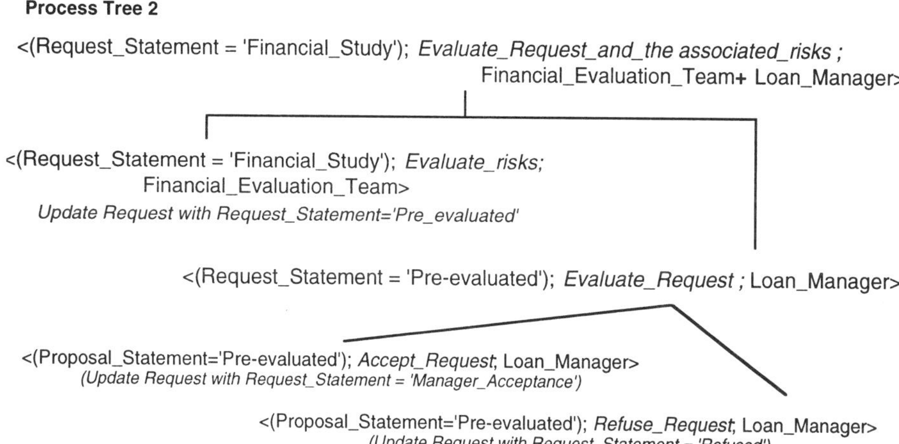

Figure 15. Way-of-working for *Evaluate_Request_and_the_associated_risks*

Figure 16. Precedence graph for *process tree 2*

Tree 3 (figure 17) represents the drafting of a refusal letter by the clerk's assistant when the request is refused. It is an executable context associated to an individual action.

Process Tree 3

<(Request_Statement='Refused'); *Draft_Refusal_Letter* ; Clerk_Assistant>

Figure 17. Executable context for *Draft_Refusal_Letter*

Tree 4 (figure 18) describes the package of the loan offer by the loan service clerk and his/her assistant when the situation corresponds to manager acceptance. This is a plan context composed of two executable contexts affected to individual roles.

Process Tree 4

<(Request_Statement='Manager_Acceptance');*Package_Offer* ; Loan_Service_Clerk+Clerk_Assistant>

<(Request_Statement='Manager_Acceptance'); *Prepare_Offer* ; Loan_Service_Clerk>
(Update Proposal with Proposal_Statement = 'Prepared')

<(Proposal _Statement='Prepared'); *Draft_Offer* ; Clerk_Assistant>

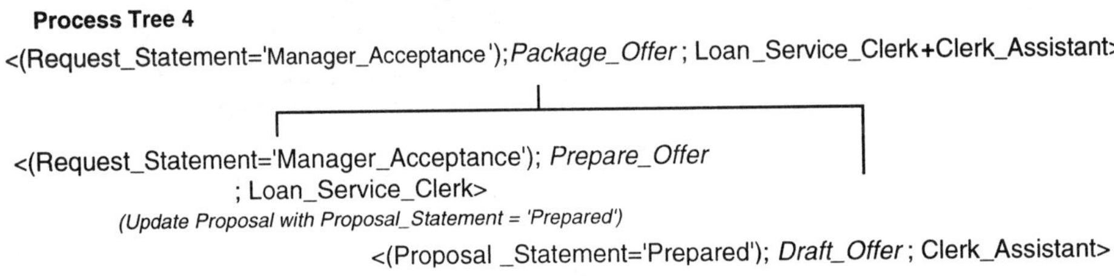

Figure 18. Way-of-working for *Package_Offer_when_accepted_by_the_manager*

When the situation corresponds to clerk acceptance, the process can be performed according to *tree 5* (figure 19). The first component context of the plan is an executable one and corresponds to the clerk's individual action in order to prepare the loan offer. The second component context of the plan represents the validation of the offer by the loan manager with three alternatives.

Process Tree 5

<(Request_Statement = 'Clerk_Acceptance'; *Package_Offer* ; Loan_Service_Clerk+Loan_Manager>

<(Request_Statement='Clerk_Acceptance'); *Prepare_Offer* ; Loan_Service_Clerk>
(Update Proposal with Proposal_Statement = 'Prepared')

<(Proposal_ Statement='Prepared'); *Validate_offer* ; Loan_Manager>

<(Proposal_Statement = 'Prepared'); *Accept_Offer* ; Loan_Manager>
(Update Proposal with Proposal_Statement = 'Validated')

<(Proposal_Statement = 'Prepared'); *Ask_for_making_offer_again* ; Loan_Manager>
(Update Proposal with Proposal_Statement = 'to_be_reviewed')

<(Proposal_Statement ='Prepared'); *go_Back_to_Pre-evaluation* ; Loan_Manager>
(Update Request with Request_Statement = 'Financial_Study')

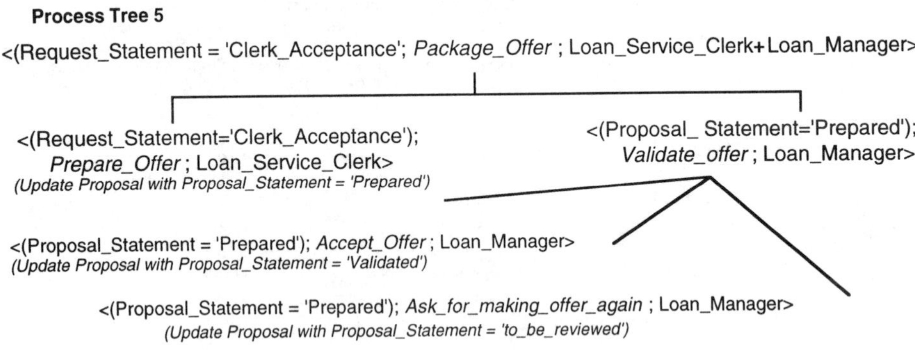

Figure 19. Way-of-working for *Package_Offer_when_accepted_by_the_clerk*

Process Tree 6

<(Proposal _Statement='Validated'); *Draft_Offer* ; Clerk_Assistant>

Figure 20. Executable context for *Draft_Offer*

Tree 6 (figure 20) represents the drafting of the offer by the clerk's assistant when the proposal is validated.

5. Conclusion

In this paper, we have presented a *cooperative process meta-model* which provides means to deal with secure and rather well-structured processes and provides the flexibility to handle ill-structured processes . It allows us:
- to represent cooperative work processes,
- to integrate conversations between agents,
- to guide and keep track of what happened in cooperative brainstorming sessions,
- to model the emergence of new contexts;

all these being made in an homogeneous manner.

An instantiation of the cooperative process meta-model results in a cooperative process model allowing to deal with a large variety of situations in a *decision-oriented* manner.

The concept of plan context enables the cooperative process meta-model to deal with well-structured cooperative processes which require the use of a control model. In fact, the corresponding precedence graph defines the ordering of the component contexts (the possible ordered transitions between contexts or their possible parallel enactment).

The alternative-based guidance of the choice context leaves freedom to users who can make a choice which is not even one of the predefined alternatives proposed by the way-of-working. This feature allows the cooperative process meta-model to deal with exception handling in cooperative processes.

The concept of conversation action allows us to represent emergent cooperative activities. It enables the cooperative process meta-model to deal with ill-structured cooperative work processes and the emergent component of globally well-structured cooperative work processes.

Our current work consists of building a cooperative environment which supports the definition of cooperative process models (in terms of ways-of-working) and provides the flexible guidance of groups in well-structured and/or ill-structured cooperative work processes. This environment is an extension of the MENTOR process centred environment [25].

References

[1]   Ang, J.S.K. and Conrath, D.W. (1993): The ITHACA Office Object Model: Modeling and Implementation, *Data Base*, November 1993, p. 5-14.

[2]   Bubenko, J. (1994): Enterprise Modelling, *Ingénierie des Systèmes d'Information*, Vol 2, N° 6, 1994.

[3]   Dumas, P. and Charbonnel, G. (1990): *La méthode OSSAD - Pour maîtriser les technologies de l'information - Tome 1: Principes*, Les Editions d'Organisation, Paris.

[4]   Dumas, P., Charbonnel, G. and Calmes, F. (1990): *La méthode OSSAD - Pour maîtriser les technologies de l'information - Tome 2: Guide pratique*, Les Editions d'Organisation, Paris.

[5]   Ellis, C. (1979): "Information Control Nets, A Mathematical Model of Office Information Flow", In *Proceedings of the ACM conference on Simulation, Measurement and Modelling of Computer Systems*, p.225-240.

[6]   Ellis, C.A., Gibbs, S.J. and Rein, G.L. (1991): "Groupware: some issues and experiences", *Communications of the ACM*, 34(1), p.38-58.

[7]   Ellis C.A. and Wainer J. (1994): "Goal-based models of collaboration", *Collaborative Computing*, Volume 1, Number 1, March, p.61-86.

[8]   Grudin, J. (1994): Computer-supported cooperative work: History and focus. *IEEE Computer, Special CSCW*, May 1994, p.19-26.

[9]   Johansen, R. (1991): *Leading business teams*, Reading, Addosn-Wesley.

[10]   Khoshafian, S., Baker, A.B., Abnous, R. and Shepherd, K. (1992): "Collaborative work and work flow in intelligent offices", *Intelligent Offices: Object-Oriented Multi-Media Information Management in Client/Serveur Architectures*, Wiley.

[11]   Loucopoulos, P. and Kavakli, E. (1995): "Enterprise Modelling and the Teleological approach to Requirements Engineering", *International Journal of Cooperative Information Systems*, Vol. 4, N° 1, p. 45-79.

[12]   McCarthy, D.R. and Sarin, S.K. (1993): "Workflow and transactions in InConcert", *Bulletin of Technical Committe on Data Engineering*, Vol. 16, N° 2, IEEE, june, *Special Issue on Workflow and Extended Transactions Systems*. p. 53-56.

[13]   Naffah, N. (1994): "Workflow: Etat de l'art et évolution", In *Proceedings of the Conference IT FORUM'94*, Télécom Paris.

[14]   Nurcan, S. and Trolliet, J.Y. (1995): "Une méthode d'analyse et de conception pour les applications workflow", In *proceedings of the 13th INFORSID congress*, May 31-June 2 1995, Grenoble, p.453-472.

[15]   Nurcan, S. and Chirac, J.L. (1995): "Quels modèles choisir pour les applications coopératives mettant en œuvre les technologies de workflow et de groupware ?", In *Proceedings of the AFCET 95 congress,* October 25-27 1995, Toulouse, p.593-602.

[16]   Nurcan, S. (1996): "A method for cooperative information systems analysis and design: CISAD", In *Proceedings of the Second International Conference on the Design of Cooperative Systems (COOP'96),* 12-14 juin 1996, Juan-Les-Pins, p.681-700.

[17]   Nurcan, S. (1996): "Analyse et conception de systèmes d'information coopératifs", *Numéro thématique "Multimédia et collecticiel" de Techniques et Sciences Informatiques,* Vol. 15, N° 9.

[18]   OVUM (1991): *Workflow Management Software.* Ovum Ltd., London, England.

[19]   Palermo, A.M. and McCready, S.C. (1992): "Workflow software: A primer", In *Proceedings of the Conference GROUPWARE'92,* London, p.155-159.

[20]   Rolland, C. (1993): "Modeling the Requirements Engineering Process", *Information Modelling and Knowledge Bases,* IOS Press.

[21]   Rolland, C. and Prakash, N. (1994): "A Contextual Approach for the Requirements Engineering Process", *Proceedings of the International IEEE Conference on Software Engineering and Knowledge Engineering (SEKE94),* Riga, 1994.

[22]   Rolland, C. (1994): "Modeling the evolution of artifacts", *1st IEEE International Conference on Requirements Engineering,* Colorado Springs, Colorado, 1994.

[23]   Rolland, C., Souveyet, C. and Moreno, M. (1995): "An approach for defining ways-of-working", In *Information Systems Journal,* Vol. 20, N° 4.

[24]   Rolland, C., Nurcan, S. and Grosz, G. (1997): "Guiding the participative design process", *Association for Information Systems 1997 Americas Conference,* August 15-17, 1997, Indianapolis, Indiana.

[25]   Si-Said, S., Rolland, C. and Grosz, G. (1996): "MENTOR : A Computer Aided Requirements Engineering Environment", *in the Proceedings of the 8th CAISE Conference Challenges In Modern Information Systems,* Heraklion, Crete, Greece, May 1996.

[26]   Solvberg, A., Krogstie, J. and Feltveit, A.H. editors (1995): *Proceedings of the IFIP Conference on Information Systems Development for Decentralized Organizations.* Chapman & Hall.

[27]   Swenson, K.D. (1993): "Visual Support for Reengineering Work Process", In *Proceedings of the Conference on Organizational Computing Systems,* ACM, Milpitas, California, p. 130-141.

[28]   Yu, E.S.K. and Mylopoulos, J. (1994): "From E-R to "A-R" - Modelling Strategic Actor Relationships for Business Process Reengineering", In *Proceedings of th 13th Int. Conference on the Entity-Relationship Approach,* December 13-16, 1994, Manchester.

Information Modelling and Knowledge Bases IX
P.-J. Charrel et al. (Eds.)
1998, IOS Press

A Class of Elementary Formal Systems That Has an Efficient Parsing Algorithm

Naoyuki HARADA*   Setsuo ARIKAWA*   Hiroki ISHIZAKA[†]

{naoyuki, arikawa}@i.kyushu-u.ac.jp
ishizaka@donald.ai.kyutech.ac.jp

*Department of Informatics,
Kyushu University, Fukuoka 812-81, Japan

†Department of Artificial Intelligence,
Kyushu Institute of Technology, Iizuka 820, Japan

Abstract

The elementary formal system(EFS, for short) is a kind of logic programs over the domain of strings. The EFS's can define various classes of formal languages, and a prover, i.e., a resolution procedure, for EFS's works as a uniform recognizer of such various classes of languages. The basic operation of the procedure is the unification as in the ordinary resolution. This paper deals with a prover for a special subclass of EFS's called regular EFS's that defines exactly the same class as context-free languages in the Chomsky hierarchy. The prover searches derivation trees for refutations. This paper first introduces a subclass of regular EFS's, called variable-separated EFS's, for which the prover becomes efficient, proves that the newly introduced EFS's are equivalent to the regular EFS's in their language defining power, and shows an experimental result on parsing some simple Japanese sentences.

1. Introduction

The elementary formal system (EFS, for short) Smullyan invented[3] to develop his recursive function theory is a kind of logic programs over the domain of strings of characters. The EFS's can define various classes of formal languages, and a resolution procedure for EFS's works as a uniform recognizer of such various classes of languages.

In the formal language theory, several classes of automata such as finite automata, pushdown automata, linear bounded automata, and Turing machines are used as recognizers of such classes of languages. Their basic mechanisms are different from one to another. Hence, we need to change the automata depending on the classes of languages we are interested in. However, as far as EFS's are concerned, we do not need to change the basic devices. We may just use the resolution principle as a uniform device.

Several subclasses of EFS's have been considered; variable-bounded EFS's, length-bounded EFS's, regular EFS's and linear EFS's and so on[4][5]. Among them the regular EFS's equivalent to the class of context-free grammars are the most important in discussing programming languages[1].

We implemented the prover, i.e., the resolution procedure, for regular EFS's. It is a kind of recognizers of the formal languages. Given a regular EFS and a string, the prover determines whether the string is proved by the regular EFS, or not. In fact, the prover searches for a refutation in a tree, a derivation tree, produced from the EFS and the string.

In case ill-formed EFS's are given, the prover does not work efficiently. The inefficiency is mainly due to *consecutiveness of variables* in clauses. The consecutive variables spread many failed branches which can not be a refutation in a derivation tree. Hence it takes a lot of time to search such trees for refutations.

To get rid of *consecutive variables* in clauses, we propose a new subclass of EFS's called variable-separated EFS's by putting a restriction on the clauses in the regular EFS's. In a variable-separated EFS, any pattern in the heads of clauses must start and end with some constant symbols, and variables in the term must be separated from each other.

In this paper first we recall some basic definitions on EFS's necessary for our discussions. In Section 3 we define derivations for EFS's and derivation trees. In Section 4, we introduce the variable-separated EFS's, and prove that the power of them is the same as that of regular EFS's although they are defined by posing some restrictions on the regular EFS's. Thus our prover for variable-separated EFS's can be applied to all context-free languages. In Section 5 we give an experimental result on parsing some simple Japanese sentences.

2. Elementary formal systems

We start with recalling the basic notions on EFS's. Let Σ, X, and Π be mutually disjoint sets, and let Σ and Π be finite. We refer to Σ as *alphabet*, and to each element of it as symbol which will be denoted by $a, b, c, \ldots$, to each element of X as *variable*, denoted by $x, y, z, x_1, x_2, \ldots$ and to each element of Π as *predicate symbol*, denoted by $p, q, q_1, q_2, \ldots$, each of which has an arity. A^+ denotes the set of all nonempty words over a set A.

Definition　　A *term* is an element of $(\Sigma \cup X)^+$. Each term is denoted by $\pi, \tau, \pi_1, \pi_2, \ldots, \tau_1, \tau_2, \ldots$. A *ground term* of S is an element of Σ^+. Terms are also called *patterns*.

Definition　　An *atomic formula* (or *atom*, for short) is an expression of the form $p(\tau_1, ..., \tau_n)$, where p is a predicate symbol in Π with arity n and $\tau_1, ..., \tau_n$ are terms. The atom is *ground* if all $\tau_1, ..., \tau_n$ are ground.

　　Clauses, empty clauses ($\square$), *ground clauses and substitutions* are defined in the ordinary way[2].

Definition　A *definite clause* is a clause of the form

$$A \leftarrow B_1, ..., B_n \quad (n \geq 0).$$

Definition   An *elementary formal system* (EFS, for short) S is a triplet (Σ, Π, Γ), where Γ is a finite set of definite clauses, which are sometimes called *axioms* of S.

We denote a substitution by $\{x_1 := \tau_1, ..., x_n := \tau_n\}$, where x_i are mutually distinct variables. We also define

$$p(\tau_1, ..., \tau_n)\theta = p(\tau_1\theta, ..., \tau_n\theta),$$
$$(A \leftarrow B_1, ..., B_m)\theta = A\theta \leftarrow (B_1\theta, ..., B_m\theta),$$

for substitution θ, an atom $p(\tau_1, ..., \tau_n)$ and a clause $A \leftarrow B_1, ..., B_m$.

Definition   Let $S = (\Sigma, \Pi, \Gamma)$ be an EFS. We define the relation $\Gamma \vdash C$ for a clause C of S inductively as follows:

(1) If $\Gamma \ni D$, then $\Gamma \vdash D$.

(2) If $\Gamma \vdash D$, then $\Gamma \vdash D\theta$ for any substitution θ.

(3) If $\Gamma \vdash A \leftarrow B_1, ..., B_n$ and $\Gamma \vdash B_n \leftarrow$, then $\Gamma \vdash A \leftarrow B_1, ..., B_{n-1}$.

C is *provable from* Γ if $\Gamma \vdash C$.

Definition   For an EFS $S = (\Sigma, \Pi, \Gamma)$ and $p \in \Pi$ with arity n, we define

$$L(S, p) = \{(\alpha_1, ..., \alpha_n) \in (\Sigma^+)^n \mid \Gamma \vdash p(\alpha_1, ..., \alpha_n) \leftarrow\}.$$

In case $n = 1$, $L(S, p)$ is a language over Σ. A language $L \subseteq \Sigma^+$ is *definable by EFS* or an *EFS language* if such S and p exist.

Now we give definition of regular EFS's which can define context-free languages.

Definition   Let $o(x, \pi)$ be the number of all occurrences of a variable x in term π. A pattern π is *regular* if $o(x, \pi) \leq 1$ for any variable x in π. A definite clause C is *regular* if C is of the form

$$p(\pi) \leftarrow q_1(x_1), ..., q_n(x_n),$$

and π is regular. An EFS $S = (\Sigma, \Pi, \Gamma)$ is *regular* if each clause in Γ is regular.

Theorem 2.1 (Arikawa et al.[5])   A language L is definable by regular EFS if and only if L is a context-free language.

Example 2.1   An EFS $S = (\{a, b\}, \{p\}, \Gamma)$ with

$$\Gamma = \left\{ \begin{array}{l} p(axb) \leftarrow p(x), \\ \quad p(ab) \leftarrow \end{array} \right\}$$

is regular. It defines a context-free language $L(S, p) = \{a^n b^n \mid n \geq 1\}$.

3. Derivations and refutations for EFS's

EFS's have an aspect of logic programs. Hence a resolution procedure for EFS's can be considered and works as a device for recognizing formal languages. In this section, we discuss the derivations and refutations for EFS's.

Definition   Let α and β be a pair of terms or atoms. Then a substitution θ is a *unifier* of α and β if $\alpha\theta = \beta\theta$.

Definition   A *goal clause* (or *goal*, for short) of EFS S is a clause of the form

$$\leftarrow\ B_1, ..., B_n \ \ (n \geq 0).$$

Definition   If clauses C and D are identical except renaming of variables, that is, $C = D\theta$ and $C\sigma = D$ for some substitutions θ and σ, we say D is a *variant* of C and write $C \equiv D$.

We assume a *computation rule R* to select an atom from a goal.

Definition   Let S be an EFS, G be a goal of S, and $v(C)$ be the set of all variables in a clause C. A *derivation from G* is a (finite or infinite) sequence of triplets (G_i, θ_i, C_i) $(i = 0, 1, ...)$ which satisfies the following conditions:

(1) G_i is a goal, θ_i is a substitution, C_i is a variant of an axiom of S, and $G_0 = G$.

(2) $v(C_i) \cap v(C_j) = \emptyset$ for every i and j ($i \neq j$), and $v(C_i) \cap v(G_i) = \emptyset$ for every i.

(3) If G_i is $\leftarrow A_1, ..., A_k$ and A_m is the atom selected by R, then C_i is $A \leftarrow B_1, ..., B_q$, and θ_i is a unifier of A and A_m, and G_{i+1} is

$$(\leftarrow A_1, \ldots, A_{m-1}, B_1, \ldots, B_q, A_{m+1}, \ldots, A_k)\,\theta_i.$$

A_m is a *selected atom* of G_i, and G_{i+1} is a *resolvent* of G_i and C_i by θ_i.

Definition   A *refutation* is a finite derivation ending with the empty goal $\square$.

Now we show a theorem, which asserts that a ground atom A is provable from EFS if and only if there is a refutation from $\leftarrow A$. Let $S = (\Sigma, \Pi, \Gamma)$ be an EFS, and $B(S)$ be the set of all ground atoms, i.e., the *Herbrand base* of S. Then we define the following sets.

$$\begin{aligned} SS(S) &= \{A \in B(S) \mid \text{there exists a refutation from } \leftarrow A\}, \\ PS(S) &= \{A \in B(S) \mid \Gamma \vdash A\}. \end{aligned}$$

Theorem 3.1 (Arikawa et al.) $SS(S) = PS(S)$ for every EFS S.

Example 3.1 For an EFS $S = (\{a, b\}, \{p\}, \Gamma)$ with

$$\Gamma = \left\{ \begin{array}{c} p(axy) \leftarrow p(x), p(y) \\ p(ab) \leftarrow \\ p(b) \leftarrow \end{array} \right\},$$

a refutation from $\leftarrow p(aabb)$ is illustrated by Fig.1, where the computation rule R selects the leftmost atom from every goal.

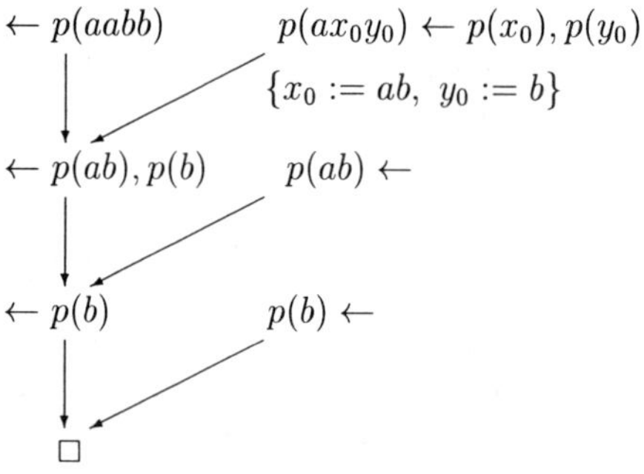

Figure 1: A refutation

There may exist two or more derivations from a goal. In the above example, if we use a substitution $\{x_0 := a,\ y_0 := bb\}$ instead of the substitution $\{x_0 := ab,\ y_0 := b\}$, we can get another derivation. Now we consider the derivation tree which expresses all such derivations together.

Definition Let S be an EFS, and G be a goal of S. Then the *derivation tree from G* is defined as follows:

(1) Each *node* of the tree is a goal.

(2) A *root node* of the tree is G.

(3) Let $\leftarrow A_1, ..., A_m, ..., A_k$ $(k \geq 1)$ be a node, and A_m be a selected atom. If $A \leftarrow B_1, ..., B_q$ is a clause of S and θ is a unifier of A and A_m, then a child of the node is

$$\leftarrow (A_1, ..., A_{m-1}, B_1, ..., B_q, A_{m+1}, ..., A_k)\theta.$$

(4) A node of empty goal does not have any children.

A derivation tree in example 3.1 is illustrated by Fig.2.

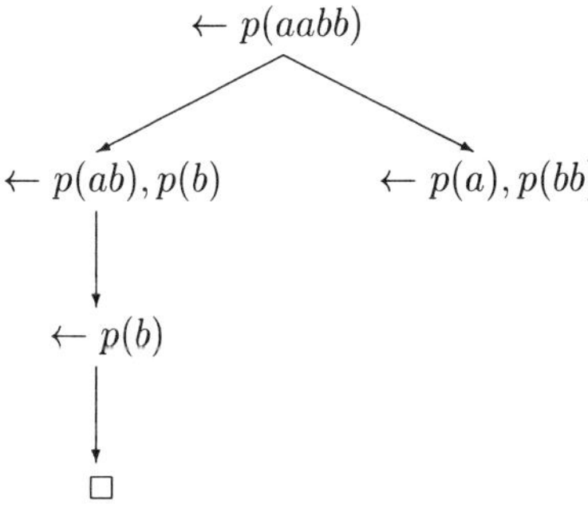

Figure 2: A derivation tree

4. Variable Separated EFS's

Given a set of axioms and a ground goal, the prover outputs "yes" and a refutation from the goal if any, otherwise it outputs "no". The prover searches a derivation tree for the empty goal by a depth-first-search. Hence if we can reduce branchings in the derivation tree, we can make the prover more efficient. A branching is caused by the following steps in derivations:

1. Selecting an axiom whose head can be unified with the goal. Two or more clauses may be selected as in the ordinary logic programming.

2. Selecting an unifier. Unlike the ordinary logic programming two or more unifiers may exist for a pair of two terms, which is due to:

    (a) Consecutiveness of variables in a head of the selected axiom. For example, in unifying two atoms $p(abba)$ and $p(axy)$, there exist two unifiers $\{x := b, \ y := ba\}$ and $\{x := bb, \ y := a\}$.

    (b) Selecting a location of constant strings in the goal which are substrings of the term in the head of the axiom. Some constant strings in an axiom may appear in several locations in a goal. For example, in unifying $p(abba)$ and $p(xby)$, a constant string b in xby locates twice in $abba$, and two unifiers $\{x := a, \ y := ba\}$ and $\{x := ab, \ y := a\}$ are obtained.

The number of branchings depends on the number of axioms in Case 1, and on the length of a term in a goal in Case 2. The number of axioms is fixed, while the lengths of the terms vary depending on the goals. The branchings due to Case 1 are common to all the logic programming. In this paper we try to reduce the branchings due to Case 2. However, we can not cope with the branchings due to Case 2(b), because the number of locations where the constant strings in the head of the selected atom appear depends on the input strings in the given goal which may range all over the Σ^+. Hence only the way we can take is to reduce the branchings due to Case 2(a). We solve this problem by transforming the given EFS's to EFS's with a good property. First we introduce a notion of such good EFS's, and show that they are equivalent to the original ones in language defining power.

Definition A regular EFS $S = (\Sigma, \Pi, \Gamma)$ is *variable-separated* if the term in the head of each clause in Γ is of the form

$$\alpha x_1 \alpha_1 \ldots x_n \alpha_n \qquad (\alpha, \alpha_i \in \Sigma^+,\ x_i \in X,\ n \geq 0).$$

In the variable-separated EFS's, every variable must be surrounded by constant strings on both sides, by virtue of which we can reduce the branchings due to Case 2(a). The variable-separated EFS's are a special class of regular EFS's. However, they are equivalent to the unrestricted ones. We prove this in the rest of this section.

By a *p-clause* we mean an axiom with predicate symbol p on its head. Then we can easily prove the following lemma.

Lemma 4.1 Let $S = (\Sigma, \Pi, \Gamma)$ be a regular EFS. Let $p(\alpha_1 x \alpha_2) \leftarrow A_1, q(x), A_2$ be an axiom in Γ and $q(\beta_1) \leftarrow B_1,\ \ldots,\ q(\beta_r) \leftarrow B_r$ be the set of all q-clause in Γ, where $\alpha_i \in (\Sigma \cup X)^*$ and $\beta_i \in (\Sigma \cup X)^+$, and A_i, B_i are finite (possibly empty) sequences of atoms. Let $S' = (\Sigma, \Pi, \Gamma')$ be a regular EFS obtained from S by deleting the axiom $p(\alpha_1 x \alpha_2) \leftarrow A_1, q(x), A_2$ from Γ and adding the axioms $p(\alpha_1 \beta_i \alpha_2) \leftarrow A_1, B_i, A_2 (1 \leq i \leq r)$. Then $L(S, p) = L(S', p)$.

We need two more lemmas.

Lemma 4.2 Let $S = (\Sigma, \Pi, \Gamma)$ be a regular EFS, $\{p(x\alpha_j) \leftarrow p(x), A_j | 1 \leq j \leq r\}$ be the set of p-clauses such that p is the leftmost predicate symbol in the body of an axiom in S, and $\{p(\beta_i) \leftarrow B_i \mid 1 \leq i \leq s\}$ be the remaining p-clauses in S. Construct an EFS $S' = (\Sigma, \Pi \cup \{q\}, \Gamma')$ by replacing all the p-clauses with the following clauses:

$$p(\beta_i) \leftarrow B_i$$
$$p(\beta_i \alpha_j) \leftarrow B_i, A_j$$
$$p(\beta_i x \alpha_j) \leftarrow B_i, q(x), A_j$$
$$q(\alpha_j) \leftarrow A_j$$
$$q(\alpha_j \alpha_k) \leftarrow A_j, A_k$$
$$q(\alpha_j x \alpha_k) \leftarrow A_j, q(x), A_k$$
$$(1 \leq i \leq s,\ 1 \leq j, k \leq r)$$

Then $L(S, p) = L(S', p)$.

Proof We first prove that if $w \in L(S, p)$ then $w \in L(S', p)$.

Suppose a goal $\leftarrow p(w)$ is given in S. If $p(\beta_i) \leftarrow B_i$ is selected at the first step, it is also selected in a refutation from $\leftarrow p(w)$ in S'. Next we consider the case that

$p(x\alpha_i) \leftarrow p(x), A_i$ is selected. The predicate symbol of leftmost atom in a resolvent is p so that the axiom of this form can be selected many times, say n times, until the axiom of the form $p(\beta_i) \leftarrow B_i$ is selected. Let $\theta_n, \ldots, \theta_1$ be the unifiers used in these n resolutions. Then the leftmost atom with a predicate symbol p is replaced with $B_j\theta$ by selecting $p(\beta_j) \leftarrow B_j$ and a unifier θ. The resolvent, i.e., the goal at this point, is $\leftarrow B_j\theta, A_{i_1}\theta_1, \ldots, A_{i_n}\theta_n$.

These resolutions in S can be traced in S' in the following way. If $n = 1$, $p(\beta_i\alpha_j) \leftarrow B_i, A_j$ is selected in a refutation from $\leftarrow p(w)$ in S'. If k is an even number, $q(\alpha_j) \leftarrow A_j$ is selected after $p(\beta_i x \alpha_j) \leftarrow B_i, q(x), A_j$ is selected, and then axioms of the form $q(\alpha_j x \alpha_k) \leftarrow A_j, q(x), A_k$ are selected $(n-2)/2$ times in the refutation. If n is an odd number, $q(\alpha_j\alpha_k) \leftarrow A_j, A_k$ is selected after $p(\beta_i x \alpha_j) \leftarrow B_i, q(x), A_j$ is selected, and then axioms of the form $q(\alpha_j x \alpha_k) \leftarrow A_j, q(x), A_k$ are selected $(n-3)/2$ times.

The other parts of refutaions in S are exactly the same as those in S'. Thus the refutations in S can be translated as those in S'. Hence we have $L(S,p) \subseteq L(S',p)$. The converse can be proved in a similar way. $\square$

Lemma 4.3   A similar statement to Lemma 4.2 is valid for p-clauses of the form $p(\alpha_j x) \leftarrow A_j, p(x)$.

By using these lemmas we can show the following theorem.

Theorem 4.1   For any regular EFS S and any predicate symbol p, there exists a variable-separated EFS S' and a predicate symbol p' in S' such that $L(S,p) = L(S',p')$.

Proof   Let $S = (\Sigma, \Pi, \Gamma)$ be a regular EFS and let $\Pi = \{p_1, \ldots, p_m\}$. First we transform S into an EFS in which clauses of the form

$$p_i(x_j\alpha x_k) \quad \leftarrow \quad p_j(x_j), A, p_k(x_k),$$

are its axioms only if $i < j, k$, where $\alpha \in (\Sigma \cup X)^*$, and A is a finite sequence of atoms.

This transformation is carried out from p_1-clauses to p_m-clauses in the following way. Suppose the clauses have been transformed so that for any i $(1 \leq i < l)$, $p_i(x_j\alpha x_k) \leftarrow p_j(x_j), A, p_k(x_k)$ is an axiom only if $i < j, k$. Now let us transform the p_l-clause. If a p_l-clause is either of the forms:

$$p_l(x_j\alpha) \quad \leftarrow \quad p_j(x_j), A,$$
$$p_l(\alpha x_k) \quad \leftarrow \quad A, p_k(x_k) \quad (l > j, k),$$

we introduce a new set of clauses by replacing $p_j(x_j)$ and $p_k(x_k)$ with bodies of p_j-clauses and p_k-clauses according to Lemma 4.1. By repeating this process at most $2(l-1)$ times, we obtain clauses of the form:

$$p_l(x_{j'}\alpha'x_{k'}) \;\leftarrow\; p_{j'}(x_{j'}), A', p_{k'}(x_{k'}) \;\;(l \le j', k'),$$

where both ends of the terms in the head may possibly be constant symbols. If $l = j'$ or $l = k'$, the p_l-clauses are replaced according to Lemma 4.2 and 4.3, introducing a new predicate symbol q_l.

By the above process, we have clauses only of the forms:

$$
\begin{aligned}
&p_i(a_1\gamma a_2) \leftarrow A,\\
&p_i(x_j\gamma a_2) \leftarrow p_j(x_j), A,\\
&p_i(a_1\gamma x_k) \leftarrow A, p_k(x_k),\\
&p_i(x_j\gamma x_k) \leftarrow p_j(x_j), A, p_k(x_k),\\
&q_i(\gamma) \leftarrow A,\\
&q_i(\gamma x_i\gamma') \leftarrow A, p_i(x_i), A',\\
&\qquad (i < j, k, \; a_1, a_2 \in \Sigma, \; \gamma, \gamma' \in (\Sigma \cup X')^*),
\end{aligned}
$$

where X' consists of variables introduced when Lemma 4.2 and 4.3 are applied, and A, A' are finite sequences of atoms whose predicate symbols are in $\Pi \cup \{q_1, ..., q_{i-1}\}$.

Both ends of terms in the heads of p_m-clauses are constant symbols, because m is the largest index of p. By using Lemma 4.1, we transform all the p_i-clauses from $m - 1$ down to 1 until constant symbols appear at the both ends of terms in the heads. Then we obtain clauses of the forms:

$$
\begin{aligned}
&p_i(a_1\gamma a_2) \leftarrow A,\\
&q_i(\gamma) \leftarrow A,\\
&q_i(\gamma x_i\gamma') \leftarrow A, p_i(x_i), A'.
\end{aligned}
$$

Now we transform p_i-clauses with bodies into variable-separated clauses, by introducing new predicate symbol r_i and replacing bodies of p_i-clauses with $r_i(x_i)$. Then all of the p_i-clauses are transformed into variable-separated clauses of the forms:

$$
\begin{aligned}
&p_i(a_1x_ia_2) \leftarrow r_i(x_i),\\
&q_i(\gamma) \leftarrow A,\\
&q_i(\gamma x_i\gamma') \leftarrow A, p_i(x_i), A',\\
&r_i(\gamma) \leftarrow A.
\end{aligned}
$$

Finally, we deal with q_i- and r_i-clauses. We can show that indices of predicate symbols in the bodies of any q_i- and r_i-clauses are less than those in their heads. Since all the predicate symbols in the bodies of q_1-clauses are p_i for some i, we can transform q_1-clauses into variable-separated clauses according to lemma 4.1. Applying this process to the clauses with $q_2, \ldots, q_m, r_1, \ldots, r_m$ as heads in this order, we can transform all the clauses into variable-separated clauses. Thus we have a variable-separated EFS S' such that $L(S, p) = L(S', p')$. $\square$

Example 4.1 Let $S = (\{a, b\}, \{p_1, p_2, p_3\}, \Gamma)$ be a regular EFS with the following Γ:

$$p_1(xy) \leftarrow p_2(x), p_3(y),$$
$$p_2(ax) \leftarrow p_2(x),$$
$$p_2(a) \leftarrow,$$
$$p_3(yb) \leftarrow p_3(y),$$
$$p_3(b) \leftarrow .$$

The EFS S defines a regular language $L(S, p_1) = \{a^m b^n \mid m, n \geq 1\}$. Let us transform S into a variable-separated the regular EFS S'. The indices of predicates in the body of the first axiom is greater than the index in its head. Hence we start with the axiom $p_2(ax) \leftarrow p_2(x)$ and $p_3(yb) \leftarrow p_3(y)$, and apply Lemma 4.2 and 4.3. Then we have the following set of clauses:

$$
\begin{array}{ll}
p_1(xy) \leftarrow p_2(x), p_3(y), & \\
p_2(a) \leftarrow, & p_3(b) \leftarrow, \\
p_2(aa) \leftarrow, & p_3(bb) \leftarrow, \\
p_2(axa) \leftarrow q_2(x), & p_3(byb) \leftarrow q_3(y), \\
q_2(a) \leftarrow, & q_3(b) \leftarrow, \\
q_2(aa) \leftarrow, & q_3(bb) \leftarrow, \\
q_2(axa) \leftarrow q_2(x), & q_3(byb) \leftarrow q_3(y).
\end{array}
$$

We now apply Lemma 4.1 to the p_1-clause. Then we have the desired set of clauses each of which is a variable-separated clause:

$$
\begin{array}{ll}
p_1(ab) \leftarrow, & p_1(aabyb) \leftarrow q_3(y), \\
p_1(abb) \leftarrow, & p_1(axab) \leftarrow q_2(x), \\
p_1(abyb) \leftarrow q_3(y), & p_1(axabb) \leftarrow q_2(x), \\
p_1(aab) \leftarrow, & p_1(axabyb) \leftarrow q_2(x), q_3(y), \\
p_1(aabb) \leftarrow, & \\
p_2(a) \leftarrow, & p_3(b) \leftarrow, \\
p_2(aa) \leftarrow, & p_3(bb) \leftarrow, \\
p_2(axa) \leftarrow q_2(x), & p_3(byb) \leftarrow q_3(y), \\
q_2(a) \leftarrow, & q_3(b) \leftarrow, \\
q_2(aa) \leftarrow, & q_3(bb) \leftarrow, \\
q_2(axa) \leftarrow q_2(x), & q_3(byb) \leftarrow q_3(y).
\end{array}
$$

As a more practical example, we have transformed all the Pascal grammar, which can be described in a regular EFS, into an equivalent variable-separated EFS. Due to limitation of space, we do not go into further detail.

By giving the prover a variable-separated EFS which is equivalent to the original regular EFS, we can reduce not only the number of branchings in the derivation tree but also the height of the tree, i.e., the length of the longest branch from the root to a leaf. Note here that given a ground goal, in general, a derivation tree for a regular EFS may be infinite. In fact, in the derivation for a regular EFS, if an axiom which does not contain any constant symbol is selected, the total length of terms in the resolvent, a new goal, does not decrease at all. In the worst case that an axiom $p(x) \leftarrow q(x)$ is selected and another axiom $q(x) \leftarrow p(x)$ exists, the tree becomes infinite. However, the trees for our variable-separated EFS's are always finite.

In this paper we are mainly interested in the refutations starting with ground goals. In such refutations the heights of trees depend on the lengths of ground goals given to the prover.

Now we compare the heights of derivation trees for regular EFS's and those for variable-separated EFS's equivalent to them. Here we deal with regular EFS's for which every derivation tree from a ground goal is finite, that is, the pathological case mentioned above may not happen.

Let n be the length of an input string, i.e., a term in the ground goal given to the prover. For a regular EFS the length of the term in the derivation tree decreases by at least one at every step of the derivation. Hence, the height of the derivation tree is n in the worst case. On the other hand, for a variable-separated EFS, the length decreases by at least two at every step, because the both ends of the term in each clause are constant symbols. Hence, the height of the tree does not exceed $n/2$. This shows that we can make the prover faster if we use the variable-separated EFS's instead of the regular EFS's.

5. An experimental result

In this section we show how the prover for variable-separated EFS's works efficiently by an example. The following are a regular EFS and a variable-separated EFS which define the same simple Japanese sentences.

The "は", "が" and "を", "に" below are Japanese postpositional particles which change (pro)nouns into the subjective cases and the objective cases, respectively. The "あなた", "彼", "彼女" and "彼ら" are Japanese stems of pronouns which make pronouns which correspond to, for example, "you", "he", "she" and "they", respectively, followed by the postpositional particles "は" or "が". The meanings of the other Japanese words are shown in the comments.

    1. A regular EFS S with the following 36 axioms.

```
sentence(XYZ)<-subject(X),pred(Y),period(Z)
subject(XYZ)<-noun(X),post(Y),comma(Z)
subject(WXYZ)<-modifier(W),noun(X),post(Y),comma(Z)
pred(X)<-verb(X)
pred(X)<-adj(X)
pred(XY)<-modifier(X),verb(Y)
pred(XY)<-modifier(X),adj(Y)
modifier(X)<-adj(X)
modifier(XY)<-noun(X),post(Y)
noun(あなた)<-
noun(彼)<-
noun(彼女)<-
noun(彼ら)<-
```

```
noun(犬)<-          /* noun(dog)<-        */
noun(鳥)<-          /* noun(bird)<-       */
noun(花)<-          /* noun(flower)<-     */
noun(大空)<-        /* noun(sky)<-        */
noun(自由)<-        /* noun(freedom)<-    */
noun(海岸)<-        /* noun(beach)<-      */
post(は)<-
post(が)<-
post(を)<-
post(に)<-
adj(おおきな)<-     /* adj(big)<-         */
adj(ひろい)<-       /* adj(wide)<-        */
adj(あおい)<-       /* adj(blue)<-        */
adj(きれいな)<-     /* adj(beautiful)<-   */
adj(ちいさい)<-     /* adj(little)<-      */
verb(飛ぶ)<-        /* verb(fly)<-        */
verb(走る)<-        /* verb(run)<-        */
verb(植える)<-      /* verb(plant)<-      */
verb(見る)<-        /* verb(see)<-        */
verb(放す)<-        /* verb(release)<-    */
verb(降る)<-        /* verb(fall)<-       */
comma(, )<-
period(. )<-
```

2. A variable-separated EFS S' with 506, some of which are listed below.

```
sentence(あなた X, Y. )<-post(X),pred(Y)
sentence(彼 X, Y. )<-post(X),pred(Y)
sentence(彼女 X, Y. )<-post(X),pred(Y)
sentence(彼ら X, Y. )<-post(X),pred(Y)
sentence(犬 X, Y. )<-post(X),pred(Y)
sentence(鳥 X, Y. )<-post(X),pred(Y)
sentence(花 X, Y. )<-post(X),pred(Y)
sentence(大空 X, Y. )<-post(X),pred(Y)
sentence(自由 X, Y. )<-post(X),pred(Y)
sentence(海岸 X, Y. )<-post(X),pred(Y)
sentence(おおきな X は, Y. )<-noun(X),pred(Y)
sentence(おおきな X が, Y. )<-noun(X),pred(Y)
sentence(おおきな X を, Y. )<-noun(X),pred(Y)
sentence(おおきな X に, Y. )<-noun(X),pred(Y)
sentence(ひろい X は, Y. )<-noun(X),pred(Y)
                 :

adj(おおきな)<-
adj(ひろい)<-
adj(あおい)<-
adj(きれいな)<-
adj(ちいさい)<-
```

```
verb(飛ぶ)<-
verb(走る)<-
verb(植える)<-
verb(見る)<-
verb(放す)<-
verb(降る)<-
comma(, )<-
period(. )<-
```

We made an experiment on Sun SPARC station 10 by giving these two EFS's and following four goals with Japanese sentences to the prover, and obtained the results in the table.

1. ←sentence(大空を飛ぶ)
   /* ←sentence(Fly in the sky.)   */
2. ←sentence(彼女は, 鳥を放す.)
   /* ←sentence(She releases a bird.)   */
3. ←sentence(ちいさい犬が, 海岸を走る.)
   /* ←sentence(A little dog runs on the beach.)   */
4. ←sentence(彼女が植えた赤い花が, 庭の花壇できれいにさいている.)
   /* ←sentence(Flowers she planted are in full
               bloom in the flower bed in the garden.) */

Sentence	Regular EFS	Variable-separated EFS
1	0.17 sec	0.60 sec
2	0.44 sec	1.04 sec
3	2.42 sec	1.62 sec
4	318.89 sec	1.90 sec

The sentences No.2 and No.3 have been accepted by the prover, while the rest have been rejected. From this table we can see that the variable-separated EFS S' makes the prover much faster than the original regular EFS.

6. Concluding remarks

In this paper, we have introduced a notion of variable-separated EFS's. Then we have proved that these two classes of EFS's are equivalent to each other in expressive power, and shown that the variable-separated EFS's make the prover for regular EFS's at least twice as fast as the original regular EFS's.

We have also given a procedure to transform regular EFS's into equivalent variable-separated EFS's in the process of proving the theorem. However, it is not always efficient. In fact, there has been observed that even a small regular EFS with just five axioms may be transformed into a variable-separated EFS with more than a thousand axioms. To make the procedure efficient is one of the future problems we should solve.

We conclude this paper by noticing that our notions and methods can be directly applied to context-free grammars, and hence the prover also works as a top-down parser for context-free grammars.

Acknowledgements

We would like to thank E. Hirowatari and S. Matsunaga for their valuable comments.

References

[1] J.E.Hopcroft and J.D.Ullman. *Introduction to Automata Theory, Languages, and Computation* . Addison-Wesley Publishing Company, 1979.

[2] J.W.Lloyd. *Foundations of Logic Programming(second edition)*. Springer-Verlag, 1987.

[3] R.M.Smullyan. *Theory of Formal Systems*. Princeton Univ. Press, Princeton, 1961.

[4] S.Arikawa, S.Miyano, A.Shinohara, T.Shinohara, and A.Yamamoto. Algorithmic learning theory with elementary formal systems. *IEICE Transactions on Information and Systems*, Vol. E75-D, No. 4, pp. 405–414, 1992.

[5] S.Arikawa, T.Shinohara, and A.Yamamoto. Learning elementary formal systems. *Theoretical Computer Science*, Vol. 95, pp. 97–113, 1992.

Information Modelling and Knowledge Bases IX
P.-J. Charrel et al. (Eds.)
1998, IOS Press

A Multi-Level Knowledge-Based Model of Diagnostic Reasoning

Antoni LIGĘZA[†] & Pilar FUSTER-PARRA[‡]

[†]*Institute of Automatics AGH, al. Mickiewicza 30, 30-059 Kraków, Poland*
[‡]*University of Balearic Islands, Ctra. de Valldemossa km 7.5, E-07071 Palma, Spain*

Abstract. This paper addresses the issues of multi-level diagnostic reasoning based on abductive analysis of causal structures. A basic, core, uniform model for a single-level representation of causal behaviour of the diagnosed system is presented; it has the form of an AND/OR/NOT causal graph allowing for specification of causality types reflecting basic logical operations. The causal graph defines the search space for diagnostic inference at some abstraction level. The diagnosis is performed as a backward search on the graph. Building on this single-level model the paper introduces the idea of a multi-level model for enabling realistic and efficient modelling of diagnostic reasoning and information processing. The paper presents ideas emerging from analysis of engineering approach to diagnosing complex systems; a diagnostic process is considered as a multi-level knowledge representation, sophisticated backward search procedure supported with sequential testing and ordering strategies. Further, use of logical constraints for pruning diagnostic hypotheses and constructive constraint propagation is discussed.

1. Introduction

Automated and computer aided diagnosis constitutes an important area of applied Artificial Intelligence (AI) and Knowledge Engineering (KE). Its main aim consists of supporting efficient failure detection (detection of abnormal behaviour) and determination of initial causes (fault isolation) in complex systems, being given only a set of symptoms of abnormal behaviour and certain auxiliary observations. After some experiences with pattern recognition, neural nets and expert systems a new, deeper insight into the nature of diagnostic reasoning is provided by the so-called *model-based approaches* [4, 5]. The attractiveness of diagnosis as a matter of research follows from non-trivial, diversified reasoning paradigms to be investigated and possibility of practical verification of the developed approaches.

Modelling information processing for efficient solution of diagnostic problems must take into account factors like multi-source and multi-form information (information coming from different sources and represented in different forms), different character and modes of reasoning applied to search for solutions, diversified credibility of accessible information, etc. Moreover, diagnostic knowledge should be represented and considered at several levels of abstraction in order to provide the possibility of efficient, hierarchical fault localization.

A basic inference mode for modelling diagnostic reasoning accepted in this paper is *abduction*. Abduction constitutes an inference mode opposite (inverse) to deduction; contrary to deduction, abduction is not a valid logical inference rule; it may result in generation of several hypotheses, while only some of them (or none) are true. In this sense abduction provides no unique, always valid result – the results constitute only *hypotheses* which normally require further validation. However, it seems to be most close to human diagnostic reasoning. Supported with the possibility of testing and verification and guided by expert knowledge it may constitute a powerful tool for diagnostic reasoning.

This paper aims at presenting a basic approach to diagnostic multi-level knowledge representation and reasoning incorporating abductive inference as a basic diagnostic tool. It is using the abductive reasoning for finding explanations of observed failure symptoms in an almost straightforward way at a single level, where abduction is considered mainly as a *backward search procedure* for appropriately defined search space. For such basic diagnostic model various mechanisms enabling multi-level knowledge representation and processing are proposed. Consistency-based reasoning can be then considered as one of these mechanisms allowing for checking of consistency and detection of conflicts using a more detailed, lower-level knowledge specification.

In fact, diagnosis of any more complex system must be performed in a hierarchical manner: first one identifies a faulty system in the diagnosed device, then perhaps a faulty subsystem and finally – the faulty element(s) themselves. The paper presents a study of several hierarchization mechanisms on the base of a uniform, single-level diagnostic model. The presented approach offers possibilities of hierarchization along three basic directions: division of the initial graph into smaller subgraphs ("geographical" hierarchization; horizontal separation, or single-level separation), use of graphs with different type of knowledge represented at different levels of reasoning (functional abstraction and hierarchization; vertical separation), and, finally, using different level of logical knowledge definitions, constraints, constraint relaxation, etc. ("level of abstraction" hierarchization w.r.t. different details incorporated at a single level). Last but not least, the proposed approach seems to be close to human engineering intuitions, which seems difficult to overestimate when it comes to diagnoses understanding, explanation and verification. The presented hierarchization mechanisms are quite general ones, and they can also be used in other information modelling and processing systems.

2. Single-Level Diagnosis

This section presents in brief some basic concepts concerning formal representation of causal modelling and diagnostic reasoning at a single level. For intuition, the basic representation structure is a graph, where the vertices are arrows indicating which items can influence other ones. These items are referred to as *symptoms*; presence or absence of some symptoms may *cause* other symptoms to occur.

2.1 Symptoms

The idea of using symptoms to represent and analyze system behaviour is a popular way for speaking about variety of phenomena, when no single, precise mathematical formalism can capture all the representational issues. A *symptom* is mostly understood to be equivalent to *propositional formula*, i.e. a statement that is assumed to take normally two truth values: *true* or *false*, i.e, to be present or absent; its current value can also stay unknown. For simplicity, such logical binary-valued interpretation of symptoms is kept throughout this paper. However, an extension to qualitative variable values or multiple-valued logics is almost straightforward.

Let $\mathbf{N}$ denote a set of symptoms of interest, i.e. ones referring to the system under analysis. An individual symptom is denoted as $n \in \mathbf{N}$. An inverse symptom (one having inversed logical value) will be denoted as $\bar{n}$. A set of symptoms all of them *true* will be denoted as N^+, while a set of *false* symptoms will be denoted as N^-.

It is convenient to distinguish among all the symptoms some *input symptoms* or *initial (elementary) causes*. Let $\mathbf{D}$ denote a set of considered input symptoms, $\mathbf{D} = \{d_1, d_2, \ldots, d_d\}$. This category may include control actions, external signals, faults of selected elements (in case of diagnostic reasoning), etc.

Similarly, one can distinguish a set of *output symptoms* or *manifestations*. The set of such symptoms will be denoted by $\mathbf{M} = \{m_1, m_2, \ldots, m_m\}$. This category may include output signals, observed effects of control actions or external events influencing the behaviour of the system, external characteristics, or failure manifestations in the case of diagnostic reasoning.

Beside symptoms which are input and output ones (i.e. belonging to $\mathbf{D}$ or $\mathbf{M}$), all the other symptoms are *intermediate* ones, i.e. they are just any symptoms, observable directly or not, helpful for expressing some intermediate events or partial system characteristics. The set of such symptoms will be denoted by $\mathbf{V} = \{v_1, v_2, \ldots, v_v\}$. It is assumed that $\mathbf{N} = \mathbf{D} \cup \mathbf{V} \cup \mathbf{M}$. For clarity, it is also assumed that the sets are pairwise disjoint, i.e. $\mathbf{D} \cap \mathbf{V} = \emptyset$, $\mathbf{V} \cap \mathbf{M} = \emptyset$, and $\mathbf{D} \cap \mathbf{M} = \emptyset$.

All symptoms are represented by the graph nodes. For simplicity, we do not distinguish between the nodes and the symptoms assigned to them. Taking into account practical diagnostic problems, any element of $\mathbf{N}$ can be regarded as *symptom*, *event*, *binary variable*, or *propositional formula*. Thus several ways of notation are possible; a symptom $n \in \mathbf{N}$ being observed can be denoted as n being *true*, $n = 1$ or simply $n \in N^+$ while the absence of it can be denoted as n being *false*, $n = 0$, or $n \in N^-$.

2.2 Causal Relations

The interrelationship among symptoms are defined by *causal relations*. In the most straightforward interpretation, *causality* means influence leading to occurrence of selected symptoms as result of appearance of some other ones. Causal relations between symptoms are expressed by arcs in the graph structure. An arc pointing from n to n' says that n *causes* n'. The semantics of causality can be further understood and defined in several ways; however, most of the papers do not deal with this subject in an explicit way [2, 3, 9, 13, 18]. In this paper, for simplicity, a straightforward logical semantics of causality is assumed, i.e. if $n \longrightarrow n'$ then $n \models n'$ (the inverse is not necessarily being true); for a more detailed semantics see [11].

A *causal relation* is understood as a function or a partial function[1] from the set of possible combinations of values of some direct cause symptoms into the set of values of another symptom being the result of them. Let $n_1, n_2, \ldots, n_k$ and n be symptoms; a causal relation defining an influence of $n_1, n_2, \ldots, n_k$ on n is any function of the form

$$\psi(n_1, n_2, \ldots, n_k) \longrightarrow n. \tag{1}$$

---

[1]A partial function is a one defined only on a subset of the set normally understood as its domain.

Selection of specific functions is a matter of arbitrary choice and it can be performed with respect to current requirements. In the case of two-valued, logical symptoms, a reasonable and straightforward choice is to take functions referring to the basic logical connectives, i.e. AND, OR, and NOT [7, 12]. The AND connection, i.e. one where simultaneous presence of all input symptoms causes the resulting symptom to occur will be denoted as $[n_1, n_2, \ldots, n_k] \longrightarrow n$. The OR connection, i.e. one where the presence of a single input symptom is enough to cause the output symptom to occur will be denoted as $n_1|n_2|\ldots n_k \longrightarrow n$. Further, the NOT connections, where the absence of symptom n causes presence of symptom n' (and vice versa) will be denoted as $n \bullet\!\!\rightarrow n'$.

2.3 Causal Graphs

A causal graph is a structure representing all the considered causal dependencies existing in a considered system in a uniform and concise way. Let $\mathbf{N} = \mathbf{D} \cup \mathbf{V} \cup \mathbf{M}$ be the set of considered symptoms and let $\mathbf{\Psi}$ denote a set of specific functions defining causal relations among the symptoms of $\mathbf{N}$. The causal graph is defined as follows:

Definition 1 *A "causal graph" is any pair of the form* $\mathbf{G} = (\mathbf{N}, \mathbf{\Psi})$.

In the graph the nodes such that no arc points to them will be referred to as *initial nodes*; for simplicity, it is assumed that the initial nodes are the ones of $\mathbf{D}$. Further, the nodes from which no arc points to other nodes will be referred to as *terminal* or *final nodes*; for simplicity, it is assumed that the set of terminal nodes is just $\mathbf{M}$. To simplify the discussion it is further assumed that there are no loops in the graph and the graph is a connected one.

The AND/OR/NOT causal graph defined as above follows the structure of classical AND/OR graphs used in problem-solving [15]. The main differences consist of the direction and interpretation of arcs (here different extensions of the basic causal interpretation are possible; see for example the MAY links in [3, 18]; for some comments see also [7]) and nodes (an initial node here means only a potential solution); the application of the graph is also different. A visible extension consists in admitting the NOT links. Further, a "solution graph" in classical problem-solving constitutes here only a "possible justification" (to be further validated) for the observed failure. The AND/OR/NOT causal graphs are also a generalization of fault trees [6] and other causal graphs used in model-based diagnosis (e.g. [1, 13]) as they admit AND and NOT connections (in general: functional causal dependencies).

Having defined causal graph as a model of system behaviour, one can define *diagnostic problem* to be solved. The definition takes into account two basic factors: the qualiative logical model of the system, i.e. the causal graph defining in fact the search space for solutions, and the current observations defining the initial state for the search. Let $\mathbf{N}$ denote a set of symptoms and $\mathbf{\Psi}$ be a set of functions defined on these symptoms, $\mathbf{N} = \mathbf{D} \cup \mathbf{V} \cup \mathbf{M}$, $\mathbf{G} = (\mathbf{N}, \mathbf{\Psi})$ be a causal graph.

Definition 2 *A "diagnostic problem" is defined by* $(\mathbf{G}, M^+, M^-, OBS^+, OBS^-)$, *where* $M^+, M^- \subseteq \mathbf{M}$ *are the sets of manifestation symptoms true and false, respectively, and* $OBS^+, OBS^- \subseteq \mathbf{N}$ *are the sets of auxiliary observation symptoms true or false, respectively.*

Manifestation symptoms M^+, M^- typically specify the abnormal behaviour to be explained while observations provide auxiliary information for controlling and refining diagnostic reasoning. Any diagnosis must be consistent with observations and must fully explain the symptoms observed to be true and false; the symptoms of observations need not necessarily be explained.

2.4 Abductive Search for Diagnoses

Let us consider a causal graph $\mathbf{G} = (\mathbf{N}, \mathbf{\Psi})$; this graph represents the structure of causal dependencies. Taking into account the current values (known e.g. by observation) of the symptoms one can define the state of the graph. A partial state (manifestations, observations, etc.) can be specified as two disjoint sets, e.g. $S^+ = \{s_1, s_2, \ldots, s_i\}$ and $S^- = \{s_{i+1}, s_{i+2}, \ldots, s_j\}$, where all the symptoms in S^+ are *true* while all the ones in S^- are *false*. This kind of specification is especially convenient for performing consistency check; inconsistency is detected if the intersection of the appropriate sets is not empty i.e. when $S^+ \cap S^- \neq \emptyset$.

Having defined a partial state one can obtain the most complete information about symptoms status by propagation of the values defined by partial state. The final state, where no further propagation is possible is a complete state. The rules for propagation are basically the ones of logical reasoning; however, depending on the interpretation of causality various modifications are possible. A most common set of such propagation rules can be found in [12] (see also [8] and [11]). If a state (S^+, S^-) follows from some state (S_0^+, S_0^-) this will be denoted as $(S_0^+, S_0^-) \vdash (S^+, S^-)$. If starting from some partial state (S_0^+, S_0^-) the state (S^+, S^-) such that no further propagation is possible is obtained, the state (S^+, S^-) is considered to be *maximal* or *fixed-point* under propagation operation and will be denoted as $(S_0^+, S_0^-)^*$. From now on when speaking about the state (the complete state), a fixed-point under the propagation possibilities will normally be taken into account. Furthermore, the discusion of diagnostic inference is naturally restricted to consistent states of the graph only.

The most important result of search is a *diagnosis*, or, more precisely, a set of *diagnoses*. For further use a diagnosis is defined as follows.

Definition 3 *Let $(\mathbf{G}, M^+, M^-, OBS^+, OBS^-)$ be a diagnostic problem defined as above. A <u>diagnosis</u> is any (minimal and consistent) pair $D = (D^+, D^-)$ of initial symptoms* true *and* false*, such that:*

- *D justifies M^+ and M^-, i.e. assuming that $\mathbf{G}$ specifies the domain theory, $(D^+, D^-) \vdash (M^+, M^-)$,*

- *D is consistent with observations w.r.t. fixed point state, i.e. if $(S^+, S^-) = (D^+ \cup OBS^+, D^- \cup OBS^-)^*$ is the maximal state implied by the diagnosis and observations, then $S^+ \cap S^- = \emptyset$.*

Obviously, any diagnosis must fully account for the observed abnormal behaviour. Further, it must be internally consistent ($D^+ \cap D^- = \emptyset$) and consistent with current observations, more precisely, the set of all logical consequences of the assumed diagnosis and observations must be consistent; all with respect to the theory of the system specified by the causal graph. Moreover, a diagnosis is normally assumed to be a minimal one. Minimality may be understood in two ways, i.e. with respect to set inclusion (this is the classical understanding in AI), or with respect to minimality of the subgraph of $\mathbf{G}$ necessary for explaining the failure [8].

The search for diagnoses is performed recursively backwards on the AND/OR/NOT graph structure, with indeterministic selection of nodes to explore and normally in the depth-first manner. The initial problem specification is given by a set of manifestation symptoms together with their logical values, M^+ and M^-. The following rules specify the principles of backward search for a selected node:

- *OR node* $n_1|n_2|\ldots n_k \longrightarrow n$ *true*: if the goal is to explain an OR node n being *true*, then one of its predecessors n_j, $j \in \{1, 2, \ldots k\}$ having the status *true* or *unknown* is selected and – if unknown – its state is set to *true*,

- *AND node* $[n_1, n_2, \ldots, n_k] \longrightarrow n$ *true*: if the goal is to explain an AND node n being *true*, then all of its predecessors $n_1, n_2, \ldots n_k$ are selected and their state is set to *true*,

- *OR node* $n_1|n_2|\ldots n_k \longrightarrow n$ *false*: if the goal is to explain an OR node n being *false*, then all of its predecessors $n_1, n_2, \ldots n_k$ are selected and their state is set to *false*,

- *AND node* $[n_1, n_2, \ldots, n_k] \longrightarrow n$ *false*: if the goal is to explain an AND node n being *false*, then one of its predecessors n_j, $j \in \{1, 2, \ldots k\}$ having the status *false* or *unknown* is selected and its state – if necessary – is set to *false*,

- *NOT node true*: if the goal is to explain a NOT node *true*, then its predecessor is selected and its status is set to *false*,

- *NOT node false*: if the goal is to explain a NOT node *false*, then its predecessor is selected and its status is set to *true*,

- *initial nodes*: initial nodes are assumed to be *true* or *false* when necessary; arriving at an initial node completes the search on the selected path.

The operations are performed only if possible (no inconsistency occurs). The node selection procedure in case of OR node *true* and AND node *false* may be any systematic, nondeterministic, or heuristic one.

3. Multi-Level Diagnostic Reasoning

Multi-level knowledge representation extends the single-level approach based on and centered around causal graphs, as presented in the former section. In order to increase the efficiency of model-based diagnosis, model representations at several levels of detail are required. Several authors have taken into account the importance of hierarchization for diagnostic inference. In [14] a hierarchical model representation is formulated. In [16] a multi-level causal description is presented. In [18] several levels of knowledge representation are considered, and a car troubleshooting example showing the frame-system hierarchy is presented.

In this section it is shown that the proposed approach offers different levels of detail as a "human oriented approach" with the goal to increase the effectiveness of model-based diagnosis. The efficiency improvements are mainly due to reduced search spaces at more abstract levels and limited search at the detailed level performed only for preselected parts of the whole system.

3.1 Abstracting and Specifying

The first issue in multi-level information modelling is the possibility to represent and deal with the knowledge about the system at several levels of details. Let us consider just two such levels, one of them referred to as *abstract* or *higher* level, and the other one, covering more details, to be referred to as *specification* level, or the *lower* level. The knowledge to be dealt with at any such level refers to the same phenomena, however even the description language can be different.

Inference is normally carried out at a certain level; passing from one level to another is a special operation required in certain circumstances. Below, a simple model of inter-level information transfer is put forward.

Let q be a propositional formula, e.g. one defining certain symptom. The formula is considered as one belonging to the upper, abstract level; it can denote a node of the causal graph. When attempting at verification of its truth-value, one may need a more detailed definition. Thus passing down to the specification level is necessary. Let ψ be a formula defining the symptom q at the lower level. The operations changing the level of inference are denoted as:

$$\bigtriangledown q = \psi \tag{2}$$

and

$$\bigtriangleup \psi = q. \tag{3}$$

The first operation, *down*, means simply that instead of q its logical definition specified with other symbols and expressed in another language (covering more details) is taken into account; an obvious choice for the more detailed language in this case is first-order logic, but other possibilities can be considered. The second operation, *up*, means that instead of considering formula ψ at the lower level, one can consider atom q at the higher level, and, in particular, if ψ has been found to hold, symptom q is set to true.

Application of the above operations in diagnostic reasoning is straightforward. Assume one attempts at verification of certain symptom, while its current truth value is neither given nor decidable at the current level. In such a case one can look for the possibility of passing to a more detailed level. If the symptom specification at the lower level is accessible, the inference at the abstract level is temporarily suspended; after succesful verification of the formula specifying the symptom at the lower level, its truth value is passed back to the abstract level and the inference is resumed. Such an operation is useful in the following four particular situations:

- *initial failure detection* – let Φ denote the detailed description of the current state of the analyzed system. Now if $\Phi \models \psi$, and $\bigtriangleup \psi = q$, then symtom q occurs. Analogously, occurrence of $\bar{q}$ can be detected. This procedure can be performed for the final nodes, i.e. the manifestation symptoms (ones belonging to $\mathbf{M}$). Thus the sets of positive and negative manifestations, M^+ and M^- can be generated in this way.

- *initial observations detection* – this can be done in similar way for nodes belonging to $\mathbf{V}$; in this way the sets of positive and negative observations, OBS^+ and OBS^- can be formed.

- *symptoms testing* – during the process of abductive reasoning, the values of certain intermediate symptoms are just hypothesized. If for some of such symptoms a lower level specification is accessible, a test of such symptom can be performed. This is done by passing to the lower level, verification of the symptom specification formula and passing the result up. If the output of the test is *true*, the occurrance of the symptom is confirmed and the current way of reasoning should be followed. In the other case, the search can be abandonned, having the effect of reducing the search space.

- *final diagnoses verification* – any potential diagnosis is composed of a set of elementary diagnoses; by appropriate use of the above mechanism verification of the elementary diagnoses can be carried out by analysis at the deailed level.

For illustration, let us consider a simple example concerning failure detection. We refer to a tank system [8], where the main failure is described with symptom m describing a situation when water is pouring out of a tank (an overflow); the abstract level causal graph of this system is presented in Fig. 6. Symptom m is further specified with a formula defining it at the lower level; there is $\nabla m = \psi$, ψ describes all the states in which overflow occurs. The formula may be of the form $\psi = \texttt{water\_level} \in (\texttt{max}, +\infty)$. The failure detection problem consists in checking if the current state satisfies this failure description; for this purpose, any automated theorem proving procedure can be applied. Assume that the level denoted symbolically as $\texttt{very\_high}$ is higher than the one of $\texttt{max}$ (in practical system these may be just ordinary numbers). Let the current state formula be $\Phi = \texttt{water\_level} \in (\texttt{very\_high}, +\infty) \wedge \phi$, where ϕ denotes another state properties at the detailed level. Thus in our case

$$\texttt{water\_level} \in (\texttt{very\_high}, +\infty) \wedge \phi \models \texttt{water\_level} \in (\texttt{max}, +\infty)$$

Since $\psi = \texttt{water\_level} \in (\texttt{max}, +\infty)$ holds, and $\triangle \psi = m$, the set of failure manifestations is formed as $M^+ = \{m\}$; the crucial element of the check consists of verifying that $(\texttt{very\_high}, +\infty) \subseteq (\texttt{max}, +\infty)$. For more details see [8].

3.2 Separation or Horizontal Hierarchization

Another possibility of making the search for diagnoses more efficient consists of dividing the search space into separated subareas, by division of the complete initial graph into smaller parts. Such a "geographical hierarchization" may be obtained by division of the initial graph into smaller subgraphs ("geographical" hierarchization; horizontal separation, or separation, for brevity), the initial system may be easily separated into subsystems. The determination of the subsystem for further analysis can be done by analysis of the signal flow from one subsystem to another (see Figure 1 and Figure 2).

In Figure 2 a top node of some subgraph becoming an elementary diagnosis of another subgraph is shown. The element $d2$ is considered to be an elementary diagnosis (or disorder) at this level of abstraction, but it is connected to $m1$ in a more detailed level, and so one can obtain more detailed diagnoses following (backwards) this line of causality.

Such an operation of separation can be denoted as $\mathbf{G} = \mathbf{G}_1 \wr \mathbf{G}_2$, or, more precisely as $\mathbf{G} = \mathbf{G}_1 \wr_U \mathbf{G}_2$; the meaning of the operation is that graph $\mathbf{G}$ is split into two simpler graphs, namely $\mathbf{G}_1$ and $\mathbf{G}_2$, where U (if present) specifies the set of common nodes, i.e. the ones through which the "separation line" goes.

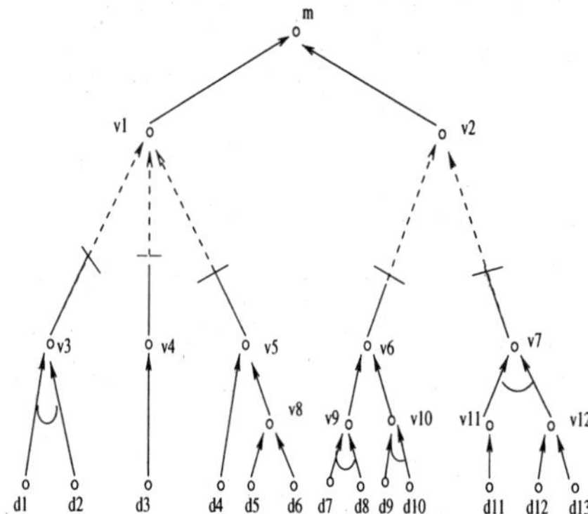

Figure 1: An example of horizontal hierarchization.

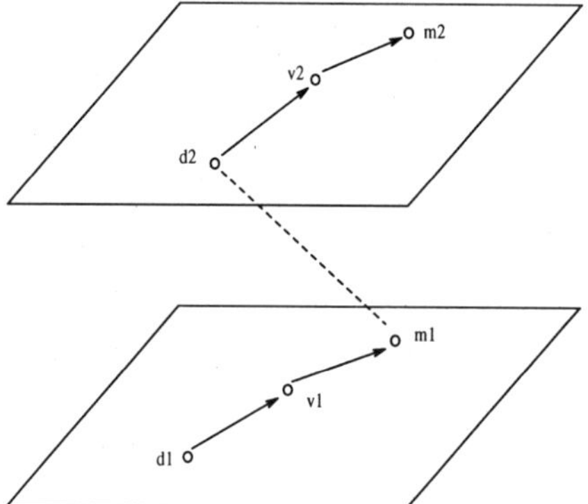

Figure 2: Another example of horizontal hierarchization.

Note that, intensionally, the separation as above can be either "mostly horizontal", when the level of knowledge representation is the same for both resulting subgraphs and the main gain consists of reducing complexity of the search, or "mostly vertical", when one of the graphs specifies diagnoses at a higher, more abstract level, and the other graph, connected to these diagnoses provides more detailed definition of them for further verification. In both cases the testing method outlined in the former subsection can be used for verification of the status of the frontier nodes (the ones of U), which may be helpful for focusing the search on one of the separated subgraphs.

3.3 Functional Abstraction or Vertical Hierarchization

The use of graphs with different details of knowledge represented at different level of reasoning (functional abstraction and hierarchization; vertical hierarchization), and use of different level of details in system description provides another natural way of introducing hierarchy into the diagnostic process; thus for any level a separate graph, representing the knowledge at desired level of abstraction should be used.

Let us consider the concept of *detailness* of knowledge specification for AND and for OR nodes. In the case of an AND node n , e.g. $[n_1, n_2, \ldots, n_k] \longrightarrow n$, if some connections to this node are removed, the node becomes more general since in this way one specifies weaker conditions (see Figure 3); formally one obtains $[n^1, n^2, \ldots, n^j] \longrightarrow$

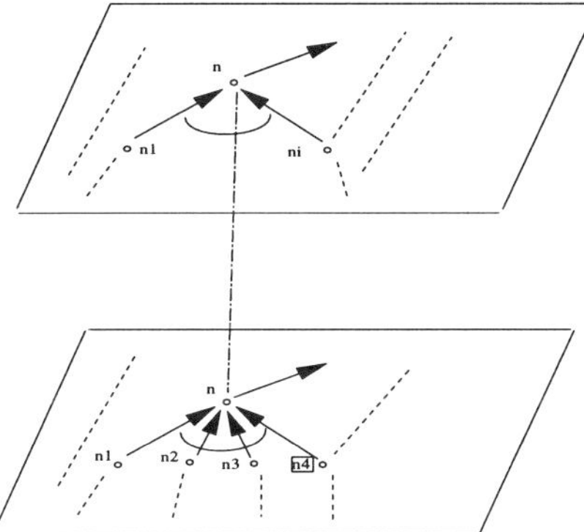

Figure 3: Removing connections in an AND node (vertical hierarchization).

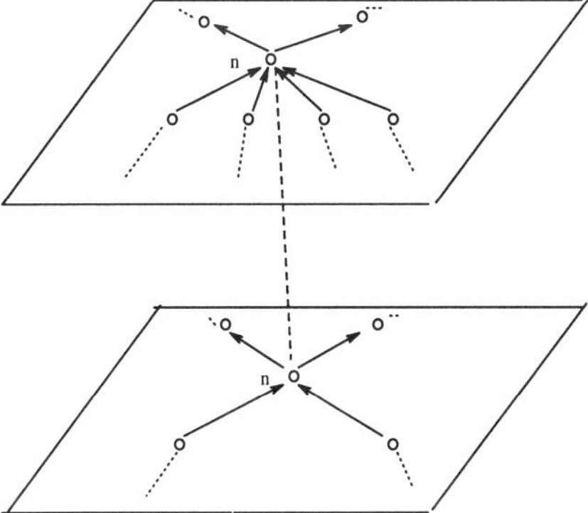

Figure 4: Deleting some connections to an OR node (vertical hierarchization).

n', where $\{n^1, n^2, \ldots, n^j\} \subseteq \{n_1, n_2, \ldots, n_k\}$. In this case one can also say that the node becomes *less informative*, or *less informed*. If n' is an AND node resulting from n by removing some arcs pointing to it, we shall say that n' is less informed than n; this will be denoted symbolically as $n' \preceq n$. For intuition, such way of abstraction may lead to smaller diagnoses – less conditions are required to satisfy the AND nodes.

On the other hand, in the case of an OR node n, $n_1|n_2|\ldots n_k \longrightarrow n$, if some connections to an OR node are deleted it makes the graph more specific (see Figure 4); formally one has $n^1|n^2|\ldots n^j \longrightarrow n'$, where $\{n^1, n^2, \ldots, n^j\} \subseteq \{n_1, n_2, \ldots, n_k\}$. However, from diagnostic point of view it becomes also less informative – there are less possible causes for the analyzed symptom. If n' is an OR node resulting from n by removing some arcs pointing to it, we shall say that n' is less informed than n; this will be denoted symbolically as $n' \preceq n$. For intuition, such way of abstraction may lead to smaller number of diagnoses – there are less possibilities of satisfying the analyzed OR node.

Another idea consists in amalgamating nodes, e.g. on a path of the form $n \longrightarrow v' \longrightarrow v'' \longrightarrow n'$ it is always possible to glue v' and v'' having v; the connection becomes $n \longrightarrow v \longrightarrow n'$, etc. (see Figure 5).

In this case one can also speak about generation of a less informed, more abstract graph; the expected number of potential diagnoses remains stable.

Let $\mathbf{G}_1$ be an upper-level graph obtained from a lower-level graph $\mathbf{G}_2$ by abstracting

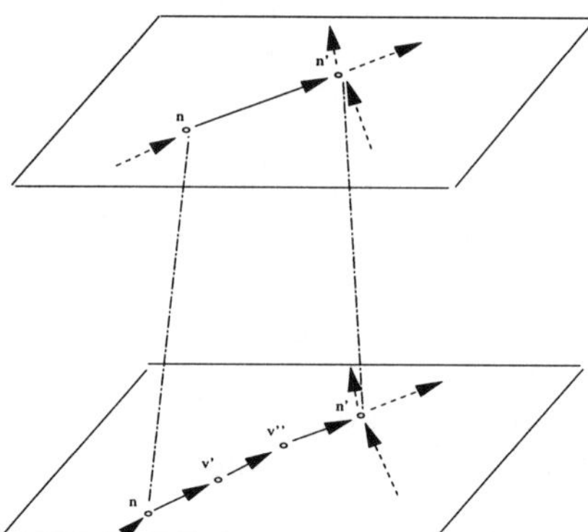

Figure 5: Amalgamating nodes in vertical hierarchization.

some of the AND and OR nodes in the above way (and deleting unnecessary nodes) or amalgamating nodes on a single path. We shall say that graph $\mathbf{G}_1$ is *less informed* than the original graph $\mathbf{G}_2$ ($\mathbf{G}_1 \preceq \mathbf{G}_2$), or that graph $\mathbf{G}_2$ is more informed than graph $\mathbf{G}_1$ ($\mathbf{G}_2 \succeq \mathbf{G}_1$). Normally, for any diagnosis found for the less informed graph $\mathbf{G}_1$ there exists a bigger diagnosis in graph $\mathbf{G}_2$; on the other hand, for some of the diagnoses for $\mathbf{G}_2$ there may be no diagnosis in $\mathbf{G}_1$.

For illustration, let us consider the causal graph for the mentioned tank systems [8]. The structure of the causal graph is presented on Figure 6.

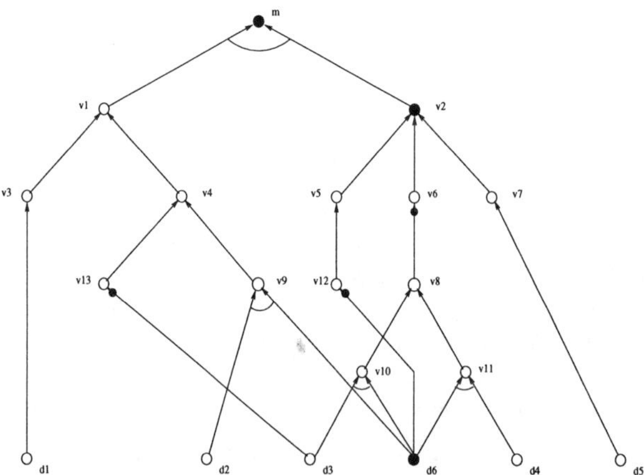

Figure 6: A causal graph for diagnostic reasoning.

On the picture symptoms (nodes) found to be *true* are marked with filled circles; the empty circles denote false symptoms or ones of unknown status. After identification of the failure, only the node marked with m is found to be true. When further observations are accessible, also $v2$ and $d6$ are marked *true*.

The sets of all possible diagnoses consistent with the observations found by the algorithm are:

(1) $D_1^+ = \{d_1\}$, $D_1^- = \{d_3, d_4\}$, (2) $D_2^+ = \{d_1, d_5\}$, $D_2^- = \emptyset$, (3) $D_3^+ = \emptyset$, $D_3^- = \{d_3, d_4\}$, (4) $D_4^+ = \{d_5\}$, $D_4^- = \{d_3\}$, (5) $D_5^+ = \{d_2, d_6\}$, $D_5^- = \{d_3, d_4\}$, (6) $D_6^+ = \{d_2, d_5, d_6\}$, $D_6^- = \emptyset$.

and only four of them are minimal diagnoses (i.e.(2), (3), (4), (6)) in the sense of set inclusion. But with respect to the generated subgraph, all the six diagnoses constitute different solutions. For information, for the above problem specified with no initial observations there are as many as 14 potential solutions, and 6 of them are minimal with respect to set inclusion.

Now consider a less informed graph obtained from the initial one by removing nodes $d6$, $v5$, and $v12$, and the appropriate links. The obtained graph is less informed, and the possible diagnoses in such a case are:

(1) $D_1^+ = \{d_1\}$, $D_1^- = \{d_3, d_4\}$, (2) $D_2^+ = \{d_1, d_5\}$, $D_2^- = \emptyset$, (3) $D_3^+ = \emptyset$, $D_3^- = \{d_3, d_4\}$, (4) $D_4^+ = \{d_5\}$, $D_4^- = \{d_3\}$, (5) $D_5^+ = \{d_2\}$, $D_5^- = \{d_3, d_4\}$, (6) $D_6^+ = \{d_2, d_5\}$, $D_6^- = \emptyset$.

Note that one obtains the same number of diagnoses, but two of them are simpler, namely (5) and (6). Eliminating $d6$ (and consequent links and nodes) resulted in simplification of the search space without violating the possibility of generating all the diagnoses. Further, since $d6$ was observed to be true, in fact the simplification has had no influence on the diagnostic process. For information, the meaning of $d6$ was that power was on, and the simplified graph referred to a situation of searching for diagnoses under this observation.

Graph abstraction may be useful for improving efficiency of search for diagnoses. Starting with a more informed graph and – basing on it – a more abstract graph for the top-level search can be built. Then the results of the search (in abstract, restricted space) can be used to guide the low-level search with use of the detailed graph.

3.4 Model-Based Reasoning and Consistency Constraints

Using different levels of logical knowledge definitions, constraints, constraint relaxation, etc. ("level of abstraction" hierarchization; with respect to different details incorporated at a single level) can provide another way of hierarchization of diagnostic process.

One can consider a causal graph at the upper level (for search) and an auxiliary more detailed level specifying logical definitions of symptoms (to be verified during the search). Such a definition can be a more precise logical formula, or a test (see Figure 7); this was discussed in the first subsection. What is most interesting here, is that some global logical constraints covering several nodes can be specified as well (e.g. if $n1$, $n2$, $n3$ are true then $n4$, $n5$ must be false; if this is not true, then the search is to backtrack, etc.). This auxiliary knowledge form an additional theory specifying certain constraints $CONS$ which are not expressible directly with the causal graph.

The causal graph structure is aimed at direct representation of causal dependencies among symptoms. However, for assuring precise knowledge representation covering also some logical constraints, it may be convenient to specify a set of logical constraints to be satisfied by any state of the graph. Such constraints may refer to further model specification of certain component involved in the diagnostic process, define system properties or specify some relationship (not the causal ones) among the symptoms.

For the sake of practical implementation, these constraints can be specified in the form of rules, such that the precondition of any rule is a formula defining some set of states of the symptoms and the conclusion is another set of symptom states. In this way one can express the propagation of values among symptoms other than the ones specified by the causal graph. A typical example may include "physical negation", i.e. a case when occurrence of some symptom may require that another symptom cannot occur. The constraints in the form of rules can also be used to specify inconsistent

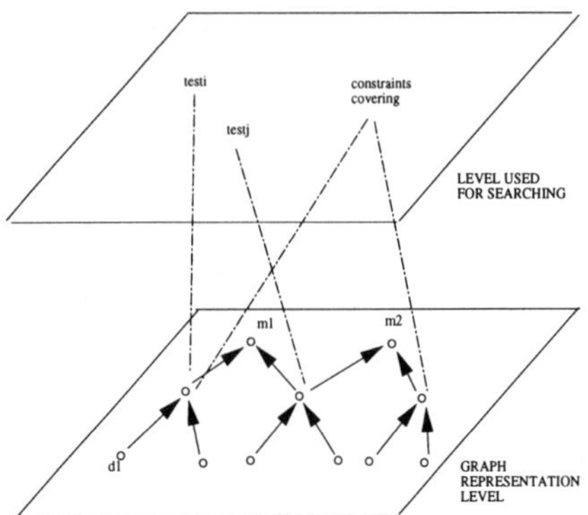

Figure 7: Logical description hierarchization.

states, by providing a special conclusion equivalent to the truth value *false* (the so-called *nogood* states). As in the case of initial observations, the use of rules specifying auxiliary constraints can be twofold:

- if, at certain stage of the search the generated state (S^+, S^-) of the symptoms violates the auxiliary constraints (i.e. $\nvDash CONS \cup (S^+, S^-)$), the information can be used to block some search possibilities; this is analogous to the case of initial observations applied to refine the search process,

- the rules can be used to generate state of some symptoms temporarily *unknown* on the base of the state of known symptoms at selected stages of the search (i.e. $CONS \cup (S^+, S^-) \models (S'^+, S'^-)$, where $S^+ \subset S'^+$ or $S^- \subset S'^-$). Thus, the auxiliary rules can be used to guide the search for solution – confirmed symptoms may be selected first if they explained the symptoms specifying the problem. In this way expert knowledge (if accessible) can be used to guide the search for diagnoses.

If such auxiliary rules are in use, the consistency verification mechanism should be used at any stage of the search so as to avoid developing inconsistent search hypotheses immediately after inconsistency occurs. This however, may slow down the search.

4. Concluding Remarks

The main objective of this paper was to discuss a multi-level inference model for diagnostic reasoning. A single-level knowledge representation formalism and an approach to single-level diagnostic reasoning were oulined in brief. This approach is based on abductive reasoning applied to search of appropriately defined causal graphs.

The presented approach supports several possible extensions and applications of efficiency enhancing tools specific for diagnostic process, such as observations, probes, tests, consistency checking or auxiliary model based reasoning for consistency detection and diagnoses verification. It can be used even in the case of incomplete knowledge specification and it does not require specification of complete model of the diagnosed system – for the sake of simplifying the diagnostic reasoning, specific, diagnosis-oriented models can be used. The approach supports also hierarchical diagnosis which is important to cut down the diagnostic procedure complexity. Last but not least, it preserves transparency of reasoning at any stage of diagnostic procedure and provides the possibility of explanation and incorporation of new incoming information at any stage.

The main contribution of this paper consists of theoretial investigation into the nature and mechanisms of the multi-level knowledge specification, passing from one level to another, and application of multi-level inference to improving diagnostic efficiency. Four basic mechanisms of multi-inference were outlined; they cover: abstraction/specification of symptoms, hierarchical separation, functional abstraction and consistency verification. Further, the hierarchization of diagnostic reasoning can be supported using different level simulation models for potential diagnoses analysis and different level theories used for auxiliary reasoning such as propagation of symptom values, symptom descriptions, etc. Note that, if a precise simulation model of the analyzed system is accessible, it can be used for testing states generated during the search for inconsistency and thus refining or guiding the search.

Acknowledgment: The research was carried out within KBN Grant No.: 8 T11A 013 08 (with respect to the first author), and was partially supported by HELIOS Esprit Project No.:22354 and by the project TAP96-1114-C03-02 with respect to the second author.

References

[1] Chang, S. J., F. DiCesare, and G. Goldbogen: Failure propagation trees for diagnosis in manufacturing systems. *IEEE Transactions on Systems, Man, and Cybernetics*, Vol. SMC-21, No.4, July/August 1991, 767-776.

[2] Chu B.-T. B.: Diagnosis with continuous and discrete causal relationships: knowledge representation. *Int. J. of Pattern Recognition and Artificial Intelligence*, 1992, 731-751.

[3] Console, L. and P. Torasso: An approach to the compilation of operational knowledge from causal models. *IEEE Transactions on Systems, Man, and Cybernetics*, Vol. SMC-22, No.4 July/August 1992, 772-789.

[4] Davis, R. and W. Hamscher: Introduction to model-based diagnosis. A chapter in: *Readings in Model-Based Diagnosis*, W. Hamscher, L. Console and J. DeKleer (Eds.), Morgan Kaufmann Publ., San Mateo, CA, 1992.

[5] DeKleer, J. and B.C. Williams: Diagnosing multiple faults. *Artificial Intelligence*, Vol. 32, 1987, 97-130.

[6] Fussell, J.B.: Computer aided fault tree construction. In Barlow, R.E., Fussell, J.B. and Singpurwalla, N.D. (Eds.) *Reliability and fault tree analysis. Theoretical and applied aspects of system reliability and safety assessment*, SIAM, Philadelphia, pp. 37-56, 1975.

[7] Fuster-Parra, P. and A. Ligęza: A Model for Representing Causal Diagnostic Reasoning. Paper presented at EMCSR'96, Vienna. In *Proceedings of the 13th*

European Meeting on Cybernetics and Systems Research, vol.:2, pp. 1222-1227, Vienna, Austria, April 1996. Also as *LAAS Report*, No.: 96186.

[8] Fuster-Parra, P.:A Model for Causal Diagnostic Reasoning. Extended Inference Modes and Efficiency Problems. Ph.D. Thesis presented at the University of Balearic Islands, 1996.

[9] Guan, J. and J.H. Graham: Diagnostic reasoning with fault propagation digraph and sequential testing. *IEEE Transactions on Systems, Man, and Cybernetics*, Vol. SMC-24, No. 10, October 1994, 1552-1558.

[10] Ligęza, A. and P. Fuster-Parra: An approach to diagnosis through search of AND/OR/ NOT causal graphs. In: J. Kocijan and R. Karba (Eds.), *Preprints of the IFAC/IMACS International Workshop on Artificial Intelligence in Real-Time Control*, Bled, Slovenia, 1995, 126-131.

[11] Ligęza, A., P. Fuster-Parra and J. Aguilar-Martin: Causal Abduction: Backward Search on Causal Logical Graphs as a Model of Diagnostic Reasoning. *LAAS Report*, No. 96316, 1996.

[12] Ligęza, A. and P. Fuster-Parra: AND/OR/NOT causal graphs – a model for diagnostic reasoning. *Applied Mathematics and Computer Science*, 1997, Vol.7, No.1, 185-203.

[13] Lunze, J. and F. Schiller: Logic-based diagnosis utilising the causal structure of dynamical systems. In IFAC/IFIP/IMACS Int. Symp. on Artificial Intelligence Real Time Control, Delft, The Netherlands, 649-654, 1992.

[14] Mozetic, I.: Hierarchical model-based diagnosis. *Int. J. of Man-Machine Studies*, Vol.35, 1991, 329-362.

[15] Nilsson, N.J.: *Problem-Solving Methods in Artificial Intelligence*. McGraw-Hill Book Company, New York, 1971.

[16] Patil, R.S.: Causal representation of patient illness for electrolyte and acid-base diagnosis. Ph.D. Thesis presented at the Massachusetts Institute of Technology, october, 1981.

[17] Reggia, J.A. and al.: Diagnostic expert systems based on a set covering model. Int. J. Man-Machine Studies, 19:437-460, 1983.

[18] Torasso, P. and L. Console: *Diagnostic Problem Solving. Combining heuristic Approximate and Causal Reasoning*. North Oxford Academic, A Division of Kogan Page, London, 1989.

Author Index